D0929505

W

470

JAN 2 8 2013

JAN 2 8 2013

WAYNE PUBLIC LIBRARY
MAIN LIBRARY
461 Valley Road
Wayne, NJ 07470

CRITICAL SURVEY
OF GRAPHIC NOVELS
MANGA

REFERENCE

CRITICAL SURVEY OF GRAPHIC NOVELS
MANGA

Editors

Bart H. Beaty
University of Calgary

Stephen Weiner
Maynard, Massachusetts

SALEM PRESS
A Division of EBSCO Publishing
Ipswich, Massachusetts   Hackensack, New Jersey

Cover: From left to right (Top Row): *Banana Fish, Barefoot Gen, Battle Angel Alita, Bleach, Boys over Flowers* (Middle Row) *Death Note, Dragon Ball, The Drifting Classroom, Fullmetal Alchemist, Golgo 13* (Bottom Row) *Hikaru no go, InuYasha, JoJo's Bizarre Adventure, Maison Ikkoku, Monster.* All courtesy of Viz Media.

Copyright © 2013, by Salem Press, A Division of EBSCO Publishing, Inc.

All rights in this book are reserved. No part of this work may be used or reproduced in any manner whatsoever or transmitted in any form or by any means, electronic or mechanical, including photocopy, recording, or any information storage and retrieval system, without written permission from the copyright owner. For permissions requests, contact proprietarypublishing@ebscohost.com.

The paper used in these volumes conforms to the American National Standard for Permanence of Paper for Printed Library materials, X39.48-1992 (R1997).

Library of Congress Cataloging-in-Publication Data

Critical survey of graphic novels : manga / editors, Bart H. Beaty, Stephen Weiner.
    p. cm. -- (Critical survey of graphic novels)
  Includes bibliographical references and indexes.
  ISBN 978-1-58765-955-3 (hardcover) -- ISBN 978-1-58765-956-0 (ebook) 1. Graphic novels. 2. Comic books, strips, etc. I. Beaty, Bart. II. Weiner, Stephen, 1955- III. Title: Manga.
  PN6725.C756 2012
  741.5'0973--dc23
                            2012019473

First Printing

Printed in the United States of America

CONTENTS

PUBLISHER'S NOTE

Graphic novels have spawned a body of literary criticism since their emergence as a specific category in the publishing field, attaining a level of respect and permanence in academia previously held by their counterparts in prose. Salem Press's *Critical Survey of Graphic Novels* series aims to collect the preeminent graphic novels and core comics series that form today's canon for academic coursework and library collection development, offering clear, concise, and accessible analysis of not only the historic and current landscape of the interdisciplinary medium and its consumption but also the wide range of genres, themes, devices, and techniques that the graphic novel medium encompasses.

The combination of visual images and text, the emphasis of art over written description, the coupling of mature themes with the comic form—these elements appeal to the graphic novel enthusiast but remain a source of reluctance to other readers. Designed for both popular and scholarly arenas and collections, the series provides unique insight and analysis into the most influential and widely-read graphic novels, with an emphasis on establishing the medium as an important academic discipline. We hope researchers and the common reader alike will gain a deeper understanding of these works, as the literary nature is presented in critical format by leading writers in the field of study.

Manga is the third title of the *Critical Survey of Graphic Novels* series, in conjunction with *Heroes and Superheroes*; *Independents and Underground Classics*; and *History, Theme, and Technique*. This title collects more than sixty-five of the most popular and studied manga graphic novels, ranging from metaseries to stand-alone books. A recent influx of translated Japanese manga into the American market has sparked a greater interest in foreign-language traditions and long-form comics. The current volume provides detailed insight into and analyses of the major works that have helped to define the manga medium, focusing on translated works that have been particularly influential in the development of the manga tradition. Stories have been compiled and dissected to provide viewpoints that are easily missed during initial readings.

Scope and Coverage

This single-volume set covers over sixty-five well-regarded works of the manga medium, summarizing plots and analyzing the works in terms of their literary integrity and overall contribution to the graphic novel landscape. Often defined by such characteristics as stylized line work, cultural-specific narratives, and compelling storytelling that often stand in contrast to the character-centric framework of American comics, manga nonetheless encompasses a broad range of genres and subgenres. Researchers will gain a better understanding of the latter, which, in the manga tradition, is represented by a wide spectrum that includes *josei* manga, which targets a mature female audience; *shoujo-ai* manga, which focuses on the spiritual, sexual, or emotional aspects of relationships; *shōnen-ai*, manga created by female authors that focuses on homoerotic or homoromantic male relationships; and *kodomo* manga, created exclusively for a young audience.

In writing these essays, contributors worked from original sources, providing new criticism and content aimed at deconstructing both centuries-old themes and concepts as well as nontraditional genres and styles, and portraying the graphic novel as literature. To that end, essays look beyond the popular-culture aspects of the medium to show the wide range of literary devices and overarching themes and styles used to convey beliefs and conflicts. Furthermore, critical attention was paid to panel selection and relevancy and to a particular work's influence on the creators' careers, other graphic novels, or literature as a whole.

The graphic novels field is defined by tremendous complexity; to that end, many important works and creators in the manga medium have been omitted. Finally, while the series has an international scope, attention has been focused on translated works that have been influential in the development of a specific graphic novel tradition.

Organization and Format

The essays in *Manga* appear alphabetically and are approximately 3 to 4 pages in length. Each essay is heavily formatted and begins with full ready-reference top matter that includes the primary author or authors, illustrators, and other artists who contributed to the work, and the first serial and book publication. This is followed by the main text, which is divided into "Publication History," "Plot," "Volumes," "Characters," "Style," "Themes," and "Impact." A list of adaptations of the graphic novel into film and television are also noted, and a user-friendly bibliography completes the essay. Cross-references direct readers to related topics, and further reading suggestions accompany all articles.

Publication History presents an overview of the work's origin and publication chronology. Specifically, dates of first serial publication, first book publication, and first translation into English are provided. Many graphic novels were first serialized in comic book form, often as a limited series, and were later collected or re-published in book format, while other graphic novels were conceptualized as novelistic works. In addition, details about the significant awards and honors won by each work are listed.

Plot provides an in-depth synopsis of the main story progression and other story arcs. As an aid to students, this section focuses on the most critically important plot turns in the series or work and why these were important.

Where applicable, *Volumes* orients the reader or researcher to the accepted reading order of the work. For series, it lists individual volumes or collections, often comprising different story arcs. The year when each collection was published is provided. Also identified are the issues that were collected within a volume, a synopsis of the volume's main focus, and its significance within the entire collection.

Characters presents detailed descriptions of major characters in the story, beginning with the main protagonists and antagonists. The section discusses physical descriptions, character traits and significant characteristics, the character's relationship with others, and the primary role a character plays in advancing the plot of the work or series. To aid readers, descriptions include "also known as" names and monikers.

Style provides analysis of the work's visual content, especially as it relates to characterization, plot, and mood; discussion of any changes in style as the story progresses; and the use of elements and devices such as dialogue, captions, panels, penciling, inking, and backgrounds.

Themes identifies the central themes in the work, how they are expressed—for example, through plot or layout—and how they relate to characterization and style. It also discusses, when applicable, whether a major thematic point is a chronicle of the author's personal development, or a projection of it, and how this may resonate with readers.

Impact covers the work's influence on the creators' careers, publishing houses, the medium of graphic novels itself, and literature in general. The section also analyzes the impact of the creation of new characters or series. Of focus is the critical reception of the work or series and whether it was atypical for its historical period.

Bibliography lists secondary print sources for further study and examination, annotated to assist readers in evaluating focus and usefulness.

Appendixes and Other Special Features

Special features help to further distinguish this reference series from other works on graphic novels. These include a general bibliography as well as a timeline discussing significant events and influential graphic novel predecessors spanning the ancient world, when woodblock printing was first brought to Japan from China, through the first use of the term "manga" in the early 1800s to the present. Another key feature of the essays in this publication are biographical sidebars on authors, illustrators, and significant publications related to the works profiled. Additionally, the single-volume set features full-page images and panels from the actual works. Four indexes round out the set, illustrating the breadth of the reference work's coverage: Works by Publisher, Works by Author, Works by Artist, and a subject index.

Acknowledgments

Many hands went into the creation of this work, and Salem Press is grateful for the effort of all involved. This includes the original contributors of these essays, whose names can be found at the end of each essay and also found in the "Contributor List" that follows the Introduction. Special mention must be paid to Marc Weidenbaum, who penned the introduction and lent his expertise to many of the volume's supplemental and complimentary materials, including the sidebars. Weidenbaum is former Editor in Chief of the American edition of *Shōnen Jump*, the best-selling manga magazine in Japan. He was Vice President of Magazines, Online, and Original Comics at Viz Media, which published the American *Shōnen Jump*. Comics he edited have appeared in books by Jessica Abel, Justin Green, Carol Swain, and Adrian Tomine, among others. He also introduced and edited the comics in *Pulse!* and *Classical Pulse!*, which were published by Tower Records, and was a contributor to the book *1001 Comics You Must Read Before You Die*. Special mention must also be paid to Lisa Schimmer, who played an invaluable role in shaping some of the reference content.

Finally, we are indebted to our editors, Bart Beaty, Professor of English at the University of Calgary, and Stephen Weiner, Director of Maynard Public Library in Maynard, Massachusetts, for their advice in selecting works and their writing contributions. Both are published in the field of comics and graphic novels studies. Beaty is the author of *Fredric Wertham and the Critique of Mass Culture, Unpopular Culture: Transforming the European Comic Book in the 1990s*, and *David Cronenberg's "A History of Violence."* Weiner is the author or co-author of *The 101 Best Graphic Novels, Faster than a Speeding Bullet: The Rise of the Graphic Novel, The Hellboy Companion, The Will Eisner Companion*, and *Using Graphic Novels in the Classroom*. Their efforts in making this resource a comprehensive and indispensible tool for students, researchers, and general readers alike is gratefully acknowledged.

INTRODUCTION

Manga is as indigenous to Japan as the *telenovela* is to Latin America and as jazz is to the United States. Which is to say, while there are things in other countries that seem to resemble manga — let's call them "comics" — the process of sorting out just how unlike manga these other mediums are can be informative, enlightening, even enthralling.

Cultural parallels are useful as a point of comparison. Soap operas remain a popular form of serialized television throughout the world, yet none follow the norms of the *telenovela*, whether in regard to received notions of story structure or consensual appreciation of cultural impact. And while there is a rich tradition of modal music around the world that comingles appropriation, group improvisation, and composition, no form has the specific literature, the accrued techniques, and the internal conflict of jazz.

Similarly, storytelling that combines concise text with static images in a sequential format is present around the globe, from the funny pages of American newspapers to the *bandes dessinées* of francophone culture. But no nation at the start of the third millennium can compare with Japan in terms of the extent to which sequential art infiltrates and informs the everyday life of the populace. This is true even as manga faces, in its native land, significant and long-running declines.

To speak of manga is not to speak of a "genre" or even a "medium." It is to speak of a cultural cycle — in fact, of several interrelated and overlapping cultural cycles.

First, there is the publication cycle. The majority of manga appears initially in thick, inexpensively printed anthologies that are published in serial form, often weekly, generally monthly. The best known of these magazines outside of Japan, titled *Weekly Shōnen Jump*, is also the best selling inside Japan. Home to *Dragon Ball*, *Naruto*, and *Slam Dunk*, among many other series, the magazine sold upwards of six million copies each week at its height in the mid-1990's—and that's based entirely on newsstand sales. (Full disclosure: I am a former editor-in-chief of the magazine's American edition, which was published from 2002 through 2012, when it moved online.)

The various series in these anthology magazines are then collected into paperbacks, called *tankōbon*, that collect around a dozen or so chapters in one volume. As of this writing, for example, the magazine *Big Comic*'s series *Golgo 13*, which debuted in 1969 and continues to be published monthly, has seen at least 160 sequential *tankōbon* volumes, which excludes art books, anime, video games, and assorted other merchandise. A successful manga in Japan isn't merely the launching pad for a franchise—it is the fuel on which the country's cultural engine runs.

Second, there is the participation cycle. Before the advent of video gaming, it was said there were two things most teenage boys in Japan wanted to do professionally: play baseball and create manga. While the tantalizing, brass-ring cultural status of manga may be diminishing slowly, the medium remains part of the everyday imagination of Japanese youth. Manga creators are often drafted, like basketball players, right out of high school—they come from the manga magazines' readership, brought to the attention of manga editors through regular drawing and storytelling competitions. Manga magazines, of which there are dozens upon dozens, compete not just with each other, but also internally; each week and month, some series will be dropped out and others added, based on reader opinion as gauged through fast-response polling. To an extent, the route from reader to manga creator, along with the status of reader-as-judge, is an illusion intended to enhance the bond between readers and the manga industry. But even allowing for a certain amount of marketing showmanship, the strategy's effectiveness is predicated on an already existing and deep cultural permeation.

The third cycle of manga is the consumption cycle. Manga entices the young and entertains the elderly and is part of mainstream Japanese life in between. There is manga for every stage of life, from toddlers through the standard peer groups associated with comics (teenage, early adulthood), up through professional life, and on to retirement. Abroad, much is made of pornography and manga (from tentacles to pedophilia), but the root of that association has less to do with an inherently sexualized medium than it does with a publishing realm in which sex is simply one of countless subjects. There is biography manga, romance manga, educational manga, business manga, and action manga. And there is populist manga and literary manga—the former arriving with the full intent to shortly thereafter have a second life as fish wrap, and the latter part of a vibrant and avant-garde exploratory art.

That is manga inside Japan.

To read manga outside Japan involves several acts of distancing. There is the translation process, in which jokes and other references are transformed with the foreign reader in mind. There is the time lag, in which cultural events to which a specific manga chapter was timed (political, seasonal) are severed and forgotten. And foremost there is, among numerous additional aspects, the general absence of the weekly/monthly serial experience—the act of consuming in relative sync with a sizable population of fellow readers over the extended period of a given manga's run.

Manga outside Japan is generally consumed in paperback *tankōbon* collections reprinted years if not decades after their original publication; removed from its initial, dynamic, magazine-based publication cycle, manga in translated paperbacks can collectively appear stolid and cumbersome. The result is that manga is seen, not entirely incorrectly, as so massive that it confounds, eludes, and overwhelms potential new readers. (Only the online manga-reading experience approaches the aura and the momentum of the indigenous Japanese magazine experience, and that online activity is largely the province of the thriving amateur translation, or "scanlation," community.)

Manga's immensity can be unwieldy. It's essential to keep in mind that Comiket, the annual Japanese convention for self-published (or *dōjinshi*) comics, attracts upwards of half a million attendees—four times the audience of the preeminent American comics convention, San Diego Comic-Con. The challenge when approaching manga is to see that immensity as evidence of cultural and literary wealth, and not as a warning sign of an impenetrable world.

CONTRIBUTOR LIST

Ted Anderson
Golden Valley, MN

Fergus Baird
Concordia University

Richard A. Becker
Pasadena, CA

David A. Beronä
Plymouth State University

Jef Burnham
FilmMonthly.com

Rachel Cantrell
Texas A&M University, Commerce

Daniel D. Clark
Cedarville University

Lan Dong
University of Illinois, Springfield

Jack Ewing
Boise, ID

Thomas R. Feller
Nashville, TN

Wendy Goldberg
University of Mississippi

Raz Greenberg
The Hebrew University

Robert Greenberger
Fairfield, CT

Josh Hechinger
Downingtown, PA

Héctor Fernández L'Hoeste
Georgia State University

R. C. Lutz
CII Group

Verena Maser
University of Trier

Roxanne McDonald
Wilmot, NH

Julia Meyers
Duquesne University

Todd S. Munson
Randolph-Macon College

Shannon Oxley
University of Leeds

Robert J. Paradowski
Rochester Institute of Technology

Marco Pellitteri
London Metropolitan University

Lyndsey Raney
Texas A&M University, College Station

Jeremy R. Ricketts
University of New Mexico

Scott Robins
Toronto Public Library

Joseph Romito
University of Pennsylvania

Robert Sabella
Budd Lake, NJ

David S. Serchay
Broward County Library System

Rik Spanjers
Utrecht, Netherlands

Akiko Sugawa-Shimada
Kansai Gaidai University, Japan

CJ Suzuki
Baruch College (CUNY)

Jonathan Thorndike
Belmont University

Shawncey Webb
Taylor University

Snow Wildsmith
Mooresville, NC

CRITICAL SURVEY OF GRAPHIC NOVELS
MANGA

A

ADOLF

Author: Tezuka, Osamu
Artist: Osamu Tezuka (illustrator)
Publisher: Bungei Shunju (Japanese); Cadence Books (English)
First serial publication: *Adorufu ni tsugu*, 1983-1985
First book publication: 1992 (English translation, 1995-1996)

Publication History

A passage in a book Osamu Tezuka once read suggested that German chancellor Adolf Hitler had Jewish roots (a theory that remains popular to this very day, even though it has been completely discredited by historians). Tezuka decided to combine the idea with a story about the famous World War II (1939-1945) spy Richard Sorge, with whom he was fascinated. The story grew into an epic series that spans many years and involves different historical and fictional figures. The story began running in the weekly political magazine *Shukan Bunshun* in 1983, but Tezuka's deteriorating health (he received a treatment for hepatitis while working on the series) meant some elements were cut from the story; these were restored in the collected edition. The collected edition was translated to English in 1995 and became the first work by Tezuka to have an American edition.

Plot

The story is set in Berlin in 1936. Sohei Toge, a Japanese reporter covering the Olympic Games, schedules a meeting with his brother, a foreign-exchange student who lives in the city. Upon arriving at his brother's apartment, Toge discovers that his brother has been murdered and that certain elements of the crime bear disturbing similarities to the murder of a popular geisha, a crime he covered in Japan several months be-

fore. His investigations into the matter get him into trouble with the oppressive authorities in Nazi Germany and his native Japan.

Toge's story intertwines with the story of two people named Adolf: the first, Adolf Kamil, is the son of a Jewish family of refugees who fled Germany and settled in the Japanese city of Kobe; the other, Adolf Kaufman, is the son of a senior Nazi official who also lives in the city. The two boys become friends after being harassed by local Japanese children for their foreign look, but their friendship turns into bitter hatred as the years pass and the war progresses; their differences become irreconcilable, and both of them fall in love with the same girl. Their rivalry, stretching throughout the war and beyond, is linked to the murder of Toge's brother by a mysterious package of documents, which carries a secret that could lead to the downfall of the story's third Adolf, the infamous tyrant Hitler, as the documents prove that he is of Jewish ancestry.

Volumes

- *Adolf: A Tale of the Twentieth Century* (1995). Covers Sohei Toge's investigation in Berlin and the tale of friendship between the two Adolfs.
- *Adolf: An Exile in Japan* (1996). Toge returns to Japan, learns of the documents, and is harassed by the police. Kaufman is sent to the Hitler Youth boarding school in Berlin and becomes a devoted Nazi.
- *Adolf: The Half-Aryan* (1996). The quest for the documents continues, and things get complicated for the two Adolfs when they both fall in love with a beautiful Jewish girl.
- *Adolf: Days of Infamy* (1996). Kamil and Toge believe that they have found a trustworthy party

to deliver the documents to when they make contact with a ring of communist spies in Japan; Kaufman is sent to Japan to retrieve the documents at any cost.

- *1945 and All That Remains* (1996). Kamil and Kaufman, now bitter enemies, clash repeatedly, first as the war draws to a close and later against the backdrop of the Arab-Israeli conflict, until their final confrontation.

Characters

- *Sohei Toge*, a Japanese journalist, is one of the series' protagonists and also serves as the story's narrator. A capable, well-built man with a strong sense of justice, Toge's involvement in the affairs described in the series comes not only from his wish to avenge his brother's death but also from his disgust with the oppressive, hateful regimes of both Nazi Germany and his own country.
- *Adolf Kamil* is a boy from a family of German Jewish refugees who settled in Kobe. In some ways, he is a younger version of Toge: physically strong, resourceful, kind, and altruistic; also, he bears deep hatred toward Nazi Germany and its leader. However, he is frustrated by the Jews' helplessness and admires the nationalistic and militaristic character of imperial Japan, believing that the Jews should follow the same example.
- *Adolf Kaufman*, the son of high-ranking Nazi official and a Japanese woman, starts the series as an innocent boy who befriends Kamil. As he is absorbed deeper into life in Nazi Germany, he becomes a stronger and more confident person but also a cunning one, capable of almost psychotic violence.
- *Acetylene Lampe* is an official with the German secret police. He is a narrow-faced, bespectacled sadist, and in charge of the investigation of the documents affair.
- *Akabane* is an officer with the Japanese secret police. A sadist much like Lampe, he is a short, unshaven bully. He becomes obsessed with tracking the documents, suspecting they are a part of communist political activity.

- *Elisa Gutheimer* is a young, pretty brunet Jewish girl, with whom Kaufman falls in love while persecuting her family in Berlin. To save her life, Kaufman sends Gutheimer to Japan, where she and Kamil fall in love.
- *Miss Ogi* was the schoolteacher for both Toge's brother and Kamil. She is described as a lean, middle-aged woman, though she is drawn as a much younger person (a rather attractive woman in her thirties). She is a communist and pacifist political activist and aids Toge in his quest for the documents.
- *Yoshio Honda* is the son of a decorated colonel in the Japanese army; he hates his father and the Japanese imperialist ideology for which he stands. He is physically well built, with a military haircut, though his facial expression always seems to reflect anger and disdain. He works for the communist spy ring to which Toge and Kamil attempt to deliver the documents.
- *Adolf Hitler*, the infamous Nazi German dictator, is often portrayed in the series as a hysterical, grotesque figure who accompanies his speeches with exaggerated gestures. His characterization poses the question of why an entire nation chose to follow such a person to its doom. The secret of Hitler's ancestry hidden in the documents is the driving force of the series' plot.

Artistic Style

Adolf is perhaps the most serious and realistic series in Tezuka's enormous body of work; its artistic style represents something of a departure from Tezuka's usual cartoony character designs and gag-ridden action drawings. The male protagonists, in particular, could pass for protagonists in an American comic book: tall, strong, realistically drawn "men of action" set to deal with the cruelty of the modern world. Female characters retain some of the cute appearances typical of Tezuka's other works but still look more like stars in classic Hollywood cinema than figures in the Walt Disney Productions and Fleischer Studios cartoons admired and imitated by Tezuka in other works.

Cartoony design and gags are mostly reserved for the minor antagonistic characters; the German investigator Lampe and the Japanese policeman Akabane, for example, are notable for being the only two characters in the series from Tezuka's "star system" of regular characters (the two characters often appear as villains in Tezuka's works). Other antagonistic characters, notably Hitler, also are drawn in a cartoony style, portraying their evil as grotesque, and linking this evil to human stupidity. Interestingly, though most characters, even Japanese characters, feature a Western appearance (not particularly unusual in Tezuka's work), some minor Asian characters, especially of the questionable type (a Chinese spy or a Japanese smuggler), feature an appearance that could be seen as stereotypically offensive had they not been drawn by an Asian artist. The detailed, well-researched background drawings that take readers from Germany to Japan and the Middle East further reflect the series' realistic tone.

Themes

The life of Tezuka, Japan's "God of Comics," is indeed a "tale of the twentieth century," much like the title of the first volume in *Adolf*. Born in 1928, Tezuka grew up as Japan became a military dictatorship that committed atrocious crimes against its neighbors and suffered a terrible defeat at the hands of Allied forces, falling into ruin and poverty after the war. Tezuka was alive during Japan's amazing recovery, in which the country became an economic superpower. He sensed that this new status led to political and environmental corruption and made Japan a pawn for the Americans in the struggle against the Soviet Union, whose early stages of collapse he saw before his death in 1989. Though Tezuka hardly endorsed communism, a degree of sympathy for Japanese communists during the war years can be felt in some of the series' chapters.

All of this led Tezuka to develop a deep suspicion of nationalism, the military, and any ideology that pretended to offer quick solutions to humanity's problems. The Jewish people, who for generations lacked their own national identity or country, seem to have fascinated Tezuka; he appears to have found this existence an ideal alternative to the ideologies that led to the great tragedies of the twentieth century. In a particularly brave move, Tezuka drew parallels between the Nazi regime in Germany and the Japanese regime during World War II and the crimes against humanity committed by both. However, he lets the Japanese population off the hook somewhat, claiming that many were ignorant of the crimes committed in their name.

The final confrontation between the two Adolfs— one an Israeli soldier and the other fighting alongside the Palestinians—demonstrates how the tragic cycle continues well into the future. The Jews have adopted the nationalistic, militant sentiment that previously led to their own persecution, and the Palestinians aspire toward the realization of the very same sentiment.

Impact

Though one of Tezuka's less influential works, produced in a decade when dealing with serious political and historical issues in manga was nothing unusual, *Adolf* is nonetheless regarded as one of the artist's most compelling and well-plotted narratives. The collected edition of the series was among the first manga to be featured in the literature rather than comic book section of Japanese bookstores.

Naoki Urasawa's acclaimed series *Monster* (1994-2001) appears to have borrowed many elements from *Adolf*, including the story of a Japanese protagonist in Germany and a murder mystery set against the political backdrop of changing times. In 1995, *Adolf* became the first series by Tezuka to be published in an American edition, and though it was not an instant success, many other titles by the author would follow, including those of a less commercial variety, such as *Buddha* and *MW*.

Raz Greenberg

Further Reading

Spiegelman, Art. *Maus: A Survivor's Tale* (1986).
_____. *Maus II: A Survivor's Tale, and Here My Troubles Began* (1991).
Tezuka, Osamu. *Ayako* (2010).
Urasawa, Naoki. *Monster* (2006-2008).

Bibliography

Kershaw, Ian. *Hitler, 1889-1936: Hubris*. New York: W. W. Norton, 1999.
McCarthy, Helen. *The Art of Osamu Tezuka: God of Manga*. New York: Abrams ComicArts, 2009.

Schodt, Frederik L. *Dreamland Japan: Writings on Modern Manga*. Berkeley, Calif.: Stone Bridge Press, 1996.

_____. *The Astro Boy Essays: Osamu Tezuka and the Manga/Anime Revolution*. Berkeley, Calif.: Stone Bridge Press, 2007.

See also: *Monster*; *Buddha* series; *MW*

AKIRA

Author: Otomo, Katsuhiro

Artist: Katsuhiro Otomo (illustrator); Steve Oliff (colorist); Saito (cover artist); Mark Cox (cover artist); Lia Ribacchi (cover artist)

Publisher: Kodansha (Japanese edition); Marvel Comics (first U.S. edition); Dark Horse Comics (second U.S. edition); Kodansha (third U.S. edition)

First serial publication: 1982-1990 (English translation, 1988-1995)

First book publication: 1984-1993 (English translation, 2000-2002; authoritative edition, 2009-2011)

Publication History

In Japan, Katsuhiro Otomo published the first *Akira* story in the December 20, 1982, issue of Kodansha's *Yangu Magajin* (*Young Magazine*). Because of the success of the series Kodansha began to publish the magazine installments in paperback collections in 1984. With the *Akira* series running strong, the Epic Comics division of Marvel Comics in the United States began publication of the *Akira* series in booklets of sixty-eight pages each in 1988.

This first American edition was based on Kodansha's ongoing paperback collections of the series. Japanese manga are read from the top right to the bottom left of the page and are bound on the right side. The American editors converted this to the familiar Western pattern of top left to bottom right by mirroring, or "flipping," the pages and binding the comic books on the left. Even though Otomo had colored only the few initial pages of each Kodansha paperback collection, the first American edition was completely computer colored by Steve Oliff, whom Otomo chose for this role.

Otomo finished the last of the 120 magazine installments of *Akira* in the June 25, 1990, issue of *Yangu Magajin*. However, he agonized over retouching his work for the paperback Kodansha collections. It took nearly three years to complete *Akira*, with the appearance of Volume 6 in this format on March 23, 1993. As the American edition was based on these collections, Epic Comics issued

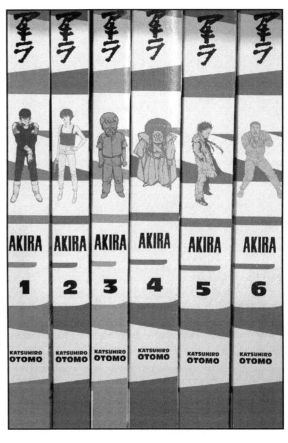

The *Akira* series, one of the earliest manga series to arrive in the United States, is collected into six volumes. (AFP/Getty Images)

the much-delayed finale of its thirty-eight issues of the colorized *Akira* in 1995. Marvel Comics began to publish both paperback and hardback collections of these issues. However, only ten of the thirteen planned paperback collections were published from 1990 to 1993, and only five of the six hardback limited editions were published. This left *Akira* unfinished in this publication run.

From December, 2000, to March, 2002, Dark Horse Comics published *Akira* in six black-and-white volumes with only the initial pages in color, as in the Japanese collections. This edition still flipped the manga to conform to Western reading habits. From October, 2009, to April, 2011, Kodansha published an American edition of *Akira* in six volumes that followed the earlier

Dark Horse Comics version, which followed closely the original Japanese six-volume collection of the *Akira* magazine installments and is discussed below. In addition to the American editions, *Akira* has been published in French, German, Dutch, Spanish, Polish, and Flemish.

Plot

At age twenty-six, Katsuhiro Otomo launched *Akira* by building on the success of his previous manga work, particularly *Domu* (2001). *Akira* was created for the same young male Japanese readership as *Domu*. Otomo set *Akira* in the postapocalyptic Neo-Tokyo of 2030. Thirty-eight years after an unexplained explosion destroyed the original Tokyo at 2:17 P.M. on December 6, 1992, and triggered World War III, Neo-Tokyo sits atop an artificial island in Tokyo Bay.

Akira rapidly launches its story of two teenage friends, Shotaro Kaneda and his sidekick Tetsuo Shima, who become bitter enemies when Tetsuo acquires vast psychic powers. Defying authorities, as is their habit, Kaneda's gang of teenagers races futuristic motorcycles and breaks through the dilapidated barrier on the bridge that connects Neo-Tokyo to the ruins of the original city. On their return, Tetsuo nearly runs over a ghostly boy, who has the facial features of an old man and is later revealed to be Takashi. Takashi is part of a group of psychics who as children were subjected to secret government experimentation. This gave them various paranormal powers but trapped them in their child's bodies while aging their faces. Tetsuo is injured when Takashi makes his motorcycle explode before he teleports from the scene. Suddenly, the military appears, and Tetsuo is taken to a hospital.

With Tetsuo away, Kaneda gets involved with a mysterious teenage girl, Kei. She belongs to a violent, secret antigovernment group that includes her older brother Ryu and Nezu, a member of parliament. They encounter Takashi again in the streets of Neo-Tokyo just as a special military unit, led by Colonel Shikishima, tries to capture him. This leads to much violence triggered by Takashi's paranormal powers and the fight between Shikishima's troops and the antigovernment forces.

Tetsuo leaves the hospital, and his new psychic powers have changed him into Kaneda's bitter enemy. He teams up with a rival gang and seeks to kill Kaneda. The price for Tetsuo's powers, as for the child-bodied psychics, is a new dependence on a powerful drug to which only the Colonel has access. As a result, the Colonel can take Tetsuo, as well as Kaneda and Kei, into custody. The Colonel reveals that Tokyo's destruction was caused by the powers of a child psychic called Akira. Akira is kept in a cryogenic chamber in cold stasis and guarded by the Colonel.

The bitter fight between Tetsuo, Kaneda, and Kei reaches a new dimension when Tetsuo decides to release Akira from his cold chamber. He succeeds in awakening Akira, who looks and acts like a rather passive boy, but Kaneda and Kei snatch Akira from Tetsuo's hands.

Soon different forces led by the Colonel, an old woman psychic called Lady Miyako, and the rebels under Nezu all chase after Akira and battle one another violently. When Nezu catches up with Akira, he shoots at him but kills Takashi instead. This shocks Akira into releasing a telekinetic shockwave that destroys Neo-Tokyo in much the same style of his earlier destruction of Tokyo. Tetsuo suddenly appears and leads away Akira.

In the ruins of Neo-Tokyo, the battles between the rival factions resume. Tetsuo sets up Akira as boy emperor for the Great Tokyo Empire and acts as his prime minister. Kei and the Colonel support Lady Miyako, while the Americans enter the scene through their spy, Japanese American George Yamada. At the climax of Tetsuo's attack on Lady Miyako's temple, the Colonel fires a powerful laser gun at Tetsuo but destroys only one of his arms. Kaneda, presumed dead, reappears and rejoins the anti-Tetsuo alliance.

Worried about the goings-on in Neo-Tokyo, the Americans and Russians send a joint force of aircraft carriers to the region. Determined to kill Tetsuo, the foreigners consider using biological weapons to kill all city dwellers. Tetsuo teleports to the lead aircraft carrier and demonstrates his power by destroying fighter jets before disappearing. More fighting ensues among Tetsuo and his Japanese and foreign opponents. Tetsuo destroys foreign battleships and even launches a nuclear weapon. He survives being hit by a missile that is psychically guided by Lady Miyako.

While Kaneda and Tetsuo fight a fierce battle at the Olympic stadium, the American-led foreign forces seek to complete the destruction of Neo-Tokyo with a laser satellite called FLOYD. Tetsuo yanks FLOYD out of its orbit. Employing her powers as psychic medium, Kei uses the combined psychic forces of the child-bodied psychics to eliminate Tetsuo's physical body in a final blast of destruction. Akira absorbs Tetsuo's psychic energy. Kaneda and Kei tell advancing foreign troops to stay out of Neo-Tokyo and ride off on their motorcycles.

Volumes

- *Akira 1* (2009). Sets up the series, launches the mortal Kaneda-Tetsuo rivalry, and introduces many main characters.
- *Akira 2* (2010). Offers the story's first climax with the reawakening of Akira; violent fights over his custody motivate explicit depictions of graphic violence.
- *Akira 3* (2010). The second climax, the destruction of Neo-Tokyo, offers a repeat of the initial apocalypse, indicating humanity has not learned much.
- *Akira 4* (2010). The rise of Akira and Tetsuo's empire draws Americans and Russians into the conflict, calling into question Japanese sovereignty.
- *Akira 5* (2011). While Japanese factions fight one another in Neo-Tokyo, foreign forces are ready to ruthlessly wipe out all inhabitants with futuristic weapons of mass destruction.
- *Akira 6* (2011). After Tetsuo's defeat, the series comes full circle as Kaneda and Kei return to life as juvenile motorcycle racers.

Characters

- *Shotaro Kaneda*, the protagonist, is a fifteen-year-old Japanese delinquent youth and leader of a teenage gang of motorcycle racers. Meeting the mysterious girl Kei changes his life as much as when his best friend Tetsuo acquires paranormal

powers and becomes his biggest enemy. Kaneda combines human decency with a desire for adventure and distrust of authorities.
- *Tetsuo Shima*, the antagonist, is a repressed teenager who changes into a power-obsessed, demonic character once he obtains paranormal powers. He represents humanity's dark side as he uses his psychic abilities brutally to seek ultimate personal power.
- *Kei*, the romantic interest of Kaneda, is an attractive and mature teenage girl involved with a violent antigovernment group. As a medium, she has no psychic powers herself but can channel those of true psychics; she helps Kaneda to defeat Tetsuo.
- *Colonel Shikishima* is a major character involved in the battle over Akira. He is a grown-up military man leading a secret government section in charge of psychics like Akira. More sinister in the beginning, he develops into an ally of Kaneda and Kei.
- *Akira*, the prized object of the series, is a powerful psychic in the body of a small boy. Passive and mild-mannered, he inadvertently destroys Tokyo twice when shocked by the violence around him. He appears to exist beyond good and evil.
- *Lady Miyako*, a supporting character, is an older female psychic who creates a temple cult and allies herself with Kaneda and Kei. She represents esoteric leaders in Japanese society.
- *George Yamada*, a spy and assassin, is an adult Japanese American sent to kill both Tetsuo and Akira. He is killed by Tetsuo.
- *Ryu* is an antigovernment rebel and ally of Kei, ostensibly her adult brother, but the series later makes this claim sound improbable. He helps to fight Tetsuo until he dies shortly before the end of *Akira*.
- *Chiyoko*, a major supporting character of Kaneda and Kei, is a middle-aged woman and weapons expert.
- *Kaori* is Tetsuo's love interest; she is shot to death by Tetsuo's jealous captain.

Artistic Style

Throughout *Akira*, Otomo's style is extremely cinematic. His panels range from vast, long shots of urban landscapes to middle shots of a group of characters drawn against a visually vivid background and impressive close-ups of weapons or characters' expressions. His illustrations create a distinctly dark atmosphere for the run-down parts of a rebuilt city transforming itself into a postapocalyptic landscape. Otomo's large panoramic panels include haunting images, such as the forbidden bridge linking Neo-Tokyo to the original city or the dilapidated concrete exteriors and vandalized interiors of Kaneda's vocational school.

Otomo's fascination with machines, particularly military hardware, stands out in the series. Kaneda's futuristic motorcycle is drawn in loving detail. Helicopters, tanks, aircraft carriers, military special-purpose vehicles, and technical apparatuses are given visual preeminence.

Depictions of graphic violence abound throughout *Akira*. When characters are killed, whether by telekinetic decapitations or by a barrage of gunfire, dark blood splatters on the panels and injuries are also depicted in graphic detail. Otomo delights in illustrating gun battles, chase scenes, and close person-to-person combat. Sound expressions almost literally explode in his panels, and violence appears ubiquitous and is the focus of much of the visual storytelling.

Otomo's characters are drawn to reflect the look of 1980's Japan rather than a truly futuristic alternative. The hairstyle of Kaneda and his fellow gangsters has a distinct 1980's look. The Colonel is drawn as a masculine leading man with crew cut, but he also has a diamond ear stud. Part of the freakishness of the psychics comes from the stark visual contrast of their child-sized and child-limbed bodies and their aged facial features. Overall, visuals and visual sound effects dominate the dialogue. There are no explanatory narrative captions after the bold, colorized introductory pages in the first volume. Generally, the reader is thrust right into the graphic action.

Themes

Even though *Akira* is set in the future, many of its themes can be traced to issues in 1980's Japanese so-

---

Katsuhiro Otomo

Katsuhiro Otomo, born in 1954, is best known for his *Akira* manga, which began serialization in Kodansha's *Young Magazine* in 1982, the same year Ridley Scott's *Blade Runner* hit movie screens. The two creations bear numerous similarities, notably their depiction of metastasized urban settings and their enduring influence on pop culture. *Akira* ended its serialization in 1990; since then, Otomo has primarily been associated with film. He directed the 2004 *Steamboy*, an ambitious European escapade, and a live-action 2006 manga adaptation, the supernatural *Mushishi*. Like many manga and anime greats, Otomo fell into the professional orbit of the late Osamu Tezuka, scripting the film adaptation of Tezuka's *Metropolis*. *Akira* remains Otomo's sole long-form manga, though in early 2012, he announced plans for a new ongoing manga series aimed at male teen readers and taking place in the Meiji period (1868-1912).

---

ciety. A key theme is rebellion against society, particularly by those like Kaneda, who resemble the generation of Japanese youths that felt left out of the "bubble economy" of the era. Kaneda and Tetsuo begin as friends in a teenage motorcycle gang that is modeled after the biker gangs popular in Japan in the 1980's, which provoked traditional society. Kaneda and Tetsuo's recreational drug use and drug dealing and their attendance at a decaying, graffiti-ridden vocational school are extrapolations of Japanese worries.

A dominant theme of *Akira* is an intense amount of violence at all levels of human interaction. Violence ranges from criminal acts of juvenile delinquency to gunfights and military and paranormal confrontation. The existence of a violent antigovernment underground, of which Kei is a member, and the violent response by the military special forces under Colonel Shikishima have historical roots in the violent clashes over the building and expansion of Tokyo's Narita International Airport from 1967 into the 1980's. Otomo's vision of the future incorporates this reemergence of political violence in Japan and widely expands it to become a central element of his dystopian future society.

The theme of paranormal power is used to comment further on possible negative trends in Japanese society. Deeply alienated from the society that has secretly created child-adults with enormous paranormal powers, many of the child-adults themselves resort to violence. Akira himself twice destroys Tokyo when he unleashes his telekinetic powers.

Finally, as *Akira* was written in the last years of the Cold War and during heightened Japanese-American political tensions, the issue of nuclear war and American military intervention in Japan is a political theme of the series. After the fight against Tetsuo is won, Kaneda and Kei insist on Japanese sovereignty and send away foreign troops.

Impact

In Japan, the popular and critical success of *Akira* established Otomo's enduring reputation as a great *mangaka*, or manga artist. His receipt of the coveted Kodansha Manga Award in the General Category in 1984 fueled the development of his series. Ironically, after completing *Akira*, Otomo turned from printed manga toward directing manga anime films.

Otomo's *Akira* inspired the next generation of manga artists, impressing them with its masterfully drawn vision of a violent future set in a decaying and destroyed city. By 2011, many important Japanese *mangaka*, such as Masashi Kishimoto, twenty years Otomo's junior, credited *Akira* as being deeply influential on their contemporary work.

In the United States, the initial publication of *Akira* in 1988 made it one of the first manga series to appear in English for a mass comics market. American audiences saw in *Akira* a powerful contribution to the cyberpunk genre. U.S. readers linked the manga to Ridley Scott's dystopian science-fiction film *Blade Runner* (1982) and literary works such as William Gibson's science-fiction novel *Neuromancer* (1984),

which Otomo did not read until well into his *Akira* series. The enduring popularity of *Akira* in the United States fueled a manga boom in the 1990's. It led to a 2009-2011 reissue of the six-volume collection of Otomo's work. *Akira* is considered a classic of the mature-audience manga genre.

Films

Akira. Directed by Katsuhiro Otomo. Tokyo Movie Shinsha, 1988. The adaptation of Otomo's manga series was the most expensively produced anime film at the time. It set new standards for high production values, featuring over 160,000 animation cels. Made while the *Akira* series was still going on, the film features most of the series' characters and follows the story with only a few alterations. The film condenses the series by ending almost immediately after the destruction of Neo-Tokyo, with Tetsuo being absorbed by Akira. Kaneda, Kei, the Colonel, and most positive characters survive.

R. C. Lutz

Further Reading

Nihei, Tsutomu. *Blame!* (1998-2003).
Shirow, Masamune. *Ghost in the Shell* (1989-1997).

Bibliography

Gravett, Paul. *Manga: Sixty Years of Japanese Comics*. London: Laurence King, 2004.

Lamarre, Thomas. "Born of Trauma: Akira and Capitalist Modes of Destruction." *positions: east asian cultures critique* 16, no. 1 (Spring, 2008): 131-156.

Napier, Susan J. *Anime from Akira to Howl's Moving Castle*. New York: Palgrave Macmillan, 2005.

_____. *The Fantastic in Modern Japanese Literature*. New York: Routledge, 1996.

Natsume, Fusanosuke. "Akira Acclaimed." *Look Japan* 46, no. 481 (April, 1996): 20-21.

See also: *Naruto* series

AMULET

Author: Kibuishi, Kazu

Artist: Kazu Kibuishi (illustrator); Amy Kim Kibuishi (colorist); Anthony Wu (colorist); Jason Caffoe (colorist)

First serial publication: 2008-2010

Publisher: Scholastic Books

Publication History

The inspiration for *Amulet* began at the end of Kazu Kibuishi's studies in college and with an idea about two children moving into a mysterious puzzle maker's house. After a short stint in animation, Kibuishi pursued a career in comics and went on to edit and contribute to *Flight* (2007-   ), an anthology of comics by creators mainly from the animation industry, and published first by Image Comics and later by Random House. Gathering stories for the fourth volume of *Flight*, Kibuishi discovered he had a collection of child-friendly comics, which he decided to publish as a separate anthology called *Flight Explorer*, featuring an original story of his Web comic *Copper*.

In 2005, Scholastic Books launched Graphix, the first graphic novel imprint from a traditional children's publishing company, and editors sought creators to follow their first group of releases, which included Jeff Smith's *Bone* (1991-2004). Raina Telgemeier, illustrator of the graphic novel adaptations of *The Baby-Sitters Club* (2006) and a previous *Flight* contributor, asked Kibuishi if she could show his work to editors at Scholastic. Kibuishi pitched *Amulet* with six completed pages and a one-page story synopsis, and the book was acquired. *Amulet* was first signed to a three-volume series, then a five-volume series.

Plot

Two years after their father's death in a tragic car accident, Emily and Navin Hayes move with their mother Karen from the city to an old house that belonged to their great-grandfather Silas Charnon, a mysterious inventor who disappeared years ago. In Silas's library, Emily finds a magical amulet that warns her to protect her family. That night, their mother is kidnapped by an

---

Kazu Kibuishi

Like Stan Sakai before him, Kazu Kibuishi is a Tokyo-born writer-artist who, despite having been raised in the United States, is often associated in readers' imaginations with manga and anime. His *Amulet* series, published by Scholastic, has drawn a substantial audience, as does his free Web comic, *Copper* (a compilation of which has also been published by Scholastic). *Amulet* is an ongoing steampunky, alternate-universe tale with teen protagonists, while *Copper* is an anecdotal "boy-and-his dog" yarn. Kibuishi's influence extends beyond his own original works: He founded the anthology journal *Flight*, initially published by Image Comics, later by Ballantine. It was created to showcase the work of his friends. Kibuishi is a graduate of the University of California, Santa Barbara, and continues to live in Southern California. He has cited Hayao Miyazaki and *Bone*'s Jeff Smith as his biggest influences.

---

arachnopod, and the children must descend beneath the basement to an underground world. After Emily attempts to free her mother from the creature using a magical bolt of energy, the voice of the amulet advises the children to seek help from their long-lost great-grandfather.

The children are brought to a mysterious house by Misket, a small rabbit-like robot and one of Silas's assistants. On his deathbed, Silas speaks of Emily's amulet and how it contains the power to rule Allendia, the alternate Earth where he has been living all these years. Emily, reluctant to accept this power and responsibility, is told by Silas that the amulet has the power to control time. Emily imagines the return of her dead father and accepts the amulet's power as Silas passes away.

Misket locates the pack of arachnopods with the children's kidnapped mother, and the trio travels to intercept them. After an initial struggle, the group fails to free Karen, who is jabbed with a poisonous stinger.

After a crash landing, Emily finds an elf creature, which has been previously spying on the children, facing down the arachnopod holding her mother. Using his own amulet, the elf creature, Prince Trellis, frees Karen from the arachnopod and captures Emily. Using a creature that can alter thoughts, he tries to coerce her into helping him destroy his father, the Elf King. Emily destroys the thought creature, and the amulet tries to convince her to kill the fallen prince; she resists and lets him go.

Back at Silas's house, Karen is in a coma, poisoned by the arachnopod. In desperate need of an antidote, the group heads to the city of Kanalis using the only transportation that remains, which transforms into a giant robot.

The *Stonekeeper's Curse* (Volume 2) opens with Trellis scolded by his father for failing to capture the two children. Convinced that Trellis is likely to fail again, the Elf King orders Luger—another elf warrior—to accompany him. In Kanalis, Emily and the others bring Karen to Dr. Weston, who describes a life-saving fruit that can be found only on the peak of Demon's Head Mountain, a treacherous journey. Leon Redbeard, a humanoid fox, overhears the doctor's instructions and offers to accompany the group on their quest. When an army of elves led by Luger and Trellis surrounds the doctor's office, Navin and others escape in an underground trolley, while Emily, Leon, and Misket take to the rooftops of the city.

Arriving at the hidden underground headquarters of the Resistance—an army that opposes the Elf King—Navin meets Father Adler, an ancient tree who has a vision in which Emily falls off a cliff to her death. Before Adler can finish explaining his vision, Navin orders the Resistance to take back the robot house from the elves so that he can use it to save his sister. The Elf King delivers new instructions to Luger: Have Prince Trellis kill the children, and if he hesitates, Luger is to kill the prince.

Reaching the forest of the ancient Godoba trees, Emily finds the fruit to cure her mother. Leaving Trellis behind, Luger reaches the forest and burns it down. He travels quickly, coming face-to-face with Emily and her friends and overpowering them. Prepared to kill Emily, Luger is attacked from behind by Trellis. Luger

allows the amulet to take him over, and he transforms into a giant beast. Luger throws Emily and Leon off a cliff, just as Father Adler had prophesied, but Navin catches them in the hand of the robot house before they fall to their deaths. Combining the strength of the robot house and the power of Emily's amulet, the house delivers a punch that seems to destroy Luger. Exhausted, Emily passes out but wakes to find that her mother is cured of the arachnopod's poison. When Karen says they can finally go home, Emily explains that she must stay and fulfill her destiny as a stonekeeper.

The Cloud Searchers (Volume 3) begins with Trellis finding a defeated Luger guarding his destroyed amulet. They both renounce their loyalty to the Elf King. At the Elf King's palace, Gabilan, an elf assassin, receives his mission: Kill both Emily and Prince Trellis.

Back in the robot house, Leon researches information on the location of the city of Cielis, home of the Guardian Council, a group of five of the most powerful stonekeepers, and the next destination for the group. The group travels to the city of Nautilis to find an airship that will take them to Cielis. At a local tavern, Emily and Leon find pilots—Enzo and Rico—and try to persuade them to shuttle the group. While the group discusses travel plans, two elf warriors find Trellis and Luger hiding in an alley behind the tavern. Emily recognizes the Elf Prince and defeats the two warriors.

Ready to head to Enzo's airship, the group, including Trellis and Luger, is faced with an elf-piloted tank, but they manage to escape. In the tavern, Gabilan confronts the two injured elf warriors and uses a memory extractor to gain information on the whereabouts of Emily and Prince Trellis. On the airship, Leon verifies the location of Cielis in the eye of a massive storm, and Enzo makes preparations to fly through it. The ship is attacked by the dragon-like creatures wyverns, damaging one of the airship's engines. Cogsley repairs the engine, but once his task is completed a wyvern pulls both Misket and Cogsley off the ship. Saddened by the loss of their friends, the group stops at a nearby fueling station to complete preparations to travel to Cielis.

Departing from the station, the group is unaware that the assassin Gabilan has stowed away on the ship. With Navin piloting through the storm, the group discovers a floating island that acts as a beacon for those wanting passage to Cielis. Trellis and Emily use their powers to piece together a puzzle that acts as a key to the beacon. Taking Karen hostage, Gabilan reveals himself. Emily and Trellis combine their powers to attack Gabilan, but his shield is able to absorb and redirect their magic. Emily causes boulders to collapse onto Gabilan and uses her powers to throw him off the island, but he is rescued by his own wyvern. With the beacon activated, a group of stonekeepers appears and guides the ship to the city of Cielis.

Volumes

- *The Stonekeeper* (2008). Emily and Navin journey to Allendia to rescue their mother.
- *The Stonekeeper's Curse* (2009). Emily and Navin must find an antidote to save their poisoned mother.
- *The Cloud Searchers* (2010). To fulfill her destiny, Emily searches for a lost city in the clouds.

Characters

- *Emily Hayes*, the protagonist, is a twelve-year-old girl with red hair. She is a natural-born leader, courageous and determined to help those she loves most. She discovers that she is a stonekeeper, a potential leader of Allendia, and possesses incredible powers she must learn to control before they take control of her.
- *Navin Hayes* is the younger brother of Emily. He looks up to her and is trying constantly to prove his worth during their adventures. He has a natural talent for piloting and discovers he is the foretold commander of the Resistance.
- *Karen Hayes* is the mother of Emily and Navin. She is kindhearted and caring. She wants the best for her two children after her husband's death. During their adventures she realizes that her two children are growing up quickly.
- *Silas Charnon* is the long-lost great-grandfather of Emily and Navin and the previous owner of the amulet that Emily now possesses. He is an inventor of amazing machines and a stonekeeper.
- *Misket* is a robot creation of Silas Charnon that resembles a pink rabbit. He is intelligent and re-

sourceful and vows to protect Emily at all costs during her adventures in Allendia.
- *Morrie* is a robot creation of Silas Charnon that looks like a traditional robot. He is often nervous and wary but is also caring and stood by Karen Hayes's bedside when she was poisoned.
- *Cogsley* is another robot creation of Silas Charnon who also looks like a traditional robot. His gruff exterior does little to hide the fact that he is hardworking, deeply loyal, and honest.
- *Trellis* is the son of the Elf King. He is mysterious, power hungry, and rebellious. At first, he hunts Emily down to coerce her to help him kill his own father, but later he shows signs of a conscience and eventually joins Emily.
- *The Elf King* is the main antagonist of the series. He is the ruler of Allendia and wears a stylized mask. He is ruthless and determined to kill Emily and her friends to prevent them from destroying him. Once a promising young stonekeeper, the Elf King was corrupted by the amulet power and is now dead. His body serves as a vessel for the dark power of the amulet.
- *Luger* is an Elf warrior whom the Elf King sends with Trellis to find and kill Emily. Luger succumbs to the power of the amulet and becomes a giant monster. He is defeated by Emily, loses his powers, becomes docile, and accompanies Trellis when the prince joins Emily's group.
- *Leon Redbeard*, a bounty hunter from the city of Kanalis, is a humanoid fox and a powerful fighter. He accompanies Emily on her journey and mentors her to control her great powers. He understands her importance in the future of Allendia and stands by her side through all dangers.
- *Gabilan*, the main antagonist of Volume 3, is a masked elf assassin hired by the Elf King to hunt down both Emily and Prince Trellis. He is crafty and without mercy and has plans of his own to take over the land of Allendia.

Artistic Style

Kibuishi's artistic style is heavily influenced by his previous career in animation and his love for Japanese comics and animation, especially the work of Hayao

Miyazaki. When placed on the book's heavy rendered backgrounds, his characters, drawn using fine lines, pop off the page, therefore resembling an animation cel. Characters are designed in bright, flat colors, creating a further juxtaposition to the lush and painterly backgrounds. Kibuishi draws on his previous experience using Photoshop for concept paintings for video games and animation to create effects that give his work a distinct, moody tone.

The first book of the series features a heavy, dark palette, symbolizing the movement from the real world to the fantasy world of Allendia. In Volumes 2 and 3, the backgrounds are brighter and more colorful than before to show off landscapes and fantastical cities. A number of single-page images and double-page spreads illustrate the scope of the world of Allendia and emphasize the world-building aspect of *Amulet*. Kibuishi employed background artists to help with more detail in these pages. The pages in *Amulet* are open but include a large amount of visual details. Kibuishi is an artist who relies heavily on images and visual clues to move the story along.

Panel layout is varied but readable, an important element for a graphic novel aimed at children. Kibuishi also uses a mix of decompressed scenes to illustrate character moments or create narrative tension, but he also uses fast-paced action scenes, making the series appealing to both children and adults. Kibuishi uses standard word balloons but plays with lettering by enlarging or stretching text when he wants to convey excitement or danger. Sound effects are also a strong element that helps to establish action and mood.

Themes

Amulet is aimed at children; thus, growing up is a major theme. Both Emily and Navin are forced into maturity at the beginning of the series by the death of their father. With their mother kidnapped and then poisoned, roles are reversed, as Emily and Navin risk their lives to save their only remaining parent. The revelation of the prophesied destinies of Emily (as potential ruler of Allendia) and Navin (as commander of the Resistance army) adds urgency to the maturation of the two children but also gives them confidence to fulfill their important roles.

The next major theme is power, as illustrated by the amulets that each stonekeeper possesses. The series explores the fine balance between controlling power and being consumed by it. Throughout the story, the amulet constantly tries to convince Emily to give in to its seductive power. Kibuishi has stated how the original *Star Wars* trilogy is an influence on *Amulet*, which also explores the nature of power from both sides, dark and light. Leon Redbeard vows to help Emily focus and control her powers and acts as mentor, in a way similar to characters like Obi-Wan Kenobi and Yoda. The Elf King provides readers with an example of what happens when power consumes all. As revealed in Volume 3, the Elf King himself is dead but the dark power of his amulet has taken complete control and animates his body. Also, with her red hair and control of pink-tinted energy from her amulet, Emily is reminiscent of Jean Grey of the X-Men, who also fought against her growing dark power in *X-Men: The Dark Phoenix Saga* (2006).

Family is also a key theme in *Amulet*. With the death of their father, Emily and Navin come to appreciate and cherish their family, and when their mother is in danger they stop at nothing to rescue her. The various characters Emily and Navin meet on their journey also become part of their extended family. Even Silas's robot assistants show love and emotion for the two children. Even though Emily is to be protected because of her potential to rule Allendia, she risks her own life in many instances to save these newfound friends. When Cogsley and Misket are snatched off the airship in Volume 3, it is devastating for Emily to leave them behind. The relationship between Trellis and the Elf King illustrates what happens when family breaks down. Even Trellis, who is an antagonist in the first and second books, comes to join Emily's family in Volume 3.

Impact

Amulet is one of the more successful children's graphic novel series published in the first decade of the twenty-first century, and it has appeared on best-seller lists in both the United States and Canada. As the number of graphic novels created specifically for children has grown, *Amulet* holds a firm place in the category, especially as an ideal follow-up to Smith's *Bone*. Kibuishi has said he hopes that *Amulet* introduces children to comics, especially after hearing from librarians, booksellers, and teachers about the need for more comics suitable and engaging for young readers. *Amulet* can be viewed as a direct extension of *Flight Explorer*, his first commitment to offering exciting stories for children, and *Flight*, which introduced readers to stories with strong narrative visuals, lush coloring, and high production values.

Published by Scholastic, the largest North American children's publishing company, *Amulet* has had the unique opportunity to reach a larger audience through Scholastic's sales channels, including traditional bookstores and the school market, book clubs and book fairs.

Amulet is indicative of the growing trend of the darkening of children's literature. The first volume opens with the tragic death of Emily and Navin's father. After crashing through a highway guardrail, the Hayeses' car remains teetering on a cliff. Emily and her mother manage to escape, but their father is trapped inside as the car plummets off the cliff. Kibuishi portrays the death honestly and with deep emotion. At the beginning of the series, Kibuishi raises the stakes for readers, preparing them for a story that is both challenging and meaningful.

The series has been generally well reviewed, especially in library journals, which have praised the series' artwork, character design, pacing, and wide appeal. In addition to winning a state award, *The Stonekeeper* was one of American Library Association's Best Books for Young Adults, selected as a Children's Choice by the International Reading Association, and nominated for an Eisner Award in the Best Publication for Kids category, all in 2009. Also, soon after the release of Volume 1, actor Will Smith optioned the film rights as a vehicle for his two children, Willow and Jaden. Since then, the rights have been reverted, and the film is no longer in development. With only the third book released by 2011 and seven more in the works, *Amulet*'s popularity is likely to grow with each book published.

Scott Robins

Further Reading

Miyazaki, Hayao. *Nausicaä of the Valley of the Wind* (2004).

Nykko and Bannister. *Elsewhere Chronicles* (2009-   ).

Smith, Jeff. *Bone* (2005-2009).

Soo, Kean. *Jellaby* (2008-2009).

Bibliography

Smith, Zack. "An Amulet Update: Checking In with Kazu Kibuishi." *Newsarama*, July 6, 2009. http://www.newsarama.com/comics/070906-Amulet2-Kazu.html

_____. "Searching the Clouds and Taking Flight with Cartoonist Kibuishi." *Newsarama*, November 10, 2010. http://www.newsarama.com/comics/amulet-flight-kazu-101110.html

See also: *Nausicaä of the Valley of the Wind*

ASTRO BOY

Author: Tezuka, Osamu
Artist: Osamu Tezuka (illustrator)
Publisher: Akita Shoten (Japanese); Dark Horse
　　Comics (English)
First serial publication: *Tetsuwan Atom*, 1952-1968
First book publication: 1981 (English translation,
　　2002-2004)

Publication History

Tetsuwan Atom, the Japanese title for *Astro Boy*, was
first published as *Atom Taishi* (literally "ambassador
atom," also known as "captain atom") from April,
1951, to March, 1952, in the weekly magazine *Shōnen*.
In this manga, Atom had a supporting role. The story
was later retouched and inserted into the *Astro Boy* series as a prequel and as an episode of the 1963-1966
animated television series. The first version of Atom
was inspired by Mitchy, the androgynous robot from
another manga by Tezuka (*Metropolis*), and by Perri, a
robot character created by manga author Fukujiro
Yokoi.

　The *Tetsuwan Atom* series was first published
weekly in *Shōnen* from April, 1952, to March, 1968,
and then in other publications until 1981: From 1967
to 1969 the series was published in a newspaper; two
other series/reeditions were published in 1972-1973
and in 1980-1981. There have been many reprints
and several reeditions of the manga, often with
changes, including the 1981 *Sun Comics* collected
edition by Akita Shoten, which is the most renowned
in Japan and abroad as it is the version used for foreign editions. The Akita Shoten collection contains,
in many stories, newly added pages drawn by Tezuka
as introductory commentary. From a philological
point of view, these editions have two negative aspects: Tezuka often intervened by retouching and re-
drawing several details of the pages, therefore even
the so-called ultimate edition is different from the
original, which is hard to find even in Japan, and the
order of publication that Tezuka and Akita Shoten
wanted was not the original order (stories from the
1960's are mixed with stories from the 1950's).

Osamu Tezuka

By the early 1960's, Osamu Tezuka had launched
an animation studio within Tezuka Productions
and brought *Astro Boy* to the small and big
screens. Other productions included anime adaptations of his *Jungle Emperor* (a.k.a. *Kimba the
Lion*) and *Dororo* manga, the latter a dark fable
about a limbless *ronin*. Tezuka's production
cycle remains largely the norm in Japan: storytelling is refined in manga (where it develops an
audience) and is then ported to animation (as
well as to merchandise and games). Tezuka
never pursued medicine as a career, but it informed his later era, more mature dramatic
manga, notably the werewolf-themed *Ode to
Kirihito* (1970-1971), the tales of mercenary
doctor *Black Jack* (1973-1983), and his final
original manga, *A Tree in the Sun* (1981-1986),
the story of a doctor modeled on his own great-
grandfather. Tezuka died in 1989.

　In the United States, the first version of *Astro Boy*
was not Tezuka's original manga but an apocryphal
version published by Gold Key in 1965, licensed by
NBC (which had been broadcasting the *Astro Boy* animated series since 1963), and based on the television
version, but which was severely criticized by Tezuka.
Whether or not Tezuka legally authorized this version
is unknown. In 1987-1988, the twenty-issue color
comic book *The Original Astro Boy* was published by
NOW Comics. In 2002, Dark Horse Comics began
translating, directly into trade-paperback volumes, the
Akita Shoten collection, recognized by Tezuka as definitive. The American edition consists of twenty-three
books published from March, 2002, to January, 2004.
Volumes 1 and 2 were later republished as one trade
paperback in September, 2008. All the volumes follow
the Japanese order of publication of the Akita Shoten
edition, and the pages are turned in order to make
reading the manga more natural for Western readers.
The American edition is translated by renowned manga

scholar Frederik L. Schodt, who offers a contextualizing introduction in the first volume.

Plot

Tetsuwan Atom is a "story manga" (a concept introduced in Japan by Tezuka) consisting of weekly episodes that form various story arcs. It is a seventy-three-episode series, formed by adventures of various lengths in which Atom (Astro in the American version) fights evil robots, solves crimes, and helps humans. The manga was created by Tezuka for children, and it is a prototype of the manga category known as "shōnen." It is also one of the first examples of science-fiction manga in the post-World War II period and offers an optimistic vision of the future.

The narrative structure is based on a prior event, which readers may rely on to understand Atom's psychology and behavior as well as those of his partners. Atom is born from a tragedy. In the early twenty-first century, Dr. Umatarō Tenma (Dr. Astor Boynton II), director general of the Japanese Ministry of Science, has a beloved son Tobio (Toby) who dies in a car accident; overwhelmed by grief, Tenma decides to build a powerful and clever robot whose appearance is identical to Tobio's and who is activated on April 7, 2003. When the scientist realizes that this robot, however sophisticated, is not Tobio and cannot grow as a normal child, he sells him to a circus. After some time, Atom is rescued by the new director general, Dr. Ochanomizu (Dr. Packadermus J. Elefun), a defender of robots' civil rights. Atom begins a new life: Ochanomizu creates two robot parents and two siblings for Atom. Among Atom's best friends are Higeoyaji (Mr. Mustachio), a detective, and young Ken'ichi, a classmate. Atom attends school and plays with other children like a normal child, but he also fights crime and injustice around the world so that robots can live in harmony with humans.

In the American edition of *Tetsuwan Atom*, identifying a coherent sequence among the story arcs is nearly impossible. Nevertheless, the story manga structure allows readers to enjoy extensive and independent self-contained narratives. Some specific stories can be pinpointed that constitute relevant plot turns. "Atlas" (Volume 18 in the Dark Horse edition) marks the introduction of the eponymous robot, which contains the "Omega Factor," a device that makes him evil; Atlas is one of the most powerful robots in the world, and the Omega Factor, which makes robots capable of hurting or killing humans, is an important element of *Tetsuwan Atom*'s mythology. "Mad Machine" (Volume 3) deals with the concept of a "day off" for robots and the subsequent problems among humans; the story is an important allegory about slavery and workers' rights. In *The Greatest Robot on Earth* (Volume 3) a powerful robot named Pluto, programmed to destroy the seven strongest robots on Earth, faces Atom after having destroyed the other robots. "The Blue Knight" (Volume 19) introduces a robot that is a hero among other mechanical men because it defends them against humans who treat them badly; the story is a significant parable about racism and discrimination.

Characters

- *Atom*, a.k.a. *Astro* (English edition), is sustained with nuclear power and has a 100,000 horsepower reactor. He understands sixty languages and has rockets coming out of his limbs, machine guns in his backside, lasers inside the fingers, and other powers and functions. He is a mechanical copy of Tobio Tenma (Astor Boynton). He tries to be as human as possible and has delicate feelings and a deep sense of justice.

- *Dr. Ochanomizu*, a.k.a. *Dr. Packadermus J. Elefun* and *Mr. Pompous*, director general of the Ministry of Science, is a stout, middle-aged man with white hair and a big nose; he is an assumed father for Atom and helps him in his adventures.

- *Higeoyaji*, a.k.a. *Old Man Moustache*, *Dr. Walrus*, and *Mr. Mustachio*, is a stout, bald, middle-aged man who declares himself a private detective. He is Tezuka's representation of the Japanese Everyman, full of common sense. Like Ochanomizu, he is like a father to Atom and often helps the little robot in his missions for peace and justice.

- *Dr Umatarō Tenma*, a.k.a. *Dr. Astor Boynton II*, is Atom's inventor and the father of late Tobio Tenma. He is a brilliant man of science and was a good soul before losing his nerve after his son's death. He has become a sort of evil scientist.

- *Uran*, a.k.a. *Zoran* or *Astro Girl*, is a robot girl created by Ochanomizu as Atom's sister.
- *Cobalt*, a.k.a. *Jet*, is Astro's brother; like Uran, he is similar to Atom but less advanced.
- *Atlas*, a somewhat dark version of Atom, was created either by Tenma or, in other versions of the manga, by other villains. He first appears in 1956. He is equipped with a program called Omega Factor, which allows robots to ignore the basic rules of not hurting or killing humans.
- *Osamu Tezuka* is a metacharacter who often appears in stories and comments on them.

Artistic Style

Tezuka's style in *Astro Boy* is most representative of manga for children in the 1950's and 1960's. From the illustrative point of view, figures are round and soft. Tezuka was inspired by American commercial animation from the 1930's and 1940's (especially Walt Disney's and Max Fleischer's); features such as eyes, faces, bodies, and hands derive directly from those styles. These kinds of figures are visually enjoyable for children, easily readable as images, and create a sense of affection. Tezuka's innovation with these types of characters is that, despite being visually cartoonish, they are mortal; people and robots in Tezuka's works can actually die, and sometimes do).

Tezuka's mise-en-scène is innovative. The composition of the panels within the page is dynamic; panels have various shapes and sizes, giving readers an impression of movement and suggesting a reading pace. In *Astro Boy*, synthesis is fundamental: Backgrounds are drawn only when necessary to the narrative, and figures are always neatly drawn at the center of the scene.

Tezuka's drawings naturally evolved from 1951 to 1968 (and in subsequent versions of *Astro Boy*), but this evolution is hardly recognizable in the American edition for two reasons: Tezuka revised most of his stories for the Akita Shoten edition, trying to homogenize the drawing style, and his preferred order of publication inhibits readers from noticing significant changes in Atom.

Video Games

Media crossover is an important part of any manga franchise, and many successful manga series have anime tie-ins, soundtracks, and video games. The following is a list of video games, for multiple gaming platforms, featuring the Astro Boy character.

- *Tetsuwan Atom* (*Mighty Atom*). Developed by Home Data. Published by Konami, 1988. Available for personal computers and Nintendo, this was the first video game devoted to *Astro Boy*.
- *Tetsuwan Atom* (*Atom*). Developed by Zamuse. Published by Banpresto, 1994. Available for Super Famicom and Nintendo. Like the previous version, this game is based on the 1963 animated series.
- *Astro Boy*. Developed by Sonic Team. Published by Sega, 2003. Available for PlayStation 2. This videogame is based on the 2003 animated series devoted to Astro Boy.
- *Astro Boy: Omega Factor*. Developed by Treasure/Hitmaker. Published by Sega, 2004. Available for Game Boy Advance. This video game uses almost the entire *Astro Boy* canon and was well-received.
- *Astro Boy: The Videogame*. Developed by High Voltage Software/Art Co. Published by D3, 2009. Available for Wii, PlayStation 2, PlayStation Portable, and Nintendo DS. This video game is based on the American 3D animated movie, and its design adheres to the movie rather than to the manga.
- *Astro Boy: Tap Tap Rush*. Developed and published by Widefos, SJ Games, and Tezuka Production, 2010. Available for iPhone, iPod touch, iPad.

Themes

In *Astro Boy*, there are three main levels of interpretation. On the first level, the manga is basically a science-fiction/adventure serial for children, in which each adventure contains a hidden moral, meaning that, thanks to Tezuka's ability to avoid pedantic storytelling, young readers will learn without even noticing.

On another level, the series offers an antiracist, pro-pacifist, and optimistic view of Japan: Many of the characters demonstrate a self-evident otherness and struggle to be accepted by so-called normal people, whether they be humans, Japanese, or earthlings. This kind of moral message is central to *Atom Taishi*.

The third level of interpretation adds both historical and political dimensions related to the international role of postwar Japan, as seen by Tezuka in the early 1950's. Because Atom was "a boy of twelve," one can interpret *Astro Boy* as a parable of Japan's emergence from the terrible defeat (and exposure to atomic weaponry) of World War II. Atom is a child-robot born from collapsed Japan and looks toward a future of peace and dialogue with the world's political powers. In this sense, *Astro Boy* is a long-running series of moral apologues for both Tezuka's generation and, above all, the generation of children born after the war who learned to live by a new set of pacifist values.

Impact

Atom/Astro is one of the most famous fictional characters in the world. In Japan, *Tetsuwan Atom* has had a deep and lasting effect on Japanese popular culture. Its general plot and symbols stimulated reflection among young readers, and its sales have been impressively constant for decades (it is one of the most reprinted and reedited manga of all time). Japanese culture and society have so deeply absorbed *Astro Boy*'s values and content that the manga is considered a national treasure.

Tetsuwan Atom was the first Japanese animated series to be broadcast in the United States, and Astro is one of the most-remembered non-American cartoon characters. Though American audiences did not initially recognize the story as a Japanese narrative, *Astro Boy* was celebrated in later years as a genuine Japanese masterwork. The *Astro Boy* franchise has remained lively in the United States, although mainly among those who watched the 1960's series.

Finally, from a narrative and graphical point of view, *Astro Boy* is an important chapter in Tezuka's long and busy career. Its impact as a series is considerable, but its innovations in style and theme are key to Tezuka's overall canon. Storytelling elements such as the "star system" (characters that recur from one manga to another), and the use of panels with dynamic shapes and visual storytelling, along with Tezuka's courageous sensibility in dealing with important values, have had strong influences on generations of readers and comics creators.

Films

Tetsuwan Atom: Uchū no yūsha (*Astro Boy*). Directed by Rintaro, Yoshitake Suzuki, Eiichi Yamamoto. Fuji TV, 1964. Features episodes 46, 56, and 71 from the original series.

Astro Boy. Directed by David Bowers. Imagi Animation Studios/Imagi Crystal/Tezuka Production, 2009. Features the voices of Nicolas Cage, Charlize Theron, and Freddie Highmore as Astro Boy.

Television Series

Tetsuwan Atom. MBS, 1959-1960. Also known as "Mighty Atom." This live-action, black-and-white series of sixty-five episodes aired in Japan on Fuji TV and starred Masato Segawa as Atom.

Tetsuwan Atom (*Astro Boy*). Directed by Osamu Tezuka, et al. Mushi Production, 1963-1966. This animated series aired in Japan on Fuji TV and NHK from January, 1963, to December, 1966. Adapted and reedited by producer Fred Ladd, 104 of the original 193 episodes aired in the United States on NBC from September, 1963, to August, 1965.

Shin Tetsuwan Atom (*Astro Boy*). Directed by Noboru Ishiguro and Osamu Tezuka. Tezuka Production, 1980-1981. This animated series (fifty-two episodes) aired in Japan from October, 1980, to December, 1981. It also aired in the United States; its title translates literally to "the new iron-arm atom." It is more modern than its predecessors thematically but full of the manga's spirit. In nine episodes, Astro fights against Atlas. The overall tone is more tragic than that of previous versions.

Tetsuwan Atom (*Astro Boy*). Directed by Kazuya Konaka. Tezuka Production, et al, 2003-2004. Fifty 25-minute episodes. This series aired in Japan from April, 2003, to March, 2004. It aired in the United States in 2004. This remake balances dark themes and playful subjects, making it more akin to the 1963-1966 series than to the 1980-1981 version.

Marco Pellitteri

Further Reading

Tezuka, Osamu. *Adolf* (1995-1996).
_____. *Black Jack* (2008-2011).
_____. *Phoenix* (2002-2008).

Bibliography

Gravett, Paul. *Manga: Sixty Years of Japanese Comics*. New York: Collins Design, 2004.

McCarthy, Helen. *The Art of Osamu Tezuka, God of Manga*. New York: Abrams ComicArts, 2009.

Onoda Power, Natsu. *God of Comics: Osamu Tezuka and the Creation of Post-World War II Manga*. Jackson: University Press of Mississippi, 2009.

Ōtsuka, Eiji. "Disarming Atom: Tezuka Osamu's Manga at War and Peace." Translated by Thomas LaMarre. In *Mechademia* 3, edited by Frenchie Lunning. Minneapolis: University of Minnesota Press, 2008.

Pellitteri, Marco. *The Dragon and the Dazzle: Models, Strategies, and Identities of Japanese Imagination*. London: John Libbey, 2010.

Schodt, Frederik L. *The Astro Boy Essays: Osamu Tezuka, Astro Boy, and the Manga/Anime Revolution*. Berkeley, Calif.: Stone Bridge Press, 2006.

See also: *Adolf*; *Black Jack*; *Phoenix*; *Pluto*

B

BANANA FISH

Author: Yoshida, Akimi
Artist: Akimi Yoshida (illustrator)
Publisher: Shogakukan (Japanese); VIZ Media (English)
First serial publication: 1985-1994
First book publication: 1996-1997 (English translation, 1998-2002, Volumes 1-7; 2004-2007, Volumes 1-19)

Publication History

Banana Fish began publication in May, 1985, in the special monthly supplement issue of the magazine *Shōjo Comic*. The magazine is aimed at adolescent girls, and many major female manga creators have made their debut in it. The art of *Banana Fish*, however, was radically different from what was appearing in the magazine at the time, eschewing the stylized character designs and flowery art and writing of early-1990's *shōjo* comics. Yoshida had published several short series prior to *Banana Fish*, but *Banana Fish* was an immediate hit and cemented her status as a great creator.

The series ran until April, 1994. Yoshida also completed three extra chapters, showing some characters' first meetings, and one epilogue chapter set years after the end of the series. *Banana Fish* was collected in Japan through Flower Comics, an imprint of Shogakukan, in nineteen volumes, an additional volume collecting the short stories, an art book, and a guidebook. VIZ Media began printing English-translated chapters in their magazines *Pulp* and *Animerica Extra* in collected volumes starting in 1998. These volumes had flipped (left-to-right) artwork at slightly larger-than-digest size; only the first seven volumes were part of the first edition. A subsequent edition had right-to-left art in a standard digest size; this edition was published from 2004 to 2007 and included two of the extra chapters.

Banana Fish (Courtesy of VIZ Media)

Plot

Banana Fish has two major plot threads: The first involves teenage gang leader Ash Lynx and his struggle for revenge against mob boss Dino "Papa" Golzine; the second centers on the mysterious "banana fish" and the underworld war that erupts over it.

In 1985 Ash Lynx, a seventeen-year-old gang leader in New York City, witnesses two of his underlings attacking a man who gives Ash a small vial, an address in Los Angeles, and the phrase "banana fish" before dying. Ash's men were acting on the orders of Dino "Papa" Golzine, a major Mafia figure who controlled Ash's life for most of his youth, training him and sexually abusing him. Golzine confronts Ash about the murder, but Ash reveals nothing. Golzine allows his men to capture and torture Ash until he reveals the truth.

Meanwhile, Ibe Shunichi, a magazine writer, and Eiji Okamura, his young photographer, arrive in New York City to do a story on youth gangs. Thanks to Ibe's friend Max Lobo, a former soldier and writer, they are able to interview Ash in person.

Ash and Eiji are captured by Golzine's men, and then Ash is briefly put in the same prison as Lobo, where they discover their connection: Ash's older brother was in the Vietnam War with Lobo and went insane, firing on his own unit and saying only the words "banana fish." Lobo was forced to cripple him in order to stop his rampage; thus, Ash swears revenge on Lobo.

When Ash is bailed out, he, Eiji, Lobo, Ibe, and Ash's friend Shorter travel to Los Angeles to track down the address. They find the home of Dr. Abraham Dawson, who has gone missing, and Dawson's adopted son, Yau-Si. Ash finds Dawson's notes on "banana fish," which is revealed to be a drug. Yau-Si is actually part of the Lee family, head of the American Chinese underworld. He captures Eiji and brings him back to New York with Shorter. Ash and the rest follow, and all are brought before Golzine, who reveals the truth about banana fish: It is a form of LSD that can brainwash a person into doing or believing anything. Golzine plans to provide the drug to the U.S. government, which will use it to destabilize communist governments in South America, providing Golzine with easy access to cocaine in exchange. Shorter is brainwashed into attacking Eiji, and Ash is forced to kill Shorter.

Ash and the others escape and begin a gangland war on Golzine. Ash allies with Sing Soo-Ling, who becomes head of the Chinese gangs after Shorter's death; Yau-Si and Golzine enter into an alliance of convenience. Ash is forced to fight Golzine's new lieutenant (and Ash's longtime rival) Arthur, and kills him in a knife fight. When Ash steals several million dol-

---

Akimi Yoshida

Akimi Yoshida, born in Japan in 1956, has to her credit one of the earliest mangas to reach a wide audience in the United States: *Banana Fish*. Though the work is categorized as *shōjo*, aimed at teen girls, it is quite different from the romances and fantasies that have come to typify the genre. Instead, it tells a tale of drug trade in an ultraviolent New York City from the point of view of a Vietnam veteran. In the United States it was originally serialized in *Pulp*, the VIZ manga magazine aimed at mature audiences. Yoshida made her debut at the age of twenty-one with a short story. Her ongoing *Umimachi Diary* series debuted in 2007 and is aimed at older (*josei*) female readers; it is serialized in the Shogakukan-published magazine *Monthly Flowers*. Her *Yasha* and *Kissho Tennyo* both won the Shogakukan Manga Award.

---

lars from the Corsican syndicate and frames Golzine as an embezzler, Golzine brings in Ash's former mentor Blanca, a master assassin. Ash realizes he cannot beat Blanca and surrenders himself and all the evidence of banana fish to Golzine in exchange for Eiji's safety. Ash is adopted by Golzine and briefly forced to work for him; however, Eiji and the gangs manage to rescue Ash.

For his final attack on Golzine's empire, Ash obtains photos, taken at Golzine's sex club, of major government figures raping young boys; Golzine held onto the photos as insurance, but Ash intends to release them to the press. In response, Golzine hires a group of mercenaries, led by the sinister Colonel Foxx, to finally eliminate Ash and his gangs. The mercenaries nearly wipe out Ash's forces, but at the last minute, Foxx betrays Golzine, intending to turn Ash into his puppet and, through him, control the Corsican syndicate. Golzine kills Foxx before succumbing to his injuries, and all samples of and information about banana fish are destroyed. Golzine's blackmail photos are published, forcing the resignation of dozens of politicians, including Golzine's co-conspirators in the banana-fish plot.

Ash puts Eiji on a plane back to Japan, hoping to spare him from a violent life. Eiji, however, sends a letter to Ash (asking him to join him in Japan) and a plane ticket. At the last minute, Ash changes his mind and races to the airport, only to be stabbed by Sing's lieutenant, who never forgave Ash for killing Shorter. In the end, Eiji flies back to Japan, while Ash dies quietly in the New York Public Library, a smile on his face.

Volumes

- *Banana Fish*, Volume 1 (2004). Eiji and Ash meet for the first time.
- *Banana Fish*, Volume 2 (2004). Ash meets Max Lobo in jail and discovers their connection.
- *Banana Fish*, Volume 3 (2004). Ash attempts to assassinate Dino. He, Lobo, Eiji, Ibe, and Shorter leave New York.
- *Banana Fish*, Volume 4 (2004). The group meets Ash's father and travels to Los Angeles, where they meet Yau-Si.
- *Banana Fish*, Volume 5 (2004). Eiji is kidnapped by Yau-Si and Shorter. Ash and the rest are taken by Dino and brought to New York City.
- *Banana Fish*, Volume 6 (2005). Shorter is brainwashed by banana fish into killing Eiji; Ash is forced to kill Shorter instead. Ash and the rest escape Dino's mansion.
- *Banana Fish*, Volume 7 (2005). Ash begins a gangland war on Golzine.
- *Banana Fish*, Volume 8 (2005). Ash takes on rival Arthur in a knife fight.
- *Banana Fish*, Volume 9 (2005). Ash kills Arthur but is captured by Golzine. Eiji is taken by Yau-Si.
- *Banana Fish*, Volume 10 (2005). Lobo and Ibe try to free Ash.
- *Banana Fish*, Volume 11 (2005). Ash escapes Golzine, who brings in Blanca to capture him. Yau-Si allies with Golzine.
- *Banana Fish*, Volume 12 (2006). Ash surrenders to Golzine in exchange for Eiji's life.
- *Banana Fish*, Volume 13 (2006). Ash becomes Golzine's protégé.
- *Banana Fish*, Volume 14 (2006). Eiji, Sing, and others rescue Ash.

- *Banana Fish*, Volume 15 (2006). Ash obtains Golzine's blackmail photos.
- *Banana Fish*, Volume 16 (2006). Golzine's mercenaries attack Ash and his gangs.
- *Banana Fish*, Volume 17 (2006). The war between Golzine and Ash continues.
- *Banana Fish*, Volume 18 (2007). The war ends, Golzine dies, and the blackmail photos are released.
- *Banana Fish*, Volume 19 (2007). Ash and Eiji say good-bye. Ash is killed by Sing's lieutenant. This volume also contains the short chapters "Angel Eyes," showing Ash and Shorter's first meeting, and "Garden of Light," an epilogue.

Characters

- *Ash Lynx*, a.k.a. *Aslan Callenreese*, a beautiful, blond teenager, is the protagonist. He is exceptionally intelligent but suffered traumatic sexual abuse at age eight and murdered his rapist at age nine. He was bought as a "toy" by Golzine, who recognized Ash's potential and had him specially trained. Ash is torn between his savage instincts and his great intelligence and his desire for revenge and the goodness he senses in Eiji.
- *Eiji Okumura* is a nineteen-year-old Japanese man. Ibe says Eiji is his assistant; in fact, Eiji is a former athlete who cannot compete after an injury. Ibe has hired him in an attempt to revitalize him. Eiji is extremely naive. Though Ash wishes to protect Eiji's innocence, Eiji wishes to learn how to shoot and fight.
- *Dino "Papa" Golzine*, the main antagonist, is a hefty, mustachioed, older man. He is a major player in the Corsican syndicate, controlling much of the criminal activity in New York City.
- *Max Lobo*, a.k.a. *Max Glenreed*, is a beefy, former soldier and former policeman turned journalist. At the beginning of the series, he is in jail for punching a cop, where he meets Ash. Coincidentally, Lobo is not only researching "banana fish," but he is also from the same unit in Vietnam as Ash's brother.
- *Yau-Si*, a.k.a. *Yut-Lung Lee*, is a slim, seventeen-year-old Chinese boy often mistaken for a

woman. He is the youngest brother in the Lee family. He is a master of poisons and is tactically skilled.

- *Shorter Wong* is a Chinese man a few years older than Ash who constantly wears sunglasses and sports either a Mohawk or a shaved head. Initially, he is the head of the Chinese gangs of New York and a close friend of Ash. Shorter resentfully and reluctantly betrays Ash.

- *Sing Soo-Ling*, a short Chinese youth, takes over the street-level Chinatown gang of New York City after Shorter's death. Nearly as smart and as skilled as Ash, he initially despises Ash for killing Shorter.

- *Blanca* is a tall, athletic, and handsome man with a cheery disposition. He is a supremely talented assassin, having taught Ash everything he knows about combat and tactics.

Artistic Style

Yoshida's style is stripped-down and realistic. Her characters have expressive features but are more recognizable by their body types and postures; even heavily muscled characters have realistic proportions, avoiding both the willowy bodies of *shōjo* and the hyperdefined anatomy of *shōnen* manga. Yoshida's environments are usually defined in a few establishing shots; most scenes focus more on the characters and their actions than on the backgrounds. Yoshida makes liberal use of speed lines in action sequences, and characters in hand-to-hand combat throw relatively realistic punches and kicks.

Overall, Yoshida's style is fairly typical for late-1980's and early-1990's *shōnen* manga. However, in context, her style is a surprising departure. For a manga that appeared in

a magazine targeting teenage girls, *Banana Fish* had a "masculine" style. Frederik L. Schodt, in his *Dreamland Japan* (1996), compares Yoshida's style to that of Katsuhiro Otomo, creator of the science-fiction manga *Akira* (1982-1990); while Yoshida's backgrounds are far simpler than Otomo's highly detailed environments, her characters have a similar degree of realism in their features and proportions.

Many of Yoshida's characters are based on real people. Ash was initially modeled after tennis player Stefan Edberg and, later, actor River Phoenix. Max

Banana Fish (Courtesy of VIZ Media)

Lobo was based on Harrison Ford. This emphasis on real-life faces adds another dimension of realism to Yoshida's art.

Themes

Banana Fish is largely a character-driven series; its major theme is the dehumanizing effect of violence. Ash is compared to either a wild animal or a divine figure. Yau-Si is obsessed with revenge; once he obtains it, he admits he no longer has a purpose in life. Blanca, the hit man, is only able to live with his actions by strictly separating his professional and personal lives. These characters and others have to deal with the disconnect that comes from living a life of violence.

As the main character, Ash most embodies the primary theme. His violent upbringing and training have made him a creature devoted solely to killing. He has resigned himself to a violent death. Ash is not truly suicidal, as he is driven to take down Golzine, but he does not value his own life.

The one hope for Ash is Eiji: a natural innocent who can look past the surface of the hardened killer and see the scared and lonely boy beneath. Ash is torn between wanting to live a "normal" life with Eiji and trying to protect Eiji from the horrors of his violent life.

The title of the series derives from a short story by J. D. Salinger, "A Perfect Day for Bananafish," which ends with the main character's inexplicable suicide. The "bananafish" of the story are fish that eat to excess and are unable to leave their den. The symbolism of the original story is unclear and there are few direct references to it in the manga; there are perhaps connections to Golzine's self-destructive greed and Ash's seemingly suicidal tendencies, but these connections are tenuous at best.

Impact

Banana Fish was highly regarded in its initial release and sold well in collections. A 1998 reader's poll in Japan's *Comic Link* magazine ranked *Banana Fish* as the top manga of all time. *Banana Fish* was part of a general "manga boom" in the mid-1980's and 1990's as new creators, series, genres, and magazines flourished and international markets opened. The series received similar praise when it was printed in the United States, where it has been regarded as an example of mature, plot-driven comics of a sort not often seen in the United States. In recent years, as more explicit *yaoi* has been printed both in Japan and the United States, *Banana Fish* has been held up as a "crossover" series: more plot-driven than most *yaoi*, but more character-focused than most action manga.

Banana Fish is a *shōnen-ai* or "boys' love" manga; it is not as explicit as *yaoi* but clearly depicts a homosexual relationship. The astute reader understands the unspoken elements of Ash and Eiji's relationship. The naive reader, however, could interpret their relationship as nothing more than a friendship. This is perhaps part of the reason the series was so quickly translated and released in the United States; its relatively tame sexual content and graphic violence fit well with American audiences' expectations.

Ted Anderson

Further Reading

Aoike, Yasuko. *From Eroica with Love* (2004-   ).
Hagio, Moto. *A, A'* (1997).
Yoshinaga, Fumi. *Ōoku: the Inner Chambers* (2009-   ).

Bibliography

Schodt, Frederik L. *Dreamland Japan: Writings on Modern Manga*. Berkeley, Calif.: Stone Bridge Press, 1996.
Welker, James. "Flower Tribes and Female Desire: Complicating Early Female Consumption of Male Homosexuality in *Shōjo* Manga." *Mechademia* 6 (2011): 211-228.

See also: *From Eroica with Love*; *Old Boy*; *Akira*

BAREFOOT GEN

Author: Nakazawa, Keiji
Artist: Keiji Nakazawa (illustrator)
Publisher: Shūeisha (Japanese); Last Gasp Books (English)
First serial publication: *Hadashi no Gen*, 1973-1974, 1975-1987
First book publication: English translation, 2004-2010

Publication History

Barefoot Gen was originally written in Japanese by Keiji Nakazawa and serialized in a Tokyo magazine beginning in 1973. Several English speakers became interested in the work and published an English version in 1978. Volunteer translators have ensured that the series has been published in several different languages. Early English-language volumes were also published by Educomics, New Society Publishers, and Penguin. Last Gasp Books of San Francisco published the complete series in ten volumes between 2004 and 2010.

Plot

Barefoot Gen tells the story of Gen Nakaoka, a boy who witnesses the August 6, 1945, atomic bombing of Hiroshima, Japan. Author Nakazawa's own life experience as a *hibakusha* ("survivor of the bomb") informs much of the narrative. The first volume relates the events leading up to the bombing of the city through Gen's eyes, and nine subsequent volumes explore Gen's life in the aftermath of the bomb, chronicling the period between 1945 and 1953.

In the beginning, Gen and his family live a happy but difficult life in Hiroshima during World War II (1939-1945). He shares a home with his father, Daikichi; his pregnant mother, Kimie; his younger brother, Shinji; two older brothers, Akira and Koji; and an older sister, Eiko. Gen's father is a vocal antiwar activist, and his opposition to the war draws unwelcome attention to the family. The narrative occasionally shifts outside of Gen's perspective to educate the audience about the history of both the war and the atomic bomb.

Barefoot Gen. (Courtesy of Last Gasp Books)

Near the end of the first volume, the atomic bomb is detonated, and Gen loses his father, sister, and brother Shinji to the ensuing fires. His brother Akira had been evacuated prior to the attack, and Koji is serving in the navy at the time of the bombing. Gen saves his mother with the help of a neighbor, the Korean-born Mr. Pak, and delivers his baby sister, Tomoko, in the horrific aftermath of the bomb.

In Volume 2, Gen tries to procure rice for his nursing mother. Along the way, he serves as a witness to the atrocities of the bomb and to the anxiety induced by its mysterious effects. As Volume 3 begins, Gen, his mother, and Tomoko find refuge at the home of Kimie's childhood friend. In an effort to make money, Gen cares for a badly burned painter whose family refuses to go near him for fear of catching radiation sickness. Gen's family also takes in a young orphan named Ryuta, who reminds them of Shinji.

In Volume 5, Kimie and Koji have found jobs, but their employers cannot pay them. Gen attends school sporadically and writes essays about the horrors of the bomb. He helps Ryuta and other orphans build a home where they can collectively work and live. Ryuta, Katsuko, and Musubi live with Natsue, a girl Gen saved from suicide, and Matsukichi, an elderly writer whose remaining life goal is to publish a novel about the atrocity of the bomb. The American occupiers are depicted as vultures who, through the auspices of the Atomic Bomb Casualty Commission (ABCC), prey on the dead and dying but give nothing in return.

Kimie soon grows ill, and in Volume 6, the family rallies around her. Koji goes to work in a coal mine, and Gen takes on various odd jobs. Koji succumbs to alcoholism, so the younger children must raise money for Kimie's medical care. Katsuko and Natsue begin to sew dresses, and Ryuta robs gangsters to get money for the dying Kimie. Gen manages to secure a publisher for Matsukichi's novel.

As Volume 7 opens, Ryuta has recently escaped from his reformatory prison, and he joins Gen in publishing Matsukichi's novel. Matsukichi dies shortly thereafter, and Gen and Ryuta are taken into American custody and interrogated about the novel and their role in its publication. After mistakenly being labeled insane, Gen and Ryuta are set free; afterward, they begin to sabotage American vehicles by putting sugar in the gas tanks. Kimie is released from the hospital but is told that she has only four months to live. The family visits Kyoto, where she dies.

In Volume 8, Gen enters junior high as the Korean War begins. The Hiroshima Carp, a local baseball team, serves as a locus of hope for Ryuta. Katsuko and Natsue make dresses that Ryuta and Musubi sell on the streets of Hiroshima, and Gen gets further schooling in political activism from his teacher, Mr. Ohta. Gen finds that his house is to be torn down to build a road and is ultimately left alone, as Akira moves to Osaka and Koji marries.

In Volume 9, Gen fights to save his house, but workers tear it down. He is further demoralized when Natsue dies from the lingering effects of radiation exposure. The ABCC comes to collect her body, but Gen refuses to let her go and buries her ashes with his family. Gen finds his calling in art and becomes determined to use the medium for ideological expression.

As Volume 10 opens, Ryuta, Katsuko, and Musubi have saved nearly enough money to open a dress shop. Gen graduates from junior high school, but he disrupts the graduation ceremony by declaring the emperor a war criminal. Musubi becomes addicted to drugs and rapidly depletes his partners' savings. Gen falls in love with a young woman named Mitsuko, whose father forbids their relationship; Mitsuko ignores her father, but she soon dies from radiation sickness. Ryuta and Katsuko forgive Musubi for taking money from their business, and he later dies from a brutal beating at the hands of gangsters. In response, Ryuta kills several members of the gang and then flees to Tokyo with Katsuko. In the end, Gen decides that to realize his dreams, he must also go to Tokyo.

Volumes

- *Barefoot Gen: A Cartoon Story of Hiroshima* (2004). Covers the events leading up the atomic bombing and the day of the bomb, focusing on the mindless devotion to the war displayed by many Japanese, the heroism of Gen's pacifist father, and the horrors of the bomb.
- *Barefoot Gen: The Day After* (2004). Details the aftermath of the bombing and highlights both atrocity and resilience.
- *Barefoot Gen: Life After the Bomb* (2005). Details life for Gen and his family in the weeks after the bombing, focusing on the horrors of war and the possibilities of embracing hope.
- *Barefoot Gen: Out of the Ashes* (2005). Covers the two years after the bombing, critiquing American hegemony while showing how active opposition can produce meaningful change.
- *Barefoot Gen: The Never-Ending War* (2007). Covers late 1947 to early 1948, depicting the struggles of the atomic-bomb orphans and analyzing the social costs of the bomb.
- *Barefoot Gen: Writing the Truth* (2008). Deals with events in 1948 and 1949, including Ryuta's incarceration and the return of Natsue.

- *Barefoot Gen: Bones into Dust* (2009). Continues to depict the events of 1949, including the death of Gen's mother, which serves as the culmination of a long-developing theme of assigning equal blame to Japanese warmongering and American acts of atrocity.
- *Barefoot Gen: Merchants of Death* (2009). Spans the latter half of 1950 and examines several lingering social issues, including the costs of drug addiction among returned soldiers and the importance of activism in securing peace in a nuclear world.
- *Barefoot Gen: Breaking Down Borders* (2010). Covers late 1950 to 1951, depicting Gen's awakening to his artistic potential.
- *Barefoot Gen: Never Give Up* (2010). Begins in March of 1953 and details the events leading up to Gen's departure for Tokyo, continuing to examine themes of peace, resilience, and the horrors of war.

Characters
- *Gen Nakaoka*, the protagonist, is a second-grader living in Hiroshima, Japan, when his world is upended by the atomic bombing of that city. While he loses family in the attack, he remains relentlessly optimistic. Nakazawa's alter ego, Gen both helps characters in need and critiques those who do not fully understand the devastating effects of the bomb.
- *Daikichi Nakaoka* is Gen's father. He dies the day of the bombing, but his memory plays an important role in Gen's development. He always told Gen to be like wheat: No matter how much he is trampled on, he must rise up again.
- *Kimie Nakaoka* is Gen's mother. She survives the bomb and gives birth that same day. She is loving and selfless, and her death from radiation sickness provokes family members to go their separate ways.
- *Koji Nakaoka* is Gen's eldest brother. He joins the navy against the wishes of his pacifist father and survives the war. He tries to work to help the family but struggles with alcoholism and gambling. He eventually marries.

Keiji Nakazawa

Keiji Nakazawa was born in Hiroshima, Japan, in 1939, and his best known work deals with the bombing by Allied forces of his native city. *Barefoot Gen* is often compared with Art Spiegelman's *Maus* for not only dealing with complicated moral and historical circumstances in comics form but also helping audiences come to appreciate that such an undertaking is a natural and acceptable one. Nakazawa moved to Tokyo at age twenty-two to pursue manga and was an assistant to manga creator Naoki Tsuji. He has dealt with the Hiroshima legacy several times. The first, *Struck by Black Rain*, he wrote within a few weeks of his mother's funeral. For many years, he gave lectures around Japan in support of peace, and he has said that he and his publishers have faced government concerns about the potential perception of an anti-American perspective in his stories.

- *Akira Nakaoka* is Gen's older brother. He is evacuated from the city with his classmates prior to the bombing, thus surviving. He ultimately leaves for Osaka to become a "peace merchant."
- *Eiko Nakaoka* is Gen's older sister. She dies the day of the bombing.
- *Shinji Nakaoka* is Gen's younger brother. He dies the day of the bombing.
- *Natsue Ohara* is a young girl who was seriously burned during the bombing and remains scarred. Gen saves her from suicide. Later, he saves her again and convinces her to move in with some other orphans, with whom she starts making dresses. She dies from radiation sickness.
- *Ryuta Kondo* is the leader of a gang of orphans. He so strongly resembles Gen's brother Shinji that Gen convinces Ryuta to live with him. He confronts various gang members throughout the series. He helps Katsuko and Natsue run their dress business and eventually leaves for Tokyo with Katsuko.

- *Katsuko* is an atom-bomb orphan who lives with the other children. She is ashamed of the scars she developed due to the bombing. She discovers a talent for dressmaking and hopes for a future with Ryuta.
- *Musubi* is an orphan who helps run the dress business. He becomes addicted to drugs and dies after an assault by gang members.
- *Mr. Pak* is Gen's Korean neighbor. He saves Gen and Kimie after the bombing and reappears throughout the series as an aid to Gen and a reminder of the difficulties Koreans faced during and after the war.
- *Tomoko Nakaoka* is Gen's baby sister, born the day of the bomb. She becomes a rallying point for hope but succumbs to radiation sickness.
- *Matsukichi Hirayama* is the orphans' adopted father. He writes a book bearing witness to the atrocity of the bomb before dying from radiation sickness.
- *The Chairman* is a leader in Gen's neighborhood who openly slanders Gen's pacifist father. He appears infrequently, but throughout the series, he serves as the embodiment of the ruling elite's hypocrisy.
- *Mitsuko Nakao* is Gen's love interest. Her death from radiation sickness causes her warmonger father to become a peaceful man.
- *Mr. Ohta* is Gen's politically involved teacher. He serves as a rallying point for student activism

Barefoot Gen. (Courtesy of Last Gasp Books)

Artistic Style

Nakazawa's artwork is in line with the modern manga style that developed after World War II, featuring starkly drawn characters with large eyes and exaggerated depictions of emotion. Antagonists are sometimes drawn without pupils and appear demonic and shadowy. Nakazawa has admitted to being influenced by legendary manga artist Osamu Tezuka, an influence that can be seen in *Barefoot Gen*. The entire series is drawn in black and white, and the images remain largely consistent throughout all ten volumes.

The panels are read in the traditional Western style (left to right), making the series accessible to newcomers to manga. Nakazawa uses the spacing of the panels to great effect. In particular, in depictions of the day of the bombing, Nakazawa's panels break wide open to better illustrate the horrors of the bomb. A burning horse literally breaks through a panel, and the mushroom cloud from the bomb rises vertically over the entire page. Nakazawa depicts the terrible impact of the bombing by drawing people with sloughed-off skin, festering wounds, and severe burns. His visual depiction of the bombing and its aftermath is the most powerful element of the series.

Themes

Barefoot Gen is a coming-of-age story that is deeply concerned with the effects of living in a nuclear world. From its explosion to its mysterious effects on people after the war, the atomic bomb haunts the entire series. Nonetheless, the series is not nihilistic. The main theme of *Barefoot Gen* is resilience, and this is emphasized by Gen's father's metaphor of a wheat stalk. Despite the death surrounding him, Gen always fights on and encourages others to do the same. "Gen" means "root" or "source" in Japanese, and Nakazawa envisioned Gen as a locus for antiwar ideologies.

The series moves beyond simple resilience to develop a deeply pacifist viewpoint. An omniscient narrator sometimes takes control of the story and provides history lessons for readers about the corruption of Japanese and American leaders and the importance of activism. At times, the narrator addresses readers directly and urges them to remain vigilant so that nuclear weapons are never used again.

Barefoot Gen also explores themes of power and hegemony and moves seamlessly from critiques of the emperor to denunciations of American occupying forces. Critiques of power are examined from multiple angles: Gen's teachers are often portrayed as mindless purveyors of militarist propaganda, and the gangsters who control the black market are depicted as selfish and heartless. Gen attacks power imbalances wherever he sees them, serving as a voice of the common people.

Impact

Barefoot Gen has been credited as the first full-length manga to be translated into English. Through the efforts of Project Gen and Last Gasp Books, all ten volumes are readily available through major retailers. The series has been translated into several languages and adapted into different media, increasing the breadth of its dissemination. It is particularly popular in Japan, where it is commonly read by schoolchildren. After the Chernobyl disaster (1986), the series also became popular with many Russians.

In the introduction to the Last Gasp Books edition of the series, American graphic novelist Art Spiegelman links *Barefoot Gen* with his own graphic novel, *Maus* (1986, 1991), characterizing both works as graphic narratives that bear witness against twentieth century mass atrocity. Despite its ideological ambitions for the eradication of nuclear weapons, *Barefoot Gen* has been unsuccessful in bringing about nuclear disarmament. Nevertheless, the series remains a powerful testimony to the lasting effects of the atomic bomb, and Nakazawa's personal history as a survivor of the bombing gives the story added credence.

Films

Barefoot Gen. Directed by Mori Masaki. Mad House/ Gen Productions, 1983. This anime adaptation comprises two volumes and is easily accessible in English. The first volume is true to the ethos of the series in that it focuses on both the atrocity of the bomb and themes of resilience; however, several characters are eliminated because the story is so condensed.

Barefoot Gen 2. Directed by Toshio Hirata and Akio Sakai. Mad House/Gen Productions, 1986. As in the first volume, Volume 2 honors the manga's themes but condenses characters to a significant extent. The anime film is often linked with Isao Takahata's influential *Grave of the Fireflies* (1988), also about World War II Japan.

Television Series

Barefoot Gen. Directed by Masaki Nishiura and Shosuke Murakami. Fuji Television, 2007. This live-action Japanese television show adapts the basic story from the manga but was constrained by the inherent time limitations of television, causing Nakazawa to complain that the program blunted the impact of his message by omitting issues such as the fallibility of the emperor system.

Jeremy R. Ricketts

Further Reading

Hasegawa, Machiko. *The Wonderful World of Sazae-San* (1997).

Spiegelman, Art. *Maus* (1986, 1991).

Tezuka, Osamu. *Apollo's Song* (2007).

Bibliography

Berndt, Jaqueline, ed. *Comic Worlds and the World of Comics: Towards Scholarship on a Global Scale.* Kyoto: International Manga Research Center, Kyoto Seika University, 2010.

Hong, Christine. "Flashforward Democracy: American Exceptionalism and the Atomic Bomb in *Barefoot Gen.*" *Comparative Literature Studies* 46, no. 1 (March, 2009): 125-155.

Nakazawa, Keiji. *Hiroshima: The Autobiography of Barefoot Gen.* Translated by Richard H. Minear. Lanham, Md.: Rowman & Littlefield, 2010.

_____. "A Note from the Author." In *Barefoot Gen: A Cartoon Story of Hiroshima.* San Francisco: Last Gasp Books, 2004.

See also: *Town of Evening Calm, Country of Cherry Blossoms*; *Astro Boy*; *A Distant Neighborhood*

BATTLE ANGEL ALITA

Author: Kishiro, Yukito
Artist: Yukito Kishiro (illustrator)
Publisher: Shūeisha (Japanese); VIZ Media (English)
First serial publication: *Gunnm*, 1991-1995
First book publication: 1991-1995 (English translation, 1995-1998)

Publication History

Battle Angel Alita was published as *Gunnm* in Japan in 1990 in the weekly magazine *Business Jump*. Starting in 1991, the series was released as nine individual volumes. It gained its English title in translation; English-language editions were released from 1995 to 1998. The author and illustrator, Yukito Kishiro, has produced other series that take place in the same universe as *Battle Angel Alita*. The manga's story was continued in a series called *Battle Angel Alita: Last Order*, which was first published in Japan in 2001 and in the United States starting in 2003. The original series received much praise from critics and fans. The author began a new series after the original *Battle Angel Alita* called *Aqua Knight* (2000-2002), but he placed that series on hold to create the revised *Battle Angel* series.

Plot

Ido Daisuke finds the remains of a cyborg in a large garbage pile. After realizing that the brain inside is still alive, he rebuilds the cyborg and names her Alita. Daisuke and Alita become hunters to support themselves. Alita's first fight is against a monster named Makaku, who eats the brains of others to sate an endorphin addiction. Alita's body is destroyed, and she is rebuilt into a mysterious alien "berserker body." Using her powers and residual memories of the ancient martial art Panzer Kunst, Alita is able to defeat Makaku.

Alita remains a hunter and meets a young man named Hugo. She quickly falls in love with him but fears that a human could not love a cyborg. Meanwhile, Hugo has been stealing spinal columns while working for a criminal named Vector. Vector has promised that if Hugo brings him 100,000 credits, he will send him to

Battle Angel Alita. (Courtesy of VIZ Media)

the midcity of Tiphares, a mysterious dreamland above the rubble.

Zapan, a hunter Alita had previously humiliated, reveals Hugo's crimes to the authorities, and a bounty is issued for him. Hugo's body is destroyed, and Alita hooks his head up to her life-support system after tricking the authorities into thinking Hugo is dead. After defeating Zapan, Alita has Ido resurrect Hugo as a cyborg. Still obsessed with Tiphares, Hugo goes mad when Vector reveals that there is no way to get there. Hugo climbs one of the cables to the city and is destroyed by the defense system.

Distraught after Hugo's death, Alita flees to the western region and becomes a star in Motorball, a dangerous, high-speed cyborg sport. Alita trades in her berserker body for a racing body and works her way to the top of the league. Meanwhile, Ido follows Alita to the west. Along the way, he saves the life of a girl named Shumira and begins living with her. Shumira's brother, Jashugan, is the Motorball champion but is slowly dying as a side effect of brain reconstruction surgery. Alita challenges Jashugan; Jashugan defeats Alita, but he also dies. The fight with Jashugan unlocks some of Alita's memories of being trained in Panzer Kuntz.

Alita returns to the Scrapyard with Ido and Shumira and becomes a singer in a bar. She learns that her berserker body had been sold by her mechanic, and Ido leaves to buy back the body from Desty Nova. Desty Nova is experimenting on Zapan's damaged brain, and it becomes fused with the berserker body. The reconstructed Zapan travels to the Scrapyard and destroys the bar and kills many of the residents. Alita uses a special liquid to battle Zapan. He is destroyed, but Alita is sentenced to death for using a handgun.

Alita is saved by a man from Tiphares and is turned into a special operative called the "tuned." Alita serves the citizens of Tiphares and fights against threats to the city, including those from the guerrilla group Barjack. She falls in love with a mercenary named Figure Four. Alita reunites with Koyomi, an orphan girl from the bar. They travel to meet Kaos, the radio host of the desert, to learn more about Barjack and its mysterious leader, the giant robot Den. Kaos proclaims his love for Alita and begins bringing her to his father, Desty Nova. They are intercepted by Barjack, and Alita battles Den. With the help of Tiphares technology, Alita defeats Den, but he persuades Koyomi to join Barjack.

Kaos reveals that he is actually a dual personality with Den, and the giant robot is remotely controlled through a unit in his chest. Alita and Kaos are washed away in a flood; when they awake, Alita is able to subdue Kaos. Alita inspires Kaos to face his father, and meanwhile she finds Ido in a small village. Ido does not recognize Alita. In a video recorded in the past, Ido states that Desty revealed the secret of Tiphares to him, driving him insane; thus, he had his memories erased.

Alita is told that if she can capture Desty Nova, she will be allowed to live freely. She breaks into Desty Nova's compound but is tripped up by one of his booby traps. She escapes the trap and attacks Desty Nova but becomes trapped in an alternate version of herself. She escapes and decapitates Desty Nova.

Meanwhile, Den has begun his destruction of the Scrapyard. Kaos turns himself into energy and helps the factory forces destroy Den. After leaving Desty's lair, Kaos and Alita go their separate ways. While driving, Alita runs over a small child. The child is actually a bomb sent by Desty Nova; Alita is destroyed in the explosion. She wakes up reborn in Tiphares and is given a new body by Desty Nova. She begins to rampage throughout the city. The riot spills into the central computer control room, where Desty releases "nanobots" that destroy the controls. Desty tells Alita that the city will fall unless she uses her body to mutate at the docking port at the top of the city. She turns her body into a living tree encompassing all of Tiphares. In the epilogue, the Scrapyard builds a tower to connect to Tiphares, and a new, more egalitarian society begins to grow.

Yukito Kishiro

Yukito Kishiro was born in Tokyo, Japan, in 1967 and spent some of his youth in Chiba, outside of Tokyo. While still in his teens, Kishiro won the best newcomer award for *Kikai* from *Shōnen Sunday* magazine. He is best known for the influential science-fiction manga *Battle Angel Alita* and, later, *Battle Angel Alita: Last Order*. The original *Battle Angel* was published by Shūeisha in its mature-readers magazine *Business Jump*. The sequel began with Shūeisha, but following a reported editorial disagreement Kishiro moved the series to rival publisher Kodansha—a fairly unusual circumstance in the world of manga. American movie director James Cameron (*Terminator*) has long been associated with the development of a feature film. Although the move from Shūeisha to Kodansha suggests that Kishiro may be a demanding creative collaborator, he has expressed comfort with the exigencies of film adaptation. He told American journalist Jonah Morgan, "The more important thing is not adherence to the original story but excellence as a complete movie" (Anime).

Volumes

- *Battle Angel Alita: Rusty Angel* (1995). Collects chapters 1-6. Features the stories of Alita's origins and her life as a hunter.
- *Battle Angel Alita: Tears of an Angel* (1994). Collects chapters 7-11. Includes Alita's love for and loss of Hugo.
- *Battle Angel Alita: Killing Angel* (1995). Collects chapters 12-17. Highlights Alita's entry into the world of Motorball.
- *Battle Angel Alita: Angel of Victory* (1995). Collects chapters 18-22. Features Alita's Motorball career and fight against Jashugan.
- *Battle Angel Alita: Angel of Redemption* (1996). Collects chapters 23-29. Features Alita's return to the Scrapyard and Zapan's resurrection.
- *Battle Angel Alita: Angel of Death* (1997). Collects chapters 30-35. Includes Alita's resurrection and her career working for Tiphares.
- *Battle Angel Alita: Angel of Chaos* (1997). Collects chapters 36-41. Features Alita's meeting with Kaos and her battle with Barjack.
- *Battle Angel Alita: Fallen Angel* (1998). Collects chapters 42-47. Includes Alita's replacement (the tuned) and Den's failure.
- *Battle Angel Alita: Angel's Ascension* (1998). Collects chapters 48-52 and "Epilogue." Alita's battle with Desty Nova reaches its conclusion.

Characters

- *Alita* is the main protagonist of the series. She is a cyborg with no memories except those concerning her ability in the cyborg martial art Panzer Kuntz. She has a petite, athletic figure and long black hair and a young appearance. She spends the majority of the series searching for her past and identity. Her combat abilities are exceptional, but she lacks battle experience.
- *Ido Daisuke* is another protagonist and an exile from Tiphares. He is kind-hearted but also enjoys battles. As the one who discovered Alita, he feels protective of her.
- *Zapan* is a mediocre hunter who is humiliated by Alita during her fight with Makaku. He constantly seeks revenge and becomes increasingly deformed and more powerful. He rampages through the Scrapyard and kills a number of minor characters.
- *Hugo* is a young human and a backbone thief. Alita falls in love with him. He is obsessed with reaching Tiphares.
- *Jashugan* is the Motorball champion. His brain was reconstructed after an accident, giving him superhuman reflexes but causing his body to gradually break down.
- *Desty Nova* is a scientist from Tiphares and a source of both aid and adversity for the protagonists. He uses his medical and mechanical skills to experiment on the cyborgs of the Scrapyard. He left Tiphares because he discovered the terrible secret of the people of the midcity.
- *Kaos* is a supporting character and the son of Desty Nova. He is a rogue DJ who broadcasts from the wastelands surrounding the Scrapyard. His frail body and constitution are the result of his psychic abilities.
- *Makaku* is the first villain Alita faces. He is a brutal murdering cyborg who was once an orphan child. He was turned into a cyborg by Desty Nova and became addicted to endorphins; therefore, he devours human and dog brains to satisfy his cravings.

Artistic Style

The style of *Battle Angel Alita* merges realism with science fiction in its depiction of industrial and cybertronic machinery. Kishiro's focus on anatomy means the characters are drawn in great detail, revealing the intriguing connection points between living tissue and machine. This connection is especially prominent in several of the main villains, including Makaku, who is a fusion of bulky, geometric machinery and human flesh. One of the most prevalent images throughout the manga is the human brain. Brain tissue represents the actual life of each individual; the brain and its destruction are depicted in high detail. Kishiro illustrates brain tissue as small, delicate, naturally folding tissue proportioned to fit into the craniums of the characters.

The female characters (especially Alita) appear particularly feminine as a result of their Lolita-like figures.

Each character has a slim frame and pointed, still faces. Alita wears uniforms that are both form-fitting and modest at the same time. The only time she is depicted without her form-fitting attire is in *Angel's Chaos*, in which she wears a wedding gown. Kishiro captures ethnic variation beautifully, as seen in his depiction of Africans and Middle Easterners. The landscapes are a combination of barren beauty and extreme industrial complexity.

Themes

The most important themes in *Battle Angel Alita* are related to either humanity or individuality. Because they are devoid of organic matter except for a brain, cyborgs raise questions about the nature of human life. The brain's organic nature and connection to mortality are placed in direct opposition to the residents of Tiphares and their electronic brains. Alita exists only because her brain has been salvaged from the Scrapyard.

Another theme is the nature of self. Alita lacks nearly all memory, so the individual who she was is not the individual who she becomes. Each memory she recovers dramatically alters her.

Hugo's connection with the body is expressed through his acquisition of his brother's hand. His inability to accept a cyborg body after his first death leads to his inevitable self-destruction; however, his death may be more attributable to a loss of hope. Ido's reaction to learning that his brain is electronic shows the deep connection between the self and the brain. The concept of gender and identity is also alluded to through the ambiguous nature of cyborg bodies and Alita's own sexuality.

Impact

Battle Angel Alita has influenced the genres of both graphic novels and modern science fiction. Alita is a strong female character, which is evident not only in her frank confrontation with each of her rivals but also in her independence and direct approach to life and love. Her personality is similar to characters in *Sailor Moon* (1998-2001); however, Alita is more mature and realistic in her approach to the tragedies of life.

The series deflates the notion of a cyborg as a symbol of technological advancement and recasts it as a symbol of slavery. The series' commentary on human nature echoes those of highly regarded authors such as Robert A. Heinlein and Isaac Asimov. The popularity of the series prompted Kishiro to revitalize and continue Alita's story and to create further characters within the world of the Scrapyard. The series also affected manga's popularity in North America. Filmmaker James Cameron has stated that he wants to produce a live-action version of the series as soon as the technology exists to convey the story.

Joseph Romito

Further Reading

Iwaaki, Hitoshi. *Parasyte* (2007).

Kitoh, Mohiro. *Bokurano: Ours* (2010-   ).

Tabata, Yoshiaki, and Yuki Yugo. *Akumetsu* (2002-2006).

Bibliography

Anime News Service. "MNS Exclusive Interview: Battle Angel (GUNNM) Creator Yukito Kishiro." Accessed March, 2012. http://www.animenewsservice. com/archives/yukito.htm.

Brenner, Robin E. *Understanding Manga and Anime*. Westport, Conn.: Greenwood, 2007.

Schodt, Frederik L. *Manga! Manga! The World of Japanese Comics*. 12th ed. Tokyo: Kodansha, 2001.

Wong, Wendy Siuyi. "Globalizing Manga: From Japan to Hong Kong and Beyond." *Mechademia* 1 (2006): 23-45.

See also: *Akira*; *Sailor Moon*; *Ghost in the Shell*

BERSERK

Author: Miura, Kentaro

Artist: Kentaro Miura (illustrator)

Publisher: Hakusensha (Japanese); Dark Horse Comics (English)

First serial publication: *Beruseruku*, 1990-

First book publication: 1990-   (English translation, 2003-   )

Publication History

A forty-eight-page prototype of Kentaro Miura's *Berserk* debuted in 1988. In November, 1990, the first volume of the manga was published in Jets Comics, an imprint of Hakusensha. After Volumes 2-4 (1991-1992), Hakusensha began serializing *Berserk* through its Young Animal division. As of September, 2011, Miura had completed thirty-six volumes, and the series continues to appear in individual volumes of eight to ten episodes each, published twice a year in Jets Comics collection. Young Animal releases episodes every two weeks, on the second and fourth Fridays of every month.

Plot

By the age of twenty, Guts has lost an eye and an arm, been branded for sacrifice, forced into the Interstice (a zone between the human world and the astral world), and rescued. He is known as the Black Swordsman, and possesses Godot's specially forged armor and the magnificent sword Dragon Slayer. Guts leaves Godot's Cave, inadvertently rescues the elf Puck, and defeats the Snake Tyrant. He then launches an epic quest.

In Misty Valley, Guts is challenged by the Apostle Rochine, a teenaged warrior who intends to free children from the adult world by terrorizing the village in which they live. Guts defeats Rochine but is then challenged to battle by Farnese, the leader of the Holy See's Holy Iron Chain Knights (H.I.C.K.s), who capture and imprison Guts. Guts escapes and flees to Godot's Cave, where he reequips himself with tools, and then departs to find and save his lover, Casca, whom he suspects is imprisoned by Femto. Guts invades Casca's prison, the

---

Kentaro Miura

Kentaro Miura, born in 1966 in Chiba, outside Tokyo, is known for a variety of violent comics, foremost *Berserk*, which in 2002 won the Award for Excellence among that year's Tezuka Osamu Cultural Prizes. It has run since 1990, serialized in the Hakusensha publisher's *Young Animal* magazine. *Berserk* appears at a rate allowing for one collected volume per year. In the late 1980's and early 1990's, Miura also served as the illustrator on two series produced in collaboration with *Fist of the North Star* writer Buronson: *Japan* and *King of Wolves*. Miura lists Tim Burton and Sam Raimi among his favorite directors and his countryman Go Nagai (*Devilman*) as one of his favorite comics artists. He has said that *Beserk* was his attempt to show the influence of the West on his work.

Tower of Retribution; the Tower topples as Guts defeats Mozgus, the Holy See chief inquisitor.

En route to Elfhelm, Puck's former hometown, Guts (joined by Casca and Puck) faces his second of many challenges with the Beast of Darkness—the powerful, inner culmination of all of his hatred and anger. The Beast of Darkness appears often, especially when Guts has donned the Berserker Armor, a malevolent energy that threatens to take over his body and mind. Resisting but not ignoring the Beast, Guts forges on, adding to his Band of the Hawk three runaways, including Isidro, Farnese, and Schierke. With the addition of more energies and equipment, Guts moves on, reaching Enoch Village, where he and his band encounter the Trolls of Qliphoth. As Schierke wipes out the Troll horde with floods by evoking the water elemental (Windinu), Guts battles with Slan, the sole female God Hand. By the time the band reaches the safety of the tree mansion of Flora, Guts appears too vulnerable to defeat the Apostle army and its leader Grunbeld.

Bestowed with the Berserker Armor again, Guts defeats the Apostle army, and, with Flora's assistance, he and his band escape safely. Arriving at the ocean shoreline outside Vritannis, Guts encounters the Skull Knight; Casca adopts a child the band has found on the beach; and the Beast makes another appearance, as Guts fights the serpentine beast Makara. Schierke goes into Vritannis, and Farnese visits her home and her father, the wealthy overlord Federico Vandimion.

Attempting to escape Vritannis, and confronting several Makara, Guts enables the Beast of Darkness to take over. In the process, he inadvertently conjures the astrally projected Schierke, who has summoned the Blaze Rod to manifest as the Dragon Slayer, which results in the annihilation of the Kushan emperor's elemental power. Guts and his team arrive at the Sea Horse, and the Band of the Hawk sets off for Puck's homeland, Elfhelm. In the interim, the Beast speaks to Guts, threatening to eventually return.

Volumes

- *Berserk*, Volume 1 (2003). Collects "Black Swordsman," "The Brand," and "The Guardians of Desire," chapter 1. Introduces Guts. The volume features the hero's first nemesis and foreshadows his destiny to perpetually fight evil and exact revenge.
- *Berserk*, Volume 2 (2004). Collects "The Guardians of Desire," chapters 2 and 3. Features the first appearance of the Beast of Darkness and introduces Puck.
- *Berserk*, Volume 3 (2004). Collects "The Guardians of Desire," chapter 4-6, and "The Golden Age," chapter 1. Features the conclusion of the battle with the Count and introduces the egg-shaped Behelit, the talismanic entity of great demonic power.
- *Berserk*, Volume 4 (2004). Collects "The Golden Age," chapters 2-6. Explores Guts's psychological makeup.
- *Berserk*, Volume 5 (2004). Collects "The Golden Age," chapters 7 and 8; "Sword Wind"; "Nosferatu Zodd," episodes 1-4; and "Master of the Sword," chapter 1. Guts seeks revenge against God Hand demon Griffith. Introduces the good-versus-evil construct with the appearance of Nosferatu Zodd.

- *Berserk*, Volume 6 (2005). Collects "Master of the Sword," chapter 2; "Assassin," chapters 1-4; "Precious Thing," "Departure for the Front," and "Engagement" episodes; and "Casca," chapters 1 and 2. Features elements of medieval kingly favoritism, princess flirtation, and dual jealousies of the feudal-era kind.
- *Berserk*, Volume 7 (2005). Collects "Casca," chapter 3; "Prepared for Death," chapters 1-3; "Survival" and "Campfire of Dreams" episodes; and "The Battle for Doldrey" chapters 1-4. Features the culmination of a century-long feudal rivalry and focuses on Guts and his sword.
- *Berserk*, Volume 8 (2005). Collects "The Battle for Doldrey," chapters 5 and 6; "Triumphant Return" and "Moment of Glory" episodes; "Tombstone of Flame," chapters 1 and 2; "One Snowy Mist" episode; and "The Morning Departure," chapters 1-3. Features courtly, political competition and power battles.
- *Berserk*, Volume 9 (2005). Collects "Knight of the Skeleton," "Start of the Everlasting Night," "The Fallen Hawk," "Demise of a Dream," "Arms Tournament," "The Fugitives," "The Fighter," "Comrades in Arms," and "Confession" episodes, as well as "Wounds," chapters 1 and 2. Demonstrates the consequences of romantic involvement with royal offspring and includes the deus ex machina rescue of Griffith by Guts.
- *Berserk*, Volume 10 (2006). Collects "Sparks from a Sword Tip"; "Infiltrating Windham," chapters 1 and 2; "Festival's Eve," chapters 1 and 2; "Thousand-Year Fifedom," "Reunion in the Abyss," and "A Way Through"; "Bakiraka," chapters 1 and 2; and "Flower of the Stone Castle." Features a strengthening of the bonds between Guts and Casca.
- *Berserk*, Volume 11 (2006). Collects "Devil Dogs," chapters 1-4; Roar of the Wild Beast" and "Forest of Tragedy"; "Mortal Combat," chapters 1 and 2; "Armor to the Heart," "The Flying One," and "The Immortal Once Again." Introduces Wyald of the Knights of the Black Dog.
- *Berserk*, Volume 12 (2006). Collects "Requiem of the Wind," "The Warriors of Twilight," "Back

Alley Boy," "Eclipse," "The Promised Time," "Advent," "The Inhuman Host," "The Castle," "Parting," and "The Feast" episodes. Emphasizes themes of camaraderie and what makes for a strong team. Introduces Guts's temptation to stray to the dark side.

- *Berserk*, Volume 13 (2006). Collects "Storm of Death," chapters 1 and 2; "God of the Abyss," "Lifeblood," "Quickening," "Birth," "Afterglow of the Right Eye," "Escape," "Awakening to a Nightmare," "The Sprint," and "Vow of Retaliation" episodes. Features the misuse of the Behelit by Griffith, the summoning of the God Hand demon lords, and the fire walk through Hell.
- *Berserk*, Volume 14 (2006). Collects "Demon Infant," "Armament," "He Who Hunts Dragons," "The Black Swordsman, Once More," "The Elves of Misty Valley," "Jill," "By Air," "Elf Bugs," and "Berserk: The Prototype." Emphasizes the original vendetta undertaken by the Black Swordsman.
- *Berserk*, Volume 15 (2007). Collects "Queen," "Elf Fire," "Red-Eyed Peekaf," "The Recollected Girl," "The World of Winged Things," "Cocoons," and "Pursuers"; "Guardians," chapters 1 and 2; and "The Misty Valley," chapters 1 and 2. Features a side trek into a deceptively quaint country village.
- *Berserk*, Volume 16 (2007). Collects "Monster," "Sky Demon," "A Bloody Night Sky," "The Space Between Demon and Man," "Firefly," "The Way Home," "Blue Sky Elf," *Conviction Arc: Binding Chain Chapter*, "The Beast of Darkness," "The Hollow Idol," and "The Holy Iron Chain Knights," parts 1 and 2. Introduces a version of Puck's genotype that perhaps explains the elf's dark side.
- *Berserk*, Volume 17 (2007). Collects *Conviction Arc: Chapter of the Birth Ceremony*, "The Unseen," "Night of Miracles," "Past and Future," "Morning of Truth," "Cracks in the Blade," "A Feeble Flame," and "To Holy Ground," parts 1 and 2. Features an enchainment of the hero by the Knights of the Holy Iron Chain.

- *Berserk*, Volume 18 (2007). Collects "Kushan Scouts," parts 1 and 2; "Tower of the Shadow," parts 1 and 2; "Children of the Shadow," "Fierce Believer," "Bowels of the Holy Ground," and "The Witch"; "Spirit Road," parts 1 and 2; and "Pillar of Flame." Features the death of Midland's king.
- *Berserk*, Volume 19 (2007). Collects "The Black Swordsman on Holy Ground," "Straying," "Ambition Boy," "Den of Evil," "The Reunion," "Ambush," "The Cliff," "Captives," "The Iron Maiden," and "Blood Flow of the Dead," parts 1 and 2. Spotlights Casca as she succumbs to pagan culture. The plot ventures into the realm of witchcraft.
- *Berserk*, Volume 20 (2007). Collects "The Spider's Thread," "Those Who Dance at the Summit, Those Who Creep in the Depths," "Hell's Angels," "One Unknown in the Depth of the Depths," "The Threatened," "Omens," "Martyrdom," "Collapse," and "Shadows of Idea," parts 1-3. Features Casca's capture and imprisonment in the Tower of Conviction.
- *Berserk*, Volume 21 (2008). Collects "Leaping Fish"; "Bestial Priest," parts 1 and 2; "Those Who Cling, Those Who Struggle"; "Tidal Wave of Darkness," parts 1 and 2; and "Resonance," "The Sky Falls," "Daybreak," "The Arrival," and "Determination and Departure." Refines, retools, and reinforces Guts's primary goal.
- *Berserk*, Volume 22 (2008). Collects *Hawk of the Millennium Empire Arc: The Holy Evil War Chapter*; "The Rent World," "Reunion of the Hill of Swords," "The Beast Swordsman vs. the Black Swordsman," "Unchanged," "Prologue to the War," and "Fierce Kushan Attack"; "War Cry of the Wind," parts 1 and 2; and "Of Snow and Flame," parts 1 and 2. Features Griffith's return and his perverted version of Midland as his personal kingdom.
- *Berserk*, Volume 23 (2008). Collects *Falcon of the Millennium Empire Arc: The Holy Evil War Chapter*; "Winter Journey," parts 1 and 2; "Scattered Time," "Fangs of Ego," "Wilderness Reunion," "The War Demons," "Banner of the

Flying Sword," "Wings of Light and Darkness," "The Night of Falling Stars," and "Like a Baby." Casca accelerates into madness.

- *Berserk*, Volume 24 (2008). Collects *Falcon of the Millennium Empire Arc: The Holy Evil War Chapter*, "Trolls," "The Witch," "The Astral World," "Magic Stone," "Elementals," "Enoch Village," "Ambition and Reflection," "Troll Raid," and "Mansion of the Spirit Tree," parts 1 and 2. Features a population of militant, predatory Trolls.
- *Berserk*, Volume 25 (2008). Collects *Falcon of the Millennium Empire Arc: The Holy Evil War Chapter*; "Magic Sword," "Mirror of Sin," "Magic," "The Arcana of Invocation," "Raging Torrent," "Shaman," "Qliphoth," "Taint," and "Evil Horde," parts 1 and 2. Introduces Schierke, who is childlike in her zeal but mature in her powers.
- *Berserk*, Volume 26 (2008). Collects *Falcon of the Millennium Empire Arc: The Holy Evil War Chapter*; "Retribution," "Redemption," "Vicinity of the Netherworld," "Whore Princess of the Uterine Sea," "Companions," and "Claw Marks"; "The Blaze," parts 1 and 2; and "The Berserker Armor," parts 1 and 2. Features Slan of the God Hand, who appears from the entrails of slain Trolls.
- *Berserk*, Volume 27 (2009). Collects *Falcon of the Millennium Empire Arc: The Holy Evil War Chapter*, "Fire Dragon," "The Depths of Hellfire," "Departure of Flame," "Demon City," "Dread Emperor," "The Daka," "Demon Knights," "Demon God," "The Sleeping Princess Awakens," *Falcon of the Millennium Empire Arc: Falconia Chapter*, and "The Sound of the Sea." Features the appearance of Grunbeld, who, in dragon form, poses a threat to Guts.
- *Berserk*, Volume 28 (2009). Collects *Falcon of the Millennium Empire Arc: Falconia Chapter*, "Proclaimed Omens," "The Boy in the Moonlight," "Familiars," "Supernatural Fog," "Sea Beast (Makara)," "The Roar of the Sea," "Superhuman (Jnanin)," "Navy Yard," "City of Humans," and "The Kite and the Owl of the Wharf."

Casca bonds with and adopts an abandoned child. Guts struggles against the Kushan-possessed Makara.

- *Berserk*, Volume 29 (2009). Collects "Bloodshed," "Warrior," "A Meager Supper," "Homing," "In the Garden," "The White Lily of the Field," "Mother," "The Ball," and "The Colonnade Chamber." Features battles against new foes. Schierke and Isidro battle pirate slavers to secure the band's passage out of Vritannis.
- *Berserk*, Volume 30 (2009). Collects "Duel," "Suzerain of the Religious Domain," "Enchanted Tiger," "Intrusion," "The Rusted Birdcage," "A Proclamation of War," "Demon Beast Invasion," "Divine Revelation," and "City of Demon Beasts," parts 1 and 2. Farnese sacrifices her freedom so the Band of the Hawk can move on.
- *Berserk*, Volume 31 (2009). Collects "Broiling Bay," "Blaze Rod," "Sword Beast," "Paramarisha Sen'an'I (Wizard General)," "Eastern Magic," "The Coiler," "Bursting Flame," "Thunder Emperor," "Attack of the Demon Army," and "Cloud Cluster." Guts must choose between leaving Farnese and summoning the strength to control the Berserker Armor to fight off the Kushan clan.
- *Berserk*, Volume 32 (2009). Collects "Human Bullet," "Setting Sail," "The Flight," "The Torn Battlefield," "Wind Coil," "The Midland Regular Army," "Hero," "On Board," and "Massive Invasion," parts 1 and 2. Features the reappearance of Griffith as Femto, demonic lord of the God Hand.
- *Berserk*, Volume 33 (2010). Collects "Bubbles of Futility," "A Howl from the Darkness," "Dream of Foresight," "Fog of Death," "Silent Darkness," "Exodus," "Shiva," "The Heavens Shook," and "Naval Battle," parts 1 and 2. Includes Guts's quest to reach Puck's homeland, to get the help of Elfhelm's king to restore Casca's sanity, and find the demonic Griffith.
- *Berserk*, Volume 34 (2010). Collects "Giant God of Blindness," "Demonic Release," "Inhuman Battlefield," "The Medium of the Hawk," "Chaos," "The Flight," "Black Lighting," "Fissure," "Creation," and "Fantasia" episodes. The

new Band of the Hawk, led by Griffith, is compelled to reveal its true beastly identities.

- *Berserk*, Volume 35 (2011). Collects "Falconia," "Solitary Island," "Girl of the Roaring Torrent," "Denizens of the Sinister Sea," "Human Tentacles," "The Tentacled Ship," and "Ghost Ship," parts 1-3. Guts and his entourage find a deceptively safe haven.

Characters

Guts, a.k.a. *the Black Swordsman*, is the tall, muscular, battle-scarred protagonist and hero of the series. He is marked by the God Hand with the Brand of Sacrifice, an actual laceration on his neck that functions as a demon beacon. With an eye missing and an arm severed at the elbow (replaced by a mechanical prosthetic equipped with a magnetic grip), he is a renegade bent on revenge and an eternal malcontent fated to suffer continual loss. As his name implies, he is a proud and wily warrior.

Griffith, a.k.a *Femto*, is the mutable and spiritually morphing antagonist. He begins as the proud and capable mercenary leader responsible for founding the first Band of the Hawk. With a name implying strength (in Welsh "griffith" means "strong chief"), he begins as a competent fighter for the king of Midland and gains Guts's sword-fighting support. He is, however, overly confident, exaggeratedly powerful, and self-serving, and his ulterior motive is to rule over a great kingdom. He begins not to gain but to lose power, and so he reincarnates as Femto, a God Hand demon. As Femto, he rapes Casca, defeats his comrade Guts in a vengeful battle, and abuses his power.

Casca, the only female to lead the Band of the Hawk, has a dark past and a foreboding future. Sold by her parents to a nobleman who immediately sexually abuses her, she seeks vengeance as a swordswoman, ranking in sword-fighting skill behind only Guts and Griffith. She becomes Griffith's lieutenant and Guts's lover and takes command of the Band when Griffith is captured. She endures being raped by Femto, being marked by an Eclipse, and giving birth to a baby. She goes mad.

Puck is a cross between a pixie, fairy, and elf. Though diminutive, he has a strong personality. He is smart-mouthed, frisky, and often silly. He is rescued by Guts and becomes immediately attached to him.

The God Hand is the collective foil to the Band of the Hawk. The five angels/demons are assigned the task of showing the purpose behind human suffering. The God Hand is summoned by Behelit.

Artistic Style

Miura's art is a familiar 1980's manga style. Set up to be read right to left and top to bottom, the individual panels are in a montage format, overlapping according to importance. Sparse dialogue, generous pencil and ink shading, and economical use of panels on the page contribute to the overall ominous tone. A calculated gradation of black juxtaposed with a sudden explosion of white combine with a mature level of detail and clean lines to create movement and action.

Early installments of *Berserk* used densely packed panels to convey action and violence. Later volumes, however, spotlight the developed central characters; thus, a longtime nemesis posing a great threat and a main character in victorious battle mode receive large spaces and are depicted in close-ups, with head shots, or with dark space extending across the larger portion of page space. In general, landscape is relegated to the background, and minor characters are marginalized or diminished in size. Only on occasion does a supporting character command an entire panel.

The dialogue bubbles, captions, and sound effects are unobtrusive. Background commentary is offset with diminished and slightly differing fonts from the foreground dialogue font, a traditional WildWords font that gives definition to primary dialogue and gives voice to primary characters.

Themes

Taking cues from a great number of literary, historical, and popular-culture sources, *Berserk* is a manga with ample intertextuality. Also, the series delivers a generous selection of major, and universal, themes. Good versus evil, duality, and the dark side of human nature are all themes present in *Berserk*. The series' hero is also an antihero: He is purportedly good and fighting against evil, but he is compelled to tap into dark sources for power and strength. The Behelit symbolizes this evil, superhuman, and immortal force, while the Beast of Darkness represents the propensity for human ambition for power gained through malevolent action.

The duality of the characters is illustrated by the inking, which demonstrates the light-dark division. The Shadow Creatures and Creatures of Light further the theme. The conflicting, constantly changing dynamic between Guts and Griffith demonstrates the challenge of dual and then dueling egos. The story traces a tortured hero who is perpetually troubled by his destiny, which he attempts to defy at every turn. Guts's duality is echoed by the presence of masks and masking, the alternating of the setting between human and astral worlds, and the Interstice, where all action plays out. This duality frames the other prominent themes of the manga, including alienation and vengeance.

Impact

Miura's *Berserk* series has resonated with readers all over the world, especially in Asia, Europe, and the United States. The critical acclaim has ranged from respect to reverence. The manga's *tankōbon* are sought after by fans of the manga, and the merchandise, which includes a unique 3D "hack and slash" Sega Dreamcast video game version, has remained popular.

Television Series

Berserk. Directed by Naohito Takahashi. OLM-Animation Studio/VAP, 1997-1998. *Berserk* aired on Japanese television under the Japanese title *Kenpû denki beruseruku* from 1997 to 1998. The twenty-five episodes cover Volumes 1-13 of the manga.

Roxanne McDonald

Further Reading

Shiono, Etrouji. *Evil Blade* (2005-   ).
Yoshida, Akimi. *Banana Fish* (1996-1997).
Yukimura, Makoto. *Vinland Saga* (2005-   ).

Bibliography

"*Berserk*: Book 1." Review of *Berserk*, by Kentaro Miura. *Publisher's Weekly* 251, no. 10 (2004): 52.
"Best Sellers: Graphic Novels." *Library Journal* 1 (October, 2004): 126.
Gravett, Paul. *Manga: Sixty Years of Japanese Comics.* New York: Collins Design, 2004.

See also: *Banana Fish*; *Blade of the Immortal*; *Monster*

BLACK JACK

Author: Tezuka, Osamu

Artist: Osamu Tezuka (illustrator)

Publishers: Akita Shoten (Japanese); Vertical (English)

First serial publication: *Burakku Jakku*, 1973-1983

First book publication: 1987-2004 (English translation, 2008-2011)

Publication History

The character of Black Jack originally appeared in the comic *Tezuka Osamu's One Man Theater Production*, written to celebrate manga creator Osamu Tezuka's thirtieth anniversary as a cartoonist. When readers clamored for more, Tezuka created the long-running comic *Black Jack*, a series of short, black-and-white stories. Published in the weekly manga magazine *Shōnen Champion* between November 19, 1973, and October 14, 1983, the 243 stories in this fast-paced medical drama average twenty pages each and are independent, self-contained adventures with no detailed plot continuity between episodes, although there is continuity of characterization. The first 230 stories were published consistently through 1978, while the last 13 appeared sporadically over the following five years. The series was collected in book form on several occasions, with a definitive collected edition, edited and arranged by Tezuka, published beginning in 1987.

Black Jack was an immediate success in Japan, but it did not appear in English until selected stories were published in *Manga Vizion*, the first English-language manga magazine, in 1995. In 2008, Vertical Publishing issued the entire series of short stories in seventeen paperbacks. This collected edition arranged the stories in Tezuka's preferred order, rather than in order of publication.

Plot

Black Jack is an unlicensed doctor who travels the world, taking on the most serious and, in some instances, most dangerous cases. Because of his lack of a medical license, Black Jack operates illegally and is frequently pursued by the law. Most people view him

Black Jack. (Courtesy of Vertical)

as a mercenary concerned only with charging extravagant fees, but he is actually altruistic, often receiving no payment or even recognition for his kindness toward others. When necessary, he teaches people important lessons while healing them.

Black Jack's background, including the childhood accident that nearly killed him and left him horribly scarred, is revealed gradually. When Black Jack's father abandoned him and his mother after the accident, Dr. Honma, the surgeon who saved his life, became Black Jack's surrogate father and lifelong mentor.

Black Jack is accompanied by Pinoko, who was a parasitic twin living inside the body of her sister before becoming Black Jack's medical assistant, partner, and housekeeper. Black Jack does not realize that she has an unfulfilled crush on him throughout the series; while he thinks of her as a daughter, she considers herself his wife.

The stories in the series combine various genres: medical drama, fantasy, horror, science fiction, comedy, philosophy, and morality tales. Each story is short, averaging twenty pages in length, and entirely self-contained. Although he established his reputation as a cartoonist with simpler comics, Tezuka drew upon his own medical training to create *Black Jack*, a sophisticated comic with more to its plot than mere surface adventures. Often Black Jack must deal with mobsters, government officials, a rival doctor who believes that euthanasia is the only humane treatment for seriously ill patients, an acupuncturist who considers surgery brutal, and psychologically scarred patients for whom he must serve as both surgeon and psychologist.

Volumes

- *Black Jack*, Volume 1 (2008). Contains the stories "Is There a Doctor?," "The First Storm of Spring," and "Teratoid Cystoma," among others. The volume introduces several important people in Black Jack's life: Pinoko, the Black Queen, Kisaragi Kei, and Dr. Honma.
- *Black Jack*, Volume 2 (2008). Contains the stories "Needle," "Granny," and "The Ballad of the Killer Whale," among others. Black Jack encounters the unlicensed acupuncturist Biwamaru, who quickly becomes an enemy. In another story, Black Jack seeks the doctor who donated the skin for his facial skin graft after his traumatic childhood accident.
- *Black Jack*, Volume 3 (2008). Contains the stories "Disowned Son," "Shrinking," and "Dingoes," among others. Black Jack meets his greatest rival, the unlicensed physician and euthanasia provider Dr. Kiriko. In another story, Black Jack is hospitalized with a broken arm, and the surgeon operating on it, only knowing of Black Jack's heartless reputation, decides to put an end to his surgical career.
- *Black Jack*, Volume 4 (2009). Contains the stories "False Image," "The Scream," and "Drifter in a Ghost Town," among others. Pinoko is in danger of dying, and Black Jack must balance his feelings for her with his objectivity as a surgeon to save her life. In another story, Black Jack receives a letter from Kei Kisaragi requesting he perform a frivolous operation that is against his principles.
- *Black Jack*, Volume 5 (2009). Contains the stories "Hospital," "Quite a Tongue," and "Asking for Water," among others. Black Jack must work with Dr. Kiriko to save the latter's father. In another story, Black Jack must save Dr. Kiriko, who has contracted a contagious disease and plans to euthanize himself to prevent it from spreading.
- *Black Jack*, Volume 6 (2009). Contains the stories "Surgical Knife," "Downpour," and "A Body Turning to Stone," among others. Black Jack is arrested for practicing medicine without a license in two stories, but he avoids punishment both times. This volume also contains the series' only two-part episode, in which Black Jack is trapped on an island with a female doctor who falls in love with him.
- *Black Jack*, Volume 7 (2009). Contains the stories "Guys and Birds," "The Gray Mansion," and "A Cat and Shozo," among others. Black Jack deals with the effects of environmental pollution and the refusal of government agencies to acknowledge them. In another story, Black Jack's life is endangered when he operates on a young boy whose grandfather owns land that is coveted by the Mafia.
- *Black Jack*, Volume 8 (2009). Contains the stories "What Lurks the Mountain," "Fits," and "A Wrong Diagnosis," among others. A killer tries to prevent Black Jack from interfering with a planned murder. In another story, Black Jack encounters an important doctor who does not make his own diagnoses.
- *Black Jack*, Volume 9 (2010). Contains the stories "Teacher and Pupil," "Pinoko Lives," and "Eyewitness," among others. Two stories illustrate the type of superficial, uncaring doctors whom Tezuka resents: In one, Black Jack encounters a doctor who orders the amputation of the arm of a talented pianist, and in the other, Black Jack's life

depends on an esteemed doctor who turns out to be a fraud.

- *Black Jack*, Volume 10 (2010). Contains the stories "Island of Avina," "The Most Beautiful Woman in the World," and "Revenge," among others. Black Jack turns down a chance to obtain a medical license because of his concern for the whereabouts of the missing Pinoko. In another story, he reunites with his father, who abandoned him years before.
- *Black Jack*, Volume 11 (2010). Contains the stories "Pneumothorax Operation," "Broken into Little Pieces," and "Days of Vanity," among others. Black Jack discovers he has an emotional problem related to his troubled childhood that prevents him from performing a particular operation. In another story, Black Jack demands an excessive fee from a patient, with unexpected consequences.
- *Black Jack*, Volume 12 (2010). Contains the stories "Wildcat Boy," "The Language of Breath," and "Invaders from Space," among others. Black Jack encounters a faith healer who challenges him to a competition to see which of them can save the life of a stillborn fetus. In another story, Black Jack encounters a group of terrorists responsible for the death of his mother.
- *Black Jack*, Volume 13 (2011). Contains the stories "A Perverse Swimmer," "The Pirate's Arm," and "Death of a Movie Star," among others. Black Jack encounters another parasitic twin, and Pinoko begs him to create a body for this unborn person as well. In other stories, Black Jack deals with life and death, encountering a would-be suicide victim who resents Black Jack for saving him and a dying girl in the care of Dr. Kiriko.
- *Black Jack*, Volume 14 (2011). Contains the stories "The Corsican Brothers," "The Phone Rings Three Times," and "Temporary Love," among others. Black Jack is forced to marry a girl dying of cancer before he can operate on her. In other stories, he performs surgery on the daughter of his childhood mentor and on a Vietnam War veteran who shows no regret for the atrocities he committed during the war.

- *Black Jack*, Volume 15 (2011). Contains the stories "Treasure Island," "A Star Is Born," and "Leaf Buds," among others. A gang leader tries to determine where Black Jack hides his profits from his operations, following the trail of the money to a mysterious island. In another story, Black Jack's fingers become mysteriously paralyzed.
- *Black Jack*, Volume 16 (2011). Contains the stories "Anaphylaxis," "Miyuki and Ben," and "Lost Youth," among others. Black Jack spends a night in a haunted mansion to prove that it is not haunted. In another story, Black Jack seeks a doctor whose reputation is even better than his own.
- *Black Jack*, Volume 17 (2011). Contains the stories "Pinoko Refuses to Leave Home," "Bird Man," and "Two Shujis," among others. Black Jack tries to find foster parents for Pinoko, but she flees from them and returns just in time to help save Black Jack's own life. In another story, Black Jack is torn between operating on a patient and returning home to help Pinoko, who is stranded without power after a typhoon.

Characters

- *Black Jack*, the protagonist, is a doctor who travels the world performing surgeries. He often wears a superhero-style cape and has two-colored hair and a strangely scarred body, hinting at a mysterious past that is revealed slowly through the series. Known for charging high fees for his services, he is considered by many to be a sort of mercenary; however, he often heals people for free, and the majority of his income goes to charity. Although he is believed to be a harsh person, he feels great empathy for his patients and always does what is morally best for all parties concerned.
- *Pinoko* is Black Jack's constant companion. She is an underdeveloped parasitic twin who lived in the body of one of Black Jack's patients for eighteen years before Black Jack removed her and gave her a plastic body of her own. She fills a variety of roles, including housekeeper and medical

assistant, and occasionally provides some comic relief in tense medical situations. She considers herself Black Jack's wife and is jealous of the other women he befriends.

- *Dr. Jotaro Honma* is Black Jack's surrogate father. He saved Black Jack's life after a tragic accident and became his mentor as well after Black Jack's father abandoned him. He dies of old age in the series.

- *Black Queen* is a doctor who primarily performs amputations and has a reputation for being harsh. She meets Black Jack when he finds her drunk, and he quickly falls in love with her. However, she is engaged to Rock, whom she eventually marries after Black Jack saves both his legs in an operation.

- *Kei Kisaragi* is a doctor who met and became attracted to Black Jack when they were both interns. Jealous of other women in Black Jack's life, Pinoko meets her and learns about their relationship.

- *Biwamaru* is a blind, unlicensed acupuncturist who charges no fees for his services but considers surgery barbaric. He becomes one of Black Jack's nemeses.

- *Dr. Kiriko* is an unlicensed physician who travels the world charging outrageous fees to perform euthanasia. He is another nemesis of Black Jack.

- *Dr. Tezuka* is a fictionalized version of Tezuka who appears periodically as a member of the official medical establishment and a supporter of Black Jack and his work.

Artistic Style

From the beginning of his career as a cartoonist, Tezuka was influenced stylistically by early Disney cartoons. While he did not invent the genre of manga, his iconic wide-eyed characters, inspired by such Disney characters as Mickey Mouse and Bambi, influenced the development of a visual

style that would come to dominate Japanese comics. This style is evident throughout *Black Jack*. Although Tezuka completed many of his projects with the assistance of a team of illustrators, as he wrote so many comics simultaneously that he was unable to draw all of them, he was reportedly so fond of *Black Jack* that he did all the drawing himself.

The art in *Black Jack* is primarily simple and cartoonish, although the characters do not have the round simplicity of those in earlier Tezuka comics. Tezuka's intent was for the characters in *Black Jack*, especially Black Jack himself, to resemble real people more than cartoon characters. His characters' faces are drawn with a few simple lines, yet they are able to display a variety of emotions, which Tezuka emphasizes with lines of motion around the characters and beads of sweat on their faces. Youthful characters, including Black Jack, have small noses, while older males have either long and sharp or large and round noses. To add to his aura of mystery, Black Jack has hair that always covers one side of his face, concealing one eye completely. Black Jack's exposed eye is not drawn in the

Black Jack. (Courtesy of Vertical)

large, round style typical of Tezuka's manga, although other characters are drawn in that style.

The main characters are the focal point of the panels, and the backgrounds are relatively sparse. This gives the panels an open, relaxed feel, which adds to the relatively rapid pacing of the stories. Like most manga, *Black Jack* consists of drawings, speech balloons, and sound effects and is printed in black and white.

Tezuka avoids depicting graphic violence in *Black Jack*, restricting himself to occasional "cartoon" violence that is neither realistic nor particularly offensive. However, he does not restrain himself in surgery scenes. Nearly every story includes at least one operation, during which Tezuka generally abandons his typical cartoonish style for a more realistic and graphic depiction of the surgery.

Themes

Although Tezuka made his reputation with manga for young readers, *Black Jack* is aimed at an older audience. The mature nature of its subject matter and themes is apparent from the first story in Tezuka's preferred order, "Is There a Doctor?," in which the spoiled son of a wealthy tycoon is injured in a devastating car accident and can only be saved if another young man sacrifices his own body.

The most prevalent themes in *Black Jack* are the sanctity of life and the necessity of fighting for it against all odds. This is shown repeatedly in Black Jack's acceptance of cases that seem hopeless and his constant battles with Dr. Kiriko, who believes euthanasia to be the most humane treatment for seriously ill patients. When Black Jack believes he has failed a patient, he becomes frustrated with his inability to foil death.

Another theme is the danger of judging people based on outward appearances and preconceptions. Black Jack charges exorbitantly high fees for his services, but unbeknownst to the public, he uses the money for mostly charitable purposes. In addition, Black Jack often deals with patients in ways that oppose the express wishes of the person hiring him yet are the morally proper actions for all concerned parties.

Tezuka was a trained doctor who never practiced, and his concerns about the medical establishment are evident throughout *Black Jack*. Black Jack rejects the

---

Osamu Tezuka

To compare manga legend Osamu Tezuka (born in 1928) to entrepreneurial American storyteller Walt Disney is not uncommon, but do so while imagining an alternate time line, in which Disney neither was so consumed by the construction of a business that he forwent the personal creation of new stories nor so fully moved beyond the printed page in favor of animation. Tezuka is said to have drawn more than 150,000 pages of manga in his life, many volumes of which became seeds of entire industries. *Astro Boy* (1952-1968) symbolizes national pride as much as it does manga for young boys. *Princess Knight*, originating a year later, is said to be the template for *shōjo*, or young girls' manga. After domestic wartime service, Tezuka trained in medicine, but forsook it in favor of the Japanese entertainment industry. He initially made his name in 1947 with the publication of the hit *New Treasure Island*.

---

hypocrisy of the medical profession, and he deliberately takes on the difficult cases no other doctors dare handle. Several stories deal with Black Jack's interactions with callous or fraudulent doctors, while several others display Tezuka's distrust of faith healing.

Impact

During his career, Tezuka was responsible for several revolutions in the field of manga. In addition to popularizing an iconic visual style that has become recognizable worldwide, he created comics that had substantial plots and emotional depth. *Astro Boy* (1952-1968) was the first popular manga based on detailed, emotional plots rather than cartoonish jokes. After creating comics featuring boys' adventures, he began the first series geared toward girls, incorporating long, detailed, and emotional story lines. Tezuka's success during the 1950's inspired other manga artists to begin writing more serious adventures for a slightly older audience. Rejecting the comics they had read as children, including the early works of Tezuka, they created the term "drama comics" to represent the level of sophistication they strove to reach. In turn, this influenced Tezuka to create comics for adult readers, including *Black Jack*.

A series of morality plays in miniature, *Black Jack* combines exciting adventures with thought-provoking ethical dilemmas. Each story in the series contains a philosophical aspect, with Black Jack either teaching someone a much-needed lesson or displaying behavior that influences someone for the better. The characters and their emotions are more complex than in Tezuka's earlier comics, representing a trend toward well-rounded manga characters that would continue to develop in the subsequent decades. A significantly successful series, *Black Jack* set the standard for the adult and young-adult manga that followed it.

Films

Black Jack: The Movie. Directed by Osamu Dezaki. Tezuka Production/Shochiku, 1996. This animated film adaptation is a science-fiction drama involving a scientist who breeds a group of superhumans. When the superhumans begin to deteriorate physically, the scientist hires Black Jack to find a cure for them. Directed by one of Tezuka's protégés, the film features dark overtones and violence generally absent from the manga.

Black Jack: The Two Doctors of Darkness. Directed by Makoto Tezuka. Tezuka Production, 2005. This animated film combines elements from several episodes of the comic to create a single story, which involves a group of researchers who kidnap Black Jack and force him to seek a cure for an epidemic that is afflicting them. To complicate matters, Dr. Kiriko plans to euthanize the researchers.

Television Series

Black Jack. Directed by Osamu Dezaki. Tezuka Production, 1993-2000. This animated adaptation is a series of ten independent episodes made for direct home release. The episodes are considerably more graphic in terms of both violence and nudity than either the original manga or subsequent dramatizations. Black Jack's origin is not explored in these episodes, nor is that of Pinoko. Black Jack's nemesis, Dr. Kiriko, appears in one story.

Black Jack: The Four Miracles of Life. Directed by Makoto Tezuka. Tezuka Production, 2003. This television special of four self-contained episodes adapts the manga stories "Is There a Doctor?," "Disowned Son," "U-18 Knew," and "Sometimes Like Pearls." The plots differ somewhat from the original stories, but the characters and themes remain faithful to the comic.

Black Jack 21. Directed by Satoshi Kuwahara. Tezuka Production, 2006. This seventeen-episode series adapts various stories from the manga and features all of the major characters, including Pinoko, Dr. Kiriko, and Dr. Honma. While more intense and slightly darker than the comic and differing somewhat in plot, it remains faithful to the spirit of the original manga.

Robert Sabella

Further Reading

Sōryō, Fuyumi. *Eternal Sabbath* (2006-2007).

Tatsumi, Yoshihiro. *A Drifting Life* (2009).

Urasawa, Naoki. *Pluto: Urasawa x Tezuka* (2009-2010).

Bibliography

Bunche, Steve, "Tezuka: Discovering a God of Manga." *Publishers Weekly*, November 24, 2009. http://www.publishersweekly.com/pw/by-topic/new-titles/adult-announcements/article/26010-tezuka-discovering-a-god-of-manga-.html.

McCarthy, Helen. *The Art of Osamu Tezuka: God of Manga*. New York: Abrams Comic Arts, 2009.

Power, Natsu Onoda. *God of Comics: Osamu Tezuka and the Creation of Post-World War II Manga*. Jackson: University Press of Mississippi, 2009.

See also: *A Drifting Life; Pluto series; Astro Boy*

BLADE OF THE IMMORTAL

Author: Samura, Hiroaki
Artist: Hiroaki Samura (illustrator); Tomoko Saito (letterer and retoucher); Wayne Truman (letterer and retoucher)
Publisher: Dark Horse Comics
First serial publication: *Mugen no Jūnin*, 1994- (English translation, 1996-2007)
First book publication: English translation, 1997-

Hiroaki Samura

Hiroaki Samura was born in 1967 in Chiba, outside Tokyo, and later attended the Tama Art University in Tokyo. Samura is best known for the ongoing samurai series *Blade of the Immortal*, which has been published by Kodansha since 1994. He has described how strong the influence of Katsuhiro Otomo (*Akira*) was and how he felt the need to distinguish his work from him. In the United States, his manga has won a readership through its publication by Dark Horse Comics, and it won the Eisner Award for Best U.S. Edition of Foreign Material in 2000. Samura's school experiences at Tama surfaced in his romantic series *Ohikkoshi*.

Publication History

Blade of the Immortal was first published in Kodansha's *Afternoon* magazine in 1994. It was picked up by Dark Horse Comics and released in pamphlets in 1996 and then collected into graphic novels, the first one appearing in 1997. The last pamphlet-style comic is issue 131 (November, 2007). Thereafter, Dark Horse Comics released only the graphic novel format.

A common practice in U.S. manga publishing in the 1990's was "flipping" in which publishers "mirrored" manga pages so that the comics would read left to right, Western style. At creator Hiroaki Samura's request, Dark Horse Comics did not use this method and instead cut up the pages, rearranged the panels, and redid the lettering. These changes were made so that the fighters would not appear to be left-handed and Manji's personal symbol would not appear to be a Nazi swastika, rather than the counterclockwise Buddhist symbol. Although Dark Horse Comics acknowledged that this process can disrupt the flow between pages and panels, the publisher accommodated Samura's wishes.

Plot

Set in the late eighteenth century, *Blade of the Immortal* follows the path of vengeance taken by Rin Asano, a sixteen-year-old girl whose family was murdered before her eyes by Anotsu and his sword school, the Ittōryū. She enlists the aid of Manji, a swordsman whose body is inhabited by *kessen-chu*, or "sacred bloodworms," that make him immortal. Because he has killed one hundred good men, he vows to kill one

thousand evil men, which will end his immortality. The first volume recounts how Manji accidentally killed his sister's husband and her resulting madness and death.

The first five volumes depict the battles between Manji and Rin's foes. Manji and Rin kill Sabato Kuroi, who killed Rin's father; the immortal Eiku Shizuma; and Araya Kawakami, the man who raped Rin's mother. Manji also fights with Ittōryū members Magatsu, who survives and reveals the secret of Manji's immortality, and Makie, who nearly kills Manji.

The next volumes, from *Dark Shadows* to *The Gathering II*, introduce members of the mysterious Mugai-ryū, who also seek to kill the Ittōryū. Meanwhile, Anotsu is offered an alliance with Habaki, an official working for the shogun. Despite their concerns about the sadistic Mugai-ryū member Shira, Rin and Manji ally with Hyakurin and the Mugai-ryū, who share the common goal of killing Anotsu. Their ambush fails, and Anotsu escapes to Kaga; the group is stymied by the fact that they lack a *tegata*—an official pass that will allow them to move through checkpoints.

Rin departs to travel by herself, and Manji ambushes several Ittōryū members with help from Hyurakin. After a fierce fight, he kills the trio, but not before the *tegata* has been ruined by the bloodshed. Master Sōri appears in the aftermath and takes Manji back to his house, revealing that he could have gotten Manji a *tegata* had he merely asked. There, Manji meets and briefly allies with Ittōryū member Magatsu, who is on the hunt for Shira.

The volumes *Secrets* through *Last Blood* follow the different characters on their paths. Anotsu's trip to Kaga is an attempt to forge an alliance with a sword school by marrying the founder's daughter. However, the government orders the school to kill Anotsu. The volume also covers Rin's struggles to cross the mountain to Kaga; she meets Anotsu accidentally and travels with him. Finally, while Rin helps an ill Anotsu in *Last Blood*, the sword school catches up with them. Manji, Magatsu, and Makie arrive to rescue the pair. Temporary alliances dissolve, and the volume concludes with Giichi taking Manji to his boss, Habaki, which begins a new story arc.

The next seven volumes, from *Trickster* to *Demon Lair II*, recount Manji's imprisonment in the catacombs under Edo castle. Habaki, the shadow leader of the Mugai-ryū, is an official under the shogun, and he permits gruesome experiments to be performed on Manji. His goal is to learn how to pass on Manji's immortality to others. Meanwhile, Rin searches for Manji and is able to do so only with the help of Dōa and Isaku, new members of the Ittōryū.

The next story arc recounts the aftermath of events under Edo castle. Habaki has been commanded to commit seppuku. Since he is given a month before he must perform the ritual suicide, he moves swiftly to destroy the Ittōryū completely. Anotsu, who only witnesses the chaos caused by the events at Edo castle, also moves to gather his forces. Meanwhile, Manji recovers from his ordeal, but he has left his hand in the dungeon. Shira has taken it and has plans of his own. The volume *Footsteps* concludes with another chance encounter between Anotsu and Rin, the former wanting to speak with the latter for unknown reasons.

Volumes

- *Blade of the Immortal: Blood of a Thousand* (1997). Collects issues 1-6, featuring Rin hiring Manji as her bodyguard.

- *Blade of the Immortal: Cry of the Worm* (1998). Collects issues 7-12, featuring Manji fighting with two members of the Ittōryū.
- *Blade of the Immortal: Dreamsong* (1999). Collects issues 12-18, featuring Manji's fight with Ittōryū swordswoman Makie.
- *Blade of the Immortal: On Silent Wings* (1999). Collects issues 19-22, featuring Rin's accidental meeting with Anotsu.
- *Blade of the Immortal: On Silent Wings II* (2000). Collects issues 23-28, featuring Araya Kawakami, who raped Rin's mother.
- *Blade of the Immortal: Dark Shadows* (2000). Collects issues 29-34, introducing the Mugai-ryū, assassins who are collecting the heads of the Ittōryū.
- *Blade of the Immortal: Heart of Darkness* (2001). Collects issues 35-42, featuring Rin and Manji's alliance with the Mugai-ryū and its consequences.
- *Blade of the Immortal: The Gathering* (2001). Collects issues 43-49, featuring Rin's departure and Manji's next difficult fight.
- *Blade of the Immortal: The Gathering II* (2001). Collects issues 51-57, featuring the conclusion of Manji's fight and chronicling Rin's solo adventure.
- *Blade of the Immortal: Secrets* (2002). Collects issues 58-65, focusing on Anotsu and the alliance offered to him by a sword school.
- *Blade of the Immortal: Beasts* (2002). Collects issues 66-72, featuring Hyakurin's rape and torture by low-ranking members of the Ittōryū and flashbacks to her past.
- *Blade of the Immortal: Autumn Frost* (2003). Collects issues 73-80, featuring the formation of temporary alliances and former Ittōryū member Magatsu's quest for revenge against the sadistic Shira.
- *Blade of the Immortal: Mirror of the Soul* (2004). Collects issues 81-89, featuring Rin's travels with Anotsu.
- *Blade of the Immortal: Last Blood* (2005). Collects issues 90-98, featuring Rin and Manji's reunion and revealing the identity of the person controlling the Mugai-ryū.

- *Blade of the Immortal: Trickster* (2006). Collects issues 99-105, featuring Manji's capture by those who want to discover the secret of his immortality.
- *Blade of the Immortal: Short Cut* (2006). Collects issues 106-111, featuring Rin's encounter with Dōa and Isaku, members of the Ittōryū, and the gruesome experiments performed on Manji.
- *Blade of the Immortal: On the Perfection of Anatomy* (2007). Collects issues 112-117, featuring the doctor Burando's struggles with the ethics of experimenting on Manji and death-row prisoners.
- *Blade of the Immortal: The Sparrow Net* (2008). Collects issues 118-126, featuring the formation of an alliance between Rin and Dōa.
- *Blade of the Immortal: Badger Hole* (2008). Collects issues 127-131, featuring Dōa and Rin's attempt to rescue Isaku, who has been taken by the same men holding Manji.
- *Blade of the Immortal: Demon Lair* (2008). Collects chapters 121-129, featuring Rin's reunion with Manji and their battle against a series of dangerous foes in the catacombs.
- *Blade of the Immortal: Demon Lair II* (2009). Collects chapters 130-136, following Rin, Manji, Dōa, and Isaku as they battle the insane creature that Burando created in his experiments.
- *Blade of the Immortal: Footsteps* (2010). Collects chapters 137-143, featuring Habaki's quest to destroy the Ittōryū and introducing his illegitimate daughter, Ryō.
- *Blade of the Immortal: Scarlet Swords* (2011). Collects chapters 144-148, featuring Anotsu and the Ittōryū's attempts to foil Habaki.

Characters

- *Manji*, a.k.a. *Killer of One Hundred*, is a tall, one-eyed swordsman who earned his nickname by killing policemen while working for his mob bosses. When all his wounds are healed by the *kessen-chu*, or sacred bloodworms, that he is given by a Buddhist nun, he vows to kill one thousand evil men to free himself from the curse of immortality. He has a cavalier attitude toward his fights, frequently acknowledging that his im-

mortal body has ruined his sword skills. He often wears a kimono decorates with a *sauvastika*, a Japanese Buddhist symbol of good fortune, and he carries an impossible number of oddly shaped swords and knives. In addition to having lost one eye, he has a wound that stretches across the bridge of his nose, his missing eye, and his forehead, which he received before he had the *kessen-chu*.

- *Rin Asano* is the daughter of the owner of the Mutenichi-ryū, a venerable sword school. Her family was murdered before her eyes by Anotsu and the Ittōryū. Though fourteen at the time, she vowed vengeance. At the age of sixteen, she persuades Manji to be her bodyguard and to aid her in her revenge. She often wears a kimono with flames on the hem and sleeves in which she hides short knives that she hurls at her targets.
- *Kagehisa Anotsu* is a tall and slender man who wields a heavy, blunt ax and is the leader of the Ittōryū. His grandfather was expelled from the Asano family sword school for using a foreign weapon, and the resulting family shame causes Anotsu to orchestrate the murder of Rin's family and seek to destroy all sword schools. He loves the swordswoman Makie, whom he met as a child, and is briefly married to Hisoka Ibane for political reasons.
- *Makie Otono-Tachibana* is a swordswoman of the Ittōryū and the best fighter in the school. She wields a three-jointed spear, which she hides in a *shamisen*, a musical instrument. She is in love with Anotsu, whose life she saved when they were children.
- *Kagimura Habaki* is an officer serving under the shogun who offers an alliance to Anotsu but secretly plots the Ittōryū's destruction. He is a tall, mustached samurai who carries traditional weapons.
- *Hyakurin* is a member of the Mugai-ryū who allies with Rin and Manji. She dyes her hair blond and uses a crossbow with poison darts. She is on death row because she murdered her samurai husband for killing their son.

- *Shira* is a member of the Mugai-ryū who allies with Rin and Manji, but his sadistic tendencies put an end to their alliance. Manji and Magatsu each cut off one of his hands. He is thought to be dead until he is discovered in the catacombs under Edo castle.

- *Eiku Shizuma* is a member of the Ittōryū who poses as a wandering monk, but in his fight with Manji, he reveals that he also possesses the *kessen-chu* and has been alive for more than two hundred years. He poisons Manji with *kessen-satsu*, literally "bloodworm killer," which opens all of the wounds that the bloodworms had healed. Manji kills him after recovering.

- *Taito Magatsu* is a member of the Ittōryū who was present the night Rin's family was murdered. He survives his first battle with Manji and reveals Manji's immortality to the rest of the Ittōryū. He wears a mask over his lower face and has spiky hair, and his sword hides a dagger in its handle.

Artistic Style

A classically trained artist, Samura has been praised for his realistic drawings of the human body and his use of perspective. His character design is anachronistic; characters have spiky, punk hairstyles and wear sunglasses. As is common in manga, the work is presented in black and white. Throughout Samura's work, he uses the "scratchiness" of his drawings to depict speed and violence.

In early volumes, Samura depicts the climaxes of the characters' fights as full-page meditations on violence featuring entangled bodies, weapons, clothing, and unrelated symbols and images. These drawings are reminiscent of Japanese wood-block prints, such as those from the famous *ukiyo-e* artist Yoshitoshi Tsukioka. Although Samura has never claimed Yoshitoshi as an influence, instead citing the influence of manga artist Katsuhiro Otomo, both use the entire page and flatten the foreground and background as if the action can barely be contained by the borders. This technique prompts the reader to pause and consider the artwork carefully in order to determine which body part belongs to which character. Later in the series, Samura abandons these full-page scenes to focus on more realistic depictions of the dramatic action. His panel layouts and pacing show great sophistication, allowing for quiet moments that illustrate the characters' reflections on past events.

Themes

The major theme of *Blade of the Immortal* is what it means to be human. The series reflects the notion of integrity in both senses of the word: physical wholeness and ethical consistency. Though Manji evokes awe and horror in his foes when they watch him rise from the dead, pull knives from his flesh, and reattach his severed limbs, he remains whole in both mind and body after every violation. His stability of mind reflects the stability of his flesh. In contrast, when Burando's test subjects survive the process of transplanting Manji's *kessen-chu*, the immortal beings they become are obscene, insane "gods."

Throughout the series, numerous characters practice body modification as a reflection of their morality. Sabato Kuroi attaches the heads of women he "loves" to his shoulders. Likewise, Shira, who loses his hand to Manji, carves off his arm's flesh and sharpens the bones into daggers; his sadism turns to masochism, as each attack causes him great pain. In contrast, the swordswoman Makie is able to demonstrate her moral integrity by not getting a drop of blood on her when slaughtering her enemies.

The body politic, as represented by the government and the dojo, forbids knowledge from the West to ensure its own integrity; no Western medicine, art, weapons, or fighting styles are permitted. However, there are members of the ruling institution who are permitted to transgress: Master Sōri becomes the shogun's ninja so he can collect taboo art, and the officer Habaki permits Burando to perform the autopsies and vivisections he has witnessed in the West. Habaki desires to use Manji's immortality to perpetuate institutional power, and the institutionalized violence that he inflicts on Manji's body transcends any violation that Manji has experienced in his previous battles. Similarly, those who reject the rigid rules of the dojo, such as Anotsu and the other members of the Ittōryū, are targeted for destruction.

Perhaps the most important rule is the one that governs revenge: Samurai may kill, but no one else has that right. Though Rin has filled out the paperwork necessary for a recognized vendetta, which is her right as a samurai's daughter, she receives no response. When asked by Makie in *Dreamsong* if killing people is the right path for her, Rin answers, "If samurai say that killing for their master is a noble cause . . . then isn't getting your hands bloody for your own parents . . . more *human*?" Rin is unable to achieve institutional justice and must make her own path. The family unit, rather than the dojo attached to it, is the foundation of true societal integrity; the government seeks only to secure its own power.

Ultimately, Rin's humanity is the central concern of the series—her revenge will not transgress her morality. Through a series of accidents, she meets her foe, Anotsu, and when given the chance to kill him with her own hands, she refuses to do so; instead, she actively helps him to survive. Though not concluded as of 2012, the story appears to be moving toward a resolution between Rin and Anotsu that may break the cycle of revenge, but the characters may also seek a redress of wrongs against corrupt institutions.

Impact

One of the first successful manga to be published in the United States, *Blade of the Immortal* proved that there was an audience for Japanese comics among American readers. Volumes of *Blade of the Immortal* have regularly appeared on the lists of the best-selling graphic novels compiled by Diamond, a comics distributor. The series paved the way for other *seinen* stories that feature graphic violence, including the *Berserk* series (2003-), to be published in the United States. *Blade of the Immortal*'s anachronistic take on Japanese history and the samurai story has also been influential, likely inspiring elements of the postmodern anime series *Samurai Champloo* (2004-2005).

Television Series

Blade of the Immortal. Anime Works (2009-2010). Originally produced by Bee Train in 2008, the series adapts thirteen stories from the manga, from *Blood of a Thousand* to *On Silent Wings*.

Wendy Goldberg

Further Reading

Koike, Kozue, and Koseki Gōjima. *Lone Wolf and Cub* (2000-2002).

Miura, Kentaro. *Berserk* (2003-).

Samura, Hiroaki. *Ohikkoshi* (2006).

Bibliography

Goldberg, Wendy. "The Manga Phenomenon in America." In *Manga: An Anthology of Global and Cultural Perspectives*, edited by Toni Johnson-Woods. New York: Continuum, 2010.

Stevenson, Jason. *Yoshitoshi's Strange Tales*. Amsterdam: Hotei, 2005.

Tong, Ng Suat. "A Swordsman's Saga: Blade of the Immortal." *The Comics Journal* 228 (November, 2000): 42-45.

See also: *Astro Boy; Adolf: A Tale of the Twentieth Century; Akira*

BLEACH

Author: Kubo, Tite

Artist: Tite Kubo (illustrator); Andy Ristaino (letterer); Sean Lee (cover artist)

First serial publication: *Burīchi*, 2001- (English serialization, 2007-)

First book publication: 2002- (English translation, 2004-)

Publisher: Shūeisha (Japanese); VIZ Media (English)

Publication History

Tite Kubo started *Bleach* in 2001; the manga continues to be serialized in *Weekly Shōnen Jump* and targets boys between ages twelve and eighteen. Because of *Bleach*'s popularity, Shūeisha made the series available in larger volumes. These *tankōbon* (paperback) volumes have sold well in Japan. *Bleach* has also been popular in the United States, where the manga is published by VIZ Media.

Plot

Ichigo, *Bleach*'s protagonist, appears to be a normal high school freshman. However, for as long as he can remember, he has been able to see ghosts. Eventually, he encounters the soul reaper Rukia, who is amazed that Ichigo can see her; she decides to explain who she is. As they talk, however, an evil spirit attacks Ichigo's family. Rukia's fight with the "hollow" (bad soul) is unsuccessful because of Ichigo's interference, and their only chance for survival is for Rukia to turn Ichigo into a substitute soul reaper. Ichigo turns out to be an incredibly strong soul reaper and defeats the hollow without much effort.

The next day, everything seems to be back to normal. However, when Ichigo gets to class, Rukia is there. She explains that she meant to give Ichigo only half of the power with which he has been endowed, but because of his strength, Ichigo drained her completely. As a result, Rukia is unable to return to Soul Society; thus, Ichigo has to help her perform her duties.

Ichigo learns that soul reapers protect the balance between Earth and Soul Society. Their mission is to guide the good souls to Soul Society and vanquish the

Bleach. (Courtesy of VIZ Media)

hollows. As Ichigo learns more about the duties of a soul reaper, he hones his combat skills by fighting several hollows. The first hollows Ichigo fights are connected to Ichigo's close friends Orihime and Chad, who both develop psychic powers later.

Ichigo meets Ishida, the last descendant of the Quincy clan, and they fight. To demonstrate the fighting prowess of his clan, Ishida challenges Ichigo to a hollow-vanquishing contest. The competition gets out of control and turns into a fight for survival. When a Menos Grande (a gigantic hollow) appears, Ichigo only barely manages to defeat it.

In the second main story arc, other soul reapers from Soul Society arrive. They are not pleased that a human possesses the power of a soul reaper and wish to kill Ichigo and take Rukia back to Soul Society's inner circle, Seireitei, to judge her for her actions. Ichigo and his friends battle the soul reapers but are not strong enough to beat their enemies; thus, Rukia is taken.

After special training designed to help him communicate with the soul of his sword, Ichigo, along with his friends, invades Soul Society to rescue Rukia. Entering Soul Society, the group fights various battles but is still not strong enough to face the soul-reaper captains. They retreat in order to regain their strength and train. Soul Society and its leaders also need to reorganize their defenses because of the mysterious murder of a captain.

Rukia's impending execution sets the plot in motion again. Ichigo and his friends struggle to free her. Ichigo even manages to defeat Rukia's stepbrother, Byakuya, one of the strongest captains. The execution has been only a distraction: Behind the scenes, Aizen and Gin, two captains, have staged a rebellion against Soul Society. They hope to steal the Hōgyoku, a mystical sword artifact used to execute soul reapers. With the Hōgyoku, Aizen and Gin escape into Hueco Mundo, the world of the hollows.

In the third story arc, Ichigo and the captains of Soul Society unite to battle Aizen. As Soul Society rebuilds, Ichigo meets a half hollow, half soul reaper named Shinji. When Karakura Town is attacked by the Arrancar (an incredibly strong breed of hollows created by Aizen), Ichigo begins training with Shinji.

Aizen is interested in Orihime powers. He sends two of the Espada, the strongest of the Arrancar, to take her to Hueco Mundo. When Ichigo finds out Orihime has been kidnapped, he sets out for Hueco Mundo.

Volumes

- *Bleach: Strawberry and the Soul Reapers* (2004). Collects issues 1-7. Ichigo meets Rukia, who is wounded when a hollow attacks Ichigo's family. Ichigo becomes a substitute soul reaper.
- *Bleach: Goodbye Parakeet, Goodnight My Sista* (2004). Collects issues 8-16. Chad is haunted by a hollow. Ichigo fights and vanquishes the malignant spirit.
- *Bleach: Memories in the Rain* (2004). Collects issues 17-25. Ichigo has memories of his mother, who died when he was a child.

- *Bleach: Quincy Archer Hates You* (2004). Collects issues 26-34. A famous psychic brings his television show to Karakura Town. Ichigo uses all his strength to prevent the psychic from getting hurt. In the process, Ichigo meets Ishida, the last descendant of the Quincy archer warriors.
- *Bleach: Right Arm of the Giant* (2005). Collects issues 35-43. Ishida challenges Ichigo to a contest to see who can kill the most hollows. In doing do, Ishida endangers the people in Karakura Town.
- *Bleach: The Death Trilogy Overture* (2005). Collects issues 44-52. As the contest continues, the balance between life and death shifts, and a huge hollow appears, whom Ichigo vanquishes.
- *Bleach: The Broken Coda* (2005). Collects issues 53-61. Soul reapers are upset to find that Rukia has given her powers to Ichigo. A group of soul reapers brings Rukia back to Soul Society.
- *Bleach: The Blade and Me* (2005). Collects issues 62-70. Ichigo is beaten by Byakuya and realizes he needs further training. He discovers that his sword has a soul and that he needs to communicate with it.
- *Bleach: Fourteen Days for Conspiracy* (2005). Collects issues 71-79. Ichigo and his friends set out to save Rukia and encounter numerous hardships along the way.
- *Bleach: Tattoo on the Sky* (2005). Collects issues 80-88. With the help of Kūkaku, Ichigo and his friends infiltrate Soul Society.
- *Bleach: A Star and a Stray Dog* (2006). Collects issues 89-98. When they enter the inner city of Soul Society, the group of friends scatters. Fights break out. Ichigo defeats his opponent and discovers where Rukia is imprisoned.
- *Bleach: Flower on the Precipice* (2006). Collects issues 99-107. While Ichigo and his friends are infiltrating Seireitei, one of the soul-reaper captains is found dead.
- *Bleach: The Undead* (2006). Collects issues 108-115. Ichigo fights a desperate battle with the captain Kenpachi.

- *Bleach: White Tower Rocks* (2006). Collects issues 116-123. After defeating Kenpachi, Ichigo goes back to training.
- *Bleach: Beginning of the Death of Tomorrow* (2006). Collects issues 124-130. Ishida faces a sadistic soul-reaper doctor. Desperate to survive, Ichida uses a move that will grant him great strength at the cost of losing his powers forever.
- *Bleach: Night of Wijnruit* (2006). Collects issues 131-139. Rukia's execution date is moved up; but additional problems seem to be developing in Seireitei.
- *Bleach: Rosa Rubicundiur, Lilio Candidior* (2007). Collects issues 140-149. Rukia's soul-reaper friends decide to help Ichigo.
- *Bleach: The Deathberry Returns* (2007). Collects issues 150-158. Tension mounts as Rukia's execution draws closer and Ichigo is nowhere to be found.
- *Bleach: The Black Moon Rising* (2007). Collects issues 159-168. Ichigo returns from his training and fights Byakuya.
- *Bleach: End of Hypnosis* (2007). Collects issues 169-178. As Ichigo defeats Byakuya, the true magnitude of the rebellion comes to the fore. Aizen and Gin have used Rukia's impending execution as a ruse.
- *Bleach: Be My Family or Not* (2007). Collects issues 179-187. Aizen and Gin have stolen Hōgyoku; they begin preparing to attack the human world. In Seireitei, new alliances form. On Earth, Ichigo meets a mysterious, strong man.
- *Bleach: Conquistadores* (2008). Collects issues 188-197. Two Arrancar arrive in Karakura Town.
- *Bleach: ¡Mala Suerte!* (2008). Collects issues 198-205. Grimmjow secretly travels to Earth in an attempt to kill Ichigo.
- *Bleach: Immanent God Blues* (2008). Collects issues 206-214. Ichigo is losing against Grimmjow, but the fight abruptly ends when Grimmjow must return to Hueco Mundo.
- *Bleach: No Shaking Throne* (2008). Collects issues 215-223. Ichigo finds that controlling his inner hollow is harder than he thought.
- *Bleach: The Mascaron Drive* (2009). Collects issues 224-233. Aizen takes interest in Orihime's powers and mounts an attack force to kidnap her.
- *Bleach: Goodbye, Halycon Days* (2009). Collects issues 234-242. The Arrancar give Orihime time to say good-bye to her friends but promise to kill her friends if she reveals their plot.
- *Bleach: Baron's Lecture Full-Course* (2009). Collects issues 243-251. Ichigo and friends decide to invade Hueco Mundo.
- *Bleach: The Slashing Opera* (2009). Collects issues 252-260. As the invaders make their way into Hueco Mundo, they make friends with three seemingly innocent hollows.
- *Bleach: There Is No Heart Without You* (2010). Collects issues 261-269. Includes more fighting between the invaders and the lesser Arrancar.

Bleach. (Courtesy of VIZ Media)

- *Bleach: Don't Kill My Volupture* (2010). Collects issues 270-278. Ichigo is beaten by Ulquiorra. As his heart is pierced, only Orihime's healing powers can save him.
- *Bleach: Howling* (2010). Collects issues 279-286. A fight breaks out between Ichigo and Grimmjow. During the fight, flashbacks reveal Grimmjow's past.
- *Bleach: The Bad Joke* (2010). Collects issues 287-295. Arrancar arrives just as the fight between Ichigo and Grimmjow finishes. Ichigo does not stand a chance against this new enemy.
- *Bleach: King of the Kill* (2011). Collects issues 296-305. The fight between Nnoitra and Nel continues.
- *Bleach: Higher than the Moon* (2011). Collects issues 306-315. Reinforcements from Seireitei help turn the tide in the fight against the Arrancar. Several captain soul reapers help Ichigo.
- *Bleach: Turn Back the Pendulum* (2011). Collects "Turn Back the Pendulum" 1-9. This volume looks to the past, revealing dramatic moments in Soul Society.
- *Bleach: Beauty Is So Solitary* (2011). Collects issues 316-322 and "Turn Back the Pendulum" 10 and 11. Shinji finds that Aizen has betrayed him. In the present, a grand battle begins.
- *Bleach: Fear for Fight* (2012). Aizen and his underlings try to destroy Karakura Town, and Ichigo and the others stand sentry over the four pillars that protect the town.
- *Bleach: El Verdugo* (2012). Features the continuation of the fight over Karakura Town. General Yamamoto joins the fight.

Characters

- *Ichigo Kurosaki*, the protagonist, is a teenage boy who is quick to anger and somewhat sarcastic but good-natured. He treasures his friends and family, and will do anything to protect them.
- *Rukia Kuchiki* is a relatively old soul reaper who looks like a teenage girl. She has dark hair and is rather small. She values duty and honor but holds friendship and sacrifice in higher regard.
- *Orihime Inoue* is a beautiful girl with red hair. She is shy and has a secret crush on Ichigo. She develops strong healing powers. She is kidnapped in the third story arc.
- *Yasutora "Chad" Sado* is a half-Spanish, half-Japanese teenage boy. His huge size and strength make him a formidable fighter. He rarely speaks and keeps to himself but always protects his friends.
- *Ishida Uryū* is a smart but silent teenager who wears glasses. He is the last descendent of the ancient human-hollow fighting clan the Quincy. Because the Quincys have been murdered by the soul reapers, he hates Soul Society.
- *Renji Abarai* is a teenage soul reaper who was raised in the poorest part of Soul Society. His personality is similar to Ichigo's.
- *Byakuya Kuchiki*, an antagonist, is the ideal image of the Japanese samurai warrior. He is silent and values duty and honor before anything else. Though he is Rukia's brother, he is the leader of the squad that takes her back to Soul Society to be executed.
- *Aizen Sōsuke*, the primary antagonist, loses his dorky hairdo and glasses and assumes the look of a true villain as he leads the rebellion. Aizen is the driving force behind the plot of the second and third story arcs.

Artistic Style

Kubo's style has become less dense as the series has progressed. The pages of the first chapters are crowded, with illustrations and text balloons fighting for panel space. Kubo has an acute eye for detail, which can be seen in his overuse of shadows and blacks in the first chapters. Initially, *Bleach* looked as much like a horror manga as it did an action-based manga. However, it has evolved into a primarily action-based manga. Thus, Kubo uses less shadow and less crowded action pages; in fact, the action often occupies many consecutive pages.

Bleach's illustrations have a somewhat different feel to them than those of other *shōnen* manga. Kubo's sharp and dark style gives *Bleach* a more mature feeling than *Fairy Tail* (2008-   ) and *Naruto*

(2003-   ), for example, and makes the series artistically more akin to manga developed for adult audiences.

Themes

Bleach is a coming-of-age story. As Ichigo and his friends fight various battles, they find out more about themselves and what is important to them. As with other *shōnen*, however, the coming-of-age process is continually thwarted by the realities of comic-book publishing and the endless expansion of the series because of its popularity. As a result, the characters make the same mistakes and often arrive at the same conclusions. In other words, *Bleach*'s characters hardly evolve; although the series has more than ten years worth of adventures, Ichigo has not really matured and has roughly the same opinions and problems that he had at the beginning.

Sword fights are the most important and appealing aspect to *Bleach*; thus, power is an important theme as well. Ichigo fights to protect his loved ones. One subtle aspect of *Bleach*, however, is that Ichigo also discovers that he is addicted to the thrill of fighting. Ichigo is somewhat disgusted by his bloodlust, an aspect of his character that is not developed thoroughly; therefore, the philosophical implications of *Bleach* are rather bleak. In the end, characters who fight to protect always vanquish those who fight just for the thrill.

Family and friends also play an important thematic role. Not only are they safe havens to which Ichigo can return after his fights, but his fights almost always involve protecting his family or friends. Whether one should also protect those that are not friends or family is referenced only briefly, when Ichigo is asked to perform the duties of a soul reaper. Ichigo finds that he cannot sit by idly as innocents get hurt.

Impact

Bleach is as much a continuation of the standard manga tropes as it is an influence on the creation of such tropes. It is influenced greatly by other successful *shōnen* manga such as *Dragon Ball* (2003-2004), *Naruto*, and *One Piece* (2003-   ). With these manga, it shares a common style and a set of morals. However, *Bleach* differs from its predecessors in

---

Tite Kubo

Tite Kubo, born 1977, is one of the most popular creators of *shōnen* manga in Japan, thanks to his ongoing series *Bleach*. The series launched in 2001 and—though only his second attempt after *Zombiepowder* in 2000—it quickly became a huge hit for *Weekly Shōnen Jump*, the Shūeisha magazine in which it is serialized. Kubo has listed *Saint Seiya: Knights of the Zodiac* as one of his favorite manga, and connections can be made between the noble figures and deep mythology of the two series, as well as *Gegege no Kitaro* by Shigeru Mizuki, whose inventive yokai (or monsters) have influenced his own dark creations. Kubo is a huge fan of American and British rock music, and references music groups including the bands Nirvana, the Who, and the Red Hot Chili Peppers in his comics.

---

the dark quality of its illustration and the increased quantity of explicit violence and bloodshed. Thus, *Bleach* has cleared the way for a breed of more violent and darker manga marketed to an adolescent audience.

Bleach has also become one of the most popular manga series in the English-speaking world. After the groundbreaking popularity of *Dragon Ball* and *Naruto*, *Bleach* has introduced many English-speaking youths to manga. Even though anime and manga had already found their way to the West by the 1980's, they mainly remained underground forms of popular culture. However, *Naruto* and *Bleach* can be bought in most bookstores in the United States, and anime adaptations have been translated and aired on Cartoon Network and have been released online by VIZ.

Rather disappointingly, there has hardly been any serious critical work done on *Bleach*. *Bleach*'s popularity and its lack of originality mean it is generally ignored by most manga critics. This is a shame, as in-depth analysis of *Bleach* might provide insights into why it is so popular and what its impact on contemporary mainstream culture is.

Films

Bleach: Memories of Nobody. Directed by Noriyuki Abe. Gekijo Ban Bleach Seisaku Iinkai/Studio Pierrot/Toho Company, 2006. This anime stars Masakazu Morita as Ichigo and Fumiko Orikasa as Rukia. Though its basic themes are the same, the film does not follow the narrative of the manga.

Bleach: The DiamondDust Rebellion. Directed by Noriyuki Abe. Gekijo Ban Bleach Seisaku Iinkei/Studio Pierrot/Toho Company, 2007. This anime stars Morita as Ichigo and Orikasa as Rukia. Ichigo and Rukia have to fight for their lives as they try to stop an unknown enemy from changing Seireitei forever.

Bleach: Fade to Black. Directed by Noriyuki Abe. Gekijo Ban Bleach Seisaku Iinkei/Studio Pierrot/Toho Company, 2008. This anime stars Morita as Ichigo and Orikasa as Rukia. Ichigo faces an enemy with the power to wipe out his friends' memories.

Bleach: The Hell Chapter. Directed by Noriyuki Abe. Gekijo Ban Bleach Seisaku Iinkai/Studio Pierrot/Toho Company, 2010. This anime stars Morita as Ichigo and Orikasa as Rukia. A new enemy appears to threaten Ichigo's family. Ichigo and his friends must save their town and friends.

Television Series

Bleach. Directed by Noriyuki Abe. Dentsu Music and Entertainment/Studio Pierrot, 2004- . Though some differences exist in the way that the story is told, this anime adaptation of *Bleach* follows the narrative of the manga.

Rik Spanjers

Further Reading

Kishimoto, Masashi. *Naruto* (2003-).
Mashima, Hiro. *Fairy Tail* (2008-).
Oda, Eiichiro. *One Piece* (2003-).

Bibliography

Born, Christopher E. "In the Footsteps of the Master: Confucian Values in Anime and Manga." *ASIANetwork Exchange* 17, no. 1 (Fall, 2009): 39-53.

Cools, Valérie. "The Phenomenology of Contemporary Mainstream Manga." *Image [&] Narrative* 12, no. 1 (2011): 63-82.

Gallacher, Lesley-Anne. *The Sleep of Reason: On Practices of Reading Shōnen Manga*. PhD diss., University of Edinburgh, 2010.

Handa, Issei, and Daniel Komen. *The Bleach Breakdown: The Unofficial Guide*. Tokyo, Japan: Cocoro Books, 2007.

Kubo, Tite. *All Colour but the Black: The Art of Bleach*. San Francisco: VIZ Media, 2008.

See also: *Naruto*; *One Piece*; *Dragon Ball*

BOYS OVER FLOWERS

Author: Kamio, Yoko
Artist: Yoko Kamio (illustrator)
Publisher: Shūeisha (Japanese); VIZ Media (English)
First serial publication: *Hana yori dango,*
    1992-2003
First book publication: English translation,
    2003-2009

Publication History

Yoko Kamio started *Boys over Flowers* in 1992. The title is a Japanese pun: *Hana yori dango* means "food over flowers," referring to those who attend flower-viewing parties but only care about the food; however, the kanji used to write "food" means "boys" in this context. The series was an instant success, winning the Shogakukan Manga Award in 1995, and continued until 2003, through five different editors.

The final chapter appeared in the September, 2003, issue of *Margaret*. An epilogue chapter set one year after the finale was printed in 2006, and two more epilogue chapters, dealing with the character Rui, were printed in 2008. English-language volumes were released in the United States beginning in 2003.

Plot

Boys over Flowers has a soap opera plot with improbable coincidences and sudden reversals of fortune that stand in the way of the characters' happiness. The protagonist is Tsukushi Makino, a sensible, lower-class girl attending Eitoku Academy. Her fellow students are upper-class and rich, and Tsukushi despises them. Eitoku is ruled by the "flowery four," or "F4," a group of four extremely wealthy and handsome boys. When Tsukushi crosses them, the F4 mark her with the "red slip," a piece of red paper that signals the entire school to terrorize her. Undaunted, Tsukushi marks the F4 with red slips of their own.

Tsukushi finds a surprising ally in her defiance: Rui Hanazawa, the cool, unflappable member of the F4. However, after seeing Rui's clear attraction to a childhood friend, Tsukushi gives up on her interest in him and finds herself instead drawn to the F4's leader,

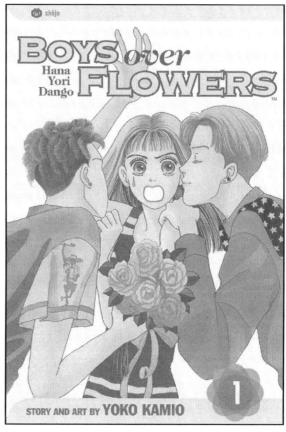

Boys over Flowers. (Courtesy of VIZ Media)

Tsukasa Domyoji. Alternately attracted to his sensitive moments, amused by his buffoonery, and repulsed by his jealous fits of rage, Tsukushi falls into a strange love-hate relationship with Tsukasa.

As the series progresses, Tsukasa is forced to face the consequences of his hedonistic lifestyle and his domineering mother Kaede, who has arranged and paid for his life so far. She decides Tsukushi is unfit for Tsukasa and tries to arrange his marriage to an upper-class girl.

Tsukushi's family is forced to move away; Tsukushi moves into the Domyoji mansion and becomes Tsukasa's personal maid. She and Tsukasa grow closer. When Kaede returns, however, Tsukushi is blackmailed into cutting ties with the Domyoji family and breaking up with Tsukasa. Tsukushi leaves to live with her family in a remote village. She eventually returns, but she does not reconcile with Tsukasa immediately.

Later, Kaede attempts to break up Tsukushi and her son once more by hiring a Tsukasa look-alike to seduce Tsukushi, but this plan fails when even the impostor is charmed by Tsukushi. Finally, with much prodding from the other members of the F4, Tsukushi admits her love for Tsukasa, and the two begin an official relationship. This is the last straw for Kaede. She brings Tsukasa to New York City, and Tsukushi follows. With help from her friends, Tsukushi goes to confront Kaede in her mansion only to be met by Tsukasa, who breaks up with her. Deeply depressed, Tsukushi is comforted by Rui. But when Tsukushi unwittingly facilitates a major business deal for the Domyoji family, Kaede offers her a gift: Tsukasa can do whatever he wants for one year, after which she will "take him back."

Shortly after Tsukushi and Tsukasa are reunited they are kidnapped and wind up on an island as part of their friends' plan. When they return to Japan, Tsukasa is stabbed by the son of a businessman ruined by the Domyoji family and is rushed to the hospital. As a result of blood loss and brief brain death, he develops a case of amnesia, forgetting Tsukushi. He briefly falls in love with a girl at the hospital; however, his memory is jogged by the taste of Tsukushi's cooking and he returns to normal.

Just before prom, when all the F4 are about to leave for college, Tsukasa proposes to Tsukushi. But he reveals that he will have to take over the company sooner than he thought, and Tsukushi will have to wait four years for him. In the end, Tsukushi says she will wait for him as long as it takes; Tsukasa leaves for New York City.

There are two epilogues. The first, set a year after the conclusion of the original series, shows Tsukushi and Tsukasa renewing their commitment to one another after meeting in Paris for a friend's wedding. The second shows how Rui has accepted his role in the lives of his friends.

Volumes

- *Boys over Flowers*, Volume 1 (2003). Collects chapters 1-5 and the unconnected short story

"The End of the Century." Tsukushi challenges the F4.

- *Boys over Flowers*, Volume 2 (2003). Collects chapters 6-11. Tsukushi continues her struggle with the F4.
- *Boys over Flowers*, Volume 3 (2003). Collects chapters 12-17. Tsukasa tells people that Tsukushi is in love with him but becomes distraught when he finds she is attracted to Rui.
- *Boys over Flowers*, Volume 4 (2004). Collects chapters 18-24. Tsukushi is tricked into thinking she has been date-raped.
- *Boys over Flowers*, Volume 5 (2004). Collects chapters 25-30. The tension mounts between Tsukushi and Tsukasa.
- *Boys over Flowers*, Volume 6 (2004). Collects chapters 31-37. Rui returns from France. Tsukushi has ambivalent feelings toward Tsukasa.
- *Boys over Flowers*, Volume 7 (2004). Collects chapters 38-44. Tsukasa is jealous because he finds Rui and Tsukushi together.
- *Boys over Flowers*, Volume 8 (2004). Collects chapters 45-51. Despite their moment together, Rui admits to Tsukushi that he cannot forget about his former love.
- *Boys over Flowers*, Volume 9 (2004). Collects chapters 52-58. Tsukasa leaves for New York. Tsukushi's family has money problems.
- *Boys over Flowers*, Volume 10 (2005). Collects chapters 59-65. To pay off her father's debt, Tsukushi enters the Miss Teen Japan competition.
- *Boys over Flowers*, Volume 11 (2005). Collects chapters 66-71. Tsukushi trains for the Miss Teen Japan competition.
- *Boys over Flowers*, Volume 12 (2005). Collects chapters 72-77. Tsukushi goes on a date with Tsukasa.
- *Boys over Flowers*, *Volume* 13 (2005). Collects chapters 78-83. The group goes to Canada for winter break, where Tsukasa saves Tsukushi's life in a snowstorm.
- *Boys over Flowers*, Volume 14 (2005). Collects chapters 84-90. By coincidence, Tsukushi gets a modeling job and appears on the cover of a magazine.

- *Boys over Flowers*, Volume 15 (2005). Collects chapters 91-97. Tsukushi attends Tsukasa's eighteenth birthday party and meets his domineering mother Kaede.
- *Boys over Flowers*, Volume 16 (2006). Collects chapters 98-104. Kaede attempts to bribe Tsukushi and her family to give up Tsukasa. Next, she tries to arrange a marriage for Tsukasa.
- *Boys over Flowers*, Volume 17 (2006). Collects chapters 105-111. Tsukasa reveals that he is in love with Tsukushi, but she is unsure about how she feels about him.
- *Boys over Flowers*, Volume 18 (2006). Collects chapters 112-118. Tsukushi is forced to work as Tsukasa's maid.
- *Boys over Flowers*, Volume 19 (2006). Collects chapters 119-125. Tsukushi becomes a maid in the Domyoji mansion.
- *Boys over Flowers*, Volume 20 (2006). Collects chapters 126-132. Tsukushi and Tsukasa become girlfriend and boyfriend, but on a temporary basis.
- *Boys over Flowers*, Volume 21 (2006). Collects chapters 133-139. Tsukasa's mother returns and kicks Tsukushi out of the mansion. To save her friends from Kaede's wrath, Tsukushi agrees to sever all ties with the Domyojis.
- *Boys over Flowers*, Volume 22 (2007). Collects chapters 140-146. Tsukushi leaves Tokyo and goes to live with her parents in a seaside village.
- *Boys over Flowers*, Volume 23 (2007). Collects chapters 147-153. Tsukushi meets Kiyonaga, who resembles Tsukasa and claims to be his cousin.
- *Boys over Flowers*, Volume 24 (2007). Collects chapters 154-160. Kiyonaga reveals he was hired by Tsukasa's mother to seduce Tsukushi.
- *Boys over Flowers*, Volume 25 (2007). Collects chapters 161-167. The drama continues between Tsukushi and the Domyojis.
- *Boys over Flowers*, Volume 26 (2007). Collects chapters 168-174. Tsukushi and Tsukasa's relationship becomes more complicated as it grows.

- *Boys over Flowers*, Volume 27 (2007). Collects chapters 175-181. Tsukushi finally admits she loves Tsukasa. Tsukushi moves into a small apartment, and Tsukasa moves in next door.
- *Boys over Flowers*, Volume 28 (2008). Collects chapters 182-188 and the extra chapter "Story of an Encounter."
- *Boys over Flowers*, Volume 29 (2008). Collects chapters 189-195. Tsukasa's funds are cut off. His mother brings him to New York City.
- *Boys over Flowers*, Volume 30 (2008). Collects chapters 196-202. Tsukushi is seemingly rejected by Tsukasa. She saves a business deal for Kaede. Tsukasa escapes to Japan with Tsukushi.
- *Boys over Flowers*, Volume 31 (2008). Collects chapters 203-207. Tsukasa decides to leave the Domyoji family but is stabbed and has to go to the hospital.
- *Boys over Flowers*, Volume 32 (2008). Collects chapters 208-214. Tsukasa develops amnesia and forgets about Tsukushi.
- *Boys over Flowers*, Volume 33 (2008). Collects chapters 215-221. Tsukasa believes that another

---

Yoko Kamio

Yoko Kamio, born in 1966, is best known for her *shōjo* series *Boys over Flowers*, which ran for more than a decade in the Shūeisha-published magazine *Margaret*. Routinely described as the best-selling *shōjo* manga of all time, *Boys over Flowers* has been adapted to television on several occasions. A reviewer for National Public Radio in the United States complimented the series for its depiction of student bullying, noting that its heroine came through "a picture of composed triumph." Other notable Kamio manga series include *Cat Street*, about a former child star; *Matsuri Special*, about a female wrestler; and *Tora to Ookami*, about a young woman working at her family's restaurant. Kamio is one of a small number of female *shōjo* manga creators selected to contribute to Shūeisha's *Jump Square* magazine.

patient is his forgotten girlfriend, but he eventually remembers Tsukushi.

- *Boys over Flowers*, Volume 34 (2009). Collects chapters 222-228. Focuses on the relationship between Yuki and Sojiro.
- *Boys over Flowers*, Volume 35 (2009). Collects chapters 229-235. Tsukasa proposes to Tsukushi, but he reveals he may not be free for four years.
- *Boys over Flowers*, Volume 36 (2009). Collects chapters 236-240 and the special "Night of the Crescent Moon." Tsukushi considers leaving Eitoku for her last year but decides against it. This volume includes prom and graduation.
- *Boys over Flowers: Jewelry Box* (2009). Collects one untitled story, the chapters "Shall I Talk About Myself" parts 1 and 2, an interview with Kamio, a summary and time line of the series, and short pieces about the main characters.

Characters

- *Tsukushi Makino*, the protagonist, is a straight-haired sixteen-year-old girl with large, expressive eyes. Naturally stubborn and protective of others, she is initially the only student who dares to stand up against the F4. Her plain-spoken and independent demeanor does not make her popular, but her few friends are fiercely loyal.
- *Tsukasa Domyoji*, Tsukushi's romantic interest for most of the series, is a curly-haired student at Eitoku, the leader of the F4, and heir to the Domyoji corporation. He is slow on the uptake, prone to malapropisms, and occasionally has violent fits of anger.
- *Rui Hanazawa*, light-haired with pensive eyes, is a member of the F4 and Tsukasa's occasional competitor for Tsukushi's affection. He seems cool and unemotional but is actually withdrawn and has difficulty connecting with others. Rui was originally intended to be Tsukushi's love interest, but Tsukasa proved more popular with readers.
- *Sojiro Nishikado* is a member of the F4; he has straight black hair and cool, untroubled looks. He is heir to a famous tea school and is a playboy. Late in the series, he has a subplot with Yuki, revealing some of his background; the two spend a

night together but mutually decide not to have a relationship.

- *Yuki Matsuoka*, a young woman with midlength wavy hair and bright, innocent eyes, is Tsukushi's closest friend. Also poor, she does not attend Eitoku; the two work together in a sweet shop. She provides stability and a sympathetic ear to Tsukushi.
- *Shizuka Todo*, a tall, strikingly beautiful young woman, is a childhood friend of the F4, particularly Rui. She is the one person able to draw Rui out of his shell. Despite being born into a wealthy family, she chooses to become a lawyer for the poor.
- *Kaede Domyoji*, a tall, domineering woman with light hair usually worn in a bun, is Tsukasa's mother and head of the Domyoji group. Although Kaede is severe and unfeeling, focused on making Tsukasa into a proper heir, Tsukushi manages to find a deeply buried compassion inside her.

Artistic Style

Boys over Flowers has a fairly classic *shōjo* look. Characters' faces are rendered in high detail, with particularly large eyes, though in comedic moments they become more cartoony and simplified. Backgrounds tend to disappear during conversations to be replaced by screentone patterns or images representative of a character's mood. Most shots are medium- or close-range and focused on the characters, with few long shots or landscapes. Kamio's art improves noticeably over the course of the series. Her faces become more realistic, and backgrounds are drawn more often and with more detail. For some of the more "exotic" locations in the series (Paris, New York City, Tuscany), Kamio used photographic references.

Her layouts tend to be dynamic, using odd angles and filling the page to emphasize characters' motions. However, Kamio also uses emptiness to good effect, reflecting the loneliness or inner turmoil of a character by surrounding them with blankness.

Characters' clothing is given careful attention, generally to highlight the difference between the working-class Tsukushi and the upper-class students of Eitoku.

Tsukushi usually wears her school uniform, but the untouchable F4 come to school wearing whatever they please, usually designer clothing in the latest styles. Kamio shows an understanding of and appreciation for fashion.

Themes

Because *Boys over Flowers* is a romance, the emphasis of the series is the relationship between Tsukushi and Tsukasa, including their initial mutual dislike, their slow understanding of each other, and the obstacles they encounter on the road to love. The emphasis of the series is their struggle to be together, and the strength and patience they need. The two are an unlikely couple, constantly butting heads and arguing, but this is how they express affection for each other.

Boys over Flowers. (Courtesy of VIZ Media)

There is a strong thread of class consciousness in the series. Tsukushi is looked down on by the rich students of Eitoku, but her poor upbringing has helped her develop a strong sense of independence and justice. Conversely, those characters born into privilege are often spoiled, self-centered, and have no sense of responsibility or consequence. However, the series is not a blanket condemnation of the wealthy; some of the major characters born into wealth are moral, upstanding individuals. Kamio's target is not the wealthy but the privileged: those who lack common sense and empathy.

Tsukushi is praised by others for her resilience and strong sense of justice; she cannot abide underhandedness or dirty tricks. She often compares herself to a weed (*tsukushi* is the name of a species of weed in Japanese), in contrast to the flowery four. She is also proud, refusing to take anything she has not earned. The series is often credited with bringing attention to bullying in Japanese schools, which became a national problem in the 1990's. Tsukushi's cruel treatment at the hands of her classmates prompted many readers to write in with stories of similar experiences, and her fortitude was an inspiration to others.

Impact

Boys over Flowers is one of the most famous *shōjo* series ever published, and one of the best-selling. The series is certainly not the first *shōjo* romance title, nor probably the best, but it is undoubtedly among the most famous. It is not a transformative or revolutionary series in any way; its story will be familiar to most *shōjo* readers and many of its elements are common in the genre. Its success lies not in its originality or novelty but its perfection of a formula that had already proven highly popular.

The series is one of the most adapted, having been made into eight live-action and animated series in three different countries, and into three separate films. (The actors portraying the F4 in the Chinese television series later formed a popular music group called F4, renamed JVKV, which was also quite popular.) The manga series has also spawned several prose novels, a number of video games, and assorted ancillary merchandise.

Films

Hana yori dango. Directed by Yasuyuki Kusuda. Fuji Television Network, 1995. This live-action film stars Yuki Uchida as Tsukushi and Shosuke Tanihara as Tsukasa. The film moves the setting from high school to university and compresses the events considerably. The actor playing Rui, Naohito Fujiki, had a cameo appearance in the 2008 live-action film.

Hana yori dango: Final. Directed by Yasuharu Ishii. Toho Company/Tokyo Broadcasting System, 2008. The film starred Mao Inoue and Jun Matsumoto and was written by Yoko Kamio.

Television Series

Hana yori dango. Directed by Shigeyasu Yamauchi. Toei Animation, 1996-1997. This animated series stars Maki Mochida as Tsukushi and Naoki Miyashita as Tsukasa. This fifty-one-episode series is faithful to the look of the manga series, and it follows the story closely up to the introduction of the character of Shigeru. However, since it was completed before the manga finished, its ending was an original creation.

Hana yori dango. Directed by Yasuharu Ishii. TBS, 2005. This live-action series stars Mai Inoue as Tsukushi and Jun Matsumoto as Domyoji. This nine-episode series rearranges some of the events of the manga and emphasizes some characters over others but is otherwise faithful to the manga's plot. A sequel series of eleven episodes and a "finale" movie in 2008 were made with the same cast.

Ted Anderson

Further Reading

Hatori, Bisco. *Ouran High School Host Club* (2005-   ).

Takaya, Natsuki. *Fruits Basket* (2004-2009).

Yazawa, Ai. *Nana* (2005-2010).

Bibliography

Mockett, Marie Matsuki. "Head over Heels for *Boys over Flowers*." *National Public Radio*, April 15, 2011. http://www.npr.org/2011/04/15/134563204/head-over-heels-for-boys-over-flowers.

Thorn, Matt. "*Shojo* Manga—Something for the Girls." *The Japan Quarterly* 48, no. 3 (July-September, 2001).

See also: *Nana*; *Fruits Basket*

BUDDHA

Author: Tezuka, Osamu

Artist: Osamu Tezuka (illustrator); Chip Kidd (cover artist)

Publisher: Ushio Shuppansha (Japanese); Vertical (English)

First serial publication: *Budda*, 1972-1983

First book publication: 1974-1984 (English translation, 2003-2005)

Publication History

Osamu Tezuka's *Buddha* was first published in the Japanese manga periodicals *Kibō no Tomo, Shōnen Warudo*, and *Komikku Tomu* from September, 1972, to December, 1983. Multivolume collected editions were published in Japan beginning in the mid-1970's and have continued to be reprinted in multiple sizes and formats. The series was introduced to Western audiences comparatively recently. A ten-volume edition entitled *Buda* was published in Spanish by Planeta De-Agostini in 2002-2003. An English-language version was published by Vertical in eight hardcover volumes from 2003 to 2005, followed by a paperback edition in 2006-2007.

Plot

Buddha is a sprawling saga of sixty-six chapters and nearly three thousand pages. At its core, the series is a heavily fictionalized biography of the historical Buddha, Siddhartha Gautama. Interwoven into Siddhartha's story are dozens of well-developed secondary characters, both historical and entirely fictional, whose narrative trajectories unfold over the course of the series. Slaves, kings, crooks, giants, ghosts, demons, princesses, prostitutes, and even the creator-god Brahma all play roles in shepherding the story toward its inevitable conclusion.

Buddha begins just prior to the birth of the Siddhartha Gautama, and over the course of its eight volumes the story follows the protagonist's biography as it is traditionally told: He is born the son of a minor king in northern India; grows up in luxury, learning only in late childhood about the presence of death and

Buddha. (Courtesy of Vertical)

disease; rejects his home and family in young adulthood and spends eight years undergoing various trials as a wandering ascetic; finds enlightenment under the *bodhi* tree; and passes his remaining decades preaching the dharma.

Interspersed in this relatively faithful account of Siddhartha's life are several wholly fictional subplots, some of which are rather brief and others which span nearly the length of the series. Foremost among the subplots is the story of Tatta, a pariah child whose family is killed by a neighboring tribe prior to the Buddha's birth. Tatta begins adult life as an infamous thief and murderer but comes to renounce violence as a disciple of the Buddha. In the end, however, he is unable to resist an opportunity to seek revenge and dies in battle, fighting the tribe that slew his family. His ultimate failure to come to terms with the Buddha's message of peace and forgiveness speaks to the conflicted nature of Tezuka's work, fraught as it is with difficult choices and fateful outcomes for so many of its characters.

Volumes

- *Buddha*: *Kapilavastu* (2003). Contains the twelve chapters of part 1, which takes place prior to, during, and shortly after the Buddha's birth. Introduces Tatta.
- *Buddha: The Four Encounters* (2003). Contains the ten chapters of part 2, in which the Buddha grows to young adulthood and rejects his family to become a wandering ascetic.
- *Buddha: Devadatta* (2004). Contains the first five chapters of part 3. Introduces Devadatta, Migaila, and Asaji.
- *Buddha*: *The Forest of Uruvela* (2004). Features the remaining chapters of part 3, in which the Buddha finally attains enlightenment.
- *Buddha: Deer Park* (2005). Contains the seven chapters of part 4, in which the Buddha gives his first sermon.
- *Buddha: Ananda* (2005). Features the first eight chapters of part 5. Introduces Ananda, a murdering thief who finds redemption in the Buddha's teachings.
- *Buddha: Prince Ajatasattu* (2005). Features the remaining two chapters of part 5 and the first seven chapters of part 6. The Buddha, now aged, returns to the place of his birth.
- *Buddha: Jetavana* (2005). Contains the remaining chapters of part 6 and part 7. Tatta falls in battle, and Shakya is destroyed; the Buddha dies and passes into nirvana.

Characters

- *Siddhartha* is the protagonist of the series. He is based on the historical Buddha, a prince of the Shakyamuni clan who rejects luxury at an early age to become a wandering ascetic. The narrative of his life in *Buddha* largely follows accepted legend. Unlike traditional representations of the character, however, Tezuka's Buddha is a very human presence throughout the series, showing fear, frustration, and anger—even after his enlightenment experience. Throughout *Buddha,* he changes visually in dramatic fashion—at the series' end, aged and bearing the traditional marks of the Buddha (elongated ears, cranial protrusion, curled hair, circular "eye of wisdom" mark on forehead), he is virtually unrecognizable from the young monk of the middle chapters.
- *Tatta* is a pariah child with the uncanny ability to enter into the minds of animals, a power he loses when he matures and becomes a bandit leader. Married to Migaila, he renounces his murdering ways and joins the royal guard of the kingdom of Magadha, a rival of the clan that killed his friends and family years before. He later joins the Buddha as a disciple. Other than the Buddha, Tatta is the most featured character in the series.
- *Migaila* is Tatta's wife. A subcaste thief who develops romantic feelings for the Buddha early in the series, she is blinded by the Buddha's father in order to discourage their relationship. She then finds lasting companionship with Tatta, bearing him several children and joining him as a disciple of the Buddha.
- *Devadatta*, based on the actual disciple of the Buddha, is said to have instituted the rules of monastic life into Buddhism. He also created a schism in the early monastic community and even attempted to kill the Buddha out of jealousy. Tezuka fictionalizes aspects of the character, including his being raised in the forest by wolves and spending much of his childhood living in nature.
- *Ananda* is, true to legend, the Buddha's devoted attendant and helper. In Tezuka's version, he begins life as an angry orphan, his mother having been killed by troops from Kosala. With the help of the evil spirit Mara, he becomes a murdering bandit invulnerable to physical harm. Later, he renounces his thieving ways, breaks free of Mara's influence, and becomes the Buddha's most loyal servant and disciple.
- *Dhepa* is an ascetic forced by the adult Tatta and Migaila to blind himself in one eye to earn his release. He accompanies the Buddha in his spiri-

tual quest and encourages him to undergo severe ascetic trials.

- *Asaji*, loosely based on the historical disciple, is a comically diminutive and meek young monk who tags along after the Buddha and Dhepa. He develops the power of prophecy and lives calmly for years knowing the precise time and date of his own death. At the appointed hour, he lies down next to a pack of starving wolves and is torn apart by their mother to provide sustenance for her cubs.

- *Crystal Prince* is a prince of the Kosala tribe who vows to eliminate the Shakya clan because they sent a slave woman to marry the Kosalan king, his father. The slave woman, the Crystal Prince's mother, is for him a source of great humiliation and suffering, as he had been raised to believe

he was of pure and noble birth. With the help of the Buddha's teaching, he comes to regret his attacks, but in the end he is unable to quell his desire for revenge and destroys the entire Shakya tribe.

- *Ajatasattu* is a prince prophesized by Asaji to kill his father, King Bimbisara, in twenty years' time. To avoid this fate, Ajatasattu is imprisoned in a tower, where he falls in love with a slave girl, who is subsequently put to death by Bimbisara to terminate their illicit relationship. Upon release, he makes his prophesized revenge, usurping the throne and imprisoning his father, who eventually starves to death.

- *Naradatta*, one of the first characters introduced in the series, is an inexperienced young monk sent by his master on a pilgrimage to find a great

Buddha. (Courtesy of Vertical)

holy man. He is punished by his master for squandering the life of several animals to save a human life and is sent into exile in the forest, where he spends his remaining decades in a mute, bestial existence. He briefly raises Devadatta before forcing the boy to return to the human world. At the close of the series, he meets the Buddha and dies peacefully, the goal of his pilgrimage having been realized at long last.

Artistic Style

A pioneer in graphic storytelling in the manner of Walt Disney or Jack Kirby, Tezuka virtually invented the visual vocabulary and grammar of the manga genre. As Tezuka had been writing and drawing professionally for more than two decades when the *Buddha* series began in 1972, his talents were in full maturity. Tezuka's so-called cinematic style, for example, is much in evidence in the series, as he uses a variety of angles, far and long shots, and close-ups to dynamically capture motion and mood.

A hallmark of Tezuka's visual aesthetic—cute, cartoonish art standing side by side with adult graphic violence and nudity—may be off-putting to Western readers, who are greeted in the series' opening pages with the self-immolation of a doe-eyed bunny drawn à la Disney. Finally, along with the artist's cartoonish images are numerous jokes and anachronisms: E.T., Yoda, and even Tezuka are among the Buddha's monkish followers, and the text makes reference to then-current events.

Themes

As is the case with Tezuka's other masterworks (such as *Phoenix*, published in English from 2003 to 2008), the overarching theme of the *Buddha* series is humanism. Tezuka had a great respect for the dignity and value of human life, and the work confronts this issue directly, as its young protagonist seeks to find the ultimate meaning and purpose of existence. Before, during, and even after his enlightenment experience, the Buddha constantly questions what purpose human lives serve in the overall scheme of the universe. "Why do humans suffer Why do they live Why should a world such as ours exist" The Buddha finally

awakens to the answer late in the series, when he sees Ajatasattu smile after three years of torment. "It is in the Heart of Man that God exists!" he exclaims, forswearing the need for rigorous training and ascetic practices in favor of profound empathy for one's fellow man.

Other themes in *Buddha* deepen and expand upon Tezuka's concern with the human condition. The Buddhist notion of the interconnectedness of all living things, for example, and the role that sacrifice plays in providing for the greatest good are featured prominently in the *Buddha* series. In fact, the series begins and ends with the same anecdote (a rabbit that immolates itself to provide food for a starving man), first related by the Brahman master Asita and later by the Buddha in one of his final sermons. This fate is echoed in the character of Asaji, a prophetic monk who performs a similar sacrifice.

Another recurring motif is the suffering and injustice caused by caste difference, a subject central to the historical Buddha's teachings. Early in his ascetic wanderings, the Buddha rejects Brahmanic concepts of the fundamental and inviolable difference between social classes. The Buddha's friendship and intimacy with persons of the lowest classes speak to his belief in equality—a belief that extends beyond humans to all life-forms.

Impact

Along with *Phoenix*, *Buddha* remains one of Tezuka's best-known and best-regarded works. In Japanese, it has been reprinted numerous times since the 1970's. The planned film trilogy also highlights the series' continued resonance in Japan. Vertical's hardcover English translation (coupled with a Spanish-language release during the same time period) brought a truly global audience to the series. In the United States, *Buddha* elicited high praise from both mainstream American sources, such as *Time* magazine, the *New York Times Book Review*, and the American Library Association, and the comic book industry, which bestowed the series with prestigious Harvey and Eisner awards from 2004 to 2006. A subsequent paperback release of the eight volumes remains in print.

Films

Buddha: The Great Departure. Directed by Kozo Morishita. Tezuka Production Company/Toei Animation Company, 2011. This animated film is the first of a planned trilogy based on the *Buddha* series. The first film covers Siddhartha's youth.

Todd S. Munson

Further Reading

Chopra, Deepak. *Buddha: A Story of Enlightenment* (2007).

Tezuka, Osamu. *Ode to Kirihito* (2006).

_____. *Phoenix* (2003-2008).

Bibliography

MacWilliams, Mark Wheeler. "Japanese Comic Books and Religion: Osamu Tezuka's Story of the Buddha." In *Japan Pop! Inside the World of Japanese Popular Culture*, edited by Timothy J. Craig. Armonk, N.Y.: M.E. Sharpe, 2000.

Power, Natsu Onoda. *God of Comics: Osamu Tezuka and the Creation of Post-World War II Manga*. Jackson: University Press of Mississippi, 2009.

Swanson, Paul L. "Osamu Tezuka's *Buddha*." Review of *Buddha*, by Osamu Tezuka. *Japanese Journal of Religious Studies* 31, no. 1 (2004): 233-240.

See also: *Phoenix*; *Astro Boy*; *Adolf*; *Ode to Kirihito*

C

CARDCAPTOR SAKURA

Author: Clamp

Artist: Mokona Apapa (illustrator); Satsuki Igarashi (illustrator); Tsubaki Nekoi (illustrator)

Publisher: Kodansha (Japanese); TOKYOPOP (English)

First serial publication: *Kādo Kyaputā Sakura,* 1996-2000

First book publication: 1996-2000 (English translation, 2000-2003)

Publication History

Cardcaptor Sakura first appeared in the monthly Japanese *shōjo* magazine *Nakayosi.* Kodansha collected the series in twelve graphic novels released between 1996 and 2000. The first English release in North America was published by TOKYOPOP from 2000 to 2003.

In 2010, Dark Horse Manga began to rerelease the series in omnibus editions containing three books each. The omnibus editions are printed on larger paper than the average graphic novel to provide a better view of the pictorial story elements presented by the all-female *mangaka* group Clamp, which includes Nanase Ohkawa, Mokona Apapa, Tsubaki Nekoi, and Satsuki Igarashi.

The series is split into two story arcs: *Cardcaptor Sakura* (Volumes 1-6), in which Sakura must capture the Clow Cards, and *Cardcaptor Sakura: Master of the Clow* (Volumes 7-12), in which she is the master of the Clow Cards.

Plot

Cardcaptor Sakura features a preadolescent female protagonist, Sakura, who possesses magical ability. Her touch unintentionally awakens the Guardian of the Seal, Cerberus (also known as Kero), and opens the Clow book, which contains cards that imprison magical entities of gold, wood, water, fire, earth, clouds, wind, rain, and electricity. Kero enlists Sakura's aid in

> ### Nakayoshi
>
> *Nakayoshi* is a classic ongoing manga anthology aimed at young girls, which is to say it publishes *shōjo* manga. These series emphasize teen romance and light fantasy, often in tandem. Even more than *shōnen* (boys) manga publications, *shōjo* magazines like *Nakayoshi* compete with each other by including small items in issues such as jewelry and toys. It has been published since 1954 by Kodansha, once of Japan's biggest comics companies. Outside Japan, *Nakayoshi,* which means "good friend," is arguably overshadowed by the success of its various series, including the *Sailor Moon* franchise, and the *Cardcaptor Sakura* phenomenon. It is in *Nakayoshi* that manga genius Osamu Tezuka published much (though not all) of his series *Princess Knight,* which is said to have set the template for *shōjo* manga. Other popular series include *I Am Here!* (*Koko ni Iru yo!*), *Kitchen Princess* (*Kitchen no Ohime-sama*), and *Magic Knight Rayearth.*

recapturing the cards. Sakura must use her magical abilities to recapture these entities while safely harnessing their power. She combines her power with that of the staff used to seal the entities back into their cards, which is formed from a key on the book's front cover.

The cards were first created hundreds of years before by a sorcerer named Clow Reed, who called the entities forth with his magic before eventually sealing them into the book. After collecting all of the cards, Sakura must pass the judgment of the cards' second guardian, Yue (also known as Yukito), to prove that she is worthy of being the cards' master and will not abuse the power the cards grant. If Sakura fails the final judgment, everyone who has encountered the Clow Cards will lose the memories of the one he or she loves the most.

Within the second story arc, *Cardcaptor Sakura: Master of the Clow*, Sakura faces new challenges. She must strengthen her powers in order to protect those she loves by transforming the Clow Cards into Sakura Cards (also known as Star Cards). As Master of the Cards, Sakura endows the cards with power. She must transform them, or they will cease to exist. Meanwhile, Eriol, a reincarnation of Clow Reed, pushes Sakura to reach her full power.

Volumes

- *Cardcaptor Sakura*, Volume 1 (2000). Collects chapters 1-5. The series opens with Sakura watching video footage of her last card battle, filmed by her best friend, Tomoyo. Sakura then tells the reader how she came to be involved with the Clow Cards.
- *Cardcaptor Sakura*, Volume 2 (2000). Collects chapters 6-10. The field-day event being held at Sakura's elementary school is threatened by a Clow Card. Revelations are made about Sakura's mother. Syaoran Li transfers to Sakura's school and seeks the Clow Cards.
- *Cardcaptor Sakura*, Volume 3 (2000). Collects chapters 11-14. Kero teaches Sakura how to do divinations with the Clow Cards while a card pretends to be Sakura and causes trouble around town.
- *Cardcaptor Sakura*, Volume 4 (2000). Collects chapters 15-18. After capturing the Maze Card, Sakura eagerly goes on her school field trip to the beach. Afterward, there is a festival at the Tsukimine Shrine, where another card awaits Sakura.
- *Cardcaptor Sakura*, Volume 5 (2001). Collects chapters 19-22. Sakura's school puts on a play and the Dark Card swallows everything. The Light and Dark Cards test Sakura's potential to become Master of the Cards. It is revealed that she must face a final judgment by the cards' second guardian, Yue.
- *Cardcaptor Sakura*, Volume 6 (2001). Collects chapters 23-26. The final judgment awaits Sakura. The text reveals that the seal on the cards

broke when Clow Reed died in Japan. After the trial, Sakura speaks to a vision of Clow Reed, who tells her that the staff now glows with the power of her own star, the strength of her heart.
- *Cardcaptor Sakura*, Volume 7 (2001). Collects chapters 27-30. Sakura discovers that her Clow Cards are useless against a new power in town. This new invading power corresponds with the arrival of a transfer student from England, Eriol Hiiragizawa.
- *Cardcaptor Sakura*, Volume 8 (2002). Collects chapters 31-34. The relationship between Syaoran and Sakura develops as the former takes care of the latter while she is ill. Kero starts to sense the presence of Clow Reed.
- *Cardcaptor Sakura*, Volume 9 (2003). Collects chapters 35-38. Yukito begins to die, as he can only exist through the power of the Master of the Cards. Sakura's failure to transform the cards fast enough is causing him to cease to be. Toya gives Yukito all of his magic in order to sustain him.
- *Cardcaptor Sakura*, Volume 10 (2003). Collects chapters 39-42. Sakura confronts her feelings for Yukito only to have him reject them. Syaoran comforts her as he struggles with his feelings for her.
- *Cardcaptor Sakura*, Volume 11 (2003). Collects chapters 43-45. Sakura faces her final battle with Clow Reed as he reveals to her his purpose in fighting her. More secrets are revealed, and Sakura must transform the final two cards, Light and Dark, to win.
- *Cardcaptor Sakura*, Volume 12 (2003). Collects chapters 46-50. Relationships come full circle as each character ends up with the person he or she loves the most: Fujitaka with Nadeshiko, Eriol with Kaho, and Yukito with Toya. Syaoran confesses his love to Sakura.

Characters

- *Sakura Kinomoto* is a ten-year-old girl in the fourth grade. She lives with her father and brother; her mother is deceased. She is the "Cardcaptor."

- *Cerberus*, a.k.a *Kero*, is the guardian of the Clow book. He appears as a miniature toy version of himself as the result of his drained power. He regains power as Sakura captures cards, especially those relating to fire.
- *Fujitaka Kinomoto* is Sakura and Toya's father. He is an archaeology professor who discovered the Clow book and a reincarnation of Clow Reed.
- *Toya Kinomoto* is Sakura's older brother and Yukito's best friend. He has psychic abilities that include being able to see ghosts and sense those with magical abilities. He struggles with romantic feelings for Yukito.
- *Yukito Tsukishiro* is Toya's best friend and love interest. He is truly Yue, a guardian of the Clow Cards, but he forgets his true identity when he takes the form of Yukito.
- *Tomoyo Daidouji* is Sakura's best friend and the first to know of her Cardcaptor status. She makes Sakura's costumes and films her card battles.
- *Nadeshiko Kinomoto* is Sakura's mother. She died at the age of twenty-seven when Sakura was three years old.
- *Sonomi Daidouji* is the mother of Tomoyo and chief executive officer of a large corporation. She was the cousin and childhood best friend of Sakura's mother. She is angry at Fujitaka for taking Nadeshiko away from her.
- *Syaoran Li* is a descendant of Clow's mother's family. His family consists of his mother and four older sisters, who all reside in Hong Kong. He is sent alone to Japan to recover the Clow Cards because he possesses the strongest magic in his family.
- *Kaho Mizuki* is Sakura's substitute math teacher in Volume 3 and a psychic. She is the only child of the head priest of the Tsukimine Shrine. She dates Toya for a year and helps him with his psychic abilities. She is in a romantic relationship with Eriol.
- *Clow Reed* is the all-powerful sorcerer who created the Clow Cards and their book.
- *Eriol Hiiragizawa* is one of the two reincarnations of Clow Reed. He holds all of Clow's orig-

inal memories and power. His true age is unknown, as he has used magic to halt his aging in order to aid Sakura.

Artistic Style

The artists of Clamp are known for their myriad art styles; each manga series the group creates is uniquely designed. *Cardcaptor Sakura* features simple lines and a youthful appeal. The series is drawn in black and white with full-color covers. Movement is depicted with varying amounts of curved lines, depending on the pace of the action. The creators use the *shōjo* conventions of full-body panels and the inclusion of flowers in the background to display and symbolize emotions. Some panels have no borders containing them; characters may cross many panels, and panels may bleed into each other. Occasionally, a panel will span two pages and include little or no dialogue.

Facial expressions are rendered in great detail, as characters' emotions are a key part of the story line. During humorous or embarrassing moments the characters may be drawn in a style that has been called "super deformed," which is similar to a caricature. This style has become common in *shōjo* manga. When not drawn in super-deformed style, both male and female characters are depicted as exceedingly beautiful. The Clow Cards are drawn in high-fantasy style with great detail, which makes them all stunningly beautiful to behold.

Sakura wears many different costumes during her battles with the enchanted cards. These costumes are made by her best friend, Tomoyo, instead of being part of a magical transformation, as is usually the case in magical *shōjo* manga. The artists have stated that they chose to depict Sakura wearing many different beautiful outfits because they felt this would mirror the desires of many preteen female readers to possess many beautiful outfits.

Themes

Relationships are a key theme within the series. Sakura prizes her relationships above all else. Every character is connected through a complex web; for example, Sakura's best friend, Tomoyo, is revealed to be her second cousin as well. Sakura recaptures the Clow

Cards in order to save her friends and family members, and it is only for the sake of preserving relationships that she battles Yue in the final judgment. Sexuality is explored through the various relationships as the characters navigate their feelings: Tomoyo loves Sakura, Sakura loves Yukito, and Yukito loves Toya.

Dreams play a major role in the series. Kero tells Sakura that dreams are important, especially the dreams of magical people. Since she possesses a great deal of raw magic, she should try to remember her dreams. Her dreams prove to be precognitive, as she dreams of events before they happen or of people before she meets them, and they give her an advantage in tough battles.

Power is also a pivotal theme. Sakura must learn to harness her own raw magical power to save the world. Each character has his or her own power, whether magical or not. The characters must master their inner power in order to overcome the darkness within their lives.

Impact

Cardcaptor Sakura exalts *shōjo* manga, a genre targeted at preteen and teenage girls, as it adheres to its main conventions. Building upon themes and concepts established in series such as *Sailor Moon* (1992-1997), which has been credited with popularizing *shōjo* manga worldwide, *Cardcaptor Sakura* encourages girls to fulfill their dreams and desires by learning to exercise their agency through their inner power. The story goes beyond the action sequences of capturing the cards, exploring relationships and emotions that emulate the *shōjo* genre ideals.

Cardcaptor Sakura became a global hit essentially because it provided its female readers with a protagonist to whom they could relate intensely. Whether through her inner struggles with power and agency or through her emerging maturity in exploring love, Sakura becomes a character to whom readers could relate. The series' multicultural approach has made it appealing to preadolescent girls around the world. In addition, the series explores questions of sexual identity faced by many preadolescent female readers. Sakura explores sexual identity through her first crush on Yukito and her love for Tomoyo and Syaoran. Sakura is

unsure whether her love for Tomoyo goes beyond friendship, and moving on from her crush on Yukito brings her attention to Syaoran. The series models acceptance for same-sex relationships and provides a safe universe in which sexual identity can be explored.

The North American release of a heavily edited English version of the *Cardcaptor Sakura* animated television series by Nelvana resulted in a massive outcry from fans who were outraged over the changes. These edits included changing the characters' names to English versions, heavily altering the story line by removing character backgrounds, and changing key plot points that were viewed by some as too mature for the North American preteen audience. Pioneer Entertainment later released an uncut version with English subtitles. This incident and others made the North American anime industry aware of the fact that English-speaking fans wanted English-language releases to be as true to the original Japanese versions as possible. As a result, companies frequently market their releases as authentic and accurate manga or anime.

Films

Cardcaptor Sakura: The Movie. Directed by Morio Asaka. Bandai Visual Company/Madhouse/NHK Enterprises, 1999. Sakura goes to Hong Kong and confronts a vengeful spirit from Clow's past. Nelvana released an English version of the film that was edited to match the story line of the dubbed television series. Pioneer Entertainment later released the uncut film with English subtitles.

Cardcaptor Sakura: The Sealed Card. Directed by Morio Asaka. Amber Film Works/Bandai Visual Company/Kodansha, 2000. The fifty-third Clow Card appears and the series concludes. First edited and dubbed by Nelvana, the film was later released unedited with English subtitles by Pioneer Entertainment.

Television Series

Cardcaptor Sakura. Directed by Clamp, et al. Clamp/Madhouse/NHK Enterprises, 1998-2000. This animated television adaptation of the series consists of seventy episodes. Nelvana released thirty-nine heavily edited dubbed episodes in North America under the title *Cardcaptors*. Pioneer Entertainment later released the complete, unedited series with English subtitles under the title *Cardcaptor Sakura*.

Rachel Cantrell

Further Reading

Takaya, Natsuki. *Fruits Basket* (1999-2006).
Takeuchi, Naoko. *Sailor Moon* (1992-1997).
Watase, Yuu. *Alice 19th* (2001-2003).

Bibliography

Cubbison, Laurie. "Anime Fans, DVDs, and the Authentic Text." *Velvet Light Trap* 56 (Fall, 2005): 45-57.

Ellis, Bill. "Folklore and Gender Inversion in Cardcaptor Sakura." In *The Japanification of Children's Popular Culture: From Godzilla to Miyazaki*, edited by Mark I. West. Lanham, Md.: Scarecrow Press, 2009.

Solomon, Charles. "Four Mothers of Manga Gain American Fans with Expertise in a Variety of Visual Styles." *The New York Times*, November 28, 2006, E5.

See also: *Sailor Moon*; *Fruits Basket*

CRYING FREEMAN

Author: Koike, Kazuo

Artist: Ryoichi Ikegami (illustrator); Wayne Truman (letterer)

Publisher: Shogakukan (Japanese); VIZ Media (English); Dark Horse Comics (English)

First serial publication: *Kuraingu Furiiman*, 1986-1988 (English translation, 1989-1990)

First book publication: 1987-1988 (English translation, 1990-1994)

Publication History

Crying Freeman, written by Kazuo Koike and illustrated by Ryoichi Ikegami, was originally serialized in Shogakukan's *Big Comic Spirits* from March 29, 1986, to July 1, 1988 (issues 7-21). As is typical for serialized manga, which tend to be collected after their original publication into larger books printed on higher quality paper, *Crying Freeman* was quickly assembled into nine individual *tankōbon* volumes released between January of 1987 and July of 1988.

VIZ Media was the first American publisher to acquire the English-language distribution rights to *Crying Freeman*; the company repackaged the manga into six volumes and began publishing the series in 1990. After the release of a second VIZ Media edition, the series went out of print for several years. In 2005, Dark Horse Comics began to republish the series in five volumes. Dark Horse Comics' Chris Warner also edited the volumes for content, bringing artist Wayne Truman to the project to handle any needed touch-up art and English-language lettering. One of Truman's tasks was to conceal some of the more graphic depictions of nudity.

Plot

Protagonist Yō Hinomura is a Japanese artist who has gained international recognition for his pottery and is invited to take a selection of his artwork to an exhibition in the United States. While Hinomura is there, a photographer spying on the crime organization the 108 Dragons hides photographs of a murder in one of Hinomura's pots. Hinomura inadvertently discovers the pictures, but he refuses to give them up when confronted

---

Kazuo Koike

Kazuo Koike, born in 1936 in Japan, is the author of several of the best-known works of manga outside Japan, all thick with themes of stylized violence and revenge. Among these are the classic samurai series *Lone Wolf and Cub*, drawn by Gōseki Kojima; *Lady Snowblood*, drawn by Kazuo Kamimura (Koike scripted the film, which was a strong influence on director Quentin Tarantino); and several landmark series with artist Ryoichi Ikegami, including *Crying Freeman* and *Wounded Man*. Numerous major manga creators came through his Gekika Sonjuku class, including *InuYasha*'s Rumiko Takahashi and *Vampire Hunter D*'s Hideyuki Kikuchi. He has said of his approach to teaching, "I've only been teaching how to develop characters—never how to construct a storyline" (Dark Horse). Koike won the Hall of Fame award at the Eisner Awards in 2004.

---

by members of the organization, part of the Chinese mafia, and instead sends the developed photographs to the police. The organization's leader, Father Dragon, decides to have Hinomura abducted and compelled to serve the 108 Dragons. Ironically, after Hinomura has been mentally altered to ensure his loyalty to the organization, it becomes apparent that he naturally possesses the traits of a perfect assassin. Also, since the leaders of the 108 Dragons are selected on the basis of exceptional ability, Father Dragon sees in Hinomura a worthy successor. Marked with the full-body tattoo that signifies his high status in the 108 Dragons, Hinomura is given his first assignment. Initially, Hinomura is horrified by the murders he is ordered to commit. After each kill, he briefly awakens from his hypnotized state and weeps from regret.

During one of his assigned assassinations, Hinomura is seen by a young woman, Emu Hino, who is charmed by his beauty and the tears he sheds when forced to kill a notorious crime boss. She asks him his name, to which he responds, simply, "Yō." Knowing her own life is in danger because she has witnessed the killing, Emu nevertheless cannot help becoming obsessed with her memories of the killer. When he comes to her house to silence her, she accepts her fate and asks only that he take her virginity so that she might feel what it would be like to be loved by him. He admits that he is attracted to her and is also a virgin, and they have sex.

Afterward, it is clear to Hinomura that he cannot kill Emu, so he takes her to Hong Kong and sponsors her entry into the 108 Dragons as his wife, with the approval of Hǔ Fēng-Líng, or Tiger Wind Chime, the female leader of the 108 Dragons. The two are embraced as future leaders. Emu is tattooed with the tiger symbols that represent her place at Hinomura's side, and both are given Chinese names: Lóng Tài-Yáng for Hinomura and Hǔ Qīng-Lán for Emu.

Hinomura and Emu's first joint mission is to travel to Macau to determine which organization is behind a string of attacks on the Dragons. Meanwhile, Bái Yá Shàn (White Ivory Fan), the granddaughter of the former female head of the 108 Dragons, insists that she be the next leader. She kidnaps Hinomura and attempts to hold him hostage. When he manages to escape and defeat her in combat, she pledges her loyalty to him.

In a later episode, professional wrestler Oshu Tohoku nearly kills Hinomura's friend, Dark Eyes, leaving Hinomura with no choice but to kill Oshu. Hinomura is challenged to a contest of strength by Oshu and religious leader Naiji. Oshu manages to catch Hinomura in a weak moment and squeezes him until he passes out. Hinomura is taken to Naiji's fortress, where he encounters a pair of men altered to look like him in order to infiltrate the 108 Dragons.

Later, Oshu's widow, the geisha Kimiryu, rejects Hinomura's attempts to provide financially for her needs. However, her son, Yujun, is sick from poison and needs an antidote held by another assassin, Tateoka. Hinomura kills the man and cures Yujun, keeping a promise made to the dying Oshu.

Volumes

- *Crying Freeman: Portrait of a Killer* (1990). Artist Emu Hino accidentally witnesses a murder, and she and her would-be killer, Yō Hinomura,

must make a difficult transition to escape their intended fates.

- *Crying Freeman: Shades of Death* (1992). Hinomura and Emu marry and begin their life together, receiving Chinese names that signal their status within the 108 Dragons.

- *Crying Freeman: The Killing Ring* (1992). Hinomura, now called Lóng Tài-Yáng (Dragon Sun), is the leader of the 108 Dragons. He and Emu are threatened by the Askari, also known as the African Tusk, a crime syndicate. Meanwhile, Emu finds a cursed *Muramasa katana* and tames it through her purity.

- *Crying Freeman: A Taste of Revenge* (1992). Religious leader Naiji Kumaga sends professional wrestler Oshu Tohgoku to attack Dark Eyes in the hope that the assault will cause Hinomura to seek out her attacker for revenge.

- *Crying Freeman: Abduction in Chinatown* (1993). The American cartel Kidnappers Organization, which uses the abduction of young children for ransom to fund its other criminal activities, comes into conflict with the 108 Dragons.

- *Crying Freeman: Journey to Freedom* (1994). Hinomura fulfills a promise made to the dying Oshu to protect his family, providing an antidote when Oshu's son is poisoned.

Characters

- *Yō Hinomura*, a.k.a. *Crying Freeman* and *Lóng Tài-Yáng* (*Dragon Sun*), is a handsome and muscular man whose training as an assassin enhances both his natural grace and his physical attractiveness. Forced into the life of a killer, he manages to keep his conscience clear by never taking a contract to kill an innocent person. His tears of pity for his victims further demonstrate his essentially good nature.

- *Emu Hino*, a.k.a. *Hǔ Qīng-Lán* (*Tiger Pure-Orchid*), is a beautiful woman with long, dark hair and a delicate frame. She was once wealthy, but her father's death left her with nothing but a rotting mansion. Her goodness touches her intended killer, Hinomura, and dramatically changes his perspective on his role in the 108

Dragons. She is stronger and more vital than she initially appears.

- *Hŭ Fēng-Líng*, a.k.a. *Tiger Wind Chime*, is the former leader of the 108 Dragons. She chooses to adopt Hinomura as her son and heir. She is elderly but still strong and vital. Although she is the wife of a Chinese mafia boss and a tough leader, she guides her followers with a balanced and fair perspective.
- *Bái Yá Shàn*, a.k.a. *White Ivory Fan*, is the granddaughter of the two former leaders of the 108 Dragons. Large and corpulent, she is nevertheless a highly dangerous opponent. She eventually acknowledges Hinomura as a charismatic and effective leader.
- *Bugnug*, a.k.a. *Dark Eyes*, is the beautiful and muscular head of the Askari. She conceals her association with the Askari by acting through others.
- *Ryuji "Blade" Hanada* is a handsome, charismatic member of the Japanese Hakushin Society. He is a schemer without a conscience. His repeated attempts to kidnap Emu cause his own death at Hinomura's hands.
- *Kimie Hanada* is the beautiful and ambitious wife, and later widow, of Ryuji Hanada. Her obsession with Hinomura, in combination with the fact that his heart is committed to Emu, causes her to act irrationally.
- *Oshu Tohgoku* is a former professional wrestler who starts contract killing to make extra money. He is physically huge and incredibly strong.

Artistic Style

One of the strengths of *Crying Freeman* is the artwork. *Crying Freeman* is a visually stunning manga that uses a great deal of fine, realistic detail. Most of the characters are drawn realistically with only slightly exaggerated proportions. Ikegami seems to have a background in classical art, as the proportions of his figures and architectural drawings seem almost drawn from life. At times, the artwork is so detailed that it does not appear to be manga at all; the style is closer to that of Golden Age American comics from the 1940's and 1950's.

One of the most interesting aspects of *Crying Freeman* is the stark contrast between its graphic portrayals of sex and violence and its highly restrained, almost "picture-pretty" artwork. The lush combination of realistic figures and intricate, detailed backgrounds contributes to the series' occasional designation as erotica. The conventions used by Japanese illustrators to represent human anatomy are, on occasion, somewhat jarring. Japanese censorship laws restrict the portrayal of nudity, yet nudes appear in a significant percentage of the splash pages. Careful concealment of genitals behind scenery and in shadow makes the composition of some of the frames seem crowded. Nevertheless, the series has well-executed scenery and visually well-balanced settings.

Themes

Despite its subject matter, the series tends to promote a distinctly positive view of life. For example, Hinomura's organization is decidedly less criminal than one might otherwise expect. Further, Hinomura's place in the organization is based solely on his natural abilities and his internal drive to be the best he can be. Even as an outsider, a man of Japanese descent in a Chinese organization, he is embraced by the 108 Dragons as a potential, and then actual, leader. His individual desires are ultimately respected by his peers as well. The plotlines of the series are decidedly escapist and sometimes border on pure fantasy. These factors highlight the protagonist's role as a vehicle for male wish fulfillment. Hinomura becomes a master assassin who conquers women's hearts as easily as he dominates his enemies, and in this respect, *Crying Freeman* seems to have much in common with the escapist male-targeted literature of other countries, such as the James Bond series of novels begun by Ian Fleming. Likewise, Hinomura appeals to female readers due to his presentation as an impossibly attractive and talented criminal who falls deeply in love with a seemingly ordinary woman.

Impact

An influential manga due to its art and subject matter, *Crying Freeman* contributed greatly to the increasing popularity of manga for adult readers in the United States. Its graphic content emphasized the fact that manga, and comics in general, are not inherently intended for young readers. In some ways reminiscent of a live-action martial-arts film, *Crying Freeman* inspired a film adaptation that was released internationally in 1995.

Films

Crying Freeman. Directed by Christophe Gans. August Entertainment, 1995. This live-action film adaptation was directed by French filmmaker Christophe Gans. Hinomura is portrayed by Mark Dacascos. The film differs from the manga in several ways, most notably changing the story's setting and the nationalities of several characters.

Crying Freeman: Complete Collection. Toei Animation/ A.D.V. Films, 2004. Collects six animated films released between 1988 and 1993: *Crying Freeman: Portrait of a Killer*, directed by Daisuke Nishio; *Crying Freeman 2: Shades of Death, Part 1*, directed by Nobutaka Nishizawa; *Crying Freeman 3: Shades of Death, Part 2*, directed by Johei Matsuura; *Crying Freeman 4: A Taste of Revenge*, directed by Shigemori Yamauchi; *Crying Freeman 5: Abduction in Chinatown*, directed by Harunisa Okamoto; *Crying Freeman 6: The Guiding Light of Memory*, directed by Yamauchi.

Julia Meyers

Further Reading

Buronson and Ryouiti Ikegami. *Strain* (1998).

Dostoyevsky, Fyodor, and Osamu Tezuka. *Crime and Punishment* (1990).

Bibliography

Dark Horse Comics Inc. "Kazuo Koike - The Dark Horse Interview 3/3/06." Accessed March, 2012. http://www.darkhorse.com/Interviews/1261/ Kazuo-Koike---The-Dark-Horse-Interview-3-3-06.

Klady, Leonard. "Crying Freeman." Review of *Crying Freeman*, by Kazuo Koike. *Variety* 360, no. 10 (October 9, 1995): 63.

Raiteri, Steve. "Crying Freeman." Review of *Crying Freeman*, by Kazuo Koike. *Library Journal* 131, no. 15 (September 15, 2006): 44.

Tse, David. "Crying Freeman." Review of *Crying Freeman*, by Kazuo Koike. *Sight and Sound* 7 (May, 1997): 40.

See also: *Lone Wolf and Cub; Mai, the Psychic Girl; Sanctuary*

D

DEATH NOTE

Author: Ohba, Tsugumi
Artist: Takeshi Obata (illustrator); Gia Cam Luc (letterer)
Publisher: Shūeisha (Japanese); VIZ Media (English)
First serial publication: *Desu Nōto*, 2003-2006
First book publication: 2004-2006 (English translation, 2005-2007)

Publication History

Death Note is the creation of the *mangaka* Tsugumi Ohba. The name is an alias, and whether Ohba is a man or a woman is not publicly known. *Death Note* was one of two "thumbnails" that Ohba submitted to Shūeisha in 2003. The story was approved, and Takeshi Obata was hired as the artist. The pilot story was published in *Weekly Shōnen Jump 2003*, issue 36. Reader reaction was positive, and *Death Note* became a weekly series, eventually comprising 108 chapters.

Ohba and Obata also created several humorous, four-panel comic strips (known as *yonkoma*) that appeared in 2004 and 2005 in various issues of *Akamaru Jump*, the seasonal edition of *Weekly Shōnen Jump*, and in the *Shōnen Jump Gag Special 2005*. The series was popular, with readership ranging from elementary school age to adults.

The English version was translated by Tetsuchiro Miyaki, Alexis Kirsh, and others into thirteen volumes published by VIZ Media from 2005 to 2007. VIZ has also packaged the thirteen volumes in a box set and published a special hardcover edition of the first volume. In December of 2010, VIZ began publishing the six-volume *Death Note: Black Edition*, each volume of which collects the contents of two of the original volumes.

Plot

Shinigami (death gods) possess books known as Death Notes, which are capable of killing a person if that

Death Note. (Courtesy of VIZ Media)

person's name is written in them. A bored Shinigami named Ryuk drops one of the books on Earth, and it is found by Light Yagami on November 28, 2003. Light picks up the book and reads the rules governing its use, which state that if one writes someone's name in the book while envisioning that person's face, then that person will die of a heart attack in forty seconds. He tests the book's powers by writing the names of some criminals he sees on the news, and the criminals die. Light soon meets Ryuk, who is invisible to all but him, and decides that he will use the Death Note to kill evildoers.

People begin to realize that the recent rash of deaths is no coincidence, and some applaud these apparent vigilante killings, referring to the perpetrator as "Kira." Law enforcement around the world—from the Japanese Police Force (JPF), of which Light's father is a deputy director, to international organizations and the mysterious and quirky detective L—become involved. L narrows Kira's location to the Kanto region of Japan.

L believes that there is a leak inside the JPF's task force and sends FBI agents to investigate. Thanks to both Ryuk and the Death Note, Light is able to identify FBI agent Raye Penber and gets him to disclose the names of the other agents. Light then kills all twelve agents. L orders additional surveillance on Light and several others, but Light is able to work around this until the surveillance is removed. L suspects Light is Kira but, knowing that Light has helped his father in the past, asks him to join the anti-Kira task force.

In April of 2004, a second Kira appears, sending video to television stations. This Kira is Misa Amane, who not only possesses a Death Note but also has made a deal with the Shinigami Rem to trade half her remaining life span for the "Shinigami Eyes," which allow her to know a person's name and life span just by seeing his or her face. She admires the original Kira and learns his true identity, and after she reveals herself to Light, they begin dating and working together. However, she is soon arrested by L, who suspects her of being the second Kira. During her interrogation, she gives up ownership of her Death Note and loses her memories of it.

Light uses this to his advantage, convincing Rem to take the book elsewhere. After giving instructions to Ryuk, he turns himself in to L, saying that he may be Kira and not even know it. He also gives up ownership of his Death Note. Nevertheless, the deaths resume after a few weeks because Rem, obeying Light's orders to help Misa, gave the book to a high-ranking employee of the Yotsuba Corporation, who uses it to kill both criminals and executives from rival corporations. Because of pressure from both Yotsuba and the public, JPF orders the investigation of Kira to stop, but most of the task force decides to work unofficially with L.

With the assistance of criminals Aiber and Wedy, L discovers that Kyosuke Higuchi is the Yotsuba Kira. Higuchi is captured, and the task force acquires the Death Note. When Light touches the Death Note, he regains his memories and uses a scrap of paper from the book to kill Higuchi. L and the task force study the book and learn its rules, but the two fake rules that Rem added under Light's orders remove suspicion from Light and Misa and ensure that the notebook will be kept.

With his memories restored, Light sends Misa to retrieve the notebook he had hidden, bringing Ryuk back. Under Light's orders, Misa resumes killing criminals and once again gets the Shinigami Eyes. L remains suspicious of Light and Misa, which troubles Rem, leading the Shinigami to use her personal Death Note to kill L and his assistant, Watari. As L dies, he realizes his suspicions about Light had been correct. Since Rem's actions extended Misa's life, something not allowed by the Death Notes, she crumbles into dust; Light grabs her notebook before the others see it and hides it. The task force decides to continue investigating Kira, and Light says that he will pose as L whenever needed. Over the course of the next five years, Aiber and Wedy are killed by the Death Note, crime rates decrease, and Light officially joins the police department.

In 2009, Near, who is L's true successor, meets with the U.S. president, telling him about the Death Note and forming the Special Provision for Kira (SPK), an anti-Kira task force made up of FBI and CIA agents. Mello, a rival of Near, begins working with the American Mafia to obtain the Death Note. They kidnap the director of the JPF and then kidnap Light's sister, Sayu, forcing Light's father to travel to the United States and give them the Death Note. Mello uses the Death Note to blackmail the president. Near contacts Light, whom he knows is not the real L, and the two exchange information. Eventually, the task force tracks down Mello and recovers the Death Note, but Mello escapes and Light's father is killed.

Near begins to suspect Light, but it is too late. After the death of the president, the new president announces that the United States will no longer pursue Kira, a decision that Japan and other countries follow. In Japan, Kira supporter Hitoshi Demegawa of Sakura TV declares himself Kira's spokesperson. To allay Near's suspicions, Light arranges for a Death Note to be given to Teru Mikami, who kills Demegawa. Light chooses newscaster Kiyomi Takada as his new spokesperson and uses her to contact Mikami. Because Mikami idolizes Light, he follows his instructions and kills more criminals. Mello later kidnaps Kiyomi, but this leads to both of their deaths.

Light thinks that he has won; however, Near outwits him, and he is exposed. After first denying he is Kira, Light admits the truth and makes a final but unsuccessful attempt to kill Near. Realizing the ruse is over, Ryuk writes Light's name in his Death Note, and forty seconds later, Light dies.

Volumes

- *Death Note*, Volume 1 (2005). Also known as *Death Note: Boredom*. Collects chapters 1-7. Light acquires the Death Note, and L and the task force investigate the Kira murders.
- *Death Note*, Volume 2 (2005). Also known as *Death Note: Confluence*. Collects chapters 8-16. Both the killings and the investigations continue.
- *Death Note*, Volume 3 (2006). Also known as *Death Note: Hard Run*. Collects chapters 17-25. Light meets L.
- *Death Note*, Volume 4 (2006). Also known as *Death Note: Love*. Collects chapters 26-34. Misa is introduced as the second Kira and meets Light.
- *Death Note*, Volume 5 (2006). Also known as *Death Note: Whiteout*. Collects chapters 35-43. A third Kira appears.
- *Death Note*, Volume 6 (2006). Also known as *Death Note: Give-and-Take*. Collects chapters 44-52. The anti-Kira task force goes after the third Kira.
- *Death Note*, Volume 7 (2006). Also known as *Death Note: Zero*. Collects chapters 53-61. Light triumphs over L, and the story moves five years into the future.
- *Death Note*, Volume 8 (2006). Also known as *Death Note: Target*. Collects chapters 62-70. Light and the task force must deal with the actions of Mello.
- *Death Note*, Volume 9 (2007). Also known as *Death Note: Contact*. Collects chapters 71-79. Near increasingly suspects that Light is Kira.

Takeshi Obata

Takeshi Obata is an illustrator for numerous mainstream manga, most released by Japanese publisher Shūeisha. He was born in 1969 and is best known for his work on *Death Note*, a brooding twelve volume series hinging on a notebook that allows its owner to kill anyone. Obata's strong, unadorned lines distinguish him, and they function in varied storytelling modes, including the lightly supernatural series *Hikaru No Go* (about a young boy possessed by an ancient master of the game go) and the sexually adventurous *Blue Dragon Ral Grad*, a spin-off of the video game *Blue Dragon*. The latter is especially interesting because it shows Obata adapting character designs by an earlier generation of Shūeisha artists, including *Dragon Ball* creator Akira Toriyama. Obata's collaborator on the *Death Note* manga writes under the pseudonym Tsugumi Ohba. They subsequently collaborated on the "behind the manga" series *Bakuman*, about aspiring young manga creators.

- *Death Note*, Volume 10 (2007). Also known as *Death Note: Deletion*. Collects chapters 80-88. Kira's power and influence grow.
- *Death Note*, Volume 11 (2007). Also known as *Death Note: Kindred Spirits*. Collects chapters 89-98. The various factions prepare for the final conflict.
- *Death Note*, Volume 12 (2007). Also known as *Death Note: Finis*. Light and Near meet for the last time.
- *Death Note*, Volume 13 (2008). Also known as *Death Note: How to Read*. Includes interviews with the creators, profiles of the characters, more information on the series, the four-panel strips, and the original "pilot" story.

Characters

- *Light Yagami*, a.k.a. *Kira* and *the second L*, the protagonist, is a teenager who finds the initial Death Note and uses it to kill criminals. He later becomes the leader of the group seeking to capture him. He dies after Ryuk writes his name in a Death Note in the penultimate chapter of the series.

- *Ryuk* is the Shinigami who possesses the Death Note owned by Light. He can only be seen by those who touch that particular notebook. Like all Shinigami, he can see a person's name and remaining life span. He kills Light.
- *L*, a.k.a. *L. Lawliet* and *Ryuzaki*, is an eccentric investigator who attempts to find and stop Kira. He works with Light even though he suspects him of being Kira. His true identity is later discovered, and he is killed by Rem.
- *Misa Amane*, a.k.a. *the second Kira*, is an actress and model who possesses a second Death Note. She trades half of her life span for the Shinigami Eyes, which enable her to learn a person's name by looking at them. An admirer of Kira, she falls in love with Light.
- *Rem* is the female Shinigami who possesses the Death Note owned by Misa. She later sacrifices herself to help Misa by killing L.
- *Near*, a.k.a. *Nate River*, is a successor to L. Working with the SPK, he puts an end to Light's career as Kira.
- *Mello*, a.k.a. *Mihael Keehl*, is a would-be successor to L who is after Kira and the Death Note. He dies after abducting Kiyomi.
- *Teru Mikami* is a prosecutor who admires Kira and is given a Death Note to continue Kira's work. His actions lead to Light's downfall, and he later kills himself.
- *Kiyomi Takada* is a college friend of Light who later becomes a television reporter and the official spokesperson for Kira. She kills Mello using a piece of the Death Note and then kills herself.
- *Sochiro Yagami* is Light's father, a deputy director in the JPF, and the leader of the group of police officers working to catch Kira.
- *Kyosuke Higuchi* is an executive at the Yotsuba Corporation who is secretly given the Death Note by Light and becomes the third Kira. He uses the book to kill executives from rival companies. Light kills him before he can be captured.

Artistic Style

Ohba created rough drafts of panel layouts and simple drawings for Obata, who made decisions about facial expressions and "camera angles" and expanded upon these thumbnails to create the final artwork. He had a great deal of artistic freedom, and he was asked to change the art only when something was missing that would be important in a later chapter. He was not made aware of most of the future plot developments and knew the story only from the five or six chapters that he was given at a time. For example, when he began drawing the scenes at the Yotsuba Corporation, he did not know which employee possessed the Death Note, and he was surprised when he found out who it was. Obata rarely met with Ohba during the creation of the story, usually meeting with the editor instead.

Obata was interested in *Death Note* because it gave him the opportunity to draw nonhuman creatures such as Shinigami, something he had not done previously. With the exception of the Shinigami, the characters are drawn in a standard style, though some of the major characters have something special about their looks. The Shinigami are drawn in many different ways; while Ryuk and Rem have similar body types, others have totally different sizes, shapes, and features and do not even look like members of the same race. While Obata created all of the major artwork, he had several assistants who handled certain details.

Themes

Basic themes of *Death Note* are good-versus-evil and moral and ethical ambiguity. Light is the protagonist of the story, but he is also a mass murderer. He thinks of himself as the "good guy" because most of his victims have performed evil acts, and he feels justified in killing anti-Kira investigators because they seek to prevent him from punishing evildoers. Misa and Mikami kill because they want to please Kira. Even Higuchi does not kill just for the sake of killing. Also, "good guys" such as L and Near are willing to break the law to stop Kira, revealing the inherent ambiguity of each character.

Death Note also touches on the willingness of some people to follow leaders blindly. Misa and Mikami obey Light's orders without question, and they and others deify Kira. Many of Kira's followers are unaware or do not seem to care that several people have spoken as "Kira."

Impact

Death Note has gained both fame and critical praise worldwide and has inspired a number of media tie-ins. An original novel, *Death Note: Another Note—The Los Angeles BB Murder Cases*, written by Niso Isin, was published in 2008. The video games *Death Note: Kira Game* and *Death Note: L o tsugumono* were released in 2007, and *L: The Prologue to Death Note—Rasen no trap* was released the following year.

Death Note has also been the subject of controversy in many countries, as some leaders and educators have worried that the series will have a negative impact on children. The books were banned in China, and in Taiwan, government officials asked elementary school teachers to monitor their students to make sure that they were not negatively affected by the series. In the United States, some schools have attempted to ban *Death Note*, and students have reportedly been suspended, expelled, and even arrested for creating their own Death Note notebooks. The most notorious *Death Note*-related event occurred in 2007 in Brussels, Belgium, where a mutilated body was found near two notes bearing the message "Watashi wa Kira dess" (roughly "I am Kira"). The murder was known as "Mangamoord," or "the Manga Murder."

Films

Death Note. Directed by Shūsuke Kaneko. Death Note Film Partners/ Nippon Television Network/Shūeisha, 2006. The first of two films that adapt the manga's main story, this live-action film stars Tatsuya Fujiwara as Light, Kenichi Matsuyama as L, and Erika Toda as Misa. The film was dubbed into English and shown in North America. Brad Swaile, Alessandro Juliani, and Shannon Chan-Kent provide the voices of Light, L, and Misa in the English version.

Death Note: The Last Name. Directed by Shūsuke Kaneko. Death Note Film Partners/Nippon Television Network/Shūeisha, 2006. This live-action film adapts the remainder of the manga and stars Fujiwara, Matsuyama, and Toda. Swaile, Juliani, and Chan-Kent provide the voices for the English version. The film eliminates the characters of Near and

Death Note. (Courtesy of VIZ Media)

Mello and makes significant changes to the story's ending.

Death Note: L Change the World. Directed by Hideo Nakata. Horipro/L Film Partners/Nikkatsu Pictures, 2008. This live-action film takes place during the events of *The Last Name.* Matsuyama reprises his role as L, and Swaile, Juliani, and Chan-Kent provide the voices for the English version.

Television Series

Death Note. Directed by Tetsurō Araki. D.N. Dream Partners/Madhouse/Nippon Television Network, 2006-2007. This thirty-seven-episode anime aired Tuesday nights on the Nippon Television Network. Mamoru Miyano, Kappei Yamaguchi, and Aya Hirano provided the voices for Light, L, and Misa. The English-dubbed version, featuring the voices of Swaile, Juliani, and Chan-Kent, aired on Canada's YTV from 2007 to 2008 and on Cartoon Network

from 2007 to 2010. Two additional animated programs, *Death Note Rewrite: Visions of a God* (2007) and *Death Note: Rewrite: L's Successors* (2008), showed parts of the episodes along with a few new scenes.

David S. Serchay

Further Reading

Mase, Motoro. *Ikigami: The Ultimate Limit* (2009-   ).
Yuki, Kaori. *Earl Cain* (2006-2008).
_____. *Godchild* (2006-2008).

Bibliography

Ohba, Tsugumi, et al. *Death Note, Volume 13: How to Read.* San Francisco: VIZ Media, 2008.
Thompson, Jeff. *Manga: The Complete Guide.* New York: Ballantine Books, 2007.

See also: *Hiraku no Go; Monster; MW*

DISTANT NEIGHBORHOOD, A

Author: Taniguchi, Jirō

Artist: Jirō Taniguchi (illustrator)

Publisher: Shogakukan (Japanese); Fanfare/Ponent Mon (English)

First book publication: *Haruka na Machi e*, 1998 (English translation, 2009)

Publication History

Jirō Taniguchi was born in Tottori Prefecture and grew up in Kurayoshi, where *A Distant Neighborhood* is set. In the early 1990's, Taniguchi decided he wanted to draw something other than action manga and created *Aruku hito* (1992; *The Walking Man*, 2004), a work presenting the simple explorations and observations of a man as he strolls through his neighborhood. One publisher, Shogakukan, suggested he create more works in this slice-of-life style. Taniguchi followed this work with *Inu wo kau* (1992; raising a dog), a collection of five short stories about his recently deceased dog. After publishing *Inu wo kau*, Taniguchi wondered if he could write similar stories about families. He toyed with an idea he believes everyone has considered at some point: returning to the past to revisit friends and family while retaining one's present memories. Taniguchi noted that he wrote *A Distant Neighborhood* to experience what might happen if he actually did return to the past.

The work was published as *Haruka na Machi e* by Shogakukan in September of 1998. It was translated and published in France by Casterman in 2002, as *Quartier lointain*; in Italy by Coconino in 2002 and 2003, as *In una lontan città*; in Spain by Ponent Mon in 2003, as *Barrio lejano*; in Germany by Carlsen in 2007, as *Vertraute Fremde*; and in the United States by Fanfare/Ponent Mon in June and October of 2009.

Plot

A hungover forty-eight-year-old Hiroshi Nakahara boards the wrong train at the Kyoto train station after a brief business trip. Instead of returning home, Hiroshi takes an express train to his boyhood hometown, Kurayoshi. While on the train, his thoughts turn to his mother, Kazue, as he realizes he is the same age

A Distant Neighborhood. (Courtesy of Ponent Mon S.L.)

as she was when she died. In Kurayoshi, Hiroshi has two hours before the next train leaves, so he decides to explore the town. He quickly discovers how much of his past has been swallowed by the present, as his old home is unrecognizable. He then walks to the Genzen Temple's cemetery to pay respect to his mother. While praying at his mother's headstone, he is mysteriously transported into the past and transformed into his fourteen-year-old self. This transformation is preceded by a butterfly floating across several panels, symbolically representing the metamorphosis that takes place.

Confused by the transformation and believing he must be dreaming, Hiroshi returns to his boyhood home, discovering his mother, father, sister, and grandmother as they were when he was a teenager. Hiroshi is deeply moved as he experiences his own past. Slowly, he embraces his transformation: He excels in school; reestablishes his friendship with Daisuke Shimada, who dreams of becoming a writer and to whom Hiroshi admits to being a forty-eight-year-old man; and develops a friendship with the beautiful Tomoko Nagase, to whom he had been too shy to speak during his first turn as a junior high school student.

Hiroshi realizes that he has returned to the year in which his father, Yoshio, abandoned the family. Never having understood why his father disappeared, Hiroshi decides to prevent his father from leaving. He begins to probe his family's past by asking his grandmother about his mother's first husband, Shinichi Kotani. He learns that Shinichi and his father both served in an artillery regiment in India during World War II and that Shinichi was killed in action while crossing the Manipur River. Yoshio survived the war and returned the ashes of his fallen friend to the Kotani family. Yoshio's plan had been to return the ashes and then move away from his home district, hoping to close the door on his past and find some sense of personal freedom. Instead, he felt bound to care for Kazue, who was left alone and was slowly ostracized by the Kotani family. When Kazue became pregnant, Yoshio married her and opened his own tailor shop. Hiroshi's family seems happy, as his friend Shimada repeatedly reminds him, but Yoshio feels trapped by his circumstances, believing his life has always been directed by others.

On the night of Yoshio's disappearance, Hiroshi confronts his father at the train station. Yoshio acknowledges his selfishness in abandoning his family but argues that he must leave if he is ever to find his real self. Upon returning home, Hiroshi tells his mother that his father has left. She acknowledges her role in forcing him to stay and expresses surprise that he had persevered so long.

Through this experience, Hiroshi realizes that he is much like his father in that he has been attempting to separate himself from his responsibilities toward his wife and two daughters. Hiroshi becomes drunk and passes out, and when he awakens, he is back at the Genzen Temple. The butterfly motif appears again, and he reverts to the present as a forty-eight-year-old man, arriving just moments after he had left. He goes home

to his wife and daughters with a fuller understanding of the consequences of selfish acts and of his importance to his family. Hiroshi questions whether his experience had been only a dream when his wife hands him a package from the famous author Daisaburo Horie, his childhood friend Daisuke Shimada. The package contains Shimada's latest book: *A Distant Neighborhood*.

Characters

- *Hiroshi Nakahara* is a life-weary forty-eight-year-old father of two. He seeks a way to escape the drudgery of his family life and considers leaving his wife and daughters. He is mysteriously transported thirty-four years into the past and is transformed into his fourteen-year-old self. Reliving his father's abandonment of his family changes his perspective on his own family relationships.

- *Yoshio Nakahara* is Hiroshi's father, who marries Kazue out of a sense of obligation and eventually abandons her and his children in search of personal fulfillment and freedom.

- *Kazue Nakahara* is Hiroshi's long-suffering mother, who blames herself for holding Yoshio back from his dreams. She dies at forty-eight from acute cardiac arrest, eight years after her husband abandons her and her children.

- *Kyoko Nakahara* is Hiroshi's high-spirited younger sister, who has many short-lived passions and dreams. As an adult, she marries at twenty and becomes a housewife, eventually having three children.

- *Grandma* is Kazue's mother, who is sickly and weak and relies heavily on Kazue and Yoshio. She informs Hiroshi of his family's past.

- *Yuko* is Hiroshi's long-suffering wife.

- *Akiko* is Hiroshi's adult daughter, who wants to move into her own apartment but is afraid to ask her father.

- *Ayako* is Hiroshi's younger daughter, who is unafraid to speak her mind and observes that her father is an alcoholic.

- *Tomoko Nagase* is one of Hiroshi's schoolmates, to whom Hirsohi was afraid to speak during his junior high school years. She is the most beautiful girl in school. She and Hiroshi develop an innocent romance, briefly fulfilling his desire to leave behind his own family relationships.

- *Daisuke Shimada* is Hiroshi's childhood friend. In adulthood, he becomes the famous author Daisaburo Horie.
- *Takashi Hamada* is Hiroshi's childhood friend. He enjoys drawing, and in adulthood, he becomes the famous manga artist Ryu Hamada.
- *Masao Harada* is Hiroshi's childhood friend, whose family owns Harada Motors. He dies in a motorcycle accident when he is in tenth grade.
- *Shinichi Kotani* is Kazue's first husband, who is killed during World War II.
- *Tamiko Osawa* is Yoshio's childhood friend, whom he visits in the hospital. Hiroshi briefly thinks that she is his father's mistress.

Artistic Style

Taniguchi's art presents highly detailed and realistic drawings, echoing the fact that the narrative is rooted in the real world despite its time-travel device. With the exception of close-up images of characters, most panels in the work include an abundance of detail. For example, when Hiroshi first steps into the *genkan* (the traditional Japanese entryway) of his family's house, one panel depicts his father's work table with its boxes of supplies, spools of thread, and swatches of cloth. Also depicted in this single panel are the room's tatami mats, *shoji* screens, small rug, extension cords, ceiling tiles, and fluorescent lights. In the background are a bicycle, a two-tiered table with books stacked on the lower tier, two chairs, an open closet with boxes stacked halfway to the ceiling, a calendar, and a poster. The characters, however, are drawn simply and iconically. The elongated legs, oversized eyes, and pointy chins of many manga characters are absent and are replaced by simple, well-proportioned faces and bodies.

Taniguchi divides each panel with clearly defined gutters; only rarely do images violate these distinctions, as when a butterfly floats over the gutters during Hiroshi's metamorphosis and when inlaid panels are used to depict the transformed Hiroshi running home. The number of panels per page varies from as many as eight to as few as one. Single, full-page panels are used

to introduce each chapter but are also occasionally used to emphasize significant moments in the narrative, such as Hiroshi's transformation and his bewilderment at returning to his past.

Themes

Taniguchi's work mixes traditional Japanese aesthetic values with a number of prominent themes. Hiroshi's transformation suggests the Japanese aesthetic of *yugen* (mysteriousness, ambiguity), as the means of his transformation remain hidden. The butterfly floating over the gutters and a full-page image of the moon are the only hints Taniguchi provides. The butterfly likely suggests metamorphosis but also may symbolize the souls of the living and the dead. The full moon indicates the passage of time, change, death, and rebirth. The mechanism for this change, however, remains veiled.

Taniguchi also displays the pleasure Hiroshi takes in the movement of the clouds, his love of natural beauty, his valuing of his younger body, and his deeply emotional response to being in the presence of his family,

---

Jirō Taniguchi

Jirō Taniguchi, born in Japan two years after the end of World War II, is a master of quotidian action and geographic detail. Outside of Japan, he is especially celebrated for *The Walking Man*, a nearly dialogue-free series of episodes in which, true to its title, a man makes his way around a neighborhood. In a medium rich with the histrionic, the fantastic, and the world-weary, Taniguchi's everyday existentialism stands out. Even when serving as illustrator for someone else's story—as in Jinpachi Mori's *Benkei in New York*—he managed to be elegant and regionally precise as well as violent. Which is not to underestimate his humor: he co-produced a manga version of Natsume Soseki's beloved novel *Botchan*. Taniguchi's numerous accolades include the Tezuka Culture Award. A sign of his renown, he won the Best Scenario award at the Angoulême International Comics Festival in 2003, beating, among others, his famous countryman Naoki Urasawa (*Monster*).

all of which reflect a sense of *mono no aware* (the pathos of things). These deep feelings toward the ordinary express the work's thematic concerns with such elements.

The work suggests the theme of *mujo* (impermanence) as Taniguchi reflects on the fleeting nature of happiness, the frailty of human beauty, and the perishability of human relationships. All of these elements take on greater value because of their impermanence, giving the work a tone of nostalgic melancholy. *A Distant Neighborhood* additionally suggests many other themes, including the inability to escape one's fate, the consequences of selfish choices, the effects of parental abandonment, the cycle of abandonment, the possibility of choosing to break such cycles, the human cost of war, patriarchal and matriarchal patterns in Japanese society, the costs of obligation, the difficulty of being free from one's obligations, and the relationship between parent and child.

Impact

Taniguchi has been associated with what Frédéric Boilet has labeled "nouvelle manga," which has involved a conscious attempt by Japanese *mangaka* and French-Belgian comics creators to learn from one another and to develop both manga and *bandes dessinées* that cross international boundaries. In this respect, Taniguchi has been successful—*A Distant Neighborhood* has been translated into multiple languages and has received both international acclaim and international awards. While Taniguchi's work has been well-received in Japan, his work may have a stronger reputation internationally.

Taniguchi's work has helped to expose the fact that realistic narratives dealing with everyday life in Japan do exist in manga. Though the work presents a pervasive Japanese aesthetic sense, it remains accessible to non-Japanese readers and provides insight into Taniguchi's view of Japanese culture and family dynamics. Some reviewers have mistaken the traditional aesthetic values at play in the work for tearful sentimentality; however, most readers seem to perceive a deeper sincerity underlying the work.

Films

Quartier lointain. Directed by Sam Garbarski. Entre Chien et Loup, 2010. This film adaptation stars Pascal Greggory as the adult Thomas Verniaz and Léo Legrand as the adolescent Verniaz. It transports the narrative from Japan to Europe. The basic structure of the original narrative remains, but changes have been made to the protagonist's age and several other elements. Taniguchi makes a cameo appearance as a passenger on the train.

Daniel D. Clark

Further Reading

Boilet, Frédéric, ed. *Japan as Viewed by Seventeen Creators* (2005).

Taniguchi, Jirō. *The Walking Man* (2004).

Bibliography

Taniguchi, Jirō. "Taniguchi Jirō." In *Manga: Masters of the Art*, edited by Timothy Lehmann. Scranton, Pa.: Collins Design, 2005.

Vollmar, Rob. "Frédéric Boilet and the Nouvelle Manga Revolution." *World Literature Today* 81, no. 2 (March/April, 2007): 34-41.

See also: *Times of Botchan*

DORORO

Author: Tezuka, Osamu
Artist: Osamu Tezuka (illustrator)
Publisher: Shogakukan (Japanese); Vertical (English)
First serial publication: 1967-1968
First book publication: 1981 (English translation, 2008)

Publication History

Osamu Tezuka began *Dororo* toward the end of his work on *Astro Boy* (1952-1968). The *Dororo* manga began as serialized chapters in *Weekly Shōnen Sunday*, a boys' manga magazine, in August of 1967 and ran into July of 1968. The final four chapters of the series were published in *Boken-o*, a rival *shōnen* magazine. *Dororo* ended abruptly, with a final chapter noticeably shorter than previous chapters. Tezuka reportedly wanted to wrap up the series quickly so he could begin work on the science-fiction series *Norman* (1968; also called *Prince Norman*) for another publisher.

Dororo was not collected until 1981, when it was released in four volumes in Japan as part of the "Complete Works" line of Tezuka's manga. In 2006, it was translated and released in France. The American publisher Vertical then acquired the English-language rights and released the series in 2008, publishing it in three volumes rather than the four released in other countries.

Plot

The story begins as cruel samurai lord Daigo Kagemitsu visits a temple containing statues of forty-eight Fiends. Daigo asks the Fiends for power to rule the entire country; in return they can have forty-eight body parts from his son, who will be born the next day. When his son is born, Daigo places the deformed child, Hyakkimaru, in a basket and floats him down the river. The child is found by the kindly Doctor Jukai, who teaches him how to use his psychic abilities to see, hear, and speak and crafts prosthetics for him so that he can look like a normal human. Years later, the adult Hyakkimaru is a wandering swordsman. He saves a "boy," Dororo, from a group of bandits and then from a demon. Dororo

Dororo. (Courtesy of Vertical)

resolves to follow Hyakkimaru and eventually steal his sword. Together the two travel the land, having adventures and confronting the Fiends.

The majority of the series is composed of unconnected, stand-alone chapters that fall within the common narrative structure of the "wandering samurai" genre popular at the time: Dororo and Hyakkimaru come to a new town or find a strange situation, discover that one or more Fiends are involved, confront them, and then leave to continue their journey. Often these stories end with the townspeople who have been saved by Hyakkimaru rejecting him, believing him to be just as monstrous as the Fiends he has slain, and forcing him and Dororo to leave.

In the story "Banmon," Hyakkimaru and Dororo arrive in a town that has been divided in two by a massive wall. The northern town is ruled by Daigo and his son, Tahomaru Kagemitsu. Hyakkimaru meets Daigo, Tahomaru, and Daigo's wife, the latter of whom tries to convince him that he is her son, which Hyakkimaru refuses to accept. Ultimately, he is forced to duel with and kill Tahomaru. Daigo sends his troops after Hyakkimaru for revenge.

Toward the end of the series, a multichapter story begins in which a bandit named Itachi, a former comrade of Dororo's parents, finds and kidnaps Dororo. Before she died, Dororo's mother tattooed a map on his back that shows the location of the fortune she and her husband stole, intending to use it to fund a full-scale rebellion against the samurai lords. Itachi, his crew, and Dororo travel to the secluded island where the money is buried, followed by Hyakkimaru. Itachi and Dororo discover the treasure chest, but there is no money inside; instead, there is a note from Dororo's father explaining that he buried the money elsewhere to keep it away from Itachi. The group is attacked by the corrupt local magistrate and his forces, Itachi sacrifices himself to save Dororo, and Hyakkimaru and Dororo are reunited. In this story, it is revealed that Dororo is truly a girl.

In the final chapter, Hyakkimaru and Dororo again meet Daigo, who has enslaved entire villages to build an enormous fort for himself. Dororo leads a rebellion against the samurai's troops. Hyakkimaru meets his mother again and tells her that he will not be her son until he has regained all his body parts. Ultimately, the rebellion is successful, but Hyakkimaru allows Daigo and his wife to flee. He then gives Dororo his sword and parts ways with her once and for all, seeking his destiny alone.

Volumes

- *Dororo*, Volume 1 (2008). Collects the chapters "The Inception," "Hyakkimaru," "The Monk," "Kanekozo," "Bandai," "The Face Tumor," "The Misery Chronicles," and "The Possessed Sword." The first chapter tells the story of Hyakkimaru's birth and childhood, while "The Misery Chronicles" depicts Dororo's early life.
- *Dororo*, Volume 2 (2008). Collects the chapters "Banmon," "The Fair Fudo," "Sabame," and

"Hell Screen." The chapter "Banmon" details Hyakkimaru's first meeting with his father and the duel with his brother, Tahomaru.
- *Dororo*, Volume 3 (2008). Collects the chapters "The Two Sharks," "Shiranui," "The Cruel Cape," "Midoro," "Donburi Belly," "The Four-Turned Bonze," and "Nueh." The first three chapters tell the story of bandit Itachi and the treasure map on Dororo's back.

Characters

- *Hyakkimaru* is a tall, strong-looking samurai with long black hair and bare feet. His father, Daigo, makes a deal with forty-eight Fiends. As a result, the Fiends take forty-eight of the infant Hyakkimaru's body parts, but he survives thanks to Doctor Jukai, who gives him prosthetic limbs and teaches him to see, hear, and speak with his "mind's eye." Every time Hyak-

---

Weekly Shōnen Sunday

The *shōnen* in the title of the long-running manga anthology *Weekly Shōnen Sunday* refers to the fact that boys are its target reader. *Sunday* refers not to the day of its release, but to the fact that Sunday is typically a day without labor or homework. The magazine, published by Shogakukan, was launched in March 1959—famously at the exact same time as its rival, *Weekly Shōnen*, which is published by Kodansha. Both magazines continue to exist, and in fact celebrated their joint fiftieth anniversaries with collaborative promotions. They remain rivals, though both generally trail *Shōnen Jump* in sales. Outside Japan, *Weekly Shōnen Sunday* is best known as the birthplace of *InuYasha*, among the first major global manga and anime hits. Other series that appeared in the magazine include *Drifting Classroom*, *Mai the Psychic Girl*, *Tuxedo Gin*, *Detective Conan*, *InuYasha* creator Rumiko Takahashi's *Ranma ½*, and Osamu Tezuka's *Dororo*.

kimaru defeats one of the Fiends, he regains a body part.

- *Dororo*, a "boy" with unruly hair, is the self-proclaimed "greatest thief in the world." He travels with Hyakkimaru, hoping to steal his sword. He is the son of two bandits who attempted to lead a rebellion against the samurai lords but were killed. Dororo is eventually revealed to be a girl, though it is unclear whether she deliberately hid this fact or had been raised unaware of it.

- *Lord Daigo Kagemitsu* is a tall, cruel-looking man with a hawkish profile and a cross burned into his forehead, a symbol of his pact with the Fiends. He hopes to rule the entire world, and to that end, he bargains with the Fiends for power. Later in the series, he is shown to be a brutal ruler, beating and enslaving his people.

- *Tahomaru Kagemitsu* is the son of Daigo and his wife, making him Hyakkimaru's younger brother. His right eye is always closed in a squint, and his black hair sticks out in eight points reminiscent of a spider's legs. He is Daigo's lieutenant and intended successor. Angry, arrogant, and hotheaded, he clashes with and ultimately fights and is killed by Hyakkimaru.

- *The blind monk* is a wandering lute player (*biwa hōshi*) and skilled swordsman. His back is twisted into a hump, and his milky white eyes are set in an old and gnarled face. He appears at various moments in Hyakkimaru's journey, occasionally acting as a mentor or guide. His name and backstory are never revealed.

- *The Fiends* are demonic monsters who strike a bargain with

Daigo: the life of his son for great power. Each of the fiends takes one of Hyakkimaru's body parts, and Hyakkimaru later regains one body part for every Fiend he kills. The Fiends appear in a variety of forms, many based on figures from Japanese mythology.

- *Doctor Jukai* is a wise healer with a heavy black beard, a bulbous nose, and a perpetually stern look. He rescues Hyakkimaru from the basket and raises him. He appears only in flashbacks.

Artistic Style

In general, *Dororo* shows the same high level of artistic quality as the rest of Tezuka's work. His lines are fluid, his layouts are both innovative and clear, and he makes great use of different styles of shading. Tezuka's distinctive style was fully developed by the mid-1960's,

Dororo. (Courtesy of Vertical)

though he continued to experiment with new tools and elements throughout his career. *Dororo* may not be his most experimental manga, but it does show the hand of a master at work.

The series demonstrates Tezuka's command of cinematic elements in his manga. Battle sequences make use of both long shots and close-ups, often alternating between a large panel showing multiple characters in conflict and many smaller panels, each showing a single sword cut. There are also cinematic "zooms" that follow a character as he or she moves toward or away from the "camera," emphasizing distance and space. However, Tezuka also manipulates images in ways that only comics can allow. For example, a character may fall through a panel border as if falling through a floor or point out something happening in the adjacent panel, his arm reaching over the panel gutter.

Tezuka is known for his "star system," in which he treated his manga characters like actors. Characters appear in different works in different capacities but with similar personalities and roles. For example, a scheming, disingenuous character would generally "play" villains, while a bearded wise man would "play" doctors, mentors, professors, or similar parts. However, *Dororo* stands somewhat apart from the star system; few of Tezuka's best-known characters make an appearance, and the characters in *Dororo* have appeared only rarely in other works.

Themes

As with much of Tezuka's work, *Dororo* places a strong emphasis on social justice, concerning itself with the plight of those crushed under the heels of the elite, in this case the peasants serving the samurai lords of feudal Japan. Although Hyakkimaru fights monsters and demons, the worst cruelties are often committed by humans, those who exploit others for their own gain. However, humans are capable of redemption, while demons are not; some of Hyakkimaru's enemies show genuine repentance and are spared, while all demons must be slain.

Dororo also demonstrates Tezuka's disgust with the horrors of war, another common theme in his works. The town of Banmon is divided into two by a massive wall—a deliberate reference to Panmunjŏm,

divided between North Korea and South Korea after the Korean War. As a result, children are kept from their parents, innocent villagers are killed as suspected traitors, and visitors are attacked by mobs of townspeople on the suspicion that they work for the samurai lords. In *Dororo*, Tezuka does not shy away from depicting cruelty and evil and places a large share of the blame for evil acts on the aggressive nature of mankind.

Hyakkimaru is the quintessential outsider: He saves lives and brings order to lawless places, but he is never accepted by those he saves. This theme is common to many of the "wandering samurai" stories. Hyakkimaru is also a cyborg, a person who is both less and more than human because technology has been used to restore parts of his body. Tezuka tackles both of these character types again in his series *Black Jack* (1973-1983).

Impact

Although period dramas (*jidaigeki*) about samurai were common in post-World War II Japanese film, *Dororo* ranks among the first manga to take on this genre. It generally follows the conventions and tropes of the genre—the wandering protagonist, the constant fights against new villains, the greedy and corrupt local government—and adds some supernatural elements. The "collection" aspect of the story—Hyakkimaru searching for his stolen body parts—may have inspired later manga with similar elements, such as the series *InuYasha* (1997-2008), in which the protagonists travel through a fantastic version of feudal Japan in search of fragments of a magical jewel. While such series may not have been inspired directly by *Dororo*, it was among the first manga to use this concept.

Dororo retains the humor and occasional metafictional elements common in Tezuka's works but includes depictions of violence that are far beyond what one might expect from the creator of *Astro Boy*. *Dororo* was certainly not the first, or the most experimental, of Tezuka's adult-oriented works, but it heralded a trend toward manga for adult readers that would continue to develop throughout Tezuka's career, both in his works and in manga in general.

Films

Dororo. Directed by Akihito Shiota. Asahi Shimbun Newspaper/Dentsu/Hokkaido Broadcasting Company, 2007. This live-action film stars Kou Shibasaki as Dororo and Satoshi Tsumabuki as Hyakkimaru. The film differs from the manga in that Dororo is much older and obviously female, and its ending is a significant departure from that of the comic. The film is reportedly intended to be the first of a trilogy.

Television Series

Dororo. Directed by Gisaburo Sugii. Mushi Productions, 1969. The title was changed to *Dororo and Hyakkimaru* after episode 14. This animated series stars Minori Matsushima as the voice of Dororo and Nachi Nozawa as the voice of Hyakkimaru. With the exception of adding a puppy companion for Dororo, the series is extremely faithful to the manga. The episodes are usually near-verbatim adaptations. Several episodes are original stories that were not present in the manga. The series was produced in black and white for budgetary reasons.

Ted Anderson

Further Reading

Koike, Kazuo, and Gōseki Kojima. *Lone Wolf and Cub* (1970-1976).

Sakai, Stan. *Usagi Yojimbo* (1987-   ).

Tezuka, Osamu. *Black Jack* (1973-1983).

Bibliography

Inuhiko, Yomota, and Hajime Nakatani, trans. "Stigmata in Tezuka Osamu's Works." *Mechademia* 3 (2008): 97-111.

McCarthy, Helen. *The Art of Osamu Tezuka: God of Manga*. New York: Abrams, 2009.

Schodt, Frederik L. *The Astro Boy Essays: Osamu Tezuka, Mighty Atom, and the Manga/Anime Revolution*. Berkeley, Calif.: Stone Bridge Press, 2007.

See also: *Lone Wolf and Cub; Black Jack; Usagi Yojimbo; Astro Boy; Phoenix*

DRAGON BALL

Author: Toriyama, Akira
Artist: Akira Toriyama (illustrator); Wayne Truman (letterer and touch-up artist)
Publisher: Shūeisha (Japanese); VIZ Media (English)
First serial publication: *Doragon bōru*, 1984-1995
First book publication: 1985-1995 (English translation, Volumes 1-16, 2003-2004)

Publication History

Having finished work on his previous series, *Dr. Slump* (1980-1984), manga creator Akira Toriyama sought to create a parody of martial arts *shōnen* manga that featured a comedic martial artist and reversed *shōnen* conventions. The result was the long-running manga *Dragon Ball*, which was serialized in *Weekly Shōnen Jump* from 1984 to 1995. The series was later collected into forty-two *tankōbon*. In 2003, VIZ Media began to publish *Dragon Ball* in the United States, releasing the first sixteen volumes as *Dragon Ball* and Volumes 17-42 as *Dragon Ball Z*, in keeping with the titles of the popular animated television adaptations.

Plot

Inspired by the Chinese classical novel *Xi You Ji* (1590; *Journey to the West*), *Dragon Ball* follows the adventures of Goku, a naïve twelve-year-old boy with a monkey-like tail. Although he is an alien, he does not realize this fact, as he was raised as a human by his adoptive grandfather, Gohan. After the death of his grandfather, Goku lives alone in the wilderness until he crosses paths with Bulma, the first girl he has ever seen. A genius heiress from the city, Bulma seeks the seven Dragon Balls, which will allow her to summon a dragon who will grant one wish. Goku refuses to relinquish his four-star Dragon Ball and agrees to join her quest only if she will return it to him afterward. Together, they explore the world in search of the other Dragon Balls. They meet other misfits and have small side adventures before the Dragon Balls are stolen by Emperor Pilaf, who seeks to rule the world. Goku's monster form, that of a giant ape, is revealed as he battles the evil within himself as well as the evil of

Dragon Ball. (Courtesy of VIZ Media)

Emperor Pilaf. Goku successfully foils Pilaf's plot by interrupting his wish, but the Dragon Balls then scatter across the globe and cannot be used for a full year.

While Goku waits for the Dragon Balls to manifest in the world again, he becomes a student of his grandfather's teacher, Master Roshi. The story line continues in a cycle of quests, training sessions, and tournaments in which Goku meets more powerful villains and teachers, developing friendships and alliances along the way. Throughout the series, Goku discovers that there is always more to learn and always someone who will be stronger than he. He learns about good and evil and takes the side of good every time, struggling repeatedly to save humanity and his friends. Kami, the guardian of Earth, states that it has been ages since he has seen anyone with such a pure heart. Goku grows into an honorable man and warrior who uses his skills to help others and save the world from myriad attackers.

Volumes

- *Dragon Ball*, Volume 1 (2003). Collects tales 1-11. Goku crosses paths with Bulma, the first human he has seen since his grandfather died. Bulma guides him through the larger world as they set out on a quest to gather the seven Dragon Balls.
- *Dragon Ball*, Volume 2 (2003). Collects tales 12-24. Goku meets his grandfather's teacher, Master Roshi, who agrees to tutor him. Emperor Pilaf steals the Dragon Balls because he wants to become emperor of the world. The quest ends temporarily.
- *Dragon Ball*, Volume 3 (2003). Collects tales 25-36. Goku trains with Master Roshi and meets a former Shaolin monk named Kuririn, who also becomes a pupil. After completing their training, Goku and Kuririn enter the Tenkaichi Budokai martial arts tournament to test their abilities.
- *Dragon Ball*, Volume 4 (2003). Collects tales 37-48. Goku and Kuririn learn their limits at the Tenkaichi Budokai tournament.
- *Dragon Ball*, Volume 5 (2003). Collects tales 49-60. Goku barely loses the Tenkaichi Budokai tournament to Master Roshi. He sets out on a new quest for the Dragon Balls. In retrieving the first two balls, he encounters the Red Ribbon Army, which also seeks the balls.
- *Dragon Ball*, Volume 6 (2003). Collects tales 61-72. Goku saves a mountain village from the Red Ribbon Army as he claims another Dragon Ball. Bulma joins him on his quest.
- *Dragon Ball*, Volume 7 (2003). Collects tales 73-84. Goku fights the Red Ribbon Army with Bulma and Kuririn's aid and retrieves another Dragon Ball. Afterward, Goku resumes his dangerous quest alone, and he sets out to defeat the Red Ribbon Army once and for all.
- *Dragon Ball*, Volume 8 (2003). Collects tales 85-96. The Red Ribbon Army dispatches its top assassin to kill Goku. Goku seeks magical water that will increase his strength.
- *Dragon Ball*, Volume 9 (2003). Collects tales 97-108. Goku defeats the Red Ribbon Army. Goku, Yamcha, Pu'ar, Kuririn, and Upa combat supernatural beings in order to learn the location of the final Dragon Ball. Goku vows to use the Dragon Balls to wish Upa's father back to life.
- *Dragon Ball*, Volume 10 (2003). Collects tales 109-120. Goku discovers that Emperor Pilaf possesses the final Dragon Ball. After summoning the dragon and fulfilling the promise to Upa, the group parts until the next Tenkaichi Budokai tournament, during which the Crane Master's pupil seeks to avenge a grudge against Master Roshi.
- *Dragon Ball*, Volume 11 (2003). Collects tales 121-132. At the Tenkaichi Budokai tournament, Goku and Kuririn struggle to defeat the three pupils of the Crane Master.
- *Dragon Ball*, Volume 12 (2003). Collects tales 133-144. King Piccolo has escaped his imprisonment and seeks the Dragon Balls. Goku and Master Roshi seek a way to stop Piccolo before he takes over the planet.
- *Dragon Ball*, Volume 13 (2003). Collects tales 145-156. King Piccolo successfully summons the dragon and wishes for the restoration of his youth and power. He tries to unseat the King of the World and take his place. Goku and Tenshinhan risk their lives to stop Piccolo.
- *Dragon Ball*, Volume 14 (2004). Collects tales 157-168. After a devastating battle, Goku kills Piccolo. Kami agrees to resurrect the dragon if Goku will live and train at the top of the world for three years. Goku wishes for everyone who has been killed by Piccolo to be brought back to life. Three years later, Goku reunites with his friends at the Tenkaichi Budokai tournament.
- *Dragon Ball*, Volume 15 (2004). Collects tales 169-180. Goku tests the limits of his new abilities at the Tenkaichi Budokai tournament. Kami possesses the body of a human contestant in an attempt to defeat Piccolo's offspring.

- *Dragon Ball*, Volume 16 (2004). Collects tales 181-194. Goku and Piccolo's offspring battle, with Goku emerging victorious.

Characters

- *Goku*, a protagonist, is a naïve twelve-year-old boy with a monkey-like tail. He is modeled after the Monkey King of Chinese legend. He has superstrength and is a skilled martial artist.
- *Bulma*, a protagonist, is a teenage heiress who uses her looks to get what she wants. She is a genius inventor who has invented a radar to track the Dragon Balls and serves as the primary holder of knowledge about the Dragon Balls throughout the quest.
- *Master Roshi*, a.k.a. *Turtle Hermit*, a protagonist, is a martial arts master known for his difficult training program and his vulgar behavior toward women. He trained Goku's grandfather and agrees to train Goku too.
- *Oolong*, a protagonist, is a cowardly shape-shifting pig who can take any form for five minutes. Bulma forces him to join the quest for the Dragon Balls, and he aids the group with his shape-shifting abilities.
- *Yamcha*, a protagonist, is a desert bandit and skilled martial artist who is terrified of girls, though he dreams of getting married. He plans to steal the Dragon Balls but instead aids Goku and Bulma on their quest.
- *Pu'ar*, a protagonist, is a shape-shifting cat who can take any form. He attended shape-shifting school with Oolong. With his shape-shifting abilities, he helps Yamcha work through his fear of women.
- *Gyū Maō*, a.k.a. the *Ox King*, a protagonist, is an enormous man with fierce martial-arts ability. He trained with Goku's grandfather and thus respects Goku for his kinship. He possesses one of the Dragon Balls.
- *Chi-Chi*, a protagonist, is a headstrong young girl with martial-arts skills. She is the daughter of Gyū Maō and becomes Goku's wife.
- *Emperor Pilaf*, an antagonist, is a short monster who wishes to rule the world. He considers

kissing and other signs of affection disgusting. He steals the Dragon Balls and summons the dragon.

- *Shenlong*, a protagonist, is an eternal dragon who will grant one wish when summoned by the seven Dragon Balls. After Shenlong grants a wish, the Dragon Balls scatter and cannot be gathered again for one year.
- *Kuririn*, a protagonist, is a short thirteen-year-old martial artist trained as a Shaolin monk. He joins Goku as one of Master Roshi's pupils and becomes Goku's best friend.
- *Lunch*, a protagonist, is a beautiful young girl whose personality goes from good to evil when she sneezes. She lives on an isolated island with Master Roshi and periodically aids the main protagonists.
- *The Red Ribbon Army* is an army of muscle-bound martial artists on a mission to find the Dragon Balls. All of the high-ranking members

---

Weekly Shōnen Jump

The weekly anthology magazine *Shōnen Jump* (*shōnen* referring to boys as its intended audience) was founded in 1968 and is, historically, the bestselling manga publication in Japan. The numbers can be startling beyond Japan, where comics are rarely as culturally pervasive. In the mid-1990s, the magazine sold over six million copies of each issue, a popularity coinciding with the publication of *Slam Dunk*, the classical basketball manga. Sales declined to half that in the subsequent decade, but the publication's prominence would only expand, thanks to a new generation of hit series, notably *One Piece* and *Naruto*. *Jump* is the flagship title for its publisher, Shūeisha, and has spun off numerous magazines, including *V Jump* (a video game magazine) and *Jump Square*, which succeeded the cancelled *Monthly Shōnen Jump*. Jump Festa is the name of an annual *Jump*-themed comics festival held in Makuhari Messe, outside Tokyo. Other classic *Jump* series include *Dragon Ball*, *Rurouni Kenshin*, and *Yu Yu Hakusho*.

are named after a color. The army is led by Commander Red, who has a Napoleon complex.

- *Upa*, a protagonist, is a young man whose father was killed by the Red Ribbon Army. Goku vows to use the Dragon Balls to bring his father back to life.
- *King Piccolo*, an antagonist, is a green alien freed from his imprisonment by Emperor Pilaf. He is pure evil and seeks to take over the world, killing anyone who gets in his way.
- *Tenshinhan*, a protagonist, is a skilled martial artist who nearly beats Goku in the Tenkaichi Budokai tournament. He becomes Goku's ally against King Piccolo.
- *Kami*, a protagonist, is the guardian of the Earth. He is identical to Piccolo, as Piccolo is the evil seed he cast out of himself in order to obtain godhood.

Artistic Style

Toriyama created all the artwork for the series. While the cover illustrations are printed in light colors, the narrative itself is rendered in black and white. The buildings and outdoor settings are drawn realistically and in great detail, and the characters are typically drawn in simple, iconic styles that allow them to be universally relatable. During funny moments, Toriyama enhances the visual comedy by drawing the characters in a style reminiscent of caricatures. He also uses panels to great effect, varying them for a variety of purposes. For example, panel frames that run off the page indicate continued high-speed movement by characters or the grandness of the setting, while characters displaying private thoughts or intense presence are depicted outside frames.

As *Dragon Ball* is ultimately a martial-arts action series, fight scenes make up a significant portion of the comic. Fighting sequences frequently take up multiple pages, with three to four frames per page on average. Martial-arts moves are frequently drawn frame by frame or in an action-to-action progression within a single panel to convey the real-time action of the movement. The illustrations often incorporate motion lines and sound effects, which intensify the depicted battles. The panels depicting a fight often run together, and at times, the lines between the panels cease to exist.

Dragon Ball. (Courtesy of VIZ Media)

Themes

Dragon Ball is a coming-of-age story in which the protagonist, Goku, evolves from a naïve child to a conscientious adult. He forges important relationships that last his entire life. While Toriyama parodies martial-arts stories in general and martial-arts coming-of-age stories in particular, Goku's journey is nevertheless a real one that resonates with readers. The initial quest for the Dragon Balls symbolizes Goku's journey into adulthood: He encounters girls for the first time and learns how to interact with people and use technology. Throughout the series, Goku learns to be true to himself as he forms relationships, discovers new powers, and battles numerous villains.

Toriyama additionally parodies the training routine undergone by the typical naïve kung fu pupil with his depiction of Goku and Kuririn's training sessions with Master Roshi. Master Roshi makes his students perform a ridiculous amount of chores that no human being could possibly accomplish or endure. He does not teach them any new martial-arts moves. Instead, the work they do gives them superstrength, super-endurance, and the ability to fly, and they must then learn how to use their newfound abilities.

Impact

Dragon Ball was the first *shōnen* series to parody martial-arts manga successfully and one of the first to defy *shōnen* conventions in its depiction of the male protagonist's journey from childhood to adulthood. An incredibly popular series responsible in part for the "Golden Age of Jump" (1985-1995), in which *Weekly Shōnen Jump* hit a record number of subscribers, *Dragon Ball* effectively replaced the martial-arts manga it once parodied, inspiring the creation of other comedic fighting manga. Japan's Agency for Cultural Affairs has named *Dragon Ball* the third-best manga of all time based on its endurance and its impact on the genre.

Films

Dragon Ball Evolution. Directed by James Wong. Twentieth Century Fox, 2009. This live-action film adaptation stars Justin Chatwin as Goku and Chow Yun Fat as Master Roshi. The film differs greatly from the manga, placing Goku in a modern-day high school and drastically changing the circumstances of his conflict with King Piccolo, the film's antagonist.

Television Series

Dragon Ball. Directed by Daisuke Nishio. TOEI Animation, 1986-1989. This animated series follows the manga series closely. The initial English release was heavily edited and aired on Cartoon Network from 2001 to 2003. In 2009, FUNimation released the uncut English version for the first time.

Dragon Ball Z. Directed by Minoru Okazaki. TOEI Animation, 1989-1996. This animated series loosely follows Volumes 17 through 42 of *Dragon Ball*, published under the title *Dragon Ball Z* in the United States. The original North American release, dubbed by Ocean Productions, was heavily edited. The series has since been redubbed and released by FUNimation.

Dragon Ball GT. Directed by Minoru Okazaki. TOEI Animation, 1996-1997. This animated series takes place after the events of the manga. FUNimation initially skipped the first sixteen episodes, which it later dubbed and released.

Rachel Cantrell

Further Reading

Kishimoto, Masashi. *Naruto* (1999-   ).
Oda, Eiichiro. *One Piece* (1997-   ).
Watsuki, Nobuhiro. *Rurouni Kenshin* (1994-1999).

Bibliography

MacWilliams, Mark W., ed. *Japanese Visual Culture: Explorations in the World of Manga and Anime.* Armonk, N.Y.: M. E. Sharp, 2008.

Martinez, D. P., ed. *The Worlds of Japanese Popular Culture: Gender, Shifting Boundaries, and Global Cultures.* New York: Cambridge University Press, 1998.

Schodt, Frederik L. *Dreamland Japan: Writings on Modern Manga.* Berkeley, Calif.: Stone Bridge Press, 1996.

See also: *Adolf: A Tale of the Twentieth Century; Black Jack; Blade of the Immortal; A Drifting Life*

DR. SLUMP

Author: Toriyama, Akira
Artist: Akira Toriyama (illustrator)
Publisher: Shūeisha (Japanese); VIZ Media (English)
First serial publication: *Dokutā Suranpu*, 1980-1984
First book publication: 1980-1985 (English translation, 2005-2009)

Publication History

From 1980 to 1984, Akira Toriyama's *Dr. Slump* was serialized in the Japanese comic magazine *Weekly Shōnen Jump*, beginning in issue 5 and concluding in issue 39. It was Toriyama's first breakout hit, inspiring a 243-episode animated series, a series of animated films and direct-to-video specials, and a vast array of merchandise, including toys and video games. The cast appeared briefly in Toriyama's even more successful follow-up, *Dragon Ball* (1984-1995). Other than *Dragon Ball*, *Dr. Slump* is the work most identified with Toriyama.

The series was originally collected in eighteen volumes by Shūeisha, with a nine-volume collector's edition released in 1990, a nine-volume novel-quality edition in 1995, and a fifteen-volume "complete collection" in 2006. Beginning in 2005, the series was translated into English and published by VIZ Media. Volume 18, matching the original Japanese collection of the series, was released in 2009.

Plot

Dr. Slump is a humorous science-fiction comic originally intended for the elementary-to-young-adult audience of Japan's *Weekly Shōnen Jump* comic magazine. The story follows Dr. Senbei Norimaki, an inventor whose perpetual personal and professional failures have earned him the nickname "Dr. Slump." Senbei lives in Penguin Village, a bizarre town occupied by humans and humanoid animals as well as robots, aliens, superheroes, and monsters. One of Senbei's few successes has been building a robot girl named Arale; however, though an undeniable technical achievement, Arale is inexplicably nearsighted and prone to inadvertently causing mayhem with the combination of her enthusiastic nature and prodigious robot strength.

Dr. Slump. (Courtesy of VIZ Media)

Following his creation of Arale, Senbei spends a significant portion of the series trying halfheartedly and unsuccessfully to teach her to pass as a normal human girl. What time Senbei does not spend humanizing Arale is spent inventing ambitious but unusable devices and trying unsuccessfully to woo attractive women such as Arale's schoolteacher, Ms. Yamabuki.

Arale, meanwhile, splits her time between attending school and getting into mischief or going on adventures with her friends: bored delinquent Akane Kimidori, harmless loudmouth Taro Soramame, and Taro's genial younger brother Peasuke. Arale is also frequently accompanied by Gatchan, a green-haired cherubic creature hatched from an egg she finds early in the series.

The series is episodic. Most stories are stand-alone installments built around a humorous situation or adventure usually involving Arale's misunderstanding of normal human behavior, Senbei's limited experience with women, or one of Senbei's inventions. Later adventures revolve around new additions to the cast, including the Tsun family and the mad scientist Dr. Mashirito. The latter frequently plots to destroy Arale, going so far as to build a male copy of her named Caramel Man 004.

The biggest change in the series comes when Senbei finally proposes marriage to Ms. Yamabuki, thinking she is out of earshot. Predictably, this is not the case, and she hears him. Unpredictably, she agrees; the two marry and start a family, having the superpowered baby Turbo. Turbo takes the spotlight as the main character for several chapters before the story returns to featuring Arale and Senbei. With the title character's central problem, bachelorhood, resolved, the series advances to features such as a metafictional question-and-answer session between Toriyama and his readers before finally concluding with a massive motorcycle race.

Volumes

- *Dr. Slump*, Volume 1 (2005). Dr. Senbei Norimaki struggles to pass off Arale as a human girl. Meanwhile, Arale makes friends in Penguin Village.
- *Dr. Slump*, Volume 2 (2005). Arale unintentionally terrorizes a bank robber who thinks he has taken her hostage. When Arale complains about not having something all the other girls have (a belly button), Senbei goes on a "research trip" with a pair of X-ray glasses.
- *Dr. Slump*, Volume 3 (2005). Arale deals with an alien invasion and a short circuit in her brain that makes her act like a normal girl. Upon recovering, she begins her strange fascination with the occasionally alive piles of feces that litter Penguin Village.
- *Dr. Slump*, Volume 4 (2005). Toriyama appears in the story to challenge his creations to a game of "kick the can" and promises to grant a wish for the winner.

- *Dr. Slump*, Volume 5 (2006). Peasuke meets the girl of his dreams but almost loses her when Arale fires a shrink ray at her to make her Peasuke's size.
- *Dr. Slump*, Volume 6 (2006). Senbei has a feces-based nightmare, and recurring mad scientist villain Dr. Mashirito makes his first appearance.
- *Dr. Slump*, Volume 7 (2006). Senbei stars in a production of *Cinderella* that is hindered when Toriyama runs out of pages. Meanwhile, Arale discovers the simple joy of poking toothpicks into snacks and applies it to all sorts of objects around the village.
- *Dr. Slump*, Volume 8 (2006). Alien invaders and a megalomaniac armed with robotic feces face Arale and friends in the "Penguin Village Wars."
- *Dr. Slump*, Volume 9 (2006). Senbei proposes to Ms. Yamabuki; a panel later, they are a married couple facing a genuinely bizarre honeymoon and multiple kidnappings of the new bride.
- *Dr. Slump*, Volume 10 (2006). The Tsun family is introduced when they crash their rocket in Penguin Village. The Tsun children quickly acclimate themselves to life in the village when they compete in the Penguin Village High School Olympics.
- *Dr. Slump*, Volume 11 (2007). Senbei and his new friend Tsuru-Ten Tsun go to the village bathhouse to peep on girls with X-ray glasses, forgetting that everyone there is already naked. Later, Senbei tries to explain Arale's existence to his grandfather.
- *Dr. Slump*, Volume 12 (2007). Senbei fixes the antigravity devices of both the Tsuns and the alien invaders from Volume 8, enabling both groups to leave. Arale and the Gatchans stow away on the invaders' ship.
- *Dr. Slump*, Volume 13 (2007). Dr. Mashirito builds Caramel Man 004 to destroy Arale and is forced to build models 005, 006, and 007 when 004 falls in love with her.
- *Dr. Slump*, Volume 14 (2008). Dr. Mashirito and his creation Caramel Man 007 finally succeed in destroying Arale, but her death is temporary.
- *Dr. Slump*, Volume 15 (2008) The Norimakis' child, Turbo, is born. Senbei finds it hard to deal

with the normal stresses of new parenting, let alone Turbo's superpowers.

- *Dr. Slump*, Volume 16 (2008). Toriyama runs an extensive question-and-answer session, fielding questions from both his readers and his characters. Meanwhile, Dr. Mashirito's latest plot involves impersonating Santa Claus.
- *Dr. Slump*, Volume 17 (2009). God reveals the Gatchans to be angels, and only Arale and friends stand between God and his wrath toward his cherubic creations.
- *Dr. Slump*, Volume 18 (2009). Toriyama indulges his love of motorcycles by throwing the characters into a massive motorcycle race.

Characters

- *Dr. Senbei Norimaki*, a.k.a. *Dr. Slump*, the protagonist, is a squat, husky man in his early thirties with curly black hair and a mustache that never seems to grow in fully or remain shaven for more than a few minutes. While he is technically skilled as an inventor, his inventions are usually flawed or unsuccessful. He is the inventor and "father" of Arale.
- *Arale Norimaki*, a.k.a. *Arale-chan*, is a robot girl designed to look roughly thirteen years old. She has straight purple hair and wears large glasses. She is a friendly, high-spirited girl and a bit of a tomboy.
- *Gadzilla Norimaki*, a.k.a. *Gatchan*, is a flying, green-haired cherub who speaks in a bubbling baby language that only Arale and Turbo Norimaki can understand. It is able to eat almost any material, clone itself, and shoot rays from its antennae. Gatchan is Arale's companion and is revealed late in the series to be an angel sent by God to keep human development under control.
- *Dr. Mashirito* becomes the recurring antagonist midway through the series. He is a lean, squinty-eyed man with sunken cheeks and an immense Afro hairstyle. His repeated failure to destroy Arale and the Norimakis forces him to replace his body parts with cybernetic ones.
- *Caramel Man 004* is an invention of Dr. Mashirito, based on stolen plans for Arale and

without those aspects of Arale that Mashirito finds annoying. Caramel Man 004 appears to be a neatly dressed, bespectacled boy about Arale's age. Though created as part of the Caramel Man series of robots, 004 falls immediately in love with Arale instead of destroying her as intended.

Artistic Style

Dr. Slump is drawn in a distinct visual style: Characters and settings are drawn squat and clear-lined, in what is known as the "super-deformed style." The characters have rounded, potbellied bodies, overly large heads, and detailed features. There is a touch of American cartooning style to the art, evident in the rounded, soft forms of the characters. Despite the cartooniness of the characters and setting, Toriyama occasionally draws in a more traditional or realistic style for comedic effect.

The chief artistic appeal of *Dr. Slump* is Toriyama's "anything goes" sense of visual inventiveness. Each chapter is packed not only with deliberate gags that drive the story but also with numerous background jokes, asides, and sequences that break the fourth wall. The line work of the series clearly evolves from a more

---

Akira Toriyama

Akira Toriyama, born in 1955 in Japan, is a massive figure in a field thick with massive figures who tell the stories of massive figures. His *Dragon Ball* helped define the words "manga" and "anime" for Earth almost as effectively as his heroes have defended it—and that series and its many spinoffs have made him a very wealthy man. His character designs have outfitted such video games as *Dragon Quest* and *Blue Dragon*. When Shūeisha, his longtime publisher, needs an icon to identify it, it is inevitably Toriyama who is called upon to lend his buoyant hand to the project. His most beloved work in his native land is arguably *Dr. Slump*, a comedic series that to Western readers is sort of a mix of *Pinocchio*, *My Fair Lady*, and a very cute *Frankenstein*. Newcomers to his work might try *Cowa!* or *Sandland*, both rare for being single-volume manga.

gag-based cartooning style to that of a skilled illustrator working in a deliberately funny style. This stylistic growth paid off in Toriyama's subsequent series, *Dragon Ball*.

Toriyama also begins a trend in *Dr. Slump* that would follow him throughout the rest of his career and become one of the most lauded aspects of his work: an attention to technical detail paid to even the most fantastic machine. Toriyama has stated that when drawing machinery, no matter how exaggerated or unreplicable in the real world, he always considers practical details such as how someone would climb aboard it, where someone would sit, and how the machine would move without falling over.

Themes

As a series primarily concerned with humor, *Dr. Slump* includes themes generally related to whatever amused or interested Toriyama when he sat down at the drawing table. While the initial story stemmed from a riff on the seminal manga series *Astro Boy* (1952-1968), the series is filtered through Toriyama's own experiences. Toriyama based Senbei on himself, and considering that Toriyama accumulated five hundred pages of rejected comics before hitting on *Dr. Slump*, one can infer a self-deprecating humor in naming an authorial doppelgänger "Dr. Slump." One can also infer that when Senbei settles down and starts a family, Toriyama is again drawing on his own experiences. Primarily, however, *Dr. Slump* seems to be a vehicle through which Toriyama explores his thoughts on popular culture and passing interests in a humorous manner, poking fun at himself and his editors, honing his craft, and delighting in "playing around" in his chosen profession.

Impact

For what is essentially a loose autobiographical parody of *Astro Boy*, *Dr. Slump* remains something of a phenomenon. The series is a popular "classic," with merchandise still produced decades after the series' conclusion. In addition to inspiring toys, animated series, and video games, *Dr. Slump* has influenced Japanese culture in at least one enduring way: The style of large glasses Arale wears in the series has come to be widely associated with her.

Ending in 1984, *Dr. Slump* helped to usher in the "Golden Age of Jump" that took place from roughly 1985 to 1995 and saw *Weekly Shōnen Jump*'s subscription numbers hit 6.5 million. *Dr. Slump* made a name for Toriyama and paved the way for his follow-up manga, *Dragon Ball*, one of the megahit series that contributed to the Golden Age. While *Dr. Slump* is dwarfed in popularity by the more story- and action-oriented *Dragon Ball*, its inventiveness is rarely matched. *Dr. Slump*'s absurdist humor is echoed in later series such as *One Piece* (1997-) and *Gin Tama* (2003-).

Films

Dr. Slump and Arale-chan: Hello! Wonder Land! Directed by Minoru Okazaki. Toei Animation, 1982. This film adaptation stars the cartoon's regular voice actors, Kenji Utsumi (Senbei Norimaki) and Mami Koyama (Arale Norimaki). The film adapts the series installments "Hello, Wonder Island" and "The Ogre-King Gyaska," wherein Senbei finds a videotape from his father detailing how to make a love potion.

Dr. Slump: "Hoyoyo!" Space Adventure. Directed by Akinori Nagaoka. Toei Animation, 1982. This film adaptation stars Utsumi and Koyama; Mariko Mukai plays Yamashita-sensei, a teacher whom Arale discovers is, in fact, an alien.

Dr. Slump and Arale-chan: The Great Race Around the World. Directed by Minoru Okazaki. Toei Animation, 1983. This film adaptation stars Utsumi and Koyama and revolves around a cross-continent race that Arale and Senbei enter. Oddly enough, the film was released before Toriyama concluded the manga series with his own massive race.

Dr. Slump and Arale-chan: Hoyoyo! The Secret of the Nanaba Castle. Directed by Hiroki Shibata. Toei Animation, 1984. This film adaptation stars Utsumi and Koyama and follows a series of thefts and counterthefts of the Eye of the Rainbow, a magical stone.

Dr. Slump and Arale-chan: Hoyoyo! The City of Dream, Mechapolis. Directed by Kazuhisa Takenouchi and Toyoo Ashida. Toei Animation, 1985. This film adaptation stars Utsumi and Koyama. Arale, the Gatchans, Akane, and Tsukutsun Tsun have an adventure in the Mechapolis and contend with the Mecha Police.

Dr. Slump and Arale-chan: Sunny Penguin Village. Directed by Yukio Kaizawa. Toei Animation, 1993. This film adaptation features Utsumi and Koyama and acts as a series reboot, reiterating the creation of Arale and adapting a Volume 4 story in which the Penguin Village police are caught between a giant monster attack and a "helpful" Arale.

Dr. Slump and Arale-chan: N-cha! From Penguin Village with Love. Directed by Mitsuo Hashimoto. Toei Animation, 1993. This film adaptation features Utsumi and Koyama. This second "reboot" film features numerous cameos from *Dragon Ball* characters and the first appearance of Nitro Norimaki, a second Norimaki child who only appears in the 1990's films. Unlike older sibling Turbo, Nitro has no superpowers.

Dr. Slump and Arale-chan: Hoyoyo!! Follow the Rescued Shark. Directed by Mitsuo Hashimoto. Toei Animation, 1994. This film adaptation features voice actors Utsumi and Koyama. Arale rescues a baby shark from some chains, and the Norimakis follow it on an undersea adventure.

Dr. Slump and Arale-chan: N-cha!! Trembling Heart of the Summer. Directed by Mitsuo Hashimoto. Toei Animation, 1994. This film features Utsumi and Koyama and is the fourth in the reboot series. Arale's summer vacation involves dealing with a group of supernatural creatures.

Dr. Slump: Arale's Surprising Burn! Directed by Shigeyasu Yamauchi. Toei Animation, 1999. This film adaptation stars Yuusaku Yara as Senbei and Taeko Kawata as Arale. Technically, this film could be considered a third reboot, as it uses the designs and voice cast from the second television series. Arale and company find a mysterious magic stone

on a picnic and have to defend it from a sudden attack by pirates and magical creatures.

Television Series

Dr. Slump. Directed by Minoru Okazaki. Toei Animation, 1981-1986. This 243-episode series stars Utsumi and Koyama. It is a fairly straight adaptation of the comic, albeit with the necessary padding and extra jokes required to turn an eighteen-page comic into a half-hour program. The series was dubbed in French, Italian, and Spanish. The first episode was

Dr. Slump. (Courtesy of VIZ Media)

dubbed by Harmony Gold for American distribution; however, the pilot was never picked up.

Dr. Slump. Directed by Shigeyasu Yamauchi. Toei Animation, 1997-1999. This 74-episode series stars Yara and Kawata and adapts the original manga story, with some story changes. It was dubbed into Italian, Spanish, and German.

Josh Hechinger

Further Reading

Graham, Brandon. *King City* (2007-2010).
Oda, Eiichiro *One Piece* (2003-   ).
Toriyama, Akira. *Dragon Ball* (1985-1989).

Bibliography

Oda, Eiichiro, and Akira Toriyama. "Monochrome Talk: Eiichiro Oda X Akira Toriyama." In *One Piece: Color Walk 1—Art of Shōnen Jump*, edited by Elizabeth Kowasaki. San Francisco, Calif.: VIZ Media, 2005.

Toriyama, Akira, and Rumiko Takahashi. "Toriyama/ Takahashi Interview." Translated by Toshiaki Yamada. *Rumic World*. http://www.furinkan.com/takahashi/takahashi4.html.

See also: *Dragon Ball; Bleach; Astro Boy; One Piece*

DRIFTING CLASSROOM, THE

Author: Umezu, Kazuo
Artist: Kazuo Umezu (illustrator); Kelle Han (letterer); Izumi Evers (cover artist)
Publisher: Shogakukan (Japanese); VIZ Media (English)
First serial publication: *Hyōryu kyōshitsu*, 1972-1974
First book publication: 1998 (English translation, 2006-2008)

Publication History

Kazuo Umezu's horror manga *The Drifting Classroom* was originally published serially in Japan under its Japanese title, *Hyōryu kyōshitsu*. The series appeared in *Shōnen Sunday* magazine from 1972 to 1974. Yuji Oniki's English translation was released by VIZ Media from 2006 to 2008, appearing as eleven bound volumes, each containing between three and five chapters of the manga. VIZ Media's English translation maintains the original Japanese right-to-left reading format, meaning Umezu's original artwork is preserved and not "reversed" as is the case with many American manga publications.

Plot

After arguing with his mother, protagonist Sho Takamatsu goes to school for the day. Yamato Elementary and everyone inside are transported into the future, appearing in a postapocalyptic wasteland. Only one student, Shinichi Yamada, is saved from this fate, as he forgot his lunch money and left school to get it prior to the event. Order at the school deteriorates rapidly in the wasteland; one student falls from the roof and dies, and teachers panic and use violence against students to silence them. A teacher named Mr. Wakahara goes insane and murders his colleagues, while Sekiya, the school lunch man, kidnaps a student and assaults several more.

Initially the children believe they have been teleported to another geographic location on Earth, but after discovering a memorial for Yamato Elementary's dead, they realize that they have been transported forward in time. The space-time barrier is permeable, and Sho is able to communicate backward through time with his

The Drifting Classroom. (Courtesy of VIZ Media)

mother, Emiko, who hides helpful survival tools in obscure places for Sho to "rediscover" in the future.

Once the majority of the adults are dead, Yamato Elementary descends into chaos reminiscent of William Golding's *Lord of the Flies* (1954). Sho leads his classmates against the mutinous efforts of bullies such as "Princess," who wants to become dictator of Yamato Elementary. At the same time, Sho must attend to basic survival needs, such as finding food. This leads the students to declare their school a "nation" led by elected representatives, with Sho as their president.

In addition to these human conflicts, the children of Yamato Elementary combat the strange forces inhabiting the future world. A giant insect attacks the school whenever Nakata, one of the students, eats. When the children return from an expedition to kill the monster, they find the school infested with the monster's babies, who swarm over the students, stripping flesh from bone instantaneously. The creatures disappear when Nakata kills himself to save his friends.

Soon afterward, an outbreak of bubonic plague hits the school. Infected, Sho and his friends go into exile to find a solution to the epidemic. Rogue students run amok in their absence and murder anyone they suspect of being infected. Sho and his friends retake the school by scaring their enemies with a mummy found in a vault. After being cured by a supply of streptomycin Emiko hid in the mummy, the children burn piles of bodies to destroy any traces of the plague.

Discovering a crack in the swimming pool, which is their primary water supply, Sho and his friends venture into the desert to find a new source. Sakiko stays behind and encourages her fellow students to pray for rain. The rain song works, but the desert is hit with a flash flood and becomes a muddy bog. Sakiko nearly dies while saving the school's plants, which begin to bear fruit.

The fruit trees become infected with a fungus that alters students who eat the fruit into scaled monsters. The transformed students worship a one-eyed deity, which visits the school and takes its devotees away. Sekiya uses this event as an opportunity to seize control of the school, enslaving the students and forcing them to dig a well. One of the students claims he saw Sho sneaking into the school with a stick of dynamite prior to the school's temporal displacement, suggesting he is to blame for the students' predicament.

While digging Sekiya's well the children find a tunnel leading underground to a subway system inhabited by mutants similar in appearance to the one-eyed deity. The mutants project a film that explains how the world became a desert as a result of overpopulation and pollution. They chase the children, who escape and find a freshwater spring that turns out to be volcanic. They run from rivers of lava to warn the school of the danger. Sho and his friends surface to find the mutants attacking the school, and Sekiya sends several children to defend the building while he escapes in a van. The mutants depart, and Sho blacks out.

Sho awakens and argues with Otomo, who believes the situation is hopeless, especially now that giant flesh-eating starfish are attacking the school. Sho and Otomo get into a knife fight, which culminates in their decision to divide the school into two halves.

Walking through the desert, the children find a derelict amusement park populated by robotic dinosaurs and cavemen, who try to kill the children. A talking computer explains how Yamato Elementary was teleported into the future: A dynamite explosion acted as a catalyst, propelling the school through a weak spot in the space-time barrier. Otomo confesses he tried to blow up the school. The children hold hands in a circle as Otomo lights his last stick of dynamite, each focusing on his or her desire to return home. In the present, Emiko goes on national television and encourages the Japanese population to join the children in this ritual.

Meanwhile, Sakiko flees from the group of survivors after realizing she does not want to return home, as she enjoys being a mother to Yu; however, Yu wants to return to his parents. The children reconvene to send Yu back to the past, hoping to utilize the force of the nearby volcano as a catalyst in place of Otomo's dynamite. Sekiya arrives seeking to kill them and is strangled by a disembodied arm. Yu returns to the present and gives Emiko Sho's notebook, which contains the details of the children's experiences in the wasteland. Emiko receives a phone call from an American scientist who wants to help send Sho supplies in the future. The manga ends with Emiko seeing Sho and his friends running through the stars.

Volumes

- *The Drifting Classroom*, Volume 1 (2006). Collects chapters 1-4. The school is teleported into the future and the protagonists are introduced.
- *The Drifting Classroom*, Volume 2 (2006). Collects chapters 5-9. The situation escalates at Yamato Elementary as the adults at the school go insane, turning against the children and one another.
- *The Drifting Classroom*, Volume 3 (2006). Collects chapters 10-13. The children venture outside of the school grounds in search of life, and

"Princess" stages a coup to take control of the school.

- *The Drifting Classroom*, Volume 4 (2007). Collects chapters 14-17. The children hold a tense democratic election and attempt to fend off an insectile invader.
- *The Drifting Classroom*, Volume 5 (2007). Collects chapters 18-22. The children attempt to escape the insect monster's babies and find a way to stop Nakata from materializing his nightmares.
- *The Drifting Classroom*, Volume 6 (2007). Collects chapters 23-25. The children struggle against the bubonic plague sweeping the halls of Yamato Elementary.
- *The Drifting Classroom*, Volume 7 (2007). Collects chapters 26-28. The school floods, and Sho and his friends wade through the desert, which turns to mud.
- *The Drifting Classroom*, Volume 8 (2007). Collects chapters 29-33. Sekiya enslaves the schoolchildren, and Sho and his friends explore the frightening world of the mutant-infested subway system.
- *The Drifting Classroom*, Volume 9 (2007). Collects chapters 34-36. Sho's and Otomo's groups come into conflict.
- *The Drifting Classroom*, Volume 10 (2008). Collects chapters 37-40. The children battle robotic dinosaurs, cavemen, and each other in a derelict amusement park.
- *The Drifting Classroom*, Volume 11 (2008). Collects chapters 41-43. Sekiya is finally defeated, and the children attempt to return to their original time.

Characters

- *Sho Takamatsu*, the protagonist, is a short sixth-grade boy with tousled hair and a furrowed brow. At first, he is a spoiled child with little sense of responsibility, but he later becomes one of the most mature characters in the series. A natural leader, he is rational and compassionate, and he is eventually voted president of the nation of Yamato Elementary.
- *Yuichi*, a.k.a. *Yu*, is a young child clad in overalls, often seen riding a tricycle. Although he is

Kazuo Umezu

Kazuo Umezu, born in 1936, is one the most acclaimed manga creators working in the field of horror. Outside Japan, he is best known for his *The Drifting Classroom* series, which ran in the early 1970's in the Shogakukan-published magazine *Weekly Shōnen Sunday*. His other notable works include *Orochi: Blood* and *Cat Eyed Boy*. Umezu was raised in rural Japan, and he has cited the legends of that region as a primary source for his own inventions. His fantastic horror creations—stark images of monstrous beings and of humans behaving monstrously—have garnered him a substantial following outside Japan. A public figure in his native country, Umezu is almost always photographed in his trademark horizontally striped shirts of wide red-and-white bands.

young, he is extremely brave and loyal to Sho. He returns to the present at the end of the manga.

- *Emiko Takamatsu* is Sho's mother. After Sho is transported into the distant future, she becomes his primary lifeline.
- *Shinichi Yamada* is one of Sho's friends and the only student to avoid transportation into the future. He has black hair with long bangs and is one of the few people in the present who believes the children of Yamato Elementary are still alive.
- *Sakiko Kawada* is a female student with a ponytail who is in love with Sho. Her younger brother is killed early in the story after running out into the desert. She becomes a surrogate mother to many students at Yamato Elementary, particularly Yu.
- *Mr. Wakahara* is a teacher at Yamato Elementary. He has wavy hair and wears a suit. He goes insane and murders all of the teachers and almost kills Sho.
- *Kyusaku Sekiya* is the man who delivers school lunches. He was popular with the students before

the school was transported, but he becomes violent and sadistic. He dies after a disembodied arm rips through the fabric of space-time and strangles him.

- *Ikegaki* is one of Sho's classmates. He has prominent front teeth and a bowl-cut hairstyle. Ikegaki is one of Sho's strongest and bravest allies and minister of defense at Yamato Elementary. He dies fighting the insect monster.

- *Ayumi Nishi* is a fifth-grade student with long blond hair and crutches. She has "prophetic" dreams that enable her to see into the past, allowing Sho to communicate with his mother. She is instrumental in returning Yu to the present.

- *Otomo* is a black-haired boy with a cowlick and one of Sho's classmates. Sho names Otomo the minister of health and welfare. He is pessimistic and easily angered. He confesses to setting off the explosion at the school.

Artistic Style

All of the drawings in *The Drifting Classroom* are black and white. The panels are strictly ordered, rectangular, and sized according to the importance of the events they contain. Umezu uses full-page spreads to emphasize important plot points and frequently uses a "zoom lens" effect in his drawings, gradually focusing on particular details or panning away from scenes for dramatic effect. VIZ Media's translation of *The Drifting Classroom* is formatted so that the

traditional right-to-left reading pattern characteristic of manga is maintained.

Umezu's artwork is characterized by liberal use of black ink. He uses aggressive shading and precise black lines to create an oppressive atmosphere appropriate to the horror genre. Backgrounds are highly detailed and drawn in a realistic mode that contrasts with

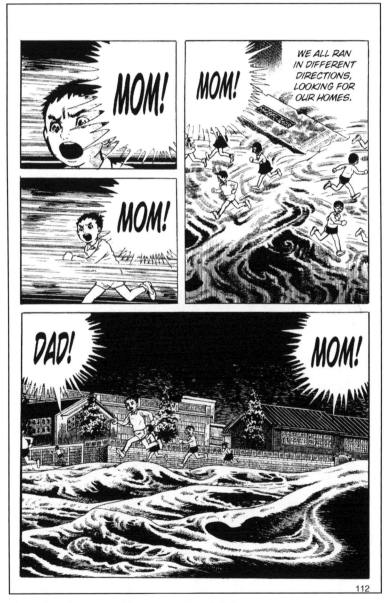

The Drifting Classroom. (Courtesy of VIZ Media)

his often-stylized characters. The incongruity between *The Drifting Classroom*'s cartoonish protagonists and the realistic environments they inhabit highlights the frighteningly alien atmosphere of the children's new world. Often, backgrounds are simply repeating patterns designed to evoke emotional responses; for example, concentric circles and small black bubbles in the background indicate fear, delusion, and madness.

Umezu draws the characters of *The Drifting Classroom* in an exaggerated manner, especially in terms of their facial features and emotions. Some characters, such as Mr. Wakahara, are drawn realistically, while others, such as the goofy Hatsuta, barely look human. Umezu amplifies the facial expressions of his characters to highlight the terror of their situation. Sho almost always has a wide-open mouth and eyes, making him look simultaneously angry and frightened. A particularly unique effect is Umezu's representation of wild eyes; at times, his characters seem to have four pupils, indicating their rapid eye movement. Heavy black lines around the eyes of the characters represent insanity or stress.

Although Umezu's characters are not always physically realistic, his embellished features differentiate the characters from one another and allow them to embody a wide variety of emotions. In many cases, realistic representation indicates a character's lack of innocence; adult characters generally look more realistic than children, whose faces are drawn with minimal lines and white space.

Themes

The Drifting Classroom is a horror manga written to evoke feelings of dread. Umezu uses dark environments and monstrous creatures to establish a frightening atmosphere. Perhaps the most horrifying aspects of *The Drifting Classroom* are the ways in which the human characters treat each another and how quickly civility devolves into anarchy. Umezu plays with group dynamics and mob psychology to show that the students of Yamato Elementary pose a greater threat to one another than carnivorous starfish, giant insects, or the bubonic plague ever could. Some members of the group consider their own lives more important than the lives of their companions and kill others to survive. As

president of Yamato Elementary, Sho negotiates a variety of problematic situations between students at the school to ensure the survival of as many of his classmates as possible. He vacillates between his sense of responsibility for his classmates and his disgust over the frequently deplorable nature of human beings.

There is an environmentalist undercurrent in *The Drifting Classroom*, as the students are transported into a barren future in which the world has been stripped of all of its natural resources and beauty. They quickly learn that resources at the school are finite: If a student breaks a window, for example, it cannot be replaced. This notion of nonrenewable resources, combined with the mutants' bleak retelling of the fall of humanity, encourages readers to consider the ecological problems facing the modern world. Tying into *The Drifting Classroom*'s environmentalist theme is its focus on the relationship between the past and the present. The children live in a barren wasteland because of the events of the past, which destroyed the future that they are forced to inhabit. Sho directly influences events in the future by calling to his mother in the present. At the end of the manga, when Yu is sent back to his original time, he promises to change people's ideas about the environment so Sho and his friends can live in a brighter future.

Impact

Much of Umezu's cultural impact in Japan is the result of his prolific output and creative approach to his art. Umezu has produced a tremendous number of manga in a variety of genres throughout his lifetime, including comedies, surrealist adventures, and ghost stories. *The Drifting Classroom* remains Umezu's most famous and widely read foray into horror manga because of its gripping and often bizarre storyline and its grim insights into the human condition. Several Japanese horror-manga writers cite Umezu as an influence, including Junji Ito and Toru Yamazaki. In Japan, Umezu is as much of a household name for the horror genre as writers such as Stephen King and Edgar Allan Poe are in the West. *The Drifting Classroom* received favorable reviews in Western periodicals and is commonly cited as a masterwork of horror manga.

Films

The Drifting Classroom. Directed by Nobuhiko Obayashi. Bandai Entertainment, 1987. This live-action film adaptation was written by Kazuo Umezu, Izō Hashimoto, Yoji Ogura, and Mitsutoshi Ishigami and stars Yasufumi Hayashi as Sho and Aiko Asano as Ayumi. The film adaptation is set at an international school in Kobe, Japan, and the characters are teenagers rather than elementary school students.

Television Series

Long Love Letter. Directed by Mizuta Narahide. Fuji Television Network, 2002. This eleven-episode live-action television drama series stars Takayuki Yamada as Sho and Tomohisa Yamashita as Otomo. The series focuses on a romantic relationship between two of the teachers at the school. *Long Love Letter* has a more optimistic plot than *The Drifting Classroom* and features an older cast of characters.

Fergus Baird

Further Reading

Ito, Junji. *Uzumaki* (2001-2002).

Ohba, Tsugumi, and Takeshi Obata. *Death Note* (2003-2006).

Yamazaki, Toru. *Octopus Girl* (2006).

Bibliography

"*The Drifting Classroom.*" Review of *The Drifting Classroom*, by Kazuo Umezu. *Publishers Weekly* 253, no. 25 (2006): 46.

Kawamoto, Saburo. "The Nightmarish Imagination." In *The Drifting Classroom, Volume 11.* San Francisco, Calif.: VIZ Media, 2008.

Macias, Patrick. "About the Artist: Kazuo Umezu." In *The Drifting Classroom, Volume 1.* San Francisco, Calif.: VIZ Media, 2006.

See also: *Death Note; Monster; Uzumaki*

DRIFTING LIFE, A
THE EPIC AUTOBIOGRAPHY OF A MANGA MASTER

Author: Tatsumi, Yoshihiro

Artist: Yoshihiro Tatsumi (illustrator); Adrian Tomine (letterer)

Publisher: Seirin Kōgeisha (Japanese); Drawn and Quarterly (English)

First serial publication: *Gekiga hyōryū*, 1995-2006

First book publication: 2008 (English translation, 2009)

Publication History

Originally serialized in a Japanese used-manga catalog issued by a publishing section of the used-manga franchise Mandarake, Yoshihiro Tatsumi's *A Drifting Life* first appeared as *Gekiga hyōryū* in *Mandarake manga mokuroku* (Mandarake manga catalog) from March of 1995 to September of 1998 (Volumes 8-22). The comic then continued in *Mandarake zenbu* (all Mandarake) from December of 1998 to December of 2006 (Volumes 1-33).

Mandarake stores sell used manga, magazines, anime videos and DVDs, video games, and related products. *Mandarake manga mokuroku* and *Mandarake zenbu* primarily promote store stock to customers, also providing interviews with creators, short reviews, columns, and event announcements. The serialization of a manga in these catalogs was rather unconventional, as manga series usually appear in manga-specific magazines.

In 2008, Seirin Kōgeisha published *Gekiga hyōryū* in book form. The work was translated into English and published as *A Drifting Life* by Canadian publisher Drawn and Quarterly in 2009. *A Drifting Life* has also been translated into Spanish and Indonesian.

Plot

This semiautobiographical graphic novel narrates the life of protagonist Hiroshi Katsumi, a veiled representation of Tatsumi, from his childhood to his later life as a manga artist. The main plot develops around the

A Drifting Life. (Courtesy of Drawn and Quarterly)

protagonist's efforts and struggles to create a new type of manga called *gekiga*, often translated into English as "dramatic pictures."

A Drifting Life opens in Osaka after World War II, when Japan was still suffering from material shortages. A thirteen-year-old boy, Hiroshi is an enthusiastic fan of the works of manga creator Osamu Tezuka. Influenced by his sickly brother, Okimasa, he begins drawing manga and soon starts sending one-frame and four-frame gag-strip manga drawn on postcards to popular manga magazine contests. At first, he is outdone by his brother, but Hiroshi gradually gets his manga accepted by several different manga magazines. Manga drawing provides a sense of comfort for him, since his childhood is wrought with difficulties, including financial adversity, his brother's chronic illness, and his parents' failed marriage. His manga, now appearing consistently in magazines, attracts the attention of a local newspaper, which leads to a meeting with Tezuka. His interactions with Tezuka and young manga creators further stimulate Hiroshi's passion for drawing manga.

Hiroshi's entrance into high school coincides with the end of the American occupation of Japan. Just before entering high school, Hiroshi begins to exchange personal correspondence with popular manga creator Noboru Ōgi and sends a story manga to him; it is eventually published. Ōgi invites Hiroshi to his Tokyo apartment, offering him a comic apprenticeship, but Hiroshi declines the invitation, feeling that he should finish high school first.

As graduation approaches, Hiroshi plans to take the entrance exam for Kyoto City University of Arts. However, he skips the exam because of a sudden lack of confidence. With the help of his brother, who has recovered from his illness, Hiroshi searches for publishers and finds Hakkō/Hinomaru-bunko, a publisher that produces *kashihon* (rental-book) manga in Osaka, which becomes a base for Hiroshi and other *kashihon* manga creators.

Publishing his manga work with Hakkō/Hinomaru-bunko and other publishers, Hiroshi encounters other rising manga creators, such as Masahiko Matsumoto, Masami Hirota, Shigeji Isojima, Susumu Yamamori, and Takao Saitō. Hiroshi's brother also starts contributing manga under the name Shōichi Sakurai. With these artists, Hiroshi studies drawings and has serious discussions about manga.

In friendly competition with the other artists, Hiroshi seeks to create a kind of manga without humor and mangalike gags. Inspired by Western and Japanese novels and films, especially hard-boiled detective fiction, Hiroshi starts drawing manga dealing with human psychology and human drama. The short manga collection *Kage* (shadow), to which Hiroshi and other creators contribute, is published; it triggers a boom for the *kashihon* industry. At the suggestion of an elderly manga creator, Hirota, Hiroshi moves into a small apartment to live with Matsumoto and Saitō, but this new working environment results in distractions, including the enticement of a female store owner who lives downstairs.

Yoshihiro Tatsumi

Yoshihiro Tatsumi, born in 1935, is a manga writer and illustrator who is widely acknowledged as the creator of the concept of *gekiga*, a more mature and literary approach to Japanese comics than the generally youth-oriented storytelling that preceded it. His manga frequently relate noir-style tales of urban life, chronicling the experiences of factory workers, prostitutes, and thieves. The mid-century, post-war settings often suggest parallels to the writings of Nelson Algren and Hubert Selby, Jr. Tatsumi is best known for his large-scale autobiography *A Drifting Life*. He has spoken frequently of the strong influence of Tezuka on his work. Tatsumi's reputation expanded internationally after Adrian Tomine, the American-born artist of Japanese descent, began editing a series of his works for the Canadian publisher Drawn & Quarterly (these include *Abandon the Old in Tokyo* as well as *The Push Man and Other Stories*). Tomine has complimented Tatsumi for his artful misanthropy.

As a result of mismanagement, Hinomaru-bunko declines. Hiroshi and other creators are invited to contribute manga to another publisher, Central Bunko in Nagoya. Soon after, Hinomaru-bunko recovers and asks Hiroshi to be an editor for the reborn *Kage*. After taking the editorship of the magazine, Hiroshi realizes that he cannot control the magazine, as publisher Shūzō Yamada intervenes often.

Hirota invites Hiroshi and Matsumoto to move to Tokyo, which, as expected, vexes Yamada. By this time, the manga creators realize that what they are drawing is no longer manga, a genre that has been associated with humorous comics. When the government begins to place restrictions on manga because of its depictions of violence, Hiroshi feels the need to create another name for the comics he is drawing. Matsumoto creates the term *komaga* for his works, while Hiroshi starts using *gekiga* for his comics. With other likeminded creators, Hiroshi establishes a creator group, the Gekiga Workshop, and publishes a short collection,

Matenrō (skyscraper). While it is successful, it also causes animosity between Hiroshi and Yamada.

The increasing pressure of being the editorial leader of the Gekiga Workshop and the constant tardiness of other creators discourages Hiroshi, and the group is disbanded after a year. As his faith in the comics genre wanes, he comes across a political demonstration led by protesters opposed to the Japanese-U.S. security treaty. He unwittingly participates in the demonstration, and while he stands in the middle of the crowd, Hiroshi rekindles his passion for *gekiga*. On the seventh anniversary of Tezuka's death, mature manga and *gekiga* creator Hiroshi muses on the past, reminiscing about a life sincerely devoted to creating *gekiga*.

Characters

- *Hiroshi Katsumi*, the protagonist, is a stand-in for author Tatsumi. He grows up with a strong passion for manga and eventually becomes a manga creator, coining the term *gekiga* and later organizing a creator group called the Gekiga Workshop. Hiroshi is the only character with a fictional name.
- *Okimasa Katsumi*, a.k.a. *Shōichi Sakurai*, is Hiroshi's older brother. As a child, he is sickly and often jealous of Hiroshi's success as a manga creator. As he grows older, he becomes more supportive, sometimes spurring Hiroshi to exercise his creativity. He also becomes a manga creator, using the pseudonym Shōichi Sakurai.
- *Shūzō Yamada* is an editor and publisher of the Osaka-based publishing company Hakkō/Hinomaru-bunko, through which Hiroshi and other manga creators publish their manga and build their careers. Yamada sometimes appears as a charlatan-like figure who tries to manipulate manga creators.
- *Masami Hirota* is an elderly manga creator working for Hakkō/Hinomaru-bunko. He was once one of the most popular manga creators in Osaka but lost

jobs because of a change in editorial policy. He becomes an adviser for Hinomaru-bunko. Although he usually helps young manga creators, he sometimes impedes them.

- *Masahiko Matsumoto* is a rival manga creator working for Hakkō/Hinomaru-bunko. Hiroshi often thinks Matsumoto surpasses him in terms of manga innovation. Later, Matsumoto coins the term *komaga*. He initially hesitates to join the Gekiga Workshop but eventually agrees to participate.
- *Takao Saitō* is a manga/*gekiga* creator who works with Hiroshi in the Gekiga Workshop. He lives with Hiroshi, but he often slacks off.

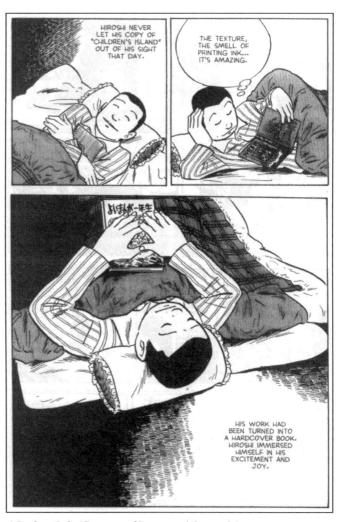

A Drifting Life. (Courtesy of Drawn and Quarterly)

Artistic Style

Gekiga is usually associated with "rough, dynamic drawing lines," "realistic depictions," or "the use of a dark background." Nonetheless, the dominant style of *A Drifting Life* is closer to the mainstream manga style influenced by the works of Tezuka. The work depicts all the characters in a simplified, cartoonish manner, but it also depicts a series of historical figures such as famous athletes, important politicians, popular entertainers, and media celebrities, all of whom are contrastingly drawn in photographic realism. Tatsumi's other *gekiga* works, especially those produced in the late 1960's and early 1970's—many of which have been collected and published in English by Drawn and Quarterly—employ dark, sullen, and realistic depictions of locations such as black markets, skid row, or other poor quarters of the urban areas. Compared to these previous works, *A Drifting Life* maintains a bright tone throughout, and it lacks the stark realism or graphic violence of some other *gekiga*.

Themes

The central theme is the personal and professional growth of the protagonist and his efforts and struggles in the manga industry. As an autobiography, *A Drifting Life* touches on many aspects of coming-of-age, including the author's transformation from a manga fan to a manga creator, childhood struggles of economic adversity and familial problems, sexual awakening and encounters, and collaborations and conflicts with publishers and other manga creators. The overall story follows a sort of bildungsroman narrative, but the majority of the work is devoted to detailing the professional careers of the protagonist and other manga creators.

Another theme is friendship. Tatsumi reminisces about his childhood and the earlier period of his professional career, focusing throughout on his relationships with other manga creators. While working as a professional manga artist, the protagonist interacts with other creators, especially with Matsumoto, whom Hiroshi feels creates better books than he. The work as a whole addresses the importance of friendly rivalry among creators.

A Drifting Life also chronicles the historical trajectory of Japan, from its surrender at the end of World War II to the 1960's. The book makes constant allusions to social and cultural moments, including the manga revolution of the period and the political demonstration that rekindles Hiroshi's devotion to *gekiga*. As a whole, the work offers a cultural history of postwar Japan, intertwined with the author's personal encounters with cultural changes.

Impact

A chronicle of manga history from the perspective of a creator who played a major role in the genre's development, *A Drifting Life* provides a close examination of some underrepresented aspects of the postwar manga movement, including the *kashihon* industry, the genesis of *gekiga*, and the internal tension and conflicts among creators, editors, and publishers of manga. Mainstream manga history has centered on the Tokyo-based manga magazine industry and culture, which Tezuka and his protégés dominated. Tatsumi's work details the less-documented Osaka-based manga publishing business, especially the *kashihon* industry, which once flourished and contributed greatly to the development of modern manga. The book also calls attention to the social biases against manga that Tatsumi faced in the 1950's and 1960's, an issue that remains relevant throughout the comics industry.

CJ (Shige) Suzuki

Further Reading

Tatsumi, Yoshihiro. *Abandon the Old in Tokyo* (2009).
_____. *Black Blizzard* (2010).
_____. *Good-Bye* (2008).

Bibliography

Garner, Dwight. "Manifesto of a Comic-Book Rebel." *The New York Times*, April 14, 2009. http://www.nytimes.com/2009/04/15/books/15garn.html.

Suter, Rebecca. "Japan/America, Man/Woman: Gender and Identity Politics in Adriane Tomine and Yoshihiro Tatsumi." *Paradoxa: Studies in World Literary Genres* 22 (2010): 101-122.

Tomine, Adrian. Introduction to *The Push-Man and Other Stories* by Yoshihiro Tatsumi. Montreal: Drawn and Quarterly, 2005.

See also: *Astro Boy; Black Jack; Blade of the Immortal; Dragon Ball*

F

FIST OF THE NORTH STAR

Author: Buronson

Artist: Tetsuo Hara (illustrator)

Publisher: Shūeisha (Japanese); VIZ Media (English); Gutsoon! Entertainment (English)

First serial publication: *Hokuto no ken*, 1983-1988 (partial English translation, 1989, 1995-1997)

First book publication: 1984-1989 (partial English translation, 1995-1997)

Publication History

Fist of the North Star (or *Hokuto no ken*, literally "fist of the big dipper") was originally serialized in the Japanese comic magazine *Weekly Shōnen Jump*, from 1983 to 1988. *Fist of the North Star* is the first major work by the writer-artist team of Buronson and Tetsuo Hara.

The series' 245 chapters were originally collected in twenty-seven volumes by Shūeisha; fifteen-volume hardcover and miniaturized editions were published during the 1990's. In 2006, publisher Shogakukan released a fourteen-volume collector's edition, featuring the original color pages from the series' *Weekly Shōnen Jump* run. The series has also been released in digital format, with downloads corresponding to the original twenty-seven-volume run.

There have been two attempts at an English translation, both unsuccessful. VIZ Media published the series as a monthly comic book in 1989, publishing enough content to produce a single collection. The series went on hiatus and was resumed in 1995, again as monthly issues, with enough content for three more volumes. Gutsoon! Entertainment revived the series from 2002 to 2004 as *Fist of the North Star: Master Edition*, which featured artwork colorized under the supervision of Hara and, beginning with Volume 4, an original cover by the artist. This version of the series lasted nine volumes before Gutsoon! En-

tertainment ended its involvement in the North American comics market. A complete translation of *Fist of the North Star* is not available in North America.

Plot

Fist of the North Star is a *shōnen* adventure and melodrama series, inspired primarily by a mixture of martial-arts films and the *Mad Max* film series (1979, 1981, 1985). It follows Kenshiro, the master of the martial art Hokuto Shinken, as he wanders the world defending, and frequently avenging, the weak from less altruistic martial artists.

Though the exact date in which the series takes place is never given, nuclear war has devastated the

---

Buronson

Buronson, also known as Sho Fumimura, is a manga writer who specializes in violent stories, particularly thrillers and crime narratives. A former Air Force mechanic, he took on the pseudonym of Buronson in honor of the hard-boiled American actor Charles Bronson. This association is true to Buronson's characterizations of masculinity: lone individuals surviving through action, immune to fear and bearing little regard for death. Born Yoshiyuki Okamura in Nagano in 1947, Buronson is the author of, among other manga, the hugely popular *Fist of the North Star*, a hyperviolent postapocalyptic battle manga, and *Sanctuary*, the story of two friends who rise to power along very different paths, one in Japanese government and the other as a *yakuza* gangster. Many of his stories, notably *Heat and Stain*, occur in the criminal underworld. He is a frequent collaborator with illustrator Ryoichi Ikegami (*Mai the Psychic Girl*, *Crying Freeman*).

---

planet, turning most cities into ruins and most of the land into barren desert. The remainder of humanity either ekes out a harsh existence trying to restore some semblance of civilization and agriculture or preys on the weak in roving gangs of marauders and slavers.

In this wasteland, Kenshiro collapses and is found by a group of villagers who imprison him until they can ascertain his motives. Kenshiro breaks free in time to rescue the village from the gang of the warlord Zeed. In the process, Kenshiro picks up two companions: the young thief Bat and the gentle child Lin.

Kenshiro is searching for Shin, a martial artist who practices Nanto Seiken. Shin was a friend of Kenshiro, but his secret and unrequited love for Kenshiro's fiancé, Yuria, drove him mad. He attacked Kenshiro, leaving him with seven scars in the shape of the Big Dipper constellation, and kidnapped Yuria. Kenshiro discovers that Shin is now "King," the leader of an army known as Southern Cross. The two former friends fight; Kenshiro emerges as the victor. Before he dies, Shin tells Kenshiro that Yuria committed suicide to escape the horrors he had perpetrated to build Southern Cross.

With his revenge taken and his reconciliation stolen, Kenshiro wanders aimlessly with the children, encountering and killing various brigands and monsters. He finds a new purpose when he meets Mamiya, a warrior woman who looks identical to Yuria, and Rei, a Nanto master who seeks revenge on "a man with seven scars on his chest," The target of Rei's revenge is actually Jagi, Kenshiro's fellow Hokuto Shinken disciple, who has been framing Kenshiro for a slaving operation. Kenshiro kills Jagi, but not before Jagi reveals that the remaining two Hokuto "brothers" are still alive.

Kenshiro, Rei, and Mamiya search for the first of these brothers, Toki. They find him in the prison city of Cassandra, slowly dying of radiation poisoning but still a formidable martial artist. The final brother, Raoh, has reinvented himself as a powerful warlord, the Fist King. He tracks down Kenshiro and companions, defeating Toki, dealing Rei a terminal blow, and fighting Kenshiro to a standstill before departing.

Rei sacrifices his life to take revenge on a slaver who had previously captured and branded Mamiya. Mamiya remains with her village and takes care of Bat and Lin. Kenshiro continues wandering, encountering Thouzer, the cruel Holy Emperor of Nanto, while Toki and Raoh watch from a distance to see if he is truly worthy of being the grandmaster of Hokuto Shinken. Kenshiro defeats Thouzer, but word reaches Raoh that the last of the Nanto have mobilized under the banner of the mysterious Last Nanto General. Raoh defeats the general's lieutenants and discovers that the general is in fact Yuria, saved from suicide by her bodyguards and kept in hiding until they could consolidate power for her. The remainder of her army gets word to Kenshiro that Yuria is alive and waiting for him, but he is too late to prevent Raoh from taking her.

Raoh and Kenshiro decide to settle things at Hokuto's sacred grounds. Both unleash the ultimate technique of Hokuto Shinken on each other: a form of enlightenment borne of loss. In Kenshiro's case, it comes from the loss of his various companions throughout his travels. In Raoh's case, it comes from the knowledge that Yuria has a terminal illness (a fact that he reveals upon being defeated); this injustice—that even if Kenshiro reunites with Yuria their time would be short—was the only thing to reach Raoh's heart. Raoh entreats Kenshiro to make the most of his time with Yuria and dies on his feet. Kenshiro and Yuria depart to finally be at peace for whatever time is allowed them.

Years later, Lin and Bat have grown up and become the leaders of a rebel force, the Hokuto Army. The widower Kenshiro returns to aid his former charges, as they become embroiled in the political intrigue taking place among the Hokuto army's enemy, the Imperial Army. Lin discovers that her long-lost sister Liu is the Celestial Empress of the army, and the conspirators involved in keeping her imprisoned are rooted out and killed. The last conspirator kidnaps Lin and escapes to the warrior nation of Asura; Kenshiro follows, discovering that Asura is ruled by his long-lost brother Hyou and Raoh's estranged brother Kaioh. Kenshiro's fight with Hyou restores the latter's memory, and Hyou rescues Lin while Kenshiro stops Kaioh. The final chapters of the series feature Kenshiro adventuring with Raoh's orphaned son, Ryu, before leaving the boy to continue his training.

Volumes

Because *Fist of the North Star* has not been translated into English in its entirety, the following is a list of the *tankōbon* published in Japanese.

- *Fist of the North Star*, Volume 1 (1984). Collects chapters 1-8. Kenshiro saves Bat and Lin's village, and then journeys with them to Southern Cross to confront Shin.
- *Fist of the North Star*, Volume 2 (1984). Collects chapters 9-17. Kenshiro and Shin conclude their battle. Kenshiro encounters the remains of the Green Berets.
- *Fist of the North Star*, Volume 3 (1984). Collects chapters 18-26. Kenshiro fails to save Bat's adopted mother from the bandit Jackal, but he is able to avenge her death despite Jackal's alliance with Devil Rebirth.
- *Fist of the North Star*, Volume 4 (1984). Collects chapters 27-35. Kenshiro and Rei are hired by Mamiya's village to fight the marauding Fang Clan after they murder her brother. Mamiya and Rei's sister Airi are used by the clan to force Kenshiro and Rei to fight to the death, but they deceive their captors and kill the entire clan.
- *Fist of the North Star*, Volume 5 (1985). Collects chapters 36-44. Kenshiro realizes that the man Rei seeks is Jagi. Kenshiro confronts and kills Jagi, but not before the latter reveals that both Toki and Raoh are still live.
- *Fist of the North Star*, Volume 6 (1985). Collects chapters 45-53. Kenshiro is shocked to discover that the previously benevolent Toki has been subjecting innocent victims to experiments. Rei reveals that "Toki" is in fact Amiba.
- *Fist of the North Star*, Volume 7 (1985). Collects chapters 54-62. Kenshiro and Mamiya rescue Toki from the prison city of Cassandra, a death camp for martial artists. Mamiya and Toki both see a star that serves as an omen of death.
- *Fist of the North Star*, *Volume 8* (1985). Collects chapters 63-71. Rei attempts to defend Mamiya's village from Raoh, but the Fist King easily defeats him, striking a blow that will kill Rei over the span of days. Toki, despite his illness, faces

Raoh in order to show Kenshiro the extent of the Fist King's power.

- *Fist of the North Star*, Volume 9 (1986). Collects chapters 72-80. Toki is defeated, and Kenshiro breaks free of Toki's paralyzing hold in order to fight Raoh. They fight to a draw that leaves both men profoundly wounded. Mamiya goes to a neighboring village to collect medicine and is captured by slavers. Rei rescues her, despite the terminal wound he received from Raoh.
- *Fist of the North Star*, Volume 10 (1986) Collects chapters 81-89. Killing Juda, Rei dies from a previous injury. Kenshiro leaves Mamiya's village and encounters Shu, a blind Nanto master whom Kenshiro knew as a child, and Thouzer, the remorseless Nanto Emperor.
- *Fist of the North Star*, Volume 11 (1986). Collects chapters 90-98. Thouzer murders Shu during the construction of a giant monument to Thouzer's deceased master. Kenshiro and Thouzer face off on the stairs of the monument.
- *Fist of the North Star*, Volume 12 (1986). Collects chapters 99-107. Thouzer relates the source of his cruelty after Kenshiro deals him a fatal blow. A warrior named Ryuuga fights and gravely wounds Toki.
- *Fist of the North Star*, Volume 13 (1986). Collects chapters 108-116. Kenshiro avenges Toki by killing Ryuuga, who reveals he is Yuria's brother. Raoh begins clashing with the five guardians protecting the Last Nanto General.
- *Fist of the North Star*, Volume 14 (1987). Collects chapters 117-125. Fudoh contacts Kenshiro and reveals that the Last Nanto General is Yuria. Raoh faces a childhood fear of Fudoh by challenging him to a duel. Raoh and Kenshiro both race to be the first to Yuria.
- *Fist of the North Star*, Volume 15 (1987). Collects chapters 126-134. Raoh reaches Yuria first and takes her to the sacred Hokuto grounds. Kenshiro and Raoh meet for their final battle, both having achieved "Unconscious Transmigration of Souls," the Hokuto Shinken ultimate technique.

- *Fist of the North Star*, Volume 16 (1987). Collects chapters 135-143. Kenshiro and Raoh conclude their battle, with Kenshiro victorious. Yuria and Kenshiro leave to live in temporary peace. Years later, Kenshiro returns to find Bat and Lin have become rebel leaders.
- *Fist of the North Star*, Volume 17 (1987). Collects chapters 144-152. Kenshiro and his allies come into conflict with Falco.
- *Fist of the North Star*, Volume 18 (1987). Collects chapters 153-161. Ein is killed in the process of restoring the Imperial Empress to her throne. Lin discovers the empress is her sister. The remaining conspirator absconds with Lin to the land of Asura.
- *Fist of the North Star*, Volume 19 (1987). Collects chapters 162-170. Kenshiro journeys to Asura to rescue Lin. He encounters and defeats various Asura masters.
- *Fist of the North Star*, Volume 20 (1988). Collects chapters 171-179. Kenshiro defeats Han, one of the three kings of Asura. He encounters the remnants of Raoh's forces in Asura when he is mistaken for the Fist King.
- *Fist of the North Star*, Volume 21 (1988). Collects chapters 180-188. Hyou, the second king of Asura and Kenshiro's long-lost brother, mobilizes to avenge Han. Kenshiro fights the remnants of Raoh's army.
- *Fist of the North Star*, Volume 22 (1988). Collects chapters 189-197. Hyou and Kenshiro clash, restoring Hyou's memory. Kaioh appears.
- *Fist of the North Star*, Volume 23 (1988). Collects chapters 198-206. Kenshiro and Kaioh clash when Kaioh learns that Hyou and Kenshiro have been reunited. Kaioh also attempts to make Lin his bride.
- *Fist of the North Star*, Volume 24 (1988). Collects chapters 207-215. The history of Hokuto Shinken is recounted. Kenshiro seeks out Raoh's son Ryu as a possible successor.
- *Fist of the North Star*, Volume 25 (1988). Collects chapters 216-225. Kenshiro and Ryu stop a former subordinate of Raoh's from hoarding food at the expense of neighboring villages be-

fore becoming embroiled in a three-way power struggle between rival princes.
- *Fist of the North Star*, Volume 26 (1989). Collects chapters 226-235. Kenshiro encounters and defeats Baran, a former general of Raoh's, who has dedicated himself to carrying on Raoh's legacy and has already conquered a kingdom.
- *Fist of the North Star*, Volume 27 (1989). Collects chapters 236-245. Learning how Raoh died, Baran repents and has himself executed for his crimes. A thug Kenshiro once blinded comes seeking revenge. Bat disguises himself as Kenshiro in the hopes that, if "Kenshiro" is killed, the actual Kenshiro can live in peace with Lin.

Characters

- *Kenshiro*, the protagonist, is a muscular Japanese man with short, shaggy hair and bushy eyebrows. He is sometimes called "the Man with Seven Scars" because of seven puncture-wound scars that cover most of his torso. He is the successor of the martial art of Hokuto Shinken, an assassin's art. Despite this, Kenshiro was a gentle man until his fiancé, Yuria, was taken from him. On his quest to reunite with her, he becomes a force for justice in the wasteland.
- *Yuria*, Kenshiro's fiancé, is a serene woman with flowing black and blue hair, widely regarded in the series as the most beautiful woman in the world. She cannot abide the suffering of others. After a long period during which she is presumed dead, she remerges as the Last Nanto General.
- *Bat*, a young thief whom Kenshiro befriends at the beginning of the series, is a rambunctious young boy with a mop of hair that covers one eye and who wears a signature pair of goggles; he later grows into a muscular martial artist. He initially joins with Kenshiro, believing Kenshiro's strength can be used for personal gain. He becomes more altruistic as the series progresses, eventually leading a rebel army alongside Lin to free the land from the tyrannical Imperial Army.
- *Lin* is a girl who was rendered mute until Kenshiro cures her. She has short hair and a tied head-

band, but she grows into a beauty that rivals Yuria's. Her sincerity and innocence can stay the hand of fiercer characters. She eventually becomes the coleader of a rebel force with Bat.

- *Shin*, the first antagonist, is a muscular man with straight blond hair and bangs. Shin is a Nanto Seiken master who was once Kenshiro's best friend and harbored a secret love for Yuria. Eventually, this love drove him mad. He beats Kenshiro in front of Yuria, giving Kenshiro his distinctive seven scars.

- *Toki*, a Hokuto Shinken practitioner, is a muscular man with sunken eyes, a thin beard, and long hair. He wears simple rags. He is one of four students of Hokuto Shinken (the others are Kenshiro, Jagi, and Raoh). While he is perhaps the most skilled of the four, he is only interested in using the pressure point techniques to heal afflictions. His health is ruined by radiation fallout, and he spends most of the series in an enervated state.

- *Raoh*, the primary antagonist for half the series, is a massive, muscular figure with piercing eyes and short cropped hair. He is a Hokuto Shinken student and Toki's brother. His ambition was to be the strongest fighter in the world, and thus he was unable to accept the law that there could only be one practitioner of Hokuto Shinken at a time. As such, when it comes time for him to lose his Hokuto training, he kills Ryuuken, the previous Hokuto master. He reinvents himself as the Fist King, amassing a mighty army and becoming a major power in the world. His ambition is ended only by a final fight with Kenshiro.

- *Hyou*, Kenshiro's long-lost brother and an antagonist in the later third of the series, has long hair and a scar on his forehead. He is one of the three rulers of Asura and is initially benevolent; the death of a loved one drives him temporarily mad. A battle with Kenshiro restores his memory and sense of self.

- *Kaioh*, the major antagonist of the last third of the series, is Raoh and Toki's estranged older brother. He looks much like Raoh, only taller and darker, with a scarred face. He is a prodigious warrior

with megalomaniacal delusions and a searing resentment of the Hokuto bloodline, represented by Kenshiro and Hyou.

Artistic Style

Fist of the North Star draws its aesthetic from the postapocalyptic cinema of the 1970's and 1980's and the martial arts cinema boom of the 1970's. While it is not wholly inaccurate to describe the look of the series as "Bruce Lee as Mad Max," *Fist of the North Star*'s visual style is one that has been frequently imitated and parodied.

The series' character designs are its distinguishing artistic features. Invariably, the characters are impossibly muscular, lantern-jawed supermen, whose eyes are either squinted with steely determination or utterly dead with cruelty. The hair styles (mullets and Mohawks abound) and the widespread use of leather, jumpsuits, and shoulder pads as the standard fashion of the day all mark the series as a product of 1980's apocalyptic pop culture. Also aging the series is Hara's figure work, which is frequently stiff; his depiction of martial arts relies less on fluidity of motion and more on speed lines and afterimages to depict the transition of a punch or kick.

Nonetheless, the stiffness of the characters seems to suit a series whose setting is a barren wasteland. It gives the series a texture of grit and heaviness that also suits the desert world and the martial arts melodrama contained within.

Whereas Hara's figures are often stiff, his expressions are anything but. Not overly given to the exaggeration often attributed to Japanese artists, Hara is a master of the cruel sneer, the pitiless glare, and the mixture of unbreakable will and profound loss that many of the characters carry with them through their battles.

The series uses the artistic convention of listing attack names; characters often shout the name of their techniques. Thus, when a technique is important enough that a character shouts its name, readers come to understand that it is a potentially fight-changing move.

Themes

Fist of the North Star is ultimately a meditation on loss. On a broad scale, the loss of civilization to atomic war forms the backdrop to the series and splits the cast into two ideologies. The heroic characters deal with the end of civilization by trying to restore, defend, and improve the lives of those around them. The villainous characters take advantage of the newly lawless age to pursue their own ambitions at the cost of their fellow man. To this end, all conflicts in the series come down to a heroic character defending the helpless from a villainous character, or punishing a villain for preying on those who cannot defend themselves.

The individual characters all find motives and origins relating in some way to the theme of loss. The loss of a loved one drives both Thouzer and Rei to cruelty; Rei is able to recover his humanity only by regaining that loved one. Jagi's loss of face to Kenshiro drives his desire for revenge. Toki is defined by a terminal illness that destroys his potential. The prospective loss of his ability to use martial arts is what spurs Raoh to kill his master and set off on his path as the Fist King. The thought of not being strong enough to keep Yuria safe imbues Shin with the mad obsession that leads him to take Yuria from Kenshiro.

The theme of loss is more defined in Kenshiro's experiences. The loss of his fiancé awakens in him a lethal sense of justice, which enables him to be a judge and executioner in the postapocalyptic wasteland. Most subsequent story arcs follow a formula of Kenshiro gaining, then losing, a companion. This companion is usually a fellow martial artist, whose death teaches Kenshiro some new technique or philosophy that then adds to his martial-arts prowess. Indeed, the final and most powerful technique of Hokuto Shinken is revealed to be a form of enlightenment derived from feeling true sorrow.

Impact
Fist of the North Star is considered to be a part of the Golden Age of Jump titles—one of the immensely popular, long-running series published during the 1985-1995 stretch in which *Weekly Shōnen Jump*'s popularity and subscription numbers skyrocketed.

Fist of the North Star's biggest impact is as a Japanese cultural reference point, elements of which are still a source of either homage or parody in modern anime and manga. The muscular, gravely

serious character designs have become visual shorthand for sudden seriousness in more lighthearted series and in parody art of more cartoonish characters.

Kenshiro's trademark attack, a series of punches thrown at such rapid speed that the afterimages imply a wave of fists coming at the target, has become a ubiquitous storytelling technique in "battle manga" to show flurries of blows. Kenshiro's rapid kung-fu shouts while throwing these punches have also become a frequently used trope. While a rich mine for parody, *Fist of the North Star* is a seminal series when it comes to fighting comics. The series' popularity has spawned numerous adaptations in animation and video games, multiple action figures and collectibles, a prequel by Hara, and a series of short side stories focusing on various supporting characters by new artists and writers.

Films
Fist of the North Star. Directed by Toyoo Ashida. Shūeisha/Toei Animation Company, 1986. This film adaptation stars Akira Kamiya as Kenshiro and Kenji Utsumi as Raoh. The film significantly condenses the events leading to Kenshiro and Raoh's first confrontation. The theatrical and home-video versions of the movie have different endings. The English-language adaptation by Streamline was poorly received and may have played a role in the series' repeated failure to connect with North American audiences.

Fist of the North Star. Directed by Tony Randel. First Look International, 1995. This live-action film adaptation stars Gary Daniels as Kenshiro and Costas Mandylor as Shin. The film is a loose retelling of the Shin arc of the comic.

Television Series
Fist of the North Star. Directed by Toyoo Ashida and Ichirō Itano. Fuji Television Network/Toei Animation/ Shūeisha, 1984-1987. This program stars Kamiya as Kenshiro and ran for 104 episodes. The series takes several liberties with the stories, especially in the first season, in which many characters and events are shuffled and retooled. The other notable change is the re-

moval of the rather graphic depictions of how Hokuto Shinken destroys a target's body.

Fist of the North Star 2. Directed by Toyoo Ashida. Toei Animation, 1987-1988. This sequel to the original series features Kamiya returning to the role of Kenshiro and ran for forty-three episodes. Whereas the original series ended with the final confrontation between Kenshiro and Raoh, *Fist of the North Star 2* begins after this event and concludes with the Asura arc.

Josh Hechinger

Further Reading

Araki, Hirohiko. *Jojo's Bizarre Adventure* (1987-1999).

Jodorowsky, Alejandro, and Juan Gimenez. *The Metabarons* (1992-2003).

Miura, Kentaro. *Berserk* (1990-   ).

Bibliography

"The Rise and Fall of Weekly Shōnen Jump: A Look at the Circulation of Weekly Jump." Comi-Press, May 6, 2007. http://comipress.com/article//1923.

Yadao, Jason S. *The Rough Guide to Manga*. New York: Rough Guides, 2009.

Zaleski, Jeff. "Fist of the Northstar." Review of Fist of the Northstar, by Buronson and Tetsuo Hara. *Publishers Weekly* 250, no. 20 (May 19, 2003): 55.

See also: *Berserk; One Piece; Blade of the Immortal*

FOUR IMMIGRANTS MANGA, THE
A JAPANESE EXPERIENCE IN SAN FRANCISCO, 1904-1924

Author: Kiyama, Henry Yoshitaka

Artist: Henry Yoshitaka Kiyama (illustrator)

Publisher: Kiyama Yoshitaka gashitsu (Japanese); Stone Bridge Press (English)

First book publication: *Manga yonin shosei*, 1931 (English translation, 1931, 1999)

The Four Immigrants Manga. (Courtesy of Stone Bridge Press)

Publication History

In February, 1927, forty-two-year-old Henry Yoshitaka Kiyama held an art exhibit in San Francisco, California, titled "Manga Hokubei Iminshi" ("a manga North American immigrant history"). In the early twentieth century, most cartoon artists serialized their work in newspapers. Kiyama, however, presented his story in its entirety at the art exhibit and then resorted to self-publication. He published his work in book format, predating what has become known as the "graphic novel" by decades.

Kiyama's *The Four Immigrants Manga: A Japanese Experience in San Francisco, 1904-1924* was printed on January 25, 1931, by Kuyama Printers in Tokyo and published on March 3, 1931, by the Yoshitaka Kiyama Studio in San Francisco. The hardcover book of more than one hundred pages was published under the title *Manga yonin shosei* (the four students comic). The book was written in English and Japanese and had a listed sale price of three dollars. Kiyama was identified as the author as well as the publisher. The book includes forewords and favorable comments from Kaname Wakasugi, the Japanese consul general in San Francisco at the time, and well-known local artists and intellectuals such as Chiura Obata, Koh Murai (known by his pen name, Hibutsu), and Kazuo Ebina (identified by his pen name, Shunshūrō), a columnist for the *Nichi Bei* (the Japanese American news).

Frederik L. Schodt, author of *Manga! Manga! The World of Japanese Comics* (1983), *Inside the Robot Kingdom* (1988), and *Native American in the Land of the Shogun* (2003), discovered Kiyama's book around 1980 while doing research on Japanese comics. A few years later, Schodt briefly introduced Kiyama's work in

his book *Manga! Manga!* Not until almost two decades later did he finally have the chance to translate Kiyama's book. Berkeley-based Stone Bridge Press released Schodt's English translation, accompanied by his introduction and notes, under the title *The Four Immigrants Manga*.

Plot

The episodic narrative begins with the arrival of four Japanese immigrants—Henry, Frank, Charlie, and Fred—in San Francisco in 1904. Henry comes to study art, Fred wants to thrive in farming, Frank is interested in business, and Charlie hopes to study the democratic system of the United States. Despite their differing career aspirations, the characters follow a path shared by many Japanese immigrants at the time: With the help of the local Buddhist temple, they become "schoolboys" who work as house servants and go to school after finishing their chores. The following nine episodes describe the schoolboys' sense of isolation and displacement as they adjust to being domestic laborers in the United States. The characters' interactions with American families and other immigrants illustrate the miscommunication and misunderstandings caused by language barriers and cultural differences. Their experience also reflects certain social issues in San Francisco at the turn of the twentieth century, including street robbery and racial discrimination.

Kiyama's work not only reflects the Japanese American experience but also documents some events in American and world history. The textual narrative and drawings tell the reader about the San Francisco earthquake of 1906, school segregation in California, the 1915 Panama Pacific International Exposition, "picture brides," World War I, and the Spanish flu in 1918, among other events and cultural developments.

As the subtitle of Kiyama's book—*A Japanese Experience in San Francisco, 1904-1924*—suggests, *The Four Immigrants Manga* documents multiple aspects of Japanese immigrant life, including the community's social standing, economic status, and relations with Caucasian Americans and other ethnic minorities in an era of increasing anti-Asian sentiment in the United States. Throughout the book, Henry's autobiographical narrative is intertwined with Frank, Fred, and Charlie's stories as well with as the experiences of other Japanese immigrants and Americans with whom they interact.

Characters
- *Henry* is loosely based on Kiyama. He comes to the United States to study art. While attending art school in San Francisco, he works mostly as a domestic laborer. He is cheerful and optimistic and usually appears with his brush and easel. At the end of the story, Henry and Frank return to Japan for a visit.
- *Charlie* is Henry's friend and loosely based on a man named Chūji Nakada. He is the tallest of the

four friends. He comes to the United States to learn about democracy and the American social system. Throughout the story, he appears to be politically conscious. He enlists during World War I and serves in the U.S. Army in Europe. After the war, his application for American citizenship is denied because of his ethnicity.
- *Frank* is loosely based on Kiyama's friend Sakuji Hida. He comes to the United States with an interest in business and hopes to make a fortune by importing goods from Japan. He and Charlie seem to be close to each other; they appear together in many of the episodes.
- *Fred* is loosely based on a man named Kiichirō Katō. He is interested in farming and becomes successful late in the story, making one million dollars with one harvest.

Artistic Style
Schodt's English edition uses the panel from the cover of Kiyama's original 1931 edition as part of its cover image. It is a portrait of the four main characters: Henry, Charlie, Frank, and Fred. The art throughout

---

Henry Yoshitaka Kiyama

Henry Yoshitaka Kiyama (1885-1951) had a unique career in comics, as the work for which he is remembered is better known today than it was during his lifetime. Kiyama was born in Japan, but his major work, *The Four Immigrants Manga*, was a version of his own life experiences while living in San Francisco for two decades, beginning in 1904 (meaning that not long after his arrival, he experienced the 1906 earthquake). While in San Francisco he attended the San Francisco Art Institute, and it's believed that, after a visit home to Japan, the start of World War II kept him from returning to the U.S. This information comes from translator Frederik L. Schodt, who discovered Kiyama's book in the Berkeley library and helped bring it to publication in the mid-1990's. A large stone memorial to Kiyama stands in his native Neu, in Japan's southerly Tottori Prefecture.

The Four Immigrants Manga is black and white, and there is no clear progression in the artistic style as the story unfolds.

Kiyama adheres to a standard layout throughout. In total, the book includes fifty-two episodes; each episode includes two pages and twelve panels, and each panel is numbered continuously from one to twelve in the lower right corner. This structure defines the nature of the book and presents a series of vignettes.

The layout of images is consistent, and the pages are not crowded with overwhelming visual details. Such a style allows the reader to engage the story without too much challenge. There are minor variations in the artist's use of dialogue bubbles, but overall, there are no drastic changes. In some cases, it is difficult to distinguish the characters from one another. As Schodt points out in his introduction to the 1999 edition, the background images are important, as they illustrate easily recognizable landmarks of San Francisco such as the Ferry Building at the end of Market Street, the California Palace of the Legion of Honor, Seal Rock, and Golden Gate Park.

The Four Immigrants Manga. (Courtesy of Stone Bridge Press)

Themes

Generally speaking, *The Four Immigrants Manga* is concerned with social issues such as immigration, racial discrimination, class, school segregation, and legislation. The list of episodes at the beginning of the book is in essence a table of contents that clearly indicates the historical coverage of Kiyama's work: It not only addresses issues and phenomena specific to Japanese immigrants at the time—such as "schoolboys," picture brides, and the Alien Land Law—but also reflects historical events at large.

Anti-Japanese legislation forms the background of the characters' stories. In the continental United States, Japanese immigrants were a racial minority in 1920, accounting for roughly 2 percent of the California population. As Kiyama's book reflects, in San Francisco, the local objection to Japanese immigrants was strong in the early twentieth century. In addition to documenting the difficulty and obstacles in Japanese immigrants' integration into American society, Kiyama's book goes further to reveal social prejudices of various kinds. Episode 12, "Working on a Farm," for example, shows how Charlie and Frank face discrimination within the Japanese American community. When the two characters seek out seasonal jobs in Stockton during harvest time, fellow Japanese immigrants inform them bluntly that they will be paid less because they are "city boys." *The Four Immigrants Manga* emphasizes the fact that discrimination can occur within every segment of society.

Impact

Initially self-published in San Francisco as a bilingual work, *The Four Immigrants Manga* is one of the first book-length comics of an autobiographical nature published in the United States. The critical reception of the book at the time of its first publication is hard to determine, as it likely had a limited readership. Nonetheless, the acclaim included in the 1931 edition seems to suggest the approval of educated Japanese Americans in the local community. Schodt's translation was a finalist for the USA Pen/West translation award in 2000. In the same year, Schodt received *Asahi Shimbun*'s Osamu Tezuka Award in a special category for helping promote manga. In March of 2000, a memorial for Kiyama was erected in Neu, Hino-cho, Tottori Prefecture, Japan.

In 2009, the First Annual Asian American ComiCon presented the inaugural Henry Y. Kiyama Award, an award intended to recognize the contribution of Asians and Asian Americans to U.S. comic book culture. Kiyama's career represented the convergence of two worlds and industries, and his work pointed the way to the future of graphic storytelling. His autobiographically inspired work predates the comics trend of graphic memoirs by decades and provides refreshing ways to evaluate the creative potential of comics.

Lan Dong

Further Reading

Eisner, Will. *Life, in Pictures: Autobiographical Stories* (2007).

Nakazawa, Keiji. *Barefoot Gen: A Cartoon Story of Hiroshima* (2004-2010).

Okubo, Miné. *Citizen 13660* (1983).

Bibliography

Arnold, Andrew D. "Coming to America." *Time*, February 19, 2005. http://www.time.com/time/columnist/arnold/article/0,9565,1029794,00.html.

Gardner, Jared. "Autography's Biography, 1972-2007." *Biography: An Interdisciplinary Quarterly* 31, no. 1 (Winter, 2008): 1-26.

Halverson, Cathryn. "'Typical Tokio Smile': Bad American Books and Bewitching Japanese Girls." *Arizona Quarterly: A Journal of American Literature, Culture, and Theory* 63, no. 1 (Spring, 2007): 49-80.

Humphrey, Robert L. "Book Notes." Review of *The Four Immigrants Manga: A Japanese Experience in San Francisco, 1904-1924* by Henry Yoshitaka Kiyama. *American Studies International* (June, 1999): 107-108.

Ichioka, Yuji. *The Issei: The World of First Generation Japanese Immigrants, 1885-1924*. New York: Free Press, 1988.

Johnson, Mark Dean. "Uncovering Asian American Art in San Francisco, 1850-1940." In *Asian American Art: A History, 1850-1970*, edited by Gordon H.

Chang, et al. Stanford, Calif.: Stanford University Press, 2008.

Schodt, Frederick L. "Henry Kiyama and *The Four Immigrants Manga*." In *The Four Immigrants Manga: A Japanese Experience in San Francisco, 1904-1924*. Berkeley, Calif.: Stone Bridge Press, 1999.

Takada, Mayumi. "The Four Immigrants Manga and the Making of Japanese Americans." *Genre: Forms of Discourse and Culture* 39, no. 4 (Winter, 2006): 125-139.

Whitlock, Gillian. "Autographics: The Seeing 'I' of the Comics." *Modern Fiction Studies* 52, no. 4 (Winter, 2006): 965-979.

From Eroica with Love

Author: Aoike, Yasuko
Artist: Yasuko Aoike (illustrator)
Publisher: Akita Shoten (Japanese); DC Comics (English)
First serial published: *Eroica yori ai o komete*, 1976-1989, 1995-2007, 2009-
First book publication: 1978- (partial English translation 2004-2010)

Publication History

Yasuko Aoike began her career as a manga artist with the short story "Sayonara Nanette" and continued to create short pieces in the *shōjo* genre until her first series appeared in the January, 1975, issue of *Princess* magazine. *Eroica yori ai o komete*, translated as *From Eroica with Love*, first appeared in the December, 1976, issue of *Viva Princess* magazine.

The first *tankōbon* book, collecting the first two and a half chapters of the series, was published in 1978. The series left *Viva Princess* magazine in April, 1979, and moved to *Princess* magazine, first appearing in the September issue. In the 1980's, *From Eroica with Love* enjoyed considerable popularity, appearing regularly in *Princess*. The occasional side story was published in *Viva Princess*, and multiple volumes collecting the magazine chapters were published.

The series stopped suddenly with the August, 1989, issue of *Viva Princess*. However, Aoike revived the series in May of 1995, and it continued to run in *Viva Princess* through December of 2007. Following a brief hiatus, it resumed publication in the January, 2009, issue of *Princess Gold* magazine.

In the United States, CMX, the manga imprint of DC Comics, published the first translated volume of *From Eroica with Love* in November, 2004. Volume 15 was published in March, 2010. Soon after, DC Comics closed CMX because of weak manga sales in the United States and ceased publication of the imprint's manga titles.

Plot

Aoike launched *From Eroica with Love* during the heyday of the *shōnen-ai* manga subgenre that emerged

Yasuko Aoike

Yasuko Aoike, born in 1948, is part of a generation of female *shōjo* artists born shortly after World War II who helped shape the manga industry. Her long-running adventure romance *From Eroica with Love* has run in the manga magazines *Viva Princess*, *Princess*, and *Princess Gold*, all published by Akita Shoten, since 1976. Her other manga include the naval series *Trafalgar* and *Eru arukon - taka* and the gay comedy *Eve no musukotachi*. Like many artists of her generation, she makes frequent use of heavily eroticized homosexual male characters intended to appeal to female rather than male readers.

in the early 1970's. Created by female manga artists for a primarily female audience, *shōnen-ai* features beautiful boys and men in generally idealized homosexual and homoerotic relationships. *Shōnen-ai* stories and series are typically published in *shōjo* manga magazines for young female readers in their late teens and early twenties. Critics have classified *shōnen-ai*, which declined in popularity in the late 1980's, as a subgenre of *yaoi*, or "boy love" (*bōizu rabu*). *Shōnen-ai* is not concerned with realistic gay relationships and is not intended for a gay audience.

Aoike's title is a deliberate allusion to Ian Fleming's James Bond novel *From Russia, with Love* (1957), indicating that the series is a spoof of the spy genre. The series' protagonist is a master art thief who leaves behind messages with his signature line, "from Eroica with love." Eroica is the pseudonym chosen by the flamboyantly dressed, highly cultured, and openly gay Englishman Dorian Red Gloria, Earl of Gloria. While Eroica's first heist only antagonizes the British police, the second chapter of the series introduces Eroica's long-standing opponent and love interest, the West German NATO major Klaus Heinz von dem Eberbach. Because Major Klaus works in intelligence during the Cold War, his various missions have classic spy themes, such as finding or protecting key classified documents or performing crucial intelligence work.

The subplots of the series derive much of their impetus from the clash of Eroica's thievery and the major's intelligence missions. Both men are young, good-looking, strong, and wealthy. Both command vast resources, from personal wealth to NATO assets. They are served by a string of comically exaggerated underlings, with the major's agents only identified by letters of the alphabet. Their opponents come from various levels of society, with the wealthy and the police lined up against Eroica and communist agents, particularly from the KGB, fighting the major. Frequently, plot twists force Eroica and the major to form a temporary alliance and combine forces to fight a common enemy, whether a master criminal or communist spies.

Chapter 2, "Iron Klaus," sets up the relationship between Eroica and the major, which drives all later plots of the series. Major Klaus is sent from West Germany to England to check on the possible telepathic powers of a teenage prodigy. His ruse is to have the art collection of his English country home appraised by this young man, Gabriel Caesar, who fell in love with Eroica in the first chapter.

The straight-laced and homophobic major clashes violently with the flamboyantly gay Eroica, who comes to visit the major's art collection. As revenge for homophobic insults, Eroica decides to steal a picture from the major. This backfires when the major takes Gabriel to Germany. After a wild chase ending on an isolated North Sea island, the major and Eroica both huddle together in a German tank to protect the fragile Gabriel from the cold. Yet when rescuers arrive at the end of the story, Eroica and the major resume their antagonism, which is sustained throughout the first fifteen volumes of the series.

Subsequent adventures bring Eroica and the major to a variety of European and Middle Eastern settings. The plots can be widely comical and exaggerated. In "Achilles' Last Stand," for example, the major must retrieve a microfilm capsule hidden by a German agent under the stone undergarment of a recently discovered ancient Greek sculpture that Eroica has set his heart on stealing. "Love in Greece" introduces the agents of the Soviet KGB, mutual enemies of Eroica and the major. "In'shallah" sends both to Iran, where Eroica tries to steal treasures and the major is tasked with locating

Russian missiles. As usual, the plot twists so that Eroica and the major must work together despite the major's distaste for Eroica's growing affection and desire for him.

With "Alaskan Front" and "The Glass Target," longer stories that stretch over more than one chapter and more than one book volume, are introduced. The plots always contain a device bringing Eroica and the major into close physical proximity. In "Seven Days in September," another multivolume story, the major seeks to retrieve a file from an English contact, while Eroica renews his attempts to steal his favorite painting from the major's collection.

In the longest story, "The Seventh Seal," featured in Volumes 12-15, Eroica plans to steal a British prince's art collection when the major forcibly persuades him to seduce a Soviet official to get information about some secret KGB accounts. Seriously wounded at the end of the story, the major recuperates in "Intermission" and "Eau de Cologne." In these stories, his attitude toward Eroica seems to become a bit more positive, but their antagonistic relationship continues as before in the subsequent volumes not yet translated into English.

Volumes

- *From Eroica with Love*, Volume 1 (2004). Features chapters 1, 2, and the beginning of 3. Chapter 1 introduces three teenagers with paranormal proclivities. Major Klaus, introduced in chapter 2, becomes Eroica's opponent and unwilling love interest.

- *From Eroica with Love*, Volume 2 (2005). Finishes chapter 3 and features chapters 4 and 5. The characters of Eroica and the major are developed, as are the outrageous plots that parody the spy genre. The volume also offers a nonseries side story.

- *From Eroica with Love*, Volumes 3-5 (2005). Collects four stories originally published in the Japanese series from 1981 to 1982. In "In'shallah," Eroica and the major involuntarily join forces in Tehran, Iran, where Eroica seeks to steal the treasures of the late shah and the major looks for hidden Russian missiles. In "Hallelujah Express," both protagonists try to break into the Vatican. This story introduces their recurring foe, KGB agent Mischa the Bear Cub. Volume 4 continues in Rome with the caper "Veni, Vidi, Vici." Eroica declares his love for the major, who rejects him. The volume concludes with part 1 of "Alaskan Front," in which both protagonists battle Mischa and the cold climate. Volume 5 finishes "Alaskan Front."

- *From Eroica with Love*, Volume 6 (2006). Collects the side story "Special Vacation Orders" and the first part of chapter 11, "The Glass Target." The major's background is revealed, and Eroica and the major come into conflict again when their missions collide.

- *From Eroica with Love*, Volumes 7-14 (2006-2009). Collects the stories originally published in Japan from 1982 to 1985. Volume 7 finishes "Glass Target" and offers the short story "Midnight Collector," which examines Eroica's childhood. "Seven Days in September" runs from Volume 8 to Volume 10. This story involves action on hijacked planes and highlights Eroica's unrequited desire for the major and their fights against Mischa. Volume 10 also introduces the next long story, "The Laughing Cardinals," which concludes in Volume 12. For different reasons, Eroica and the major save a Swiss abbey from being turned into a supermarket. Volume 12 also includes two short stories: In "A Tale of Alaska," the major finally sends his bumbling agents to Alaska as punishment. "From Lawrence with Love" gives a starring role to British agent Charles Lawrence, the author's spoof on James Bond. The volume also introduces the four-part story "The Seventh Seal." This story runs through Volumes 13 and 14 and contains all the classic elements of the series, with the major becoming less antagonistic toward Eroica.

- *From Eroica with Love*, Volume 15 (2010). Finishes the long story "The Seventh Seal" and includes several short stories. After being injured during the events of "The Seventh Seal," Major Klaus tries to escape the boredom of a medical recuperation. Some copies of this book were misprinted and included pages from a different manga; these have become collector's items.

Characters

- *Dorian Red Gloria, Earl of Gloria*, a.k.a. *Eroica*, the protagonist, is a tall English nobleman with long, curly blond hair whose physical looks were inspired, according to Aoike, by Robert Plant, the lead singer of the British rock band Led Zeppelin. His first name alludes to Dorian Gray, the title character of British author Oscar Wilde's novel *The Picture of Dorian Gray* (1891). He is an openly gay man apparently in his twenties who dresses flamboyantly, often wearing necklaces, bracelets, and rings. He is wealthy, cultured, and educated, but his secret profession is that of an art thief. He falls in love with Major Klaus.

- *Major Klaus Heinz von dem Eberbach*, a.k.a. *Iron Klaus*, is a young, tall, and lean aristocratic West German intelligence officer with black, shoulder-length hair. He often wears his uniform but is also depicted wearing civilian clothing appropriate to his missions. He is a straight-laced and somewhat homophobic but is also young, elegant, and attractive.

- *Mischa the Bear Cub*, an antagonist, is a strongly built Russian man and a former Soviet boxing champion who has become the leader of a KGB section fighting Western intelligence. His name alludes to the mascot of the 1980 Moscow Olympics. He is the sworn enemy of the major but is generally defeated by him.

- *James* is Eroica's accountant, a young British man with long, wavy black hair that obscures his right eye. His long-lashed left eye often sheds a tear. He is driven by greed and a desire to endear himself to Eroica and is jealous of Eroica's other love interests, particularly the major.

- *Agents A, B, G,* and *Z* are German agents and subordinates of Major Klaus. A is the most competent, B is somewhat rotund and bumbling, G likes to cross-dress, and Z, the youngest, appears to be the favorite of the major.

- *Charles Lawrence* is an inept middle-aged British intelligence agent who resembles James Bond. He shares Bond's fondness for gadgets, though they do not work well for him. He provides some comic relief in his bumbling.

Artistic Style

Aoike has spent considerable artistic energy in drawing her two main characters, Eroica and the major. Her color covers, prominent full-page black-and-white portraits at the beginning of chapters, and regular black-and-white panels feature Eroica in all his splendor. Aoike gives loving attention to his long, curly blond hair, which frames an unrealistic, stylized oval face with a prominent chin and long-lashed eyes. Eroica's personal jewelry is drawn in detail, as are his outrageous clothes, such as satin gowns and red blouses. His legs are impossibly, disproportionally long and extended to enhance the picture of a tall but slender young man.

In contrast, Major Klaus is drawn with more clearcut, straight lines and features. His straight black hair falls down to his shoulders. When the series was featured in Germany's army magazine, soldiers immediately commented that the major's hair was much too long. Similarly, his uniform does not show the insignia of his rank and lacks the silver trimmings that would distinguish him as an officer, thus appearing to be a common soldier's military outfit. Despite these inaccuracies, his uniform has remained unchanged throughout the series. However, because the major often dons civilian clothes, Aoike gives him a variety of masculine outfits, ranging from leather jackets to well-cut suits and casual clothes that emphasize his youthful splendor.

Eroica and the major are the most prominently drawn characters of the series. The covers, which differ slightly for the American edition but adhere in principle to the Japanese originals, feature either Eroica or the major alone or both together in a wild clash of style. This clash is first seen on the cover of Volume 2: Eroica's long blond hair hovers over the major, who wears an elegant civilian suit. Aoike starts to incorporate homoerotic overtones more strongly on the cover of Volume 4, which depicts Eroica, standing to the right in a billowing blouse with a rose between his lips, nearly touching the buttocks of the major, who wears a trench coat and is shown from behind. The cover of Volume 13 shows them walking next to each other, perhaps indicating their closer relationship, with Eroica's red blouse contrasting with the major's dark suit.

Supporting characters are drawn in a mix of manga style and Western style, in keeping with the theme of spoofing a James Bond-style story. Aoike draws in great detail some special gadgets, military hardware, and vehicles essential to her plots. As Eroica is an art thief, classic paintings and sculptures are also drawn in stylized resemblance to their originals. The many different geographic settings depicted are drawn with care as well, providing the readers with detailed illustrations of locales ranging from Bavaria to the Kurdish desert.

Themes

The major theme of *From Eroica with Love* is the relationship between Eroica and Major Klaus. Eroica's flamboyant, open homosexuality establishes the theme of homoerotic love, with the major as the unwilling target of Eroica's developing affections. Thus, the series is considered part of the *shōnen-ai* genre. Here, Eroica plays the role of the beautiful, cultured, and outrageous young man attracted to the sterner, yet still very handsome Major Klaus, whom he also admires for his strength and intellect.

The key theme of homoerotic love is highlighted further by Eroica's increasing pursuit of the major, who is homophobic to the point of initially calling Eroica a degenerate. However, as Aoike never provides a female love interest for the major, who, in fact, rejects all attempts by his superiors to set him up, enough imaginative space is provided for the relationship between him and Eroica to develop. Aoike cleverly uses plot twists that put Eroica in close physical contact with Major Klaus during their various adventures.

Another theme of the series is spoofing typical spy or heist stories. The flamboyant homosexuality of art thief Eroica serves well to introduce a comic and gender-bending element to these genres that are traditionally characterized by an exclusively heterosexual atmosphere. Here, Aoike explodes some conventions of the spy genre by creating hilarious plots.

Impact

From Eroica with Love is considered a classic of the *shōnen-ai* manga subgenre, which flourished in the 1970's and 1980's. The series is often used to illustrate the best of the conventions of this unique subgenre. Throughout the years, the series has attracted a large, loyal fan base in Japan.

Because of its lasting popularity with its fans, the series survived a long hiatus after it stopped suddenly in August of 1989. This break from publication may have been related to the end of the antagonism between the United States and the Soviet Union, which had provided much material for the spy-spoofing plots. However, other spy series, most notably the James Bond franchise, survived by finding new antagonists for their heroes, and *From Eroica with Love* did as well. When the series was revived in May of 1995, it proved popular again, despite the fact that both the golden age of *shōnen-ai* and the Cold War had ended.

In Germany, *From Eroica with Love* has become a cult favorite. Eberbach, the real German town from which Major Klaus hails, has even made Aoike an honorary citizen. In the United States, the termination of the CMX imprint has put further translation of the series into English in jeopardy.

R. C. Lutz

Further Reading

Tomoki, Hori. *Crimson Snow* (2011).
Yoneda, Kou. *No Touching at All* (2010).

Bibliography

Cornog, Martha. "*From Eroica with Love*." Review of *From Eroica with Love*, by Yasuko Aoike. *Library Journal* 133, no. 15 (September 15, 2008): 39.

Gravett, Paul. *Manga: Sixty Years of Japanese Comics*. New York: Harper Design, 2004.

Suzuki, Kazuko. "Pornography or Therapy? Japanese Girls Creating the Yaoi Phenomenon." In *Millennium Girls: Today's Girls Around the World*, edited by Sherrie Inness. Lanham, Md.: Rowman, 1998.

See also: *Banana Fish*; *MW*

FRUITS BASKET

Author: Takaya, Natsuki

Artist: Natsuki Takaya (illustrator)

Publisher: Hakusensha (Japanese); TOKYOPOP (English)

First serial publication: *Furūtsu basuketto*, 1998-2000, 2001-2006

First book publication: 1999-2007 (English translation, 2004-2009)

Publication History

Natsuki Takaya's *Fruits Basket* was serialized in the Japanese biweekly girls' manga magazine *Hana to yume* (flowers and dreams), published by Hakusensha, from 1998 to 2006, though Takaya took a year-long sabbatical from 2000 to 2001 because of a hand injury. The series was collected in book form and published by Hakusensha beginning in 1999. The English translation was first published in 2004 by TOKYOPOP.

Takaya first planned to finish the series in twenty volumes; however, she eventually expanded the story line and finalized it to fit into twenty-three volumes. Because of the series' great success, three related books were published: a *Fruits Basket* character book (2001), *Furūtsu basuketto fan bukku* (2005; *Fruits Basket Fan Book—Cat*, 2007), and *Furūtsu basuketto fan bukku—En* (2007; *Fruits Basket Banquet*, 2007). The latter two were translated into English. An English book with Japanese annotation collecting chapters 1-3 of Volume 1 was published by Hakusensha in 2003 as a tool for Japanese readers studying English.

Plot

Although it employs a common plot structure of *shōjo* manga, in which an ordinary teenage female protagonist seeks happiness while growing up and overcoming typical adolescent hardships, *Fruits Basket* explores some of the most serious problems in modern Japanese society: child abuse, child abandonment, bullying, dysfunctional families, and identity crises. The story focuses on the lives of three high school students: Tohru Honda, Yuki Sohma, and Kyo Sohma.

Natsuki Takaya

Natsuki Takaya, born in 1973, is a manga creator best known for the *shōjo* (or girls') series *Fruits Basket*. The series ran from 1999 to 2006 in the Hakusensha-published magazine *Hana to Yume* and became one of the best-selling manga series in the United States following its publication in English by TOKYOPOP. Takaya's other manga include *Hoshi wa utau*, about young stargazers; the postapocalyptic *Tsubasa: Those with Wings*; and the fantasy *Phantom Dream*. Takaya told the magazine *Time* that unlike many manga creators, she has never worked as an artist's assistant, nor has she created *dōjinshi*, amateur self-published manga.

Tohru lives by herself in a tent, having been orphaned by the recent death of her mother (her father died when she was a child). Tohru's classmate Yuki happens to see her living in the woods near his family's residence. He invites her to stay in his wealthy family's house, where she meets his cousins Shigure and Kyo and works as a housekeeper.

Tohru soon discovers that Yuki, Kyo, Shigure, and ten other members of the Sohma family have been cursed by animal spirits of the Chinese zodiac. As a result of the curse, when the Sohmas are embraced by a person of the opposite gender or feel sick, they turn into the animals that possessed them. Most of the cursed Sohmas were feared, neglected, or abused by their parents; therefore, Yuki and Kyo live away from their parents. Kyo is most deeply cursed and is destined to be imprisoned within the Sohmas' "cage" after graduating from high school. The twelve other cursed family members use him as a scapegoat, discriminating against him and feeling superior to him.

Through Yuki and Kyo, Tohru meets the other cursed family members and learns how they cope with both general struggles and conflicts with Akito, the intolerant head of the Sohma family. Because Akito is admired as a "god" by the animal spirits, no one can disobey Akito's orders. However, Tohru accepts the cursed family members as they are, which gradually eases their suffering. Knowing Kyo's destiny, Tohru seeks a way to solve the curse and confronts Akito. However, she eventually realizes that Akito has been hurt by her mother and forced to live as a man, which is a crucial secret of the Sohma family and the reason for Akito's cruelty. Tohru's understanding and acceptance free Kyo, Yuki, and the other family members from the curse.

Volumes

- *Fruits Basket*, Volume 1 (2004). Tohru begins to live with Yuki and his cousins Shigure and Kyo, who are cursed by animals. She meets Kagura, who is in love with Kyo.
- *Fruits Basket*, Volume 2 (2004). Tohru meets Momiji and Hatori. Hatori tells her not to get involved with the Sohma family.
- *Fruits Basket*, Volume 3 (2004). Tohru meets Yuki's cousin Hatsuharu, who tells her about Yuki's childhood. Tohru, Yuki, Kyo, and Momiji go to a hot spring.
- *Fruits Basket*, Volume 4 (2004). Tohru, Yuki, and Kyo become sophomores, and Momiji and Haru enter Tohru's high school. Tohru meets Akito and Ayame.
- *Fruits Basket*, Volume 5 (2004). Tohru meets Kisa, who is unable to speak because of being bullied at school.
- *Fruits Basket*, Volume 6 (2004). Kyo's guardian and master, Kazuma, returns from his journey and meets Tohru. He tests her to determine whether she can accept Kyo as he is.
- *Fruits Basket*, Volume 7 (2005). Tohru meets Hiro, who is in love with Kisa. Arisa Uotani becomes Tohru's best friend.
- *Fruits Basket*, Volume 8 (2005). Tohru meets Ritsu, and Yuki, Kyo, Haru, Ritsu, and Tohru try to tackle their problems.
- *Fruits Basket*, Volume 9 (2005). Yuki becomes the president of the student council and meets new members Machi and Kakeru. The story of Tohru's psychic friend, Saki Hanajima, is revealed.
- *Fruits Basket*, Volume 10 (2005). Tohru, Kyo, Haru, and Momiji go to the Sohmas' summer cottage and are joined by Kisa, Hiro, Shigure, and, later, Akito.
- *Fruits Basket*, Volume 11 (2005). At the cottage, Tohru meets Isuzu (or Rin), who is Haru's girlfriend. Akito attempts to blackmail Tohru.
- *Fruits Basket*, Volume 12 (2005). Tohru secretly seeks a way to dissolve the Sohmas' animal curse for Kyo, while Rin does the same for Haru.
- *Fruits Basket*, Volume 13 (2006). Yuki's selfish mother irritates him during their meeting with his teacher. Tohru and her classmates make a school excursion to Kyoto.
- *Fruits Basket*, Volume 14 (2006). Rin's past is revealed. During the activities of the student council, Yuki learns of Machi's problems with her family.
- *Fruits Basket*, Volume 15 (2006). While talking to Kakeru, Yuki remembers his childhood encounter with Tohru. In the school festival, Tohru and her classmates perform a comedic "Cinderella" play.
- *Fruits Basket*, Volume 16 (2007). Kyo remembers Tohru's mother, Kyoko, whom he met in his childhood. The story of how Tohru's parents met is revealed.
- *Fruits Basket*, Volume 17 (2007). Tohru meets Kureno, who tells her the incredible truth about Akito.
- *Fruits Basket*, Volume 18 (2007). Rin is missing, and Haru desperately searches for her. Rin has been confined in a shed by Akito and is eventually rescued by Kureno.
- *Fruits Basket*, Volume 19 (2008). Tohru realizes her true feelings for Kyo, who will soon disappear. Yuki finds out about a fatal relationship between Tohru and Kakeru.
- *Fruits Basket*, Volume 20 (2008). Because of a quarrel with her unaffectionate mother, Ren, Akito stabs Kureno. Kyo confesses to Tohru the secret of her mother's death.

- *Fruits Basket*, Volume 21 (2008). Tohru reveals her feelings to Kyo, who refuses her. She is later injured in a fall.
- *Fruits Basket*, Volume 22 (2009). When Tohru gets out of the hospital, Kyo tells her that he is in love with her. His curse is lifted, and the other family members are released from their curses.
- *Fruits Basket*, Volume 23 (2009). Tohru, Yuki, and Kyo graduate from high school. Tohru and Kyo find a new home together and live happily ever after.

Characters

- *Tohru Honda*, the protagonist, is an orphaned sixteen-year-old girl with dark brown hair and large round eyes. She is extremely polite and is characterized as unrealistically generous and optimistic. Toward the end of the manga, she realizes that she is in love with Kyo.
- *Yuki Sohma*, cursed by the rat, is Tohru's classmate and later the student-council president. He has a feminine face and short silver hair and is called "Prince" by his admirers. Because of his curse, he isolates himself from those around him, especially girls. He was abandoned by his mother and abused by Akito, and he fears "opening the lid" of his childhood memories to resolve his trauma. Thanks to Tohru, he accepts his weakness and attempts to overcome it. When he ultimately overcomes his trauma and confesses his love for Machi, his curse disappears.
- *Kyo Sohma*, cursed by the cat, is Tohru's classmate and Yuki's cousin. A tall athlete with orange hair, he is short-tempered but warmhearted. He was raised by his cousin Kazuma after his mother's suicide, for which his father blamed him. He feels his future is hopeless because he is to be imprisoned after high school. However, his outlook changes due to his love for Tohru. The curse leaves him when he overcomes his trauma.
- *Shigure Sohma*, cursed by the dog, is a twenty-seven-year-old cousin of Yuki and Kyo. A kind and easygoing novelist, he typically wears a kimono. He secretly uses Tohru to end the curse on the Sohma family so he can be with Akito, whom he has loved since his childhood.
- *Akito Sohma* is the head of the Sohma family. In her early twenties, she is a sickly, short-tempered, violent, and mysterious woman with short black hair and black eyes. She was raised as a boy and suffers from an identity crisis. Possessed by a zodiac god, she manipulates the cursed family members and has absolute power over them.
- *Kagura Sohma*, cursed by the boar, is an eighteen-year-old cousin of Yuki and Kyo and Kyo's childhood friend. She has dark brown hair and is short, slim, and feminine; however, when she is excited, she turns tremendously violent.
- *Momiji Sohma*, cursed by the rabbit, is a fifteen-year-old cousin of Yuki and Kyo. He is half German and often speaks German. He has a sunny, childlike disposition and has short, curly blond hair and blue eyes.
- *Hatori Sohma*, cursed by the dragon, is a twenty-seven-year-old cousin of Yuki and Kyo and a close friend of Shigure and Ayame. He is tall, slim, intelligent, and reserved and works as the doctor for the Sohmas. He is nearly blind in his left eye. He has the ability to erase memories through hypnosis.
- *Ayame Sohma*, cursed by the snake, is Yuki's older brother. He is a tall, handsome, talkative, and narcissistic man with long silver hair. He feels guilty for having neglected Yuki when Yuki asked him for help as a child.

Artistic Style

Fruits Basket uses an intricate narrative structure featuring changes of viewpoints and streams of consciousness, panels portraying flashbacks, flowers and animals as indicators of the characters' mental states, and an exquisite balance of comedic and serious tones. For the most part, Tohru narrates the events from her point of view, often addressing her deceased mother or the reader. However, beginning in chapter 10, different characters often take over the narrator's role, expressing their feelings toward Tohru or exposing their inner voices. These multilayered viewpoints facilitate the reader's ability to identify with various characters.

One of the most prominent techniques Takaya uses is the insertion of a panel depicting vaguely drawn, dotted characters between the sequential panels, signifying a character's memory of past sorrows or traumatic experiences. For example, a dark-colored panel or a sliced panel formed by thin lines in which Tohru's mother is standing alone is inserted between panels that show details seen from Tohru's point of view. Stream-of-consciousness narrative is interspersed with more realist forms of narration. The flashbacks are enigmas that are gradually unveiled as the story progresses.

Takaya also uses flowers and animals to signal characters' emotions and the consequences of characters' actions. A bird and red camellias drawn with Akito, for example, symbolize her desire to be free from her ambiguous gender identity; in Japan, camellias represent "outstanding beauty" and "beheading." Animals and objects also appear in text bubbles to indicate who is talking: A text bubble with a rice ball signifies Tohru's voice, while one with a cat signifies Kyo. This technique produces comical moments in the narrative. The change between a serious and a comical mode is often represented by the appearance of characters drawn in a simplified or deformed style.

Themes

The major themes of *Fruits Basket* are love, friendship, family, and coping with trauma. "Fruits Basket" is a popular children's game in Japan in which players are assigned names of fruits and then form a circle. One player (*oni*) stands in the center of the circle. When the *oni* calls out a name of a fruit, those who were named that fruit must move to other chairs, while the *oni* tries to sit in a free chair. In the manga, Tohru is bullied by classmates who dub her *onigiri* (rice ball) in the game, and she waits in vain for her name to be called. This represents Tohru's initial position in the story. Tohru has no family on whom she can rely and is an outsider among the Sohmas. Therefore, she seeks a home in which she belongs. Through her interactions with her friends and the cursed Sohma family members, she eventually realizes that she belongs with the people she loves.

The inserted anecdote "A Tale of a Stupid Traveler" symbolizes the way in which the characters should confront their hardships. In the tale, the traveler gives everything he has, from money to body parts, to those who beg him. In the end, after offering his eyes to a monster in the forest, he receives a piece of paper from the monster as a "gift"; the paper reads "Idiot." The traveler is unable to see it without his eyes but feels happiness because of the monster's thoughtful gift. This allegory represents Tohru's altruism. Furthermore, it critiques the self-centered attitudes of Yuki, Kyo, and other characters who have blamed their hardships on someone else and have avoided facing their own traumas. Ultimately, the book asks readers to consider how devotion to someone serves to produce self-confidence and courage to confront suffering.

Impact

Fruits Basket became one of the best-selling *shōjo* manga not only in Japan but also in the United States, Singapore, France, and Mexico. The series particularly appealed to young female readers who wanted to read romantic, emotion-centered stories or stories more realistic and relevant to their lives than those in many male-dominated American comics. In this sense, *Fruits Basket* helped popularize *shōjo* manga in the U.S. market. The success of the 2001 anime adaptation also served to lead new readers to the genre. *Fruits Basket* is remembered for exploring serious adolescent issues with both sensitivity and humor.

Television Series

Fruits Basket. Directed by Nagisa Miyazaki. FUNimation Entertainment/Studio DEEN, 2001. This twenty-six-episode animated adaptation features the voices of Yui Horie as Tohru, Aya Hisakawa as Yuki, and Tomokazu Seki as Kyo. Laura Bailey, Eric Vale, and Jerry Jewell provide the voices for the English version. The show adapts Volumes 1-6 and parts of Volumes 7 and 8. It differs from the manga in several ways, including its treatment of Akito's gender and Kyo's secret identity.

Akiko Sugawa-Shimada

Further Reading

Hino, Matsuri. *Vampire Knight* (2005-　).

Midorikawa, Yuki. *Natsume's Books of Friends* (2005-　).

Takaya, Natsuki. *Tsubasa: Those with Wings* (1995-1998).

Bibliography

Choo, Kukhee. "Girls Return Home: Portrayal of Femininity in Popular Japanese Girl's Manga and Anime Texts During the 1990's in *Hana yori dango* and *Fruits Basket*." *Women: A Cultural Review* 19, no. 3 (2008): 275-296.

Shamoon, Deborah. "Situating the *Shōjo* in *Shōjo* Manga: Teenage Girls, Romance Comics, and Contemporary Japanese Culture." In *Japanese Visual Culture*, edited by Mark W. MacWilliams. Armonk, N.Y.: M. E. Sharpe, 2008.

Spies, Alwyn. *Studying Shōjo Manga: Global Education, Narratives of Self and the Pathologization of the Feminine*. PhD diss., University of British Columbia. 2003. https://circle.ubc.ca/handle/2429/15104.

See also: *Tsubasa; Boys over Flowers; Nana*

FULLMETAL ALCHEMIST

Author: Arakawa, Hiromu

Artist: Hiromu Arakawa (illustrator)

Publisher: Enix (Japanese); Square Enix (Japanese); VIZ Media (English)

First serial publication: *Hagane no renkinjutsushi*, 2001-2010

First book publication: 2002-2010 (English translation, 2005-2011)

Publication History

Fullmetal Alchemist, written and illustrated by Hiromu Arakawa, was first published in one of Enix's monthly manga magazines, *Shōnen Gangan*. (The publisher merged with Square, becoming Square Enix in 2003.) In the almost nine years that it ran (the story was serialized from July, 2001, to June, 2010) *Fullmetal Alchemist* comprised 108 chapters, not including the *gaiden* (bonus) stories included in some of the collected volumes. Almost immediately after its initial serial publication, it was gathered into twenty-seven *tankōbon* volumes beginning in January, 2002.

Fullmetal Alchemist's commercial success in Japan attracted the interest of American audiences seeking manga with dark themes and complex characters. VIZ Media published an English-language edition of *Fullmetal Alchemist* from May, 2005, to December, 2011.

Plot

Fullmetal Alchemist is a complex story that has many intersecting arcs occurring in both the present and the distant past. The series opens with two boys, Alphonse and Edward Elric, who are in search of the fabled "Philosopher's Stone"—a stone that can cure any disease or injury. The backstory of the alchemical experiment that changed them so dramatically is told in a series of asides and flashbacks during the first nine chapters. As children, they try to resurrect their deceased mother. But because of the alchemical law of "Equivalent Exchange," the reanimation of their mother's body causes the dissolution of Alphonse's body and Edward's left leg. As he sees his brother disappear before his eyes,

Fullmetal Alchemist. (Courtesy of VIZ Media)

Edward sacrifices his right arm to bind his brother's soul to a nearby suit of armor.

The Elric brothers' act of human transmutation is illegal, attracting the attention of the alchemical division of the state military. Recognizing that the boys have talent, Colonel Roy Mustang approaches them, offering them the opportunity to join the military and research a method to recover their lost bodies. Having few alternatives, Edward agrees. His left leg and right arm are replaced with "automail" (controllable prosthetic limbs), and he learns to alter the structure of metal (hence his code name, "the Fullmetal Alchemist").

The role of state alchemists is not always well regarded by citizens. In response to religious extremism practiced in the Ishbal Province (to the northwest of the capital), the state military of Amestris decides that the rioting in Ishbalan would be best handled through genocide. Edward and Alphonse's quest for rejuvenation is constantly sidetracked by the political machinations of the military; the murderous intentions of Scar, one of a handful of Ishbalan survivors, who seeks vengeance; and the monstrous plots of the homunculi, the artificially created agents of the Father.

Volumes

- *Fullmetal Alchemist*, Volume 1 (2005). Collects issues 1-4. The Elric brothers search for the Philosophers Stone.
- *Fullmetal Alchemist*, Volume 2 (2005). Collects issues 5-8. Edward begins his work as a state alchemist. Roy Mustang sends the Elric brothers to Shou Tucker, the "Life-Binder Alchemist," who claims that he is able to create new life-forms.
- *Fullmetal Alchemist*, Volume 3 (2005). Collects issues 9-12. The brothers look for Winry Rockbell. They discover the secret of the Philosopher's Stone.
- *Fullmetal Alchemist*, Volume 4 (2005). Collects issues 13-16. Showcases the value of Dr. Marcoh and his research to the brothers. Alphonse begins to question his humanity because he can no longer recall what his childhood was like. Envy, one of the Father's homunculi, kills Lieutenant Colonel Maes Hughes.
- *Fullmetal Alchemist*, Volume 5 (2006). Collects issues 17-21. Includes a flashback that relates how the brothers learned to practice alchemy.
- *Fullmetal Alchemist*, Volume 6 (2006). Collects issues 22-25. Provides background on the relationship between the Elric brothers and their teacher, Izumi Curtis.
- *Fullmetal Alchemist*, Volume 7 (2006). Collects issues 26-29. Alphonse is kidnapped, and Elric goes in search of him. He has to fight a homunculus along the way.
- *Fullmetal Alchemist*, Volume 8 (2006). Collects issues 30-33. Edward and Izumi learn that King Bradley is not what he appears to be. Edward undergoes a formal assessment of his research on the Philosopher's Stone. Chimeras lure Alphonse

away from Izumi, offering to provide information about reversing transmutations. Edward and Izumi learn that King Bradley is the homunculus Wrath.

- *Fullmetal Alchemist*, Volume 9 (2006). Collects issues 34-37. Wrath punishes the rebellious Greed by taking him to the Father, who kills him and consumes his body. Meanwhile, Edward and Alphonse go back to Rush Valley and meet Prince Lin Yao, the ruler of Xing Valley.
- *Fullmetal Alchemist*, Volume 10 (2006). Collects issues 38-41. Alphonse, Prince Lin Yao, Lin's bodyguard, Lan Fan, and Roy Mustang's soldiers fight against Lust, Envy, Gluttony, and Pride. Roy Mustang uses his alchemical fire to "burn out" Lust's Philosopher's Stone. Edward and Roy Mustang take Ross to Xing.
- *Fullmetal Alchemist*, Volume 11 (2007). Collects issues 42-45. Alphonse and Edward meet Hohenheim, their long-absent father. They do not reveal their mother's transmutation.
- *Fullmetal Alchemist*, Volume 12 (2007). Collects issues 46-49. With the assistance of Prince Lin, the brothers capture Gluttony. Wrath discovers their plot and attacks the prince.
- *Fullmetal Alchemist*, Volume 13 (2007). Collects issues 50-53. Despite his appearance, Gluttony is utterly inhuman. A fight between Edward, Prince Lin, and Envy results in Gluttony swallowing the three combatants. While inside Gluttony, Envy reveals that Gluttony's original purpose was to act as a gate between the lands of the living and the dead. Using Envy's internal Philosopher's Stone, the three are transported outside Gluttony.
- *Fullmetal Alchemist*, Volume 14 (2007). Collects issues 54-57. Recognizing that Edward and Alphonse are the sons of Hohenheim, Father uses his alchemical abilities to heal them. He hands over Edward and Alphonse to King Bradley, who admits that he is Wrath. He tells Edward that if he tries to leave the state military, he will murder Winry Rockbell. In the meantime, Scar finds Tim Marcoh and forces him to reveal the original deception that started the Ishbal Civil War.

- *Fullmetal Alchemist*, Volume 15 (2007). Collects issues 58-61. Edward learns the role that the alchemists played in the Ishbalan campaign, the tragic consequences of which are still felt.
- *Fullmetal Alchemist*, Volume 16 (2008). Collects issues 62-65. Riza Hawkeye confirms that the alchemy division of the state military conducted the Ishbalan genocide. She recalls that an attempted surrender offered by the Ishbalan resistance was rejected. The brothers discover the homunculus Sloth while digging a tunnel under Amestris.
- *Fullmetal Alchemist*, Volume 17 (2008). Collects issues 66-69. The brothers combat Sloth. Kimblee fights Scar and is wounded. He is healed by a doctor who possesses a Philosopher's Stone.
- *Fullmetal Alchemist*, Volume 18 (2009). Collects issues 70-73. Sloth has been involved in creating a massive transmutation circle under Amestris. The only option the brothers have to slow his progress is to freeze him. Wrath's adopted son is the homunculus Pride. They both threaten Riza. Kimblee continues to hold Winry Rockbell hostage to ensure the Elric's loyalty to the state military.
- *Fullmetal Alchemist*, Volume 19 (2009). Collects issues 74-78. Major General Armstrong and President Bradley (a homunculus) meet. Edward is badly hurt.
- *Fullmetal Alchemist*, Volume 20 (2009). Collects issues 79-83. Reveals that Hohenheim, Edward and Alphonse's father, achieved immortality by being implanted with a Philosopher's Stone formed by the destruction of the city of Cselkcess. Envy is destroyed by Dr. Marcoh. Envy's remains are then confined to a jar, intended to be taken to Xing for safekeeping. At the same time, Prince Lin is briefly able to regain control of his body from the parasitic Philosopher's Stone within him.
- *Fullmetal Alchemist*, Volume 21 (2009). Collects issues 84-87. Mustang and his soldiers attack King Bradley as he travels by train. Al-

phonse is abducted by Pride and loses control of his armor. Edward, Heinkel, Greed, and Darius, along with Prince Lin's servants, finally force Pride to release him. Pride devours Gluttony and absorbs his Philosopher's Stone.
- *Fullmetal Alchemist*, Volume 22 (2010). Collects issues 88-91. Alphonse and his father force Pride into a cave, holding him captive. Edward and his group overtake Father. Roy Mustang hopes to make public the true nature of the military.
- *Fullmetal Alchemist*, Volume 23 (2010). Collects issues 92-95. Chimera Heinkel attempts to assist the Elric brothers against the nearly impervious homunculi. Heinkel's stone not only helps Alphonse during his combat with Pride, but also proves useful when Dr. Marcoh uses it to heal the injured Chimera.
- *Fullmetal Alchemist*, Volume 24 (2011). Collects issues 96-99. Hohenheim confronts Father, and the latter must return to his shadow state. Sloth is killed.
- *Fullmetal Alchemist*, Volume 25 (2011). Collects issues 100-103. Wrath remains loyal to his cre-

---

Hiromu Arakawa

Hiromu Arakawa, born in 1973, is the creator of the manga *Fullmetal Alchemist*, which ran in the Square Enix magazine *Monthly Shōnen Gangan* for nearly a decade beginning in 2001. Her ongoing *Silver Spoon*, serialized in Shogakukan's *Weekly Shōnen Sunday*, is about a boy attending an agricultural school; for it she drew from her experiences with her parents, who are dairy farmers in her native Hokkaido. Her *Hero Tale*, authored by Huang Jin Zhou, is a period fantasy. While such artists are not entirely rare, it is worth noting that Arakawa is a woman who made her fame in boys' (*shōnen*) manga.

ator, but Greed joins Edward. Wrath manages to activate the transmutation circle beneath Amestris, which sends Edward, Izumi, and Alphonse to the Gate of Truth. Alphonse is brought back into contact with his original body for a short time.

- *Fullmetal Alchemist*, Volume 26 (2011). Collects issues 104-106. Father undertakes his "master plan," which reconfigures the world. The brothers attack Father.
- *Fullmetal Alchemist*, Volume 27 (2011). Collects issues 107-108. Alphonse makes a final gamble and offers his soul to the divine essence of Truth in exchange for Edward's original arm. This allows Edward to fight Father more effectively. Greed offers his own destruction as a means of keeping Father trapped in the circle. Edward offers the ultimate exchange—his alchemical ability for the body and soul of his brother.

Characters

- *Edward Elric* is blond, short, and hotheaded. He is the older of the two Elric brothers. He and his brother, Alphonse, become interested in alchemy after their father abandons them and their mother dies. Edward is the youngest applicant to ever pass the state examinations for alchemists.
- *Alphonse Elric* is the younger of the Elric brothers. Although temperamentally calmer and the intellectual equal of Edward, he decides not to become an alchemist, primarily because his lack of a conventional body would prevent him from passing the required physical examinations. On the other hand, the suit of armor that comprises his "self" makes him extremely strong and difficult to damage.
- *Father* is a small, shadowy creature and the villain of *Fullmetal Alchemist*. He is a homunculus—a humanoid created artificially through illicit use of the Philosopher's Stone—and he creates a series of other homunculi to serve his purposes.
- *King Bradley* is the king of Amestris and führer of the state military. He is a tall and dark-haired

man who wears an eye patch to conceal the Ouroboros mark that identifies him as the homunculus Wrath.
- *Lust*, an attractive, curvaceous female, is one of the seven homunculi who act as physical manifestations of the Father's traits. She uses her fingers as weapons, extending them into spear-like points. Like all of the major homunculi, she is marked with the sign of the Ouroboros and can quickly recover from most types of damage.
- *Gluttony*, a short and stocky figure with strong jaws, is Lust's constant companion. His original purpose—to act as a portal for the Father—has become subverted to his perennial hunger.
- *Envy* is a slim, dark-haired youth who can change his appearance at will. He frequently acts as a spy for the Father, assuming any identity needed to gain an advantage over an opponent.
- *Greed*, who appears in the guise of an attractive, dark-haired man, is unable to control his desire to possess whatever appeals to him. In pursuit of his desires he is incapable of being loyal to the Father or other homunculi.
- *Sloth* is a large, powerful man easily controlled by the Father. His lack of intelligence or introspection makes him a perfect tool for the other homunculi because he fails to question the purpose behind his assigned tasks.
- *Pride* appears in the persona of King Bradley's young son, Selim. Although he can only exist within the transmutation circle underlying Amestris, he has the ability to mimic the abilities of any individual he consumes.
- *Lt. Colonel Roy Mustang* is an attractive, youthful man. He is known as the "Flame Alchemist" because of his ability to create and control fire.
- *Riza Hawkeye*, a slim, blond woman, is Roy Mustang's assistant and closest companion. She has deadly aim with any handheld weapon.

Artistic Style

Arakawa's bold, expressive style seems to explode off the pages. She presents the characters' emotional states in bold lines and frequently draws dialogue to duplicate, visually, the content of an utterance. At the end of each manga chapter, Arakawa draws comic "interludes" that poke fun at the more serious themes within the respective chapter. These interludes provide a welcome relief from the intense and often horrific occurrences that dominate the primary events of the series. For example, in the "Binding-Life Alchemist," Shou Tucker, turns his beloved daughter, a mere child, into a grotesque blend of a little girl and a dog; Ultimately, both are destroyed by the Ishbal rebel, Scar, as a way of purifying the evil of Tucker's alchemical act. Arakawa ends the chapter by cartooning the young girl, presenting her as an angel with a little halo, while her monstrous father is slipping downward into a cartoony "hell." In another example, Arakawa pokes fun at Roy Mustang's immense ego when she has him attempt to hijack the role of the central protagonist from Edward Elric. Edward can be observed glowering in the background. These touches bring much-needed humor to a rather dark series.

Themes

Arakawa uses her exaggerated world to present lessons in humanity to her readers. The value of life, both human and animal, is presented through the analogy of transmutation. Grotesqueries, like the homunculi, seem to represent traits inherent in all human beings to a lesser or greater extent, but their continual symbolic presence in the background of the plotlines suggests the presence of lust, envy, wrath, and the other deadly sins within the human characters. Shou Tucker is as driven by pride and envy as the two homunculi who bear those titles. Lust rears her head not only in her tight, black dress but also in the form of the lustful Cornello, who eyes his worshipper Rose inappropriately. The fact that King Bradley initially appears to be a decent and evenhanded leader is undercut by the reality of his dual role as Wrath. Appearances can be deceiving. Both Edward and Alphonse learn repeatedly that individ-

uals have hidden sides to their personalities, which define their behaviors more clearly than the "outer" self they present to the world.

Impact

Fullmetal Alchemist presents concepts that have universal appeal. In many ways, *Fullmetal Alchemist* is a typical example of Japanese fantasy-based manga. It subverts what many Americans regard as a literary form for adolescents (a series of "comic-strip" images,

Fullmetal Alchemist. (Courtesy of VIZ Media)

and utterances appearing to be hand-drawn and hand-lettered) into a vehicle intended as much for the presentation of graphic violence, dark themes, and contemplative philosophies as comedy and lighthearted amusement. Intuitively, Western audiences realize that they are witnessing a profound difference between the two cultures' use of literary form, but they still have difficulty absorbing that a Japanese audience can present the annihilation of humanity in a graphic form without flinching at the subject matter.

Films

Fullmetal Alchemist: The Movie—Conqueror of Shamballa. Directed by Seiji Mizushima. Aniplex/Bones/Dentsu, 2005. FUNimation Entertainment released the English-language version of *Fullmetal Alchemist: The Movie—Conqueror of Shamballa* in August, 2006, and then on DVD.

Fullmetal Alchemist: The Sacred Star of Milos. Directed by Kazuya Murata. Aniplex/Bones/Dentsu, 2011. This film premiered in Japan in July, 2011. FUNimation Entertainment has acquired licensing rights to an English-language version for distribution in the United States and Canada in 2012.

Television Series

Fullmetal Alchemist. Directed by Seiji Mizushima. Aniplex/Bones/Mainichi Broadcasting System, 2003-2004. Bones Studio adapted the manga characters and plot into fifty-one episodes released between October, 2003, and October, 2004. The series, which differed significantly from the original manga series, still retained the appeal of Hiromu Arakawa's original. FUNimation Entertainment took on the challenge of dubbing the Japanese anime series and distributing it for English-speaking audiences.

Fullmetal Alchemist: Brotherhood. Directed by Yasuhiro Irie, et al. Bones/Square Enix, 2009-2010. This anime series follows the plot of the manga (the first series used an original story line). The English version aired on Cartoon Network from 2010 to 2011.

Julia Meyers

Further Reading

Shirow, Masamune. *Ghost in the Shell* (1989-1991).

Yoshiyuki, Tomino, and Yoshikazu Yasuhiko. *Mobile Suit Gundam* (2002-2003).

Bibliography

Solomon, Charles. "For Manga, a Novel Approach." Los Angeles Times, April 29, 2007. http://articles.latimes.com/2007/apr/29/entertainment/ca-manga29

Yadao, Jason S. *The Rough Guide to Manga*. New York: Rough Guides, 2009.

See also: *Ghost in the Shell*; *Fist of the North Star*

G

GHOST IN THE SHELL

Author: Shirow, Masamune
Artist: Masamune Shirow (illustrator)
Publisher: Kodansha (Japanese); Dark Horse Comics (English)
First serial publication: *Kōkaku kidōtai*, 1989-1991
First book publication: 1991 (English translation, 1995)

Publication History

First published in *Young Magazine* in 1989, *Ghost in the Shell* is the creation of writer and illustrator Masamune Shirow, famed for manga cult classics *Appleseed* (1985-1989), *Black Magic* (1983), and *Dominion* (1985). *Ghost in the Shell* is considered a *seinen* manga, targeting Japanese businessmen between the ages of eighteen and thirty. The English translation was produced by Dark Horse Comics, which released the first full volume of the collected work in 1995. The manga proved popular in the West, where it attained such a cult status throughout the 1990's that second and third volumes were released in 2003 and 2005; the latter contains an addendum of four chapters that were originally intended for the first volume.

Plot

The various plots of *Ghost in the Shell* have to do with the work of Public Security Section 9, a government agency dedicated to locating and capturing cyberwarlords. Two of the chief cybercriminals are Puppet Master and Laughing Man, world-class hackers who possess capabilities beyond those of the best employees of Section 9. Cyberhacking allows the perpetrator to overtake a person's mind and, thus, control that person's body. During these hacking instances, the hacker can make victims commit suicide or criminal acts. Puppet Master is able to hijack the minds of top-level officials; the Laughing Man takes over the minds of large groups of people and is able to hide his face under the camouflage

Masamune Shirow

Masamune Shirow, born in 1961, is the creator of the influential manga *Ghost in the Shell*, which ran for nearly a decade in the Kodansha-published *Young Magazine*. The manga is one of Japan's major contributions to pop cultural contemplation of the spiritual and interpersonal consequences of artificial intelligence. His other major works include the ambitious series *Appleseed*, *Orion*, and *Dominion*. Manga ambassador and translator Frederik L. Schodt has noted that Shirow continued to be employed as a high school art teacher throughout his early career. In interviews, Shirow tends to posit science fiction less as predictive and more as admonitory. He once noted, "The history of industrialized societies is rather short, as a part of mankind's history, so we need to take a long range view to establish that level of tolerance" (Smith).

of a special seal. In each instance, the team at Section 9 is forced to respond quickly and use the most technologically advanced equipment to take down the cybercriminals, who prove almost unbeatable.

Volumes

- *Ghost in the Shell* (1995). Collects issues 1-8. In the year 2029 in Newport City, Japan, Major Kusanagi and the others of Section 9 seek to stop Puppet Master. They are stunned when they realize the hacker is actually a project for government department Section 6. In the end, Kusanagi merges with the Puppet Master on the Web.
- *Ghost in the Shell 1.5: Human-Error Processor* (2003). Collects issues 1-8 of *Ghost in the Shell 1.5: Human-Error Processor*. Technically the third installment, though released in the United

States before the collected *Ghost in the Shell 2*, it contains material that was meant to be included in the original publication. A politician named Mr. Hayasaka is kidnapped and murdered; his corpse is controlled remotely by a hacker. Azuma and Togusa investigate.

- *Ghost in the Shell 2: Man-Machine Interface* (2005). Collects issues 1-11 of *Ghost in the Shell 2: Man-Machine Interface*. Motoko Aramaki, a composite version of Major Kusanagi and Puppet Master, works for Section 9 and seeks to capture cybercriminals, spies, and hackers.

Characters

- *Major Motoko Kusanagi*, the protagonist, is a female cyborg with an organic brain and spinal cord. She is always connected to the Internet; therefore, she can hack into other people's interfaces and direct other versions of herself remotely. Emotionally, she is often represented in a brooding manner, philosophizing about her sense of self. She is the tactical commander for Section 9 and is also bisexual. She appears in *Ghost in the Shell 2* as Motoko Aramaki.
- *Batou*, second-in-command of Section 9, is a male cyborg with cybernetically enhanced eyes, through which he is able to connect to the Web. He is physically powerful yet down-to-earth and spends his free time working out at the gym or with his basset hound.
- *Togusa* is one of the few noncyborgs of Section 9 at the start of the series. He is a family man and has a penchant for antiquated weaponry.
- *Ishikawa* is the warfare technologist of Section 9. Like Togusa and Saito, he has little (if any) cybernetic enhancement. He is a master hacker and contributes to the missions from behind the computer, rather than serving actively.
- *Saito* is the sniper for Section 9. He has a cybernetically enhanced arm and eye, which are useful for precise handling of heavy submachine guns.
- *Pazu* is the team investigator. He spends his time on the streets interviewing old connections from the underworld, where it is rumored he was pre-

viously part of the *yakuza* street gangs of Tokyo. He is also a notorious womanizer.
- *Boma* is the weapons specialist of the team. His job is to fight synthetic threats and cyberorganic threats such as viruses. He has an imposing physique and cybernetically enhanced eyes.
- *Chief Daisuke Aramaki* is a male cyborg and the chief of Section 9. His crew has several epithets to describe his half-man, half-ape face. He is a loyal, fatherly figure.
- *Hideo Kuze* is a male cyborg who was with Kusanagi in the plane crash that left them both paralyzed and in need of cyborg bodies.

Artistic Style

The style of *Ghost in the Shell* is often referred to as "cyberpunk," a term that describes the futuristic, artificial world in which the characters reside. There is also an overriding sexual subtext to the work, and a parental advisory warning is often displayed on the cover of the Dark Horse versions of the manga due in part to this characteristic. Kusanagi is often presented in skin-tight clothing and thigh-high boots, on her knees, and connected to the Web via a series of cables that calls to mind a bondage scene. Despite being sexualized, Kusanagi is the leader of her police unit and is physically and mentally capable.

The series usually employs the *yonkoma* vertical four-panel splash effect, and scenes are often dramatized using no captions or bubbles. During the scenes in which characters have philosophical soliloquies, the line drawings are more open and the usage of narrative bubbles limited, inviting readers to participate in the characters' search for identity and meaning. At the beginning of a new sequel chapter, a page is often dedicated to bringing readers up to speed on the events that occurred previously; this will sometimes be done in a different artistic style than the rest of the manga. These catch-up diaries depict the characters as shorter, with rounder faces, and the dialogue and plot are truncated to give a brief summary of events.

The manga is primarily presented in black and white, but the first several pages are colored. Shirow's original watercolor illustrations are reproduced exactly in the English version and help to depict the artificial world the characters inhabit. The mood of the watercolors is muted, and they contribute to the dreamy, futuristic, and sometimes dark mood of the series. Eventually, Shirow abandoned the watercolor method and began to use computer-created animation. At times, he also uses photographs changed only by the imprint of his graphics. His illustrations are renowned for consistently portraying minute details, which are often accompanied by footnotes, helping readers understand scientific details or technical definitions. In some instances, the footnotes are direct editorials in which Shirow speaks to the readers to explain his choices in relation to the technology.

Themes

The primary theme of the *Ghost in the Shell* series has to do with the defining elements of humanity. The series poses several philosophical questions to readers regarding what it means to be human. Kusanagi often wonders if it is possible to be human when the majority of one's body is nonorganic. She consistently debates whether she is truly human and wonders if she has any real memories or if her few memories are fabricated. Kusanagi is also known to be one of several versions of her mechanical self, which reflects on her need for individualism. These are all subjects to which most readers can relate, and they endear the characters and the series to readers.

Impact

Produced in the Modern Age of comics, *Ghost in the Shell* is considered to have inspired the futuristic film *The Matrix* (1999) and its sequels. The directors of the film have commented that they were inspired by the world created by Shirow and tried to duplicate the atmosphere. Both the manga and the film are concerned with alternative realities and the connection to a virtual world. In its own right, *Ghost in the Shell* has been one of the most popular manga in Asia and the West, and the franchise has moved from graphic art to other media, including film and television.

Films

Ghost in the Shell. Directed by Mamoru Oshii. Bandai Visual Company/Kodansha, 1995. This animated film features the voices of Atsuko Tanaka as Motoko Kusanagi and Akio Otsuka as Batou and adapts part of the manga's plot dealing with the Puppet Master.

Ghost in the Shell 2: Innocence. Directed by Mamoru Oshii. Bandai Visual Company/Buena Vista Home Entertainment, 2004. This animated film adaptation stars Tanaka and Otsuka and features Batou as the protagonist. The film is set in 2032, and its plot focuses on a character named Locus Solus, referencing the eponymous 1914 French novel by Raymond Roussel. The plot mirrors Roussel's novel in that the characters watch different versions of themselves through a window. The film became a Selection Officielle at the Cannes Film Festival and also won the Orient Express Award at the Catalonian International Film Festival.

Ghost in the Shell: Stand Alone Complex—Solid State Society. Directed by Kenji Kamiyama. Production I.G., 2006. This film spin-off of the television series stars Tanaka and Otsuka. The Puppet Master returns and hacks into people's cyberbrains, forcing them to commit suicide. He also kidnaps children by hacking into their parents' brains. However, the Puppet Master goes to Section 9 to seek amnesty, claiming that he had been committing the crimes against his will.

Television Series

Ghost in the Shell: Stand Alone Complex. Directed by Kenji Kamayama. Bandai Visual Company, 2002-2003. This series stars Tanaka and Otsuka and follows Section 9 as they search for the criminal known as the Laughing Man, who is discovered to be a hacker known as Aoi. Section 9 uncovers the truth about Aoi and offers him a position on the team.

Ghost in the Shell: Stand Alone Complex, 2nd Gig. Directed by Kenji Kamayama. Bandai Visual Company, 2003-2004. This series stars Tanaka and Otsuka. Section 9 is being manipulated in a plot to use terrorists to cover up a government conspiracy to rid the nation of refugees. Section 9 turns against its government to uncover the truth about the prime minister.

Shannon Oxley

Further Reading

Miura, Kentaro. *Berserk* (2003-   ).

Oku, Hiroya. *Gantz* (2008-   ).

Otomo, Katsuhiro. *Akira* (1988-1995).

Bibliography

Brenner, Robin E. *Understanding Manga and Anime*. Westport, Conn.: Libraries Unlimited, 2007.

Cavallaro, Dani. *Magic as Metaphor in Anime: A Critical Study*. Jefferson, N.C.: McFarland, 2010.

Napier, Susan J. *Anime from Akira to Princess Mononoke: Experiencing Contemporary Japanese Animation*. New York: Palgrave, 2000.

Ryberg, Jesper, Thomas S. Petersen, and Clark Wolf. *New Waves in Applied Ethics*. New York: Palgrave McMillan, 2007.

Smith, Toren. "Interview with Masamune Shirow." *Manga Mania* 1 , no. 8, February, 1994.

Wong Kin Yuen. "On the Edge of Spaces: *Blade Runner, Ghost in the Shell*, and Hong Kong's Cityscape." *Science Fiction Studies* 27, no. 1 (March, 2000): 1-21.

See also: *Akira; Berserk*

Golgo 13

Author: Saito, Takao

Artist: Takao Saito (illustrator); Mark McMurray (letterer); Yukiko Whitley (letterer)

Publisher: Shogakukan (Japanese); LEED (English); VIZ Media (English)

First serial publication: 1969-

First book publication: 1973-   (partial English translation, 1986-1987)

Publication History

Takao Saito published his first manga, *Baron Air*, in 1955. In order to spread out the massive amount of work associated with a first-class manga, he founded a manga production studio with seven colleagues in 1958, which became Saito Production in 1960. That year, he and his studio created a four-issue James Bond manga, which inspired Saito to develop a series about a master Japanese assassin. The first *Golgo 13* story was published in the January, 1969, issue of Shogakukan's *Big Comic* magazine. As the magazine was on sale in November, 1968, that year is sometimes given as the beginning of the series.

Big Comic magazine has typically published one assassination story per issue, with longer stories split into installments. Originally planned for a limited run only, *Golgo 13* proved extraordinarily successful and popular. The first *tankōbon* was published in June, 1973. By the end of 2011, 160 *tankōbon* volumes of *Golgo 13* had been published, and the series was ongoing. There were also 132 *bunkoban*, or small paperback, volumes collecting *Golgo 13* stories. In general, the volumes do not publish the magazine stories strictly in order of their publication. Instead, the books rearrange the stories, often inserting an older story among newer ones. Because of their controversial subject matter, four stories have not been published in book collections.

In English, Saito's LEED Publishing Company published four trade paperback volumes of *Golgo 13* stories from 1986 to 1987. The originally black-and-white pages were colorized and "flipped" so the comic could be read from left to right in the traditional Western style. As a product tie-in with the *Golgo 13*

Golgo 13. (Courtesy of VIZ Media)

video game, two graphic novels of *Golgo 13* stories translated into English were published in 1989 and 1990. LEED also published a three-part series, *The Professional: Golgo 13*, between 1991 and 1992. From 2006 to 2008, VIZ Media published a thirteen-volume collection of select *Golgo 13* stories, retaining the original black-and-white illustrations and the original right-to-left reading order.

Plot

From the beginning of the series, each Golgo story has focused on a particular contract for which the superassassin has been hired. For both the right fee and the proper justification, Golgo 13 will carry out an assignment, typically an assassination. The assignment must be related to sniping, though the target does not have to be a person. Professional pride prevents Golgo from taking on double contracts or doing nonsniping work, such as exclusively gathering intelligence. As a rule, Golgo never accepts a contract from the same person twice. This rule has been broken somewhat, as Golgo has repeatedly worked for intelligence agencies such as the CIA or Great Britain's MI6. However, he always has a different primary client within such an organization.

The plots of the individual stories fall into two general categories. The first focuses directly on Golgo carrying out his assignment and the means, strategy, and tactics he employs to that effect. The second category focuses more strongly on the person, institution, or organization that hires Golgo and on their choice of target. Here, Golgo often makes a brief but climactic appearance as he fulfills his mission. Stories have also featured Golgo's reputation only, with characters using it to instill fear in targets who are not even killed or impersonating Golgo to achieve their ends. Golgo has also used sniping to destroy key inanimate objects, ranging from an Iraqi supergun to disputed Florida ballots in the 2000 U.S. presidential election. Some stories have suggested a possible origin for the Golgo character. However, Saito has always avoided giving a definite history and has written more than one possible origin story.

Throughout the series, Saito has been imaginative in creating exciting and cutting-edge plots for Golgo's assignments. He has created many plots based on current events. The VIZ Media edition warns that historical persons are used in an entirely fictional context.

In general, plots have featured rather unsympathetic targets for Golgo, ranging from surviving Nazis to neo-Nazis and enemies of the West during the Cold War, and they often include members of crime or terrorist organizations. Targets are never completely innocent, and Golgo takes on only those assignments for which he sees a proper justification. Even though Golgo has stretched his definition for justification at times, never has he performed assignments for outright evil people.

While there have been some plot developments that reach across multiple stories, such as the birth and death of Golgo's son, Saito has not developed Golgo much through the decades. Most noticeably, Golgo's age has remained the same, though some wounds have been added to his body over the years. In essence, each new Golgo story can stand on its own, with cross-references to earlier stories exceedingly rare. Individual story plots are unique, while Golgo remains a powerful, constant force in each of them.

Volumes

- *Golgo 13: Supergun*, Volume 1 (2006). The first of VIZ Media's thirteen-volume translation of select *Golgo 13* stories. Each volume contains two stories, which were chosen from the original, ongoing Japanese series for their potential appeal to American audiences. The stories are not arranged chronologically, and the years of their original creation cover a long period. The volumes constitute the first edition in English that maintains the manga's original black-and-white illustrations and the Japanese right-to-left reading order. Volume 1 features an assignment in Saddam Hussein's Iraq and a contract against a hit-and-run driver in San Francisco.

- *Golgo 13: Hydra*, Volume 2 (2006); *Golgo 13: Power to the People*, Volume 3 (2006); *Golgo 13: Orbital Hit*, Volume 4 (2006). Each volume typically includes episodes that feature assignments related to pivotal historical events, such as the Tiananmen Square protests in China in June, 1989. Volume 3 includes a cameo by former South African president Nelson Mandela; Golgo confronts a Mandela impostor in the second story. In Volume 4, Golgo goes into space. He also appears at the site of Princess Diana's death in Paris, in an episode originally published in Japan just three months after the event.

- *Golgo 13: Wiseguy*, Volume 5 (2006). The selected stories feature an assignment involving the Mafia and an intrigue after the fall of the Berlin Wall in 1989.

- *Golgo 13: One Minute Past Midnight*, Volume 6 (2006); *Golgo 13: Eye of God*, Volume 7 (2007); *Golgo 13: Gravestone in Sicily*, Volume 8 (2007); *Golgo 13: Headhunter*, Volume 9 (2007); *Golgo 13: Wasteland*, Volume 10 (2007); *Golgo 13: The Wrong Man*, Volume 11 (2007); *Golgo 13:*

Shadow of Death, Volume 12 (2007). Volume 6 includes a story with an American setting and one in which Golgo is contracted to kill a false pope in Italy. Volume 7 features two double-cross stories. Volume 8 features the only story in which Golgo misses his target, reducing his much-acclaimed success rate from 100 to 99 percent. In Volume 9, Golgo's gun misfires, making him wonder if the bullets delivered to him for his contract were deliberately flawed. In the first story of Volume 10, Golgo is hired to prevent a nuclear power plant disaster in Los Angeles. The second story focuses on mobsters in Nevada and is one of Saito's personal favorites. Volume 11 features a story set in Okinawa, Japan, and another in which a surprised salesman is mistaken for Golgo. Volume 12 features two stories from the 1970's. Golgo is hired to destroy evidence of a CIA chemical-weapons lab, and then he impersonates an African American man to fulfill his contract to assassinate a racist Caucasian mayor in Mississippi.

- *Golgo 13: Flagburner*, Volume 13 (2008). Golgo's background is explored in one of the Golgo origin stories, which ends ambiguously. In the last story, Golgo is contracted to affect the outcome of the Florida ballot recounting in the 2000 U.S. presidential elections.

Characters

- *Duke Togo,* a.k.a. *Golgo 13*, the protagonist, is a tall, athletic Japanese (or possibly part Japanese) man with dark, straight hair and dark eyes. His real name and age are unknown, but his professional alias refers to Golgotha, the site of the crucifixion of Jesus, and the number of Jesus' disciples including the traitor Judas Iscariot. He appears to be in his thirties. A professional sniper for hire, he dresses elegantly but also appropriately for each assignment. His weapon of choice is an M16, especially the sniper version M16A2, but he can use almost any other weapon. He is taciturn but a master linguist, extremely self-composed, and attractive to women and acts according to his own code of conduct.

Takao Saito

Takao Saito was born in 1936. He has been cited by Yoshihiro Tatsumi (*A Drifting Life*), as one of the original creators of *gekiga*, or artistically ambitious manga for mature readers. Saito is known primarily for his long-running creation: a heartless, extremely talented, and sexually aggressive assassin in the James Bond mode whose anecdotal adventures are published as *Golgo 13*. The *Golgo 13* assassin, also known as Duke Togo, has been likened to a modern-day samurai. The series has run continuously since 1969 in the Shogakukan magazine *Big Comic*, targeted at mature readers. Prior to creating *Golgo 13*, Saito developed a short-lived James Bond manga, and he also produced a manga adaptation of the classic Japanese disaster novel *Japan Sinks*, written by Sakyō Komatsu.

- *Golgo's Clients* differ for each story and thus number in the hundreds. They must be able both to pay Golgo's professional fee and to provide him with a justification for his assignment. They have ranged from members of the intelligence community to government institutions, organized crime organizations, individuals with grievances, and persons as unlikely as a White House gardener.

- *Golgo's Human Targets* differ in each story. Generally, they are unsympathetic characters ranging from Nazis to criminals, terrorists, and aspiring dictators; sometimes, however, they are morally neutral but stand in the way of Golgo's clients. In rare instances, clients have hired Golgo to kill them as their own targets. Occasionally the targets are meant to be intimidated rather than killed. Targets also include historical persons with an alternate history, such as Argentine president Juan Perón.

Artistic Style

From the beginning, Saito employed his professional staff of Saito Production to provide each story of *Golgo 13* with high visual production values. While Saito has been generally in charge of plotting each individual story, Fumiyasu Ishikawa, or sometimes his deputy, has been responsible for coordinating all elements of the illustrations, working much like a movie director editing the visuals of a film.

As *Golgo 13* was inspired by Ian Fleming's James Bond character, the series has been drawn in a classic, Western realist style, forgoing typical manga elements such as exaggerated eyes or childishly drawn characters. Golgo is drawn with attention to his trademark black hair, cut short but with long sideburns, reflecting his origin in the late 1960's. He is drawn either wearing a suit and tie or attire appropriate for his assignments. Some fans and critics have been quick to point out occasional flaws in the drawing of Golgo when Saito Production did not meet its high graphic standards for the protagonist.

Each book of the series features the logo of a skeleton wearing a crown of thorns, shown from behind and walking across the Japanese characters spelling *Golgo 13*. This visualizes the idea of the protagonist sacrificing himself for the ills of society in allusion to the biblical Jesus. However, the series is generally free of religious references, though its depiction of Islamic characters has occasionally stirred controversy.

In general, *Golgo 13* follows a restrained graphic style that often keeps to regular panels. A significant feature of the series has been the elaborate background illustrations, ranging from the deserts of Iraq to orbital space and the cityscape of an American metropolis. Historical characters, such as former U.S. president Bill Clinton and members of his cabinet or former Iraqi president Hussein, have also been featured and drawn in realistic graphic style. Weaponry is depicted in loving detail. Golgo's exploits as a sniper are often highlighted by close-ups of bullets on their exactly calculated trajectory toward their targets.

A major merit of the VIZ Media edition has been the preservation of the original Japanese right-to-left orientation of the manga. Similarly, the stark contrasts of black and white of the original have been maintained, suggesting Golgo's existence in a world of violently clashing ideas and characters.

Themes

A key theme of *Golgo 13* is the idea that in the modern, morally ambiguous world, personal autonomy may express itself successfully in the professional choice of being an assassin. Remarkably, Golgo 13 is consistently modeled, and drawn, in the style of a Western character. He has virtually nothing to do with a traditional Japanese ninja assassin. Quite to the contrary, Golgo's adamant refusal to work twice for a single client highlights his autonomy. His insistence on personal self-determination makes him a modern, Western-style character with no higher loyalty than to his own code of conduct.

Another theme concerns Golgo's ability to carry out some next-to-impossible exploits as a sniper. Golgo's perfect, ultimate mastery of the weapons he uses celebrates the triumph of humanity over both forces of nature and human physical limitations. Golgo's brilliant physical and psychological performance is not limited to weaponry, as he also controls his body and is able to carry out astonishing physical feats. These are complemented by his ability to perform well sexually.

In many aspects, Golgo symbolizes a fantasy of near absolute power and skill. This is tempered by the theme that Golgo inevitably serves his clients. As his name suggests, he may sacrifice his life for the sins of society. There are almost no scenes depicting Golgo enjoying the fruits of his labor. Golgo is not shown to luxuriate privately in material comfort; rather, he appears always focused on his assignment at hand.

Throughout Golgo's various assignments, the stories of the series also offer a reflection on current political and social events. Here, Golgo emerges as a powerful executioner of the will of his clients. Golgo embodies the ultimate professional, and he ensures he is beholden to no single other person. Perhaps this severe theme of autonomy has also prevented Golgo from developing much as a character. Even as the world turns around him, Golgo remains essentially the same.

Impact

Golgo 13 immediately rose to popularity in Japan. As a kind of indigenous James Bond character, Golgo struck a chord with the readers of *Big Comic* magazine.

Clearly modeled after a Western character, Golgo fascinated his readers at a time during the 1970's and 1980's when Japan looked closely to the West for inspiration and pop-culture ideas. This focus on bringing Western styles, images, and ideas to a Japanese audience, and the relative downplaying of Japanese themes in the series, may explain why Golgo took some time to catch on with American readers, who may have preferred a more typical manga.

With *Golgo 13*, Saito also promoted manga for a more mature audience as well as manga with high production values. By the end of 2011, *Golgo 13*'s loyal readership in Japan had bought more than 200 million copies of the books in all available formats. With 160 book titles, *Golgo 13* ranks third in terms of individual book titles published for a manga series, behind the long-running baseball manga series *Dokaben* and the comic cop series *Kochikame*. *Golgo 13* is Japan's longest-running manga series.

Films

Golgo 13. Directed by Junya Sato. Toei Company, 1973. This live-action film stars Ken Takakura as Golgo 13 and is a dark assassination story that captures the spirit of the series.

Golgo 13. Directed by Yukio Noda. Toei Company, 1977. This live-action film stars Sonny Chiba as Golgo 13. An action-packed assassination story set in Hong Kong, Japan, and a Pacific island, the film features a rare miss by Golgo. This happens when another assassin reaches the assigned target before Golgo can fire his shot. Golgo redeems himself at the end, shooting his next target out of a flying helicopter while hanging from a cliff.

The Professional: Golgo 13. Directed by Osamu Dezaki. Tokyo Movie Shinsha, 1983. This animated film stars Tetsuro Sagawa as the voice of Golgo; the English dub features the voice of Greg Snegoff. Set primarily in San Francisco and New York City, the film includes an unusual twist: The first target orders his own killing, a plot device that is similar to the conclusion of the Golgo origin story "The Serizawa Family Murders," collected in the thirteenth volume of VIZ Media's English edition.

Golgo 13: Queen Bee. Directed by Osamu Dezaki. Urban Vision, 1998. This animated film stars Tessho Genda (pseudonym of Mitsuo Yokoi) as the voice of Golgo; the English dub features the voice of John DiMaggio. The film was not well received and was considered by some viewers to be contrived and excessively sexual.

Television Series

Golgo 13. Directed by Mitsuru Nasukawa, Masahiro Takada, and Shunji Oga. Answer Studio, 2008-2009. This animated television series stars Hiroshi Tachi as the voice of Golgo 13. The series ran for fifty episodes, covering typical *Golgo 13* assassination stories. The last episode offers an unusual twist in which Golgo assassinates his target by firing a modified M16 rifle with his left

Golgo 13. (Courtesy of VIZ Media)

hand and then killing his client by using his usual right-hand trigger finger on another M16. Two DVD collections were released in the United States in 2010, featuring episodes 1-13 and 14-26, respectively.

R. C. Lutz

Further Reading

Koike, Kazu, and Goseki Kojima. *Path of the Assassin* (1978-1984).

Miller, Frank, and Bill Sienkiewicz. *Elektra: Assassin* (1986-1987).

Bibliography

Gravett, Paul. *Manga: Sixty Years of Japanese Comics*. New York: Harper Design, 2004.

Johnson-Woods, Toni, ed. *Manga: An Anthology of Global and Cultural Perspectives.* New York: Continuum, 2010.

Schodt, Frederik. *Dreamland Japan: Writings on Modern Manga.* Berkeley, Calif.: Stone Bridge Press, 1996.

Thompson, Jason. *Manga: The Complete Guide.* New York: Del Rey, 2007.

See also: *Monster; Berserk*

GON

Author: Tanaka, Masashi

Artist: Masashi Tanaka (illustrator)

Publisher: Kodansha (Japanese); DC Comics (English)

First serial publication: 1991-2002

First book publication: 1992-2002 (English translation 2007-2009)

Publication History

Gon, a black-and-white series by Masashi Tanaka, was first introduced to the Japanese public in 1991 in the thirty-ninth issue of Kodansha's *Weekly Morning* magazine. The tremendous success of the comic resulted in its trade publication by Kodansha beginning in 1992. In the early 1990's, dinosaurs were prevalent in popular culture, from the zany children's television character Barney, a purple, anthropomorphic *Tyrannosaurus rex*, to the fiercely realistic dinosaurs in Steven Spielberg's 1993 film *Jurassic Park*, an adaptation of the novel by Michael Crichton. This public interest in dinosaurs extended to comics, and in 1996, Paradox Press (DC Comics) began publishing the first U.S. version of *Gon*. The pages of the manga were reversed so that the comic could be read in the standard Western left-to-right reading order. The series included a color issue, *Gon Color Spectacular*, published in 1998. Later, in 2007, this highly popular series was published in its original format (reading right to left) by CMX (WildStorm, also an imprint of DC Comics). Kodansha Comics USA began to reprint the series in 2011.

Plot

The twenty-four wordless episodes in *Gon* follow a small but tough anthropomorphic dinosaur named Gon who lives in the modern animal world. There are no humans in these stories. Gon's adventures involve conflict with a variety of animals indigenous to specific regions on every continent. Readers experience the beauty and drama of nature through Tanaka's rich portrayal of flora and fauna.

Gon is a free spirit who roams the earth and defends animals from easily identifiable antagonists. He always

---

Weekly Morning

Weekly Morning is a *seinen* manga magazine published by Kodansha and targeted at adult male readers. The magazine launched in 1982 and has published its longest-running series, Tochi Ueyama's *Cooking Papa*, since 1985. *Gon*, the silent dinosaur manga by Masashi Tanaka, ran for a decade beginning in 1992. *Weekly Morning* also publishes *Billy Bat*, a period piece about a comic-book character that is the center of a mystery, by renowned manga creator Naoki Urasawa (*20th Century Boys*, *Pluto*) and longtime collaborator Takashi Nagasaki. Among the publication's best-known series are the science-fiction epic *Planetes*, the time-traveling military naval series *Zipang*, and the swordsman tale *Vagabond*.

---

subdues his foes with his indomitable spirit and a ferociousness that crushes the most powerful beasts, from grizzly bears to tiger sharks, and sends a shiver of fear through the onlooking animals. Because of his size, he befriends young animals that are often the prey of larger animals.

In the early episodes, Gon is portrayed in a gritty manner, with a determined gaze and an annoyed expression. He is intent on dispensing retribution for injustice and does not rest until the antagonist is punished in what appears to be a savage and cruel manner. One example from "Gon Goes Flying" involves a hungry bobcat who attempts to kill one of the young golden eagles that Gon has befriended. Gon pursues the bobcat relentlessly and finally, in a falling flight from the sky, crashes through tall trees that fall on the bobcat, pinning him helplessly under their weight.

Gon evolves after the first few episodes, developing a more playful nature; however, his true, savage nature resurfaces when he is threatened or disturbed. Many of the episodes show Gon coming to the aid of unfortunate animals.

Gon serves as a guide through the brutal animal world in stories that include a mix of humor and violence. In the episode "Gon Glares," a hungry dingo chases after a koala. The koala escapes the dingo's snapping jaws by climbing a tree, where it joins hundreds of other koalas and Gon, who looks menacingly down on the dingo. Resembling a swarm of bees, the koalas follow Gon's lead and plummet down on the dingo. With his exceptionally large feet, Gon kicks the dingo out of the jungle. In a series of vaudevillian events, the dingo is surprised to find Gon wherever he goes; the dinosaur emerges from a kangaroo's pouch and leads an army of gnashing crocodiles. In the final scene, the dingo prepares to fight Gon but cowers in fear. The dingo is humiliated in front of his cubs, and in a gesture of peace, Gon tosses a large fish out to the dingo. His cubs run to eat the fish until their father growls; in a show of pride, the cubs follow their father, turning their backs on Gon's offering and walking away.

In one uncharacteristic episode, "Gon Builds a Mansion," Gon destroys an entire forest as he attempts to replicate a beaver dam on a large scale. This destruction results in extensive flooding, leaving the animals in the forest homeless and angry at Gon's indifference.

Volumes

- *Gon*, Volume 1 (2007). Includes "Gon Eats and Sleeps," featuring grizzly bear, sockeye salmon, and American black bear; "Gon Goes Hunting," featuring spotted hyena, blue wildebeest, and lion; "Gon Builds a Mansion," featuring three-toed woodpecker, coyote, and North American beaver; and "Gon Goes Flying," featuring golden eagle and bobcat.
- *Gon*, Volume 2 (2007). Includes "Gon Plays with a Giant Shark," featuring giant tortoise, white shark, and giant sand tiger shark; "Gon Struggles Against a Tick," featuring African elephant, savanna baboon, hard tick, South African hedgehog, and warthog; "Gon Gets Angry at the Forest," featuring squirrel monkey, tamandua, tarantula, ocelot, and green anaconda; and "Gon Lives with the Penguins," featuring southern giant petrel, Weddell seal, and Adélie penguin.
- *Gon*, Volume 3 (2008). Includes "Gon Goes Down the Big River," featuring piranha, fin whale, and Amazon dolphin; "Gon Glares," featuring dingo, koala, and red kangaroo; "Gon Goes Mushroom Hunting," featuring raccoon, emperor mushroom, and poisonous mushroom; and "Gon Fights with Wolf Brothers," featuring tundra wolf and Siberian tiger.
- *Gon*, Volume 4 (2008). Includes "Gon Becomes a Turtle," featuring white-nosed coati, swordfish, and squid; "Gon Journeys into the Desert," featuring savanna monkey and impala; and "Gon and His Posse," featuring caracal and serval.
- *Gon*, Volume 5 (2008). Includes "Gon Goes Through the Underground," featuring prairie dog, giant termite, spider, giant mayfly, king salamander, hog-nosed bat, and pill bug.
- *Gon*, Volume 6 (2008). "Gon with the Huge Wise Elephant," featuring spotted hyena, red-tailed monkey, and African grand elephant; "Gon and the Bird Nest on His Head," featuring brown hyena, wondering locust, giraffe, and weaver bird; "Gon and His Wounded Fellows," featuring wolf, puma, beaver, marten cat, and eagle; and "Gon Climbs a Mountain" featuring ibex and snow leopard.
- *Gon*, Volume 7 (2009). Includes "Gon Raises a Chick," featuring shearwater and monitor; "Gon Has Fun with an Orangutan Family," featuring albatross, orangutan, and gibbon; "Gon Does Some Physical Training," featuring orangutan; and "Gon Collects Honey with his Friends in the Forest," featuring honeybee, flying fox, cockatoo, Malayan porcupine, tarsier, and Indian muntjac.

Characters

- *Gon*, the protagonist, is a tiny *Tyrannosaurus rex* with abnormally large jaws and feet who has survived the extinction of other dinosaurs and lives in the modern animal world. He has unusual strength and exhibits unrelenting aggression in response to any assault from larger animals. His gentle and humorous nature surfaces after the initial episodes, and this playful side balances his aggressive behavior.

- *Other animals* are supporting characters whose presence emphasizes various aspects of Gon's personality and his role in their lives.

Artistic Style

Tanaka's skillful black-and-white line work is breathtaking, with its realistic and detailed depiction of animals and nature. The focus on detail with little white space in the panels is unusual in comics, which rely generally on caricature and visual suggestion. The intricate drawings, featuring fine lines and crosshatching, pull readers inside each natural setting and make the dubious action and events seem plausible. Tanaka's animals are provided with anthropomorphic expressions that are worthy of consideration. He displays a depth of emotion in Gon and the various animals, depicting a range of what American comics theorist Scott McCloud has identified as "pure expressions," including those of anger, disgust, fear, joy, sadness, and surprise. These recognizable human expressions personalize the characters and create a visually captivating story. This element is particularly evident in one of the more tender episodes, "Gon with the Huge Wise Elephant," in which Gon escorts the wise elephant to an ancestral elephant burial cave to die. The wise elephant's facial expression, which exhibits both his determination to reach the cave and his tears of gratitude for Gon, shows Tanaka's ability to illustrate heartfelt emotions. Another element that Tanaka conveys effectively is motion, expressed through the use of speed lines. Gon is forever bouncing from one battle to the next, diving from the sky, swimming intently after prey, or ricocheting through the forest from tree to tree.

Tanaka patiently develops every wordless story with a variety of panel sizes, using full-page and two-page spreads to deliver the greatest visual impact. For example, in "Gon Plays with a Giant Shark," Tanaka displays a calm underwater scene, with a variety of fish casually swimming, in a large panel covering two-thirds of the page. The bottom third shows an expression of fear in faces of the fish and a few speed lines. The next page is broken into three horizontal panels, and a shark appears in the first. The fish swim franti-

cally away in the second panel, and the shark chases after the fish in the third. Tanaka uses numerous speed lines during the chase and dramatically increases the size of the shark in the last panel. On the next page, Tanaka presents an extreme close-up of the shark's open mouth, displayed as though it were coming right out at the reader.

In addition to his diversity of panel displays, Tanaka makes full use of changing angles within the panel, using low-angle and extreme-low-angle views of Gon consistently throughout the episodes to show the dinosaur's power over his foes. An extreme-low-angle view and close-up of Gon's glaring eyes displayed in a horizontal panel across the page is a clear signal of an upcoming burst of aggression.

Tanaka's mix of panel displays and angle views results in a unique visual experience in every episode. One of the more innovative approaches to angle views is in "Gon Gets Angry at the Forest." In this story, a squirrel eats a nut that Gon was saving for his dessert. In a rage, Gon chases after the squirrel, inciting the surprise and anger of other animals and reptiles. To provide a glimpse of the towering trees in the forest, Tanaka displays Gon from a low-angle long shot; his small figure gazes up into the canopy of the forest, and through a small opening, a bird can be seen high in the sky. Another scene is viewed from a high angle, from the back of a green anaconda poised to pounce on Gon. In a two-page spread, Tanaka uses a high-angle view that reveals Gon's feeble figure in relationship to the thick jungle foliage. Later, Gon rams his head solidly into a tree that Tanaka displays in an extreme low angle from behind Gon. He gazes up into the tall tree as many nuts fall and cover him. In a fit of frustration, he chomps on a nut and finds it tasty. The squirrel he was chasing joins him in the feast, and in the last full-page panel, Tanaka, from another extreme low angle, shows Gon sleeping soundly next to the squirrel at the base of the towering tree that rises majestically into the sky. The stunning collection of angles through which Tanaka displays the action is not only visually stimulating but also provides clear relationships between characters and settings.

Themes

The major theme of *Gon* is the use of personal strength and power to overcome injustice. Despite his small size, Gon does not hesitate to do the right thing, especially in protecting the helpless from nasty predators. On another level, the theme of friendship and the strength of family are consistent throughout these episodes. "Gon Has Fun with an Orangutan Family" is about a happy family of orangutans who wholeheartedly accept Gon, despite his species, and enjoy an afternoon of playfulness in the jungle. Gon's survival as a dinosaur is the result of his ability to integrate with nature and other species, which is constantly displayed in the series through an assortment of animals and global surroundings.

Another theme is the role of the environment. "Gon Builds a Mansion" exemplifies the effect that indifference has on the environment. It touches on the issue of human responsibility for keeping the environment in a natural state and seems to ask if people are aware of their impact on the environment. Finally, perhaps one of the more important themes is the value of simple outdoor play enjoyed by Gon and the animals. This theme is in contrast to the modern dependence on technological games and devices for entertainment and fun.

Impact

Published amid increasing media interest in dinosaurs in the 1990's, *Gon* provides an entertaining view of the animal world through the eyes of an indestructible little dinosaur. It was initially published in English at a time when interest in manga was on the rise in the United States. With Tanaka's realistic visual depictions and *Gon*'s entertainment value, the series started to shrink the separation between comics and children's picture books in publishing, a trend that eventually led to the publication of comics such as Sara Varon's *Robot Dreams* (2006), which received a Publisher's Weekly Best Children's Book of the Year award in 2008.

David A. Beronä

Further Reading

Bissette, Steve. *Tyrant* (1994-1996).

Delgado, Ricardo. *Age of Reptiles Omnibus* (2011).

Murphy, Matthew H. et al. *Turok, Son of Stone* (1954-1982; reprint 2009-   ).

Bibliography

McCloud, Scott. *Making Comics: Storytelling Secrets of Comics, Manga, and Graphic Novels*. New York: Harper, 2006.

Molotiu, Andrei. "Masashi Tanaka's Gon Series." *The Comics Journal* 242 (April, 2002): 71-74.

Rust, David. "Like Nothing Else Going: Gon." *The Comics Journal* 201 (January, 1998): 41-42.

See also: *Astro Boy*; *Nausicaä of the Valley of the Wind*

H

HIKARU NO GO

Author: Hotta, Yumi
Artist: Takeshi Obata (illustrator)
Publisher: Shūeisha (Japanese); VIZ Media (English)
First serial publication: 1998-2003
First book publication: 1999-2003 (English translation, 2004-2011)

Publication History

Author Yumi Hotta got the idea for *Hikaru no go* after playing a game of Go with her father-in-law in the 1990's. Her idea won the Story King Award of Shūeisha's manga magazine *Weekly Shōnen Jump*. The magazine teamed her with the up-and-coming manga artist Takeshi Obata. Hotta wrote the story for *Hikaru no go*, and Obata did the major artwork. As is common for manga art production, Obata was assisted by a creative staff, and the twenty-two support artists are credited in the final volume of the manga. They include Hotta's husband, Kiyonari Hotta, with whom she had worked on a four-panel manga about horse racing. Yukari Umezawa, a young Go master, supervised the drawings of the moves and board positions of the many Go matches featured in the manga. She was also assisted by a staff of twelve Go players and the Japanese Go Association.

The series ran in *Weekly Shōnen Jump* from December, 1998, to July, 2003. It comprised 189 chapters, called games. Because of the series' success, from April, 1999, to September, 2003, all episodes were published in a total of twenty-three *tankōbon* volumes. The books added a total of eleven extra stories. They also featured special pages in which Hotta addressed the readers directly to make casual comments on different aspects related to the series.

In the United States, VIZ Media published all twenty-three books from June, 2004, to May, 2011. Some fans were angered by VIZ Media's decision to censor all refer-

Hikaru no go. (Courtesy of VIZ Media)

ences to smoking by characters. Visually, cigarettes were erased and replaced with drawings of chewing gum; also, dialogue was altered. This was done to adjust the manga for a young-adult audience in the United States. However, the occasional visual or verbal reference to smoking slipped by the censors, such as "smoking permitted" signs in areas where characters gathered.

Plot

In *Hikaru no go*, Hotta brings a mischievous twelve-year-old boy in touch with the game through an encounter with the ghost of a young Go teacher from Japan's medieval ages. Hotta's idea was intended for the young male readership of *Weekly Shōnen Jump*.

When his parents cut his allowance as a result of poor grades, sixth-grader Hikaru Shindo ransacks his grandfather's attic for some antiques to sell. He and his friend, Akari Fujisaki, stumble upon an old Go board. Only Hikaru can see that blood has been spilled on the board. The ghost of Fujiwara-no-Sai appears and speaks to Hikaru. The first encounter shocks Hikaru into unconsciousness. Soon Sai contacts Hikaru again and tells Hikaru that he was a young Go teacher in Japan's medieval Heian period. Accordingly, Sai dresses and behaves like a Heian nobleman. Because Sai was cheated and died too young to play a perfect game, he seeks a human medium through which he can fulfill his wish to play again. According to the manga, Sai was behind the triumphs of the legendary nineteenth century Go master Honinbo Shusaku.

At first, Hikaru is reluctant to play Go. When he does, all his moves are directed by Sai. Only the promise of winning money at the game motivates Hikaru. Sai finds Hikaru's motivations abominable but goes along nevertheless. Hikaru soon becomes the rival, and later the friend, of one of the strongest young Go players, fellow teenager Akira Toya. Akira is trained by his father, Go master Toya Meijin.

Hikaru and Akira go to different middle schools and join their schools' Go clubs. Their rivalry continues as they are supported by a different cast of teammates. In addition, they have to fight a variety of bullies and classmates who are jealous of their Go skills.

Even though his wins are directed by Sai, Hikaru grows to like Go. When he plays without Sai's directions, however, he loses. This earns him a reputation as an unpredictable, maverick player. Eventually, Hikaru uses the Internet to let Sai play Go under his own name in cyberspace. Toya Meijin joins the Internet Go games seeking to defeat Sai. Some Go players assume Sai is Hikaru's screen name as their game styles are similar.

After Akira becomes a professional Go player—which in Japan is a decision to be made before turning eighteen—Hikaru sets the same goal for himself. To prove his merits he has to join a pro-Go school, which is known as an *insei* school. Without Sai's help, Hikaru

loses his games. Hikaru begins to win on his own, however, by relying on his increasingly good instincts for the game.

Once Hikaru turns professional, he often teams with Sai, who has become a steady Go presence on the Internet. Their opponents include Akira, who plays Hikaru, and Toya Meijin, who takes on Sai. In Sai and Toya's climactic game, Toya loses by overlooking a brilliant move of the kind Sai sought to make to fulfill his career. Soon afterward Hikaru refuses to let Sai play more Internet games. Because of this, Sai disappears, never to return in the series' present.

Left on his own, Hikaru gives up Go. Later, he struggles to come back. He has to rely on his own skills, and he slowly establishes his reputation. At this point, the series turns to an interlude. It offers six episodes called side stories, featuring the series' top players, excluding Hikaru, and ending with Sai. After this interlude, the plot moves toward preparations for the climactic Hokuto Cup—a tournament for the best under-eighteen Go players from China, South Korea, and Japan.

As part of the three-member team representing Japan, Hikaru and Akira are finally joined on the same side. The games against China come first. Only Akira can win his game. On the final day of the tournament, Hikaru faces South Korea's best player, Kong Yong Ha. Surprisingly, Hikaru loses. Nonetheless, Hikaru discovers that ultimately he and Kong play for the same reason: to link the past with the future. With this insight, *Hikaru no go* ends, leaving Hikaru to look for more games in the future.

Volumes

- *Hikaru no go: Descent of the Go Master*, Volume 1 (2004). Collects issues 1-7. Introduces key characters and the main premises of the series: Teenage boy Hikaru Shindo connects with the spirit of an ancient Go teacher, Fujiwara-no-Sai. Sai persuades Hikaru to pick up Go, at first directing his every move.
- *Hikaru no go*, Volumes 2-22 (2004-2011). Each volume collects about eight to nine of the original episodes, or games. Sai disappears in volume 15 after having guided Hikaru to become a profes-

sional Go player. Volume 18 stands out, offering six episodes called side stories that highlight major characters. With volume 20, preparations and preliminary games begin, leading up to the climactic three-nation Hokuto Cup that ends the series.

- *Hikaru no go: Endgame*, Volume 23 (2011). On the final day of the Hokuto Cup, Hikaru plays against the Korean champion, Ko Yong Ha. Hikaru loses, but both players are united in their love for Go, a game that links the past with the future.

Characters

- *Hikaru Shindo*, the protagonist, is a gangly Japanese adolescent with a trademark two-tone hairstyle, blond in front and naturally black in back. During the series, he grows from an eleven-year-old to a nearly eighteen-year-old boy. His clothing style changes from casual to formal for the Hokuto Cup tournament. He is basically good-natured and mischievous. His relationship with Sai and his Go matches drive the story of the series.

- *Fujiwara-no-Sai*, mentor of Hikaru, is the ghost of a medieval Go instructor of Japan's Heian period. He is dressed in the style of his time with a prominent black cap and multilayered kimono. His features are drawn to look feminine; many readers mistook him for a woman at first. He appears to Hikaru and begs him to play Go, the great unfulfilled passion of his life. After playing on the Internet for a time, Sai disappears in volume 18.

- *Akira Toya*, Hikaru's key opponent and, later, his teammate, is a black-haired teenager of Hikaru's age, dressed conservatively throughout his adolescence. He is a serious, accomplished Go player who is trained by his father. His rivalry with Hikaru drives much of the action of the story.

- *Toya Meijin* is Akira's father and the key contemporary adult of the series. He is an elegant, lean, middle-aged man with expressive hands. He has medium-length hair that is dyed blond, strands of

---

Gaming in Manga

Though a hit in Japan, *Hikaru no go* presents challenges outside its country of origin due to its focus on a board game. The series contrasts greatly with popular *Shōnen Jump* manga such as *Bleach* and *Dragon Ball Z*, which feature life-threatening battles, as well as with titles featuring *Hikaru no go* illustrator Takeshi Obata, including the thriller *Death Note* and video-game spinoff *Blue Dragon Ral Grad*. Still, it is helpful to recognize parallels between *Hikaru no go* and its teen-manga ilk, many of which focus on high-stakes gaming. Think of *Yu-Gi-Oh!*'s magical cards, *Eyeshield 21*'s comically exaggerated football, or *Toriko*'s culinary adventures. *Shōnen* manga is about mastery, be it of martial arts (*Naruto*), basketball (*Slam Dunk*), or an ancient board game.

---

which fall into his forehead. He is mentor to Akira. He is fascinated by Hikaru's play, which is really that of Sai, whom he battles on the Internet.

- *Ko Yong Ha*, leader of the South Korean team at the Hokuto Cup, is an elegant Korean adolescent just under eighteen years old. He dresses in a suit and tie for the tournament. He is passionate about Go and certain of his invincibility. His final match against Hikaru provides the climax of the series.

- *Akari Fujisaki* is one of the few developed female characters of the series. She is the same age as Hikaru and Akira and dresses conservatively. She seems to have romantic feelings for Hikaru that never blossom. Out of her affection for him, she becomes a Go player and leader of her middle school's girls' Go team.

- *Tesuo Kaga*, the Japanese antagonist of Hikaru and Akari, is a lean teenager who goes to the same middle school as Akari. He is captain of the rival shogi (Japanese chess) team. He hates to play Go because his father forbade him from playing shogi and forced him into Go (he loses all his matches to Akira). He smokes as a sign of his rebellious nature in the Japanese original and chews gum instead in the edited American version.

Artistic Style

Unusual for a manga, *Hikaru no go* features an artist, Obata, who drew but did not write the story. Instead Obata collaborated with Hotta, who wrote the story. Throughout the series, Obata followed the basic stylistic elements of manga. Namely, characters have large, expressive eyes and faces that can contort to comic proportions to represent their emotions, whether good or bad.

Of particular visual interest is that throughout the series, the teenage characters grow up by some six to seven years. Obata's drawings reflect these changes. While Hikaru keeps his two-tone haircut, his features become more adult. He is also drawn to act more stylishly, particularly when placing a Go stone on the board. The clothing of the characters is important to Obata. Hikaru's fashion style changes as he grows up. The original manga showed names of certain brands, which the American version edited out.

Fujiwara-no-Sai is drawn to look almost like a woman, befitting the style of a medieval Japanese nobleman. This led even Japanese readers to mistake him for a woman. His clothes and visual gestures, however, are in line with the historical tradition of his era.

A particular challenge was drawing the Go board for the various matches. In these cases, Go master Umezawa supervised Obata's drawings. She, Obata, and Hotta felt it was crucial to show correct, believable positions of the black-and-white Go stones on the board. Occasionally, a mistake in the drawing of a Go position was discovered only at the last moment of copy editing the weekly manga pages.

Obata likes to include occasional, detailed scenes featuring aspects of contemporary Japanese settings. When the action of the Go matches heats up, there is often a close-up focus on hands placing stones on the board with great panache. Obata's style is generally vivid, and his panels show variation in tune with the tempo of the storytelling. As is common for manga, all interior pages are in black and white. Only the covers of the books are in color.

Themes

Hikaru no go is a coming-of-age story. This theme is fueled by the ghostly presence of the mischievous Fujiwara-no-Sai, who acts like an older brother or mentor to Hikaru. From a somewhat lackadaisical sixth grader, Hikaru grows into an ambitious Go player, who uses self-discipline and study to achieve his goal of becoming a great player. This theme is developed through a plot that features many of Hikaru's matches, first as a puppet of Sai, and then as forceful player of his own. Akari serves as a foil for Hikaru because he achieves his strength as a player by normal rather than supernatural means. Akari is trained by his father instead of a spirit.

Hikaru's identification with Go is sometimes expressed through his wearing clothes with the number five on them (as on the cover of volume 1). This is a play on the Japanese pronunciation of five, "go."

Hikaru no go. (Courtesy of VIZ Media)

Hikaru becomes fascinated with the elegance of dropping Go stones on the board. Many panels focus on this movement. His growth is also expressed by his more mature facial features and his more conservative clothes as he moves from elementary to middle to high school.

Apart from featuring Go as a way for adolescents to find a higher, more spiritual goal in their lives, *Hikaru no go* is also concerned with issues facing Japanese teenagers, particularly bullying. The series features quite a few bullies and cheaters. Hikaru and his friends overcome them all. In these instances, the visuals often show detailed scenes of contemporary Japanese settings, such as school buildings, Go salons, or the homes of the teenagers.

The splendor of the past is visualized in the many lavish drawings of Sai in Heian-era court attire. As Sai is drawn in what modern readers view as a feminine look, the series also touches on questions of gender and the changing display of masculinity through the ages.

Impact

In Japan, *Hikaru no go* fueled a tremendous interest in the game of Go among adolescents fascinated by the series. Go lost its somewhat stuffy image as a game for older people. As a result, Go has become fashionable among young Japanese of both sexes. When the series was translated, it also created interest in Go in the United States.

Among manga, *Hikaru no go* extended the range of the popular subgenre of sports manga to include non-physical games that relied on mental strength and skills alone. The animated television series proved popular and reinforced the attraction of Go among young viewers. This was aided by the inclusion of Umezawa's one-minute Go lessons at the end of each episode.

The success of *Hikaru no go* also justified the uncommon collaboration of a writer and a graphic artist in creating a manga series. Typically, in manga, one artist would be responsible for both aspects of the graphic novel—a marked difference from the American and European model. Ohba collaborated with a manga writer, Tsugumi Ohba, for his next two series, *Death Note* (2003-2006) and *Bakuman* (2008-   ).

Television Series:

Hikaru no go. Directed by Shin Nishizawa. Studio Pierrot, 2001-2003. This animated TV series stars the voice of Tomoko Kawakami as Hikaru Shindo. In terms of plot, the seventy-five episodes of the animated television series generally adhere to the manga, but they only cover the events up to volume 19. A final New Year's special, which aired in Japan on January 3, 2004, shows the events leading to the Hokuto Cup that ends the manga. All episodes have been dubbed in English.

R. C. Lutz

Further Reading

Clamp. *Cardcaptor Sakura* (1996-2000).

Ohba, Tsugumi, and Takeshi Obata. *Bakuman* (2008-   ).

_____. *Death Note* (2003-2006).

Bibliography

Cha, Kai-Ming. "Sports Manga Gets in the Game." *Publishers Weekly* 252 (April 18, 2005): 25-26.

Exner, Nina. "Basic Reader's Advisory for Manga: Select Popular Titles and Similar Works." *Young Adult Library Services* 5 (Spring, 2007): 13-21.

Johnson-Woods, Toni, ed. *Manga: An Anthology of Global and Cultural Perspectives*. New York: Continuum, 2010.

Raiteri, Steve. "Graphic Novels." *Library Journal* 130 (May 15, 2005): 98-103.

Shimatsuka, Yoko. "Do Not Pass Go." *Asiaweek* 27 (June 29, 2001): 54-55.

I

InuYasha: A Feudal Fairy Tale

Author: Takahashi, Rumiko
Artist: Rumiko Takahashi (illustrator)
Publisher: Shogakukan (Japanese); VIZ Media (English)
First serial publication: 1996-2008
First book publication: 1997-2009 (English translation, 1998-2011)

Publication History

InuYasha, written and illustrated by Rumiko Takahashi, was featured in the Japanese magazine *Weekly Shōnen Sunday* from November, 1996, to June, 2008. *Tankōbon* volumes of the series were published by Shogakukan from 1997 to 2009. After initially trying to serialize the story in English, VIZ Media began publishing paperback versions in North America beginning in 1998. At first, the English-language versions were "flipped," reading left-to-right; this practice was done halfway through the series. VIZ originally published the first-edition graphic novels with the subtitle "A Feudal Fairy Tale" but dropped it in the subsequent editions. In 2009, VIZ Media started reprinting the series in large collections called VIZBIG Editions, collecting previous volumes. The VIZBIG Editions featured larger pages than before to provide a closer look at both the artistic details and the beautiful color artwork pages.

InuYasha. (Courtesy of VIZ Media)

Plot

Kagome Higurashi is an average Japanese schoolgirl. She dismisses the legends surrounding her family's Shinto shrine until her fifteenth birthday, when the legends take hold of her destiny. A demonic spirit pulls her inside the family well, and she is transported to the Sengoku period, a world full of demonic spirits. The spirit that pulled her through the well tries to remove the Shikon Jewel hidden within Kagome's body. Kagome awakens the half demon InuYasha from his enchanted slumber in order to save her life. He triumphs, but the Shikon Jewel is shattered. Both Kagome and InuYasha learn that Kagome is the reincarnation of the *miko* (priestess) Kikyo, who first guarded the jewel and sealed InuYasha in the enchanted slumber. The text reveals that Kikyo and InuYasha were in love, a love that was corrupted by the half demon Naraku's quest for power.

Naraku is Kagome and InuYasha's main foe, as he seeks to gather the jewel shards for his own power base. Naraku will use anyone he can as a pawn, even children. Kagome and InuYasha's secondary foe is Inu-Yasha's half brother Sesshomaru, a full-blooded demon who sees InuYasha as a family disgrace who must be eradicated. Sesshomaru and InuYasha find a common enemy in Naraku when the latter tries to manipulate Sesshomaru for his own purposes.

Along the way, Kikyo is partially resurrected from her old bones; however, whose side she is on is unclear. InuYasha struggles with his old love for Kikyo and his new love for Kagome, who feels that she cannot compete with her past self. A twisted love triangle forms, as the three struggle with their own tumultuous inner emotions.

Kagome uses the well as a doorway between the past and the present in order to complete the quest, while her grandfather tries to cover for her school absences with several ludicrous medical excuses that horrify her classmates. The series is a dark action story that combines the *shōnen* (boy) and *shōjo* (girl) genres to provide a world in which both subgenres interact; this type of subgenre pollination was popular in the 1990's.

Volumes

- *InuYasha*, Volume 1 (1998). Collects issues 1-8. Kagome is transported five hundred years into the past and discovers she is the reincarnation of *miko* Kikyo. She awakens InuYasha during her fight with a demon. The Shikon Jewel shatters, beginning the main characters' quest to recover all the shards before they fall into evil hands.
- *InuYasha*, Volume 2 (1998). Collects issues 9-18. InuYasha recovers his dead father's sword, the Tetsusaiga, while battling his half brother, Sesshomaru.
- *InuYasha*, Volume 3 (1999). Collects issues 19-28. In the present, a cursed mask has Kagome calling for InuYasha's aid. In the past, Shippo steals Kagome's shards.
- *InuYasha*, Volume 4 (1999). Collects issues 29-38. The Tetsusaiga breaks during battle, breaking the only seal on InuYasha's demon self. It has to

be repaired before his demon half takes over his human half.

- *InuYasha*, Volume 5 (2000). Collects issues 39-48. The new moon strips InuYasha of his demonic powers, temporarily leaving him in human form. The ogress Urasue partially resurrects Kikyo through her ashes.
- *InuYasha*, Volume 6 (2000). Collects issues 49-58. Kagome attempts to recover her soul from the resurrected Kikyo. Miroku allies with Kagome and Inuyasha against their common enemy: Naraku.
- *InuYasha*, Volume 7 (2000). Collects issues 59-68. Sesshomaru accepts aid from Naraku before challenging InuYasha for the Tetsusaiga. Sesshomaru seeks to kill rather than serve Naraku.
- *InuYasha*, Volume 8 (2001). Collects issues 69-78. InuYasha defeats Royakan. Naraku admits his part in getting Kikyo and InuYasha to betray each other 500 years ago.
- *InuYasha*, Volume 9 (2001). Collects issues 79-88. The protagonists face off against Tokajin. They hear of Sango's demon conquest and try to find her. Naraku manipulates her brother Kohaku and has the inhabitants of their village slaughtered.
- *InuYasha*, Volume 10 (2002). Collects issues 89-98. Naraku tries to use Sango to kill InuYasha by implanting a shard in her back. Sango discovers Naraku is responsible for the village slaughter and joins InuYasha and company against him.
- *InuYasha*, Volume 11 (2002). Collects issues 99-108. Naraku tries to separate Miroku from the others when he leaves to have Mushin repair his wind tunnel. Naraku resurrects Kohaku. Sango betrays InuYasha in an attempt to bargain with Naraku for Kohaku.
- *InuYasha*, Volume 12 (2002). Collects issues 109-118. Kagome destroys Naraku's body, leaving only his head. Naraku is forced to find an alternative body. InuYasha and company fight to clear the name of a half demon wrongly accused of eating his fellow villagers.
- *InuYasha*, Volume 13 (2003). Collects issues 119-128. Naraku claims a new body before

striking out at InuYasha and company. Kikyo gives Naraku the jewel shard. InuYasha's right to wield the Tetsusaiga is questioned by its swordsmith, Toto-sai.

- *InuYasha*, Volume 14 (2003). Collects issues 129-138. InuYasha defeats Sesshomaru with a new Tetsusaiga attack called the Wind Scar. Rin nurses the wounded Sesshomaru. InuYasha faces off against Koga after he kidnaps Kagome.
- *InuYasha*, Volume 15 (2003). Collects issues 139-148. Kagome and InuYasha disagree about Koga's actions. Kagome, InuYasha, and Koga battle Kagura. Miroku encounters a girl from his past.
- *InuYasha*, Volume 16 (2003). Collects issues 149-158. InuYasha and company battle Kanna, who tries to fit Kagome's soul into a mirror. They discover that Naraku's power to create detached parts of himself comes from possessing nearly all of the jewel shards.
- *InuYasha*, Volume 17 (2004). Collects issues 159-168. InuYasha is attacked during the new

moon, when he is most vulnerable. Later, he is separated from the Tetsusaiga when Sesshomaru tests his full demon form.

- *InuYasha*, Volume 18 (2004). Collects issues 169-178. InuYasha engages in a gruesome battle with Kageromaru. Kagome struggles with her love for InuYasha and her feelings of inadequacy.
- *InuYasha*, Volume 19 (2004). Collects issues 179-188. InuYasha and company must defend an attack led by Kagura. There is a mole in their group whose task is to kill Kagome. Sesshomaru gains insight into InuYasha's transformation. InuYasha seeks greater control over his full demon form in order to protect Kagome from himself.
- *InuYasha*, Volume 20 (2005). Collects issues 179-188. InuYasha faces off against Ryukotsusei. Naraku has nearly completed the jewel. He offers its power to Kikyo's former rival, Tsubaki. She tries to make Kagome kill InuYasha.
- *InuYasha*, Volume 21 (2005). Collects issues 199-208. Shippo discovers an orphan girl, Satsuki, in possession of a jewel shard. Kagura tries to steal Koga's shards. Miroku and Sango discover a princess who is stealing men's youth. InuYasha battles Muso.
- *InuYasha*, Volume 22 (2005). Collects issues 209-218. It is revealed that Muso is Naraku's original human core, as he struggles to regain the memories of his former self, Onigumo. He tells InuYasha that Onigumo did not want Kikyo to die before Naraku recaptures him. InuYasha seeks to learn how to break barriers with the Tetsusaiga.
- *InuYasha*, Volume 23 (2005). Collects issues 219-229. Naraku's blackmail attempt against Sesshomaru backfires. InuYasha attacks Naraku's castle, inadvertently saving Sesshomaru's life.
- *InuYasha*, Volume 24 (2006). Collects issues 229-238. InuYasha battles the ogres again before saving a village from monkeys. Koga encounters the Band of Seven.
- *InuYasha*, Volume 25 (2006). Collects issues 239-248. After a battle with Mukotsu, InuYasha struggles to find a safe place for Kagome, Sango,

---

Rumiko Takahashi

Rumiko Takahashi, born in 1957, is the creator of the internationally popular manga *InuYasha*. The feudal fantasy series ran from 1996 through 2008 in *Weekly Shōnen Sunday*, published by Shogakukan, and inspired an animated series as well as several films and video games. Takahashi could be considered a legend based on the strength of *InuYasha*'s success alone, but she has far more to her credit, including the romance *Maison Ikkoku*, the cross-gender martial-arts comedy *Ranma 1/2*, and the boxing comedy *One-Pound Gospel*. Takahashi has also produced *Rumic Theater*, a series of short stories that run in *Big Comic Original*, and *Rin-ne*, a story about ghosts that runs in *Weekly Shōnen Sunday*. *Rin-ne* may be the first manga to be published simultaneously in Japan and the United States. Takahashi studied at the famed manga school run by Kazuo Koike (*Lone Wolf and Cub*, *Crying Freeman*).

and Miroku to recover. InuYasha battles Ginkotsu and Renkotsu. Kikyo finds a member of the Band of Seven who is doing honorable work.

- *InuYasha*, Volume 26 (2006). Collects issues 249-258. Unlike InuYasha and company, Kikyo and her allies cannot enter Mount Hakurei. InuYasha battles the Band of Seven before following Bankotsu to Hijiri Island.
- *InuYasha*, Volume 27 (2006). Collects issues 259-268. Koga kills Ginkotsu. Rin is once again held hostage in an attempt to hurt Sesshomaru.
- *InuYasha*, Volume 28 (2007). Collects issues 269-278. While in human form, InuYasha faces Jakotsu. They break the barrier protecting Naraku. Naraku acquires all the shards and finishes his transformation.
- *InuYasha*, Volume 29 (2007). Collects issues 279-288. InuYasha and Kikyo battle Naraku. Sesshomaru attempts to kill Naraku. Naraku removes his human heart.
- *InuYasha*, Volume 30 (2007). Collects issues 289-298. Miroku gets trapped in an enchanted shrine scroll, where a demon tries to kill him. Naraku's infant is split into two people: Akago and Hakudoshi.
- *InuYasha*, Volume 31 (2007). Collects issues 299-308. InuYasha and company go to the gate of the afterlife.
- *InuYasha*, Volume 32 (2008). Collects issues 309-318. InuYasha and company help Kohaku defend the castle.
- *InuYasha*, Volume 33 (2008). Collects issues 319-328. InuYasha fights Hosenki. Naraku gets the last shard of the sacred jewel.
- *InuYasha*, Volume 34 (2008). Collects issues 329-338. Shippo is possessed by a nymph. Koga fights a demon made of corpses.
- *InuYasha*, Volume 35 (2008). Collects issues 339-348. InuYasha and company battle Hakudoshi and Moryomaru. Kagura gives Sesshomaru a tool to find Naraku's heart.
- *InuYasha*, Volume 36 (2009). Collects issues 349-358. The group battle Goryomaru at the

temple and then encounter a medicine man who supposedly has a potion to counteract all poisons.

- *InuYasha*, Volume 37 (2009). Collects issues 359-368. Kohaku chases Hitoukon, while Mouryoumaru seeks his jewel shard. Sesshomaru reveals a crystal that can detect demonic power.
- *InuYasha*, Volume 38 (2009). Collects issues 369-378. InuYasha and company fight Hakudoshi with aid from Naraku, who then kills Kagura for revealing the location of his heart, inside Moryomaru. Kikyo discovers that only the Shikon Jewel can defeat Naraku.
- *InuYasha*, Volume 39 (2009). Collects issues 379-388. Koga receives the claw weapon called the Goraishi. InuYasha battles Mujina, who holds a sword capable of absorbing demonic energy.
- *InuYasha*, Volume 40 (2009). Collects issues 389-398.
- *InuYasha*, Volume 41 (2009). Collects issues 399-408. InuYasha struggles with the Tetsusaiga. Mouryoumaru increases his power, causing InuYasha and company to team up with Sesshomaru, Kikyo, and Kokahu.
- *InuYasha*, Volume 42 (2009). Collects issues 409-418. Totosai gives the Tensaiga the ability to travel between the living and the dead. InuYasha is attacked by Nikosen while in his vulnerable human form. Mouryoumaru learns of two brothers whose blood would strengthen his defenses.
- *InuYasha*, Volume 43 (2009). Collects issues 419-428. InuYasha thwarts Mouryoumaru's plans by absorbing one of the brothers. Tetsusaiga later fails InuYasha in a battle.
- *InuYasha*, Volume 44 (2010). Collects issues 429-438. Koga must save two clan members from a Byakuya's *youkai* who wants Koga's shards.
- *InuYasha*, Volume 45 (2010). Collects issues 439-448. Mouromaru absorbs Naraku, allowing Naraku to reclaim his heart. Miroku tries to capture Naraku's heart at the expense of his own life.
- *InuYasha*, Volume 46 (2010). Collects issues 449-458. InuYasha, Kagome, and Kikyo get en-

snared in Naraku's spider webs. Kagome quests to Mount Azusa for an arrow that will save Kikyo.

- *InuYasha*, Volume 47 (2010). Collects issues 459-468. Naraku uses his spider webs to put the Shikon Jewel into Kikyo's body, causing the jewel to be purified when Kagome saves her with the arrow. Naraku reclaims the jewel, killing Kikyo. A hellhound is released from Sesshomaru's father's Meidou stone.
- *InuYasha*, Volume 48 (2010). Collects issues 469-478. Rin is retrieved from the underworld. InuYasha's demon blood takes control as he battles Kanna.
- *InuYasha*, Volume 49 (2010). Collects issues 479-488. InuYasha destroys the Tetsusaiga copy. InuYasha and company aid Miroku and Sango in a battle against a bone-seeking *youkai*.
- *InuYasha*, Volume 50 (2010). Collects issues 489-498. InuYasha and Sesshomaru fight Shishinki in order to retrieve the Meidou Zangetsuha power. Sango battles Naraku for Kohaku's shard, while InuYasha battles Byakuya.
- *InuYasha*, Volume 51 (2010). Collects issues 499-508. Sesshomaru attempts to take the Meidou Zangetsuha power from the Tetsusaiga. InuYasha and company track down a Naraku spider web.
- *InuYasha*, Volume 52 (2010). Collects issues 509-518. Kagome escapes Hitomiko while Naraku unleashes the dark spirit of the Shikon Jewel in the form of Magatsuhi.
- *InuYasha*, Volume 53 (2010). Collects issues 519-528. InuYasha and Kagome return from present-day Tokyo to find their friends have fallen victim to Magatsuhi.
- *InuYasha*, Volume 54 (2010). Collects issues 529-538. Naraku attempts to absorb the Shikon Jewel while InuYasha and company try to stop him.
- *InuYasha*, Volume 55 (2010). Collects issues 539-548. InuYasha and Sesshomaru continue to attack Naraku.
- *InuYasha*, Volume 56 (2011). Collects issues 549-558. The final battle over the Shikon Jewel.

This volume summarizes the three years after the final battle.

Characters
- Kagome, a protagonist, is a fifteen-year-old Japanese girl skilled in archery. She is the reincarnation of Kikyo, guardian of the Shikon Jewel, and a love interest of InuYasha.
- InuYasha, a protagonist, is half-demon, half-human with a dog-man appearance. He is hot-tempered and deadly with the Tetsusaiga sword. He joins Kagome in reclaiming the Shikon Jewel and defeating Naraku.
- Kikyo, a protagonist, is originally the *miko* charged with the task of protecting the Shikon Jewel. She is resurrected and must consume the souls of dead women in order to keep her physical form.
- Shippo, a protagonist, is a young orphan fox demon who joins Kagome and InuYasha. He can shape-shift but usually takes the form of a boy with a foxtail. True to Japanese folklore, his powers relate to him being a trickster.
- Sango, a protagonist, is an adolescent demon slayer from a prominent slaying family. Naraku convinces her to attack InuYasha after her family is killed by a demon. She joins InuYasha and company after she realizes Naraku was using her.
- Kohaku, a protagonist and Sango's younger brother, is controlled by Naraku. When freed from Naraku's control, he initially joins Kikyo.
- Kirara, a protagonist, is a demon-cat serving Sango and can adjust her size to Sango's needs.
- Miroku, a protagonist, is a lecherous Buddhist monk who has a cursed wind tunnel on his hand that will consume anything when unbound. He allies with InuYasha.
- Sesshomaru, a protagonist, is InuYasha's half brother and a full-blooded demon. He hates InuYasha for his mixed blood and for inheriting the Tetsusaiga.
- Rin, a protagonist, is an orphan girl who becomes attached to Sesshomaru after he saves her life.

- Jaken, a protagonist, is a green demon who masters the Staff of Two Heads and serves Sesshomaru.
- Koga, a protagonist, is a leader of the eastern yokai-wolf tribe who has shards of the Shikon Jewel embedded in his limbs. He initially fights InuYasha but later becomes his ally.
- Ah-Un, a protagonist, is a two-headed dragon demon who serves Sesshomaru. He frequently transports Sesshomaru.
- Kaede, a protagonist, is Kikyo's surviving younger sister who advises InuYasha and company as she continues to protect her village from demons.
- Myoga, a protagonist, is a flea demon who advises InuYasha and serves as an informant. He guards the Tetsusaiga until InuYasha claims it.
- Totosai, a protagonist, is the blacksmith who forged the Tetsusaiga and Tenseiga.
- Naraku, an antagonist, is the demon who drives the plot in his quest to gain the full power of the Shikon Jewel. He is a human who forged himself with demons.
- Kanna, an antagonist, is the first detachment of Naraku and takes the form of a young girl in white. She can conceal her demon energy and possesses a soul-stealing mirror.
- Kagura, an antagonist, is the second detachment of Naraku and despises Naraku for his control over her.
- Muso, an antagonist, is the faceless sixth detachment of Naraku.
- The Infant, an antagonist, is the seventh detachment of Naraku.
- Hakudoshi, an antagonist, is the eighth detachment of Naraku who places Naraku's heart within Moryomaru. He turns against Naraku.
- Byakuya, an antagonist, is Naraku's final detachment and spies on InuYasha and Moryomaru.

- Tsubaki, an antagonist, is a dark priestess from Kikyo's time. She has retained her youth and beauty by communing with demons. Naraku uses her against Kagome and InuYasha.
- The Band of Seven, antagonists, are mercenaries resurrected by Naraku for their deadly skills.
- Moryomaru, an antagonist, is a demonic golem created by Hakudoshi to hold Naraku's heart. He absorbs demonic energy and seeks the Jewel shards for his own purposes.

InuYasha. (Courtesy of VIZ Media)

Artistic Style

Takahashi incorporates the artistic styles typical of both the *shōjo* and *shōnen* manga genres. As is typical of the *shōjo* genre, she uses full-body illustrations of female characters that exceed panel boundaries. She also uses frame-by-frame shots of faces with expressive eyes in order to show emotion and the psychologically complex relationships between characters. Head shots of either Kagome and InuYasha or Kikyo and InuYasha are paralleled on the same page to convey the tense and often unspoken feelings between them.

Action sequences are typical of those found within the *shōnen* genre, in which vertical lines are used to indicate motion, full-page or two-panels-per-page shots of important moments within the fight, and sequence-by-sequence frames of fighting action. Nature backgrounds are intensely realistic, while characters are not, which is conventional of manga style. Onomatopoeia is used throughout the series both to incorporate sounds and indicate movement, and, during action scenes, to indicate the power behind an action. Jagged thought bubbles indicate yelling or dialogue with intense emotion. Takahashi successfully blends the unique artistic styles of two definitive genres to create a visually complex narrative that captivates audiences of both genders.

Themes

InuYasha is immersed in spiritual themes. It combines Shinto and Buddhist philosophies in a way that mirrors the blending of these spiritualities within Japanese culture. In her construction of demons within the text, Takahashi draws on Shinto constructions of spirit lore in regards to spirits' diversity and power levels. Kikyo's reincarnation as Kagome draws on both Buddhist and Shinto beliefs of reincarnation for the purpose of furthering good. The main female protagonists, Kagome and Kikyo, are Shinto *mikos*. The theme of good versus evil is also built on Shinto and Buddhist ideologies, as Kagome and Kikyo are Shinto priestesses who fight to keep the demonic evil from consuming the world.

True love that transcends time is another theme. For example, Kagome is the reincarnation of Kikyo, InuYasha's love. He falls in love with Kagome because he feels the continuing connection between them. He loves both Kagome and the resurrected Kikyo because they are of the same soul.

Impact

Takahashi is praised for her ability to combine *shōnen* and *shōjo* genres to create an action-packed adventure story that also focuses on relationships, incorporating fierce female protagonist to create an overall story that is accessible to both genders. Her use of Buddhist and Shinto philosophies and her combination of past and present settings connects readers with Japan's spiritual roots and, thus, is an example of how the art form can reappropriate classic Japanese legends for modern readers. Takahashi's beautiful fairy tale crosses time lines and transcends genres as she blends action, adventure, comedy, romance, and fantasy into a vast series.

Films

InuYasha the Movie: Affections Touching Across Time. Directed by Toshiya Shinohara. Sunrise, 2001. This film adaptation stars Kappei Yamaguchi (Richard Ian Cox in the English version) as InuYasha and Satsuki Yukino (Moneca Stori in the English version) as Kagome. The son of a fallen demon defeated by InuYasha's father has come for revenge.

InuYasha the Movie 2: The Castle Beyond the Looking Glass. Directed by Toshiya Shinohara. Shogakukan Production/Sunrise, 2002. This film adaptation stars Yamaguchi as InuYasha and Yukino as Kagome. Cox and Stori return in the English versions. Naraku fakes his death in order to try to absorb Kaguya as the remaining protagonists set to reclaim the Jewel shards, while the antagonists seek to free Kaguya from her mirror prison.

InuYasha the Movie 3: Swords of an Honorable Ruler. Directed by Toshiya Shinohara. Kyoto Animation/Nippon Television Network Corporation/Shogakukan Production, 2003. Yamaguchi and Cox voice InuYasha; Yukino and Stori voice Kagome. The sword So'unga, the third and strongest sword of InuYasha's father, tries to possess InuYasha.

InuYasha the Movie 4: Fire of the Mystic Island. Directed by Toshiya Shinohara. Kyoto Animation/

Shogakukan Production/Sunrise, 2004. Kappei Yamaguchi and Yukino (and Cox and Stori) return to voice the main characters. A demonic child, Ai, escapes the Horai Island. InuYasha and company go to the island to investigate the strange happenings.

Television Series

InuYasha. Directed by Megumi Yamamoto, Naoya Aoki, and Yasunao Aoki. Yomiuri Telecasting Corporation/Sunrise 2000-2004. Cox and Stori provide English voices for InuYasha and Kagome. The series covers only a portion of the graphic novels. It caught up to the manga production twice, the first time resulting in filler episodes; the second time it caught up, the anime was halted.

Rachel Cantrell

Further Reading

Takahashi, Rumiko. *Ranma 1/2* (1987-1996).

Watase, Yu. *Alice 19th* (2001-2003).

Watsuki, Nobuhiro. *Rurouni Kenshin* (1994-1999).

Bibliography

Allison, Brent. "Interviews with Adolescent Animé Fans." In *The Japanification of Children's Popular Culture: From Godzilla to Miyazaki*, edited by Mark I. West. Lanham, Md.: Scarecrow Press, 2009.

Bryce, Mio, and Jason Davis. "An Overview of Manga Genres." In *Manga: An Anthology of Global and Cultural Perspectives*, edited by Toni Johnson-Woods. New York: Continuum, 2010.

Orbaugh, Sharalyn. "Busty Battlin' Babes: The Evolution of the *Shojo* in the 1990s Visual Culture." In *Gender and Power in the Japanese Visual Field*, edited by Joshua S. Mostow, Norman Bryson, and Maribeth Graybill. Honolulu: University of Hawaii Press, 2003.

See also: *Ranma 1/2*; *Rurouni Kenshin*

J

JAPAN AI: A TALL GIRL'S ADVENTURES IN JAPAN

Author: Steinberger, Aimee Major
Artist: Aimee Major Steinberger (illustrator)
Publisher: Go! Comi
First book publication: 2007

Publication History

In 2002, Aimee Major Steinberger was surfing the World Wide Web when she discovered a Web site for a ball-jointed doll called the "Super Dollfie," manufactured by Volks, a Japanese company. Each doll is custom-made, and the buyer is provided with an "adoption" certificate. At that time, the dolls were not sold in the United States. Steinberger helped start another Web site dedicated to these dolls and went on to become a part-time staff writer for *Haute Doll* magazine.

When Steinberger decided to take a vacation in Japan, she contacted the management of Volks, and they agreed to a meeting. Steinberger then persuaded two of her friends to join her for the trip. She kept a diary in the form of drawings, and when she returned to the United States she considered publishing them herself in a book-length format. She mentioned her idea to a friend, an employee of Go! Comi, an American manga publisher, who then expressed an interest in publishing it. Designer James Dashiell of Go! Comi helped Steinberger edit and lay out the material and shape it into a coherent story, deleting some of the redundant drawings and having her draw additional ones for parts of her trip that he felt she had neglected. The first edition came out in December, 2007.

Plot

The story is a simple, illustrated trip report, and each chapter corresponds to roughly one day of the trip. On their first full day in Japan, Steinberger and her two friends tour Kyoto, the capital of Japan until 1868, and visit its temples, including Kiyomizu, which was

---

Westerners and Manga

Aimee Steinberger, author of *Japan Ai: A Tall Girl's Adventures in Japan*, is an example of a generation of non-Japanese comic artists for whom manga is virtually a first language. The Japanese manga industry is tough enough for a native, and tougher still for a visitor. Yet some have managed the transition with varying degrees of success. Takeshi Miyazawa, a Canadian, did high-profile work for Marvel Comics (*Uncanny X-Men, Mary Jane*) before electing to move to Japan, where he found work with Dengeki Comics. Felipe Smith (whose background includes Jamaican, Argentine, and American roots) wrote *MBQ* for the U.S. publisher TOKYOPOP before moving to Japan, where he published several volumes of *Peepo Choo* for Kodansha. Shūeisha's *Weekly Shōnen Jump* publishes *Ultimo*, a collaboration between Hiroyuki Takei (*Shaman King*) and Marvel legend Stan Lee.

---

founded in 780 C.E. The following day, they visit the Yasaka Shrine (established 656 C.E.) and arrive in the middle of Setsubun, a celebration of the beginning of spring in which people dress in costumes; during this celebration, they watch two geishas perform a traditional dance.

On the third day, Steinberger and her friends visit a photography studio, where they dress in geisha costumes to have their pictures taken. On the fourth day, they take a train to visit an *onsen* (a hot-springs resort), where they stay in a traditional Japanese inn. On their fifth day, they attend the Takarazuka Revue, an all-female theater group that was founded in 1913. The company performs both Japanese and Western plays, but the cast always ends the show with a Las Vegas-style kick line and wear costumes featuring feathers and sequins. They also visit a costume salon where Steinberger dresses as Marie Antoinette and again has her photograph taken.

On the sixth day, the three are supposed to visit the Volks office but board the wrong train, an express to Tokyo, and have to reschedule. On the seventh day, they return to Tokyo by train, this time on purpose, and rent a small apartment. On days eight and nine, they visit the Tokyo Tower, an Internet café, Nakano Broadway, a mall, a "maid" café where the waitresses dress as maids, and another café called the Lockup, which is decorated like a dungeon and whose patrons are handcuffed. On the tenth day, a Sunday, they visit Harajuku Street, a neighborhood in Tokyo where people dress in costume every Sunday. They had brought "Lolita" costumes from the United States so they could join in. On their last full day in Japan, they finally visit the Volks office, which is located in the same building as the company's largest store, a doll-themed café, and a doll museum. They also meet the president of Volks, Mr. Shigeta, and, on their last night in Japan they have dinner with him and his daughters at a traditional Japanese restaurant.

Characters

- *Aimee Major Steinberger*, the narrator, is an American writer, layout artist, and animator. A self-proclaimed "geek," she likes video games; science-fiction television shows and films; costuming, for which she has won awards at conventions; dolls; and comic books, especially manga. She is also administrator for denofangels.com, an English-language Web site devoted to ball-jointed dolls such as Dollfies. She is 6 feet tall, which causes many Japanese to stare at her. She lives in California with her husband Mitch and is a 2001 graduate of the California Institute of the Arts.
- *A. J.*, one of Aimee's companions on her trip to Japan, is a Chinese American software engineer who sings in Chinese operas and likes pants with chains. She suffers from narcolepsy and has many tattoos. Since, according to Steinberger,

only samurai and members of the *yakuza* (organized crime) have tattoos in Japan, she is given considerable attention. Like Aimee, she is a costumer and a self-proclaimed geek.
- *Judy*, Aimee's other companion on the trip, is a Croatian American estate planner who likes Victorian dresses, making hats, and chain mail. She does not like Japanese teas, finding them too bitter, and finds that her breasts are too large for kimonos to fit her comfortably. Like Aimee and A. J., she is a costumer and a self-proclaimed geek.
- *Mr. Shigeta* is the president of Volks, which is owned by his family.

Artistic Style

The simplest way to describe Steinberger's artistic style is "cute." Her style in the narrative sections is minimalist, casual, clean, simple, and cartoonish, occasionally showing the influence of old Disney cartoons. The drawings are mostly black against a plain white background and are done using pencils, not pens or brushes. Her style is so minimal that in her drawings people do not have noses. Nonetheless, her characters express a wide range of emotion. Her emphasis is on character and action, and she only shows those backgrounds that are absolutely necessary to tell her story. Even though she mentions crowds frequently, she rarely depicts one. The sections explaining Japanese culture and showing Japanese landscapes are more detailed, but her transitions between the two styles are smooth.

Only some of the illustrations are in color, and even these are drawn in Steinberger's minimalist style; examples include the pages in which she introduces herself, her husband, and her companions. Among the costumes illustrated in color are traditional geisha and *maiko* (a geisha's apprentice) wardrobes, the ones worn at the Takarazuka Revue, Lolita costumes, and ones worn by cross-dressing male rock-and-roll singers. One scene that is not drawn in color depicts Steinberger inadvertently wandering into an S and M shop.

The book has a sparkling pink cover, which some readers may find too feminine. There is even some controversy over whether *Japan Ai* should really be considered a graphic novel. While every page is illustrated, it is not broken down into panels and, in fact, some pages are mostly text with one small illustration. Other pages consist of maps or diagrams.

Themes

In Japanese, *ai* means "love," which describes Steinberger's feelings for and enthusiasm toward Japanese popular culture. As with most personal-trip reports, the author focuses on the parts of the places she visits that interest her rather than trying to be comprehensive, as in a formal travel guide. It is not a voyage of self-discovery, as Steinberger is the same person before and after the trip, so to call the book "travel literature" would be rather pretentious. It is light in its tone and definitely oriented toward women and fans of manga and anime. It would be more accurate to call the work an illustrated travel journal.

The conflict of cultures occurs many times, such as when Aimee, A. J., and Judy insist on wearing bathing suits at the communal bath where everyone else is naked. The author also comments on the small bathrooms and crowded trains. Because she is 6 feet tall, she has a hard time fitting into some restrooms and is never comfortable having to squat to urinate, as opposed to sitting, since few toilets have seats. The vending machines sell teas, coffees, and hot chocolate, but rarely soft drinks. The three friends did like the idea of women-only train cars, a policy implemented because sexual harassment is a problem on trains in Japan.

There are also comparisons between older Japan, represented by Kyoto, and the newer Japan, represented by Tokyo. In Kyoto, they visit temples and shrines that are more than one thousand years old and see geishas perform a traditional dance. In Tokyo, they visit stores, malls, and themed cafés. They dress in geisha costumes for one day in Kyoto and in Lolita costumes for one day in Tokyo.

Impact

In 2009, the Young Adult Library Service Association selected *Japan Ai* for its list of "Top Ten Great Graphic Novels for Teens," and its list of "2009 Quick Picks for Reluctant Young Adult Readers." *Japan Ai* was the only book to make both lists. With those kinds of endorsements, *Japan Ai* gained considerable respectability among librarians, and copies can be found in many libraries around the country. Since the book comes with a glossary, it can also serve as an introduction to manga and anime for people not familiar with those art forms. Examples of manga and anime given within the text and in the glossary are *Bleach* (2002-), *Chobits* (2001-2002), *Fruits Basket* (1999-2007), *InuYasha* (1996-2008), and *Revolution Girl Utena* (1996-1997).

Thomas R. Feller

Further Reading

Cleveland, Ann. *It's Better with Your Shoes Off* (1955).
Steinberger, Aimee Major. *Cosplay Ai* (2009).
Williamson, Kate T. *A Year in Japan* (2006).

Bibliography

Goldsmith, Francisca. "*Japan Ai: A Tall Girl's Adventures in Japan*." Review of *Japan Ai: A Tall Girl's Adventures in Japan*, by Aimee Major Steinberger. *Booklist* 104, no. 15 (April 1, 2008): 39.
"*Japan Ai: A Tall Girl's Adventures in Japan*." Review of *Japan Ai: A Tall Girl's Adventures in Japan*, by Aimee Major Steinberger. *Publisher's Weekly* 254, no. 50 (December 17, 2007): 40.
Kan, Kat. "Pirates, Zombies, Racing, and Being a Stranger in a Strange Land." *Voice of Youth Advocates* 31, no. 1 (April, 2008): 36.

See also: *Bleach*; *Fruits Basket*; *InuYasha*

JoJo's Bizarre Adventure

Author: Araki, Hirohiko
Artist: Hirohiko Araki (illustrator); Sean McCoy (letterer)
Publisher: Shūeisha (Japanese); VIZ Media (English)
First serial publication: *JoJo no kimyō na bōken*, 1987-
First book publication: 1987-   (English translation, 2005-2010)

Publication History

Hirohiko Araki launched *JoJo's Bizarre Adventure* in 1987 in Japan's *Weekly Shōnen Jump* magazine. The first five parts of the series, consisting of 594 chapters later collected in sixty-three volumes, were published in *Weekly Shōnen Jump* from 1987 to 1997. Strictly speaking, these first sixty-three volumes are the only ones published under the series title of *JoJo's Bizarre Adventure*. However, as Araki has used the same characters, ideas, settings, and background in later works, he has, in fact, continued the JoJo story under different titles. For that reason, the series is considered to be ongoing.

From 1998 to 2002, *Weekly Shōnen Jump* published seventeen volumes under the new series title *Stone Ocean*. In 2004, the series moved to Shūeisha's *Ultra Jump*, a *seinen* magazine, and ran for another twenty-four volumes under the title *Steel Ball Run*. After Japan's devastating Tohoku earthquake on March 11, 2011, Araki launched a new version of his series, *JoJolion*, for *Ultra Jump*. *JoJolion* is set in a fictional Japanese town affected by the earthquake and tsunami and features some of the familiar JoJo characters.

VIZ Media began to publish the series in English under the title *JoJo's Bizarre Adventure* in 2005. The VIZ volumes begin with the last chapter of the original volume 12 and extend to the end of the original volume 28. For the English edition, Araki created an eight-page prologue summarizing the story up to the point at which VIZ's first volume begins.

Plot

Targeted to a teenage male audience, *JoJo's Bizarre Adventure* combines an action-adventure story beginning in nineteenth century England with supernatural

JoJo's Bizarre Adventure. (Courtesy of VIZ Media)

elements. As the series develops, Araki introduces new protagonists for each different story arc, all of whom are given names that fit the nickname of JoJo.

As summarized by Araki in his introduction, part 1 of the series begins in 1868, when a carriage accident kills the wife of English lord George Joestar. A bandit prowling for loot, Dario Brando, rescues Lord George and his infant son, Jonathan. Out of gratitude, George raises Dario's son, Dio, as his own. However, evil Dio plots to take over the Joestar family.

At age twenty, Jonathan Joestar fights Dio. Jonathan has been trained in the supernatural martial art of Hamon, or Ripple, by an itinerant teacher. Hamon uses solar energy and is most effective against vampires. This is fortunate, as Dio becomes a vampire after he puts on a magic South American stone mask.

After Dio kills Jonathan's father, he severs his own head. This saves his head from being destroyed by Jonathan's Hamon attack. Later, at sea, Dio's head attacks Jonathan. Both appear to die as Jonathan grips Dio's head and they sink to the bottom of the Atlantic.

Part 2 develops another story arc bypassed in the English version. It features the fight, ultimately victorious, of young Joseph Joestar, grandson of the late Jonathan, against Nazis and vampire gods in 1938.

The English edition begins with part 3 of the series. Part 3 opens as seventeen-year-old Jotaro Kujo sits in a jail cell in Tokyo in 1989. Jotaro is the half-Japanese grandson of Joseph Joestar. A punk-style rebel, he was arrested after winning a street fight against four armed thugs. However, as Jotaro believes he is possessed by an evil spirit, he refuses to leave jail.

A flashback reveals that vampire Dio was brought back to life four years before when sea treasure hunters raised and opened a chest containing Dio's head, now fused with Jonathan's body. Aware of this, Jotaro's grandfather Joseph arrives in Japan to prepare Jotaro for the battle against Dio. Joseph tells Jotaro that he has acquired special psychic powers. The manifestation of these powers is called a "Stand," because it stands beside the person who can command and control it. Jotaro's Stand is Star Platinum, and Joseph's is Hermit Purple; the first part of each Stand's name comes from a distinctive card in the Western tarot deck.

Jotaro leaves jail with Joseph and his grandfather's Egyptian friend, Mohammed Avdol, who also has a Stand. The fight against Dio becomes more urgent when Jotaro's mother and Joseph's daughter, Holly, develops a plantlike Stand on her back. This Stand will consume Holly's life unless Dio dies.

Jotaro and Joseph embark on a quest to fight Dio, who has come to reside in Egypt. The airplane meant to transport them there crashes during an onboard fight with one of Dio's henchmen, who also controls a Stand of his own, a giant stag beetle. Jotaro, Joseph, and their allies fight their way from Hong Kong to Egypt. On this quest, many new characters with unique Stands of their own join, or oppose, Jotaro and Joseph. By the time Jotaro confronts Dio in Cairo, many of his closest friends have died as the result of fights with Dio's allies.

Hirohiko Araki

Hirohiko Araki, born in 1960, is best known for his ongoing maverick, multigenerational saga *JoJo's Bizarre Adventure*, which has been running in Shūeisha's *Weekly Shōnen Jump* on and off since 1987. Araki frequently employs names from Western rock 'n' roll to give additional color to his characters, and many of his non-*JoJo* manga are actually *JoJo* manga under a different cover (*Battle Tendency*, *Phantom Blood*, *Steel Ball Run*). So popular is *JoJo* that a widespread cultural joke, or meme, emerged in which groups of people imitate various histrionic poses from the manga. His other manga include *Baoh*, named after a parasite that gives a man powers, and a collection of stories about such "eccentric" historical figures as Nikola Tesla, Typhoid Mary, and the creator of the Winchester Mystery House.

In Cairo, Jotaro discovers that Dio's Stand, The World, enables Dio to stop time for his opponent for a few seconds, rendering his opponent defenseless for this period. The two fight, and Dio initially seems to overpower Jotaro. However, after Dio stops time for nine seconds, Jotaro manages to stop Dio's time for two seconds and escape his trap. Jotaro defeats Dio and allows the sun to destroy the vampire's remains. Reunited with Joseph, Jotaro relishes his well-earned victory.

Though the VIZ volumes end with Jotaro's victory, the original series continues past this point. Part 4 features the adventures of Joseph's illegitimate son, Josuke Higashikata. Part 5 introduces Dio's son Giorno Giovana, who seeks to become a Mafia don. The original series ends after part 5, but parts 6 through 8 are also set in the JoJo universe, employing alternate time lines and different versions of the familiar characters. The setting of the ongoing series then moves to the fictional Japanese town of Morio, which is suffering from the aftermath of the Tohoku earthquake and tsunami.

Volumes

- *JoJo's Bizarre Adventure: The Evil Spirit*, Volume 1 (2005). Collects original Japanese chapters 114-123 (renumbered 1-10). Jotaro Kujo is introduced, as is the concept of the Stands. The series moves from a domestic Japanese setting to an international one.

- *JoJo's Bizarre Adventure: Silver Chariot*, Volume 2 (2006). Collects original chapters 124-132 (renumbered 11-19). Jotaro's journey to Egypt is interrupted when his plane crashes near Hong Kong. This plot device stretches the travel time to allow for the development of a multitude of adventures featuring good and evil characters and their Stands.

- *JoJo's Bizarre Adventure*, Volumes 3-10 (2006-2008). Each volume collects nine to ten of the original chapters, ranging from chapter 133 to 210 (renumbered 20-97). The adventures move from Asia to the climactic location of Egypt. In Egypt, Jotaro and his allies battle enemies using Stands based on ancient Egyptian gods. Jotaro is helped by a sympathetic animal character, the Boston terrier Iggy, who commands a Stand of his own.

- *JoJo's Bizarre Adventure*, Volumes 11-15 (2009-2010). Collects original chapters 211-246 (renumbered 98-143). Jotaro and his friends move in on Dio, who is defended by the flamboyant D'Arby brothers. Several prominent characters are killed, including Avdol, Iggy, and Kakyoin.

- *JoJo's Bizarre Adventure: Journey's End*, Volume 16 (2010). Collects original chapters 257-265 (renumbered 144-152). The story arc ends with the climactic showdown between Jotaro and Dio.

Characters

- *Jotaro Kujo*, the protagonist, is a seventeen-year-old high school student living in Japan. He has an English American mother and a Japanese father and likes to dress in punk-style clothing, wearing a black leather cap and piercing the collar of his black high school uniform overcoat with a short chain. He is a rebel and commands the Stand Star

Platinum, which delivers powerful punches to any opponent. His quest to defeat Dio and save his mother drives the plot.

- *Dio Brando*, the antagonist, is a blond vampire from Victorian England. He commands the Stand The World. He desires to rule the world and seeks to destroy the Joestar family.

- *Holly Kujo* is Jotaro's loving mother and the daughter of Joseph Joestar. A pretty English American woman, she is married to a Japanese jazz musician. Her unnamed Stand will kill her unless Jotaro defeats Dio.

- *Joseph Joestar* is Jotaro's grandfather, a bearded older man who wears a hat and cloak. His Stand is Hermit Purple. He is kind but determined to kill Dio. He mentors Jotaro in the use of his Stand and seeks to save Holly from hers.

- *Mohammed Avdol* is a middle-aged Egyptian magician with the Stand Magician's Red. A friend of Joseph, he trains and supports Jotaro until he dies in battle.

- *Noriaki Kakyoin* is a tall, somewhat arrogant Japanese high school student with flowing brown hair and pierced ears. He hides a warm heart under a cold posture and commands the Stand Hierophant Green. Although he initially seems to be an enemy, he becomes a close friend of Jotaro until his death.

- *Gray Fly* is an elderly, balding Japanese man who commands the Stand Tower of Gray and is allied with Dio. His attack on Jotaro brings down the plane on which he is traveling, setting the stage for an adventure-filled journey to Egypt.

- *Jean Pierre Polnareff* is a young Frenchman with white hair. His ears are pierced with broken heart ornaments in memory of his sister.

- *Captain Tennille's Impersonator* is an assassin in league with Dio and impersonates a ship captain to try to kill Jotaro.

- *Soul Sacrifice* is a sadistic Native American shaman and assassin.

- *J. Geil* is an ally of Dio with a deformed body and two right hands. He commands the Stand the Hanged Man and is killed by Polnareff in retribution for the murder of Polnareff's sister.

- *Iggy* is a Boston terrier tamed by Avdol. His Stand, the Fool, helps Jotaro and his friends battle Dio and his allies.
- *Daniel J.* and *Terence Trent D'Arby* are brothers and powerful allies of Dio. One is a cheating poker player, and the other is a skilled video-game player.
- *Vanilla Ice* is an ally of Dio who commands the Stand Cream. He is defeated by Polnareff, Avdol, and Iggy.

Artistic Style

Perhaps because of the series' origin as a vampire story set in England, Araki draws *JoJo's Bizarre Adventure* in a Western-influenced style that does not feature many of the stylistic elements common in manga, such as exaggerated wide eyes. Major characters are drawn extravagantly, often breaking out of their panels and occasionally filling up more than half a page. Araki takes great pride in creating detailed drawings of the elaborate costumes of his characters. Jotaro, for instance, stands out by wearing a black leather outfit resembling a punk version of a traditional Japanese boy's high school uniform. This emphasis on black leather clothing may remind Western readers of the figures drawn by Tom of Finland (pseudonym of Finnish artist Touko Laaksonen).

The supernatural Stands offer Araki the opportunity to exercise artistic freedom to stunning visual effect. The many Stands depicted within the series range in look from human-shaped martial-arts experts to insect and other animal shapes and the robotlike The World. The World, commanded by Dio, has sensuously drawn lips similar to those of his master, who somewhat resembles the Joker of the *Batman* series.

Araki's exuberant graphic style rarely follows traditional, static arrangements of panels. Instead, he seems to enjoy splashing his human and animal characters and their Stands wildly across double pages. Blood and body parts often splatter the panels. It is not uncommon for minor characters to endure brutal violence. Some of the graphic violence against animals, particularly dogs, has been toned down by Araki for the English version of the series.

The story is told through pictures, dialogue, and bursts of sound effects, which are occasionally written in Japanese characters. Plot information is provided on introductory pages for each English volume. For his covers, Araki uses bold, splashy colors that contrast with the black-and-white content of the interior pages. On the color covers, Jotaro's leather coat is depicted as dark blue, and the links of his chain are painted gold.

Themes

The core themes of part 3 of *JoJo's Bizarre Adventure* are good versus evil and coming-of-age. At the center of the story is Jotaro, who has obvious problems fitting into regular Japanese society. With his outsized leather coat and torn leather cap, Jotaro is the very image of a teenage rebel verging on juvenile delinquency. He feels stifled by the affection of his mother and seems disparaging of the many female high school classmates who adore him.

JoJo's Bizarre Adventure. (Courtesy of VIZ Media)

What makes Jotaro special is his discovery of the magic powers of his Stand and his obligation to carry on the fight inherited from his maternal grandfather. When Jotaro learns he must fight the evil vampire Dio to save the life of his mother and ensure the survival of the Joestar family, the knowledge gives the young man a new sense of purpose in life.

Jotaro is guided by his English grandfather, Joseph, who takes the place of Jotaro's absent Japanese father, who is touring Japan as a jazz musician and never makes an appearance. This aspect has been noted as a critique of contemporary Japanese family and society. In the course of his quest to defeat Dio, Jotaro gains new friends and ends his initial social isolation. As a consequence of his supernatural adventure, he matures as a person.

Many characters are named after real-life pop stars and music groups. For copyright reasons, a few of these names were changed in the English version. Most Stands are based on Tarot cards. However, both of these artistic choices seem to lack a discernible deeper motivation or effect.

Impact

Part 3 of *JoJo's Bizarre Adventure* proved to be the most popular segment of Araki's multigenerational adventure story, and the invention of the Stands gave the manga a unique edge with its young male readers. Despite its popularity in Japan, the series was not as well received in the United States; as of 2012, part 3 remains the only part of the series translated into English. Its publication in the United States was additionally hindered by a one-year hiatus between volume 10 and 11, from April of 2008 to April of 2009. The hiatus came about because of complaints from viewers of the animated adaptation who objected to a scene in which Dio is shown reading the Qur'ān. Nevertheless, Araki has continued the manga in Japan, creating new story arcs

and characters that expand the JoJo universe. By including the 2011 Tohoku earthquake in his plot, Araki has also made his ongoing series very topical.

Films

JoJo's Bizarre Adventure. Directed by Hideki Futamura and Hiroyuki Kitakubo (first season) and Kazufumi Nomura and Noboru Furuse (second season). A.P.P.P., 1993-1994, 2001-2002. This thirteen-episode original video animation stars Jurota Kosugi as the voice of Jotaro Kujo and Nobuo Tanaka as Dio Brando. The first season covers the middle of the story to its end, with the second season adapting the beginning of the story. In the United States, Super Techno Arts released the entire story arc in chronological order in six DVD volumes between 2003 and 2005.

JoJo's Bizarre Adventure: Phantom Blood. Directed by Junichi Hayama. A.P.P.P., 2007. This animated film stars Katsuyuki Konishi as the voice of Jonathan Joestar and Kenji Nojima as Dio Brando. It follows the plot of the first story arc quite faithfully.

R. C. Lutz

Further Reading

Araki, Hirohiko. *Baoh* (1985-1986).
Miura, Kentaro. *Berserk* (1990-   ).

Bibliography

Gravett, Paul. *Manga: Sixty Years of Japanese Comics*. New York: Harper Design, 2004.

Johnson-Woods, Toni, ed. *Manga: An Anthology of Global and Cultural Perspectives*. New York: Continuum, 2010.

Thompson, Jason. *Manga: The Complete Guide*. New York: Del Rey, 2007.

See also: *Berserk*; *InuYasha*

L

LONE WOLF AND CUB

Author: Koike, Kazuo

Artist: Gōseki Kojima (illustrator); Guy Davis (cover artist); Darin Fabrick (cover artist); Vince Locke (cover artist); Frank Miller (cover artist); Bill Sienkiewicz (cover artist); Matt Wagner (cover artist)

Publisher: Dark Horse Comics

First serial publication: *Kozure ōkami*, 1970-1976 (partial English translation, 1987-1991)

First book publication: English translation, 2000-2002

Publication History

Lone Wolf and Cub was originally serialized from 1970 to 1976 in the Japanese magazine *Manga akushon* (manga action), published by Futabasha. This manga magazine, first published in 1967, was one of the earliest magazines to publish *seinen* manga aimed at adult male readers. Writer Kazuo Koike researched the samurai feudal culture and everyday life of commoners during the Edo period and authentically re-created the historical setting in this epic manga, working in collaboration with self-taught painter and manga artist Gōseki Kojima. Koike made his name with this work, earning the respect of other creators and artists. The immense popularity of the *Lone Wolf and Cub* series led to a series of film adaptations, television serials, and even theatrical plays within Japan.

The first partial English translation was published from 1987 to 1991 by First Comics, an American comic book publisher that was active from 1983 to 1991. American comic artist Frank Miller was assigned to draw the covers for the first twelve issues of the First Comics edition, which helped popularized the series among readers in the United States. After First Comics ceased business, Dark Horse Comics began to publish the series in a trade paperback edition in 2000, releasing all twenty-eight volumes by 2002.

Gōseki Kojima

Gōseki Kojima, who passed away in 2000, was famously born on the same day as manga legend Osamu Tezuka (*Astro Boy*): November 3, 1928. He was the illustrator of some of the most renowned work by manga writer Kazuo Koike. These titles include *Lone Wolf and Cub*, *Samurai Executioner*, and *Path of the Assassin*, which together ran almost continuously from 1970 to 1984; all were published by Kodansha. *Lone Wolf*, in particular, was a major influence on the American comic-book artist and writer Frank Miller (*Batman: The Dark Knight Returns*, *Sin City*). Kojima witnessed the transitions that led to the origins of contemporary manga, having worked first in *kamishibai* (or "paper drama"), wherein street storytellers use sheets of drawings. Toward the end of his life he adapted films by Akira Kurosawa in manga form.

Plot

The main plot of *Lone Wolf and Cub* concerns a vengeance journey against the Yagyū clan by protagonist Ittō Ogami and his three-year-old son, Daigoro, but the series is also full of episodes about the people whom Ittō encounters on the road and Ittō's work as an assassin. Flashbacks, inserted occasionally, reveal the past events that have led to the protagonist and his son's current status.

The story is set in the Edo period, during which the Tokugawa shogunate rules over Japan by defeating other feudal lords throughout the country. To secure its rule, the shogunate implements a strict punitive system that demands the discharge of positions and termination of clans that exhibit the slightest sign of defiance against the government. To maintain the reign of terror, three different organizations are established: *tansakunin*, the network of ninja spies (the Kurokuwa clan); *shikyakunin*, the secret assassins (the Yagyū clan); and *kaishakunin*, the executioners at a feudal lord's seppuku, or ritual suicide (the Ogami clan). Ittō Ogami is the *kōgi kaishakunin*, the shogun's executioner, and is allowed to wear a robe with the Tokugawa hollyhock crest on it, which signifies that he is the proxy of the shogun himself. This balanced system is destroyed when the Yagyū clan begins to take over the powers of other clans, secretly aiming to gain control of the Tokugawa government.

After taking control of the Kurokuwa clan, Retsudō Yagyū, the leader of the Ura-Yagyū (shadow Yagyū), attempts to obtain the position of *kaishakunin*. Ittō becomes a victim of Retsudō's ploy; his wife is murdered and he is considered a betrayer of the shogunate. Discovering Retsudō's ruse, Ittō escapes from the scene and vows vengeance against the Yagyū clan. Becoming an assassin for hire, Ittō roams Japan with his son, Daigoro. Forsaking the ethos of Bushido, Ittō decides that he and his son will keep the way of *meifumadō*, the Buddhist path of hell, the way of demons and damnation.

Noticing the governmental investigation of the feud between Ittō and the Yagyū clan and seeking to clarify that there is no "personal grudge" involved, Retsudō officially proclaims that the Yagyū will not attack Ittō unless he enters the city of Edo. However, Retsudō uses different official authorities, clandestine groups of ninja and assassins, and minions under the control of the Yagyū to try to hunt down and destroy Ittō. All of Retsudō's attempts fail, resulting in the abolition of the Kurokuwa clan as well as the deaths of all Retsudō's sons and daughters, who are slain by Ittō.

On his journey, Ittō acquires one of the secret documents of the Yagyū. Realizing that Ittō has acquired the document, Retsudō begins to attack Ittō outright. In a battle between the two, Retsudō loses an eye via an arrow thrown by Ittō.

Finally, Ittō travels to Edo to achieve his long-sought revenge. There, the manipulative Tanomo Abe serves as a food tester for the shogun. Knowing of the feud between Ittō and Retsudō, Tanomo plots to use it to destroy them both. Because of Tanomo's miscalcula-

tions, however, the city of Edo is almost submerged in a flood. Because of this crisis, Ittō and Retsudō agree to make a temporary truce and save the city together by detonating a bomb to create a dam. Soon after, Tanomo finds the secret document and reports it to the shogun, who places Retsudō in custody within Edo castle. Even in this confinement, Retsudō succeeds in summoning all the ninjas in Japan to Edo, instructing them to carry out a final attack against Ittō. Retsudō sends a sword polisher to Ittō under the pretense that it is a proper samurai gesture before a duel, but the sword polisher is truly a minion of the Yagyū. The group of ninjas attack, and Ittō's *dōtanuki* sword is broken.

The climax of the series is a duel between Ittō and Retsudō by the riverside. This final fight, which continues for more than 150 pages, ends with Ittō's defeat. *Lone Wolf and Cub* closes with a sequence in which Daigoro, after his father's death, grasps a spear and runs toward Retsudō. Holding Daigoro tightly with both hands, Retsudō allows the blade of the spear to penetrate his body and tearfully calls Daigoro "grandson of my heart," a statement that concludes the series.

Volumes

- *Lone Wolf and Cub*, Volume 1: *The Assassin's Road* (2000). Collects the stories "Son for Hire, Sword for Hire" and "A Father Knows His Child's Heart, as Only a Child Can Know His Father's," among others.
- *Lone Wolf and Cub*, Volume 2: *The Gateless Barrier* (2000). Collects the stories "Red Cat" and "The Coming of the Cold," among others.
- *Lone Wolf and Cub*, Volume 3: *The Flute of the Fallen Tiger* (2000). Collects the stories "The Flute of the Fallen Tiger" and "Half Mat, One Mat, a Fistful of Rice," among others.
- *Lone Wolf and Cub*, Volume 4: *The Bell Warden* (2000). Collects the stories "The Bell Warden" and "Unfaithful Retainers," among others.
- *Lone Wolf and Cub*, Volume 5: *Black Wind* (2001). Collects the stories "Trail Markers" and "Executioner's Hill," among others.
- *Lone Wolf and Cub*, Volume 6: *Lanterns for the Dead* (2001). Collects the stories "Lanterns for the Dead" and "Deer Chaser," among others.

- *Lone Wolf and Cub*, Volume 7: *Cloud Dragon, Wind Tiger* (2001). Collects the stories "Dragnet" and "Night Stalker," among others.
- *Lone Wolf and Cub*, Volume 8: *Chains of Death* (2001). Collects the stories "Tidings of the Geese" and "The Frozen Crane," among others.
- *Lone Wolf and Cub*, Volume 9: *Echo of the Assassin* (2001). Collects the stories "Wife of the Heart" and "Wandering Samurai," among others.
- *Lone Wolf and Cub*, Volume 10: *Hostage Child* (2001). Collects the stories "The Yagyū Letter" and "The Tears of Daigoro," among others.
- *Lone Wolf and Cub*, Volume 11: *Talisman of Hades* (2001). Collects the stories "Talisman of Hades" and "Ailing Star," among others.
- *Lone Wolf and Cub*, Volume 12: *Shattered Stones* (2001). Collects the stories "Nameless Penniless, Lifeless" and "Body Check," among others.
- *Lone Wolf and Cub*, Volume 13: *The Moon in the East, the Sun in the West* (2001). Collects the stories "The Moon in the East, the Sun in the West" and "'Marohoshi' Mamesho," among others.
- *Lone Wolf and Cub*, Volume 14: *The Day of the Demons* (2001). Collects the stories "One Rainy Day" and "O-Shichiri Man," among others.
- *Lone Wolf and Cub*, Volume 15: *Brothers of the Grass* (2001). Collects the stories "The Castle of Women" and "The Women of Sodeshi," among others.
- *Lone Wolf and Cub*, Volume 16: *The Gateway into Winter* (2001). Collects the stories "Umbrella" and "Sayaka," among others.
- *Lone Wolf and Cub*, Volume 17: *The Will of the Fang* (2002). Collects the stories "To a Tomorrow That Never Comes" and "Bounty Demons," among others.
- *Lone Wolf and Cub*, Volume 18: *Twilight of the Kurokuwa* (2002). Collects the stories "Firewatchers of the Black Gate" and "The Immortal Firewatchers," among others.
- *Lone Wolf and Cub*, Volume 19: *The Moon in Our Hearts* (2002). Collects the stories "Four Seasons of Death" and "Wives and Lovers," among others.

- *Lone Wolf and Cub*, Volume 20: *A Taste of Poison* (2002). Collects the stories "Good Fortune, Ill Fortune" and "Lair of the Nighthawks," among others.
- *Lone Wolf and Cub*, Volume 21: *Fragrance of Death* (2002). Collects the stories "Poison Currents" and "Flood of Fire," among others.
- *Lone Wolf and Cub*, Volume 22: *Heaven and Earth* (2002). Collects the stories "The Last Fistful" and "Totekirai," among others.
- *Lone Wolf and Cub*, Volume 23: *Tears of Ice* (2002). Collects the stories "Frozen Edo" and "Tears of Ice," among others.
- *Lone Wolf and Cub*, Volume 24: *In These Small Hands* (2002). Collects the stories "Child of the Fields" and "In These Small Hands," among others.
- *Lone Wolf and Cub*, Volume 25: *Perhaps in Death* (2002). Collects the stories "Perhaps in Death" and "Tales of the Grass: Oyamada Shume," among others.
- *Lone Wolf and Cub*, Volume 26: *Struggle in the Dark* (2002). Collects the stories "Tales of the Grass: Nindo Ukon" and "Struggle in the Dark," among others.
- *Lone Wolf and Cub*, Volume 27: *Battle's Eve* (2002). Collects the stories "To Protect and Defend" and "For Whom to Die," among others.
- *Lone Wolf and Cub*, Volume 28: *The Lotus Throne* (2002). Collects the stories "Corpse Tree" and "Flute and Wave," among others.

Characters

- *Ittō Ogami*, the protagonist, is a traveling assassin for hire who vows to destroy the Yagyū clan. Formerly appointed the shogun's executioner, he is the master of *suiō-ryū* swordsmanship and carries a *dōtanuki* sword. He is trapped by the Yagyū clan's ploy to seize power and punished as a betrayer of the Tokugawa shogunate. To fulfill his revenge against the Yagyū clan, he roams around Japan with his young son, Daigoro. Read in the Japanese name order, his name, Ogami Ittō, sounds similar to *ōkami ittō*, which means "lone wolf."

- *Retsudō Yagyū*, the primary antagonist, is the leader of the *Ura-Yagyū*. He attempts covertly to control the shogunate by managing the other clans and entraps the Ogami clan with his scheme. He is an elderly man with a long white beard, but he is a superb swordsman.

- *Daigoro Ogami* is Ittō's son, a three-year-old child with a top-knotted hair bun. Generally taciturn, except when calling for his father with a shout of "chan!," he travels in a wooden cart pulled by Ittō. When asked to choose between a Japanese handball or a sword, he approaches the sword and reaches for its hilt, which signifies his fate as a samurai.

- *Tanomo Abe*, a.k.a. *Kaii*, is the food taster of the shogun. He has been trained to concoct poisons, with which he repeatedly plots to kill Ittō and Retsudō. He manipulates people through the use of opium. He is a clownlike figure and a fat, sleazy, greedy, and lecherous coward.

Artistic Style

In contrast to the simplified, cartoonlike illustrations common in manga, the art of *Lone Wolf and Cub* is characterized by the abundant use of dynamic and thick drawing lines. Some critics call such a style *gekiga*. Kojima uses this style extensively to depict violent and graphic fight scenes, with the contrapuntal depiction of the static tranquility of natural features such as rivers, deep woods, and snowy plains. *Lone Wolf and Cub* also features various cinematic techniques, such as switching angles, different framings, and deliberate use of mise-en-scène. Using pens and brushes with India ink for calligraphy, Kojima creates the appropriate mise-en-scène for each scene.

Both creators tell a story skillfully using only visuals. In some instances, the reader does not encounter a monologue or dialogue for several pages; instead, a narrative sequence develops visually, without any words. Most notable among these examples are the fight scenes, but the introductory expositions of the characters and settings are also conducted without words. Comic artist Miller has noted that when he col-

lected the complete set of *Lone Wolf and Cub* volumes published in Japan, he enjoyed the series without any knowledge of the Japanese language.

Themes

One of the main themes of *Lone Wolf and Cub* is vengeance, which, by definition, is a quest for retribution as a response to grief. In Ittō's case, the death of his wife and the stripping of his official position fuel his need for revenge. The degradation of his noble status, which turns him from an honorable samurai into a drifting *rōnin*, is part of a traditional Japanese narrative structure that literary critic and folklorist Shinobu Origuchi calls the *kishu-ryūri-tan*, or the "exile of the young noble." Seen in Japanese mythology and *Genji monogatari* (c. 1004; *The Tale of Genji*, 1925-1933), this literary trope encompasses a young aristocrat's (or a god figure's) journey into a distant, hostile place, where he experiences a series of hardships, and his eventual return to his homeland as a hero. With its classic narrative of revenge, *Lone Wolf and Cub* aligns itself with this Japanese literary tradition.

Another theme is the importance of the samurai code. Ittō declares that in order to achieve his revenge, he must abandon the ethos of Bushido and become a demon, walking in *meifumadō*, or the Buddhist hell. However, he offers help to others who are in similar situations. Also, he inherits the spirit of the samurai warriors who die for what they believe. Even in his duel with his archenemy, Retsudō, Ittō maintains the authentic manner of samurai, following the proper procedures in fighting. The final duel is observed with courtesy by all the officials, including the shogun himself, signifying Ittō's acceptance as a genuine samurai.

The father-son relationship is also a central motif throughout the work. Ittō claims that Daigoro is ready to die anytime on the journey; indeed, on one occasion, Ittō does not try to save his son even when he is drowning. However, throughout the series, the strong bond between the protagonist and his son is implicit. In the last section of the series, this motif becomes explicit, with a Buddhist implication. Ittō tells his son, "In my next life, I will be your father and you will be my son. We are eternally father and son."

Impact

Lone Wolf and Cub became a best seller, selling more than 8.3 million copies following its publication in Japan. Its impact went beyond the limited audience of manga readers, with film adaptations of *Lone Wolf and Cub* created soon after the series' publication.

As the creator of many influential manga, Koike has had a tremendous influence on a generation of manga artists and writers. In 1977, he established *Gekiga sonjuku* (gekiga school) with the intention of training and educating future manga/*gekiga* writers and artists. Several popular contemporary manga creators studied at this school, including Tetsuo Hara, illustrator of *Hokuto no Ken* (1989, 1995-1997; *Fist of the North Star*, partial translation 1983-1988) and Rumiko Takahashi, creator of *InuYasha* (1996-2008; English translation 1998-   ). The success of *Lone Wolf and Cub* gained considerable attention from creators and artists who later played major roles in its reproduction and adaptation through different mediums of popular entertainment.

Lone Wolf and Cub has also influenced American comic book artists, most notably Miller, who has identified Koike and Kojima's work as a major inspiration for his graphic novel *Ronin* (1983-1984). Max Allan Collins has also remarked that his graphic novel *Road to Perdition* (1998) is an "unabashed homage" to the manga. In 2002, writer Mike Kennedy and artist Francisco Ruiz Velasco reimagined the original manga epic in the graphic novel *Lone Wolfe 2100*, which features characters with similar names but has several differences in story lines and characters. Explicit homages and allusions to *Lone Wolf and Cub* also occur in Quentin Tarantino's *Kill Bill* films (2003-2004), in which the daughter of the female protagonist insists on watching *Shogun Assassin* (1980), an American edition of the film adaptation of *Lone Wolf and Cub*, as a bedtime film.

Films

Lone Wolf and Cub: Sword of Vengeance (*Kozure ōkami: Kowokashi udekashi tsukamatsuru*). Directed by Kenji Misumi. Katsu Production, 1972. This live-action film adaptation is the first in a series of six films starring Tomisaburō Wakayama as Ittō Ogami.

Lone Wolf and Cub: Baby Cart at the River Styx (*Kozure ōkami: Sanzu no kawa no ubaguruma*). Directed by Kenji Misumi. Katsu Production, 1972.

Lone Wolf and Cub: Baby Cart to Hades (*Kozure ōkami: Shinikazeni mukau ubaguruma*). Directed by Kenji Misumi. Katsu Production, 1972.

Lone Wolf and Cub: Baby Cart in Peril (*Kozure ōkami: Oya no kokoro ko no kokoro*). Directed by Buichi Saito. Katsu Production, 1972.

Lone Wolf and Cub: Baby Cart in the Land of Demons (*Kozure ōkami: Meifumadō*). Directed by Kenji Misumi. Katsu Production, 1973.

Lone Wolf and Cub: White Heaven in Hell (*Kozure ōkami: Jigoku e ikuzo! Daigorō*). Directed by Yoshiyuki Kuroda. Katsu Production, 1974.

Shogun Assassin. Directed by Robert Houston. Anim-Eigo, 1980. This film is an edited compilation of footage from the first two films in the 1972 *Lone Wolf and Cub* series. It has been dubbed in English.

Television Series

Lone Wolf and Cub. Nippon Television, 1973-1976. This live-action television program stars Kinnosuke Yorozuya as Ittō Ogami.

Lone Wolf and Cub. TV Asahi, 2002-2004. This live-action series stars Kinya Kitaōji as Ittō Ogami. The program differs from the manga in that it does not feature the character Tanomo Abe.

CJ (Shige) Suzuki

Further Reading

Koike, Kazuo, and Gōseki Kojima. *Path of the Assassin* (2006-2009).

_____. *Samurai Executioner* (2005-2006).

Koike, Kazuo, and Kazuo Kamimura. *Lady Snowblood* (2005-2006).

Bibliography

Gravett, Paul. *Manga: Sixty Years of Japanese Comics*. London: Collins Design, 2004.

Koike, Kazuo. "Kazuo Koike: The Dark Horse Interview." Interview by Carl Horn. *Dark Horse Comics*, March 3, 2006. http://www.darkhorse. com/Interviews/1261/Kazuo-Koike--The-Dark-Horse-Interview-3-3-06.

O'Rourke, Shawn. "*Lone Wolf and Cub* Part 1: History and Influences." *Popmatters*, December 2, 2009. http://www.popmatters.com/pm/feature/116502-lone-wolf-and-cub-part-1-history-and-influences.

Schodt, Frederik L. *Manga! Manga! The World of Japanese Comics*. New York: Kodansha International, 1986.

See also: *Blade of the Immortal; Fist of the North Star*

Lupin III

Author: Monkey Punch (pseudonym of Kazuhiko Kato)

Artist: Monkey Punch (pseudonym of Kazuhiko Kato, illustrator); Monalisa De Asis (letterer); Patrick Hook (cover artist)

Publisher: Futabasha (Japanese); TOKYOPOP (English)

First serial publication: *Rupan sansei*, 1967-1972

First book publication: 1974-1975 (English translation, 2002-2004)

Publication History

Lupin III, with stories and artwork entirely by Monkey Punch (Kazuhiko Kato), debuted in serialized form in August, 1967, in *Weekly Manga Action*, published by Futabasha. The series ran in ninety-four installments, until May, 1969, and in thirty-six chapters (as *The New Adventures*) in 1971-1972. Futabasha periodically collected chapters of the series in *tankōbon*. Power Comics published the series in fourteen Japanese-language volumes in 1974-1975, and Futabasha's Action Comics reprinted *Lupin III* in eleven volumes in 1984-1985. An additional twenty-four-page story was originally published in March, 1970, as *Lupin the Third Gaiden*.

In 1977, Monkey Punch began writing and illustrating a second series, *Lupin III: World's Most Wanted* (*known as Lupin III: Most Wanted* in English). This ran until 1981 in 188 installments (plus two extra chapters) in *Weekly Manga Action* and was reprinted by Action Comics in sixteen volumes. The series was renewed in 1997 as *Lupin III S*, written by Satozumi Takaguchi, illustrated by Shusay, under the creative control of Monkey Punch. *Weekly Manga Action* and *2 Action* magazines published five complete *Lupin III S* stories, which Action Comics and Futabasha reprinted in a single volume in 1988 and 2001, respectively.

Lupin III Y, with multipart stories from Monkey Punch and art by Manatsuki Yamakami, appeared in *Weekly Manga Action* between 1998 and 2003. Futabasha reproduced the entire *Lupin III Y* series in twenty volumes between 1999 and 2004 and completed a second printing of the series with new covers from

---

Monkey Punch

Monkey Punch is the pseudonym of Kazuhiko Kato, born in 1937 and the creator of Lupin III, an accomplished thief whose tales have filled numerous manga, anime, and films. Kato has likened the character to d'Artagnan of the Three Musketeers. The first ever feature-length motion picture by legendary filmmaker Hayao Miyazaki was *Lupin III: The Castle of Cagliostro*. In an interview with the Anime News Network, Kato listed numerous Western cultural influences on his work, including Agatha Christie, *Treasure Island*, *Columbo*, and *Mission: Impossible*. Among the many anime to Monkey Punch's credit are *Cinderella Boy*, a futuristic detective story adopted from his manga, and *Musashi Gundoh*, a feudal epic.

2001 to 2005; Action Comics began a new printing, featuring a third set of covers, in 2010.

Lupin III M, with longer, self-contained stories by Monkey Punch and illustrations by Yukio Miyama, has appeared since 2005 in *Lupin the Third Official Magazine*. Action Comics began reprinting these stories in volumes form in 2005; Futaba Bunko has done so since 2009. A sixth series, with illustrations by Naoya Hayakawa, *Lupin III H*, began in 2010.

English-language versions of the first *Lupin III* series have been available since 2002, when TOKYOPOP released the first of fourteen black-and-white paperbound volumes in "unflipped" format. Toshi Yokoyama did translations, and Matt Yamashita handled English adaptations. TOKYOPOP also published English versions of the first nine volumes of *Lupin III: World's Most Wanted*, between 2004 and 2007, before the translations were discontinued. Italian-, Spanish-, and German-language versions of various *Lupin III* imprints are also available.

Both Action Comics and Comic Bunko have released several *Best of Lupin the Third* compilations since 2004. A spin-off, called *Lupin III Millennium*, produced in Italy and with the approval of Monkey

Punch, featuring many different artists and styles, has appeared since the mid-1990's. Kappa Edizioni has reprinted the Italian version in ten volumes, beginning in 2001.

Plot

Lupin III does not present a unified plot but individual, nonsequential chapters that are frenetic, often difficult to follow, and seldom logical. The series as a whole consists of brief, convoluted stories that serve to illustrate the cleverness and resourcefulness of the central character in executing thefts, scams, or other illegal schemes and in escaping detection, death, or capture. A typical Lupin tale involves the theft of a precious stone, the recovery of a hidden microfilm, the search for treasure, or an assassination or prevention thereof. There are usually multiple complications before Lupin can achieve his goal. No matter the catalyst for the story, a woman is invariably connected with the plot, and Lupin usually winds up in bed with her, often to his detriment.

Relationships are important throughout the series, not only between Lupin and his accomplices or love interests but also with his antagonists. Lupin seldom reveals his full plans, even to henchmen Jigen or Ishikawa, and they must trust him to do what is right for the team. Lupin's lascivious nature frequently derails his schemes, because women, especially Fujiko, often betray him.

Humor plays a significant part in the series, in which crimes are treated in a light-hearted, matter-of-fact manner. Some of the gags are accessible to Western readers, while other jokes referring to cultural differences are subtler, and perhaps best understood by a Japanese audience.

Volumes

This section includes volumes published in English by TOKYOPOP.

- *Lupin III*, Volume 1 (2002). Collects issues 1-10. Arsène Lupin III, his grandfather, Inspector Zenigata, Fujiko Mine, and Daisuke Jigen are introduced over the course of several capers.
- *Lupin III*, Volume 2 (2003). Collects issues 11-19. Lupin combats a competing thief.
- *Lupin III*, Volume 3 (2003). Collects issues 20-31. Goemon Ishikawa XIII is introduced.
- *Lupin III*, Volume 4 (2003). Collects issues 32-43. Features Lupin III's childhood and training for a life of crime.
- *Lupin III*, Volume 5 (2003), Collects issues 44-51. Focuses on both the relationship between Lupin III and his father and how Lupin III and Goemon met.
- *Lupin III*, Volume 6 (2003). Collects issues 52-61. Highlights Lupin's history, concentrating on the time when he actually held a job.
- *Lupin III*, Volume 7 (2003). Collects issues 62-71. Lupin cons his way into college.
- *Lupin III*, Volume 8 (2003). Collects issues 73-80. Charts more Lupin capers, including a chapter told in first person.
- *Lupin III*, Volume 9 (2003). Collects issues 81-89. Features surrealistic sequences in which Lupin III time travels.
- *Lupin III,* Volume 10 (2003). Collects issues 90-98. Charts more Lupin capers, focusing on the interactions among Zenigata, Lupin, Jigen, and Goemon.
- *Lupin III*, Volume 11 (2003). Collects issues 99-106. Highlights Lupin's efforts to escape imprisonment.
- *Lupin III*, Volume 12 (2003). Collects issues 107-114. Showcases Lupin's vendetta against a publication that is writing an exposé about him.
- *Lupin III*, Volume 13 (2003). Collects issues 115-122. Highlights Lupin's battle against a worthy opponent named Rasputin.
- *Lupin III*, Volume 14 (2003). Collects issues 123-130. Includes a variety of Lupin adventures, including the hero's apparent death.
- *Lupin III: Most Wanted*, Volume 1 (2004). Collects chapters 1-10. Lupin and his gang reunite for fresh capers, involving secret weapons and diamonds. New antagonist Melon Cop is introduced.

- *Lupin III: Most Wanted*, Volume 2 (2004). Collects chapters 11-20. Lupin avoids an assassination attempt.
- *Lupin III: Most Wanted*, Volume 3 (2005). Collects chapters 21-31. Lupin escapes prison and plans to steal a monarch's jewels.
- *Lupin III: Most Wanted*, Volume 4 (2005). Collects chapters 32-42. Includes more trickery from Lupin.
- *Lupin III: Most Wanted*, Volume 5 (2005). Collects chapters 43-54. A fortune-teller sees Lupin stealing a piece of valuable art.
- *Lupin III: Most Wanted*, Volume 6 (2005). Collects chapters 55-66. Lupin and Goemon foil a filmmaker's deadly trap.
- *Lupin III: Most Wanted*, Volume 7 (2006). Collects chapters 67-78. Lupin outdoes himself with a plot to execute five crimes at once.
- *Lupin III: Most Wanted*, Volume 8 (2007). Collects chapters 79-90. Focuses on Lupin's capabilities with disguises.
- *Lupin III: Most Wanted*, Volume 9 (2007). Collects chapters 91-102. Inspector Zenigata tests a disguise-penetrating machine against Lupin.

Characters

- *Arsène Lupin III* is the grandson of Arsène Lupin, a fictional creation of French author Maurice Leblanc that first appeared in 1905. Like his grandfather, Lupin is a sophisticated "super-thief," spy, and rogue who usually wears a coat and tie and uses Japan as his base of operations. Dark-haired, handsome, slender, and in his thirties, he typically sports long sideburns. A womanizer, a wit, and a meticulous planner of capers, he is known for his audacity, his ability as a ventriloquist, and his many disguises.
- *Daisuke Jigen* is Lupin's best friend and frequent partner in crime. A former Chicago mobster who took sanctuary in Japan and changed his name, he is slender, thirty years old, and a deadly shot with any type of firearm. He is bearded and foulmouthed, dresses in black, wears a hat, and smokes incessantly.
- *Goemon Ishikawa XIII*, another of Lupin's accomplices, is a samurai and a descendent of a sixteenth century Japanese personage executed for thievery. He has long hair and dresses in traditional samurai garb. He lives a spartan existence and is recognized both for his skills in a variety of martial arts and for his mastery with his sword, Zantetsu.
- *Fujiko Mine*, a beautiful, busty young Japanese woman, sometimes joins Lupin and sometimes opposes him in the commission of crimes. Completely untrustworthy and amoral, she often betrays Lupin to achieve her own agenda, but he usually forgives her for the sake of their uninhibited make-up sex.
- *Inspector Kouichi Zenigata* is Lupin's trench-coat-wearing nemesis. Black-haired, black-eyed, Japanese-born, and middle-aged, he was a Tokyo Metropolitan Police officer before joining Interpol. An emotional, physically fit man, a deadly shot, and a master of martial arts, he is totally dedicated to the capture of Lupin. The two adversaries have grudging respect for each other's skills.

Artistic Style

While the subject matter of *Lupin III* springs from many sources—original Arsène Lupin stories, adventure tales of Alexandre Dumas, mysteries of Agatha Christie, James Bond movies, and such action-oriented television programs as "Mission Impossible"—the style of the first manga series owes much to *MAD* magazine of the 1960's. Monkey Punch has publicly acknowledged his debt to three longtime *MAD* artists: Mort Drucker, Don Martin, and Sergio Aragonés.

Most of the main characters in *Lupin III* are drawn in loose, sketchy, semirealistic line art. Human figures are sometimes enhanced with high-contrast inking, occasional crosshatching to emphasize details, watercolorlike washes to underscore mood, or silhouettes to add drama. Male characters are subject to comical exaggeration: impossibly wide eyes to indicate surprise, gritted teeth to show anger or frustration, or broad, humorously treated gestures that help readers understand and appreciate particular emotions. Female characters, however—always beautiful, big-breasted and with willowy limbs—do not suffer from the same distortions, and their portrayals are handled with reverence, even as their characters are abused or demeaned. Visual interest is added through specific touches: the pattern of a shirt or tie or the lacy borders of women's lingerie. Inanimate objects—guns, automobiles, planes, trains, or architectural structures—are typically rendered realistically and in great detail.

Because *Lupin III* concentrates on action to carry the stories, the series does not rely on lengthy narration blocks to explain events. Speech and thought balloons are kept short to provide lively interplay between characters; many scenes are entirely wordless. Three to twelve panels (typically six or seven per page) are creatively employed to vary layouts and keep reader interest high. Monkey Punch seldom employs the same design scheme on consecutive pages, which range from double-page, across-the-gutter horizontal panels to narrow top-to-bottom panels and a multitude of small rectangular panels when characters interact. Though the majority of the stories are presented in medium-length depictions, close-ups and long shots are included to provide telling details or overviews to help explain the action.

Lupin III: World's Most Wanted continues the same types of storylines as the previous incarnation. The artwork, however, is considerably more refined, making it possible to more easily distinguish between characters. Likewise, *Lupin III Y* and *S* continue the updating process, giving the series a crisper, more simplified look more consistent with modern manga than with the 1960's vintage cartoons that provided the original inspiration. Monkey Punch's *Lupin III M* and *H* versions complete the transformation of the series' look from outmoded to modern, thanks to slick, full-bodied drawings accented with highlights and shadows that add realism and dimensionality.

Themes

A constant and recurring theme in *Lupin III* is the conflict between good and evil, and the blurring of the lines between the two extremes in a world full of contradictions. An antihero who is admired for his boldness and ingenuity even as he applies his skills in doing wrong, Lupin is a modern version of many fictional predecessors in the gentleman thief tradition. However, more so than most of his predecessors, Lupin III is the modern embodiment of the trickster. An archetype found in the folklore and mythology of most cultures; the trickster does mischief simply for the challenge of planning a prank and the fun of carrying it out.

A second major theme is Monkey Punch's homage to the 1960's, the decade during which he started his cartooning career and achieved his first successes. Lupin is essentially stuck in a time warp from a bygone era. His clothing, haircut, and devil-may-care attitude, particularly toward women as sexual objects, all preserve the morality of the freewheeling 1960's.

Impact

Lupin III is a paradigm of the late Silver Age/early Bronze Ages of comics: hip, cool, irreverent, crude, and vulgar. The series offers enough imagination, humor, and dynamic artistry to offset politically incorrect factors such as rampant chauvinism, violence, and the glorification of crime and to lend *Lupin III* staying power in the Modern Age.

Though the prolific Monkey Punch has not garnered any major awards for his work, his *Lupin III* series has been hugely popular since its introduction and is yearly included in Japanese polls of the top fifty manga. A whole *Lupin* industry has sprung up in Japan, with films, television series, and annual made-for-TV specials, as well as video games, soundtracks, posters, T-shirts, and other specialty items. There are numerous Web sites devoted to Money Punch and *Lupin III*. In recognition of his influence and longevity, Monkey Punch has been a member of the jury of the Ministry of Foreign Affairs of Japan International Manga Award. Dubbed versions of many of the *Lupin III* anime films and original video animations (OVA) are sold worldwide.

Films

Lupin III Secret Files. Directed by Masaaki Osumi. Tokyo Movie Shinsha, 1969. This is an animated pilot film inspired by the original manga series. Completed in theatrical and television versions in 1969 but not released until 1989, this forty-minute film was shown only on television.

Lupin the Third: Strange Psychokinetic Strategy. Directed by Takashi Tsuboshima. Toho, 1974. A live-action theatrical release adapted from the series, this film focuses on slapstick humor and spectacular stunts. This film stars Yuki Meguro as Lupin. Lupin helps a beautiful woman escape from jail and contemplates following in the footsteps of his grandfather.

Lupin III: The Secret of Mamo. Directed by Soji Yoshikawa and Yasuo Otsuka. TMS, 1978. This animated feature stars Yasuo Yamada as the voice of Lupin. The film opens with the apparent death of Lupin and includes a quest for the philosopher's stone. Dubbed several times into English, the movie was released on DVD in 2003.

Lupin the Third: The Castle of Cagliostro. Directed by Hayao Miyazaki. TMS, 1979. This is a feature-length animated film based on an Arsène Lupin novel by Leblanc, updated as a vehicle for Lupin. The plot follows Lupin's heist of a Monaco casino. Dubbed into English on numerous occasions, the film was well-received both commercially and critically.

Lupin III: The Legend of the Gold of Babylon. Directed by Seijun Suzuki and Shigetsugu Yoshida. Toho Columbia Pictures, 1985. This full-length animated feature focuses on the quest for ancient hidden gold. The film was later reissued with subtitles.

Lupin the Third: The Fuma Conspiracy. Directed by Masayuki Ozeki. Toho, 1987. This direct-to-video full-length OVA features Toshio Furukawa as Lupin. The plot involves the rescue of Goemon's fiancé.

Lupin III: Die Nostradamus. Directed by Shunya Ito, Takeshi Shirado, and Nobuo Tomizawa. TMS, 1995. Monkey Punch wrote the screenplay for this feature-length animated film, which features Kanichi Kurita as the voice of Lupin. The bizarre plot involves Richard Nixon, a new Tower of Babel, a vicious cult, and the Brazilian soccer team.

Lupin III: Dead or Alive. Directed by Monkey Punch. Toho, 1996. This the fifth full-length animated film and the last theatrical release. Cowritten by the director and Hiroshi Sakakibara, the film is about a heist of loot located on a heavily guarded fictional Middle Eastern island.

Return of the Magician. Directed by Mamoru Hamatsu. TMS, 2002. This direct-to-video OVA is a fifty-minute production that brings back Pycal, a villain from the original television series.

Lupin III: Green vs. Red. Directed by Shigeyuki Miya. TMS, 2008. A third OVA with the voice actors from the other movies, this film features a story in which Lupin battles a legion of impersonators.

Television Series

Lupin III. Directed by Soji Yoshikawa, et al. TMS, 1971-1972. This anime series based on the original manga ran for twenty-three episodes.

Lupin III, Part II. Directed by nine different individuals. TMS, 1977-1980. This anime series ran for 155 episodes and was dubbed for DVDs in English-speaking countries.

Lupin III, Part III. Directed by Seijun Suzuki. TMS, 1984-1985. This anime series ran for fifty episodes.

Bye Bye, Liberty Crisis. Directed by Osamu Dezaki. TMS, 1989. This is the first of more than twenty annual TMS-produced original animated television specials. Each was dubbed into English for worldwide release. The others in the series are *Mystery of the Hemingway Papers* (1990), *Steal Napoleon's Dictionary!* (1991), *From Russia with Love* (1992), *Voyage to Danger* (1993), *Dragon of Doom* (1994), *The Pursuit of Harimao's Treasure* (1995), *The Secret of Twilight Gemini* (1996), *Island of Assassins* (1997), *Burning Memory—Tokyo Crisis* (1998), *Da Capo of Love—Fujiko's Unlucky Days* (1999), *Missed by a Dollar* (2000), *Alcatraz Connection* (2001), *Episode 0—First Contact* (2002), *Operation Return the Treasure* (2003), *Stolen Lupin* (2004), *An Angel's Tactics—Fragments of a Dream Are the Scent of Murder* (2005), *Seven Days Rhapsody* (2006), *Elusiveness of the Fog* (2007), *Sweet Lost Night—Magic Lamp's Nightmare Premonition* (2008), *Lupin III vs. Detective Conan* (2009), and *Lupin III: The Last Job* (2010)

Jack Ewing

Further Reading

Miwa, Shirow. *Dogs: Stray Dogs Howling in the Dark* (2001).

Tatsumi, Yoshihiro. *Black Blizzard* (2010).

Tezuka, Osamu. *Swallowing the Earth* (1968-1969).

Bibliography

Gravett, Paul. *Manga: Sixty Years of Japanese Comics.* New York: Harper Design, 2004.

Patten, Fred. *Watching Anime, Reading Manga: Twenty-Five Years of Essays and Reviews.* Berkeley, Calif.: Stone Bridge Press, 2004.

Thompson, Jason. *Manga: The Complete Guide.* New York: Del Rey, 2007.

See also: *MW*; *Golgo 13*

M

MAISON IKKOKU

Author: Takahashi, Rumiko
Artist: Rumiko Takahashi (illustrator)
Publisher: Shogakukan (Japanese); VIZ Media (English)
First serial publication: *Mezon ikkoku*, 1980-1987 (English translation, 1993)
First book publication: 1982-1987 (partial English translation, 1994-2000)

Publication History
Rumiko Takahashi's *Maison Ikkoku* (the house of the fleeting moment) was serialized in the weekly manga magazine *Big Comic Spirits*, published by Shogakukan, from November, 1980, to April, 1987. The series was successful enough to be collected in *tankōbon* volumes before its serialization was finished; it was published in fifteen volumes under the Big S Comics label between May, 1982, and July, 1987. Between September, 1992, and June, 1993, Shogakukan released a ten-volume edition of the manga.

In the United States, *Maison Ikkoku* first appeared as seven monthly comic books (June to December, 1993) published by VIZ Comics in an abridged version, with several episodes changed in either content or order. Later, VIZ republished the manga as a fourteen-volume paperback series beginning in April, 2001. The publication of a complete trade paperback edition that followed the format of the original manga began in November, 2003, when VIZ Media published the first issue of *Maison Ikkoku* under the label Editor's Choice; this release ended with the publication of the last volume of the series in November, 2006.

Plot
Maison Ikkoku is a romantic comedy that takes place in a modern Japanese setting and cultural context. The story is set in a quiet, suburban part of 1980's Tokyo.

Maison Ikkoku. (Courtesy of VIZ Media)

Almost all the main characters live in an old apartment building, a two-story house with seven small apartments, one of which is occupied by the building's guardian. The house's owner is Mr. Otonashi. As the series begins, a new guardian has just arrived: Kyoko Otonashi, Mr. Otonashi's daughter-in-law. Kyoko is the young widow of Soichiro Otonashi. After the sudden death of her husband, Kyoko has remained attached to her father-in-law, and she has decided to become the building's guardian, taking along her big, clever dog, Soichiro.

Upon her arrival, she meets the people living in the house, including Yusaku Godai, a twenty-year-old man who falls in love with her at first sight. Yusaku is shy and unresolved and has trouble passing his university entrance exam. He is the continuous target of jokes from the other tenants.

Funny gags, often based on misunderstandings, are the core of the series, but several scenes and story arcs stress the love story and the drama. Yusaku cannot manage to declare his love to Kyoko, and the beautiful widow also attracts the attention of other men, especially the handsome tennis instructor Mitaka. Yusaku is loved by several girls, but he has eyes for Kyoko only. After several years of friendship, fights, misunderstandings, arguments, and reconciliations, Kyoko and Yusaku finally develop mature feelings of love for each other. Yusaku finds his place in life, becoming a beloved kindergarten teacher and educator after earning his master's degree, and Kyoko reacquires an inner serenity after her first husband's death. The two eventually marry and have a daughter, Haruka.

Volumes

- *Maison Ikkoku*, Volume 1 (2003). Collects chapters 1-10. The main characters, their psychologies, and the general plot are introduced.
- *Maison Ikkoku*, Volume 2 (2003). Collects chapters 11-21. New characters are introduced, and Yusaku and Kyoko grow closer to each other, despite a misunderstanding.
- *Maison Ikkoku*, Volume 3 (2004). Collects chapters 22-32. Numerous subplots and secondary characters are presented. Kyoko's parents meet Yusaku and dislike him.
- *Maison Ikkoku*, Volume 4 (2004). Collects chapters 33-43. The neighbors create problems in the friendship between Yusaku and Kyoko.
- *Maison Ikkoku*, Volume 5 (2004). Collects chapters 44-53. Kozue vies for Yusaku's affections.
- *Maison Ikkoku*, Volume 6 (2004). Collects chapters 54-63. Yusaku's grandmother is introduced; she helps him get closer to Kyoko.
- *Maison Ikkoku*, Volume 7 (2004). Collects chapters 64-73. Yusaku gets injured and must share a

hospital room with Mitaka, his competitor for Kyoko's love.
- *Maison Ikkoku*, Volume 8 (2004). Collects chapters 74-84. Yusaku's sloppiness causes him to misunderstand Kyoko again. A new tenant arrives at the apartment building.
- *Maison Ikkoku*, Volume 9 (2005). Collects chapters 85-95. Yusaku works some part-time jobs and meets schoolgirl Yagami, a cousin of Kyoko.
- *Maison Ikkoku*, Volume 10 (2005). Collects chapters 96-106. Yagami's fight for Yusaku's heart gets him into trouble. Mitaka tries to get over his fear of dogs.
- *Maison Ikkoku*, Volume 11 (2005). Collects chapters 107-117. Kyoko goes on vacation and is followed by Yusaku, who wants to make peace with her after yet another misunderstanding.
- *Maison Ikkoku*, Volume 12 (2005). Collects chapters 118-129. A misunderstanding leads Mitaka to propose to young heiress and dog-lover Asuna.
- *Maison Ikkoku*, Volume 13 (2005). Collects chapters 130-140. Yusaku's search for a job inadvertently leads him to work in a strip club, where he also babysits the child of a stripper.
- *Maison Ikkoku*, Volume 14 (2005). Collects chapters 141-151. The love story reaches its crucial point, and the characters reveal their feelings.
- *Maison Ikkoku*, Volume 15 (2006). Collects chapters 152-161. Kyoko and Yusaku marry and begin their life together.

Characters

- *Yusaku Godai* is a twenty-year-old man who is trying to enter college. He does not know how to communicate with women. He is the target of the other tenants, who often invade his privacy and have parties in his room. He is infatuated with Kyoko and ultimately falls deeply in love with her.
- *Kyoko Otonashi* is twenty-two years old, has long black hair, and is beautiful in every aspect. She is a young widow who is trying to rebuild her life as the new guardian of Mr. Otonashi's house.

She has a sweet disposition but can also become grumpy. She is an independent woman but also relies on a wide set of typical Japanese values.

- *Hanae Ichinose* is a cheerful, energetic, fat woman who lives in room 1 with her husband and son. She often joins Akemi and Yotsuya in throwing noisy parties in Yusaku's room.

- *Akemi Roppongi* is a voluptuous and attractive but somewhat vulgar red-haired woman who lives in room 6. She works as a bar hostess at the Cha-Cha Maru. She usually walks through the building in sexy underwear, sometimes teasing Yusaku. She marries her boss.

- *Yotsuya* is a mysterious man who lives in room 4 and is always ready to drink beer and party in Yusaku's room with the other tenants. He has a mysterious, but legal, job.

- *Mr. Otonashi* is a kind old man and the father of Soichiro, the late husband of Kyoko. He is fond of her but hopes she will marry again and find the happiness she lost with the death of Soichiro.

- *Soichiro* is Kyoko's big, white, funny dog. He is named for her late husband.

- *Kozue Nanao* is a young friend of Yusaku. She is in love with him, and they often spend time together platonically. For the most of the series, she does not know about Yusaku's feelings for Kyoko, which causes several misunderstandings among the three of them.

- *Shun Mitaka* is a handsome twenty-six-year-old tennis instructor from a wealthy family. He meets Kyoko when she takes tennis lessons. He falls in love with her, but he is too sophisticated for her. In the end, he marries Asuna.

- *Asuna Kujo* is a sweet young girl from a rich family. She is "promised" to Mitaka by their parents, according to a traditional Japanese arrangement. They do not initially love each other but eventually fall in love.

- *Ibuki Yagami* is a student from a wealthy family. Yusaku meets her when he is a student teacher. She has a crush on him, idealizing him as a sort of tragic hero.

- *Ikuko Otonashi* is Kyoko's ten-year-old niece. Yusaku becomes her tutor.

- *Yukari Godai* is Yusaku's grandmother. She lives with Yusaku's parents but occasionally visits Yusaku. She helps his love situation.

- *Mr. Chigusa* and *Ritsuko Chigusa* are Kyoko's parents. They are a bourgeois couple and would prefer for Kyoko to marry Mitaka. At first, they do not accept Yusaku as a good fiancé for Kyoko, but they eventually change their minds.

- *Sayako Kuroki* is one of Yusaku's college classmates. She helps him find a part-time teaching job.

Artistic Style

Takahashi belongs to a generation of manga artists who began their careers in the late 1970's and were directly or indirectly influenced by the masters of the previous generations, such as Osamu Tezuka, Shotaro Ishino-

Maison Ikkoku. (Courtesy of VIZ Media)

mori, Mitsuteru Yokoyama, and the Year 24 Group. Her graphic style is neither particularly elegant nor original, and her drawings are linear and readable but not especially distinguished from the styles of the other manga artists of her generation. Settings, bodies, and faces are always simple but profoundly functional.

Maison Ikkoku features two important stylistic features: Takahashi's command of emotional expressions on characters' faces and her mastery of gag timing. *Maison Ikkoku*'s average page is clear and easy to look at, with few black areas and a simple panel structure. The fictional time in the series goes by approximately as it would in the real world, and Takahashi's main characters evolve as the series progresses. Kyoko and Yusaku in 1987 look more mature than they do in 1980. Though Takahashi's style is not outstanding from a strictly artistic point of view, the softness of her drawings and the cleverness of her evolving design strategy make *Maison Ikkoku* stand out.

Themes

Maison Ikkoku is a Japanese love story and a bildungsroman that chronicles the personal journeys of an insecure young man and a young woman who idealizes her late husband. It is also the story of quiet suburban life in Japan in the 1980's, a period in which the country was a major economic and cultural force. In addition to the main romance story line, the manga explores how Japanese universities work, how difficult it is to find a job compatible with one's predispositions, and how hard it can be to express true emotions. For Western readers, *Maison Ikkoku* is one of the most revealing manga in terms of explaining Japanese culture.

Impact

In Japan, *Maison Ikkoku* was hugely successful in serialization. Takahashi was already much appreciated for *Urusei Yatsura* (1978-1987), and after the publication of *Maison Ikkoku*, she became known as "the queen of manga." In the United States, *Maison Ikkoku* was one the first manga to earn a large fan base and contributed to the "manga fad" of the late 1980's and early 1990's. Thus, *Maison Ikkoku* helped open the door for other manga in the West. From a cultural point of view, *Maison Ikkoku*'s impact is remarkable:

It has shown Western readers a realistic, funny, and romantic image of contemporary Japan and of Japanese people in a period when other portrayals were rather stereotypical.

Films

Maison Ikkoku. Directed by Shinichiro Sawai. Toei, 1986. Starring Mariko Ishihara as Kyoko and Ken Ishiguro as Yusaku, this live-action film is a short adaptation of the manga and animation series and synthesizes the main story lines and gags.

Maison Ikkoku: Kanketsu-hen. Directed by Tomomi Mochizuki. Ajiado/Kitty Film, 1988. This animated film is the conclusion of the series, presenting the protagonists' wedding.

Maison Ikkoku: Through the Passing of the Seasons. Kitty Films, 1988. This animated film features footage from the anime series.

Maison Ikkoku: Shipwrecked on Ikkoku Island. Directed by Kenichi Maejima. Kitty Films, 1990. This animated film is based on a chapter of the manga in which the characters are shipwrecked.

Prelude Maison Ikkoku: When the Cherry Blossoms Return in the Spring. Kitty Films, 1992. This animated film features footage from the anime series and focuses on Kyoko's late husband.

Television Series

Maison Ikkoku. Directed by Kazuo Yamazaki, Takashi Anno, and Naoyuki Yoshinaga. Studio Deen, 1986-1988. This anime series consists of ninety-six episodes.

Marco Pellitteri

Further Reading

Katsura, Masakazu. *Video Girl Ai* (1989-1992).
Matsumoto, Izumi. *Kimagure Orange Road* (1984-1987).
Takahashi, Rumiko. *Ranma 1/2* (1987-1996).

Bibliography

Ceglia, Simonetta, and Valerio Caldesi Valeri. "Maison Ikkoku." *Image [&] Narrative* 1 (August, 2000). http://www.imageandnarrative.be/inarchive/narratology/cegliavaleri.htm.

Miller, John Jackson, and Maggie Thompson. *Warman's Comic Book Field Guide*. Iola, Wisc.: Krause, 2004.

Yadao, Jason. *The Rough Guide to Manga*. New York: Rough Guides, 2009.

See also: *Ranma 1/2*; *InuYasha*

Mai, the Psychic Girl

Author: Kudo, Kazuya

Artist: Ryoichi Ikegami (illustrator); Bill Person (letterer); Wayne Truman (letterer)

Publisher: VIZ Media

First serial publication: *Mai*, 1985-1986 (English translation, 1987-1989)

First book publication: 1985-1986 (English translation, 1989)

Publication History

When *Mai* debuted in 1985 in *Weekly Shōnen Sunday*, a male-leaning weekly, the series was notable for featuring a female lead character. The feature ran for fifty-three installments, ending in 1986.

VIZ Media selected *Mai* as one of three properties it would package for American audiences under a deal struck with Eclipse Comics. *Mai, the Psychic Girl*, issue 1, had a May, 1987, cover date and was published twice a month, ending in July, 1989. The black-and-white artwork, shortened page count, and increased issue frequency were ways to call attention to the content. The plan worked; the first two issues had second printings.

After Eclipse collapsed, VIZ took control of the property and collected the serial into four volumes, helping to introduce to Americans the digest size that has become the norm for manga. The series was also released to bookstores through Simon & Schuster and was a forerunner of the manga explosion of the 2000's. VIZ adapted the artwork, restoring aspects that had been edited out of the initial Eclipse releases, including one brief nude scene. In 1995, VIZ repackaged the four volumes into three "Perfect Collections," which have had multiple printings.

Plot

Mai Kuju is a teenage schoolgirl, a fairly typical protagonist for manga. Unlike her comic peers, however, she manifests psychic powers. Once they appear, Mai is propelled into a rapid-fire adventure in which she is sought by the Wisdom Alliance, a global conspiracy that wants to use those with psychic abilities as agents in its efforts to influence history.

Mai the Psychic Girl. (Courtesy of VIZ Media)

Fourteen-year-old Mai did not ask for her telepathic and telekinetic abilities, and she thinks they can be used for fun.

She would prefer to hang out with Yumiko Sugimoto and Rie Ikenami, but she soon finds herself on the run with her father, Shuichi. Her strong telekinetic abilities allow her to fly or hurl mental blasts with destructive force.

When Mai's powers become obvious, she is brought to the Alliance's attention. In turn, the group dispatches the Kaieda Intelligence Agency (KIA) to capture Mai and add her to the four children already under its control. As Mai learns to control her powers, she also learns that she is the latest in her family to have these abilities and that her revered ancestors used their gifts to protect Japan.

Without an instructor, using the powers proves problematic at first. For example, in order to protect a puppy she stops a car without taking kinetic force into account, propelling the driver through the windshield. She adopts the puppy and names him Ron.

Shuichi takes Mai to meet Madarao Idei, whose family has been protecting Mai's family for generations. Shuichi displays a mastery of martial arts, keeping the KIA agents away from his daughter. Needing to eliminate Shuichi, the KIA takes Tsukiro, a giant of a man, out of cryogenic suspension and unleashes him. At this point, Mai is led to believe that her father died after falling off a narrow ledge into a deep gorge. Tsukiro's right arm has been permanently mangled but he still is a threat to Mai, until she is rescued by Intetsu, a college student hiking in the vicinity. When Mai falls ill, Intetsu takes her to his dorm and finds a doctor.

Intetsu keeps Mai safe. She falls for him and does not want to endanger him, so she goes home on her own. Soon after she is confronted by Senzo Kaieda, and over tea he explains that he has been working for the Alliance. She goes to stay under his protection, where she finds some measure of happiness.

With Tsukiro unable to find Mai on his own, the Alliance dispatches after her its four teen agents—Baion Yuwomn, David Perry, Turm Garten, and Grail Hong. Turm strikes first, attacking her at the college. He is attempting to prove she is the most powerful of the quartet working for the Alliance, which is when Mai learns that the Wisdom Alliance, not KIA, is the real threat.

Mai eludes one psychic teen after another and winds up discovering that her father is not dead but injured and amnesic; however, her psychic abilities restore his memories. As Mai attempts to prevent worldwide destruction, she discovers everyone has secrets. Senzo Kaieda, for example, approved an experiment that turned her son Tsukiro into a monster. Turm claims to be descended from a god who protected her home of Dresden, Germany, during World War II and suspects Mai is also descended from a god that protected the Togakushi portion of Japan.

After defeating Turm and reuniting with her father, Mai returns home and to school. Soon after, Grail Hong

is enrolled as a new student, becoming Mai's friend. A few days later, Sogen Ryu, the Alliance's leader, decides that Mai is better off dead. He dispatches Baion Yuwomn and David Perry to track her down, beginning a climactic battle over the city. One by one, Mai defeats Baion, David, and Grail and then confronts Ryu. He explains the Alliance's goal: to ignite a global nuclear conflict at 9:09 A.M., September 9, 1999. With humanity largely wiped out, the Alliance would use the children under its control to become the parents of a new human race.

Mai's determination impresses Grail. She explains her legacy and that she will die before Ryu is allowed to destroy the world. Acknowledging her position, Ryu withdraws, telling her it is only a matter of time before Japan, and then the world, bows to the Alliance's will. Mai returns home and happily resumes her life.

Volumes

* *Mai, the Psychic Girl: Perfect Collection*, Volume 1 (1995). Collects the first seventeen installments, which appeared originally in issues of *Weekly Shōnen Sunday*, beginning in 1985. These were then reprinted for American audiences in *Mai, the Psychic Girl*, issues 1-17, from Eclipse Comics, beginning in June, 1987.
* *Mai, the Psychic Girl: Perfect Collection*, Volume 2 (1995). Collects installments 18-35, which appeared originally in issues of *Weekly Shōnen Sunday*, beginning in 1985. These were then reprinted for American audiences in *Mai, the Psychic Girl*, issues 18-35, from Eclipse Comics, beginning in 1987.
* *Mai, the Psychic Girl: Perfect Collection*, Volume 3 (1996). Collects the final eighteen installments, which appeared originally in issues of *Weekly Shōnen Sunday*, beginning in 1986. These were then reprinted for American audiences in *Mai, the Psychic Girl*, issues 36-53, from Eclipse Comics in 1988-1989.

Characters

* *Mai Kuju* is a fourteen-year-old girl of average height and build who is obsessed with boys and her adolescent body. She attends Otani Junior

High School in Shinjuku. One day, when she orders a baseball to stop its flight, she realizes that she has telekinetic abilities. Soon after, she discovers that she can read minds.

- *Shuichi Kuju* appears to be the director of New Energy Resource Development for Marbushi Trading and travels for business. He is keenly aware of the Wisdom Alliance, however, and becomes suspicious when he realizes that Mai had been given a psychokinetic test. He takes her from home and runs to protect her from the Kaieda Information Service thugs. He is a master martial artist with a fierce determination to protect his family and the world.

- *Maki Kuju* is descended from the Mihiro family, which has used its telepathic and telekinetic gifts to protect their homeland for generations. Her ancestors built the Togakushi Shrine, and the power is considered a sacred trust.

- *Sogen Ryu* is the leader of the Wisdom Alliance, an international cartel determined to shape mankind's destiny. Smart and cunning, he wears an eye patch, has a goatee, and can be suave, domineering, and ruthless.

- *Senzo Kaieda* governs Kaieda Information Systems. He was a secret agent during World War II. His son, Tsukiro, was an experiment gone wrong and was kept in suspended animation until needed.

- *Tsukiro* is a huge brute with a wild mane of hair, but he is also nimble and agile. When his arm was permanently mangled, he was given a robotic prosthesis.

- *Baion Yuwomn* is a slovenly, obese teen with poor manners and a horrible attitude. He is kept essentially as Ryu's pet.

- *David Perry* is an American student playing soccer in Japan when he comes under Ryu's sway. Arrogant and vain, he believes himself to be better than anyone until he is defeated by Mai.

- *Turm Garten* comes to Ryu's attention when she uses her powers to destroy an airplane containing a rival for a piano competition. Ryu brings her to the World Alliance and turns her into a weapon.

Kazuya Kudo

Kazuya Kudo is the author of *Mai, the Psychic Girl*. It is one of the earliest manga to be published in English, having been brought over from Japan shortly after the founding, in the late 1980's, of VIZ Media, the largest American translator of Japanese comics and anime. The work is a collaboration with Ryoichi Ikegami, who is best known for *Crying Freeman*, *Wounded Man*, and *Sanctuary*. He also collaborated with Ikegami on *Nobunaga*. Kudo wrote *Pineapple Army*, an early work by illustrator and sometime author Naoki Urasawa (*Monster*, *20th Century Boys*).

Petulant and petty, she believes herself more powerful than she actually is and is easily defeated by Mai.

- *Grail Hong* is short for his age but is friendly and seemingly well-adjusted, making him the perfect sleeper agent to infiltrate Mai's social circle. Seeing Mai in action, he comes to her rescue in defiance of Ryu and is ultimately returned to his native Vietnam after Mai's standoff with the Alliance.

- *Intetsu* is a college student who is hiking when he comes to Mai's rescue. He is her protector when she falls ill, and he becomes her friend.

Artistic Style

Illustrator Ryoichi Ikegami has been a popular artist in Japan since the 1970's. He illustrates with a realistic style. He began his career with *AIUEO Boy* and *Otoko Gumi*, later collaborating with Japan's top writers. He also illustrated Japan's *Spider-Man* manga, which Marvel printed in the 1990's.

His style for *Mai* is typical of the manga of its day, with many close-ups and varied page layouts, allowing for plenty of emotion and detail. He uses thin line work for shading and texture but, for the most part, leaves faces simple, letting a few lines offer up the emotion. His characters have a natural feel and fluidity to them, with many silent panels devoted to a person's head reacting to the moment.

Mixed with his realistic style are the more traditional, comically exaggerated expressions associated with manga. These are used sparingly but are done for emotional effect, giving visual punctuation to scenes.

Ikegami's work also uses Zip-A-Tone for effect and texture, adding depth to the images. Cityscapes appear to be photographs altered into line art, giving a photorealistic look to the settings. There is a clear American influence to many of the action sequences, and Ryu, the villain, is clearly modeled after Max von Sydow's Ming the Merciless from the 1980 *Flash Gordon* film.

Ikegami's style was ideal for bringing manga to American audiences and was well-received. Thus, his

Sanctuary (1993-1998) was among the second wave of manga that VIZ published in the United States.

Themes

Ikegami conceived *Mai* as a character based on the Buddhist figure Maitreya, a Bodhisattva who comes to Earth at the wrong time and as a girl. From that notion, Kazuya Kudō and Ikegami spun a modern-day tale that reflected the conspiracy fears that had been made popular in fiction. The Wisdom Alliance is a shadowy organization attempting to control the world's destiny, and is willing to kill mankind to achieve its ends. Its international makeup shows its global reach. The idea

Mai the Psychic Girl. (Courtesy of VIZ Media)

of bringing the world to the brink of annihilation is nothing new, but it is freshened by Ryu's desire to oversee the development of a new race entirely gifted with psychic abilities.

A secondary theme is that of the legendary line of powered protectors, a common enough theme in Japanese and American literature and pop culture. Mai's coming into her inheritance and only then learning of her gifts and legacy is a trope used repeatedly. Her yearning for a normal life with friends denotes her Everywoman character.

Adolescents becoming the adult they are destined to be is a subtextual theme, as exemplified by Mai and the four teens sent to oppose her. Three of the others are nasty, vain, and morally corrupt before Ryu even gets to them. Only Grail Hong is caught between his obligations to Ryu and the influence of Mai.

The father-daughter relationship is a rare theme in manga and American comics, so its presence in *Mai* is notable. Shuichi and Mai risk everything for one another, and the genuine love between them is one of the series' strengths.

Impact

Weekly Shōnen Sunday was filled with *shōnen* stories aimed at male readers, so it was eye-opening when Mai arrived in 1985. She was a teen heroine with superpowers, which was unusual at the time in Japan. More importantly, *Mai* was perfectly suited in terms of plot, characters, and art style to introduce American comic readers to manga.

Ikegami has admitted that he and Kudō were influenced by Stephen King's novel *Firestarter* (1980), which was also a film starring Drew Barrymore that played in Japan not long before work began on *Mai*. Similarly, the mutated Tsukiro was influenced by American science-fiction films.

American readers were charmed by the innocent and cute Mai, and were also no doubt titillated by Ikegami's decision to have Mai enter her climactic battle in the skies over the city essentially topless and mostly unselfconscious about it. The success of the semimonthly Mai title encouraged VIZ to publish more of Ikegami's works in the United States, beginning with *Crying Freeman* (1986-1988). The series also proved enticing to Hollywood, leading Sony to option the film for a live action adaptation; at that time, few comics and almost no manga generated interest from Hollywood film studios. As a result, *Mai* is a pioneering manga in American and Japanese comics history.

Robert Greenberger

Further Reading

Buronson and Ryoichi Ikegami. *Strain* (1999-2002).

Fumimura, Sho, and Ryoichi Ikegami. *Sanctuary* (1993-1998).

Koike, Kazuo, and Ryoichi Ikegami. *Crying Freeman* (1986-1988).

Bibliography

Gravett, Paul. *Manga: Sixty Years of Japanese Comics.* New York: Collins, 2004.

Misiroglu, Gina, ed. *The Superhero Book.* Detroit: Visible Ink Press, 2004.

Napier, Susan. "Vampires, Psychic Girls, Flying Women, and Sailor Scouts." In *The Worlds of Japanese Popular Culture: Gender, Shifting Boundaries, and Global Culture*, edited by Dolores P. Martinez. New York: Cambridge University Press, 1998.

See also: *Sanctuary; Crying Freeman*

MONSTER

Author: Urasawa, Naoki
Artist: Naoki Urasawa (illustrator)
Publisher: Shogakukan (Japanese); VIZ Media (English)
First serial publication: *Monsutā*, 1994-2001
First book publication: 1995-2001 (English translation, 2006-2008)

Publication History

Monster was originally published by Shogakukan in *Big Comic Original*, a semimonthly *seinen* manga magazine. Shogakukan also reprinted the series in eighteen *tankōbon*, or collected volumes. Beginning in 2006, an English translation of *Monster* was published in the United States by VIZ Media.

Plot

Monster tells the tale of Dr. Kenzo Tenma, a neurosurgeon working in Eisler Memorial Hospital in Dusseldorf, Germany, during the 1980's. Brilliant and on the fast track to success, he has just asked Eva Heinemann to marry him. However, Tenma begins to notice that the hospital's rich patients receive preference over poor ones. He finds himself removed from surgeries deemed less important and assigned only to those that heighten the hospital's reputation.

Tenma's dissatisfaction with this corruption comes to a head with the arrival of the Liebert twins, Johan and Anna, at the hospital. Defying the hospital director's orders to operate on the mayor of Dusseldorf, Tenma chooses to operate on Johan instead. Johan survives, the mayor dies, and the director blackballs Tenma. Soon after, the director and two other associates of the hospital are found dead, having been poisoned. Inspector Heinrich Lunge from the Bundeskriminalamt (BKA), the Federal Criminal Police Office of Germany, is called in to investigate. While he suspects Tenma from the beginning, there is no evidence to support his beliefs.

Nine years later, Tenma is chief of surgery. He operates on Adolf Junkers, a thief who had been hit by a car. Tenma befriends Junkers, and just as the man begins to open up to Tenma, he is shot dead. The killer reveals

Monster. (Courtesy of VIZ Media)

himself to be Johan. Tenma is appalled he saved the life of such a person. He flees Dusseldorf, intending to find and put an end to this "monster" he has created.

The next three volumes introduce the many mysteries surrounding Johan. Tenma tracks down Johan's sister, now named Nina, though the two quickly separate. They stumble upon a neo-Nazi organization intent on making Johan the next Adolf Hitler. Tenma begins to investigate Johan's origins, starting with Kinderheim 511, a facility that carried out experiments on children. He must also constantly evade Lunge, who is obsessed with him. Nina conducts her own search for Johan in order to learn about her forgotten past. Their searches lead them to Prague, where they uncover evidence that the twins were subjects of a eugenics experiment. Nina finds she was subjected to mental conditioning at Red Rose Mansion under the direction of Franz Bonaparta.

Tenma is arrested and extradited to Germany; he manages to escape with Gunther Milch's assistance. The final conflict occurs in Ruhenheim, where Johan has planned a massacre. Tenma, Lunge, Nina, and Grimmer manage to thwart the plan. A random citizen shoots Johan, and Tenma saves the boy's life a second time.

The story ends with Tenma joining Doctors Without Borders and Nina graduating from college. The twins' mother is discovered alive. Johan's end is ambiguous; he has either escaped the police or died.

Volumes

- *Monster*, Volume 1: *Herr Dr. Tenma* (2006). Collects chapters 1-8. Features Tenma's decision to save the life of a boy, Johan, and the consequences of saving someone who turns out to be a killer.
- *Monster*, Volume 2: *Surprise Party* (2006). Collects chapters 9-16. Features the reintroduction of Johan's sister, now named Nina, and Tenma's initial search for her and Johan.
- *Monster*, Volume 3: *511 Kinderheim* (2006). Collects chapters 17-24. Features the history of Kinderheim 511, where children were subjected to psychological experiments.
- *Monster*, Volume 4: *Ayse's Friend* (2006). Collects chapters 25-32. Features a neo-Nazi organization eager for Johan to become the next Hitler.
- *Monster*, Volume 5: *After the Carnival* (2006). Collects chapters 33-41. Features Nina's investigation and a confrontation between Lunge and Tenma.
- *Monster*, Volume 6: *The Secret Woods* (2006). Collects chapters 42-50. Features Eva's confession that she has seen Johan's face.
- *Monster*, Volume 7: *Richard* (2007). Collects chapters 51-59. Features Richard Braun, his investigation of a suicide, and his discovery that a string of unsolved murders are connected.
- *Monster*, Volume 8: *My Nameless Hero* (2007). Collects chapters 60-68. Features Tenma's ar-

rival in Munich and Reichwein's investigations of Johan.

- *Monster*, Volume 9: *A Nameless Monster* (2007). Collects chapters 69-77. Features a confrontation between Tenma and Roberto and also tells the children's story "The Nameless Monster."
- *Monster*, Volume 10: *Picnic* (2007). Collects chapters 78-86. Features Grimmer and the "Magnificent Steiner" as well as Jan Suk's investigation of corruption in the Prague Police Department.
- *Monster*, Volume 11: *Blind Spot* (2007). Collects chapters 87-95. Features a murder accusation and reveals Grimmer's origins.
- *Monster*, Volume 12: *The Rose Mansion* (2007). Collects chapters 96-104. Features Lunge's arrival in Prague and Tenma's arrest.
- *Monster*, Volume 13: *The Escape* (2008). Collects chapters 105-113. Features Tenma's escape from police custody to protect Eva from Roberto.
- *Monster*, Volume 14: *That Night* (2008). Collects chapters 114-122. Features the mystery of the Red Rose Mansion.
- *Monster*, Volume 15: *The Door to Memories* (2008). Collects chapters 123-131. Features the full recovery of Nina's memories.
- *Monster*, Volume 16: *Welcome Home* (2008). Collects chapters 132-141. Features Dr. Gillen's discovery of Johan's ties with numerous serial killers.
- *Monster*, Volume 17: *I'm Back* (2008). Collects chapters 142-151. Features Nina's reunion with Johan and introduces the mysterious Franz Bonaparta.
- *Monster*, Volume 18: *Scenery for a Doomsday* (2008). Collects chapters 152-162. Features the massacre at Ruhenheim and the aftermath of Johan's plans.

Characters

- *Kenzo Tenma*, the protagonist, is a middle-aged Japanese man. Noble and kind, he considers all lives to be equal and never hesitates to help others. Throughout the series, he feels responsible for Johan's actions and decides to atone by stopping the monster he feels he created.

- *Johan Liebert*, the primary antagonist, is young, blond, and handsome. Extremely charismatic and intelligent, he is manipulative and deceitful and a remorseless killer. However, he harbors a deep love for his sister, is shown to be kind to children, and considers Tenma his "father."
- *Nina Fortner*, a.k.a. *Anna Liebert*, is Johan's twin sister. While she is as good-looking as Johan, the similarities between the siblings end there. She is sweet, caring, hardworking, and intelligent. As her memories return, they provide clues about the mental experiments and conditioning to which she and Johan were subjected as children.
- *Eva Heinemann* is Tenma's former fiancé. Her father was the director of Eisler Memorial Hospital. She is blond, curvaceous, and stylish but is also spoiled, shallow, demeaning, and haughty. After her father's murder and three failed marriages, she becomes an embittered alcoholic. Despite her wealth, she lives a lonely life.
- *Heinrich Lunge* is an inspector for the BKA assigned to the murders that occur at Eisler Memorial Hospital. A tall and looming man with severe features and a receding hairline, he appears devoid of emotion. His pursuit of Tenma resembles Inspector Javert's search for Jean Valjean in Victor Hugo's *Les Misérables* (1862; English translation, 1862). He sacrifices everything in his pursuit of Tenma, letting his relationships with his wife and daughter erode to the point that his own grandson does not know him.
- *Dieter* is a young boy Tenma rescues from an abusive home. He has great fortitude, is supportive of his makeshift family, and is brave.
- *Director Heinemann* is the former director of Eisler Memorial Hospital and Tenma's boss at the start of the series. He is an older man, has a thick neck, and wears glasses. He is strict, egotistical, and demanding.
- *Dr. Oppenheim* is the chief of surgery at the hospital. He has a receding hairline, a slightly overweight figure, and a neatly trimmed mustache.

He reports Tenma for defying the director's wishes.

- *Dr. Boyer* is a neurosurgeon with a protruding, hawklike nose and dark hair. He blames Tenma for the mayor's death and later becomes head of neurosurgery.
- *Otto Heckel* is a short, bucktoothed thief who teams with Tenma early in his search for Johan. Selfish and cowardly, Heckel never shows interest in anything beyond ways to make money.
- *The Baby* is a short, elderly man who leads a neo-Nazi organization. Racist, cruel, manipulative, cunning, and violent, he is one of four men who want Johan to lead them as a successor to Hitler.
- *Helmut Wolfe* is an elderly soldier who found the Liebert twins wandering the Czech border. Johan murdered all of his friends and family. He is terrified of Johan and desperate for any kind of social contact.
- *Rudy Gillen* is a short, square-faced man and a criminal psychologist who attended medical school with Tenma. He is calm, clever, and secretly jealous of Tenma's brilliance.
- *Roberto* is an orphan who was at Kinderheim 511 as a child. A big, burly man with shoulder-length hair, he is calculating, smug, and cold. It is implied that he was once a child named Adolf Reinhart.
- *Hans Georg Schuwald* is a blind, elderly man and one of the richest people in Europe. He once had an affair with a prostitute named Margot Langer, which resulted in a son, Karl.
- *Karl Neumann* is a student at the University of Munich and an employee of Schuwald. Tall, awkward, and soft-spoken with curly black hair, he is actually Schuwald's son.
- *Lotte Frank* is an anthropology student at the University of Munich. She has short brown hair and wears glasses. She is nosy and pushy but also imaginative and caring.
- *Julius Reichwein* is a psychologist. He is short and balding and wears glasses. He is perceptive, strict, and forthright in his opinions but also fair and kind. As a counselor, he is experienced when it comes to reading people.

Monster. (Courtesy of VIZ Media)

pily dressed. Gruff and weary, he shows disdain for Eva; like her, his mother was an alcoholic. He is an ex-convict who served an eight-year term for murdering his former girlfriend.

- *Jan Suk* is a young detective with the Prague police. He has boyish good looks and wears his hair slicked back. Idealistic and naïve, Suk dreamed since childhood of being a police officer. His professional career has been stalled by corruption.
- *Petr Capek*, the fourth member of the neo-Nazi organization, has white hair and wears glasses. An egotistical control freak, he worked as an apprentice to Franz Bonaparta in his youth.
- *Franz Bonaparta* is the man responsible for the eugenics experiment that created the Liebert twins. He authored several children's books with the purpose of brainwashing children.

Artistic Style

While his early work in the manga industry had more cartoonlike proportions and action, Urasawa's *Monster* is steeped in realism. As the series takes place throughout Germany and the Czech Republic, the backgrounds vary from crowded city streets to quaint hamlets, all with detailed architecture. They give the series a grounded quality; what might have felt more fantastical if it had been drawn in a cartoonlike style feels closer to reality.

In addition to the drawn backgrounds, Urasawa uses actual photographs of different locations, superimposing them with his drawings to blend the fictional story tightly with real-world locations. Such a firm grounding in actual locations lends a sense of realism to the plot, even when it seems outlandish or improbable. Later in the series, Urasawa distorts the photographs to give them a fuzzy, dreamlike quality.

Like his backgrounds, Urasawa's characters are portrayed in a realistic style, with a wide variety of facial features, body types, and ages. Their appearances communicate economic standing as well as ethnic heritage through culture-specific styles of dress or hairstyle. While this helps the reader remember the vast array of characters, Urasawa uses all of these tools to communicate different facets of his characters visually; Tenma's increasingly haggard appearance, for ex-

- *Richard Braun* is a private investigator who was fired from his previous position as a police officer due to his alcoholism. A tall man with curly dark hair and a square jaw, he is intelligent and determined. He is haunted by his mistakes but strives to move on with his life.
- *Wolfgang Grimmer* is a journalist researching Kinderheim 511. Grimmer has blond, stringy hair and is so tall he towers over many of the other characters. He appears to be pleasant and polite and gets along well with children. There is a darker side to his personality, which he calls "The Magnificent Steiner," that emerges when he is angry or in danger.
- *Martin* is a bodyguard hired by Petr Capek to protect Eva Heinemann. Of average height with short hair, he is perpetually unshaven and slop-

ample, shows the strain he feels while trying to stop Johan. In contrast, Johan's utter perfection makes him look otherworldly and frightening.

Urasawa also incorporates many panels without dialogue and uses these "silent" pages to build tension in the reader, a technique similar to that used in horror films. Another filmlike quality of the work is the frequent use of close-ups of characters' faces; these panels indicate key moments of discovery, tension, or internal struggle. Despite the many murders that occur, *Monster*'s action begins and ends quickly; the murderers waste no time toying with victims when they have grander goals to achieve, and the bulk of the murders occur offscreen. However, characters' reactions to the violence allow the reader's imagination to fill in the blanks vividly.

Themes

Monster's overarching themes concern the nature of good and evil; the text asks, quite simply, "What makes a monster?" The plot explores how a person such as Johan could have come into existence. When Bonaparta admits to experimenting on the twins, he seems to provide the final explanation for Johan's twisted mind: Bonaparta and his companions cultivated this monster.

However, Urasawa soon introduces new story threads that counter this explanation. The director of Kinderheim 511 blames Johan for ruining the orphanage by introducing evil into it. Nina's memories reveal that she, not Johan, was the twin exposed to the brainwashing of the Red Rose Mansion, and Wolfe comments that even as a child, Johan was remorseless and cruel. Perhaps he was born a monster. The twins' mother admits to hoping her offspring would seek revenge against Bonaparta; however, in Nina's memories, their mother was gentle, protective, and loving. Nina herself foils any concrete explanation for Johan. By all accounts, she should be equally manipulative and disassociated, yet she strives to be a better person and is something of a pacifist. While Kinderheim 511 did create monsters such as Roberto, it also produced Grimmer, a man who struggles to express emotions but still makes the correct moral choices.

Ultimately, the key theme of *Monster* is that of choice. While outside stimuli are influential, the choices people make are what truly define them. Tenma could have chosen a more politically acceptable career in the hospital, but he chooses instead to take a more moral path. Rather than succumb to her personal demons, Nina chooses to move on and become a lawyer. Characters with shady pasts decide to atone—alcoholics give up drinking, for example—and presumed paragons of virtue lie, cheat, steal, or blackmail innocent people. *Monster* makes the argument that horrible people can exist and even be created; in the end, though, every individual must choose whether to defy the conditions of his or her upbringing or give in.

Impact

Monster marked a period of growth for Urasawa; his art style improved so drastically that he requested the publication of English-language editions of his series *Twentieth Century Boys* be delayed until after *Monster* was finished. The series also features several references to works by the "god of manga," famed artist and writer Osamu Tezuka. Tezuka was

---

Naoki Urasawa

Naoki Urasawa, born in 1960, is one of the most admired manga creators in Japan. His strong, realistic character designs have made his drawing style highly recognizable, and his stories often feature complicated mythologies and narratives. These include *Twentieth Century Boys*, in which childhood friends watch as an increasingly threatening present comes to resemble the stories that fed their youthful games, and *Monster*, a complicated suspense tale. His early work includes *Yawara!*, a manga about a young girl who practices judo. From 2003 to 2009, Urasawa produced *Pluto*, an extrapolative remake of an early *Astro Boy* story by Osamu Tezuka; it was a rare instance in which one manga creator's work was adopted by another, posthumously or otherwise. His current efforts include *Billy Bat*, running in Kodansha's *Weekly Morning*, and *Master Keaton Remastered*, running in Shogakukan's *Big Comic Original*. It's a sign of his prominence that his work is handled simultaneously by two competing publishers.

known for being critical of the medical establishment and its unfair treatment of people from lower socioeconomic classes. He, like Tenma in *Monster*, believed that all lives were equal and all people deserved equal medical care. Reichwein was modeled after Shunsaku Ban from *Astro Boy*, while Johan resembles Michio Yuki from *MW*. Readers of *Monster* find the series to be evidence of a blossoming talent, with strong inspiration from one of the most popular manga artists.

Television Series

Monster. Directed by Masayuki Kojima. Madhouse, 2004-2005. This animated adaptation stars Hidenobu Kiuchi as Tenma, Nozomu Sasaki as Johan, and Mamiko Noto as Nina.

Lyndsey Nicole Raney

Further Reading

Ohba, Tsugumi, and Takeshi Obata. *Death Note* (2003-2006).

Tezuka, Osamu. *Black Jack* (1973-1983)

Urasawa, Naoki. *Twentieth Century Boys* (2009-2010).

Bibliography

Cornog, Martha. "Monster." *Library Journal* 134, no. 12 (July, 2009): 78.

Diaz, Junot. "The Psychotic Japanese Monster." *Time* 172, no. 4 (July, 2008): 50.

Fleming, Michael. "VIZ Media Enters Movie Biz." *Daily Variety*, July 20, 2008, p. 8.

Ishii, Anne. "Medical Manga Comes to America." *CMAJ: Canadian Medical Association Journal* 180, no. 5 (March, 2009): 542-543.

Mautner, Chris. "Chris Mautner Reviews *Pluto*, Volumes 1-3 by Naoki Urasawa." *The Comics Journal*, December 29, 2009. http://classic.tcj.com/manga/chris-mautner-reviews-pluto-vols-1-3-by-naoki-urasawa.

O'Luanaigh, Cian. "Osamu Tezuka: Father of Manga and Scourge of the Medical Establishment." *The Guardian*, July 21, 2010. http://www.guardian.co.uk/science/blog/2010/jul/21/medical-manga-osamu-tezuka.

Taylor, Stephen. "Urasawa's Mesmerizing *Monster*." *The Daily Yomiuri*, April 13, 2008, p. 13.

See also: *Death Note; MW; Pluto; Twentieth Century Boys; Astro Boy*

MW

Author: Tezuka, Osamu

Artist: Osamu Tezuka (illustrator); Chip Kidd (cover artist)

Publisher: Shogakukan (Japanese); Vertical (English)

First serial publication: *Muu*, 1976-1978

First book publication: 1981 (English translation, 2007)

Publication History

MW was first published serially in the *seinen* manga magazine *Biggu komikku* (*Big Comic*), from September, 1976, to January, 1978. Since 1981, *MW* has been collected and printed in several different two- and three-volume Japanese editions. In 2007, American publisher Vertical published a single-volume hardcover edition of *MW*. A paperback edition was published in 2010.

Plot

MW is a psychological thriller about a sociopath bent on exterminating humankind. Yuki Michio is captured as a young boy by a group of vagabonds on a rural island in southern Japan. Among his captors is Iwao Garai, a brawny teen who sexually assaults Yuki in a remote cave. During this encounter, an accidental discharge of a poisonous gas known by the code name "MW" kills the rest of the gang and the entire population of the island. Though exposure does not prove fatal for either character, the gas leaves Yuki a sociopath and motivates Garai, tortured by the devastation he witnesses, to join the Catholic clergy.

Years later, Father Garai and Yuki—now a dashing bank executive—maintain a tortured romance, a source of much shame and suffering for the priest. The remainder of the novel details Yuki's efforts to destroy those responsible for the MW leak, both the personnel from "Nation X" (the United States) who developed and stored the gas on the island facility and the Japanese who collaborated in the subsequent cover-up. Yuki rises through the banking ranks in order to gain the favor of his manager—one of the few survivors of the disaster—and the politician Eikaku Nakata, the

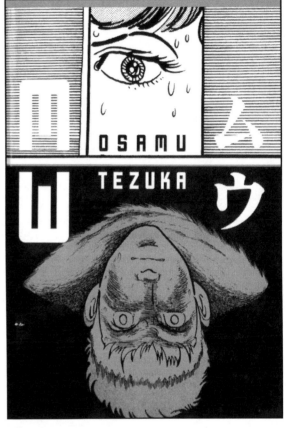

MW. (Courtesy of Vertical)

mastermind behind the cover-up. Yuki inveigles himself into Nakata's inner circle and even marries his daughter in order to achieve his goal. Finally, Yuki orchestrates the theft of the original MW gas stores, taking hostages onboard an airplane piloted by the Nation X officer who had originally overseen the transfer of the MW to Tokyo. At the close of the novel, Garai sacrifices himself to save the world—but a twist ending suggests the danger may not be over.

Characters

- *Yuki Michio*, later known as *Yuki Nakata*, the protagonist, is a tall, trim, and charismatic bank executive in his twenties. As a boy, he is kidnapped, sexually assaulted, and exposed to the MW gas, which leaves him "completely stripped of any shred of morality and decency," in the words of Garai. His life narrative from that point forward becomes one of murder, rape, and plans for the annihilation of the world's population by means of MW. He is a remorseless killer who wishes only for the eradication of all humankind.

- *Iwao Garai* is a Catholic priest with a square jaw and an athletic build. As a counterculture youth in the 1960's, he falls in with a gang called the Crows, following them from Tokyo to a remote island where they plan to start a commune. Garai instigates a physical relationship with the kidnapped Yuki in a cave, thus inadvertently saving both their lives as the deadly gas wafts below. His guilt over this act of pederasty and shock at the devastation caused by the MW leak lead him to the priesthood. He is tormented by his continuing sexual relationship with Yuki as well as his inaction in the face of the latter's pattern of rape and murder. In the novel's denouement, he jumps to his death with the stolen MW gas, which harmlessly disperses in the ocean.

- *The bank manager* is an overweight man who shepherds Yuki's career as an up-and-coming bank executive. He is originally from the island and was paid to keep quiet about the MW gas leak. Yuki rapes and kills his daughter and then murders him.

- *Miho* is the bank manager's daughter, an attractive and sexually aggressive young woman. Yuki rapes her and then injects her in the thigh with a lethal poison that kills while simultaneously producing an intense orgasm.

- *Tamanojo Kawamoto* is Yuki's identical twin brother, a famous Kabuki actor in the Kansai theater. He impersonates Yuki during a final confrontation and is mistakenly shot and killed.

- *Eikaku Nakata* is a double-chinned representative of the fictitious Liberty Party with ties to the bank manager. He relies on Yuki to manage the financial aspects of his reelection campaign and arranges for Yuki to marry his daughter, with predictably tragic results. Upon learning of his daughter's death, he suffers a cerebral hemorrhage.

Big Comic

Since 1968, *Big Comic* has been a powerhouse in manga aimed at young men who have outgrown *shōnen*, or boys', manga. This publishing realm is called *seinen*, meaning "young man." The magazine, an anthology of serialized stories, is released twice monthly. Its publisher, Shogakukan, benefits from having creators work in both *Big Comic* and *Weekly Shōnen Sunday*, which encourages readers to transition from one Shogakukan publication to the other as they mature rather than switch to other publishers' magazines. These creators include Osamu Tezuka, whose *MW* ran in *Big Comic*, and Rumiko Takahashi, who serialized *Maison Ikkoku* in the magazine. *Big Comic* is the home of the long-running series *Golgo 13*, which since 1969 has told the story of an absurdly skilled international assassin. Notable former *Big Comic* series include *Eagle: The Making of an Asian-American President*, *Galaxy Express 999*, and *A Distant Neighborhood*.

- *Mika* is Eikaku Nakata's attractive young daughter and, later, Yuki's wife. Shortly after they return from their honeymoon, Yuki strangles her and throws her body in front of a bullet train.

- *Sumiko* is an attractive former associate of Garai who goes to Tokyo in the hope of kindling a romance with the priest. Yuki preys on her weakness and naïveté, raping her twice. Sumiko falls under Yuki's spell and agrees to marry him, only to be jilted.

- *Aohata* is a newspaper reporter who, with Garai's help, writes an exposé revealing the MW scandal to the world. He escapes Yuki's first assassination attempt unharmed, but a second attack on his life renders him nearly comatose.

- *Lieutenant General Minch* is a burly, lantern-jawed officer in the army of Nation X who orders the removal of the MW gas to a base near Tokyo after the accident on the island. Years later, he meets Yuki at the latter's wedding reception, and the two commence a sexual relationship. Minch is tortured into revealing the location of the MW gas and piloting the escape airplane.

Artistic Style

Known alternately as the "god of comics" and the "Walt Disney of Japan," Tezuka created the visual grammar for modern manga. Though perhaps secondary in relation to his massive body of work, *MW* clearly demonstrates the master's many talents. The artist's so-called cinematic style, for example, is much in evidence in the work, as Tezuka uses a variety of angles, far and long shots, and close-ups to capture motion and mood dynamically. In other respects, *MW* may be seen as a departure from Tezuka's typical style: His trademark visual aesthetic of cute, Disney-style art accompanied by "adult" graphic violence and nudity is largely missing in this brooding and violent novel, as he eschews the more lighthearted visuals for a darker and more realistic tone. Remarkable are Tezuka's near-photorealistic depictions of the victims of the MW gas in a mosaic of panels surrounding the tormented Garai.

This photorealistic effect is again used in a scene depicting a protest against the MW gas, in which Tezuka reproduces a photograph possibly taken during an anti-American protest in the 1960's. Another hallmark of Tezuka's style evidenced in this work is a playful, or at least fanciful, flight from standard cartooning into abstraction and absurdity; for example, a two-page spread of Garai and Yuki nude in bed morphs into a surreal homage to the Art Nouveau illustrator Aubrey Beardsley. Finally, Tezuka's striking use of panel composition is notable: He effectively veers away from standard rectangular presentations at moments of high drama, favoring instead panels featuring sharp, sometime ragged, edges.

Themes

MW's nihilistic antihero, exploration of Christianity and homosexuality, and absence of lighthearted and "cartoony" elements make it a marked departure from Tezuka's frequent themes of humanism and justice. In other respects, however, *MW* is pure Tezuka, as his

MW. (Courtesy of Vertical)

trademark themes of antimilitarism (and anti-Americanism) and deep distrust of science and technology are reified in the eponymous gas of the title. Another characteristic of his work is use of real-life incidents as source material: Sarin and mustard gas were inadvertently leaked from an American military facility in Okinawa in 1968, sickening several service personnel. That the Japanese government was complicit in the storage of such an abhorrent weapon, and that similar chemicals were being used in Vietnam, only compounded Tezuka's antagonism toward the United States. When Detective Meguro shouts "Where the hell is our sovereignty?" while on an off-limits Nation X military base, he expresses the anger of many Japanese over the continued foreign military presence in Japan.

Homosexuality is another controversial theme in *MW*. Though pederastic homosexual relationships were an accepted cultural practice in Japan for centuries, Western influence in the nineteenth century gradually displaced such long-standing attitudes. In fact, by Tezuka's time, homosexual relationships were more generally accepted in the United States than in Japan, a point the author references in the text. Though Father Garai and Yuki begin their relationship in pederastic form, Tezuka, consistent with Japanese tradition, depicts their union as both consensual and mutually pleasurable. Of related note is a brief scene in which Yuki attempts to discredit Garai by staging photos of him at a gay bar. However, the female newspaper editor Yuki solicits to publish the photos declines to purchase them. This mystery is resolved on the next page, as the editor is seen at home later that day. "You'll never believe the good deed I did today," she says while embracing her female lover.

Impact

MW is generally regarded as a minor work in Tezuka's oeuvre, ranking not only below such acknowledged masterworks as *Phoenix* (1954-1988), *Astro Boy* (1952-1968), and *Black Jack* (1973-1983) but also beneath midcareer works such as *Ode to Kirihito* (1970-1971), to which it is often compared because of its length, Christian themes, and availability in

English. As such, the impact of *MW* remains minimal outside of Japan. Though the translated volume published by Vertical earned an Eisner Award nomination in 2008 for Best U.S. Edition of International Material—Japan, the work was ultimately lost in the shuffle of similar releases such as *Ode to Kirihito*, published to acclaim in 2006, and *Apollo's Song*, published in 2007. In Japan, interest in the work was sufficient to merit a live-action film, released in 2009, though it was not received well, either critically or at the box office.

Films

MW. Directed by Hitoshi Iwamoto. Amuse Soft Entertainment/D.N. Dream Partners/Eisei Gekijo Company, 2009. This live-action adaptation stars Hiroshi Tamaki as Yuki and Takayuki Yamada as Garai. The film departs from the manga in several salient aspects; most prominently, the sexual relationship between Yuki and Garai is muted, as the two are depicted to have grown up together as friends on Okino Mafune Island. *MW* received mixed reviews from critics.

Todd S. Munson

Further Reading

Tatsumi, Yoshihiro. *The Push Man and Other Stories* (2005).
Tezuka, Osamu. *Ode to Kirihito* (2006).
_____. *Phoenix* (2002-2008).

Bibliography
Johnson-Woods, Toni, ed. *Manga: An Anthology of Global and Cultural Perspectives.* New York: Continuum, 2010.
"*MW*." Review of *MW*, by Osamu Tezuka. *The Complete Review*, n.d. http://www.complete-review.com/reviews/comics/tezukao2.htm.
Power, Natsu Onoda. *God of Comics: Osamu Tezuka and the Creation of Post-World War II Manga.* Jackson: University Press of Mississippi, 2009.

See also: *Phoenix*; *Ode to Kirihito*; *Black Jack*

N

Nana

Author: Yazawa, Ai

Artist: Ai Yazawa (illustrator)

Publisher: Shūeisha (Japanese); VIZ Media (English)

First serial publication: 2000-   (English translation, 2005-2007)

First book publication: 2000-2009 (English translation, 2005-2010)

Publication History

Ai Yazawa had published a number of well-received *shōjo* series since her debut in 1985, most of them in the magazine *Ribon*, marketed toward nine- to thirteen-year-old girls. *Nana* began in *Ribon*'s sister magazine *Cookie* in 2000; *Cookie* is aimed at an older female audience.

The first two chapters of the series are not directly connected and instead give the backstories of the two main characters. According to Yazawa, this was to provide a satisfying stand-alone book if the series was not picked up for serialization. However, *Nana* proved to be one of *Cookie*'s most popular series and continued for nearly a decade. In June of 2009, Yazawa developed a sudden illness and put *Nana* on hiatus. She returned from the hospital in April of 2010 but had not restarted the series as of 2012 or given any indication of her future plans for it.

VIZ Media began publishing *Nana* in English in July of 2005, serializing the chapters in the American manga magazine *Shojo Beat*, and released the collected volumes beginning in December of that year. *Nana* has been collected in a total of twenty-one volumes and released in both Japan and the United States.

Plot

The story revolves around two women, Nana Osaki and Nana Komatsu, who meet accidentally on a train heading to Tokyo and again when apartment hunting. Despite their differences, they decide to move in to-

Nana. (Courtesy of VIZ Media)

gether and quickly become friends. (*Nana* is the Japanese word for "seven," and the characters end up renting apartment 707, one of many references to the number.) Nana O. is an aspiring punk-rock musician in the band Black Stones ("Blast" for short) who has come to Tokyo to pursue her musical goals. Nana K., nicknamed "Hachi," has followed her boyfriend to Tokyo. (From this point on, Nana K. will be referred to as Hachi and Nana O. as Nana.) The other members of Blast, Yasu and Nobu, join Nana in Tokyo and re-form Blast, along with new bassist Shin.

After being dumped by her boyfriend, Hachi takes an interest in Nana's love life. Hachi receives tickets to a Trapnest concert and goes with Nana, only to discover that Nana's boyfriend is Ren Honjo, the former bassist for Blast and current guitarist for Trapnest. Nana and Ren are reunited, and he and the other members of Trapnest (singer Reira, bassist Takumi, and drummer Naoki) join the cast.

Nana and Ren still love and need each other but cannot be seen together in public because of the paparazzi. Hachi is torn between suave Takumi and passionate Nobu. Tired of Takumi's coldness, Hachi breaks up with him and begins dating Nobu, but she discovers she is pregnant. Takumi forces out Nobu and declares his intention to raise Hachi's child as his own. Takumi and Hachi move into an expensive apartment with heavy security.

Blast is signed by Gaia Music. Paparazzi who have staked out Ren's apartment publish photographs of Nana and Ren together and set off a media frenzy. Gaia capitalizes on the buzz to sell Blast's debut single but moves the band to a private dormitory owned by the company. Ren and Nana can see each other only infrequently, and Hachi and Nana can hardly see each other at all.

The manga then jumps forward to a point several years later. Hachi is married to Takumi but is clearly unhappy and attracted to Nobu; she has two children, Satsuki, who resembles Takumi, and the older Ren, who looks more like Nobu. Trapnest and Blast have broken up, and Nana has disappeared.

Back in the present, both bands' singles are released on the same day, and Ren and Nana announce in a press conference that they are engaged. Takumi delays his marriage to Hachi in order to simplify the media situation. Hachi is depressed and unable to see Nana; conversely, Nana is suffering panic attacks. When a magazine takes apparently compromising pictures of Ren and Reira, Takumi decides to "sacrifice" himself in exchange for the magazine dropping the story, allowing it to write about him and Hachi instead. They are quickly married. The same magazine later releases a story revealing that Nana's mother, who abandoned her, is not only still alive but also remarried and has a daughter. Nana dismisses the story as a hoax but is secretly curious and worried about her mother.

On the eve of Blast's first concert tour, Shin is arrested for marijuana possession. The tour is canceled, and Gaia's president asks Nana to become a solo act. Ren attempts to quit drugs but suffers from withdrawal. Takumi begins sleeping with Reira in an attempt to keep her happy. However, Reira runs away, and when Ren drives after her, he is killed in a car accident.

The members of Trapnest and Blast are all devastated, Nana especially. At the funeral, it becomes obvious that virtually everyone's hopes and dreams have been shattered by Ren's death. In the last flash-forward sequence, the group has finally found Nana's trail after years of searching and are planning to find her.

Ai Yazawa

Ai Yazawa, born in 1967, is the creator of the major hit *Nana*. A *shōjo* series about two girls making a go of it in the big city, *Nana* ran in the Shūeisha-published magazine *Cookie* from 2000 until 2009, when Yazawa contracted an illness and put work on hiatus. Yazawa has said that she read the magazine *Ribon* heavily when she was growing up. The fashions that appear in her manga are often of her own design. *Tenshi Nanka Ja Nai*, a high-school romance from the early 1990's. Other manga include *Neighborhood Story* and *Paradise Kiss*. Many of her works have been adapted for animated and live-action film.

Volumes

- *Nana*, Volume 1 (2005). Collects the chapters "Nana Komatsu" and "Nana Osaki." The lives of Nana and Hachi prior to their first meeting are explored.
- *Nana*, Volume 2 (2006). Collects chapters 1-4. The two Nanas meet and decide to share an apartment.

- *Nana*, Volume 3 (2006). Collects chapters 5-8. Nana begins to put Blast together in Tokyo.
- *Nana*, Volume 4 (2006). Collects chapters 9-12. Black Stones perform their first concert. Nana and Hachi go to a Trapnest concert.
- *Nana*, Volume 5 (2007). Collects chapters 13-16. Nana and Ren are reunited. Hachi and Takumi have a one-night stand.
- *Nana*, Volume 6 (2007). Collects chapters 17-20. Nobu and Takumi compete for Hachi's affection.
- *Nana*, Volume 7 (2007). Collects chapters 21-24. Hachi breaks up with Takumi and begins seeing Nobu. Blast is scouted by Gaia Music.
- *Nana*, Volume 8 (2008). Collects chapters 25-28. Hachi discovers she is pregnant, prompting Takumi to return and force out Nobu.
- *Nana*, Volume 9 (2008). Collects chapters 29-32 and the bonus story "Naoki." Blast begins recording. Nana begins to have blackouts. Hachi moves in with Takumi.
- *Nana*, Volume 10 (2008). Collects chapters 33-36. Paparazzi publish photos of Nana and Ren together.
- *Nana*, Volume 11 (2008). Collects chapters 37-41. Blast is moved into a private dorm. Blast and Trapnest appear on a television show together. Ren proposes to Nana.
- *Nana*, Volume 12 (2008). Collects chapters 42-45. The first of the flash-forward sequences occurs. Ren and Nana announce their engagement.
- *Nana*, Volume 13 (2008). Collects chapters 46-49. Hachi, Blast, and Trapnest all meet at a party.
- *Nana*, Volume 14 (2009). Collects chapters 50-53. Seemingly incriminating photos of Ren and Reira are sent to Nana and Takumi.
- *Nana*, Volume 15 (2009). Collects chapters 54-57. Hachi and Takumi are married; Hachi remains uncertain about her future but is committed to Takumi.
- *Nana*, Volume 16 (2009). Collects chapters 58-61 and the bonus story "Nobu." A magazine investigates Nana's mother.
- *Nana*, Volume 17 (2009). Collects chapters 62-65. The magazine story is published, sending Nana's mother into hiding.
- *Nana*, Volume 18 (2009). Collects chapters 66-69

and the bonus story "Takumi." Blast's tour is canceled. Nana agrees to become a solo act.
- *Nana*, Volume 19 (2009). Collects chapters 70-73. The article about Nana's mother continues to have far-reaching effects. Shin is released from jail.
- *Nana*, Volume 20 (2010). Collects chapters 74-77. Ren dies in a car accident.
- *Nana*, Volume 21 (2010). Collects chapters 78 and 79. The band members and others attend Ren's funeral.

Characters

- *Nana Osaki*, a protagonist, is a willowy young woman with black hair and mischievous eyes. She is a talented singer and guitarist who wants to make it as a musician. When she was four, her mother left her with her grandmother, who died when Nana was fifteen. Her relationship with Ren is stormy and passionate; they are clearly in love, but their self-destructive behaviors feed each other. She wants nothing more than to sing and become famous for her music.
- *Nana Komatsu*, a.k.a. *Hachi*, a protagonist, is a bubbly, light-haired girl who falls in love easily. Though she is Nana's opposite in many ways, the two become close friends, and their relationship is the focal point of the series. Nana gives her the nickname "Hachi," which is a double pun: In Japanese, the number seven, *nana*, is followed by eight, *hachi*, and "Hachi" is also the nickname of a famously loyal dog in Japanese history, referring to Nana K.'s loyalty and devotion.
- *Ren Honjo* is a tall, thin man with short black hair. He is Nana's boyfriend and former bandmate in Blast. Shortly before the story begins, he is scouted by the group Trapnest. He is in love with Nana but is often unable to be with her. Other characters compare him to Sid Vicious of the Sex Pistols, both for his punk style and his drug habit. In chapter 77, he dies in a car accident.
- *Nobuo "Nobu" Terashima* is Blast's guitarist. He has blond spiky hair and large, expressive eyes. He quickly develops a crush on Hachi and vies with Takumi for her affection. When Hachi becomes pregnant, Takumi gives Nobu an ulti-

matum, and Nobu breaks up with her. However, he and Hachi remain attracted to one another.

- *Takumi Ichinose* is a tall, severe-looking man with long black hair. He is Trapnest's guitarist, composer, and producer and a domineering musician who writes virtually all of the band's music and tightly controls all aspects of production. He is a womanizer and initially only meets with Hachi for casual sex. However, once she becomes pregnant, he treats their relationship much more seriously. He is cold and calculating, putting Trapnest before all other concerns, and is sometimes cruel to Hachi, even forcing himself on her more than once.
- *Yasushi "Yasu" Takagi* is Blast's drummer. He is a tall, bald man who usually wears sunglasses and has an aura of seriousness. He is the most mature and careful member of Blast and the most involved in their long-term planning. He takes special care of Nana, and it is implied they have a mutual attraction, but nothing comes of it.

Artistic Style

Nana skirts the line between *shōjo* manga, which is usually about romance and aimed at young girls, and *josei* manga, which features more complex plots for teenage and adult women. This dichotomy is seen in the art as well. Yazawa makes use of elaborate patterns and prints as backgrounds for some sequences to represent characters' emotions in a visual manner, a technique that is a hallmark of *shōjo* manga, as it simplifies and speeds up the process of drawing pages. However, she also regularly draws complex backgrounds or large crowd scenes and generally draws with more detail than most *shōjo* artists.

Yazawa's layouts tend to be more varied than those in many *shōjo* manga. Conversation sequences have many small panels that emphasize characters' expressions and movements, but Yazawa also uses long, wordless sequences to convey emotion. Storytelling is more multilayered and mature than in most *shōjo* series.

Yazawa's characters tend to be thin and lanky, with long arms and legs. Movement and position is realistically depicted, with carefully observed posture and gesture. Characters' eyes tend to be large and expres-

sive, though smaller than the cartoonishly enormous eyes of most *shōjo* characters. Yazawa puts great detail into characters' clothes, assembling outfits that are stylish yet plausible and reflect the wearer's personality. Many of the outfits worn by members of Blast are punk-inspired and feature spiked collars, leather, metal studs, and similar accessories. Nana also has a love for fashion designer Vivienne Westwood and is seen carrying a Westwood handbag.

Themes

As previously noted, *Nana* treads a fine line between age groups: Although it is about romance and relationships, as most *shōjo* is, it is dense, deep, and complex enough to fall into the category of *josei* manga. The characters are more mature (or, at least, older), their relationships more explicit, and their problems more difficult to solve. Hachi's journey reflects this complexity:

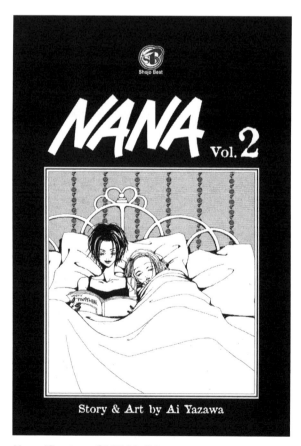

Nana. (Courtesy of VIZ Media)

She comes to Tokyo with the naïve wish of finding love and getting married, only to find herself enmeshed in a tangled web of desire and jealousy. Her naïveté and immaturity cause her to become pregnant and force her to make tough decisions about her future.

Nana is largely about the intersection of love, desire, dreams, and ambitions and what happens when these impulses conflict. Nana is in love with Ren, but she has too much pride to be simply the girlfriend of a rock star. She wants to prove herself as a musician and star in her own right first. This separation, however, hurts them both deeply, leading to Ren's self-destructive behavior. Conversely, Hachi comes to Tokyo to follow her boyfriend; when he leaves her, she tries to find another boyfriend. She idolizes the suave Takumi from afar, but her dreams of him cannot match reality. Only after spending time with Nana, who is driven by her dreams of success, does Hachi begin to question what, exactly, she wants in life.

The theme of female friendship may be the most important in the series. At the core of *Nana* is the friendship between the two Nanas. Despite, or perhaps because of, their differences, the two characters are incredibly close. When they are separated for long periods of time, neither can think of anything but the other. Their relationship is nonsexual: Characters joke about them sleeping together, but they both express disgust at the idea, and both are clearly more sexually interested in men. Hachi describes her feelings for Nana as more passionate than love. While their relationships with other characters change as the series progresses, the bond between the two Nanas stays strong.

Impact

Nana is part of a modern *shōjo* boom within the expanding and diversifying manga market that began in the 1990's. It has been popular among both teenage and adult female readers and has had enormous success in Japan and worldwide. Volumes have regularly appeared on manga best-seller lists and critics' lists. It has been popular enough to spawn an anime adaptation and two live-action film adaptations, all of which have been released in the United States as well.

In addition, the music from the various adaptations has proven popular. Several anime soundtracks were released, and the actors who portray Nana and Reira in the films both released singles related to the first movie; the songs debuted first and second, respectively, on the Japanese Oricon music chart. The sequel and the accompanying music releases were successful as well.

Films

Nana. Directed by Kentaro Otani. IMJ Entertainment, 2005. This film adaptation stars Mika Nakashima as Nana, Aoi Miyazaki as Hachi, and Ryuhei Matsuda as Ren. The film is largely faithful to the manga, particularly in its costuming and set design, though it compresses some scenes and removes some subplots. It ends shortly after Nana and Hachi attend the first Trapnest concert and Hachi meets Takumi, corresponding to the end of chapter 14 (volume 5).

Nana 2. Directed by Kentaro Otani. IMJ Entertainment, 2006. This film adaptation stars Nakashima as Nana, Yui Ichikawa as Hachi, and Nobuo Kyou as Ren. The sequel starts almost immediately after the first movie ends and continues through approximately volume 11 of the manga. The film focuses on Hachi and Takumi's relationship and the beginning of Blast's debut. Overall, the sequel was not as well received as the first film.

Television Series

Nana. Directed by Morio Asaka. Madhouse Studios, 2006-2007. This animated series stars Romi Park as the voice of Nana and KAORI (real name Midori Kawana) as the voice of Hachi. The television series is a faithful adaptation of the manga; there are no major changes to the story and only minor changes to dialogue. Forty-seven episodes were made, covering up to the end of chapter 42 of the manga.

Ted Anderson

Further Reading

Hernandez, Gilbert, Jaime Hernandez, and Mario Hernandez. *Love and Rockets* (1985-).

Ogawa, Yayoi. *Tramps Like Us* (2000-2005).

Umino, Chica. *Honey and Clover* (2000-2006).

Bibliography

Fujie, Kazuhisa, and Onno van't Hot. *Nana Essentials: The Ultimate Fanbook*. Tokyo: DH, 2008.

Macias, Patric. "Manga and the NANA Phenomenon." *Kateigaho: Japan's Arts and Culture*, 2006. http://nana-nana.net/news69.html.

Toku, Masami. "*Shojo* Manga! Girls' Comics! A Mirror of Girls' Dreams." *Mechademia* 2 (2007): 19-33.

See also: *Boys over Flowers*; *Mai the Psychic Girl*

Naruto

Author: Kishimoto, Masashi
Artist: Masashi Kishimoto (illustrator)
Publisher: Shūeisha (Japanese); VIZ Media (English)
First serial publication: 1999-   (English translation, 2003-   )
First book publication: 2000-   (English translation, 2003-   )

Naruto. (Courtesy of VIZ Media)

Publication History

The *Naruto* series is based on a pilot that appeared in the August, 1997, issue of *Akamaru Jump*. In 1999, *Naruto* began to be serialized in one of the most popular manga magazines in Japan, *Weekly Shōnen Jump*. Both of the magazines are published by Shūeisha. *Naruto*'s creator, Masashi Kishimoto, has remained in artistic control of *Naruto* by writing and illustrating the entire series throughout its long run. *Naruto* quickly became one of the most popular manga franchises in both Japan and the rest of the world. In the United States and Europe, the series has been published by VIZ Media in *Shonen Jump* magazine as well as in volumes since 2003.

Plot

Naruto is an action-comedy *shōnen* manga set in a fictional land that is loosely based on Japanese feudal society. As the narrative commences, Naruto is a mischievous twelve-year-old boy attending the ninja academy in the village of Konoha. He pulls many pranks to get the attention of the villagers and his teachers. Unbeknownst to Naruto, the villagers shun contact with him because the fourth Hokage (an honorary title granted to the protector of the village) sealed a nine-tailed demon fox in Naruto's body in a desperate attempt to save the village twelve years before.

When Naruto finishes his education at the ninja academy, he is teamed with Sakura, the girl he secretly loves, and his rival, Sasuke. Kakashi, the team captain, attempts to teach the young ninja that teamwork is the most important value for a ninja. As the team goes on its first missions, friendship evolves from the rivalry between Naruto and Sasuke.

The next step in Naruto's coming-of-age as a ninja is an exam to gain the higher ninja rank of Chunin. However, during the exam, one of Konoha's most dangerous enemies attacks the village and attempts to lure Sasuke to him with the promise of power. The fifth Hokage saves the village but dies in the process. While the village rebuilds, Sasuke and Naruto grow apart. Sasuke aims to kill his brother, who left the village after ostensibly killing his whole family. This quest for vengeance consumes Sasuke, and he decides to seek Orochimaru. Sakura, who is in love with Sasuke, asks Naruto to attempt to bring Sasuke back to Konoha. In a climactic battle, Naruto and Sasuke fight each other. During this fight, Naruto is overwhelmed by his inner demon and becomes much stronger. Sasuke, however, has grown as a ninja also and defeats Naruto.

Naruto returns to Konoha for a time before beginning to train with Jiraiya, an old ninja sage who has much sympathy for the young boy. After two years of training, Naruto has partially learned to use the powers of the demon within him. Once more, he sets out to find Sasuke, but his search is overshadowed by other important events.

A group of renegade ninja called the Akatsuki aims to extract all the tailed beasts, such as Naruto's demon fox, from the humans in whom they are sealed. Most of the ninja villages have possession of one or two of the tailed beasts. The Akatsuki hunt Naruto and others and engage in fierce battles with the Konoha ninja. Pain, the alleged leader of the Akatsuki, kills Jiraiya and sets out to destroy Konoha. This time, however, Naruto succeeds in defending the village and is finally recognized as a hero by his fellow villagers.

As Pain is defeated, a new enemy appears. Madara Uchiha, one of the legendary founders of Konoha, is revealed to be the real leader of the Akatsuki. This manipulative new enemy, who has lured Sasuke into the Akatsuki, aims to use the power of the tailed beasts to destroy all the ninja villages and become the new ruler of the ninja world. In the meantime, Naruto trains to become even stronger, as he will be one of the most important factors in deciding the outcome of the coming ninja war.

Volumes

- *Naruto: The Tests of the Ninja* (2003). Collects chapters 1-7. Naruto attempts to graduate from the ninja academy.
- *Naruto: The Worst Client* (2003). Collects chapters 8-17. Naruto goes on his first important mission with his teammates, Sasuke and Sakura, and captain, Kakashi.
- *Naruto: Bridge of Courage* (2004). Collects chapters 18-27. The mission becomes difficult and dangerous after an encounter with the rogue ninja Zabuza.
- *Naruto: The Next Level* (2004). Collects chapters 28-36. The fight with Zabuza comes to a conclu-

sion. Upon returning to Konoha, the team meets young ninja from the sand country.
- *Naruto: Challengers* (2004). Collects chapters 37-45. A new story arc in which Naruto, Sasuke, and Sakura take an exam to become higher-ranked ninja begins.
- *Naruto: The Forest of Death* (2005). Collects chapters 46-54. The first phase of the exam begins.
- *Naruto: Orochimaru's Curse* (2005). Collects chapters 55-63. During the exam, Sasuke is marked with a curse by one of Konoha's archenemies, Orochimaru.
- *Naruto: Life-and-Death Battles* (2005). Collects chapters 63-72. The exam's second phase begins. In a series of one-on-one battles, Sasuke is more and more affected by the curse mark.
- *Naruto: Turning the Tables* (2006). Collects chapters 73-81. The preliminary matches continue.
- *Naruto: A Splendid Ninja* (2006). Collects chapters 82-90. Gaara from the village of the sand brutally injures Konoha's Lee in a preliminary match.
- *Naruto: Impassioned Efforts* (2006). Collects chapters 91-99. While Naruto trains for the final stage of the exam, the other villages in the world seem to scheme against Konoha.
- *Naruto: The Great Fight* (2006). Collects chapters 100-108. Naruto fights and defeats Neji.
- *Naruto: The Chunin Exam, Concluded!* (2007). Collects chapters 109-117. While Sasuke fights Gaara in the last matchup of the exam, it is revealed that Gaara harbors a demonic "tailed beast" just like Naruto.
- *Naruto: Hokage vs. Hokage!* (2007). Collects chapters 118-126. Orochimaru attempts to destroy Konoha.
- *Naruto: Naruto's Ninja Handbook* (2007). Collects chapters 127-135. During the confusion of Orochimaru's attack, Naruto faces off with Gaara.
- *Naruto: Eulogy* (2007). Collects chapters 136-144. While the village recuperates from the at-

tack and mourns its deceased leader, new enemies encroach on the village.

- *Naruto: Itachi's Power* (2007). Collects chapters 145-153. Sasuke's older brother comes to Konoha to search for Naruto. Aspects of Konoha's past and Naruto's destiny are unveiled.
- *Naruto: Tsunade's Choice* (2007). Collects chapters 154-162. Naruto trains with Jiraiya and meets Tsunade, Jiraiya's old teammate.
- *Naruto: Successor* (2007). Collects chapters 163-171. Jiraiya, Tsunade, and Naruto battle Orochimaru. When the battle concludes, Tsunade decides to accept the invitation to become Konoha's new leader.
- *Naruto: Naruto vs. Sasuke* (2007). Collects chapters 172-180. Naruto and Sasuke grow apart.
- *Naruto: Pursuit* (2007). Collects chapters 181-190. As Sasuke seeks Orochimaru in his pursuit of power, Naruto attempts to stop him.
- *Naruto: Comrades* (2007). Collects chapters 191-199. While the young ninja from Konoha follow Sasuke, they must battle Orochimaru's henchmen.
- *Naruto: Predicament* (2007). Collects chapters 200-208. Naruto fights Kimimaro.
- *Naruto: Unorthodox* (2007). Collects chapters 209-217. Gaara and his team come to the aid of Naruto and his friends.
- *Naruto: Brothers* (2007). Collects chapters 218-226. Naruto and Sasuke fight.
- *Naruto: Awakening* (2007). Collects chapters 227-235. During the fight, Naruto's inner demon grants him strength, but there may be a cost. Sasuke awakens the next level of his ocular power, the Sharingan.
- *Naruto: Departure* (2007). Collects chapters 236-244. Naruto fails in his attempt to prevent Sasuke from going to Orochimaru and returns to Konoha disillusioned. Shortly after, Naruto, Sasuke, and Sakura depart to train with their respective teachers.
- *Naruto: Homecoming* (2008). Collects chapters 245-253. After two years of training with Jiraiya, Naruto returns to Konoha. This volume begins

the second part of the *Naruto* series, known as *Naruto Shippuden*.

- *Naruto: Kakashi vs. Itachi* (2008). Collects chapters 254-262. As Kakashi fights Itachi, Naruto finds out more about a new enemy: the Akatsuki.
- *Naruto: Puppet Masters* (2008). Collects chapters 263-271. Sakura helps Naruto by fighting Sasori, an Akatsuki member seeking to capture Naruto and extract the demon fox.
- *Naruto: Final Battle* (2008). Collects chapters 272-280. Naruto and other Konoha ninja fight a dangerous battle with Akatsuki members.
- *Naruto: The Search for Sasuke* (2008). Collects chapters 281-289. The search for Sasuke continues.
- *Naruto: The Secret Mission* (2008). Collects chapters 290-299. Naruto loses control of his inner demon and, in the process, himself. Enraged, the demon fox turns on Naruto's teammates.
- *Naruto: The Reunion* (2009). Collects chapters 300-309. Sasuke is found, but he still does not want to return to Konoha.
- *Naruto: The New Two* (2009). Collects chapters 310-319. The Akatsuki hunt the ninja in whom tailed beasts are sealed, while Naruto intensifies his training.
- *Naruto: Cell Number 10* (2009). Collects chapters 320-329. Naruto's friends Shikamaru, Choji, and Ino fight the dangerous Akatsuki member Hidan.
- *Naruto: Shikamaru's Battle* (2009). Collects chapters 330-339. In the battle against Hidan, Shikamaru's teacher is murdered. Shikamaru has his revenge.
- *Naruto: Practice Makes Perfect* (2009). Collects chapters 340-349. Naruto and Sasuke continue to grow apart, and the friendship between the two seems to be lost forever.
- *Naruto: On the Move* (2009). Collects chapters 350-359. Sasuke defeats Orochimaru and forms a ninja team.
- *Naruto: The Ultimate Art* (2009). Collects chapters 360-369. Sasuke encounters Deidera, an Akatsuki member, and does battle with him in an

attempt to find out more about his brother's whereabouts.

- *Naruto: Jiraiya's Decision* (2009). Collects chapters 370-379. Jiraiya's experiences as a young ninja are revealed.
- *Naruto: The Secret of the Mangekyo* (2009). Collects chapters 380-389. Jiraiya is killed while spying on Pain. Sasuke gets closer to his brother.
- *Naruto: The Man with the Truth* (2009). Collects chapters 390-402. Sasuke fights his brother. During the fight, secrets of the past are revealed.
- *Naruto: Senjutsu Heir* (2009). Collects chapters 403-412. Naruto aims to find out more about Pain by looking at his master's last words to him.
- *Naruto: Battlefield, Konoha* (2009). Collects chapters 413-422. Pain launches an attack on Konoha while Naruto is away training to become a ninja sage.
- *Naruto: Naruto Returns* (2009). Collects chapters 423-432. Naruto returns from his training stronger than ever and fights Pain.
- *Naruto: The Seal Destroyed* (2010). Collects chapters 433-442. During his fight with Pain, Naruto temporarily loses control over his inner demon.
- *Naruto: The Cheering Village* (2010). Collects chapters 443-453. Naruto convinces Pain to stop attacking Konoha and undo the damage he has done. Because of this victory, Naruto is finally seen as the village hero.
- *Naruto: The Gokage Summit Commences* (2010). Collects chapters 454-463. The Akatsuki's real leader, Madara Uchiha, reveals himself in the meeting of the five Hokages. As a result of the plan Madara reveals, the ninja villages decide to join forces and declare war on the Akatsuki.
- *Naruto: Water Prison Death Match* (2011). Collects chapters 464-473. Another tailed beast fights with one of the members of the Akatsuki and defeats him.
- *Naruto: Sasuke vs. Danzo!* (2011). Collects chapters 474-483. Sasuke seeks out and fights Konoha's temporary Hokage, Danzo.
- *Naruto: Cell Seven Reunion* (2011). Collects chapters 484-494. Naruto arrives near the end of the battle between Danzo and Sasuke.

- *Naruto: The Birth of Naruto* (2011). Collects chapters 495-504. As Naruto starts training to be able to control the demon fox inside him, he meets his mother and finds out about his birth.
- *Naruto: Viaduct to Peace* (2012). Collects chapters 505-514. As both factions prepare for the inevitable war, fighting breaks out all over the continent.
- *Naruto: The Great War, Outbreak* (2012). Collects chapters 515-524. The great war between the ninja villages and the Akatsuki begins.

Characters

- *Naruto Uzumaki*, the protagonist, is a young boy with blond hair. He is cheerful, loyal to his village and friends, and determined. He hopes to end hatred in a world in which ninja from different villages constantly battle. His childishness is also the source of his greatest strength: His unfaltering resolve to end the hatred between ninja might open a path to a new future.

Masashi Kishimoto

Masashi Kishimoto, born in 1974, is the creator of the massive hit *Naruto*, a ninja manga, which has been serialized in *Weekly Shōnen Jump* since 1999. Kishimoto has said that an underwhelming childhood helped him understand the "underdog" status of the central character he created for *Naruto*. He did a few short mangas in advance of *Naruto*, but since then, he has rarely taken a break. In 2010, he did a one-shot, special-occasion baseball manga titled *Bench*. He has referenced Akira Toriyama as the manga creator whose work first inspired him to draw manga and lists Katsuhiro Otomo's *Akira* as his favorite movie. Among his former assistants is Osamu Kajisa, who had some success with the manga *Tattoo Hearts*. Kishimoto is the twin brother of manga creator Seishi Kishimoto, best known for the series *0-Parts Hunter* (a.k.a. "666 Satan").

- *Sasuke Uchiha*, an antagonist, is a dark-haired boy who is lonely despite his extreme popularity. He craves revenge for the murder of his parents. Even after he kills his brother, the person responsible, his lust for revenge does not falter. Thus, he can easily be used by those who mean ill, and he becomes increasingly evil.
- *Sakura Haruno* is a pretty, free-spirited girl. She is in love with Sasuke, while Naruto is secretly in love with her. After Sasuke leaves Konoha, Sakura asks Naruto to bring him back.
- *Kakashi Hatake* is the captain of the team in which Naruto, Sakura, and Sasuke begin as ninja. He is a quiet and reserved man who believes that teamwork is the cornerstone of the ninja existence.
- *Orochimaru*, an antagonist, is the evil mastermind behind the first large attack on Konoha. His appearance resembles that of a snake. After being expelled from Konoha for conducting illegal experiments concerning forbidden ninja powers, he gathers allies in preparation for his revenge.
- *Jiraiya* is an awkward-looking man with white hair who becomes Naruto's trainer and mentor. Despite his looks and behavior, he is a great ninja who has tried to do nothing but good. After training Naruto, he is killed while on a spying mission.
- *Tsunade* is a beautiful woman who becomes Konoha's new Hokage halfway through the series. She is sometimes quick to anger but has learned not to act rashly when this might harm the village.
- *Madara Uchiha*, an antagonist, is a mysterious man who keeps his face hidden behind a mask. He persuades Sasuke to fight at his side during his war against the ninja villages. His aim is to use the tailed beasts to unlock a new ninja power with which he can rule the world.

Artistic Style

Because of both the length of the *Naruto* series and the fact that he is the only artist working on it, Kishimoto

Naruto. (Courtesy of VIZ Media)

has not produced many other series. The style of *Naruto* is less convoluted and more stylized that that of Kishimoto's first manga, *Karakuri* (1998). This transition to a more open style can also be witnessed in *Naruto*, as the illustrations have become less dense as the series has progressed.

Kishimoto deploys an artistic style akin to that of the other *shōnen* manga published in *Weekly Shōnen Jump*, such as *Bleach* (2001-). Speed and pacing are of the utmost importance for *shōnen* manga, and Kishimoto masterfully composes pages and frames that facilitate the fast reading to which *shōnen* manga readers are accustomed. The fight scenes are exciting because of Kishimoto's ability to render powerful movements in the stable images that compose the manga. He finds ways to deliver an action-packed reading experience with relatively calm and open pages, and the simplicity and clarity of the images can even be said to be constituents of the action-packed reading experience. Kishimoto often uses clear white backgrounds in his frames, and these frames are mostly surrounded and divided by white gutters. An exception to this style is when Kishimoto illustrates the numerous flashbacks in the narrative. To underscore the temporal difference between a flashback and the present narrative, Kishimoto sets frames that represent flashbacks against black backgrounds instead of white ones. Only in the comical scenes does the tone of the illustrations change significantly, with the style becoming less realistic and more cartoonish.

Themes

A coming-of-age story about an orphan, *Naruto* is an optimistic tale in spite of the adversities the protagonist encounters. Naruto's optimism, which might sometimes be mistaken for naïveté, is pitted against Sasuke's grief and hunger for revenge and the ninja world's distrust and hatred. Both Sasuke and Naruto are outsiders without families in the pleasant village of Konoha, and as they come of age as ninja, they deal with the pains of their youth differently. While Sasuke becomes strong to avenge his parents, Naruto chooses to become strong so that he can protect the villagers and be recognized as one of them.

Within the coming-of-age framework, the importance of friendship and family is constantly underlined. Sasuke is Naruto's first friend, and for this reason, Naruto does not want to give up on him even though he has done horrible things. In the course of the narrative, however, Naruto makes new friends and becomes a respected member of the village community. Naruto's strength grows as he gains more loved ones to protect, while Sasuke remains alone and is increasingly absorbed by his quest for revenge.

As the plot unfolds, it becomes clear that the tragic relationship between Naruto and Sasuke, and their respective clans, goes far back into history. The fight between the avenger and the protector has taken place countless times. Nonetheless, Naruto remains optimistic and believes that he might have the power to change the ninja world and rid it of its hate.

Impact

Read by millions of people in Japan, the United States, and elsewhere, *Naruto* is one of the most popular *shōnen* manga series in the world. As a typical example of a *shōnen* action manga, *Naruto* does not deviate much from the standard format of action-packed chapters accompanied by a somewhat flat cast of characters. Because of its popularity, however, Naruto can also be said to dictate the format of the *shōnen* action manga genre as much as it has borrowed from it.

Despite its enormous popularity, *Naruto* has not received much critical attention from Western scholars. Reasons for the lack of critical attention are its enormous popularity and its lack of innovation. However, an entire panel of the Cologne conference organized by the International Manga Research Center from the Kyoto Seika University was devoted to the *Naruto* franchise.

Films

Naruto the Movie: Ninja Clash in the Land of Snow. Directed by Tensai Okamura. Studio Pierrot, 2004. This animated film and the subsequent films follow original story lines not based on the manga.

Naruto the Movie 2: Legend of the Stone Gelel. Directed by Hirosugu Kawasaki. Studio Pierrot, 2006.

Naruto the Movie 3: Guardians of the Crescent Moon Kingdom. Directed by Toshiyuki Tsuru. Studio Pierrot, 2006.

Naruto Shippuden: The Movie. Directed by Hajime Kamegaki. Studio Pierrot, 2007.

Naruto Shippuden 2: Bonds. Directed by Masahiko Murata. Studio Pierrot, 2008.

Naruto Shippuden 3: Inheritors of the Will of Fire. Directed by Murata. Studio Pierrot, 2009.

Naruto Shippuden 4: The Lost Tower. Directed by Murata. Studio Pierrot, 2010.

Naruto Shippuden 5: Blood Prison. Directed by Murata. Studio Pierrot, 2011.

Television Series

Naruto. Directed by Hayato Date. Studio Pierrot, 2002-2007. This anime follows the plot of the manga with the exception of a number of "filler episodes," which feature stand-alone stories that do not influence the true plot of the manga.

Naruto: Shippuden. Directed by Date. Studio Pierrot, 2007- . This anime follows the second phase of the manga, in which Naruto has become an adolescent.

Rik Spanjers

Further Reading

Kubo, Noriaki. *Bleach* (2001-).
Mashima, Hiro. *Fairy Tail* (2006-).
Oda, Eiichiro. *One Piece* (2003-).

Bibliography

Born, Christopher E. "In the Footsteps of the Master: Confucian Values in Anime and Manga." ASIANetwork *Exchange* 17, no. 1 (Fall, 2009): 39-53.

Brenner, Robin E. *Understanding Manga and Anime*. Westport, Conn.: Libraries Unlimited, 2007.

Kishimoto, Masashi. *The Art of Naruto: Uzumaki*. San Francisco: VIZ Media, 2007.

Rubin, Lawrence. "Big Heroes on the Small Screen: Naruto and the Struggle Within." In *Popular Culture in Counseling, Psychotherapy, and Play-Based Interventions*. New York: Springer, 2008.

See also: *One Piece*; *Bleach*; *Dragon Ball*

NAUSICAÄ OF THE VALLEY OF THE WIND

Author: Miyazaki, Hayao

Artist: Hayao Miyazaki (illustrator);
   Walden Wong (letterer)

Publisher: Tokuma Shoten (Japanese); VIZ Media
   (English)

First serial publication: *Kaze no tani no Naushika*,
   1982-1994 (English translation, 1988-1996)

First book publication: 1982-1995 (English translation, 1990-1997)

Publication History

Hayao Miyazaki spent almost thirteen years on the
Nausicaä of the Valley of the Wind series, which was
first published by Tokuma Shoten in monthly installments in Japan's *Animage* magazine beginning in
1982. The broad appeal of the film based on the manga
led to the establishment of a new animation studio,
Studio Ghibli, which Miyazaki founded with Isao
Takahata.

Miyazaki had been fascinated for many years by the
Nausicaä character in Greek mythology. Nausicaä was
the daughter of the Phaeacian king Alcinoös and Queen
Arete from Homer's *Odyssey*. Nausicaä comforts Odysseus when he shows up nearly drowned on the shore
of her island after he is shipwrecked by Poseidon.
When Miyazaki read the description of Nausicaä in a
Japanese translation of a reference work on Greek mythology, he was captivated by the heroine's qualities:
She is beautiful, sensitive, attuned to animals and the
natural world, quick on her feet, and loves playing her
harp and singing more than she likes seeking attention
from boys. She composes a song specifically for Odysseus when he departs. She occupies a special place in
the heart of the great voyager even after he returns
home to Ithaca and his wife Penelope. While her father
offers Nausicaä's hand in marriage to Odysseus if he
would stay in Phaeacia, Nausicaä never marries but
travels from court to court as the first female minstrel,
singing songs about the Trojan War.

The character of Nausicaä reminded Miyazaki of a
Japanese heroine from the Heian era called "the princess who loved insects." She was considered an eccen-

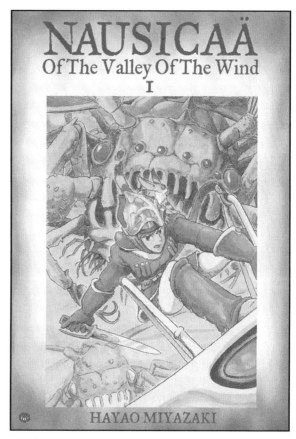

Nausicaä. (Courtesy of VIZ Media)

tric in the formal, aristocratic world of ninth century
Japan. She did not dye her teeth black, shave off her
eyebrows, or stay indoors, as was the custom.

Plot

On the simplest level, *Nausicaä of the Valley of the
Wind* is about the invasion of the kingdom of Dorok by
the kingdom of Torumekia. With its military background, the story resembles Homer's *Iliad*, the ancient
Greek epic about the Trojan War.

The story begins one thousand years after a massive
conflagration called the Seven Days of Fire, during
which the God Soldiers annihilated the human population and pollution destroyed the natural environment. A
highly complex, industrial civilization had spread from

Western Eurasia to cover the planet. As Earth became increasingly polluted, huge cities began to deteriorate, expelling clouds of toxic smoke into the air and spewing waste and chemical contaminants in every direction. High technology and urban infrastructure collapsed, and Earth was transformed into a wasteland covered by the Sea of Corruption, a mysterious toxic soup made of fumes, fungi, spores, and giant plants, constantly growing and changing shape. It was populated by giant insects, including the fourteen-eyed caterpillar-like Ohmu and other mutated species. Surviving humans fought over the small patches of inhabitable land remaining around the fringes of the Sea of Corruption.

Nausicaä is a skilled fighter, but she hates to kill sentient creatures and is attuned to the needs of people and even ugly insects. Her primary challenge is to solve the mystery of the Sea of Corruption and to lead her kingdom toward the "Pure Blue Land," where people might live free from war and pollution.

Nausicaä is the daughter of King Jhil, leader of a 500 person kingdom called the Valley of the Wind, located on the edge of the frontier. The Valley of the Wind is constantly buffeted by the Sea of Corruption. Two powerful nations, the Kingdom of Torumekia and the Dorok Empire, are about to go to war. The Valley of the Wind has managed to remain independent. Both Pejite City and the Valley of the Wind are allies of Torumekia. King Jhil dies as a result of inhaling the contaminated air, prompting Nausicaä and her soldiers to join the Torumekians, as the two groups are obligated by an ancient treaty to help each other. Jhil had hoped for a son as his heir because there was no record of a woman ever becoming chieftain.

One day, Nausicaä sees a discarded shell of an Ohmu in the jungle, and she speculates on how the insects survived in such a hostile environment. Nausicaä saves Master Yupa from an approaching Ohmu. Her former teacher marvels at what a skilled rider she has become. Like Nausicaä, Yupa wants to solve the mystery of the Sea of Corruption and figure out a way for civilization to survive. According to a prophecy, a person wearing blue and standing in a golden field would heal the bond between humans and Earth and save the world.

Back at the castle of the Valley of the Wind, Uncle Mito helps Nausicaä get her gunship ready to fly. Mito and Nausicaä travel to Pejite City, where they find corpses and devastation because the kingdom has been covered by the Sea of Corruption. Prince Rastel gives Nausicaä a secret stone for safekeeping and tells her that the emperor of Torumekia must never have it.

Torumekian soldiers invade the Valley of the Wind, searching for the stone that is the key to awakening one of the Giant Soldiers that destroyed the world one thousand years ago. Kushana, the Princess of Torumekia, attempts to get the Torumekian throne by reviving the Giant Soldier with the help of the secret stone. Princess Kushana and her nefarious chief of staff, Kurotowa, attempt to enslave the citizens of the Valley of the Wind in their quest to conquer the kingdom of Dorok and subdue the Sea of Corruption.

Nausicaä engages in several battles on the Torumekian side, but her gunship is brought down by Asbel, the last survivor of Pejite City, who despises Kushana and all Torumekians. Nausicaä rescues Asbel from an attack of the giant insects, and they escape together; however, they are taken prisoner by warriors of the Dorok Empire. The Dorok Empire is a theocracy ruled by two monks, Miralupa and Namulis, the sons of the First Holy Emperor.

Nausicaä escapes again and travels south because the Ohmu are stampeding in a *daikaisho*, or tidal wave, and she needs to determine the reason. Nausicaä lands in a small lake and meets The Holy One of Mani, a monk who believes that the Seven Days of Fire are inspired by some divine force. The Holy One thinks that Nausicaä might be the fabled savior in blue.

Nausicaä discovers that the Dorok ships are emitting toxins released by a mutant fungus engineered to control the Sea of Corruption. The Dorokians are attempting to use the poison fungus to gain the upper hand in the war with Torumekia. Charuka, the commander of the Dorokian army, tries to destroy his battleship because he can no longer control the fungus. Charuka gives up trying to employ this ultimate weapon when he realizes the fungus would kill everyone's soldiers. Charuka is persuaded that Nausicaä is not the enemy, and she helps him to rescue his soldiers. The mutant fungus keeps growing and expanding;

Nausicaä worries that Earth is nearing total devastation. She wonders if the destruction might signal a new birth and purification through death.

Nausicaä starts a quest to find the Crypts of Shuwa to unlock the secret of the fungus and the Sea of Corruption. She wants to seal the doors for eternity to stop future war and destruction. She enlists the help of the revived God Warrior, whom she names "Ohma." Ohma thinks Nausicaä is his mother. The God Warrior gives off a poisonous light that kills everything in its path, and he begins to assume the role of dispenser of justice. Nausicaä, Yupa, and Ohma race to the Crypts of Shuwa against King Vu of Torumekia and his armies.

Meanwhile, the Dorok Council of Priests starts several stampedes of giant forest insects in an attempt to defeat Torumekia through their genetically engineered strain of forest mold. Yupa dies in a battle between the clashing armies. Nausicaä learns from the Master of the Garden that at the time of Earth's destruction, a group of scientists engineered human beings, plants, and creatures such as the Ohmu and Heedra in a desperate plan to survive. The Sea of Corruption is actually attempting to resuscitate a barren Earth. The deadly gases and spores are the forest's attempt to cleanse Earth of its toxins and to recreate a new pure planet.

The story ends with the death of the Torumekian King Vu, but Princess Kushana refuses to assume the throne. Nausicaä lives with the Dorok people and does not return to the Valley of the Wind. Many see Nausicaä as the fulfillment of the prophecy about a person dressed in blue standing in a golden field who saved the world.

Volumes
- *Kaze no tani no Naushika, 1* (1982). This tells the beginning of the story of the Valley of the Wind and Nausicaä's relationship with Jhil.
- *Kaze no tani no Naushika, 2* (1983). Features the death of Jhil and Nausicaä's learning about the Torumekians and Kushana.
- *Kaze no tani no Naushika, 3* (1984). Highlights rising tides of battle between Dorok and Torumekia, with Nausicaä finding ways she can help Kushana.

- *Kaze no tani no Naushika, 4* (1987). Features much political intrigue within Torumekia about succession and rule.
- *Kaze no tani no Naushika, 5* (1991). Nausicaä meets the "Holy One of Mani," who gives her a new idea about the state of the world and how it might revive itself.
- *Kaze no tani no Naushika, 6* (1993). Nausicaä continues her search for the purpose of the Sea of Corruption.
- *Kaze no tani no Naushika, 7* (1995). Yupa dies in battle. The revived God Soldier begins his work to end the war. At the end of the story, King Vu is killed, and Nausicaä goes to live with the Dorok people.

Characters
- *Nausicaä*, the protagonist, is the daughter of King Jhil, the leader of a small fiefdom called the Valley of the Wind. She flies around on a glider with a jet engine to survey the conditions of the environment, people, and insects. She tries to solve the mystery of the Sea of Corruption by learning from the giant insects, including the Ohmu.
- *King Jhil*, the king of the Valley of the Wind. He succumbs to poisonous gases and dies in bed after a final conversation with his daughter and Yupa, his closest adviser. He worries that no woman has ever become monarch and does not know if Nausicaä is up to the task.
- *Master Yupa*, Nausicaä's instructor and the confidante of Jhil. He is regarded as the most skilled warrior in the Valley of the Wind, able to handle all kinds of combat with short and long swords and daggers. Like Nausicaä, he is on a mission to discover the secret of the Sea of Corruption.
- *Mito* is the most important of the castle guards and is the field marshal for the Valley of the Wind army. He is the copilot of the Valley of the Wind gunship and loyal to Nausicaä.
- *Kushana* is the fourth princess of Torumekia. She is the only princess of Torumekia who is biologically related to King Vu, and she quarrels with her brothers and father about proper rule and suc-

cession. She is emotionally fragile but a gifted military leader. She asks for Nausicaä's help in the war against Dorok.

- *Kurotawa* is Kushana's chief of staff. He is not related to the royal family and has a secret mision given to him by King Vu. He provides offbeat comments and comic quips during moments of tension, and he is weaker by nature than Kushana.
- *King Vu* is the evil king of Torumekia who desires to conquer the world and destroy Dorok. He dies at the end of the story and attempts to give the throne to Kushana, who will not accept it because of her father's corruption.
- *Namulis* is the purported emperor of Dorok and the older brother of Miralupa. He desires to conquer the world by harnessing the powers of the Giant Soldier and the Heedra monsters, but he lacks any psychic ability and has been a prisoner in his own palace for one hundred years. He loses ruling power to his brother.
- *Miralupa* is Namulis's younger brother and the actual ruler of the Dorok Empire. He has strong psychic powers and is feared by the people, who think he is merciless and bloodthirsty.
- *Charuka* is the commander of the Dorokian army and leader of Dorok's religious practices. He was an adviser to the power-hungry Miralupa, but after Nausicaä saved him, he changed his mind about her and helped her to save his people and to solve the mystery of the fungus.

Artistic Style

Miyazaki's artistry is unmistakable. *Nausicaä*'s seven volumes show Miyazaki's trademark style: epic storytelling, detailed facial expressions, and dynamic transitions between cells. Many great battle scenes, aerial combat maneuvers, flyovers, and interactions among mysterious animals and people highlight the central narrative of Nausicaä's quest to solve the riddle of the Sea of Corruption.

Miyazaki employs movement, subtle shading, and careful character development through close-ups on individual faces. There is no color, just the aesthetically simple Japanese pen-and-ink style, with its precise modeling and subtle shading of faces, landscapes, cas-

---

Hayao Miyazaki

Hayao Miyazaki, born in 1941, is among Japan's most celebrated artists, a reputation that took on global proportions when his film *Spirited Away* won the Academy Award for Best Animated Feature in 2003. Miyazaki got his start in Japanese television. In 1984, he directed a full-length adaptation of his own manga serial *Nausicaä*, widely considered to be his greatest work. The next year he founded Studio Ghibli, initiating an ongoing series of animated tales rich with fantastic creatures, ambiguous threats, and magical transformations. "When I talk about traditions, I'm not talking about temples, which we got from China anyway," he told the *New York Times*. "There is an indigenous Japan, and elements of that are what I'm trying to capture in my work" (Scott). Key among Miyazaki's works are *My Neighbor Totoro*, *Kiki's Delivery Service*, and *Princess Mononoke*. His father manufactured airplane parts, and he studied political science and economics in college.

---

tles, and battle scenes. Over the length of the series, major characters such as King Vu of Torumekia and Charuka of Dorok gradually reveal their qualities of either hidden evil or benign intentions that are capable of change.

Arguably the greatest artistic accomplishment of the *Nausicaä* series is the revived God Warrior, whom Nausicaä names Ohma. Once part of an invincible force of destructive giants engineered to destroy the world, Ohma emerges from the pages as still formidable, mysterious, huge, but also curiously sensitive and shy, like a wounded child whom Nausicaä takes under her wing to comfort and transform into an agent of justice.

All of Miyazaki's skills are employed in the development of Nausicaä, one of the first great female action heroes of the manga genre. A highlight of the artistic style is the detailed backgrounds. Miyazaki handles deftly the depiction of the degraded natural world of the postapocalypse and the hope for some future solution. The empires of Dorok and Torumekia and the small community of the Valley of the Wind are skill-fully contrasted through panoramic scenes and smaller portraits of lesser citizens. Miyazaki adds depth to the cultural differences between Torumekia and Dorok in the way he illustrates the major characters: the milita-ristic castles and large armies of Torumekia versus the individual tribes and mystical religious practices of the monks who rule over Dorok. Not to be overlooked is the style Miyazaki uses in creating the ominous Sea of Corruption, a stew of poisonous gasses and effluents, and the bizarre assortment of creatures that live in it, such as the Ohmu, the worm handlers, and the forest people.

Themes

Nausicaä of the Valley of the Wind con-cerns the inevitable follies that come from one person trying to control others, which are compounded in a world that verges on environmental destruction. Miyazaki writes about the outcomes of war, good and evil, and the loss of a clear distinction between the two. Dorok did not incite the invasion by Torumekia, but ethically its counterattack is no better than the action of the aggressors.

Set against the worst possible back-ground of political scheming, Nausicaä dis-plays the best qualities of human nature. She is self-confident, proud, and a good leader, and she cares deeply for the de-caying world. She carries on the legacies of her father, King Jhil, and her teacher, Master Yupa, as she finds out the true reasons be-hind Torumekian aggression.

Earth has become an impossibly pol-luted and corrupt place, yet *Nausicaä of the Valley of the Wind* holds out hope for the human race. Though in general the leaders are driven by a quest for power and the societies are rife with politics, there are people who will aid one another unconditionally and look for solutions to end senseless violence. The fact that Earth is resilient and able to withstand the

most horrific mutant life-forms and biological warfare is evidence that Miyazaki aims for a message of hope.

Nausicaä shows all of the best attributes of the Heian character known as "the princess who loved insects." She refused to follow conventions and re-mains true to her ethics of integrity and respect for all living things, even those defaced and malformed through human bioengineering. Nausicaä earns the trust of everyone she meets, orchestrates an end to the war, and fulfills the prophecy about the person dressed in blue who would be the savior of the world.

Nausicaä. (Courtesy of VIZ Media)

Impact

The film based on Miyazaki's manga series *Nausicaä of the Valley of the Wind* routinely shows up in lists of the ten best animated films of all time, so it is not surprising that the graphic novel series is regarded as a classic. Miyazaki worked on the series for almost ten years after the film was released, enriching and deepening the mythology of the characters. *Nausicaä* made a tremendous impact on the reading public because Miyazaki showed the length and depth to which he could develop an important female hero against the backdrop of global catastrophe and war.

The sales of the manga generated so much interest in the film that Miyazaki knew the story needed to go deeper. There are many characters in the manga, such as Namulis, Miralupa, and Charuka, that never made it into the film. The story is so complex that it comes close to collapsing under its own weight, yet the Nausicaä character provides the resiliency and warmth that carries reader's interest and keeps the story moving toward its conclusion. Miyazaki demonstrated how much emotional depth and variety a manga series was capable of supporting, and the finished work is breathtaking in its scope. This long-running series captured the imagination of readers worldwide. The *Nausicaä* series sold more than ten million books in Japan alone and became one of the most admired manga fantasy stories of all time.

Films

Nausicaä of the Valley of the Wind. Directed by Hayao Miyazaki. Topcraft, 1984. The film was made because of the success of the manga. Its popular acclaim and high ticket sales led to the establishment of Studio Ghibli, for which Miyazaki directed five feature-length films and produced another three films in the years between 1986 and 1997. Many of Miyazaki's adaptations produced box-office success and critical accolades.

Jonathan Thorndike

Further Reading

Nakazawa, Keiji. *Barefoot Gen: A Cartoon of Hiroshima* (2004).

Otomo, Katsuhiro. *Akira* (2000).

Samura, Hiroaki. *Blade of the Immortal* (1995).

Bibliography

Drazen, Patrick. *Anime Explosion! The What? Why? and Wow! of Japanese Animation.* Berkeley, Calif.: Stone Bridge Press, 2002.

McCarthy, Helen. *Hayao Miyazaki: Master of Japanese Animation.* Berkeley, Calif.: Stone Bridge Press, 2002.

Napier, Susan J. *Anime from "Akira" to "Howl's Moving Castle": Experiencing Contemporary Japanese Animation.* New York: Macmillan, 2005.

Scott, A.O. "Where the Wild Things Are: The Miyazaki Menagerie." *The New York Times*, June 12, 2005.

See also: *Barefoot Gen*; *Akira*; *Blade of the Immortal*

O

ODE TO KIRIHITO

Author: Tezuka, Osamu
Artist: Osamu Tezuka (illustrator)
Publisher: Shogakukan (Japanese); Vertical (English)
First serial publication: *Kirihito sanka*, 1970-1971
First book publication: 1972 (English translation, 2006)

Publication History

Ode to Kirihito was serialized in the *seinen* manga magazine *Big Comic*, published by Shogakukan, from 1970 to 1971. The work was later collected and published in several different Japanese editions. In 2006, North American publisher Vertical made this classic manga available to Western audiences in a single-volume paperback edition. Vertical reprinted *Ode to Kirihito* in two paperback volumes in 2010.

Plot

The doctors of M University Hospital are baffled by a disease they have not encountered before. The proud and important Dr. Tatsugaura believes that this strange disease, which is known as Monmow and changes normal men and women into doglike creatures, is viral. The young and talented Dr. Kirihito Osanai, however, believes the disease to be endemic. After some arguments, Tatsugaura asks Kirihito to go to the rural village Doggoddale, where the disease originated, to gather more information. Even though Kirihito's fiancé, Izumi, protests, Kirihito decides to go.

After some time in the village, Kirihito is stricken with the Monmow disease. Tazu, a woman from the village, takes care of Kirihito when he goes through the first agonizing phase of the disease. Tazu and Kirihito grow increasingly close and decide to leave the village together. However, while traveling, Tazu is raped and killed. Kirihito wanders Japan, but his appearance shocks people wherever he goes. He is eventually cap-

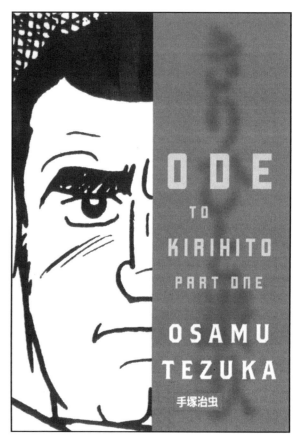

Ode to Kirihito. (Courtesy of Vertical)

tured and shipped to China, where he is forced to perform in a freak show.

Meanwhile, the people whom Kirihito left behind go on their own adventures. In shock because of her fiancé's sudden disappearance, Izumi sets out to gather information about what happened to Kirihito. Dr. Urabe, one of Kirihito's colleagues, helps her in her search. Urabe, however, has his own agenda as well as an unstable mental constitution. He is torn between his allegiance to Tatsugaura, who promises him an important career in medicine, and his desire to find out the truth about what happened to Kirihito.

Urabe travels to South Africa to present Tatsugaura's paper on the viral causes of Monmow disease. While there, he discovers that Tatsugaura sent Kirihito to Doggoddale as a human test subject. Before he can present his findings to the medical association in Japan, however, Urabe loses his mind because of his lust for both Izumi and a German nun who has contracted Monmow disease. In a state of crisis, Urabe is hit by a car and dies.

Kirihito escapes from the freak show and attempts to travel back to Japan via Taiwan, but because of his appearance, he is shunned and unable to travel freely. Then, he is abducted again and transported to the Middle East. He finds a place for himself as a respected doctor in a small village of refugees. However, he still wants to confront Tatsugaura because he believes more strongly than ever in his initial diagnosis of Monmow as an endemic disease.

Tatsugaura aims to become the president of the Japan Medical Association. His published paper on the viral causes of Monmow disease is of the utmost importance to the upcoming election, and he fears that if his thesis concerning the viral cause of the disease is invalidated, he will lose. For this reason, he tries to silence Urabe and Kirihito. His plans come to fruition, and he attains the position for which he has been striving.

Kirihito returns to Japan to present at the Japan Medical Association presidential election ceremony. He explains his findings concerning the endemic causes of Monmow and also reveals Tatsugaura's unethical behavior and research practices to the medical community. His audience, however, is not directly persuaded.

Kirihito finally finds Tatsugaura and has a heated discussion with him about the causes of Monmow. By this time, however, Tatsugaura has also been struck with the disease. As the two doctors argue, a television airs a report about a paper on Monmow published by a respected German doctor; the doctor's thesis confirms Kirihito's findings.

Tatsugaura does not change his initial diagnosis of Monmow even on his deathbed, but Kirihito is satis-fied. Even though Kirihito again becomes a respected doctor in Japan, he decides to return to the village in the Middle East where he was first accepted despite his looks. Izumi finds out where Kirihito has gone and goes after him.

Characters

- *Dr. Kirihito Osanai*, the protagonist, is a good-looking and talented doctor. He is sent to Doggoddale, where he contracts Monmow disease. Because of the change in his appearance, he goes from being a respected member of society to being an outcast. During his initial travels as a doglike creature, he is quick to anger because of his self-pity. Only when he accepts his fate do others accept him despite his appearance.

- *Dr. Tatsugaura*, the antagonist, is a small man who resembles a bulldog. He is proud, stubborn, manipulative, and ambitious. His ambition is more important to him than the lives of his co-workers, and he forces the people around him into terrible positions. Only at the end of the work does his manipulative and evil nature become known to his colleagues.

- *Dr. Urabe* is a thin and jealous man. Like Kirihito, he is ambitious, but he is less talented than his colleague. Throughout the story, he slowly loses his mind because of the pressure put on him by Tatsugaura. He rapes Izumi and, later, Sister Helen Friese.

- *Izumi* is a beautiful Japanese woman and Kirihito's fiancé. She remains deeply in love with Kirihito throughout the story. Even when she learns that he has married Tazu, she tries desperately to find out what happened to him.

- *Tazu* is a beautiful woman from the village of Doggoddale. When Kirihito arrives in the village, she forces herself on him. She takes care of him when he contracts the disease, and love slowly develops between the two. Shortly after, however, she is raped and killed.

- *Sister Helen Friese* is a German nun living in South Africa who suffers from Monmow disease. The South African authorities try to keep her a secret because they want the public to believe that only people of color can contract the disease. She is used as a test subject by Tatsugaura but later escapes to a slum, where she treats people with contagious diseases and is greatly respected.

- *Reika* is a beautiful woman whom Kirihito meets while in the freak show. After she and Kirihito escape together, she imprisons Kirihito in a mountain cabin and forces him to have sex with her. She dies trying to raise money for Kirihito by performing a dangerous stunt.

Artistic Style

Tezuka's style is heavily influenced by cinema, and he noted at times that he particularly modeled his techniques on French and German films that he had seen as boy. *Ode to Kirihito* corresponds to Tezuka's cinematic style. He uses close-ups and alternates angles to optimize the impact of both emotional and action-packed scenes.

In comparison with Tezuka's most famous manga, *Astro Boy* (1952-1968), *Ode to Kirihito*'s style is more realistic. Also, though the style is recognizably Tezuka's, the characters are not drawn with the large eyes featured in most of his other works. Nevertheless, they still have a distinctly cartoonlike feel to them. Tezuka often juxtaposes these cartoonlike characters with highly realistic backgrounds.

Throughout *Ode to Kirihito*, Tezuka experiments with the manga form. Although most pages are somewhat traditionally laid out, there are also many pages with unorthodox compositions. He particularly succeeds in visualizing the thought processes of his main characters. Two pages in *Ode to Kirihito* are especially

Ode to Kirihito. (Courtesy of Vertical)

interesting in this respect. Depicting characters who are losing grip on the situations in which they find themselves, the pages are organized in a spiral, and the narrative proceeds from the outside of the spiral to the center of the page.

Tezuka's highly original and dramatic style makes possible the depiction of a narrative as complex as *Ode to Kirihito*. The constant shifts in narrative speed, tone, and composition are constructed by Tezuka's art at least as much as by his writing.

Themes

Ode to Kirihito is a story about the difference between being normal and being abnormal, a division that is framed from a medical perspective. As Tezuka was formally educated as a doctor, he was acutely aware both that doctors deal with different forms of abnormality on a daily basis and that they are respected members of the community. When Kirihito contracts Monmow and changes into a doglike creature, he shifts from being normal to being abnormal. Suddenly finding himself on the periphery of society, Kirihito struggles with his new appearance and the hardships he suffers because of it. The people he meets while traveling also suffer because they are, in one way or another, not part of "normal" society. The different locations of the narrative—South Africa, the Middle East, and China/Taiwan—also show Tezuka's concern with the normal/abnormal divide. Those who desperately try to find some kind of normality in themselves exploit the abnormal people in *Ode to Kirihito*. There are several rapes in the story, and each seems to occur because of the perpetrator's desire for control and normality.

Tatsugaura's goal of becoming the president of the Japan Medical Association requires a spotless reputation and complete "normality," which is in complete opposition to Kirihito's abnormality. Thus, after Tatsugaura contracts Monmow, he is removed from his position as president. Often in *Ode to Kirihito*, "normal" men are more beastly than those who look like animals. In the end, Kirihito can only be at home with refugees: a group of people formally existing outside society.

Another important theme in *Ode to Kirihito* is Christianity. Sister Helen Friese bears her disease as Christ bears the cross and, through her courage, becomes an inspiration for the other characters. Keenly aware of Christian imagery and themes, Tezuka masterfully uses them to enrich the story.

Impact

Ode to Kirihito does not represent one of the major shifts in Tezuka's oeuvre, as do *Astro Boy*, which made him famous around the world, and *Princess Knight* (1953-1956), which was his first manga for girls. It also was not his first complex narrative aimed at an older audience. However, it is an enticing story both narratively and visually, and it represents Tezuka's attempts to experiment more radically with the manga medium. For these reasons, it was well received in Japan. When the work was translated into English in 2006, Western critics and readers also marked it with approval, and it was among the top fifty best-selling manga books in the United States that year.

Tezuka has had an enormous influence on the many different forms of manga. He is frequently cited as a major influence by manga artists and has even been credited with inspiring artists to begin creating manga in the first place. Though it is difficult to discern the extent to which *Ode to Kirihito* has affected the manga industry as a whole, the work has been hugely influential for manga artists, such as Yoshihiro Tatsumi or Yoshiharu Tsuge, who play with or challenge manga's stylistic and narrative boundaries.

Rik Spanjers

Further Reading

Tatsumi, Yoshihiro. *Abandon the Old in Tokyo* (2006).

Tezuka, Osamu. *Apollo's Song* (1970).

_____. *Black Jack* (1973-1983).

Bibliography

Bird, Lawrence. "States of Emergency: Urban Space and the Robotic Body in the Metropolic Tales." *Mechademia* 3 (2008): 127-149.

Cohn. Neil. "A Different Kind of Cultural Frame: An Analysis of Panels in American Comics and Japanese Manga." *Image [&] Narrative* 12, no. 1 (2011): 120-134.

Eiji, Ōtsuka. "Disarming Atom: Tezuka Osamu's Manga at War and Peace." *Mechademia* 3 (2008): 111-126.

Inuhiko, Yomoto. "Stigmata in Tezuka Osamu's Works." *Mechademia* 3 (2008): 97-110.

Power, Natsu Onoda. *God of Comics: Osamu Tezuka and the Creation of Post-World War II Manga*. Mississippi: University Press of Mississippi, 2009.

See also: *Black Jack*; *MW*; *Astro Boy*

OH MY GODDESS!

Author: Fujishima, Kosuke
Artist: Kosuke Fujishima (illustrator); L. Lois Buhalis (letterer); Chris Chalenor (letterer); Betty Dong (letterer); Pat Duke (letterer); Susie Lee (letterer); PC Orz (letterer); Tom Orzechowski (letterer); Tom2K (letterer)
Publisher: Kodansha (Japanese); Dark Horse Comics (English)
First serial publication: *Aa, megami sama*, 1988- (English translation, 1994-2004)
First book publication: 1989-   (English translation, 2002-)

Publication History

Oh My Goddess! was first serialized in the magazine *Afternoon* in 1988 and then in graphic novel form by Kodansha. The English translation of the series was initially published by Dark Horse Comics in 1994. This translation was flipped to allow for right-to-left reading; thus, the artwork had to be flipped also. This caused certain inconsistencies. The demand by North American manga readers for an authentic, uncut manga resulted in a change in the middle of the series. According to Dark Horse Comics, *Oh My Goddess!* is the longest-running manga in the United States.

Dark Horse Comics combined Volumes 19 and 20, announcing that all future volumes would be published "unflipped," with the volume's contents corresponding to its Japanese counterpart volume. Originally, Dark Horse combined two Japanese volumes into one English volume to ensure a full story arc, as seen in the publication of Volumes 19 and 20 in one book. Volume 21 showcases a format that more closely matches the original Japanese volumes. Beginning with Volume 21, the volumes have been printed in a smaller, more traditional and cheaper paperback size than their predecessors. Production time between volumes was also cut. Overall, fans praised Dark Horse Comics' decision to mimic as closely as possible the Japanese volumes. The previous volumes were later rereleased with the new format.

Kosuke Fujishima

Kosuke Fujishima, born outside of Tokyo in 1964, is widely admired for *Oh My Goddess!* The manga has, since 1988, run in *Super Manga Blast!*, the *seinen* (mature male reader) magazine published by Kodansha. To have such a long-running series begin when its creator is merely twenty-four translates to something of a limited bibliography. Fujishima has, nonetheless, managed other projects, including contributions to video games, most notably character design for *Sakura Taisen*—or, as it is known outside of Japan, *Sakura Wars*—a popular steampunk franchise with anime and other spinoff products. His *éX-Driver* (2000) is a single-volume manga about cars with artificial intelligence. In 2009, he launched a new regular series, *Paradise Residence*, about a girls' dormitory.

Plot

Keiichi, a college student at Nekomi Institute of Technology (NIT), accidentally calls the Goddess Technical Helpline. When a real-life goddess, Belldandy, appears and offers to grant him one wish, he is certain that his roommates are playing a practical joke. He wishes that a pretty girl like her would remain with him forever. She grants his wish and becomes his girlfriend. Keiichi is both surprised and horrified when he finds out that his wish is not a joke. This proves problematic in many ways; first, he lives in a men's dormitory and must find a new residence. Belldandy is unusual enough, but her sisters are even more so. Keiichi's life is never the same again, as his ordinary life experiences are altered by heavenly and demonic beings.

Volumes

- *Oh My Goddess*, Volume 1 (1996). Keiichi dials the wrong number, which results in the appearance of the goddess Belldandy. His wish to have her stay with him is granted, and life as he knows it is turned upside down.

- *Oh My Goddess*, Volume 2 (1996). Keiichi and Belldandy pose nude together in a life-drawing class in order to raise money for the NIT Motor Club.
- *Oh My Goddess*, Volume 3 (1997). Urd, another goddess, attempts to push Belldandy and Keiichi, only to have her attempt blow up in her face. Keiichi faces competition when a new recruit from the Nekomi Motor Club sets his eyes on Belldandy.
- *Oh My Goddess*, Volume 4 (1997). Urd creates a love potion to target Keiichi. A CD turns out to be a portal from the underworld used by wicked beings.
- *Oh My Goddess*, Volume 5 (1998). Belldandy wants to give a special Valentine's Day treat to Keiichi by making him traditional homemade chocolate. This volume introduces the third goddess, Skuld.
- *Oh My Goddess*, Volume 6 (1999). Urd enters "Terrible Master" mode as she frees the Fenrir wolf, triggering the activation of the Ultimate Destruction Program. Belldandy and Skuld must stop Urd and the program before the known world is destroyed.
- *Oh My Goddess*, Volume 7 (1999). Urd's love potions cause further trouble. The motor club gets a female member, Sora Hasegawa.
- *Oh My Goddess*, Volume 8 (2000). Keiichi and the goddesses join the NIT Motor Club on a vacation, during which the ghost of a young maid tries to hold Keiichi to a promise made by his grandfather.
- *Oh My Goddess*, Volume 9 (2000). Urd and Skuld are called away to heaven for training. Belldandy has an unknown illness. Keiichi searches for a possible cure among Urd's medicines only to be turned into a woman.
- *Oh My Goddess*, Volume 10 (2001). The goddesses help the NIT Softball Club of Keiichi's sister win a game against its campus rivals. Afterward, they try to relax on a hot-springs vacation only to have Mara return and challenge Urd to karaoke.
- *Oh My Goddess*, Volume 11 (2001). Keiichi dials "p," accidentally summoning Belldandy's rival,

Peorth, who insists she can provide Keiichi better service.
- *Oh My Goddess*, Volume 12 (2001). Peorth studies dating customs through *shōjo* manga and tries to drag Keiichi on a date.
- *Oh My Goddess*, Volume 13 (2002). Skuld learns how to ride a bicycle and falls in love for the first time.
- *Oh My Goddess*, Volume 14 (2002). As Keiichi approaches graduation, he tries working at a custom bike shop, discovering it is harder then he imagined.
- *Oh My Goddess*, Volume 15 (2003). Mara and Sayoko continue to battle for the minds of the NIT students.
- *Oh My Goddess*, Volume 16 (2003). Keiichi and Belldandy cannot stop holding hands, and the robot Banpei falls in love.
- *Oh My Goddess*, Volume 17 (2003). The boy who arrived in the previous volume is a demon obsessed with Belldandy. Peorth helps reverse the slowdown of time caused by the demon boy.
- *Oh My Goddess*, Volume 18 (2004). Skuld's inventions go awry as her experiments with the time-space continuum leave Keiichi and Belldandy trapped in their resized living room. Afterward, Keiichi and Belldandy take a nighttime train ride to solve the mystery of the ghost haunting the mountain pass between NIT campuses.
- *Oh My Goddess*, Volumes 19-20 (2005). Dr. Moreau kidnaps Banpei's girlfriend to aid his dreams of making machines that can walk like humans. Keiichi and Sora race to decide who will become the next president of the motor club.
- *Oh My Goddess*, Volume 21 (2005). Peorth is trapped in the form of a girl. The only one who can help Peorth is Hild, chief of the demon realm.
- *Oh My Goddess*, Volume 22 (2006). Hild and Urd struggle to restore Peorth's true form.
- *Oh My Goddess*, Volume 23 (2006). Urd's mother leaves, as do Keiichi's and Megumi's parents.
- *Oh My Goddess*, Volume 24 (2006). Keiichi's mother beats the goddesses at mah-jongg. Takano-

san suspects that the goddesses are no ordinary girls. Chihiro, Keiichi, and Belldandy take a road trip to the hot springs and encounter the fifth goddess.

- *Oh My Goddess*, Volume 25 (2007). Hild unleashes the beast Tenshikui, the Eater of Angels. Tenshikui strips the angelic forms from Urd and Peorth's bodies. Without their angelic forms, their bodies cannot survive long. The fifth goddess, Lind, appears ready to defend her sisters. She turns out to be a Valkyrie.
- *Oh My Goddess*, Volume 26 (2007). The goddesses continue to face the wrath of Hild. Keiichi struggles to save Belldandy from the Demon Angels.
- *Oh My Goddess*, Volume 27 (2007). Keiichi hosts the demonic angel that Hild had previously placed inside Belldandy. He seeks to place it within Velsper.
- *Oh My Goddess*, Volume 28 (2008). Keiichi and the goddesses return to Nekomi Tech for the campus festival.
- *Oh My Goddess*, Volume 29 (2008). A race ensues as Belldandy tries to get the secret to curing Velsper's magical mange.
- *Oh My Goddess*, Volume 30 (2008). Urd faces a challenge from Peorth in order to become a Goddess First Class.
- *Oh My Goddess*, Volume 31 (2009). Peorth is summoned to Heaven only to discover that the girl at the gate is on strike.
- *Oh My Goddess*, Volume 32 (2009). Chihiro leads Keiichi, Belldandy, Urd, and Skuld on a training retreat.
- *Oh My Goddess*, Volume 33 (2009). The training retreat continues as Chihiro and Keiichi build two bikes.
- *Oh My Goddess*, Volume 34 (2010). The group returns from the retreat to discover the store in chaos. Skuld has a reunion with her former boyfriend Sentaro.
- *Oh My Goddess*, Volume 35 (2010). Keiichi finds an old photograph of a girl inside the vintage Camaro given to him by his senior students. He and

Belldandy set out to learn more about the girl in the photo.

- *Oh My Goddess*, Volume 36 (2010). A rival attempts to help Megumi's bad memory and inadvertently erases Keiichi's and the goddesses' memories by mistake.
- *Oh My Goddess*, Volume 37 (2011). A new goddess, Chromo, appears to give Belldandy a significant program, only to have things go horribly wrong.
- *Oh My Goddess*, Volume 38 (2011). Chrono is met with demon opposition as she struggles to recover remnants of the program. Because of an uprising in Hell, Hild shows up at Keiichi's birthday unannounced.
- *Oh My Goddess*, Volume 39 (2011). The power between Heaven and Hell is out of balance because of Belldandy's relationship with Keiichi. Peorth and Lind must rebalance the power and put Hild back on her throne.
- *Oh My Goddess*, Volume 40 (2011). Keiichi joins the goddesses on a trip to Hell in order to overthrow the usurper and restore the throne to Hild.
- *Oh My Goddess*, Volume 41 (2012). Keiichi and the goddesses continue on their journey through Hell to free Hild and restore her to the throne.

Characters
- *Belldandy*, a protagonist, is a beautiful Goddess First Class. She is a Norn (fate) goddess whose relationship with Keiichi propels the plot.
- *Keiichi Morisato*, a protagonist, is the accidental boyfriend of Belldandy. He is mechanically inclined and socially awkward.
- *Urd* is a Norn goddess and half demon and is the second goddess to appear.
- *Skuld* is Belldandy's younger sister and a Norn goddess. She is an adolescent girl and is the brains of the group. She aids Belldandy and Keiichi in the progression of their relationship.
- *Peorth* is a Goddess First Class. She is voluptuous and often scantily clad. She has a temper and is Belldandy's rival.

- *Lind*, the protagonist, is a Valkyrie (warrior) goddess. She is strong and rushes to the aid of Belldandy and her sisters when necessary.
- *Hild*, an antagonist, is the demon who rules Hell and Urd's mother. She is the ultimate opposition to Kami-Sama. She leaves a *chibi* (miniature) version of herself on Earth.
- *Chromo* is a clumsy, airheaded goddess. She has hopes of becoming a Valkyrie goddess.
- *Kami-Sama*, a.k.a. *The Almighty One*, a protagonist, is king of heaven. He is an unseen character to whom the goddesses must answer.
- *Velsper*, an antagonist, is a demon who is Belldandy's doublet (twin soul) in a pact between Heaven and Hell. He tries to defy this agreement, for which he is turned into a cat.
- *Hagall*, an antagonist, is an ambitious demon who leads the revolt against Hild in Hell.

Artistic Style

The initial volumes of *Oh My Goddess!* have been criticized for their crude artwork; however, the artwork has improved as the series has progressed. Sequences of movement are often shown in two or more panels. The backgrounds displaying the setting are highly detailed. The characters are primarily displayed from the torso up to offer a clear view of the emotions expressed by their faces; however, some full-body panels are incorporated. Full-body panels are used frequently in action scenes.

Themes

Good versus evil is a prominent theme throughout the series, as the goddesses face off against both demons and the devil. However, who and what are good and evil is not black and white, as the goddesses sometimes fight one another.

Keiichi appears to have every man's dream: a harem of beautiful women. However, he is not having sexual relations with all of them. He is rarely left alone with Belldandy because other goddesses are constantly arriving and leaving, most frequently Urd, Skuld, and Peorth. He is always surrounded by these beautiful goddesses.

Impact

Oh My Goddess! takes a typical *shōnen* (boys') story in Keiichi's pursuit for beautiful girls and incorporates *shōjo* (girls') story elements by having the series focus on relationships. Keiichi values his relationship with Belldandy, and they form an inseparable bond that grows as the story unfolds. Belldandy's bond with her sisters and fellow goddesses is also important.

At the time of the initial publication of *Oh My Goddess!* the combination of *shōnen* and *shōjo* genres was not typical. Author Sharalyn Orbaugh credits the 1990's as the decade of the hybrid genre boom, and *Oh My Goddess!* was the leader of the trend. The ongoing series continues to be popular.

Films

Ah! My Goddess—The Movie. Directed by Hiroaki Goda. Anime International Company/ADV Films, 2000. This film adaptation stars the voices of Masami Kikuchi as Keiichi and Kikuko Inoue as Belldandy. The film and the novels have different timelines.

Television Series

Ah! My Goddess! Directed by Hiroaki Goda. Anime International Company/TBS (Japan), 2005. This film adaption stars the voices of Kikuchi (Drew Aaron in the English translation) as Keiichi and Inoue (Eileen Stevens) as Belldandy. The series remains true to the core of the text but creates an alternate-universe story line.

The Adventures of the Mini Goddesses. Directed by Hiroko Kazui and Yasuhiro Matsumura. FUNimation, 1998-2003. The series differs completely from the manga. In this series, Belldandy, Urd, and Skuld shrink themselves to the size of rats and have numerous adventures while Keiichi is in class.

Rachel Cantrell

Further Reading

Akamatsu, Ken. *Love Hina* (2002-2003).
Clamp. *Chobits* (2002-2003).
Okuda, Hitoshi. *Tenchi Muyo* (2003-2006).

Bibliography

Clements, Jonathan, and Helen McCarthy. *The Anime Encyclopedia: A Guide to Japanese Animation Since 1917*. Berkeley, Calif.: Stone Bridge Press, 2001.

Lyga, Allyson A. W., and Barry Lyga. *Graphic Novels in Your Media Center: A Definitive Guide*. Westport, Conn.: Libraries Unlimited, 2004.

Orbaugh, Sharalyn. "Busty Battlin' Babes: The Evolution of the *Shōjo* in 1990's Visual Culture." In *Gender and Power in the Japanese Visual Field*, edited by Norman Bryson, Maribeth Graybill, and Joshua S. Mostow. Honolulu: University of Hawai'i Press, 2003.

See also: *Tsubasa*; *Ranma 1/2*; *Mai the Psychic Girl*

Old Boy

Author: Tsuchiya, Garon

Artist: Nobuaki Minegishi (illustrator); Kathryn Renta (letterer)

Publisher: Futabasha (Japanese); Dark Horse Comics (English)

First serial published: *Ōrudo Bōi*, 1996-1998

First book publication: 1997-1998 (English translation, 2006-2007)

Publication History

Old Boy, written by Garon Tsuchiya and illustrated by Nobuaki Minegishi, was initially serialized in Japan by Futabasha in its magazine *Weekly Manga Action* from 1996 to 1998. The series eventually had seventy-nine chapters, and these were published in eight books, or collected volumes (*tankōbon*). Volume 1 was released in May, 1997, and Volume 2 in December, 1997. Volumes 3 through 8 appeared in 1998, with the culminating volume released in October. The series was very popular in Japan, and its popularity was later enhanced by a successful and award-winning South Korean film based on the manga, which appeared in 2003. This led Dark Horse Comics, an American publisher, to purchase the rights for an English version in 2005. The first volume of the English translation appeared in July, 2006; Volumes 2 and 3 were released in the latter months of 2006, and the remaining Volumes (4-8) were published in 2007. The editor of the English version is Chris Warner, with Darin Fabrick as collection designer and Kumar Sivasubramanian as translator. The film version continued to produce interest in the manga, and Futabasha rereleased the series in five volumes in June and July, 2007.

Plot

The driving predicament of *Old Boy* is the central character's obsessive quest to discover why he has been kidnapped and privately imprisoned for ten years and suddenly freed. The manga opens with the delivery of noodles to the "man on floor 7.5" in a Tokyo office building. The man's windowless chambers contain little more than a bed, a television set, and a toilet, but

---

Garon Tsuchiya

Garon Tsuchiya, born in 1947, is a manga writer best known for the series *Old Boy*, about a man who tries to figure out why he was sealed in a private prison for a decade. A collaborative work with illustrator Nobuaki Minegishi, the manga ran in the late 1990's in the magazine *Weekly Manga Action*, published by Futabasha, and was made into a quite different, though celebrated, film by Korean director Park Chan-wook. *Old Boy* won an Eisner Award for Best U.S. Edition of International Material. Tsuchiya's *Shoujo Nemu* (with illustrator Hirosuke Kizaki) tells the story of a young female manga artist who befriends a grizzled and self-doubting creator. Under the pen name "Marginal," Tsuchiya wrote *Astral Project: Tsuki no Hikari*, drawn by Syuji Takeya, about a man sorting out the mystery of his sister's death while under the spell of music that initiates out-of-body experiences.

---

to maintain his sanity he has practiced vigorous exercises to keep himself physically fit, with the hope that he might ultimately be able to exact vengeance for his meaningless suffering. Soon after the food is delivered via a narrow slot, three men wearing dark glasses enter the room to inform the prisoner that he has been released from the "private penitentiary" after serving his ten-year sentence. The man takes out his pent-up rage on his releasers, who knock him out and stuff him into a suitcase. They bring him to a park, empty him onto the ground, and shove some money into his pocket.

When the man regains consciousness he looks up and sees the moon and stars, exulting in his newfound freedom. But this feeling is short-lived, as he becomes disoriented by the teeming life of Tokyo. He abandons an attempt to make a telephone call to access someone from his past, reasoning that no one will believe him. Nevertheless, he decides that he will fight back. As a test, he pretends to be intoxicated to tempt four hooligans to take advantage of him, and when they try to, he knocks each of them senseless; instead of taking all their money, however, he modestly pockets only what he will need to live for a few days, including some food and his first beer in ten years. His waitress, Eri, notices a cut on his face and bandages it. She later invites him back to her place to spend the night. She senses a kindness in him and proceeds to lose her virginity to this "man with no name," who has not experienced the warmth of a woman for a decade.

The man may think he is free to enjoy life and plan his vengeance, but he is followed by an ugly man sent by a banker to track him. The banker, it turns out, has provided the funds for the nameless man's abduction and imprisonment. Meanwhile, the relationship between Eri and her "mister" deepens, and he confesses to her the details of his ten-year imprisonment, though he cannot remember anyone who hated him enough to do such a thing. Eri discovers a scar on his back, and he forces her to use a knife to dig out a tracking device beneath it. When he gets a construction job, he uses an alias, Yamashita, while trying to deceive his pursuers by placing the device from his back in confusing locations. He also had come across a clue while he was imprisoned: A paper scrap with the name "Blue Dragon" in one of his noodle dishes.

Using this clue and others, Yamashita discovers the building where he was imprisoned, and employing violence, he attempts to wrest from his former captors the reason for his captivity. In a repetition of his earlier plight, however, he is recaptured and then released. Yamashita, whose real name is Shinichi Goto, exchanges his tracking device with a vagrant for a cell phone, which provides him with a choice: either use it to talk with his torturer or destroy it. Seeing the phone as yet another tool of his master manipulator, he destroys it, but the battle of wits between Goto and his unknown tormentor continues through both a boxing match and the story of a woman willing to bargain sexual favors for information about the man who controls her. Goto discovers that his predicament involves a person from his youth, whom he meets at a bar but is unable to recognize through voice or visage.

Goto follows up on the clue that a former school classmate might be the person who engineered his abduction and imprisonment. He meets with a woman who taught both Goto and the unknown tormentor.

Through her, Goto comes to realize that his dilemma might be the result of somehow offending his former classmate, but he cannot remember anything that occurred during his adolescence that would warrant the monumental vendetta. The tormentor then reveals to Goto how serious the stakes are in their deadly game, which involves not only Goto's life but also the lives of his friends.

As this contest of wits continues, Goto learns the name of his mastermind manipulator, Takaaki Kakinuma, who is willing to employ extreme measures to exact his revenge, including the hypnotic conditioning of Goto's friends and lovers, so that he does not know whom to trust. Since he was similarly conditioned during his imprisonment, he cannot trust even his own memories and his plan for revenge. Kakinuma informs Goto that he will sacrifice his own life if Goto can discover which of his judgments and memories are genuine, and the ultimate meaning behind Kakinuma's manipulations. In their final, anticlimactic encounter, Goto comes to realize that he had inadvertently wounded Kakinuma's prodigious pride by expressing sorrow for his classmate's humiliation when he broke down in tears during a music class. This display of public emotion, unacceptable for Japanese men, coupled with Goto's response, was the traumatic event that precipitated Kakinuma's vendetta. In the end, Kakinuma commits suicide. But Kakinuma's death has not totally freed Goto, who now has to contend with his own unreliable memories and those of Eri, the woman he thinks he loves.

Volumes

- *Old Boy*, Volume 1 (2006). Freed from a private prison for an unknown offense, Goto plots his revenge and starts to reclaim his life.
- *Old Boy*, Volume 2 (2006). Using knowledge he gleaned while imprisoned, Goto discovers where he had been held and seeks answers for why he was incarcerated.
- *Old Boy*, Volume 3 (2006). Through friends he meets, clues he pursues, and activities he becomes involved with, Goto begins to realize that he is being manipulated by his former tormentor.

- *Old Boy*, Volume 4 (2007). Goto learns that the person responsible for his torment is a former schoolmate. The two meet, but Goto, surprisingly, fails to recognize him.
- *Old Boy*, Volume 5 (2007). Goto meets with the woman who taught both him and his tormentor, and he learns that he had in some way offended his classmate.
- *Old Boy*, Volume 6 (2007). Goto finally understands that his nemesis is Takaaki Kakinuma, who informs Goto that his vendetta stems from an emotional trauma he attributes to Goto.
- *Old Boy*, Volume 7 (2007). Goto learns that his memories and those of his friends have been hypnotically conditioned by Kakinuma.
- *Old Boy*, Volume 8 (2007). In the endgame, Goto discovers how he caused Kakinuma's emotional trauma, which leads to his torturer's suicide and to Goto being left with a diseased mind and heart that he may or may not be able to cure.

Characters

- *Shinichi Goto*, the protagonist, is a handsome, physically fit man in his midthirties at the story's beginning. He was a somewhat insensitive adolescent, and a ten-year imprisonment has left him pathologically obsessed with wreaking revenge on those responsible for his suffering. He falls in love with Eri but becomes distrustful of her, as she may have been hypnotically conditioned by his tormentor. Goto's strong will and clever mind allow him to avoid madness and solve the mystery behind his imprisonment.
- *Takaaki Kakinuma,* the antagonist, is a wealthy banker and businessman who is surrounded by hirelings rather than friends. His slit-like eyes and somber countenance reveal a man obsessed with revenge for an emotional trauma experienced in childhood. He is the man responsible for Goto's imprisonment and for the manipulation of him and his friends after his release.
- *Eri* is a young and pretty waitress in a restaurant, where she meets Goto and bandages his wounds. Eri was hypnotically conditioned to seduce Goto so that Kakinuma's confederates could conduct

surveillance on Goto. Though Goto falls in love with her, he later becomes uncertain of the genuineness of their love.
- *Yukio Kusama*, an elementary school teacher, who later becomes a writer. She taught both Goto and Kakinuma in her sixth-grade class.
- *Tsukamoto,* a bartender who was Goto's friend in the days before his imprisonment and then becomes an acquaintance, albeit a troubled one, as Goto attempts to unravel the mystery behind his imprisonment.
- *Kyoko Kataoka,* Kakinuma's chief assistant, was responsible for the hypnotic conditioning of Goto, Eri, and others.

Artistic Style

Tsuchiya was responsible for the story, and Minegishi was responsible for the art, though there was much collaborative cooperation between them. Critics have described Tsuchiya's storytelling as slow and deliberate, whereas they generally find Minegishi's black-and-white (with gray wash) drawings clear, simple, and gritty. For example, in the love scene between Goto and Eri, the nudity is handled tastefully, with only secondary sexual characteristics briefly on display, the emphasis instead placed on characterization (Goto's powerful desire for sexual comfort after ten years of imprisonment and Eri's need to lose her virginity). The story is told mostly through rectangular panels, although double-page illustrations introduce each chapter and sometimes are used to emphasize important plot points (occasionally nonrectangular panels and half-page panels are used to set scenes).

In the English version, the Japanese text in the speech balloons has been translated, but the text in various drawings has been left unaltered from the original (with English translations in small print above the panels). The style of panels that set scenes, such as panels of Tokyo buildings and nightlife, are nearly photographic, whereas the panels depicting the story in dialogue or action are like traditional comics. When violence is depicted, it is not glamorized, and the viewer is made aware of the real pain that the characters feel. The drawings tend to humanize Goto more than Kakinuma, who is presented, for the most part, as a classic villain.

Some critics have compared Minegishi's style in *Old Boy* to film noir because of his use of shadows, silhouettes, and night scenes (Kakinuma's hirelings are even depicted like American gangsters). Tsuchiya also makes use of film-noir techniques in his narrative; for example, he uses a partially amnesiac protagonist who is being manipulated by an antagonist. The use of periodic flashbacks to gradually clarify plot points is also common in film noir. Finally, the narrative and drawings combine to create sympathy for the protagonist and antipathy for the villain, who gets his comeuppance in the end, though the ambiguous conclusion is typically noirish since it leaves the reader wondering if Goto has really regained his freedom and identity.

Themes

The major theme of *Old Boy* is revenge. Unlike many classic revenge stories, vengeance is not sweet for either the protagonist or the antagonist. After causing much pain to Goto, others, and himself, Kakinuma dies, unsatisfied and by his own hand. Goto, in his own personal vendetta, also causes pain to the guilty, innocent, and himself, and ends up uncertain of who he is and what he has become.

A secondary theme, tied to the major one, is the search for truth, meaning, and identity. Besides seeking revenge, Goto wants to discover the truth about his condition and himself. His situation is reminiscent of K in Franz Kafka's *Der Prozess* (1925; *The Trial*, 1937); Goto seeks justice in a world in which justice is problematic, illusory, and mysterious. Like the protagonists in many existentialist novels, Goto has been thrown into a meaningless world, and he must forge some kind of personal meaning through actions that may or may not be free. The manga's ending, which the authors admit was left deliberately ambiguous, leaves room for both nihilist and optimistic interpretations.

Impact

Old Boy revealed the power of the comic-book form to tell extremely complex and profound stories. While some characters are little more than caricatures, the principal ones, especially Goto, are realistically conceived and fully developed. Some critics found that

parts of the story strained believability, especially the antagonist's elaborate vendetta. Nevertheless, *Old Boy* has commanded a worldwide influence, especially because of the successful film based on its basic story idea. In the United States, a planned film adaptation of the manga will most likely expand and deepen the story's popularity.

Films

Old Boy. Directed by Chan-wook Park. Egg Films/Show East, 2003. South Korean director Park released his film version of *Old Boy* in 2003. He changed the location from Tokyo to Seoul, the chief characters' names (as well as, to a certain extent, their defining traits), and many aspects of the plot, though the principal idea stayed the same. Those who found the end of the manga anticlimactic tended to think that the film was a vast improvement, with the ultimate mystery involving an incest theme. The film has much more graphic violence than the manga, leading some readers to prefer the gentler and more probing storytelling of Tsuchiya and Minegishi. Despite these differences, the film received overwhelmingly positive reviews from critics around the world. The film won numerous South Korean and international awards, including the Grand Prix at the fifty-seventh Cannes Film Festival.

Robert J. Paradowski

Further Reading

Marginal (Garon Tsuchiya), and Takeya Syuji. *Astral Project* (2008).

Millar, Mark, and Steve McNiven. *Nemesis* (2011).

Miller, Frank. *Sin City* (1991-2000).

Bibliography

Gravett, Paul. *Manga: Sixty Years of Japanese Comics.* New York: Collins Design, 2004.

Petersen, Robert. *Comics, Manga, and Graphic Novels: A History of Graphic Narratives.* Santa Barbara, Calif.: Praeger, 2010.

Thompson, Jason. *Manga: The Complete Guide.* New York: Ballantine Books, 2007.

See also: *Berserk*; *Pluto*

ONE PIECE

Author: Oda, Eiichiro
Artist: Eiichiro Oda (illustrator)
Publisher: Shūeisha (Japanese); VIZ Media (English)
First serial publication: *Wan pīsu*, 1997-   (English translation, 2002-   )
First book publication: 1997-   (English translation, 2003-   )

Publication History

One Piece was first published in *Weekly Shōnen Jump* in August, 1997. The manga was based on one-shots published under the title *Romance Dawn* the previous year. Because of the series' popularity, publisher Shūeisha began to collect the weekly chapters into *tankōbon* in December, 1997. Creator Eiichiro Oda initially intended to end the series in 2001, but both the popularity of the series and Oda's enjoyment in writing it have compelled him to continue indefinitely.

The manga has also been sold in collected volumes in North America, the United Kingdom, and Australia. The translations of the manga from Japanese into English preserve the manga panel layout, which reads from right to left, in order to preserve the integrity of the connected scenes. The manga's humor often revolves around puns and jokes involving misheard statements, so translators often change the phrasing to preserve the humor rather than follow the most literal interpretation.

Plot

As a child, Monkey D. Luffy idolizes a group of pirates resting at his hometown and decides to become a pirate. He accidentally eats a cursed fruit and gains rubber powers. At fifteen, he sets out in a small ship to find One Piece, the treasure of the Pirate King. Luffy quickly finds a swordsman, Zolo; a navigator, Nami; a sharpshooter, Usopp; and a chef, Sanji, and establishes the Straw Hat crew. Nami is trapped in a deal with a brutal fishman pirate named Arlong. The Straw Hat crew follows Nami to her hometown and defeats Arlong and his crew. This battle fully unifies the crew and gains Luffy a bounty from the Marines.

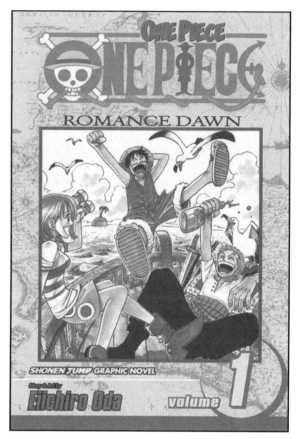

One Piece. (Courtesy of VIZ Media)

The crew travels to Loguetown, and readers learn that Luffy is the son of the Revolutionary Dragon. The crew then heads to the Grand Line, the ocean on which most of the adventures take place, and is immediately attacked by a secret group called Baroque Works. They are enlisted by Princess Vivi to destroy Baroque Works and save the kingdom of Alabasta. Along the way, they meet and recruit the reindeer doctor Tony Tony Chopper. The battle with Baroque Works requires all crew members to fight and forces Luffy to face Crocodile, a member of the Shichibukai. Luffy defeats Crocodile.

The crew then travels to an island in the sky called Skypeia, where the inhabitants use a technology based on special shells called dials. The people there are ruled by Eneru, who uses his powers of advanced hearing and electricity to destroy anyone who speaks against him. Luffy is able to defeat him because his rubber body is insulated against Eneru's electrical attacks.

The crew leaves Skypiea loaded with treasure; however, their ship, *Merry Go*, must undergo major repairs in Water Seven, land of the shipbuilders. Nico Robin's past as a witness of government brutality is revealed, and she is captured by a special government force, CP-9. Luffy declares war on the World Government and attacks the Marine base where Robin is being held. The Straw Hats defeat CP-9, with Luffy using techniques that increase his speed and size but also damage his body in order to defeat CP-9's top fighter, Rob Lucci, and rescue his crewmate.

The old ship is beyond repair, and it is replaced with *Thousand Sunny*. The Straw Hats travel into a deep fog, where they find the talking skeleton musician Brook. Brook tells the crew of a ghost island where someone is experimenting on pirates to create powerful undead warriors. The process removes an individual's shadow and places it in a corpse; however, once a person's shadow is removed, that person will be destroyed by the light of the sun. Brook asks for Luffy's help in regaining his shadow, so the Straw Hats head to the ghost island of Thriller Bark. The island is controlled by the Shichibukai pirate Gecko Moria and is covered with hundreds of undead and surgically altered monsters. Moria steals Luffy's shadow and plants it in the body of a giant monster named Oars. Meanwhile, the crew fights zombie swordsmen, invisible monsters, and a girl with the power to destroy one's sense of self-worth. These monsters are defeated, and all of the stolen shadows are restored to their owners.

The Straw Hat crew travels to the Sabaody archipelago, which is at the base of the Red Line, a mountain range marking the halfway point of the Grand Line. The crew meets Rayleigh, the Pirate King's first mate, who explains the nature of the second half of the Grand Line, a place called the New World.

While in Sabaody, Luffy is enraged when he finds out that fishmen are being sold as slaves, and he fights to stop the auction. He attacks a member of the World Nobles, privileged descendents of the founders of the World Government, and provokes a full Marine response. The crew is separated and flung to different is-

lands of the Grand Line. During this period of separation, Luffy learns that his brother, Ace, has been captured and sentenced to be executed. He breaks into Impel Down, an underwater prison, and releases all of its prisoners, only to learn that Ace has already been transferred to the capitol for his execution. Ace's captain, Whitebeard, gathers a fleet of pirates, who help Luffy and the horde of freed prisoners assault the capitol. The pirates prevent Ace's execution. However, as they are escaping, Whitebeard is killed by his own son, and Ace sacrifices himself to save Luffy from an admiral's fatal attack. Luffy is emotionally shattered, and the series spends a volume revealing Luffy's childhood with Ace. Luffy sends a message to his crew stating that they are to meet again in two years; thus, each member begins a training regime under a different master. Two years later, the crew reassembles at the archipelago and continues its journey.

Volumes

- *One Piece: Romance Dawn, Buggy the Clown, Don't Get Fooled Again, The Black Cat Pirates, For Whom the Bell Tolls, The Oath, The Crap-Geezer,* and *I Won't Die* (2003-2005). Volumes 1-8. Collects issues 1-71. Luffy leaves his hometown and recruits a crew of pirates. He also meets

---

Eiichiro Oda

Eiichiro Oda, born in 1975, is the creator of the pirate manga *One Piece*, which has been published since 1997 in *Weekly Shōnen Jump* and is one of the magazine's great successes. Like many manga creators, Oda began his career as an assistant, working under, among others, Nobuhiro Watsuki, creator of the samurai hit *Rurouni Kenshin*. Oda has cited Akira Toriyama, of *Dragon Ball*, as his greatest manga hero and has mentioned *Vicke the Little Viking*, a 1970's cartoon, as a strong early influence on the development of *One Piece*. In a unique case of life imitating art, he met his wife, Chiaki Inaba, when she was a professional cosplayer acting as Nami, one of the major *One Piece* characters.

and defeats the pirates Buggy the Clown and Don Krieg.

- *One Piece: Tears, "OK, Let's Stand Up!,"* and *The Meanest Man in the East* (2006). Volumes 9-11. Collects issues 72-99. Luffy must defeat Captain Arlong and the fishmen pirates to rescue Nami. After his victory over Arlong, Luffy heads to the entrance of the Grand Line, the strip of ocean he must travel to find One Piece.
- *One Piece: The Legend Begins, It's All Right!!!!, Instinct, Straight Ahead!!!!, Carrying on His Will,* and *Hiruluk's Cherry Blossoms* (2006-2008). Volumes 12-17. Collects issues 100-155. The Straw Hat crew makes it to the Grand Line and befriends a giant whale named Laboon. The crew meets secretive agents Miss Wednesday and Mr. 9 from the organization Baroque Works. The Straw Hats defeat King Walpol and recruit the talking, shape-shifting reindeer Tony Tony Chopper as the ship's doctor.
- *One Piece: Ace Arrives, Rebellion, Showdown at Alubarna, Utopia, Hope!!,* and *Vivi's Adventure* (2008-2009). Volumes 18-23. Collects issues 156-216. Princess Vivi, who was Miss Wednesday, brings the crew to Alabasta, her kingdom, where the members aid her in defeating the rest of Baroque Works. After saving Alabasta, Vivi leaves the crew. Nico Robin joins the crew.
- *One Piece: People's Dreams, The One Hundred Million Berry Man Adventure on Kami's Island, Overture, Wyper the Berserker, Oratorio, Capriccio, We'll Be Here Love Song,* and *Davy Back Fight* (2010). Volumes 24-33. Collects issues 217-316. Luffy meets Mont Blanc Cricket and learns about Skypiea. The Straw Hat crew goes to Skypiea, where the members learn about dial technology and confront and defeat Eneru. The people in the sky try to reward the Straw Hat crew, but there is a misunderstanding; thus, the Straw Hat crew flees with whatever treasure the members can grab.
- *One Piece: The City of Water, Water Seven; Captain; The Ninth Justice; Tom; Rocketman!!; Scramble; Gear; Declaration of War; Pirates vs. CP9; Legend of a Hero; Let's Go Back;* and *You*

Have My Sympathies (2010). Volumes 34-45. Collects issues 317-440. The Straw Hat crew goes to Water Seven to repair the ship. Nico Robin is captured by the Marines. The Straw Hat crew heads to the judicial island of Enies Lobby, where it attacks and defeats the elite Marine group CP9. Franky joins the Straw Hats, and the crew gets a new ship, *Thousand Sunny*.

- *One Piece: Adventure on Ghost Island; Cloudy, Partly Bony; Adventures of Oars; Nightmare Luffy;* and *Arriving Again* (2010). Volumes 46-50. Collects issues 441-491. The Straw Hat crew meets Brook and goes to the ghost island Thriller Bark. On the island, the warlord Gecko Moria removes the souls of some of the characters to create an army of zombies. The crew defeats the strongest zombies, and Brook joins the crew.
- *One Piece: The Eleven Supernovas, Roger and Rayleigh, Natural Born King, Unstoppable, A Ray of Hope, Thank You, Summit Battle, The Name of This Era Is "Whitebeard," The Death of Portgaz D. Ace,* and *My Brother* (2010-2012). Volumes 51-60. Collects issues 492-594. The Straw Hat crew makes it to Sabaody Park. Luffy assaults a Celestial Dragon. The crew goes to different islands through the teleportation powers of Bartholomew Kuma. Luffy lands on the Isle of Women, where the pirate empress Boa Hancock falls in love with him. He finds out Ace is in prison and tries to free him. He then joins Whitebeard and many others in an attack against Oris Plaza.
- *One Piece: Romance Dawn—For the New World, Adventure on Fish-Man Island, Otohime and Tiger* and *100,000 vs. 10* (2012). Volumes 61-64. Collects issues 595-631. The crew meets at Sabaody Park and travels to Fishman Island. They fight the fishman pirate captains Vander Decken IX and Hodi Jones.

Characters

- *Monkey D. Luffy,* the protagonist, is a young man who accidently ate the Gomu Gomu devil fruit, which turned his body into rubber. Having idolized pirates since his childhood, he gathers a crew of pirates to try to find the greatest pirate treasure, One Piece.

- *Roronoa Zolo* is the first member of Luffy's Straw Hat crew. He is a master swordsman who uses three *katana* simultaneously.
- *Nami* is a thief and expert navigator for the Straw Hat pirates. She began her career as a thief to buy back her hometown from Arlong. She initially hated all pirates because of Arlong's merciless murder of her guardian, Bellmare.
- *Usopp* is the sniper and gunnery expert of the Straw Hat pirates. He is a chronic liar and substantially weaker than most of the other members of the crew. His goal is simply to become strong enough to be recognized as a great man.
- *Sanji* is the cook of the Straw Hat pirates and a master of a martial art that uses leg techniques only. He is obsessed with beautiful women and will never fight one. His goal is to find a mythical sea called the All Blue, which contains fish from every ocean of the world.
- *Tony Tony Chopper* is a reindeer who ate a devil fruit that gave him the intelligence and capabilities of a human as well as shape-shifting abilities. He is the ship's doctor, and his goal is to find a medicine that can treat any disease or injury.
- *Franky* is a cyborg and the shipwright. He built the Straw Hat pirates' second ship and decides to travel with the pirates to discover new technologies.
- *Brook* is a living skeleton who ate a devil fruit that gave him immortality. He is a swordsman and musician and is capable of controlling the emotions of those who hear him play. His goal is to return to an old friend.
- *Nico Robin* is the ship's archaeologist and one of the most levelheaded members of the crew. She has been hunted by the government since her childhood as the sole survivor of a government-sanctioned massacre. She ate a devil fruit that gave

her the power to multiply her limbs and cause copies of her limbs to sprout from other surfaces near her. Her goal is to decipher the secrets of an ancient civilization that may be linked to One Piece.

- *Portgaz D. Ace* is Luffy's adopted brother. He ate a devil fruit that gave him the power to control fire. He is a far more infamous pirate than Luffy and the first mate to the legendary pirate White-beard. He is also the son of the Pirate King.
- *The Shichibukai*, the Seven Warlords of the Sea, is a group made up of seven powerful pirate captains who work for the Marines and control the influx of new pirates. Members include Croco-

One Piece. (Courtesy of VIZ Media)

dile, Hawkeye Mihawk, Donquixote Dofla-
mingo, Gecko Moria, Bartholomew Kuma, and
Boa Hancock. The seventh pirate, Jinbe, was removed from his position and was replaced only
briefly.

- *Gol D. Roger* was the Pirate King, a legendary
pirate who created the strongest crew and gathered One Piece. His death started the great age of
pirates, as people clamored to reach the treasure
at the end of the long stretch of ocean known as
the Grand Line.

Artistic Style

One Piece's artistic style has a certain simplicity
characteristic of *shōnen* comics; however, the large
mouths and eyes of characters allow the creator to include scenes that convey larger-than-life emotions
and reactions. Most characters have slim limbs, but
certain large characters possess wide shoulders with
pronounced recesses around the collarbones. The
style lends itself to the overall lighthearted nature of
the series; however, the detail and complexity of action scenes convey the speed and power of individual
characters and the tension of the combatants. Certain
stylistic elements distinct to manga, such as throb-
bing veins of anger and swirling lines of confusion,
are used to establish atmosphere and indicate emotion. Oda also uses unique framing on body parts
under strain to convey, in a suspenseful manner, the
effort characters are exerting or the injuries they have
received. Another interesting element in the series,
given that it is drawn in black and white, is the way in
which Oda depicts blood as either droplets or streams
depending on the severity and persistence of an
injury. Action within the comic often utilizes extreme
angles to capture characters' abilities to distort
themselves.

Themes

One Piece is about a group of friends who work together to achieve their dreams. The themes of friendship and the power of teamwork are central to the series. Luffy is rather dim and impulsive; thus, he must
be assisted by his crew, otherwise his goals are unat-
tainable. This point is reinforced from the perspectives

of the other characters, each of whom is limited in his
or her own skills but trusts the crew unwaveringly.

Another major theme is the importance of independent
thought and dedication to personal principles, as opposed
to unwavering support of the government. While the main
characters are pirates, each crew member adheres to personal rules that any heroic figure would follow.

Impact

One Piece has been extremely popular in both Japan
and the United States and in 2012 became the best-
selling manga of all time. While the characters fall into
traditional adventure manga roles, the dynamics between the characters are original in a subgenre often
cluttered with cliché story lines and thus appeal to a
wide range of readers. Manga has become an increasingly popular literary format among young audiences
in the United States, and *One Piece* continues a tradition of intriguing graphic literature.

Television Series

One Piece. Directed by Konosuke Uda. Toei Anima-
tion/FUNimation Entertainment, 1999-   . This animated adaptation of the manga is true to the source
material, though certain additional episodes have
been added to compensate for the delays in the
manga production.

Joseph Romito

Further Reading

Kubo, Tite. *Bleach* (2001–   ).
Matsuena, Syun. *Kenichi: The Mightiest Disciple*
(2002-   ).

Bibliography

Brenner, Robin E. *Understanding Manga and Anime*.
Westport, Conn.: Libraries Unlimited, 2007.
Schodt, Frederik L. *Manga! Manga! The World of Japanese Comics*. New York: Kodansha International,
1983.
Wong, Wendy Siuyi. "Globalizing Manga: From Japan
to Hong Kong and Beyond." *Mechademia* 1 (2006):
23-45.

See also: *Bleach*; *Dragon Ball*

P

PHOENIX

Author: Tezuka, Osamu
Artist: Osamu Tezuka (illustrator); Izumi Evers (cover artist); Courtney Utt (cover artist)
Publisher: Kodansha (Japanese), VIZ Media (English)
First serial publication: *Hi no tori*, 1954-1988 (English translation, 2002-2008)

Publication History

As a longtime fan of Igor Stravinsky's ballet *L'Oiseau de feu* (1910; *The Firebird*), Japan's "God of Manga" Osamu Tezuka aspired to draw a tale about the legendary Phoenix from an early stage of his career. His first attempt appeared in the boys' comics magazine *Manga Shōnen*, but he did not manage to complete the story. Another attempt followed in 1956 in the girls' comics magazine *Shōjo Club*. At the time, Tezuka had a passion for Hollywood-style romantic period epics; set in ancient times in Egypt, Greece, and Rome, the story reflected this sensibility.

A decade later, when Tezuka turned to producing long-form, adult-oriented stories, he rewrote and redrew "Dawn," the story that originally appeared in *Manga Shōnen* as a tragic tale about the life-and-death cycle, which became a recurring theme in the following stories of the series. "Dawn" was published in *COM* magazine, founded by Tezuka as a platform for experimental works. Subsequent chapters were serialized in *Manga Shōnen* (following the bankruptcy of Tezuka's production company, Mushi); *The Wild Age Comic* magazine later collected different editions.

Tezuka kept drawing stories in the series until his death in 1989, but the comic remains unfinished, as he had plans for further stories beyond those that had been published. In 2002, the second chapter in the series, "Future," was published in North America as a large-size, stand-alone volume. Later that year, "Dawn" was published in a small-sized volume to clearly identify it

Phoenix. (Courtesy of VIZ Media)

as the first in a series; subsequent editions of "Future" were published in the new format. By 2008, all the volumes in the series were translated and published in North America.

Plot

In the year 240 C.E. Nagi, a boy from a small village, watches as his people are slaughtered by the unstoppable army of Himiko, the legendary queen of Japan. He then becomes entangled in the dying queen's plot to capture the Phoenix, the bird of fire whose blood can grant eternal life. Saruta, an officer in the queen's army, gets attached to the boy and suffers a grim fate.

Over three millennia later, on a postapocalyptic Earth, the forbidden love between the human Masato and the alien Tamami forces both to flee the giant underground metropolis of Yamato to the uninhabitable surface, where they are offered refuge by Saruta—a genius scientist with questionable ethics who bears a suspicious resemblance to the soldier from Queen Himiko's army, thousands of years ago. Saruta's plan to restore Earth involves the mythological firebird.

Thus start the two major plotlines of *Phoenix*, one moving forward from the dawn of time, the other backward from the distant future. The stories are interconnected, though each can be read individually. Along the way, the protagonists in each story cross paths with the Firebird, which symbolizes their (often forbidden) ambitions, dreams, and desires. Peasants and kings, workers and tycoons, in the bloody battlefields of the past and the enormous cities of the future, clash in this great tale of the human race.

Volumes

- *Phoenix: Dawn* (2003). Queen Himiko sends her armies to capture the Phoenix, and one of her spies triggers a series of tragic events.
- *Phoenix: A Tale of the Future* (2002). Saruta, a genius scientist, plans on reviving the dying Earth with the unwilling help of two desperate lovers.
- *Phoenix: Yamato/Space* (2003). This volume collects two stories: The first is set in the fifth century, relaying the king of Yamato's plans for his subjects to accompany him on his death; the second story takes place in 2577, following a group of astronauts who find themselves on a mysterious planet where the firebird resides.
- *Phoenix: Karma* (2004). A gifted sculptor and an armless bandit clash over the construction of a giant Buddha statue in eighth century Japan.
- *Phoenix: Resurrection* (2005). Leona, a young man who was resurrected after dying in a car accident in the year 2483, falls in love with an industrial robot called Chihiro, who then begins to develop feelings of her own.

- *Phoenix: Nostalgia* (2006). A woman named Romi who finds herself abandoned on a remote planet is revealed to have played a major part in the future-history of the human race.
- *Phoenix: Civil War, Part One* (2006). Benta, a hunter from a small village, searches for his beloved Obuu and finds himself in the middle of the murderous struggle between the Taira and Genji clans in twelfth century Japan.
- *Phoenix: Civil War, Part Two/Robe of Feathers* (2006). This volume features the conclusion of the Civil War chapter and the short story "Robe of Feathers," about Zuku, a hunter who finds a mysterious robe that changes his life.
- *Phoenix: Strange Beings/Life* (2006). This volume collects two stories. The first, "Strange Beings," is about Sakon-Nosuke, a seventh century noblewoman who wishes to get even with her father for raising her as a man. The second, "Life," follows the unfortunate victims of the twenty-second century cloning and entertainment industry.
- *Phoenix: Sun, Part One* (2007) and *Phoenix: Sun, Part Two* (2007). Two volumes that feature the last chapter of *Phoenix* that Tezuka completed before his death. They tell the parallel stories of Suguru, a twenty-first century mercenary, and Harima, a Korean soldier who is forced to live in a wolf's skin and struggle against the mass conversion of Japan to Buddhism during the seventh century.
- *Phoenix: Early Works* (2008). This volume collects the first stories Tezuka attempted to draw in the series during the 1950's. They follow a crown prince and Daia, a slave girl, and the role they played throughout the history of ancient Egypt, Greece, and Rome.

Characters

- *The Phoenix* is the mythical firebird whose blood can grant eternal life to anyone who drinks it. The Phoenix is presented as a huge peacock-like creature, and the hunt for it and its blood is the driving force behind many of the stories in the series.

- *Saruta* plays many different roles in different incarnations throughout the series. He is portrayed as a hero and a villain, a savior and a destroyer, and both selfless and selfish. He appears as a short man with a grotesquely large head and a big, scarred nose. His character often crosses paths with many of the Firebird's aspiring hunters in the past and the future.
- *Queen Himiko*, featured in *Phoenix: Dawn*, is queen of Japan in 240 C.E. She tries to capture the Phoenix for her own gain.
- *Leona* is resurrected from the dead after a car accident and later falls for Chihiro, a robot.
- *Romi*, featured in *Phoenix: Nostalgia*, learns she has played an important role in the future of humanity.
- *Benta*, a hunter, becomes entangled in the rivalry between the Taira and Genji clans in twelfth century Japan.
- *Harima* is a Korean soldier during the seventh century, when Japan converted to Buddhism.
- *Daia* is a slave whose story is told against the backdrop of ancient Egypt, Greece, and Rome.

Artistic Style

Phoenix serves as one of the best examples of Tezuka's enormously large pool of styles and influences. It features human and animal characters of the cartoony, cute design inspired by the animated films of Walt Disney and the Fleischer brothers alongside realistically designed characters that bring to mind protagonists from American comic books.

Another important influence on the series is *The Little Humpbacked Horse* (1947), the first Soviet feature-length animated film, which inspired the firebird's design. The series' detailed historical backgrounds were initially inspired by Hollywood epics but later drew their influence from authentic Japanese landscapes when the location of the series' historical chapters became exclusively Japanese.

The backgrounds for the futuristic chapters also show a wide variety of influences, from the dystopian vision of Fritz Lang's *Metropolis* (1927) to cover illustration from the golden age of American science-fiction magazines. Tezuka also experimented with different styles of page layout and panel design to portray characters drifting between different stages of consciousness (as in "Space") and to represent the passage of time (as in "Robe of Feathers").

The narrative and textual structure of the series is likewise varied; it is not uncommon to find a verbal or physical gag in the midst of a serious and even tragic plot. Tezuka has also filled the series with deliberate anachronisms, and often he breaks in the fourth wall,

Phoenix. (Courtesy of VIZ Media)

enhancing the feeling that his characters are merely actors, playing their role in the great theater show of human history.

Themes

Above all else, *Phoenix* appears to be about the karma of humanity—the endless, tragic cycle in which the human race repeats the mistakes that bring suffering upon itself. The immortality that many characters pursue throughout the series is a metaphor for the human need to cheat death evident throughout history, and to maintain a presence in the world through cruel actions and through monuments often built at the cost of human lives.

In the passage back and forth between the past and the future, an unflattering picture of the human race is presented: Times change, as do technologies and societies, but humans will always retain their greedy, selfish, warlike nature. The partly satirical tone of the dystopian futuristic characters has a universal feeling to it, but the historical chapters are surprisingly critical of Japan, Tezuka's homeland, and its growth throughout the ages. Japan is presented as a having a history of constant violence, tyrannical regimes, and religious fundamentalism. Even Buddhist faith in Japan (Tezuka himself was a Buddhist) is portrayed at times in an unflattering manner. Indeed, before dying, Tezuka left behind a draft for a new story in the series that was to take place in China during the late 1930's, dealing with the behavior of the Japanese army in Asia (a theme he also touched on in another masterpiece, *Adolf*, 1983-1985). The history of Japan—a country that achieved great accomplishments at the cost of great cruelty—might have been seen by Tezuka as the perfect example of the karma of humanity he wanted to depict in *Phoenix*.

Impact

Phoenix is a transitional work for Tezuka, and it marks his move from his early period of adventure stories and romantic epics to adult works that explore serious themes and often experiment with new styles. The *gekiga* ("dramatic pictures") genre of stories, which deals with crime, sex, and politics, was gaining popularity throughout the 1960's. The maturing of comic readers and the rise of rebellious student movements in

the same decade eventually led the artists of such works to find their place within the mainstream manga industry. However, *Phoenix* went a step beyond other artists, not only in introducing Tezuka's old-school artistic and storytelling techniques to a mature audience but also in attempting to transcend storytelling itself and reach for the abstract concepts that existed beyond narrative through experimentation with a variety of new techniques; ostensibly, Tezuka attempted to turn comics into a higher form of art. *Phoenix* encouraged other Japanese artists to explore the more experimental possibilities of art and narrative in comics. Tezuka himself drew other stories that aimed for a deeper exploration of human nature, but *Phoenix* remains the forerunner among his works, his unfinished magnum opus.

During the 1970's, a group of American students made first attempts to translate the series into English, and a member of that group, Frederik L. Schodt, went on to become one of the most prominent scholars and translators of Japanese comics in the English-speaking world. A segment of the translated *Karma* volume appeared in Schodt's seminal 1983 book *Manga! Manga! The World of Japanese Comics*, and the attempts at translation during the late 1970's served as a basis for the English editions of the twentieth century.

Films

The Phoenix. Directed by Kon Ichikawa. Hi no Tori Productions, 1979. The first theatrical adaptation of *Phoenix* was a live-action retelling of the "Dawn" chapter, featuring the firebird as an animated character. The film was directed by Ichikawa, one of the pioneering film directors to emerge in post-World War II Japan. By the time the film was made and released, Ichikawa was well past his prime, and *The Phoenix*, as it was known in its English release, was considered to be little more than a curious footnote in his career.

Space Firebird 2772. Directed by Taku Sugiyama. Tezuka Production Company, 1980. An animated adaptation, *Space Firebird 2772* fared much better than *The Phoenix*. Produced by Tezuka's own company, this animated feature borrows elements from different chapters in the series to tell a new story about a hunt for the firebird through space. The film's opening ten minutes are nothing short of an animated masterpiece, delivering its protagonist's coming-of-age story through images and music alone and no dialogue, in a manner doubtlessly inspired by Disney's *Fantasia* (1940). The rest of the film, though, is a disappointingly conventional chase story, in which the firebird's mean attitude feels very out of place for readers familiar with the original series. However, the film remains an imaginative and entertaining take on Tezuka's original source material, with a worthy guest appearance by Black Jack, the brilliant unlicensed doctor and star of the Tezuka manga *Black Jack* (1973-1983). An English-dubbed, heavily edited North American release was issued on VHS, and an uncut English-subtitled DVD release is available in Australia.

Television Series

The Phoenix. Anime Works, 2007. A thirteen-episode animated adaptation, this was originally produced and broadcasted in Japan in 2004. The series features impressive designs that honor Tezuka's original work, with the addition of a rich and delicate color palate, beautiful animation, and an epic musical score. The first episodes are a faithful adaptation of the "Dawn" chapter, though the following adaptations of the "Resurrection" and "Sun" chapters feel a bit condensed. Overall, it is a respectful adaptation that will satisfy fans of the original series, though its insistence on focusing on the serious elements of the comic while ignoring its many lighter moments gives it a somewhat stiff feeling.

Raz Greenberg

Further Reading

Tezuka, Osamu. *Apollo's Song* (2007).
_____. *Astro Boy* (1952-1968).
_____. *Buddha* (2006-2007).
_____. *Ode to Kirihito* (2006).
Urasawa, Naoki, and Takashi Nagasaki. *Pluto: Urasawa ′ Tezuka* (2003-2009).

Bibliography

McCarthy, Helen. *The Art of Osamu Tezuka: God of Manga*. New York: Abrams ComicArts, 2009.
Schodt, Frederik L. *Dreamland Japan: Writings on Modern Manga*. Berkeley, Calif.: Stone Bridge Press, 1996.
_____. *Manga! Manga! The World of Japanese Comics*. New York: Kodansha International, 1988.
Tezuka, Osamu. *Phoenix Volume 2: A Tale of the Future*. San-Francisco: VIZ Media LLC, 2002.

See also: *Astro Boy*; *Black Jack*; *Buddha* series; *Pluto* series

PLUTO
URASAWA ´ TEZUKA

Author: Nagasaki, Takashi; Tezuka, Osamu; Urasawa, Naoki

Artist: Naoki Urasawa (illustrator); James Gaubatz (letterer); Mikiyo Kobayashi (cover artist)

Publisher: Shogakukan (Japanese); VIZ Media (English)

First serial publication: *Purūtō*, 2003-2009 (English translation, 2009-2010)

Publication History

In 2002, award-winning manga artist Naoki Urasawa, along with his producer, Takashi Nagasaki, approached Tezuka Productions with the concept of adapting the "Greatest Robot on Earth" story line from Osamu Tezuka's *Astro Boy* (1952-1968) in commemoration of Astro Boy's fictional birthday. "The Greatest Robot on Earth" was originally serialized in the Japanese manga *Shōnen Magazine* under the title "The Greatest Robot in History" from June, 1964, to January, 1965. It also marked Urasawa's introduction to manga as a child.

Makoto Tezuka, Tezuka's son, initially rejected Urasawa and Nagasaki's proposal; however, the team persisted, and the project got the green light after an in-person presentation for Tezuka on March 28, 2003. This adaptation was originally proposed as a single installment. However, the concept was expanded, and *Pluto* was published in sixty-five installments in *Shogakukan*'s biweekly *Big Comic Original* from September, 2003, to April, 2009, with Tezuka acting as series supervisor. The series was collected in eight volumes (released in the United States by VIZ Media between 2009 and 2010 as Signature Editions) featuring a discussion between Urasawa and Tezuka, and "Postscript" essays by Tezuka, Nagasaki, and others. The series was translated into English by Jared Cook with manga scholar and longtime *Astro Boy* translator Frederik L. Schodt.

Plot

Pluto was conceived as a murder mystery featuring the German detective-robot Gesicht, one of "The Greatest Robot on Earth's" secondary characters, as the series'

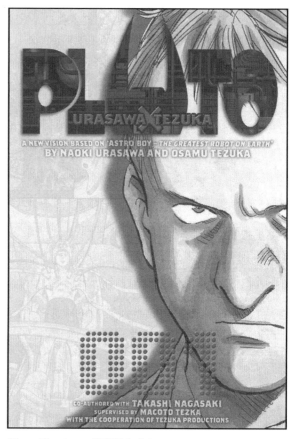

Pluto. (Courtesy of VIZ Media)

protagonist. The series is intended for older audiences and provides a self-contained narrative so that no previous knowledge of Tezuka or *Astro Boy* is required to understand the story.

The series begins with the destruction of the robot Mont Blanc in Switzerland, followed by the murder of robot-law preservationist Bernard Lanke in Germany. Special Investigator Gesicht of Europol is assigned to the Lanke case and immediately discovers a link between the destruction of Mont Blanc and the Lanke death. Both sets of remains had been desecrated postmortem by the addition of horns.

Gesicht travels to the Artificial Intelligence Correctional Facility to consult robot criminal Brau 1589, who links the horns to the Roman god of death, Pluto. He also predicts that the remaining six most advanced robots on Earth, including Gesicht, will be targeted. The murder of North No. 2 helps to confirm this theory, and afterward Gesicht warns the robot Brando and seeks the robot Atom in Japan.

Atom assists Gesicht from Japan when Junichiro Tasaki, the creator of the robot laws, is murdered. Atom learns that Lanke and Tasaki had served together on the Bora Survey Group, which had been sent to Persia to determine whether the kingdom was producing robots capable of being used as weapons of mass destruction. Despite the survey group's total lack of findings, the United States of Thracia invades Persia, beginning the thirty-ninth Central Asian War, or Persian War. Persia is ultimately overwhelmed by the peacekeeping forces, when six of the world's seven most advanced robots become involved in the conflict. In the present, Brando of Turkey confronts the killer of Mont Blanc and North No. 2 but is himself destroyed. As Brando's functions cease, he signals the other robots that his enemy has been defeated; however, a search funded by the robot Hercules produces only Brando's severed arms, positioned like horns on a rock.

In Germany, Adolf Haas, a member of a robot hate group KR, discovers that his criminal brother was killed three years previously by Gesicht, which was in direct conflict with robot laws prohibiting the murder of humans. Gesicht has no knowledge of the event, as the data were removed from his memory banks by Europol. KR decides to use this information against the robot community, and orders the assassination of Adolf should he interfere.

Meanwhile, in Tokyo City, Atom's sister Uran befriends a robot who is an extension of the robot-killer Pluto, and who has the ability to manipulate the natural world. The head of Persia's Ministry of Science, Professor Abullah, is revealed to be Pluto's creator.

A blackmail attempt on Professor Ochanomizu of Japan's Ministry of Science results in Atom's defeat by Pluto. However, Atom's body is not destroyed in the battle. Gesicht is temporarily taken off the Pluto case and charged with protecting Adolf Haas and his family after an attempt on Adolf's life by KR. Adolf attempts to rid himself of Gesicht by showing the detective a video linking Persia's former ruler, Darius XIV, to the murders of the Bora Survey Group members.

Gesicht is subsequently damaged by a cluster-cannon blast while preventing a second assassination attempt on Adolf. In Greece, the robot Hercules is destroyed by Pluto. Professor Tenma arrives in Japan, where Ochanomizu has been unable to revive Atom. The only way to revive Atom, Tenma reveals, is to introduce an emotional bias such as hate or anger. After repairs, Gesicht returns to his investigation severely weakened. He discovers a connection between Pluto and a Persian robot named Sahad.

In his search for Sahad, Gesicht travels to the Netherlands, where he learns that Abullah created Sahad. He learns, however, that news of Abullah's death had prompted Sahad to return to Persia, where his artificial intelligence (AI) was installed in Pluto. Gesicht locates and subdues Pluto but refuses to destroy Pluto per Europol commands. Suffering from severe metal fatigue, Gesicht is killed shortly thereafter by a robot child sent by Abullah. Gesicht's wife Helena gives her husband's memory chip to Professor Tenma.

A flashback at the beginning of Volume 7 reveals that, prior to the Persian War, Tenma, and Abullah created a robot with perfect AI. It was programmed with records of all six billion people on Earth and was to awaken as a result of Abullah's hatred for Thracia in his dying moments. The robot awoke believing himself to be the real Abullah and created Pluto to get revenge on mankind for the Persian War.

In the present, Epsilon, the only super-advanced robot of the seven not involved in the Persian War, defeats Pluto but does not destroy him. During their second encounter, Pluto pleads with Epsilon to kill him. Epsilon hesitates and is destroyed. In Tokyo City, Tenma revives Atom using the hatred stored in Gesicht's memory chip as an emotional bias. Atom awakens, having received Epsilon's final transmission about a threat far greater than Pluto: the robot Bora, who has the power to manipulate the world itself.

In the final volume, Abullah's AI is installed in Bora. Having disposed of the world's most advanced robots, Abullah/Bora plans to detonate the massive caldera below Thracia's Eden National Park using an antiproton bomb and wipe out mankind. Atom flies to Eden where he briefly engages Pluto in battle. The two make peace and descend into the caldera in an attempt to disarm the antiproton bomb. Failing to do so, Pluto hurls Atom to safety before sacrificing himself to freeze the exploding caldera and save mankind.

Volumes

- *Pluto: Urasawa ′ Tezuka*, Volume 1 (2009). Collects acts 1-7. Covers the murders of Mont Blanc, Bernard Lanke, and North No. 2. Gesicht is assigned to the investigation.
- *Pluto: Urasawa ′ Tezuka*, Volume 2 (2009). Collects acts 8-15. The thirty-ninth Central Asian War is detailed. Brando and Junichiro Tasaki are killed.
- *Pluto: Urasawa ′ Tezuka*, Volume 3 (2009). Collects acts 16-23. Gesicht's murder of a human is revealed. Uran temporarily befriends Pluto.
- *Pluto: Urasawa ′ Tezuka*, Volume 4 (2009). Collects acts 24-31. Atom is killed. Gesicht is assigned to protect Adolf Haas and learns of the Persian involvement in the murders.
- *Pluto: Urasawa ′ Tezuka*, Volume 5 (2009). Collects acts 32-39. Gesicht is damaged in the line of duty, and Tenma arrives in Japan to find Atom in stasis.
- *Pluto: Urasawa ′ Tezuka*, Volume 6 (2009). Collects acts 40-47. Gesicht learns the true identity of Pluto, battles Pluto, and is subsequently killed.
- *Pluto: Urasawa ′ Tezuka*, Volume 7 (2010). Collects acts 48-55. Abullah's origin is revealed. Epsilon battles Pluto twice and is killed in the second encounter. Atom is revived.
- *Pluto: Urasawa ′ Tezuka*, Volume 8 (2010). Collects acts 56-65. Abullah's plan reaches its final stage. Atom and Pluto team up to stop Bora. Pluto dies.

Characters

- *Special Investigator Gesicht*, the protagonist, is one of the world's seven most advanced robots and is composed of the virtually indestructible "zeronium" alloy. He is a detective serving the German division of Europol and appears as a slightly balding, fair-haired, middle-aged human with a large nose. He lives with his wife Helena and has nightmares linked to deleted memories.

He heads the investigation into the Pluto murders. Although he is killed in Volume 6, his memory chip is used to revive Atom, resulting in the series' resolution.

- *Atom of Japan* is one of the seven most advanced robots and is virtually indistinguishable from a human, even to sensors. He appears as a small boy with cowlicked hair and displays emotions uncharacteristic of robots. After being killed by Pluto in Volume 4, he is revived in Volume 7, and later teams up with Pluto to stop Bora.
- *Pluto* is a powerful robot capable of manipulating nature. Created by Professor Abullah using the AI of the peaceful robot Sahad, he is forced to battle the seven most advanced robots. He is large and monstrous, with two flexible horns that he uses as weapons. He sacrifices himself to stop Bora.
- *Professor Abullah* is the mastermind behind a plan to destroy humanity using the robots Pluto and Bora. He appears human and is registered by sensors as human, but until the final volume he is a robot believing himself to be the deceased Abullah. His AI is used to operate Bora.
- *Brando of Turkey* is one of the seven most advanced robots and appears as a stocky, middle-aged human when not wearing his pankration battle armor. He is the ESKKKR robot fighting champion, and for a time after his death he is believed to have destroyed Pluto in battle.
- *Hercules of Greece* is one of the seven most advanced robots and appears as a muscular human with a crew cut and rugged facial features when not wearing his pankration battle armor. Known as "the God of Battle," he is the WPKKKR robot fighting champion. His death in battle against Pluto in Volume 5 provides Epsilon with valuable data about their adversary.
- *Uran* is Atom's sister. Created by Professor Ochanomizu, she appears as a small Japanese girl with short pigtails. She has the ability to sense powerful emotions and invariably seeks to aid those in distress. Through her contact with an extension of Pluto's AI, it is revealed that she is being manipulated by Abullah.

- *Adolf Haas* is a robot hater whose brother was murdered by Gesicht. He is possessed by an overwhelming drive for vengeance, but lacks the willpower to deliver the fatal blow against Gesicht. He provides Gesicht with the evidence to link the former Persian government to the murders of the human robotics experts.
- *Epsilon of Australia* is the only one of the seven most advanced robots not to serve in the Persian War. He is human in appearance; he is slim with long hair and wears a black turtleneck and black pants. He operates a home for orphans of the Persian War and discovers the purpose of Bora before his death in Volume 7.
- *Professor Tenma* is a Japanese AI expert. He is self-absorbed and cynical and thin with a chin beard. He has black hair that curls in the front and wears tinted glasses. He created both Atom and the robot Abullah, and is responsible for Atom's revival in Volume 7.

Artistic Style

From the earliest stages of *Pluto*'s development, Makoto Tezuka challenged Urasawa to make the series a distinct work and to deviate from Osamu Tezuka's Walt Disney-influenced style wherever possible. As such, the series is drawn with Urasawa's typical realistic flair. Physics in the world of *Pluto* operate in approximate accordance to real-world physics, placing the series in marked contrast to *Astro Boy*. Human characters are drawn with less over-exaggerated features, and the robots are designed with greater emphasis on functionality and social status. As such, many of the more advanced robots are virtually indistinguishable from humans, while robots of lesser social importance, such as servants, are more machinelike in appearance. Urasawa does, however, stray from realism in his depiction of westerners as possessing large, hooked noses, per Japanese caricatures of Americans dating back to the 1850's.

Urasawa's realism is also characterized by a cinematic approach to panels and panel layouts. Urasawa employs cinematic aesthetics within his panels to create a dynamic visual experience, utilizing a wide variety of angles and compositions to the same end as their cinematic equivalents. Urasawa's approach to panel layouts closely resembles cinematic editing: Small panels inserted in conversations act as cutaways to combat tedium; the largest panels expand time much

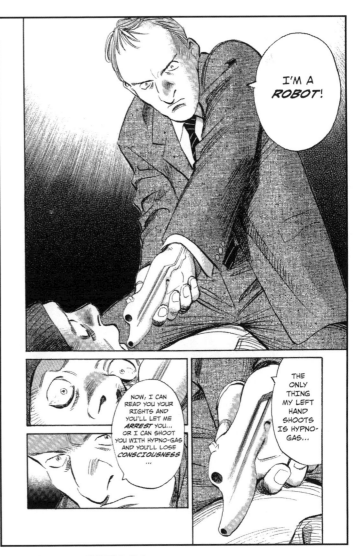

Pluto. (Courtesy of VIZ Media)

like the long take in cinema; and sequences such as the robot battles are composed entirely of smaller panels to create the impression of speed and draw the reader's eye quickly across the page.

Themes

The primary theme of *Pluto* is the absurdity of war and hate. In the first volume, although North No. 2 rejects war and wishes only to play the piano, he is lured into battle with Pluto and destroyed, leaving his blind, human master alone and unattended. In Volume 6, Gesicht learns that Pluto, built specifically for battle, was bestowed with an AI belonging to a robot who would otherwise have brought vegetation to Persia's deserts. In the last two volumes, it is revealed that the thirty-ninth Central Asian War, intended to relieve the world of the threat posed by Persia, resulted instead in the near eradication of mankind.

As in *Astro Boy*, the relationship between humans and robots is strained by discrimination. While assisting Tokyo City's Metropolitan Police Department in the investigation into the murder of Junichiro Tasaki in Volume 2, Atom is subjected to constant insults regarding his robot nature from the department's superintendent Tawashi. Volumes 3 and 4 depict members of the antirobot group KR—modeled after the Ku Klux Klan—dressed in white robes and pointed hoods. Certain of human superiority, KR assassinates the world's first robot judge and plots to ruin Gesicht in the media to create antirobot sentiment.

Another major thematic concern is memory. Throughout the series, numerous robots are implanted with others' memories or are offered the opportunity to delete painful memories, since robot memories never fade. North No. 2 aids his master Paul Duncan in correcting the inaccurate memory of his mother, and Volumes 4 through 6 find Gesicht struggling with the recovered memories of his lost child and subsequent murder of Adolf Haas's brother.

Impact

In the original *Astro Boy* manga, Osamu Tezuka attributed the date April 7, 2003, to Astro's creation by Pro-

fessor Tenma. Although *Pluto* would not begin publication until September of 2003, Urasawa and Nagasaki intended the series as a work commemorating Astro Boy's birthday. Urasawa had previously won, among other prizes, the Tezuka Osamu Cultural Award and three Shogakukan Manga Awards for his original manga. With *Pluto*, however, he sought to pursue his first adaptation in order to inspire young readers to explore those works of Tezuka that had influenced him as a child. As such, Urasawa not only drew from various *Astro Boy* story lines in addition to "The Greatest Robot on Earth" but also referenced other Tezuka works throughout the series such as *Black Jack* (1973-1983), *Kimba the White Lion*, and *Phoenix* (1954-1988).

Pluto has received near universal critical praise. Japanese critics Torohiko Murakami and Gorot Yamada even provided the postscripts for Volumes 5 and 6, respectively. The series' most significant contribution to the graphic novel is, as recognized by Makoto Tezuka, its standing as the first *Astro Boy*-related work to transcend simple homage or parody. Manga scholar Schodt predicts that *Pluto* is but the first of many liberal adaptations of *Astro Boy* to come.

Jef Burnham

Further Reading

Tezuka, Osamu. *Astro Boy* (1952-1968).

_____. *Black Jack* (1973-1983).

Urasawa, Naoki. *Twentieth Century Boys* (2009-2010).

Bibliography

Davis, Jason, Christie Barber, and Mio Bryce. "Why Do They Look White?" In *Manga and Philosophy: Fullmetal Metaphysician*, edited by Josef Steiff and Adam Barkman. Chicago: Open Court, 2010.

"The Legacy of *Astro Boy*: A Discussion between Naoki Urasawa and Makoto Tezuka." In *Pluto: Urasawa ´ Tezuka Volume 1*. San Francisco: VIZ Media, 2009.

Nagasaki, Takashi. "Postscript." In *Pluto: Urasawa ´ Tezuka Volume 8*. San Francisco: VIZ Media, 2010.

Natsume, Fusanosuke. "Postscript: Why Is *Pluto* So Interesting?" In *Pluto: Urasawa ´ Tezuka Volume 3*. San Francisco: VIZ Media, 2009.

Schodt, Frederik L. *The Astro Boy Essays: Osamu Tezuka, Mighty Atom, and the Manga/Amine Revolution*. Berkeley, Calif.: Stone Bridge Press, 2007.

Tezuka, Makoto. "Postscript." In *Pluto: Urasawa x Tezuka Volume 2*. San Francisco: VIZ Media, 2009.

See also: *Astro Boy*; *Black Jack*; *Twentieth Century Boys*; *Monster*

R

RANMA 1/2

Author: Takahashi, Rumiko
Artist: Rumiko Takahashi (illustrator)
Publisher: Shogakukan (Japanese); VIZ Media (English)
First serial publication: *Ranma nibun no ichi*, 1987-1996
First book publication: 1988-1996 (English translation, 1993-2006)

Publication History

Ranma 1/2 is the third manga series by Japan's accomplished and widely read manga artist Rumiko Takahashi. It was first published in *Weekly Shōnen Sunday* magazine beginning in September, 1987. As with her two prior series, *Urusei yatsura* (those obnoxious aliens) and *Maison Ikkoku*, Takahashi tells the story of a vexed love relationship between unlikely, quarrelsome romantic partners.

Because of its success, *Ranma 1/2* ran in original weekly installments for nine years. The final episode appeared in Volume 12 of *Weekly Shōnen Sunday* in March, 1996. As is common for successful manga, episodes of *Ranma 1/2* were collected and published in a multivolume book series that began in 1988. In 1996, Volume 38 collected the final episodes. Reader demand persuaded the Japanese publisher Shogakukan to republish the thirty-eight volumes with a different cover and a few extras in 2002. From December, 2009, to May, 2011, all 407 chapters of *Ranma 1/2* were republished in twenty-eight volumes for the *My First Big Special* edition in Japan.

In the United States, VIZ Media published *Ranma 1/2* in thirty-six book volumes from 1993 to 2006. In 2004, VIZ Media decreased both the format and price of the volumes and reprinted older volumes in the new format. VIZ Media decided to publish the manga in a mirrored layout, from left to right, with the book spine on the left instead of on

Ranma 1/2. (Courtesy of VIZ Media)

the right, as in the Japanese original. This was done to accommodate Western reading patterns. Thus, all graphics were reversed and right-handed characters became left-handed.

Plot

For *Ranma 1/2,* Takahashi wanted to create a fairy-tale scenario that would appeal to children, young adults, and women. Just as animals change into humans in fairy tales, in Takahashi's manga the protagonist

Ranma changes from a sixteen-year-old boy to a buxom teenage girl. This has happened ever since the outset of the series, when Ranma fell into a cursed spring in China. Contact with cold water turns Ranma into a girl, and hot water returns Ranma to his original male form. Even though the series was published in a weekly manga magazine directed primarily at young male adults (the *shōnen* genre), it became vastly more popular with teenage girls.

The series opens when martial artist Genma Saotome returns to Japan with his sixteen-years-old son Ranma to visit his old friend Soun Tendo, father of three teenage daughters. Years ago, the two men agreed that Genma's son should marry one of Soun's daughters. Because of cold rain in Tokyo, Genma is transformed into a panda, and Ranma becomes a girl; both had fallen into a different pool of the cursed Jusenkyo Springs in China.

The Tendo daughters seem relieved that there is no boy to marry one of them. The youngest, Akane, challenges Ranma to a martial-arts bout, which she loses. Taking hot baths, however, returns Genma and Ranma to their human forms. Afterward, the deal of the fathers is enacted. Ranma becomes engaged to Akane, but both show their displeasure at this development.

Takahashi's series is motivated by the love-hate relationship of Ranma and Akane. The relationship is complicated by Ranma's water-borne sex changes, which constitute the unique plot device of *Ranma 1/2.* The plot continues to contrast the ordinary with the supernatural. Ranma and Akane attend Furinkan High School together. There, they face the bully Tatewaki Kuno. Kuno fancies himself a poetic lover. He romances both Akane and Ranma (in the female incarnation), while fighting the male incarnation of Ranma. Akane's two older teenage sisters, the materialistic Nabiki and the domestic Kasumi, tend to support Akane. Kasumi is loved by Dr. Tofu Ono, a kindly chiropractor whom she does not love back.

Other characters are introduced in rapid succession to create more plot twists as the series progresses. Many of these characters also fell into a pool of Jusenkyo Springs, and, thus, they change into different creatures when splashed with cold water as well. Often this change is rather comical, as in the case of Ryoga

Hibiki. Ryoga is an ardent suitor of Akane, but cold water turns him into a piglet. Ironically, Akane likes him only in pig form.

In Volume 3 of the U.S. edition, Takahashi introduces the Chinese girl Shampoo. She is a serious rival of Akane for Ranma's love. Back in China, the girl version of Ranma fought and beat Shampoo. Shampoo's honor requires her to kill the girl Ranma, and she travels to Japan to search for her, but Shampoo inadvertently falls in love with Ranma in his boy incarnation. The rivalry between Akane and Shampoo drives many episodes. Shampoo is assisted by her grandmother, Cologne, a martial-arts expert. Like Akane, Shampoo also has a suitor, Mousse, whom she does not love. Cold water turns Shampoo into a cat. This makes her relationship with Ranma more problematic because Ranma has a cat phobia.

As the series progresses, Takahashi adds a variety of comic characters who are generally used to poke fun at the martial-arts genre. For example, the old martial-arts master Happogai is made ludicrous through his weakness for stealing women's panties.

Takahashi introduces Ranma's original fiancée about one-third into the series. Ukyo Kuonji was betrothed to Ranma by her father, but Ranma rejected her. Ukyo seeks to win back Ranma's love, fighting over him with Akane and Shampoo. Ukyo also has a boy in love with her whom she does not care about, the teenage ninja Konatsu.

For the climax of the series, the plot eventually moves to China, where a race of phoenix people, led by their ruler Saffron, seeks to control the waters of Jusenkyo Springs. Ranma and his friends go to China on the invitation of Plum, the daughter of the Jusenkyo guide. Akane is kidnapped by the phoenix people and brought to Jusenkyo. Ranma battles Saffron for control of the spring waters, and when Ranma is about to lose, Akane intervenes. She touches the Kinjakan, a martial-arts weapon, to turn off the hot water that strengthens Saffron. Akane succeeds, but touching the Kinjakan injures her and turns her into a little living doll.

Ranma and his friends do everything to save Akane. Ranma finally defeats Saffron. Cold water from the spring washes over Ranma and Akane, restoring her human body. Ranma confesses his love for the apparently dead Akane. This embarrasses him when Akane mentions it as she wakes up. Ranma and his friends accept that their curses can never be lifted because the spring waters changed permanently after the final battle.

Back in Japan, preparations are on for the wedding of Ranma and Akane. Almost all characters from the series are invited, or simply show up. As Ranma and Akane quarrel again, a free-for-all fight breaks out among the various guests; in the end, the wedding is postponed indefinitely. In the last panel, Ranma and Akane go back to school together.

Volumes

- *Ranma 1/2*, Volume 1 (1993). Introduces protagonists and explains the reason for Ranma's condition. Sets up the basic conflict between Ranma, Akane, and the bully Kuno. Introduces key supporting characters and their roles in the story. The American version collects the first fourteen episodes rather than just the first eight, as in the Japanese volume, to provide a longer start to the series.
- *Ranma 1/2*, Volumes 2-35 (1994-2006). Both the original Japanese book volumes and the American volumes collect about eight to eleven episodes each, covering about two to three months' worth of the original weekly installments. There is a slight difference in organization between the Japanese book collections and the American volumes. Generally, the volumes collect a connected story arc. Individual episodes and story arcs cover a wide range of settings, from contemporary Japan to fantasy lands. Depictions of martial-arts fights are a key feature of all volumes.
- *Ranma 1/2*, Volume 36 (2006). The American version collects all 407 episodes in thirty-six volumes (rather than the thirty-eight volumes of the Japanese editions). A climactic fight in China leaves all characters with their individual curses, and the wedding of Ranma and Akane is aborted. This returns them to the beginning, when they were reluctant high school sweethearts.

Characters

- *Ranma Saotome*, the protagonist, is a sixteen-year-old teenager dedicated to martial arts. On a trip to China, he falls into a cursed spring. Afterward, whenever he is splashed with cold water, he turns into a buxom girl; hot water returns him to a boy. He spends his life in an uneasy relationship with his fiancée, Akane Tendo.
- *Akane Tendo*, Ranma's love interest, is a cute sixteen-year-old girl. She prefers martial arts over boys but is drawn against her will to Ranma. With him, she shares most adventures of the series.
- *Shampoo*, Akane's prime rival for Ranma's love, is a teenage Chinese Amazon martial artist. She vows to kill Ranma in his female form for defeating her in a duel. She wants to marry Ranma in his male form but ultimately lets him go. She changes into a cat when touched by cold water.
- *Ryoga Hibiki*, Ranma's rival for Akane, is a teenager devoted to martial arts but is hopeless with directions. He changes into a black piglet.
- *Genma Saotome* is Ranma's father. His fall in Jusenkyo Springs turns him into a giant panda bear. He provides humor and initiates Ranma's betrothal.
- *Soun Tendo* is the father of three daughters and the owner of a martial-arts studio. He agrees to marry one of his daughters to Ranma.
- *Nabiki* and *Kasumi Tendo* are Akane sisters. Seventeen-year-old Nabiki is greedy and selfish, and nineteen-year-old Kasumi is a traditional young Japanese woman.
- *Happogai* is an old martial-arts master with a comic desire to steal women's panties. He helps Ranma but also represents a satirization of the martial-arts genre because of his strange habit.
- *Tatewaki Kuno*, antagonist of Ranma and Akane, is an upperclassman captain of the high school kendo team.
- *Jusenkyo Guide*, the kindly guardian of the cursed spring in China, is a middle-aged man in a Mao Zedong-style suit. His warnings usually come too late.
- *Saffron* is the leader of the phoenix people of Ho'o Mountain near Jusenkyo Springs. He fights

with Ranma and Akane over the waters of the springs.

- *Ukyo Kuonji* is Ranma's original fiancée, who he rejected. A teenage pancake chef who dresses like a boy, she studies martial arts and often fights with Shampoo over Ranma in his boy shape.
- *Cologne* is Shampoo's grandmother and an accomplished martial artist.
- *Mousse* is a Chinese teenage martial artist who is in love with Shampoo. He is first an enemy and then friend of Ranma.
- *Konatsu* is male ninja raised as a female fighter and often dresses as a woman.
- *Dr. Tofu Ono* is a bespectacled young chiropractor who treats Akane and Ranma when they are injured in battle.

Artistic Style

Takahashi created the main drawings of all 407 chapters of the black-and-white manga herself, as well as different color covers for all three book volume editions. She employed assistants only for backgrounds and minor details. Her style is that of classic manga, featuring wide-eyed characters with tiny noses; the characters' small mouths become big only when they show major emotions. As the series progresses, Takahashi's characters are drawn more precisely and in finer lines. They keep their characteristic visual features throughout the series. An exception is Akane, whose ponytail is chopped off in the first volume and never grows back.

A key visual element is the transformation of characters by cold water. Takahashi draws full upper-torso frontal nudity to emphasize Ranma's two incarnations, and also draws other female characters in this fashion. American censorship did not obliterate these drawings, which were essential to the story line. To emphasize his masculinity as a boy, Ranma often wears a tank top in his genuine incarnation.

Takahashi takes delight in depicting scenes of everyday life in Japan, such as the interior of the Tendo's martial-arts studio or the high school attended by Ranma and Akane. At the same time, she draws images of the fantastic, which range from Genma's transformation into a giant panda to the climactic battle scenes with the phoenix people.

Takahashi's panels usually vary per page. Large panels are used particularly for the many fight scenes. *Ranma 1/2* delights in surprising the reader with a fluid style of visual storytelling. There are many comic elements and ironic allusions to icons of popular Japanese culture.

Even though the American edition is reversed in terms of how it is read, the editing of signs and ubiquitous sound effects has been done quite carefully. An attentive reader will spot that, surprisingly, many characters are left-handed, which is due to the mirroring.

Themes

The key theme is the transformation of Ranma's gender. The title *Ranma 1/2* refers to the fact that Ranma can be either one of two genders.

Takahashi has stated, in a somewhat tongue-in-cheek manner, that she got the idea for the gender change from the reversible cloth pennants at a Japanese spa, where reversible pennants indicate whether the spa is open for men or women at any given time. Even though Ranma sees himself as a boy, he does not have any qualms accepting his girl incarnation. In fact, he sometimes changes into a girl for his advantage. Romantically, however, Ranma is attracted to girls only.

This theme of characters changing is enlarged for comic effect as many of the other characters are affected by the Jusenkyo Springs. The silent acceptance of these magical changes against a generally realistically drawn backdrop of modern Japan creates surprise and irony.

Martial arts are central to the storytelling and the visuals of *Ranma 1/2*. There is, however, a great degree of gentle spoofing. For example, fighting styles are often given hilarious names. The fighters themselves vary from dedicated teenagers, like Ranma, Akane, and Shampoo, to dirty old men like Happogai and supernatural beings like Saffron.

Another theme is love triangles. This is a theme featured in Takahashi's previous series, especially *Maison Ikkoku*. In *Ranma 1/2*, there is much unrequited love. Girls love boys who reject them, and girls are pursued by boys whose romantic advances they dislike.

The mix of realism and fantasy is a trademark of Takahashi's manga. Most fantasy episodes occur in China, but there are also some in Japan. Nobody seems to mind that a giant panda occasionally assists at Dr. Tofu's chiropractic clinic.

Impact

In Japan, *Ranma 1/2* proved especially popular with teenage girls. Perhaps the relative ease with which Ranma accepts his transformations between boy and girl was more appealing to a female audience.

Ranma 1/2 solidified the reputation of Takahashi as prime *mangaka* who could live well from her art. By November, 2006, sales of the series' book volumes reached the impressive number of forty-nine million. *Ranma 1/2* created a huge fan base. For the fans, some special volumes were released after the series had ended. A special memorial book was published in 1996 and rereleased in 2003. By 2011, Takahashi had become the world's most widely published female comic book artist.

In interviews, Takahashi expressed her positive surprise at the international success of *Ranma 1/2*. Even though the story is visually grounded in modern Japan, foreign audiences took to the story line with great appreciation. In the United States the series ran for thirteen years, topping the original Japanese run of nine years because of a slower publication schedule.

Films

Ranma 1/2 the Movie: Big Trouble in Nekonron, China. Directed by Shūji Iuchi. Kitty Films, 1991. This animated film brings the manga's central characters on a journey to China in an original story. One day, the Chinese girl Lychee visits the Tendo martial-arts studio. There, her long-awaited Prince Kirin arrives only to kidnap Akane and fly with her to China on his fantasy barge. Ranma and his friends follow him and free Akane from his grasp after battling the seven gods of martial arts.

Ranma 1/2 the Movie 2: Nihao My Concubine. Directed by Akira Suzuki. Kitty Films/Shogakukan Productions/Pony Canyon, 1992. In another animated film with an original story, Ranma and his friends are invited by Tatewaki Kuno onto his father's yacht. They land on an island with a magic spring that turns all who come into contact with it into men. Lacking women, the island prince, Toma, starts kidnapping all the Japanese girls, including Akane. Ranma and his friends free Akane and the others and leave the cursed island.

Team Ranma vs. the Legendary Phoenix. Directed by Junji Nishimura, 1994. An anime film that is loosely based on an episode in Volume 27 of the American manga publication. A giant phoenix rises from an egg atop the head of Tatewaki Kuno. As the phoenix begins to wreak havoc on Tokyo in the style of Godzilla, Ranma and his friends battle and defeat him.

Television Series

Ranma 1/2. Directed by Tomomi Mochizuki. Kitty Films/Studio Deen, 1989. This animated series ran for only one season in Japan. It generally followed the opening of the manga series and starred the voices of Kappei Yamaguchi as boy Ranma and Megumi Hayashibara as girl Ranma. Akane Tendo's lines were spoken by Noriko Hidata.

Ranma 1/2 Nettô-hen. Directed by Tsutomu Shibayama, Koji Sawai, and Junji Nishimura. Kitty Films/Studio Deen, 1989-1992. In Japan, this series followed the first series, picking up where the story left off and using the same voice actors. This series follows the story of the manga quite faithfully, only occasionally rearranging story arcs. It introduces only one new major character, Sasuka Sagurakure, a ninja retainer of the Kuno family. This anime series runs up to chapter 266 of the manga, collected in Volume 25 of the American edition, far from the climactic battle in China. In the United States, all seven seasons were released together on video under the title *Ranma 1/2*.

R. C. Lutz

Further Reading

Takahashi, Rumiko. *InuYasha* (1996-2008).

_____. *Maison Ikkoku* (1980-1987).

_____. *Rin-ne* (2009-   ).

Bibliography

Cornog, Martha, and Steve Raiteri. "Japan's J. K. Rowling." *Library Journal* 132 (May 15, 2007): 73.

Johnson-Woods, Toni, ed. *Manga: An Anthology of Global and Cultural Perspectives.* New York: Continuum, 2010.

Raiteri, Steve. "Graphic Novels." *Library Journal* 130 (November 15, 2005): 51.

_____. "*Ranma 1/2: Vol. 1.*" *Library Journal* 128 (September 1, 2003): 144.

See also: *InuYasha*; *Maison Ikkoku*

ROSE OF VERSAILLES, THE

Author: Ikeda, Riyoko
Artist: Riyoko Ikeda (illustrator)
Publisher: Shūeisha (Japanese); Sanyusha (English)
First serial publication: *Berusaiyu no bara*, 1972-1973
First book publication: 1972-1974 (partial English translation, 1981)

Publication History

Riyoko Ikeda's *The Rose of Versailles* originally appeared in the Japanese magazine *Margaret*, published by Shūeisha, and was serialized in the magazine in weekly installments from 1972 to 1973. Although the magazine primarily publishes *shōjo*, *Margaret*'s audience often includes adult women. The original Japanese version of *The Rose of Versailles* runs to seventeen hundred pages and was first published in *tankōbon* form in 1972. The work has been published in an eleven-volume paperback edition and a five-volume hardcover set.

In 1981, Frederik L. Schodt translated the first two volumes of the work into English. The Tokyo publishing house Sanyusha published them as textbooks to be used in teaching English to Japanese students. Sanyusha also published the volumes in the United States, making *The Rose of Versailles* the first manga translated into English to be commercially released in the country. However, the rest of the manga was not translated and published in English, and the two 1981 volumes went out of print. The work was eventually translated into French and German.

Plot

The Rose of Versailles, also known as *Lady Oscar*, is a *shōjo* manga written for a female teenage audience. The work combines an accurate account of the history of France from 1770 through the French Revolution with the fictional story of Oscar François de Jarjayes, a woman who has been reared as a boy and who becomes the commander of the Royal Guard at the French court. The plot is composed of three major story lines: the life of Marie Antoinette, Oscar's discovery of her true self and her love for André Grandier, and Oscar's realiza-

Riyoko Ikeda

Riyoko Ikeda, born in 1947, is the creator of one of the most beloved manga of all time, the historical romance *The Rose of Versailles*, set during and after the French Revolution. Ikeda is part of a core generation of female manga creators who helped shape the industry and literature in their own storytelling image. Despite its outsize reputation, *The Rose of Versailles* ran for just two years in the Shogakukan-published *shōjo* manga magazine *Margaret*. Ikeda took time off to pursue a career in music, and she has adapted opera by Richard Wagner to manga form. Among her various series are the transgender story *Claudine. . . !*; *Orpheus no Madon* (the window of Orpheus), which occurs during the Russian Revolution; and *Eikou no Napoleon—Eroica*, a sequel to *The Rose of Versailles*.

tion of the plight of the poor and participation in the revolution.

Having read Stefan Zweig's biography of Marie Antoinette while in high school, Ikeda decided to retell the story in a manga for girls. The manga is accurate in its portrayal of historical events and cleverly weaves in the fictional story of Oscar without distorting the historical reality. The work depicts Marie Antoinette's childhood in Austria, her marriage to Louis XVI, her quarrel with Madame du Barry (the mistress of Louis XV), the necklace scandal that damaged her reputation, and her love affair with Count Hans Axel von Fersen.

To this historical background Ikeda adds the fictional story of Oscar. General Jarjayes, a fictionalized version of a historical French nobleman, has no sons, and Oscar is his sixth daughter. He decides to raise her as a boy and prepare her for a military career. Oscar spends her youth learning fencing, horsemanship, and other skills essential to a nobleman's education. She shares her early years with her nanny's grandson, André Grandier, but their relationship changes as they grow older. Oscar belongs to the nobility, and André is a commoner; thus, the boundaries of social class come between them. Oscar becomes a member and, eventually, the commander of the Royal Guard, while André becomes her servant. Oscar's life at the palace introduces additional fictional and fictionalized characters into the story.

As Oscar becomes increasingly aware of the plight of the French people and the lack of compassion of the nobility, she begins to feel the need to change her allegiance. Eventually, she gives up her post as commander of the Royal Guard and becomes captain of a troop of soldiers. The faithful André follows her. When the troop discovers she is a woman, she must prove herself by fighting a duel.

Oscar's father, aware of the growing unrest and danger, decides to arrange a marriage for her. Oscar rejects this idea, although she is tempted by the life that would be afforded her by the marriage. Instead, Oscar decides to join the revolutionaries. Her soldiers follow her, and she fights against the king's soldiers. André, who has declared his love for her, is killed, and Oscar dies during the attack on the Bastille. The manga concludes with an account of the imprisonment and execution of the king and queen and Fersen's death at the hands of a mob after his return to Sweden.

Characters

- *Oscar François de Jarjayes*, the protagonist, is young, blond, slim, and beautiful. The sixth daughter of General de Jarjayes, she is reared as a boy and becomes a soldier. She faces many problems because she is torn between her loyalty to the queen and her outrage at the exploitation of the people by the French court. Eventually, she confronts problems of class discrimination as she realizes she loves her servant and aide, André Grandier.

- *André Grandier* is the grandson of Oscar's nanny. He falls in love with Oscar, for whom he works as a servant and aide, and eventually wins her love. However, during most of the story, he wrestles with his social inferiority, Oscar's inability or refusal to recognize his feelings for her, and the knowledge that her soldiering abilities are superior to his. He loses sight in one eye and slowly loses sight in the other.

- *Marie Antoinette* is an Austrian princess who becomes the wife of Louis XVI and the queen of France. Oscar admires her and is totally devoted to her, but her love affair with Count Fersen and her lack of sympathy for the French people cause Oscar to rethink this loyalty. Marie Antoinette was to be the heroine of the manga, but Ikeda's insistence on historical accuracy made her unsuitable for the role. Blamed for the suffering of the impoverished populace of France, she is guillotined during the revolution.

- *Hans Axel von Fersen* is a Swedish count who becomes Marie Antoinette's lover. Oscar is highly opposed to his love affair with the queen and persuades him to go to the United States. His absence causes the queen great sorrow, which she seeks to alleviate through excessive spending.

- *Rosalie Lamorlière* is Marie Antoinette's chambermaid. She spent her childhood in the slums of Paris with her sister, Jeanne. She is sweet and good and marries the Black Knight, a Robin Hood-like character who helps the cause of the people.

- *Madame du Barry* is the mistress of Louis XV and an enemy of Marie Antoinette. She is sent into exile following the death of Louis XV.

- *Jeanne de Valois-Rémy, Comtesse de la Motte* is Rosalie's sister. She acquires her place at the court through murder. She becomes a close friend of Marie Antoinette and brings about the infamous necklace scandal that almost destroys the queen. While much of her scandalous behavior is historically accurate, the historical Jeanne was not related to Rosalie.

Artistic Style

Ikeda's artistic style is typical of *josei* and *shōjo* manga. In terms of storytelling, the visual narrative is of far greater importance than the written narration. The pages are rendered in black and white, and color appears only on the covers. Objects and decorations such as flowers and jewelry reveal the emotions and social statuses of the characters and set the tone of the work. For example, Madame du Barry is surrounded by drawings of jewelry. There is an attention to both historical accuracy and detail in the depiction of the characters' clothing. The characters, both male and female, are drawn with a certain delicacy that reiterates the sexual ambiguity of the story.

Facial expression and body position play key roles in the visual narration. The female characters have incredibly large eyes, long eyelashes, thin eyebrows, and full wavy or curly hair. Ikeda often adds stars to the eyes of the female characters, giving them a dreamy appearance. Anger is expressed by narrowed eyes, frowns, and fanglike teeth. Disappointed and sad characters are drawn bent forward, symbolically weighed down by their emotion. Oscar is almost always drawn straight and vertical, indicating authority, self-control, and success.

Themes

Role reversal is a major theme of *The Rose of Versailles*. The manga portrays a woman freed from the social constraints imposed on her by society. However, as Oscar is freed from the limitations of being a woman, she is confined by another prescribed role, that of a young nobleman. From childhood, she is destined to become a military officer. As the political situation in France deteriorates and Oscar becomes ever more aware of the plight of the French people, she is forced to consider the moral consequences of her loyalty to the monarchy. As a noblewoman, she would not have faced this dilemma; she would have led a sheltered life similar to that of Marie Antoinette, who is not exposed to the misery of the people.

Ikeda also explores the importance of love and romantic relationships. André lives an unfulfilled life of unrequited love, and Oscar is unaware of his love for her. When he finally confesses his feelings, she rejects him; however, shortly before he is killed, she realizes that she loves him. The most developed love affair is the historical one between Marie Antoinette and Fersen, and the only love affair that ends happily is that of Rosalie and the Black Knight.

Impact

In Japan, *The Rose of Versailles* is regarded as a classic and one of the most important *shōjo* manga. It is also one of the most well-known manga outside of Japan. Although the editors of *Margaret* were reluctant to publish a girls' comic that retold historical events, Ikeda's work was well received immediately. *The Rose of Versailles* has also enjoyed enormous success in adaptation to other mediums. In 1974, the all-female Takarazuka Revue theater troupe performed a musical version of the manga. The play was highly successful and even saved the theater from bankruptcy. In 1979, a film version, *Lady Oscar*, was released in Japan and enjoyed an excellent reception. *The Rose of Versailles* was subsequently made into an anime and aired on Japanese television.

In creating *The Rose of Versailles*, Ikeda was strongly influenced by Osamu Tezuka's *Princess Knight* (1953-1956), which is recognized as the first girls' comic. The two manga share similar plot devices: a love affair, a heroine who lives as a man, and a foreign setting. However, *The Rose of Versailles* introduced important new features to girls' comics. Ikeda's use of historical settings, stars in the eyes of the heroines, and extremely detailed drawings of fashionable costumes transformed the genre.

Films

Lady Oscar. Directed by Jacques Demy. Kitty Films/ Shiseido/Nippon Television Network Corporation, 1979. This film adaptation stars Catriona MacColl as Oscar, Barry Stokes as André, Christine Böhm as Marie Antoinette, and Jonas Bergström as Fersen. The film differs considerably from the manga: André is a more dominant character than Oscar, and while André dies at the end of the film, Oscar does not. Produced in English and filmed in France, the film was well received in Japan, where it was released with subtitles. It was also released in France and the United States but was largely unsuccessful.

Television Series

The Rose of Versailles. Directed by Osamu Dezaki, et al. Tokyo Movie Shinsha, 1979-1980. This Japanese television series ran for forty-one episodes and was extremely popular in Japan. It has also enjoyed popularity in France, Italy, Spain, Taiwan, South Korea, and various Middle Eastern countries in translated versions.

Shawncey Jay Webb

Further Reading

Ikeda, Riyoko. *Orpheus no Mado* (1975-1981).
Tezuka, Osamu. *Princess Knight* (1953-1956).

Bibliography

Groensteen, Thierry. *The System of Comics*. Translated by Bart Beaty and Nick Nguyen. Jackson: University Press of Mississippi, 2007.

McCloud, Scott. *Making Comics: Storytelling Secrets of Comics, Manga, and Graphic Novels*. New York: Harper, 2006.

Schodt, Frederik L. *Dreamland Japan: Writings on Modern Manga*. Berkeley, Calif.: Stone Bridge Press, 1996.

_____. *Manga! Manga! The World of Japanese Comics*. New York: Kodansha, 1983.

See also: *From Eroica with Love*; *Oh My Goddess*

RUROUNI KENSHIN
MEIJI SWORDSMAN ROMANTIC STORY

Author: Watsuki, Nobuhiro
Artist: Nobuhiro Watsuki (illustrator)
Publisher: Shūeisha (Japanese); VIZ Media (English)
First serial publication: *Rurōni kenshin meiji kenkaku rōmantan*, 1994-1999
First book publication: 1994-1999 (English translation, 2003-2006)

Publication History

Nobuhiro Watsuki established the world in which *Rurouni Kenshin* would be set in his first professional work as a manga artist, *Crescent Moon in the Warring States*, published in a special issue of *Weekly Shōnen Jump* in the spring of 1992. Two subsequent stand-alone episodes under the title *Rurouni, Meiji Swordsman Romantic Story*, published in *Weekly Shōnen Jump* specials in 1992 and 1993, acted as pilots for the series. In *Rurouni*, Watsuki established the character of Kenshin Himura and introduced prototypical versions of some of the series' other main characters.

When production began on *Rurouni Kenshin*, Watsuki anticipated it would be approximately 30 chapters in length. Instead, the series ran for 255 chapters, which were serialized in *Weekly Shōnen Jump* between 1994 and 1999. Upon completion of the series, Watsuki authored two epilogue stories, including the side story *Yahiko no sakabatō*, published in *Weekly Shōnen Jump* in 2000, and the series' official endpoint, *Haru ni sakura* (*Cherry Blossoms in Spring*), published in the art book *Kenshin kaden* in late 1999.

The 255 chapters of *Rurouni Kenshin*, along with *Crescent Moon* and the two entries of *Rurouni*, were released in North America in twenty-eight volumes by VIZ Media between 2003 and 2006. VIZ further condensed the series into nine VIZBIG Editions, which also included *Yahiko no Sakabato* and *Cherry Blossoms in Spring*.

Plot

Rurouni Kenshin was inspired by Watsuki's passion for historical novels, particularly *Moeyo Ken* (1964;

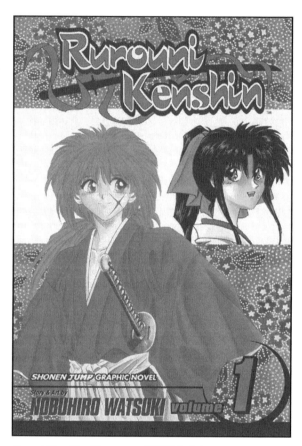

Ruroni Kenshin. (Courtesy of VIZ Media)

Burn, O Sword) by Ryōtarō Shiba and *Sugata Sanshirō* (c. 1943) by Tsuneo Tomita. *Rurouni Kenshin* follows a wandering swordsman in Meiji-period Japan through a series of escalating conflicts. It is intended for young male readers, although a consistently large portion of its readership has been female.

Rurouni Kenshin is set in 1878 Tokyo, following the 1867 defeat of the pro-Tokugawa shogunate Shinsengumi by the pro-imperialist Ishin Shishi, marking the end of Japan's Edo period and the beginning of the Meiji period. Kenshin, a wandering swordsman sworn never to kill again, is revealed to have been the Ishin Shishi's foremost assassin, Hitokiri Battōsai. He takes up residence with Kaoru Kamiya at the Kamiya

Kasshin-ryū Kenjutsu dojo. They are joined by Sano-suke Sagara and Kaoru's only pupil, Yahiko Myōjin.

In the "Megumi arc," Kenshin and friends agree to protect Megumi Takani from Kanryū Takeda, a crooked industrialist with the Oniwabanshū ninja clan in his employ. The Oniwabanshū attack Kamiya dojo, and it is revealed that Megumi was forced to produce opium for Kanryū. Megumi returns to Kanryū after he threatens to burn down the dojo, but Kenshin, Sano-suke, and Yahiko travel to Edo Castle, where they battle the Oniwabanshū for Megumi's freedom.

The Meiji government sends former Shinsengumi captain Hajime Saitō to assess Kenshin's abilities in the "Hajime Saitō arc." Satisfied with Kenshin's skills, the government requests that Kenshin assassinate former Ishin Shishi assassin Makoto Shishio, who plots to overthrow the government, beginning the "Kyoto arc." Kenshin travels to Kyoto alone but is joined thereafter by his friends and Saitō. With assistance from the remaining members of the Oniwabanshū, Kenshin and his companions defeat Shishio and his group of assassins, the Juppongatana (Ten Swords).

In the "Jinchū arc," the Kamiya dojo comes under assault by Enishi Yukishiro and his five comrades, who seek revenge against Kenshin for his actions as Hito-kiri Battōsai. In retribution for his sister's accidental murder by Kenshin during the Bakumatsu (the end of the Edo period), Enishi stages Kaoru's death. Kenshin almost dies of starvation in his near-comatose state of grieving. However, his allies discover that Kaoru's death has been faked. They, along with Kenshin, travel to Enishi's island, where Enishi is defeated and Kaoru is rescued. Four years later, Kenshin and Kaoru are married and have a son. Kenshin passes on his sword to Yahiko.

Volumes

- *Rurouni Kenshin*, Volume 1, VIZBIG Edition (2008). Collects Volumes 1-3 and the pilot stories *Rurouni, Meiji Swordsman Romantic Story*. Kenshin's core group of allies is established and the Megumi arc begins.
- *Rurouni Kenshin*, Volume 2, VIZBIG Edition (2008). Collects Volumes 4-6 and includes *Crescent Moon in the Warring States*. The Megumi

arc concludes. Kenshin and his friends have a brief rivalry with a murderer claiming to defend the future of *kenjutsu* (Japanese swordsmanship).

- *Rurouni Kenshin*, Volume 3, VIZBIG Edition (2008). Collects Volumes 7-9. Saitō tests Kenshin's abilities, and the Kyoto arc begins. En route to Kyoto, Kenshin frees a village from the Juppongatana.
- *Rurouni Kenshin*, Volume 4, VIZBIG Edition (2008). Collects Volumes 10-12. The Kyoto arc continues. Kenshin's allies arrive in Kyoto. Kenshin completes his Hiten Mitsurugi-ryū training in preparation for the battle with Shishio.
- *Rurouni Kenshin*, Volume 5, VIZBIG Edition (2009). Collects Volumes 13-15. The Kyoto arc continues, featuring battles between Kenshin's allies and the Juppongatana. Kenshin fights Aoshi Shinomori of the Oniwabanshū.
- *Rurouni Kenshin*, Volume 6, VIZBIG Edition (2009). Collects Volumes 16-18. The Kyoto arc concludes, and the Jinchū arc begins.
- *Rurouni Kenshin*, Volume 7, VIZBIG Edition (2009). Collects Volumes 19-21. The Jinchū arc continues. The fourteen-chapter "Remembrance" story line relates the events that led to Kenshin becoming a wandering swordsman.
- *Rurouni Kenshin*, Volume 8, VIZBIG Edition (2009). Collects Volumes 22-24. The Jinchū arc continues. Kenshin and his allies battle Enishi and his comrades at the Kamiya dojo. Enishi retires to his island with Kaoru.
- *Rurouni Kenshin*, Volume 9, VIZBIG Edition (2010). Collects Volumes 25-28 and follow-up episodes *Yahiko no Sakabato* and *Cherry Blossoms in Spring*. The Jinchū arc concludes. Five years later, the characters reunite.

Characters

- *Kenshin Himura*, a.k.a. *Hitokiri Battōsai*, the protagonist, is an effeminate-looking man with long, red hair pulled back into a ponytail and an *x*-shaped scar on his left cheek. He is a wandering swordsman seeking redemption for his crimes as Hitokiri Battōsai. A practitioner of the Hiten Mitsurugi-ryū style of sword fighting, he wields a sword with a reversed blade to prevent the death of his foes.

- *Kaoru Kamiya* is Kenshin's love interest and master of the Kamiya dojo. She wears a simple kimono, and her dark hair is often pulled back in a ponytail. She falls in love with Kenshin, although she vehemently denies her love for him. Her staged death in the Jinchū arc destroys Kenshin's fighting spirit.

- *Yahiko Myōjin* is the fierce-eyed, messy-haired orphan of a samurai family. He desperately yearns to be as strong and skilled as Kenshin and becomes a student of the Kamiya dojo. He is quick to fight those stronger than him and learns Hiten Mitsurugi-ryū by sight. He aids Kenshin in defeating members of the Juppongatana and Enishi's comrades.

- *Sanosuke Sagara* is tall, has spiked black hair, and wears a bandana around his head. *Aku*, the kanji for evil, is emblazoned on his back. He is headstrong and fights without regard for his own well-being. Sanosuke is Kenshin's first major opponent in the series, but he aids Kenshin in every major conflict thereafter.

- *Aoshi Shinomori* is tall and thin, has long bangs, and wears a trench coat. He has a stoic disposition and is selflessly devoted to his comrades. He is head of the Oniwabanshū and leads them in battle during the Megumi arc. He later joins forces with Shishio to fight Kenshin, only to turn against Shishio and aid Kenshin in battle thereafter.

- *Hajime Saitō* is a former Shinsengumi captain who works as a spy for the Meiji police force. He lacks compassion and believes in swift death for his opponents. He is introduced as one of Kenshin's foes, but because of his duty to the police, he reluctantly assists Kenshin in both the Kyoto and Jinchū arcs.

- *Makoto Shishio*, the antagonist of the Kyoto arc, was Kenshin's successor as Hitokiri Battōsai. He is covered in burns and completely wrapped in bandages as a result. He is ruthless and desires absolute power. He leads the Juppongatana in an attempt to seize control of Japan.

- *Enishi Yukishiro*, the antagonist of the Jinchū arc, has spiked white hair and wears Chinese-style clothing and small, circular sunglasses. He has an obsessive personality and suffers from severe

Ruroni Kenshin. (Courtesy of VIZ Media)

psychological trauma. He stages Kaoru's death but cannot murder her because she resembles his sister.

Artistic Style

Many of Watsuki's character models are based on existing photographs of key Meiji-era figures. Other models reference the creations of other artists working in manga, anime, video games, and American comic books. Watsuki places these patchwork characters in realistically rendered cities and landscapes of historical Japan. This juxtaposition draws the reader's attention to the purposely incongruous characters, reinforcing the character-driven nature of the series. As is typical of *shōnen* manga, these landscapes tend to disappear during battles in favor of backgrounds characterized by dynamic motion lines. This emphasizes the intensity of the confrontations, while the lines draw the eye to specific parts of the frame. Moreover, the reader is encouraged to proceed quickly from one frame to the next by Watsuki's minimalist art during the battle sequences, creating the impression of frenzy.

The series' few color pages are dominated by reds, browns, and metallic blues. The simplicity of Watsuki's color palette and his extensive use of white backgrounds allow for smooth transitions to and from the brief color passages. Watsuki initially uses color ink for these pages but later switches to Copic markers to save time. Characters and backgrounds also undergo revisions in the interest of time efficiency, making them easier to draw. The most drastic revisions occur mid-series, when Watsuki alters his character models to have smaller eyes and decreases the number of lines used in drawing hair and clothing. These changes give the characters a slightly more cartoonish appearance in the later chapters.

Themes

The primary theme of *Rurouni Kenshin* is responsibility. Kenshin's actions throughout the entire series reflect his deep sense of responsibility for the lives he took as Hitokiri Battōsai. He has since sworn to use his sword only as a means to protect the lives of others. However, a conflict arises between Kenshin's quest for atonement and his newfound responsibilities to his

---

Nobuhiro Watsuki

Nobuhiro Watsuki, born in 1970, is the creator of the samurai comedy-action manga *Rurouni Kenshin*, set during the Meiji period. Among notable manga-artist assistants who worked under him were Eiichiro Oda, creator of *One Piece*, and Hiroyuki Takei, creator of *Shaman King*. Watsuki trained in manga by working under Takeshi Obata (illustrator of *Hikaru no go* and *Death Note*). Watsuki's other manga include a Western (*Gun Blaze West*), an alchemy-themed adventure (*Buso renkin*), and a reworking of the Frankenstein story (*Embalming: The Another Tale of Frankenstein*). In May, 2012, Watsuki debuted a "reboot" version of *Rurouni Kenshin*. While in high school, Watsuki got his start with *Weekly Shōnen Jump* after winning the publication's Hop Step award for amateur submissions.

---

friends, whom he cannot abandon even though they face constant danger as a result of their association with him. This conflict results in Kenshin's incapacitation in the Jinchū arc. At the conclusion of the Megumi arc, Megumi undertakes a similar quest when she becomes a doctor to atone for her production of opium while enslaved by Kanryū.

Another major theme in *Rurouni Kenshin* is power, which is expressed in terms of both physical and political power. Sanosuke and Yahiko's quest for power is linked to the theme of responsibility, for they strive to increase their physical power throughout the series out of a sense of responsibility to fight alongside Kenshin. In both the Hajime Saitō arc and the Kyoto arc, former soldiers of the Bakumatsu are contracted by the Meiji government to assassinate former Ishin Shishi assassins so that the true methods of the new regime's ascent to political power may remain hidden from the public.

In the Jinchū arc, Enishi believes his dead sister has been urging him to kill Kenshin. Thus, revenge becomes an important theme in the series' final arc. Once Enishi has successfully carried out his revenge plot, he finds his hallucinations of his dead sister have not been appeased. Thus, revenge in *Rurouni Kenshin* is portrayed as hollow and unrewarding.

Impact

The people and events of the Bakumatsu period have spawned countless popular texts in Japan, including Shiba's *Moeyo Ken*. Drawing inspiration from such texts, Watsuki modeled many of the characters in *Rurouni Kenshin* on real-world figures of the Bakumatsu, and he appropriated major events of the era for the construction of his narrative. While Japanese audiences were well-acquainted with many of these people and events prior to the publication of *Rurouni Kenshin*, the specifics of the Bakumatsu and Meiji periods remained relatively unknown to most audiences outside of Japan.

Within half a year of the manga's publication, *Rurouni Kenshin* was already slated to cross media platforms with the release of a CD book chronicling the first four chapters of the manga. The series subsequently inspired video games, action figures, art books, novelizations, an anime, and a feature film spin-off of the anime. *Rurouni Kenshin* also became an international multimedia success and even established anime as a marketable form of entertainment in Indonesia in 1996. Thus, Watsuki introduced many international audiences to the key players and events of the Bakumatsu and Meiji periods for the first time. In addition, *Rurouni Kenshin* encouraged historical objectivity among the preexisting fans of Bakumatsu literature by presenting both the positive and negative aspects of the Shinsengumi and Ishin Shishi.

Films

Samurai X: The Motion Picture. Directed by Tsuji Hatsuki. Fuji Television Network/SPE Visual Works, 1997. The English-language version of this animated film stars J. Shannon Weaver as the voice of Kenshin Himura and Kara Bliss as the voice of Kaoru Kamiya. The film's story line does not appear in the manga. In this theatrically released spin-off of the *Rurouni Kenshin* anime, Kenshin and friends must quell a samurai uprising against the Meiji government.

Television Series

Rurouni Kenshin. Directed by Kazuhiro Furuhashi. Aniplex/Fuji TV, 1996-1998. The English-language version of this anime stars Richard Cansino as the voice of Kenshin Himura and Dorothy Elias-Fahn as the voice of Kaoru Kamiya. Many of the manga's chapters are omitted or condensed to accommodate the inclusion of original story lines. Most significant among these alterations is the complete absence of the Jinchū arc. The series spawned two original video animations and the feature film *Samurai X*.

Jef Burnham

Further Reading

Chrono, Nanae. *Peacemaker Kurogane* (2002-2005).
Watsuki, Nobuhiro. *Buso Renkin* (2006-2008).

Bibliography

Watsuki, Nobuhiro. "Free Talk." In *Rurouni Kenshin*, by Nobuhiro Watsuki. Vol. 5. VIZBIG Ed. San Francisco: VIZ Media, 2009.

_____. "Rurouni Secrets: An Interview with *Rurouni Kenshin* Author Nobuhiro Watsuki." In *Rurouni Kenshin Profiles*, edited by Kit Fox. San Francisco: VIZ Media, 2005.

Wyman, Walt, and Kazuhisa Fujie. *The Rurouni Kenshin Companion: The Unofficial Guide.* Denver, Colo.: DH, 2006.

See also: *Blade of the Immortal*; *Lone Wolf and Cub*; *Dragon Ball*

S

SAILOR MOON

Author: Takeuchi, Naoko

Artist: Naoko Takeuchi (illustrator)

Publisher: Kodansha (Japanese); TOKYOPOP (English); Kodansha Comics USA (English)

First serial publication: *Bishōjo senshi sērā mūn*, 1992-1997 (English translation, 1998-2001)

First book publication: 1992-1997 (English translation 1998-2001)

Publication History

Naoko Takeuchi's *Sailor Moon* was first published as *Bishōjo senshi sērā mūn* (beautiful warrior sailor moon) in the monthly *shōjo* manga magazine *Nakayoshi* beginning in 1992; it was collected in eighteen paperback volumes from 1992 to 1997. A fourteen-volume, newly bound edition was issued by Kodansha under the KCDX label from 2003 to 2004. For this edition, the English subtitle of the original series was changed from *Pretty Soldier Sailor Moon* to *Pretty Guardian Sailor Moon*.

In the United States, the first seven chapters appeared in the manga magazine *MixxZine*, published by Mixx Entertainment (TOKYOPOP), in 1998; the remaining chapters of the first, second, and third arcs were published in comic book format and later bound into paperbacks. Simultaneously, the fourth and fifth arcs were published in TOKYOPOP's manga magazine *Smile* and then bound into paperbacks. In contrast to the original Japanese version, all pages were mirrored so that the manga could be read from left to right. In the first two arcs, the names of the characters were changed in order to match the names used in the anime; characters in ensuing arcs mostly kept their original names. The TOKYOPOP edition has been out of print since 2005. In 2011, Kodansha Comics USA began publishing a fourteen-volume edition of the manga.

Naoko Takeuchi

Naoko Takeuchi, born in 1967, is the creator of the international sensation manga and anime *Sailor Moon*. She has said that the inspiration was the *sentai* (or teen TV shows) featuring superhero teams, and that she wanted to create one focused on powerful girls. It was serialized in the early 1990's in *Nakayoshi* and *Run Run*, both published by Kodansha. Her other manga include *The Cherry Project*, about figure skating, and *PQ Angels*, about girls from outer space who turn into cockroaches. From 1998 to 2004, she wrote an autobiographical series titled *Return-to-Society Punch!!* While the *Sailor Moon* manga had been aimed at teenage girls, this story of her life was aimed at adult women readers who could relate to her experiences, and thus *Return-to-Society Punch!!* appeared in *Young You*, a Shūeisha-published *josei* magazine. Takeuchi was educated as a pharmacist before entering manga.

Plot

Sailor Moon is one of the most popular and prominent representatives of *shōjo* manga and belongs to the *mahō shōjo* (magical girls) genre. The series is set in Tokyo and recounts the story of teenager Bunny Tsukino, who can transform into Sailor Moon. The name "Sailor Moon" derives from the fact that the uniforms of the Sailor Scouts are modeled on school uniforms, known in Japan as *sērā fuku* (sailor clothing). The series contains various references to Japanese, ancient Greek, ancient Roman, Celtic, and Germanic myths and legends and can broadly be divided into five arcs, with each arc having a particular villain.

The first arc (sometimes referred to as the "Dark Kingdom" arc) follows Bunny as she encounters the talking cat Luna, who reveals that Bunny is Sailor Moon and that she must find the Silver Imperium Crystal and protect the princess. As Sailor Moon fights the warriors Jadeite, Nephrite, Zoisite, and Kunzite, she meets her fellow Sailor Scouts, Mercury, Mars, Jupiter, and Venus. She also encounters the mysterious Tuxedo Mask, who is revealed to be Darien Shields.

Bunny learns she is Princess Serenity of the Moon Kingdom, holder of the Silver Imperium Crystal. In the past, she was in love with the crown prince of Earth, Endymion, but when he was killed in battle, she committed suicide. Her mother resurrected her to rebuild the kingdom. Darien, the reincarnation of Endymion, is abducted and turned evil by Queen Beryl, who acts on behalf of Queen Metallia, the empress of the night. In the end, Sailor Moon defeats her enemies and returns to Earth with Endymion.

In the second arc ("Black Moon"), the future child of Bunny/Neo Queen Serenity and Darien/King Endymion, Rini, travels to the past seeking Sailor Moon's assistance when a group known as Black Moon attacks thirtieth century Crystal Tokyo. Sailor Moon follows Rini to the future, where they fight Black Moon on the planet Nemesis. The group's leader turns Rini into the evil Black Lady; however, when she sees Sailor Pluto dying, she transforms into Sailor Chibi Moon. She and Sailor Moon destroy Nemesis.

The third arc ("Infinity") introduces the remaining Outer Scouts, Uranus, Neptune, and Saturn. The primary antagonists, the Death Busters, come from the Tau System in another dimension. The group's leader, Pharaoh 90, wants to merge with Earth so it can become a new home planet for the group. He is assisted by Professor Soichi Tomoe, who turns his daughter, Hotaru, into Mistress 9; she tries to help Pharaoh 90 complete his transformation. With the help of the Holy Grail, Sailor Moon and Sailor Chibi Moon evolve to Super Sailor Moon and Super Sailor Chibi Moon. The three Talismans held by Uranus, Neptune, and Pluto call to Sailor Saturn, hidden inside Mistress 9. Hotaru is reborn as a baby and given into the care of Uranus, Neptune, and Pluto.

In the fourth arc ("Dream"), Bunny and her friends attend high school. During a solar eclipse, the Dead Moon Circus descends to Earth and prevents Rini from returning to the future. In a dream, Rini encounters a winged unicorn named Helios; in his human form, he is the priest of Elysion, the heart of the Earth. He is held captive by Queen Nephrenia, who wants to conquer Earth. To defeat her, Hotaru quickly grows up and becomes Sailor Saturn to fight alongside the other Sailor Scouts. With the aid of the Sailors' united power and Darien's Golden Crystal, Sailor Moon evolves into Eternal Sailor Moon. After defeating Nephrenia, she frees the Amazoness Quartet from their spell, and they become the Sailor Quartet: Sailor Ceres, Sailor Palis, Sailor Juno, and Sailor Vesta.

In the final arc ("Sailor Stars"), Rini leaves for the thirtieth century, and Darien studies abroad. Sailor Galaxia steals his Golden Crystal, and he dies. Bunny collapses and is saved by the boy band Three Lights. Its members—Seiya, Taiki, and Yaten—transfer to her school and reveal themselves to be the Sailor Starlights. Sailor Galaxia's servants continue to attack the Sailor Scouts, killing them one by one. When only Bunny is left, Princess Kakyu appears. The Sailor Starlights are killed, but Sailor Chibi Moon and the Sailor Quartet rescue Sailor Moon, Kakyu, and Chibi Chibi. Sailor Moon defeats Galaxia and sacrifices herself to defeat Chaos. Chibi Chibi transforms into her real self, Sailor Cosmos, and revives all of the Sailors. The series ends with the wedding of Bunny and Darien.

Volumes

- *Sailor Moon*, Volume 1 (1998). Collects chapters 1-5. Bunny finds out about her Sailor Moon identity and meets Amy, Raye, and Lita.
- *Sailor Moon*, Volume 2 (1998). Collects chapters 6-9. Bunny meets Darien and Mina and finds out her true identity.
- *Sailor Moon*, Volume 3 (1999). Collects chapters 10-12. Sailor Moon and her team fight Darien, turned evil by Queen Beryl.
- *Sailor Moon*, Volume 4 (1999). Collects chapters 13-16. The victory over the Dark Kingdom ends the first arc. The second arc begins with the ar-

rival of Rini. Mars, Mercury, and Jupiter are abducted.

- *Sailor Moon*, Volume 5 (1999). Collects chapters 17-19. The remaining Sailor team meets Sailor Pluto and travels to the thirtieth century. This volume also contains the short story "Rini's Picture Diary 1."
- *Sailor Moon*, Volume 6 (2000). Collects chapters 20-22. Sailor Moon is abducted and reunites with Mercury, Mars, and Jupiter. Together, they fight Black Lady.
- *Sailor Moon*, Volume 7 (2000). Collects chapters 23-24. The victory over Black Moon ends the second arc. The third arc begins with the arrival of Haruka and Michiru. Rini meets Hotaru.
- *Sailor Moon*, Volume 8 (2000). Collects chapters 25-28. Haruka and Michiru are revealed to be Sailor Scouts, and Setsuna returns.
- *Sailor Moon*, Volume 9 (2001). Collects chapters 29-32. Sailor Moon becomes Super Sailor Moon, and Hotaru is revealed to be Sailor Saturn.
- *Sailor Moon*, Volume 10 (2001). Collects chapter 33. The victory over the Death Busters ends the third arc. This volume also contains the short story "Rini's Picture Diary 2."
- *Sailor Moon*, Volume 11 (2001). Recounts the story of the second anime movie, *Sailor Moon S: The Movie*, and also contains the short story "Casablanca Memory."
- *Sailor Moon SuperS*, Volume 1 (1999). Collects chapters 34-36. The fourth arc begins with the appearance of Helios and the Dead Moon Circus.
- *Sailor Moon SuperS*, Volume 2 (1999). Collects chapters 37-38. Helios reveals the truth about Elysion and Queen Nephrenia. This volume also contains three short stories about Lita, Amy, Raye, and Mina.
- *Sailor Moon SuperS*, Volume 3 (2000). Collects chapters 39-40. Hotaru becomes Sailor Saturn; the final fight against the Dead Moon Circus begins.
- *Sailor Moon SuperS*, Volume 4 (2000). Collects chapters 41-42. The victory over Queen Nephrenia ends the fourth arc. This volume also contains the short story "Rini's Picture Diary 3."

- *Sailor Moon StarS*, Volume 1 (2001). Collects chapters 43-45. The fifth arc begins with the arrival of the Sailor Starlights, Chibi Chibi, and Princess Kakyu.
- *Sailor Moon StarS*, Volume 2 (2001). Collects chapters 46-48. Sailor Moon, the Sailor Starlights, Chibi Chibi, and Princess Kakyu travel to the center of the galaxy. This volume also contains the short story "Rini's Picture Diary 4."
- *Sailor Moon StarS*, Volume 3 (2001). Collects chapters 49-52. Galaxia and Chaos are defeated; Bunny and Darien marry.

Characters

- *Serena "Bunny" Tsukino* (*Usagi Tsukino* in the Japanese version), a.k.a. *Sailor Moon*, the protagonist, is a teenager with long blond hair tied into two ponytails with two buns on top. She is clumsy and anxious but becomes mature and self-confident. She was Serenity, princess of the moon, in her past life and will be Neo Queen Serenity, queen of the moon, in the thirtieth century.
- *Darien Shields* (*Mamoru Chiba*) is Bunny's love interest. He is a tall, good-looking boy with short black hair. He often teases Bunny but is nevertheless gentle to her. He is the reincarnation of Endymion and transforms into Tuxedo Mask to support Sailor Moon during her fights.
- *Bunny* (*Chibi Usa*), a.k.a. *Rini*, is the future child of Bunny and Darien. She has long pink hair tied into ponytails with two oval buns on top. She often fights with Bunny, especially about Darien. She transforms into Sailor Chibi Moon.
- *Inner Scouts* are the Sailor Scouts who represent the inner planets of the solar system. They are *Amy* (*Sailor Mercury*), *Raye Hino* (*Sailor Mars*), *Lita Kino* (*Sailor Jupiter*), and *Mina* (*Sailor Venus*).
- *Outer Scouts* are the Sailor Scouts who represent the outer planets of the solar system. They are *Setsuna Meioh* (*Sailor Pluto*), *Haruka Tenoh* (*Sailor Uranus*), *Michiru Kaioh* (*Sailor Neptune*), and *Hotaru Tomoe* (*Sailor Saturn*).
- *Sailor Starlights* are three Sailor Scouts from another galaxy: *Seiya Lights* (*Sailor Star Fighter*),

Taiki Lights (*Sailor Star Maker*), and *Yaten Lights* (*Sailor Star Healer*). In their human forms, they appear as boy band Three Lights; when they transform, they become female.

- *The Dark Kingdom* consists of *Queen Metallia*, *Queen Beryl*, and the four male warriors *Jadeite*, *Nephrite*, *Zoisite*, and *Kunzite*, who were once servants of Prince Endymion.
- *Black Moon* consists of leader *Wiseman/Death Phantom* and his group of rebels, which includes *Prince Diamond*, *Prince Sapphire*, *Crimson Rubeus*, *Emerald*, and the Four Sisters of Deception: *Catzi*, *Bertie*, *Prizma* and *Avery*.
- *Death Busters* come from the Tau System and are led by *Pharaoh 90*. The group includes *Professor Soichi Tomoe*, *Kaori Night*, and the Witches 5 (*Eudial*, *Mimete*, *Viluy*, *Tellu*, and *Cyprine* and her twin sister, *Petite Roll*).
- *Dead Moon Circus* consists of *Queen Nephrenia*, *Zirconia*, and the *Amazoness Quartet*, four girls who are actually Sailor Scouts: *JunJun* (*Juno*), *CereCere* (*Ceres*), *VesVes* (*Vesta*) and *PallaPalla* (*Palis/Pallas*).
- *Chaos* and *Sailor Galaxia* are the antagonists of the fourth arc.

Artistic Style

A self-taught artist, Takeuchi wrote and drew *Sailor Moon* with the help of two anonymous assistants, a common practice in the manga industry. *Sailor Moon* features black-and-white drawings; gray shading is added with the help of screentones. The title pages of all chapters were originally rendered in color, though this practice was not retained in the paperback edition.

Sailor Moon is drawn in a typical *shōjo* manga style. Almost all characters are tall and slender and have long limbs, large eyes, and long, flowing hair. Takeuchi draws angled figures in fine lines and has a rather simple style; compared to those drawn by classic *shōjo* manga artists such as Riyoko Ikeda, her backgrounds and clothing do not have much detail. Instead, Takeuchi relies heavily on screentones, which create atmosphere in her work. Her techniques make for an overall impression of a floating world, where pages resemble collages and the overall mood is more important than the

story. Characters often break through the boundaries of the panels, and important scenes are drawn across double-page spreads. While Takeuchi mostly uses word balloons for the speech of her characters, in important scenes, speech is placed freely within the panels or enclosed in Art Nouveau-style frames.

Themes

Coming-of-age is one of the major themes of *Sailor Moon* and is presented in multiple ways. First of all, the characters grow up over the course of the story. Bunny becomes less anxious and more mature, which is mirrored in her abilities as a Sailor Scout and in her evolution from Sailor Moon to Eternal Sailor Moon. The other Sailor Scouts mature throughout the series as well. The characters must also decide their personal futures, reflecting the teenage female readers' wishes to grow up and become adult women.

Friendship is also a major theme. At first, Sailor Moon fights alone; only when she assembles her team, however, does she become capable of defeating her enemies. The power of friendship is emphasized in the third arc, when the Outer Scouts initially refuse to cooperate with Sailor Moon and the Inner Scouts. In the end, however, only their combined power can defeat their enemies. Likewise, in the fifth arc, Sailor Moon's belief in friendship wins over Galaxia's pursuit of power. In other words, in *Sailor Moon*, strength comes from teamwork.

Family is also a theme in *Sailor Moon*, especially for Rini and Hotaru. The former is the child of Bunny and Darien; the latter is raised by Setsuna, Haruka, and Michiru. As can be seen in this example, *Sailor Moon* presents families that do not conform to the standard pattern but are presented as valuable. While marriage is presented as the ideal outcome of romantic love, not all characters have such an ideal family background; Amy's parents are divorced, and Lita's parents died in a plane crash.

Another important theme is romantic love, one of the most important topics in modern *shōjo* manga. Bunny and Darien's love endures from past to present and future, and Sailor Moon fights in the name of love and justice. Sexuality is also a minor but nonetheless important topic in *Sailor Moon*. The series features examples of nonheterosexual characters, though this aspect is never directly discussed within the framework of homosexuality, bisexuality, or transgenderism. This ambiguity might be the result of the young target audience; however, it is common in manga to avoid discussing the topic of sexuality directly. The most important characters in terms of sexuality are Haruka and Michiru, who are in a romantic relationship, and the Sailor Starlights, who transform from male to female. Takeuchi has said that the topic allows for exploration as an author, and she compares Haruka to actors in the famous Japanese all-female theater troupe Takarazuka.

Impact

In Japan, *Sailor Moon* was one of the biggest hits of the 1990's and represented an important turning point in the magical girl genre. Bunny is not the first girl in Japanese popular culture to transform into a superhero and fight enemies; however, until the appearance of *Sailor Moon*, girl superheroes in manga fought alone. Takeuchi introduced into the genre the concept of a team of female warriors, and female teams in which each member represents something specific remained popular in Japan afterward.

Outside Japan, particularly in North America and Europe, *Sailor Moon* popularized manga among younger generations. Many fans got to know the series through the anime version before buying the manga. *Sailor Moon* was the first successfully translated *shōjo* manga in the United States, and many credit it with attracting female readers to comics. It also developed a devoted, mostly female fan base that campaigned to keep the anime series on the air in the United States.

Sailor Moon has been criticized for a several reasons. For one, the characters are said to possess no psychological depth and to be stereotypical. Another point of criticism has been TOKYOPOP's inconsistent translation of the manga. Spellings of names change, and in some cases, English names are used instead of the already introduced Japanese ones. Nevertheless, the series has greatly influenced the manga industry in Japan and elsewhere.

Films

Sailor Moon R: The Movie. Directed by Kunihiko Ikuhara. Toei Animation, 1993. This animated film fea-

tures an original story not based on the manga. Bunny and her friends visit a botanical garden where they are attacked by an alien named Fiore and his demonic flower, Xenian.

Sailor Moon S: The Movie—Hearts in Ice. Directed by Hiroki Shibata. Toei Animation, 1994. This animated film is based on a story featured in the eleventh manga volume. Luna falls in love with an astronomer while the Sailor Scouts fight Princess Snow Kaguya.

Sailor Moon Super S: The Movie—Black Dream Hole. Directed by Shibata. Toei Animation, 1995. This animated film features an original story not based on the manga. Rini is abducted. Sailors Pluto, Uranus, and Neptune appear even though they were not in the *Super S* television season.

Television Series

Sailor Moon. Directed by Junichi Sato, et al. Toei Animation, 1992-1993. The *Sailor Moon* anime series consists of five seasons, each aired under a different title. The first season of the anime series comprises forty-six episodes and differs from the manga in a number of ways. Seasons 1-4 were broadcast in the United States between 1995 and 2000. They were heavily censored and, for the first two seasons, included short "Sailor Says" moral instructions at the end of each episode.

Sailor Moon R. Directed by Kunihiko Ikuhara. Toei Animation, 1993-1994. This anime differs from the manga in that the first part introduces two alien villains, Eiru and An, who do not appear in the manga.

Sailor Moon S. Directed by Ikuhara. Toei Animation, 1994-1995. This anime differs from the manga in that Uranus and Neptune do not initially know that they hold two of the Talismans.

Sailor Moon Super S. Directed by Ikuhara. Toei Animation, 1995-1996. This anime differs from the manga in that the Outer Scouts do not appear in the regular episodes and the members of the Amazoness Quartet are not Sailor Scouts.

Bishōjo senshi sērā mūn sērā sutāzu. Directed by Takuya Igarashi. Toei Animation, 1996-1997. This anime series differs from the manga in that Nephrenia returns in the first six episodes and the Sailor Starlights do not appear until episode 7.

Pretty Guardian Sailor Moon. Directed by Ryūta Tasaki, et al. Toei, 2003-2004. This forty-nine-episode live-action series is loosely based on the first arc of the manga.

Verena Maser

Further Reading

Clamp. *Cardcaptor Sakura* (2000-2003).

Yazawa, Nao, and Sukehiro Tomita. *Wedding Peach* (2003-2004).

Yoshida, Reiko, and Mia Ikumi. *Tokyo Mew Mew* (2003-2004).

Bibliography

Allison, Anne. "Fierce Flesh: Sexy Schoolgirls in the Action Fantasy of *Sailor Moon*." In *Millennial Monsters: Japanese Toys and the Global Imagination*. Berkeley: University of California Press, 2006.

_____. "Sailor Moon: Japanese Superheroes for Global Girls." In *Japan Pop! Inside the World of Japanese Popular Culture*, edited by Timothy J. Craig. Armonk, N.Y.: M. E. Sharpe, 2000.

Napier, Susan J. "Vampires, Psychic Girls, Flying Women, and Sailor Scouts: Four Faces of the Young Female in Japanese Popular Culture." In *The Worlds of Japanese Popular Culture: Gender, Shifting Boundaries, and Global Cultures*, edited by Dolores P. Martinez. New York: Cambridge University Press, 1998.

Navok, Jay, and Sushil K. Rudranath. *Warriors of Legend: Reflections of Japan in "Sailor Moon."* North Charleston, S.C.: BookSurge, 2005.

See also: *Cardcaptor Sakura*; *Fruits Basket*; *The Rose of Versailles*

Saint Seiya
Knights of the Zodiac

Author: Kurumada, Masami
Artist: Masami Kurumada (illustrator)
Publisher: Shūeisha (Japanese); VIZ Media (English)
First serial publication: *Seinto seiya*, 1986-1990
First book publication: 1986-1991 (English translation, 2004-2010)

Publication History

Saint Seiya was created, written, and illustrated by Masami Kurumada. It was first published in *Weekly Shōnen Jump* from 1986 to 1990 and was compiled into twenty-eight volumes from 1986 to 1991. *Saint Seiya* has been reprinted several times in Japan and has been translated into numerous languages. The first international market in which *Saint Seiya* was published was France, where it was published by Kana as *Les Chevaliers du zodiaque* (knights of the zodiac) beginning in the late 1980's. As a result, *Saint Seiya* also became known globally as "knights of the zodiac"; the characters known as "saints" in the original manga are referred to as "knights" in a number of international translations. VIZ Media adapted the manga series for the North American market, publishing the series from 2004 to 2010 under the title *Saint Seiya: Knights of the Zodiac.*

Plot

Saint Seiya is a *shōnen* manga that follows five primary knights sworn to serve the Greek goddess Athena, who has taken human form and protects Earth from other deities. The knights must rise to certain power levels and prove their worth to gain their magical armor, which is called cloth. Each cloth possesses the attributes of a guardian constellation. The cloth works together with the knights' life energy, similar to chi, which they have learned to harness to become superbeings. The plot focuses on Seiya, the primary protagonist.

The manga can be divided into three main arcs: "Sanctuary," "Poseidon," and "Hades." In the Sanctuary arc, the knights train to achieve the necessary

Saint Seiya Knights of the Zodiac. (Courtesy of VIZ Media)

power levels to earn their cloths. They enter a fighting tournament to win a gold cloth. The plot is driven by corruption, as Ikki betrays his fellow knights. The knights fight against this corruption and try to save the dying Athena.

In the Poseidon arc, Poseidon threatens to destroy humanity unless Athena sacrifices herself in its place. She makes a pact with him to save humanity and allows herself to be imprisoned. The knights must work together to save her before she drowns within her prison. Once freed, Athena is able to imprison Poseidon.

Hades breaks free of the Underworld in the Hades arc and resurrects fallen enemy soldiers to defeat the knights. Athena sacrifices herself to repair the cloths.

The knights work with Poseidon to resurrect Athena, and she ultimately defeats Hades.

Volumes

- *Saint Seiya: Knights of the Zodiac—The Knights Of Athena* (2004). Collects chapters 1-4. In Greece, Seiya wins the Pegasus cloth, becoming a Bronze Knight. He must fight an old nemesis, Shaina, to keep it.
- *Saint Seiya: Knights of the Zodiac—Pegasus vs. Dragon* (2004). Collects chapters 5-8. Hyoga obtains the cloth of Cygnus in Russia before receiving orders to travel to Japan.
- *Saint Seiya: Knights of the Zodiac—Phoenix! The Warrior from Hell* (2004). Collects chapters 9-12. Ikki appears at the tournament. He steals the victor's prize, a gold cloth. Seiya, Shun, Hyoga, and Shiryu set out to retrieve the cloth.
- *Saint Seiya: Knights of the Zodiac—Phoenix! The Warrior from Hell* (2004). Collects chapters 13-17. The knights face off against Ikki's Black Knights.
- *Saint Seiya: Knights of the Zodiac—Execution!* (2004). Collects chapters 18-21. Ikki reveals his tortured training before Seiya defeats him. Ikki sees the error of his ways and joins the knights against a new enemy.
- *Saint Seiya: Knights of the Zodiac—Resurrection!* (2004). Collects chapters 22-24. The knights continue to battle the Silver Knights as they learn of the corruption at Athena's sanctuary. They meet Athena's human form, Princess Sienna.
- *Saint Seiya: Knights of the Zodiac—Medusa's Shield* (2005). Collects chapters 25-27. The Gold Knight Leo Aiolia battles the Bronze Knights until Athena reveals the pope's role in his brother's death.
- *Saint Seiya: Knights of the Zodiac—The Twelve Palaces* (2005). Collects chapters 28-30. Saori is injured by a Silver Knight's golden arrow. The Bronze Knights frantically seek the corrupt pope to save Athena. Seiya reaches the seventh sense power level.
- *Saint Seiya: Knights of the Zodiac—For the Sake of Our Goddess* (2005). Collects chapters 31-33. The Bronze Knights get caught in Gemini's illusions and go to different zodiac temples. Cassios allows Aiolia to kill him to stop the pope's corruption.
- *Saint Seiya: Knights of the Zodiac—Shaka, Close to Godhood!* (2005). Collects chapters 34-36. The Bronze Knights continue to work through the zodiac temples. Ikki reaches the seventh sense power level.
- *Saint Seiya: Knights of the Zodiac—To You I Entrust Athena* (2005). Collects chapters 37-40. The Bronze Knights continue through the zodiac temples. Hyoga awakens his seventh sense power level.
- *Saint Seiya: Knights of the Zodiac—Death Match in the Master's Chamber!* (2005). Collects chapters 41-43. Seiya and Shun arrive at the last zodiac temple; Shun fights Aphrodite, while Seiya confronts the pope.
- *Saint Seiya: Knights of the Zodiac—Athena Revived!* (2006). Collects chapters 44-45. Ikki battles the Gemini knight while trying to save Seiya.
- *Saint Seiya: Knights of the Zodiac—The Magic Flute* (2006). Collects chapters 46-49. Poseidon's Mariners make a failed attempt to kidnap Athena. Poseidon threatens to kill humankind if Athena does not sacrifice herself.
- *Saint Seiya: Knights of the Zodiac—The Undersea Shrine* (2006). Collects chapters 50-53. Both Seiya and Shun borrow the Libra cloth to demolish the South Pacific Ocean Pillar.
- *Saint Seiya: Knights of the Zodiac—The Soul Hunter* (2006). Collects chapters 54-57. Shiryu demolishes the Indian Ocean Mammoth Pillar. Ikki demolishes the Antarctic Ocean Mammoth Pillar.
- *Saint Seiya: Knights of the Zodiac—Athena's Prayers* (2006). Collects chapters 58-61. Hyoga demolishes the Pillar of the South Atlantic Ocean. Ikki is sent to another dimension.
- *Saint Seiya: Knights of the Zodiac—The End of the Azure Waves* (2006). Collects chapters 62-66. The Bronze Knights join forces and stun

Poseidon. Before Poseidon can kill the Bronze Knights for interfering, Athena imprisons him.

- *Saint Seiya: Knights of the Zodiac—108 Stars of Darkness* (2007). Collects chapters 67-70. The seal confining Hades to the Underworld is broken.
- *Saint Seiya: Knights of the Zodiac—Battle for the Twelve Palaces* (2007). Collects chapters 71-73. The knights battle the Specters.
- *Saint Seiya: Knights of the Zodiac—Under the Sala Trees* (2007). Collects chapters 74-77. Six Gold Knights use the forbidden Athena Exclamation technique to kill Shaka at the risk of demolishing the sanctuary.
- *Saint Seiya: Knights of the Zodiac—Awaken!! The Eighth Sense* (2008). Collects chapters 78-82. Shiryu aids the Gold Knights in using the Athena Exclamation against Saga and company. Athena commits suicide, and her blood is used to repair the Bronze Knights' cloths.
- *Saint Seiya: Knights of the Zodiac—Underworld, The Gate of Despair* (2008). Collects chapters 83-86. Seiya and Shun journey through the Underworld towards Hades' castle.
- *Saint Seiya: Knights of the Zodiac—Hades Reawakens* (2008). Collects chapters 87-90. Orphée rebels against Hades by joining Seiya and Shun as retribution for what was done to his lover, Eurydice.
- *Saint Seiya: Knights of the Zodiac—The Greatest Eclipse* (2009). Collects chapters 91-94. Ikki arrives at Hades' palace and fights Hades.
- *Saint Seiya: Knights of the Zodiac,* Volume 26 (2009). Collects chapters 95-99. Athena protects Shun's physical form before Hades takes her to Elysium. The Gold Knights join with the Bronze Knights.
- *Saint Seiya: Knights of the Zodiac,* Volume 27 (2009). Collects chapters 100-105. Pandora betrays Hades by giving Ikki the tools to enter Elysium. Poseidon attempts to aid the Bronze Knights against Hades.
- *Saint Seiya: Knights of the Zodiac,* Volume 28 (2010). Collects chapters 106-109. Seiya is bru-

---

Masami Kurumada

Masami Kurumada, born 1953, is the creator, writer, and illustrator of the widely popular *Saint Seiya: Knights of the Zodiac*, which was serialized in *Weekly Shōnen Jump* between 1986 and 1991. It is one of the magazine's most popular series, and continues to spin off collectible items, like plushie figurines and cigarette lighters, decades after its completed publication. It is a wild and loose appropriation of Greek mythology in the service of drama, intrigue, and mystical fighting. Kurumada has also explored boxing in *Ring ni Kakero*, ninja in *Fuma no Kojiro*, and science fiction (specifically robots and artificial intelligence) in *B't X*, among his numerous publications. *Ring ni Kakero* is his longest running work, having appeared in two runs, the first from 1977 to 1981, the second from 2000 to 2009, for a total of fifty-one volumes.

---

tally defeated, leaving the remaining Bronze Knights to face Hades. Athena defeats Hades.

Characters

- *Seiya*, a protagonist, is an orphaned young man with a great destiny: to be continuously reincarnated in order to guard the goddess Athena. He initially wears the bronze cloth of Pegasus and then works up to the gold cloth of Sagittarius. He is the jokester of the group and has superstrength and superspeed.
- *Shiryu*, a protagonist, is a Bronze Knight who wears the dragon cloth. He is considered the wisest of the main protagonists, and his strength lies in defense. He is temporarily allowed to wear the gold cloth of Libra.
- *Hyoga*, a protagonist, is a Bronze Knight who wears the cloth of Cygnus. He is stoic with a kind heart. He has the ability to conjure ice or snow.
- *Shun*, a protagonist, is a Bronze Knight who wears the cloth of Andromeda. He is a pacifist but has great strength. His older brother is Ikki.

- *Ikki*, a protagonist, is a Bronze Knight who wears the cloth of Phoenix. He is a hard-edged loner and the older brother of Shun.
- *Athena*, a.k.a. *Princess Sienna*, a protagonist, is the Greek goddess of wisdom and battle. She reincarnates every 250 years to save the Earth from the forces of darkness.
- *Thanatos*, an antagonist, is the incarnation of Hades, god of death. He is the primary opponent of Athena and the knights.
- *Hypnos*, an antagonist, is the god of sleep and is Hades' twin brother.
- *Black Knights*, antagonists, are the dark doppelgängers of the Bronze Knights. They serve Ikki. The main ones are Black Pegasus, Black Andromeda, Black Dragon, and Black Swan.
- *Blue Warriors*, antagonists, are similar in power to the Bronze Knights. They reside in the ice lands of Sinigrad.
- *Poseidon's Mariners*, antagonists, are seven warriors who follow Poseidon.
- *Pandora*, an antagonist, is incarnated as Hades' brother to protect him until the final battle against the knights, after which she will be rewarded with immortality.
- *The Specters*, antagonists, are Hades' equivalent of knights.
- *The Olympian's Angels*, antagonists, are soldiers of Olympian gods.

Artistic Style

Saint Seiya is drawn in black, white, and gray. Black and white are often utilized in sharp contrast to add emphasis or emotion. Backgrounds, especially those depicting nature and celestial scenes, are often more detailed than characters, which is typical of Japanese manga style. Characters' faces are expressive, and eyes serve as the primary vehicle for projecting emotion. However, deities have blank white eyes that are devoid of emotional expressions.

The armor worn by the knights is often highly stylized and harks back to Japan's ancient samurai armor. It is depicted in great detail during intense battles, a technique that emphasizes the damage received or

dealt and the severity of wounds. Blood and wounds are displayed in generous detail.

Backgrounds include horizontal or vertical lines that represent quick movement or rising power levels during battle. Fighting segments often have elements, such as sound, light, or movement, that go beyond the panels. The action-packed fight scenes feature large panels with full images of the fight and smaller panels that show close-ups of characters' facial expressions. Some action sequences are displayed in a series of panels that resembles a film strip, manipulating readers' conception of time and movement within the text. Important battle sequences may take up an entire page on which the images are presented in great detail. When Seiya uses intense power levels, they are emphasized with a solar-system background. In general, images are contained within neat frames unless they are important or intense, in which case they may take up an entire page or escape their panel frame.

During fights, dialogue bubbles are jagged, which shows the tension as or before a blow is delivered. When characters have intense wounds or there is great tension, dialogue appears in black bubbles resembling spilled blood. The shape of the bubbles echoes the softness or hardness of the characters' emotions. A tense situation may have sharp-edged bubbles.

When creating characters, Kurumada uses a technique similar to the "Star System" of famed manga artist Osamu Tezuka, reusing character designs from previous series. The physical characteristics of Seiya are similar to those of Ryuji in Kurumada's earlier series *Ring ni kakero* (1977-1981).

Themes

Saint Seiya is a coming-of-age story; the knights graduate from adolescence to adulthood through training and accession into knighthood. Athena plays a mother's role to the orphan boys. The major thematic point in the manga has to do with dichotomies of power. The knights have different power levels to which they can ascend, while the deities they confront have a separate power base. The knights and deities are separate from humans, who are essentially powerless and must be protected. Echoing the Shinto philosophy that teams or groups are more powerful than individuals, the text emphasizes that battles are won through team, rather than individual, effort. The power struggle among Athena, Poseidon, and Hades relates to the power struggle in Greek mythology among the brothers Zeus (Athena's father), Poseidon, and Hades.

Saint Seiya provides a complex representation of several religious ideologies. Kurumada's use of the term "saint" in the original text relates to Catholicism, and the term "knight" also has Christian connotations, prompting readers to think of the knights of the Crusades. Athena, Poseidon, and Hades are adaptations of ancient Greek deities. The reincarnation of the knights relates to the Buddhist and Shinto belief that ascended beings can choose to be reincarnated to further the enlightenment of humankind, and their use of life energy relates to the philosophies that all life forces are connected and that energy can be tapped into.

Impact

The complex molding of diverse religious elements into a new mythos, as demonstrated in *Saint Seiya*, became a common technique in 1990's manga such as *Sailor Moon* (1992-1997). The blending of religious philosophies creates a cross-cultural text that is accessible to a global audience, contributing to the international emergence of manga. The Buddhist and Shinto concept of universal energy is echoed in the manga that followed *Saint Seiya* and has been used in numerous *shōnen* and *shōjo* series. The concept of a team of male adolescents being thrust into adulthood via war helped make this series a hit and was a motif copied by later series such as *Mobile Suit Gundam Wing* (1995-1996).

Films

Saint Seiya: Gekijoban. Directed by Kozo Morishita. Toei Animation, 1987. This animated film features an original story not based on the manga. Eri is possessed by Eris (Discord), who kidnaps Athena with the intention of using her power to rule the world.

Saint Seiya: Kamigami no atsuki tatakai. Directed by Shigeyasu Yamauchi. Toei Animation, 1988. This animated film features an original story that was later incorporated into the anime plot. The Bronze Knights fight members of the Norse pantheon.

Saint Seiya: Shinku no shōnen densetsu. Directed by Masayuki Akehi. Toei Animation, 1988. This animated film continues the anime story line. Abel threatens to destroy both humanity and Athena.

Saint Seiya: Saishu seisen no senshitachi. Directed by Akehi. Toei Animation, 1989. Lucifer and his soldiers threaten to overturn the knights' power.

Saint Seiya: Tenkai-hen joso—Overture. Directed by Yamauchi. Toei Animation, 2004. This film adaptation takes place after the Hades arc. Athena struggles to find a way to heal Seiya's battle-incurred injuries.

Television Series

Saint Seiya (*Knights of the Zodiac*). Directed by Morishita and Kazuhito Kikuchi. Toei Animation, 1986-1989. This anime stars Tōru Furuya as the voice of Seiya. The series differs from the manga in that it includes a story arc ("Asgard") not included in the original comic.

Rachel Cantrell

Further Reading

Clamp. *Magic Knight Rayearth* (1993-1995).
Kubo, Tite. *Bleach* (2001-   ).
Takeuchi, Naoko. *Sailor Moon* (1991-1997).

Bibliography

Clements, Jonathan, and Helen McCarthy. *The Anime Encyclopedia: A Guide to Japanese Animation Since 1917*. Berkeley, Calif.: Stone Bridge Press, 2001.

McCloud, Scott. *Understanding Comics: The Invisible Art*. New York: HarperPerennial, 1993.

Phillipps, Susanne. "Characters, Themes, and Narrative Patterns in the Manga of Osamu Tezuka." In *Japanese Visual Culture: Explorations in the World of Manga and Anime*, edited by Mark W. MacWilliams. Armonk: M.E. Sharpe, 2008.

See also: *Bleach*; *Sailor Moon*

SANCTUARY

Author: Fumimura, Sho

Artist: Ryoichi Ikegami (illustrator); Mary Kelleher (letterer)

Publisher: Shogakukan (Japanese); VIZ Media (English)

First serial publication: *Sankuchuari*, 1990-1995

First book publication: 1990-1995 (English translation, 1993-1997)

Publication History

Sanctuary is a manga series authored by Sho Fumimura (also known as Buronson), perhaps best known for his work as the writer of *Fist of the North Star* (1983-1988), and illustrated by Ryoichi Ikegami, a professor of arts at Osaka University and lead artist for *Heat* (1999-2004). *Sanctuary* was initially serialized from 1990 to 1995 in Shogakukan's semimonthly *Big Comic Superior*. Later, it was compiled and published in twelve volumes. Eventually, it was published as forty-six comic books and released in the United States in nine volumes by VIZ Communications (later VIZ Media) from 1993 to 1997. A bestseller in Japan, *Sanctuary* was successfully adapted into a live-action film and an animated feature.

Plot

Sanctuary narrates the story of two childhood friends, Akira Hojo and Chiaki Asami, who are involved in an organized crime network and a political party, respectively. The story is a thriller, using the obscure dealings of the Japanese *yakuza* underworld and Japan's insular political system as a backdrop. The story's main thread is its heroes' quest to bring Japan out of its economic and cultural isolation, effectively opening its borders to foreign products and attitudes. Initially, the two friends come from Cambodia, where their parents labored as part of Japanese interest. Under the regime of dictator Pol Pot, the boys are separated from their families and sent to the so-called killing fields.

Having survived and returned to Japan, the pair decides its initial path with a game of rock-paper-scissors. Hojo chooses a life of crime, free from customary social conventions, while Asami joins the Japanese po-

Sanctuary. (Courtesy of VIZ Media)

litical machine, striving to become the youngest member of the national diet. Given their experiences in Cambodia, which forced them to hone their survival instincts, the friends set out on the path to shake Japan to its foundations and bring it back from its stupor as the second largest economy in the world (during the 1990's). Thus, the title of the story represents the desire of both main characters to make Japan a sanctuary protected from international intervention and financial instability.

The story chronicles Hojo's and Asami's rises to power by way of astute negotiations and clever posturing. While Hojo is adept at strategy in a world of action, Asami displays a more intellectual bent. Another key element within the story is the sexual tension between Hojo and Deputy Chief Kyoko Ishihara of the Metropolitan Police Department.

Within the first two volumes, Hojo manages to become a *yakuza* don. Asami's rise to power, on the other hand, is much more protracted and convoluted, despite Hojo's continued assistance. The political establishment, the figure head of which is the aging prime minister, Isaoka, is more entrenched and savvy than Asami originally envisioned. On the political side, Hojo and Asami resort to blackmail, threats, and the creation of a new political bloc to counteract the influence of the Liberal Democratic Party. In the criminal sphere, Hojo begins to operate in China and Hong Kong and subsequently attempts to bring his *yakuza* dealings into the open, operating as a legitimate businessman.

By the end of the series, both Hojo and Asami have succeeded in their ambitions. Hojo's plan to create a future for the *yakuza* and envision opportunities overseas becomes real. He unites all the main *yakuza* families under his leadership, hoping to increase their profile within Japanese society. After successfully promoting an electoral reform bill that he hopes will change the nature of the diet forever, introducing popular elections and thus granting responsibility to the general population, Asami becomes the youngest nominee ever for the position of prime minister. However, a somber secret darkens their triumph. The last volume shows the pair of friends in Cambodia, with a dying Asami sitting next to Hojo under a tree.

Volumes

- *Sanctuary*, Volume 1 (1995). Collects part 1, issues 1-4. The main characters and the basic plot are introduced. Hojo blackmails Sakura, a member of the diet, to speed up Asami's rise to political power.
- *Sanctuary*, Volume 2 (1995). Collects part 1, issues 5-9. Hojo becomes the don of the Sagara Alliance with the help of Tokai and makes inroads into China, planning to take over other locations. Asami runs for the diet.
- *Sanctuary*, Volume 3 (1995). Collects part 2, issues 1-5. Asami is elected to the diet and joins forces with some freshmen members. Hojo uses

attacks from an Okinawa *yakuza* faction to advance his plans.
- *Sanctuary*, Volume 4 (1995). Collects part 2, issues 5-9. Asami befriends a U.S. trade representative and uncovers some of Isaoka's dirty deeds. Assisted by Tokai, Hojo continues to work to unify *yakuza* leadership, but a Chinese adversary shoots him down.
- *Sanctuary*, Volume 5 (1996). Collects part 3, issues 1-7. Hojo recovers at the hospital, while Asami seeks to amend the constitution thanks to a new political coalition. Tokai escapes an attempt to kill him.
- *Sanctuary*, Volume 6 (1996). Collects part 3, issues 7-8, and part 4, issues 1-5. Hojo engages the Hobe Sannon Association, while Isaoka thwarts Asami's efforts to incriminate him. Isaoka starts digging into Asami's past, looking for weakness.
- *Sanctuary*, Volume 7 (1997). Collects part 4, issues 5-7, and part 5, issues 1-3. Isaoka confronts Hojo and Asami and tries unsuccessfully to bribe Asami. After Asami's connection to the *yakuza* is revealed, the diet is dissolved; Hojo runs for office, effectively legalizing the *yakuza*.
- *Sanctuary*, Volume 8 (1997). Collects part 5, issues 3-8. Asami falls ill, but the U.S. president pays him a surprise visit, boosting his campaign. Tokai deals with gang rebellion in Hokkaido, supported by the Russian Mafia.
- *Sanctuary*, Volume 9 (1997). Collects part 5, issues 8-13. Isaoka's party loses the election, and Asami and Hojo's coalition comes to power, eventually passing a bill that makes Asami the first popularly elected secretary general. However, Asami dies before taking power, leaving Hojo to carry on their dream in the form of *yakuza* working abroad.

Characters

- *Akira Hojo*, a protagonist, is the don of the Sagara Alliance. He is politically skillful and dashingly attractive. He is always well dressed and neatly groomed. As Asami's friend, he shares the pain and brutality of life in Cambodia's killing fields, thus acquiring a rugged, deeply individualistic temperament. He is ruthless in the attainment of his objectives and generous to his subordinates.

- *Chiaki Asami*, a protagonist, is as ambitious and strong-willed as Hojo. However, he focuses his efforts on politics, not crime. He exhibits a more intellectual air than Hojo and moves easily through the halls of the diet and the corridors of the University of Tokyo. He dies in Cambodia after a historic political victory.

- *Kyoko Ishihara* is a graduate of Tokyo University and a member of Japan's elite. She is a competent, upright member of the police force and an exception in a world almost entirely ruled by men. Thoroughly disciplined and angelically beautiful, she emerges as Hojo's main romantic interest, despite their obvious ethical differences. Toward the end, she becomes Hojo's companion.

- *Mr. Tokai* is the embodiment of the hardcore *yakuza*, with a tattoo covering his entire back. All brawn and little brains, he recognizes Hojo's preeminence as a leader. His loyalty to Hojo is unquestionable and even betrays a slight sense of homoerotism.

- *Secretary General Isaoka* is a shrewd, old-school politician. He is particularly adept as a quick-witted adversary, and he embodies all the corruption and treachery disdained by Asami. His short height and thick eyebrows give him a Yoda-like air, but he has a mean streak. Toward the end, he admits defeat and gives in to a new generation of politicians.

- *Mr. Ichijima* is the elder of the Japanese underworld. He spends a good amount of his time in Hokkaido, where he engages in more leisurely activities, such as raising horses. A veteran chief of organized crime, he has seemingly endless connections. In the final episode, he is in dialogue with Isaoka, revealing links between the *yakuza* and the political establishment. He favors traditional Japanese attire, hinting at his preference for the more feudal order of the pre-Meiji period.

- *Osaki* is Ishihara's subordinate. His sense of respect and loyalty to her is tinged with infatuation.

However, as a police officer, he is a competent underling.

- *Tashiro* is Hojo's young assistant. He is profoundly loyal to his boss and acknowledges an enormous debt of gratitude toward him, as Hojo saved Tashiro's newborn child when he was just starting as a *yakuza*.

Artistic Style

Sanctuary first appeared as a serialized narrative in *Big Comic Superior*, a publication dedicated to a slightly more adult audience than other manga publications. Still, it follows the customary size and appearance of most manga productions of its kind: black-and-white pages divided into six to eight frames per page, with occasional full-body frames. A key consideration in *Sanctuary*'s art is the accurate depiction of Japan in the early 1990's, with special attention to architecture and setting. Many buildings in contemporary Tokyo, such as those at the university or belonging to the government, are easily identifiable. This aspect grants *Sanctuary* a relevant, culturally charged condition, highly compatible with its narrative inclinations as a thriller.

Big Comic Superior

Big Comic Superior, published by Shogakukan, is a *seinen* magazine featuring manga aimed at mature male readers. Such magazines generally offer a mix of brutal violence, tightly plotted thrillers, and corporate drama, along with pictures of doe-eyed young women in year-round swimsuits. Much as a successful manga becomes a franchise in Japan, so too do manga magazines. Just as there is a *V Jump* and a *Jump Square* and other offshoots of publisher Shūeisha's *Weekly Shōnen Jump*, *Big Comic Superior* is part of a portfolio of magazines aimed at mature readers, among them *Big Comic*, *Big Comic Original*, and *Big Comic Spirits*. Manga that have appeared in *Big Comic Superior* include *Azumi* by Yu Koyama, *Moonlight Mile* by Yasuo Otagaki, and *Sprite* by Yūgo Ishikawa as well as various titles penned by Buronson, including *Heat*, *Sanctuary*, and *Strain*.

Along the same lines, the fact that it is possible to recognize many of the locations in the story gives *Sanctuary* a cinematic quality.

Ikegami's style of drawing is clean and neatly laid out, with well-contoured silhouettes and debonair profiles. Realism is a strong priority in the illustrations, from modern luxury vehicles to the spatial meticulousness of its scenery, with almost postcard acuity. Images are also thematically informed, with a degree of bodily allure directly proportional to the quality of each role in the story. Thus, evildoers are illustrated as ugly or grotesque, while heroes are represented as good-looking and elegant.

Additionally, the orderly framing of events, with well-organized panels arranged in easy-to-follow sequences, contributes to the clean sense of evolution in a demanding plot, with plenty of twists and turns. In a way, the story is easier to follow thanks to Ikegami's phenomenal sense of graphic orientation, guiding the reader into a world of intrigue in modern Japanese society.

When it comes to the main characters of the story, a key feature of Ikegami's art is an almost narcissistic propensity for well-delineated (particularly male) human physiques. Hojo, Asami, Tokai, and deputy chief Ishihara are repeatedly depicted as extraordinarily fine-looking, physically striking individuals with quasi-Caucasian features, usually in dramatic full-page panels that underscore the male magnetism and male and female eroticism of the characters. Recurrent conventions of race in Japanese manga are rampant, with Okinawan and Chinese characters depicted more in alignment with concrete physiognomic features. On the other hand, Hojo, Tokai, and many *yakuza* are impeccably attired, adding to the formal nature of the account. Once all these aspects are taken into consideration, it becomes evident that Ikegami's art is highly charged with an acute degree of homoeroticism, fittingly representing a male-centric milieu. In general, men are portrayed in an appealing light, while women, though also physically alluring, are almost exclusively pictured as objects of desire or commoditization—with the possible exception of a few matriarchs.

Strategically located word balloons and lettering add to the sense of drama of this narrative, with abundant use of exclamation points. At times, the histrionic bent is excessive, subtracting from the fluidity of the narrative. Too many high points make for a systemically dull evolution of the plot, which Ikegami fights through rhythm and intermittent Zen-like breaks. Though generally described as intellectual forces, Hojo and Asami are frequently portrayed with contrasting backgrounds, highlighting the melodramatic nature of their participation in the narrative. In all, *Sanctuary* behaves like a thriller, with an added sense of importance, given the pressing nature of its imagery.

Themes

Stylistically, *Sanctuary* incorporates elements of criminal fiction in its mode of representation. Beneath the veneer of modernity and social justice, Fumimura and Ikegami introduce a fashionable Japan deeply immersed in dishonesty and isolation, and, in the case of organized crime, one that serves as a dated remnant of romanticized feudal honor. This is an upside-down world in which delinquents play the role of heroes and the establishment plays the part of obstacle. The narrative's object is to explore the innards of politics and organized crime and essentially to equate them, denouncing the scope of complacency and corruption widespread in Japanese society.

Nevertheless, the real novelty of *Sanctuary*'s account resides in its thematic approach, positing a fierce critique of an economy and culture fearful of difference and change. Hojo and Asami are bent on truly modernizing the nation, opening its borders, and pushing the population toward a fully blown trade war, in exchange for the assimilation of benefits emanating from the importation of human capital and resources. Even the main characters' past posits a constructive critique of the risks of engagement at a multinational level, as it has prepared both heroes well to bring the nation back from its slumber. Also, the story's portrayal of pre-1997 Hong Kong as an available piece of commercial interest betrays Japanese anxieties of geopolitical expansion. As an economically and culturally focused narrative, *Sanctuary* could play well in any college course centered on the study of globalization.

Traces of Japan's feudal order are keenly evident in the *yakuza*, with leaders who inspire a radical sense of allegiance. The shifts in the relation between Hojo and Tokai, having gone from subordinate to master and from mentor to underling, respectively, reproduce closely the medieval mindset: The spoils must go to the victor, regardless of societal considerations and any sense of equity. In the realm of contemporary politics, which allegedly underline the significance of sagacity and negotiation, modern imperatives are profoundly thwarted.

Fumimura is at his best when he exposes the thinly veiled fashion in which Japan has embraced modernity, through the cult of technology and social stability, without questioning any of the most primordial tenets of its collective way of thinking, based on cultural ho-

mogeneity. Thus, the heroes willing to embrace globalization behave like *ronin*, while modern politicians behave like thugs. In this way, being true to its heritage, Japan finds a more likely way to be modern, beyond polished facades and technical gimmickry. Through it all, a strong undercurrent is the concept of generational renewal, as Hojo and Asami personify a new kind of national identity, more self-assured and unwilling to put up with the torpid way of elders.

Impact

Sanctuary set the pace for Fumimura and Ikegami's subsequent production. Most important, it showed that a culturally determined narrative with a more mature

Sanctuary. (Courtesy of VIZ Media)

bent could be translated and marketed successfully across the world, opening spaces for the Japanese comics industry. Though manga usually focus on action-driven narratives, the political and societal contexts of *Sanctuary* add to its sense of cultural sophistication.

In a way, it is almost ironic that the Japanese produced a story of this kind, in the early 1990's, warning of the multiple risks associated with cultural and economic isolation amid a world bent on globalization. Following the real-estate crisis of the late 1980's and the 1990's, the Japanese economy has been in the doldrums. Had Japanese society embraced the advice offered by Fumimura's characters, it is likely Japan's national standing would have found firmer footing.

As a thriller exposing the ugly underbelly of one of the strongest economies on the planet, *Sanctuary* stands as a high point of the Japanese comics industry. Defying some of the conventions of its medium and genre, it is a veritable anomaly, very difficult to emulate in its scale of naïveté and admonition and fiercely correlated to a time and moment: the impending decay of a mighty economic power. From a certain perspective, this is a series that reads as a history lesson.

Films

Sankuchuari. Directed by Yukio Fuji. Cine Wave Productions, 1995. Starring Azusa Nakamura and Takahiro Tamura, this live-action Japanese film is a fairly close adaptation of the comic.

Sanctuary. Directed by Takashi Watanabe. VIZ Video, 1995. This animated film adapts the manga's tale of organized crime, high-level politics, and big business in 1990's Japan.

Héctor Fernández L'Hoeste

Further Reading

Buronson and Ryoichi Ikegami. *Fist of the North Star* (1983-1988).

Buronson and Kentarou Miura. *Japan* (1992).

Bibliography

Schodt, Frederik. *Dreamland Japan: Writings on Modern Manga*. Berkeley, Calif.: Stone Bridge Press, 1996.

Thompson, Jason. *Manga: The Complete Guide*. New York: Del Rey, 2007.

See also: *Fist of the North Star*; *Mai the Psychic Girl*; *Crying Freeman*

SLAM DUNK

Author: Inoue, Takehiko

Artist: Takehiko Inoue (illustrator); James Gaubatz (letterer); Sean Lee (cover artist)

Publisher: Shūeisha (Japanese); Gutsoon! Entertainment (English); VIZ Media (English)

First serial publication: *Suramu danku*, 1990-1996 (English translation, 2002-2004)

First book publication: 1991-1996 (partial English translation, 2003-2004)

Publication History

Slam Dunk debuted in 1990 in *Weekly Shōnen Jump* and ran for 276 chapters until 1996. Shūeisha, via Jump Comics, collected and published chapters in thirty-one paperbound *tankōbon* volumes between 1991 and 1996. Shūeisha reprinted *Slam Dunk* between 2001 and 2002 in twenty-four *kanzenban* volumes for its large-format Jump Comics Deluxe line.

Between 2002 and 2004, Gutsoon! Entertainment published an English-language version of *Slam Dunk* in a monthly manga anthology, *Raijin Comics*. Gutsoon, via Raijin Graphic Novels, published five collected volumes of the series in 2003-2004 before the company went bankrupt. Afterward, VIZ Media acquired licensing rights for *Slam Dunk* and began serializing the manga in English in the monthly North American edition of *Shonen Jump* in early 2008. Later that year, VIZ released the first volume of the collected series, featuring English adaptations by Kelly Sue DeConnick, translations by Joe Yamazaki, touch-up art and lettering by James Gaubatz, and covers and graphic design by Sean Lee.

Plot

A Japanese-style *Hoop Dreams* (1994), *Slam Dunk* presents the high school experience in all its joy and humiliation. A saga of teen angst, complete with peer pressure, individual rivalries, and the bloom of romance, the semiautobiographical series centers on the unifying power of sport. Specifically, it deals with the game of basketball, which serves as a metaphor for the trials of youth and the process of growing up.

Slam Dunk. (Courtesy of VIZ Media)

The viewpoint character of *Slam Dunk* is Hanamichi Sakuragi, a gangling, redheaded bad boy. A gang leader, Sakuragi is often shunned by girls in junior high school and is desperate to have a girlfriend. On his first day at Shohoku High School, he meets pretty Haruko Akagi, younger sister of Takenori, the star of the school's basketball team. Smitten, Sakuragi joins the team, hoping to win Haruko's affections (though she has eyes for another player, the talented, enigmatic Kaede Rukawa) and ends up enjoying the competition and camaraderie of team play on its own merits. Along the way, the athletic but undisciplined Sakuragi must learn not only the rudiments of his new sport but also to sacrifice his innate egotism in order to play as part of an effective unit.

Slam Dunk covers a season of play as the Shohoku team coalesces from a motley, sometimes immature group of individuals to a smooth-running team capable of great feats. The ultimate goal is to improve on a game-by-game basis in order to qualify for play in the national tournament. For that to happen, Sakuragi and his teammates have to accomplish a difficult task: set aside personal differences for the sake of a common cause.

Volumes

This list reflects VIZ Media's publication of the series, which began in 2008 and is ongoing.

- *Slam Dunk*, Volume 1 (2008). Collects chapters 1-9. Sakuragi endures numerous rejections from junior high school girls before entering Shohoku High School, where love interest Haruko Akagi suggests he try out for basketball.
- *Slam Dunk*, Volume 2 (2009). Collects chapters 10-18. Sakuragi begins learning basketball fundamentals and resists an offer to become a member of the school judo team.
- *Slam Dunk*, Volume 3 (2009). Collects chapters 19-26. Sakuragi learns to shoot a simple layup and how to rebound.
- *Slam Dunk*, Volume 4 (2009). Collects chapters 27-35. Sakuragi chafes to play in an exhibition game against rival Ryonan.
- *Slam Dunk*, Volume 5 (2009). Collects chapters 36-44. Though inexperienced, Sakuragi shows flashes of brilliance during an exhibition game.
- *Slam Dunk*, Volume 6 (2009). Collects chapters 45-53. Shohoku loses a game by one point, despite heroics from rapidly improving Sakuragi.
- *Slam Dunk*, Volume 7 (2009). Collects chapters 54-62. Sakuragi and Myagi become friends after confessing their bad luck with girls. The team has a run-in at the school gym with Mitsui's punk gang.
- *Slam Dunk*, Volume 8 (2010). Collects chapters 63-71. The fight between the street punks and the basketball team escalates until everybody is bloodied.
- *Slam Dunk*, Volume 9 (2010). Collects chapters 72-80. The fight results in suspensions. Shohoku advances to the tournament quarterfinals.
- *Slam Dunk*, Volume 10 (2010). Collects chapters 81-89. Shohoku is bracketed against powerhouse Shoyo. Sakuragi begins to dominate in rebounding.
- *Slam Dunk*, Volume 11 (2010). Collects chapters 90-98. Sakuragi inspires the team to the Final Four against perennial nationals qualifier Kainan.
- *Slam Dunk*, Volume 12 (2010). Collects chapters 99-107. Shohoku goes against formidable Kainan. Meanwhile, Ryonan's Sendoh leads his team against Takezato.
- *Slam Dunk*, Volume 13 (2010). Collects chapters 108-116. Sakuragi helps rally Shohoku, to a tie game.
- *Slam Dunk*, Volume 14 (2011). Collects chapters 117-125. The game against Kainan is still in doubt, as Shohoku trails with just two minutes left.
- *Slam Dunk*, Volume 15 (2011). Collects chapters 126-134. Shohoku loses but can still advance. Sakuragi gets a buzz cut because he feels he lost the game for his team.
- *Slam Dunk*, Volume 16 (2011). Collects chapters 135-143. Sakuragi learns to shoot. Shohoku beats Takezato as Ryonan and Kainan face off.
- *Slam Dunk*, Volume 17 (2011). Collects chapters 144-152. Kainan defeats Ryonan, despite Sendoh's heroics, to qualify for the nationals. Shohoku begins play against Ryonan.
- *Slam Dunk*, Volume 18 (2011). Collects chapters 153-161. Shohoku and Ryonan's rivalry continues. Sakuragi is injured, though his team leads by halftime.
- *Slam Dunk*, Volume 19 (2011). Collects chapters 162-170. In a back-and-forth game, Shohoku takes a significant lead with just eight minutes left.
- *Slam Dunk*, Volume 20 (2012). Collects chapters 171-179. Shohoku extends its lead against Ryonan, but Sendoh's deadly shooting and outstanding defense cut the deficit with two minutes left.
- *Slam Dunk*, Volume 21 (2012). Collects chapters 180-188). Mitsui collapses from exhaustion. With key blocks from Sakuragi and Akagi, Shohoku wins by four points.

Characters

- *Hanamichi Sakuragi* is the hot-tempered main character of the series. Tall, red-haired, arrogant yet sensitive, he is smitten with classmate Haruko Akagi. He takes up basketball hoping to impress her and proves to be a natural athlete.

- *Haruko Akugi* is a pretty freshman and the sister of Takenori Akagi, who admires basketball player Kaede Rukawa.

- *Takenori Akagi*, Haruko's brother, is a third-year player at Shohoku, nicknamed "the Gorilla." Tall and powerful, he is the star, the center, and the captain of the basketball team.

- *Kaede Rukawa*, an outstanding basketball player since junior high, is a new member of the Shohoku basketball team. A strong, silent power forward, he is shaggy-haired and attractive to girls.

- *Ayako* is the pert, tomboyish manager of the basketball team, who usually wears a baseball cap turned backward for team practices.

- *Yuki Ohkusu, Yohei Mito, Nozomi Takamiya*, and *Chuichiro Noma* are members of Sakuragi's gang.

- *Coach Anzai* is the team coach. An older, fat man who wears glasses, he is nicknamed "the White-Haired Buddha." He once played on the Japanese national basketball team.

- *Kiminobu Kogure*, a member of the basketball team, is a small forward that wears glasses and is nicknamed "Four-Eyes."

- *Tatsuhiko Aota*, captain of the Shohoku judo team, tries to recruit Sakuragi.

- *Sendoh Hikoichi*, a skilled but modest rival basketball player from Ryonan, recognizes Sakuragi's raw talent.

- *Ryota Miyagi*, a quick, earring-wearing sophomore guard, sustains a knee injury before returning to the team. He is fond of Ayako.

- *Hisashi Mitsui*, a long-haired punk, once a junior high most valuable player and former member of the basketball team, returns to play for Shohoku.

Artistic Style

Inoue's predominant style in *Slam Dunk* is realistic line art, enhanced with cross-hatching and shading to pro-

Slam Dunk. (Courtesy of VIZ Media)

duce lifelike, easily readable renderings of individual characters. The illustrator's strengths are particularly evident in action scenes of basketball games, where full pages or panels take on the quality of snapshots from a sports magazine, freezing the heroic, samurai-like players in midshot. Such scenes are highly detailed, showing sweat on players' foreheads and looks of determination in players' eyes. Sound effects, such as the squeak of rubber soles on hardwood, the thump of a dribbled ball, the referee's whistle, or the roar of the crowd, are often underlaid within the panels. Starbursts focus the reader's attention on important details of scenes, and background motion lines are used to direct the eye in specific directions. Perspective changes often; Inoue uses close-ups and long shot and mixes in low-angle or overhead viewpoints to keep visual interest high.

When players (especially Sakuragi) are acting less than heroic or juvenile, they are shown in crude, cartoony fashion, with stylized features: mere slashes for eyes, dots to indicate noses, and blank ovals for mouths

---

Takehiko Inoue

Takehiko Inoue was born in 1967. His *Slam Dunk* is often cited as the most popular manga of all time in Japan. Its run in the best-selling weekly manga anthology *Weekly Shōnen Jump* between 1990 and 1996 coincided with the rapid expansion of that magazine's newsstand sales—and those same sales began a long decline once the series had come to its inevitable close. (As a sign of his popularity and cultural clout, Inoue has done commercials for Shiseido cosmetics featuring "live painting" and artfully rough animation.) Inoue also explored basketball in the science fiction series *Buzzer Beater* and continues to in the starkly told *Real*, which is about the wheelchair variation of the sport. His ongoing *Vagabond* series employs rich brushstrokes and is often silent in its portrayal of the life of a swordsman, broadly based on the legendary seventeenth century figure Miyamoto Musashi.

---

shaped to express joy, sorrow, or anger. Female characters are idealized and typically have large eyes, button noses, and shapely lips.

Over the course of the series, Inoue became more skilled in varying the dynamics of his work from page to page. In quiet, nonaction scenes he establishes an irregular succession of small rectangular panels (typically five to seven per page) that effectively advance the narration. When capturing the excitement of basketball games, however, he explodes the pattern with numerous full-page illustrations, occasional across-the-gutter scenes, and infusions of diagonal lines that produce trapezoidal panels to effectively increase the tension depicted in the story.

Themes

A major theme throughout the *Slam Dunk* series is the healing power of sports. When introduced, Sakuragi is shown to be a self-centered troublemaker obsessed with romance. Though he joins Shohoku's basketball team for purely selfish reasons, he eventually sublimates his desire through play. Though he does not succeed in his initial quest, he gains newfound capabilities and is thus victorious in maturing as an individual.

A related theme is the synergistic effect of teamwork. Though Sakuragi is naturally athletic, he must learn to channel his abilities by studying the rudiments of his new sport. A complete neophyte, he has to be schooled in dribbling, shooting, passing, and rebounding. Only in the last of these skills does he truly excel, and only by accepting his limitations and working to improve his rebounding can he significantly contribute to the efforts of the Shohoku team. Sakuragi's triumph is shared, rather than personal, which reflects the collaborative nature of most sports.

To Inoue, sports in general, and basketball in particular, are a kind of warfare. The game features strategy and capitalizes on a full range of skills, from the finesse of the playmaker to the brute power of the slam dunker. The lessons learned on the basketball court, the author seems to say, can be applied elsewhere in the battlefield of life.

Impact

From its debut, *Slam Dunk* has proved to be a highly popular manga. More than 100 million copies of the magazines and collections have sold worldwide since the early 1990's. The series also inspired four anime films and an animated television series in the mid-1990's. Inoue won a major manga award for his work and, in 2010, was recognized by the Japanese Basketball Association for stimulating basketball as a sport in his native country.

To help build upon the momentum he helped create, Inoue established a Slam Dunk Scholarship through Shūeisha, which is funded through royalties and contributions from the publisher. The scholarship aids second-year Japanese high school students with tuition and living expenses so promising basketball players can attend American prep schools to improve their skills.

In 1997, Inoue began a second basketball-based manga series: *Buzzer Beater*, with a new set of characters and a new story line involving intergalactic competition, which appeared in *Monthly Shōnen Jump,* was reprinted in four volumes, and spawned two anime television series between 2005 and 2007. Inoue's third sports-oriented manga series, the award-winning *Real*, which began in 2001 in Shūeisha's *Weekly Young Jump* magazine, focuses on a group of individuals who play wheelchair basketball and is aimed at a *seinen* audience. In 2004, Inoue also creatively continued *Slam Dunk*, with a chalk-drawn sequel, *Slam Dunk: Ten Days After*, which was reproduced in 2005 in *Switch,* a Japanese arts and media magazine.

Films

Slam Dunk. Directed by Nobutaka Nishizawa. Toei Animation, 1994. An anime adaptation of the series, this thirty-minute film stars Takeshi Kusao as the voice of Sakuragi, Akiko Hiramatsu as Haruko, Hideyuki Tanaka as Kogure, Hikaru Midorikawa as Rukawa, and Kiyoyuki Yanada as Takenori. Sakuragi leads Shohoku in a game against Takezono High in a film that captures the look, feel, and spirit of the original manga.

Slam Dunk 2. Directed by Toshihiko Arisako. Toei Animation, 1994. A forty-five-minute anime featuring the same voice actors in the primary roles as the previous film, this sequel centers on Shohoku's game against Tsukubu High School.

Slam Dunk 3. Directed by Hiroyuki Kakudo. Toei Animation, 1995. A second sequel with the regular cast of voice actors. After losing to Kainan, Shohoku faces a strong opponent in Ryokufu in this forty-minute animated film.

Slam Dunk 4. Directed by Masayuki Akihi. Toei Animation, 1995. Featuring the regular cast of voice actors, this forty-minute animated sequel provides background on Sakuragi's teammate Rukawa, as the players set out to fulfill the wishes of a former basketball player crippled by disease.

Television Series

Slam Dunk. Directed by Nobutaka Nishizawa and Nobuto Sakamoto. Toei Animation, 1993-1996. This animated, full-color 101-episode series stars many of the same voice actors featured in the *Slam Dunk* films. The television series expanded upon and supplemented the manga with more basketball tales detailing Sakuragi's growth as both a player and a person.

Jack Ewing

Further Reading

Higuchi, Daisuke. *Whistle!* (1998-2003).

Hotta, Yumi, and Takeshi Obata. *Hikaru no go* (1999-2003).

Konomi, Takeshi. *The Prince of Tennis* (1999-2008).

Bibliography

Gravett, Paul. *Manga: Sixty Years of Japanese Comics*. New York: Harper Design, 2004.

Hart, Christopher. *Mangamania Shonen: Drawing Action-Style Japanese Comics*. New York: Chris Hart Books, 2008.

Thompson, Jason. *Manga: The Complete Guide*. New York: Del Rey, 2007.

See also: *Hikaru no go*; *Speed Racer*

SOLANIN

Author: Asano, Inio
Artist: Inio Asano (illustrator)
Publisher: Shogakukan (Japanese); VIZ Media (English)
First serial publication: 2005-2006
First book publication: 2005, 2006 (English translation, 2008)

Publication History

Solanin is creator Inio Asano's first manga to be translated into English. His other works have generally been a combination of slice-of-life, Magical Realism, and understated horror. As he notes in the afterword to *Solanin*, he drew the book when he was twenty-four, about the same age as his characters, having just graduated from college and feeling insecure about his abilities as a manga creator. The issues with which he was dealing at the time grew into the themes, characters, and plot of *Solanin*.

Solanin was serialized in the manga magazine *Weekly Young Sunday* from 2005 to 2006. *Weekly Young Sunday* is a *seinen* manga magazine aimed at eighteen- to thirty-year-old men. The manga was collected in two volumes in Japan (the first was printed while the manga was still running) but was combined into a single volume for the English-language market when it was released in 2008. The French and Taiwanese versions maintained the two-volume format. A film adaptation was released in Japan in 2010.

Plot

Meiko Inoue and Naruo Taneda have been dating since they started college six years ago and have been living together in Tokyo since graduation, one year ago. Meiko is an office worker, and Taneda is a part-time graphic designer. Taneda is also a member of a band, Rotti, with Rip and Kato, friends from the college pop-music club. The three still regularly practice together.

Meiko is unhappy with her job and depressed by adulthood. Taneda promises to support them both and stand by her forever. Hearing this, Meiko decides to quit her job. After two weeks of aimless freedom, how-

Solanin. (Courtesy of VIZ Media)

ever, Meiko feels no better, and Taneda is nervous because he has become the sole source of income.

Meiko decides to encourage Taneda to pursue his dream of making music and begin taking Rotti more seriously. Fired up with passion, Taneda quits his job. The group records an album, which it sends to record companies. However, the only company that calls them back is looking for a backup band for an actress who wants to get into music; Rotti would not perform its own music. The group refuses, though Taneda agonizes over the decision.

Taneda disappears for five days. Meiko believes he has left her and becomes depressed. Taneda finally calls and reveals he begged for his old job back and has been working to rebuild their savings. He says he does not necessarily want to be famous, just in a band with his friends, and he tells Meiko that he loves her. However, as he heads home, Taneda is struck by a car and killed.

The story flashes back to just before the characters' college graduation. Rotti performs its final concert, at which Taneda forgets the words to a song and delivers an impromptu, impassioned speech about adulthood and the loss of youth. Afterward, he and Meiko promise to stay together and find their way through adulthood.

The story then jumps to two months after Taneda's death. Meiko is working at a flower shop but is still deeply depressed. Taneda's father visits to pick up his son's belongings. He tells Meiko that when Taneda disappeared for five days, he called his parents and said he would be coming back to live with them but then called later and said he had found something precious (Meiko) and would stay in Tokyo.

Inspired, Meiko picks up Taneda's guitar. She calls Rip and Kato and tells them she wants to join Rotti. They begin rehearsing. A classmate of Kato has an upcoming concert and needs an opening band; Meiko promises Rotti will perform. After much rehearsing, the group finally performs, ending with Taneda's song "Solanin."

The story flashes back to the beginning of college, when all the main characters first met in the pop-music club. Though Meiko initially wants to sing, she notices Taneda's eagerness and lets him sing instead. Afterward, she and Taneda share an emotional moment and promise never to part.

The final chapter takes place six months after the concert. Meiko is moving to a smaller apartment, and the other characters are helping her pack. Rotti has not played since, though the three continue to practice; the possibility of playing live again is left open. In the end, there are no final conflicts, no grand changes for the characters. Their lives continue, and they look toward the future with hope.

Characters

- *Meiko Inoue*, the protagonist, is a petite young woman with short black hair and freckles. She is twenty-three at the start of the story, having been out of college for one year. She is depressed by her job and reluctant to enter the world of adult-

hood. She supports, and is supported by, Taneda. Devastated by his death, she eventually draws inspiration from his life.

- *Naruo Taneda* is Meiko's boyfriend. He has shaggy, light brown hair and wears glasses. Although he loves playing and creating music, he initially lacks the confidence to devote himself to it. Only with Meiko's support does he find the courage to put his music into the world. His death occurs midway through the book.

- *Jiro Yamada*, a.k.a. *Rip*, is a tall, lanky young man with a thin mustache and beard and sleepy, half-lidded eyes. He is the drummer in Rotti and works at his family's drugstore. He and Kato are close friends.

- *Kato Kenichi* is chubby young man with glasses, thick lips, and a goatee. He is in his sixth year of college, having failed to graduate with his friends. He is the bassist in Rotti. By the end of the manga, he has graduated and found a job.

- *Ai Kotani* is Kato's girlfriend, a tall, slim woman with light hair. She works in sales at a local company. During the series, she considers taking a

---

Inio Asano

Inio Asano, born in 1980, is best known for the manga series *Solanin*, a single-volume *seinen* (or young men's) title that earned a following (along with several award nominations) among English-speaking readers. It tells the bittersweet story of two young university graduates making their way in post-boom Japan. It cemented Asano's reputation for an emotional realism. (The film version starred Aoi Miyazaki, who played the non-punk half of the movie adaptation of the *shōjo* manga *Nana*.) Asano got his first big break in *Big Comics Spirits*, which led to *Solanin*'s serialization in its sibling Shogakukan publication, *Weekly Young Sunday*. He has referred to Kyoko Okazaki, who has helped push the boundaries of the *shōjo* genre, as a major influence, and has been described by the Japanese newspaper the *Daily Yomiuri* as "one of the voices of his generation" (Ozaki).

management position in another city, but she ultimately decides to stay near her friends.

- *Ohashi* is an earnest eighteen-year-old with a mop of black hair. He is the other part-time employee at the flower shop where Meiko works after Taneda's death. He is attracted to Meiko, eventually confessing his feelings to her, but she gently turns him down. He is also an aspiring guitar player.

Artistic Style

The art in *Solanin* is highly detailed. With its realistically proportioned characters and richly textured backgrounds, it does not resemble a "typical" manga. Asano makes great use of shading: Shadows are carefully rendered to indicate time of day and light sources as well as intangible factors such as characters' moods. Characters' facial expressions are realistic and well-observed, showing their emotional states clearly.

There are a handful of fantasy or dream sequences in the book. For example, when Taneda is trying to make a difficult decision, readers see inside his head, where representatives of the different parts of his personality (wearing T-shirts that say "Cooperation," "Suspicion," "Apathy," and so forth) argue among themselves. These sequences are rendered in the same highly detailed style as the rest of the manga, although with surreal or impossible creatures and backgrounds.

Asano's pacing is careful and deliberate. There are no action scenes in *Solanin*; events happen at a measured pace. In one sequence, just after Taneda dies, silent panels of Meiko alone in her apartment alternate with solid black panels in which she describes her depression and her guilt over Taneda's death. Even the scenes in which Rotti performs are high energy and include close-ups of the faces of the band members, with their hands constantly in motion over their instruments. However, motion lines are used sparingly,

making the panels seem more like still photographs, slowing down the pace of the scene. Actual photographs are used on two occasions, showing a crowd scene in Tokyo and the face of a television announcer; the first gives a real-world weight to the scene, and the second is an almost surreal bit of humor.

Themes

Solanin can be thought of as a reversal of the classic coming-of-age story, as the characters resist the transition into adulthood. However, it is not just a story of angst and alienation. While the characters grow up and lose some of their innocence, they also learn to value

Solanin. (Courtesy of VIZ Media)

their youth and seize the energy of the moment. Most of the cast are dismissive of adulthood and adult responsibilities. As Meiko says in an early chapter, "The way I see it, adults are made of 'who cares?'" The main characters are not particularly eager to enter the workforce; while they are all employed, they are doing part-time, temporary, or entry-level work, nothing that could be called a "career." They are disgusted by the adults they see, most of whom have given up on their dreams and seem to live purposeless lives; thus, the characters do not want to grow up. This theme of seizing the moment is symbolized by the packages of vegetables that Meiko's parents keep sending her. Meiko and Taneda cook a few of them, but, inevitably, the remainder is left to spoil. Like youth itself, the vegetables are only valuable for a short time; after that they are useless.

Connected to the theme of the transience of youth is the importance of self-transformation. The characters are all in their early twenties, a period considered to be a transition between adolescence and adulthood, but none of them is eager to become an adult (or, at least, the kind of adult they see around them). Meiko and her friends know they must change, and they even want to change, but they are unsure of what they will become. Meiko initially interprets the titular song as being about "lovers parting"; she later realizes it is about parting with the person one used to be.

Impact

Solanin will likely be remembered as a successful examination of postcollege angst and indecision. The book has been praised by both Japanese and American reviewers. Although set in modern-day Tokyo, the themes of transition into adulthood and chasing one's dreams are universal and require little translation. The book has been compared favorably to English-language graphic novels in the semiautobiographical/alternative genre. Reviewers have also noted the perhaps surprising popularity of a book with a female protagonist and a focus on emotional introspection among adult males. Although Taneda's struggles are the driving force of the first half of the plot, Meiko is ultimately the protagonist and the most interesting character in the book.

After its release in the United States, *Solanin* was nominated for the 2009 Eisner Award for Best U.S. Edition of International Material–Japan; however, it lost to Osamu Tezuka's series *Dororo* (English translation, 2008). In Japan, the book was popular enough to inspire a film adaptation. While the film was not as well received as the book, it earned praise as a faithful adaptation.

Films

Solanin. Directed by Miki Takahiro. IMJ Entertainment, 2010. This film stars Aoi Miyazaki as Meiko Inoue and Kengo Koura as Naruo Taneda. Produced shortly after the completion of the manga, the film adaptation is extremely faithful to the book. Though some scenes were trimmed and others removed entirely (notably, the fantasy sequences), some shots are almost exact re-creations of panels from the manga. The music of Rotti is provided by the Japanese rock group Asian Kung-Fu Generation.

Ted Anderson

Further Reading

Thompson, Craig. *Blankets* (2003).
Umino, Chika. *Honey and Clover* (2000-2006).
Yazawa, Ai. *Nana* (2000-   ).

Bibliography

Dacey, Katherine. "*Solanin*." Review of *Solanin*, by Inio Asano. *Pop Culture Shock*, November 19, 2008. http://www.popcultureshock.com/manga/index.php/reviews/manga-reviews/solanin.

Drury, Molly. "Manga Review: *Solanin*." Review of *Solanin*, by Inio Asano. *UK Anime Network*, December 15, 2009. http://www.uk-anime.net/manga/Solanin.html.

Ozaki, Mio. "The disaffected world of Inio Asano." *Yomiuri Shimbun*, April 16, 2010.

Stephanides, Adam. "Adam Stephanides Reviews *Solanin* by Inio Asano." Review of *Solanin*, by Inio Asano. *The Comics Journal*, January 15, 2010. http://classic.tcj.com/manga/adam-stephanides-reviews-solanin-by-inio-asano.

See also: *Nana*; *We Were There*

SPEED RACER
MACH GO GO GO

Author: Yoshida, Tatsuo

Artist: Tatsuo Yoshida (illustrator); Daryl Kuxhouse (letterer); Geoff Porter (letterer); Tawnie Wilson (letterer)

Publisher: Shūeisha (Japanese); Sun Wide Comics (Japanese); Fusosha (Japanese); NOW Comics (English); DC Comics (English); Digital Manga (English)

First serial publication: *Mahha gō gō gō*, 1966-1968 (partial English translation, 1987-1990, 1992)

First book publication: 1966-1968 (English translation, 2008)

Publication History

Tatsuo Yoshida was a pioneer of anime but began his career as a manga artist. To build support for his second anime series, *Mahha gō gō gō*, released in English as *Speed Racer*, Yoshida drew and wrote a manga with the same title. In developing his characters and initial episodes, Yoshida drew heavily on his earlier manga series featuring car and motorcycle racing themes, in particular *Pilot Ace* (1960-1964). *Mahha gō gō gō* first appeared in Shūeisha's *Shōnen Book* magazine in June of 1966 and ran until May of 1968. The individual episodes were collected in *tankōbon* books by Japan's Sun Wide Comics beginning in 1966. In 2000, long after Yoshida's death from cancer in 1977, Fusosha reprinted all of the episodes in a two-volume box set.

In the United States, *Speed Racer* debuted as a fifty-two-episode anime series that first aired from September, 1967, to September, 1968. Beginning in 1987, NOW Comics published select translated chapters of the manga as *Speed Racer Classics*. DC Comics' imprint WildStorm published more episodes as *Speed Racer: The Original Manga*. In 2008, Digital Manga published the entire original series in two volumes based on the 2000 Fusosha edition. Titled *Speed Racer: Mach Go Go Go*, this edition is considered the canonical version in English.

Tatsuo Yoshida

The Japanese manga and anime legend Tatsuo Yoshida died in 1977 at the relatively young age of forty-five, but he left behind several important legacies. Foremost is *Mach Go Go Go*, better known outside Japan as *Speed Racer*, the famed racetrack franchise. (It was later adopted as a major Hollywood movie by Andy and Lana Wachowski, creators of *The Matrix*.) *Mach Go Go Go* was one of the first series to be developed by Tatsunoko Production, the company Yoshida co-founded with his two younger brothers. They joined Yoshida in Tokyo from their native Kyoto after he gained prominence in the manga industry. Yoshida also helped create the superhero team *Gatchaman*, which had a major impact on English-speaking audiences in the 1970's and 1980's under the name *G-Force*. Despite Yoshida's death, Tatsunoko Production prospered, and continues to exist into the twenty-first century.

Plot

Tatsuo Yoshida created *Speed Racer: Mach Go Go Go* in the hope that the manga would build a fan base for his planned anime series of the same title and convince potential sponsors to support the anime. Because car racing was popular in Japan in the mid-1960's, Yoshida thought that young male readers would enjoy a fast-paced, action-packed series centered on this theme.

The first episode, aptly titled "Speed Racer Arrives!!," introduces the protagonist, Speed Racer, and his friends and supporters. Speed Racer's vehicle is the Mach 5, a superb racing car with an engine developed by his father. The special abilities of the Mach 5, which enable the car to jump over obstacles, drive underwater, and race on ultrajets, are introduced gradually in the series.

Initially, the plot of the series focuses primarily on car racing. Every race featured is marred by foul play. Speed shows an absolute desire to win and dreams of becoming a professional racer. However, his father, Pops, is adamantly opposed to his son's chosen profession. When Pops, an engineer, quits his job to develop a special engine on his own, thugs try to steal his plans. There is a violent showdown, and Speed wins thanks to his girlfriend, Trixie, who intervenes from her trademark helicopter.

Next, Speed enters his first competition, the Sword Mountain Race, hoping to support his father's engine research with the expected prize money. Typical of the racing episodes of the series, Speed is pitted against both an official competitor and some thugs who try to manipulate the race. Outracing and outwitting all of his opponents, Speed wins his race. However, the race is disqualified for irregularities.

The second chapter introduces Racer X, a masked racer who challenges Speed to a private race but is secretly supportive of him. When Speed and Racer X are pitted against Captain Terror and his minions, the Car Acrobatic Team, they win the race together. After Speed is temporarily blinded in an accident, Racer X takes the copilot's seat in the Mach 5 and directs Speed to victory.

In chapter 3, Flash Marker Junior, the son of a car racer killed by thugs fifteen years previous, tries to kill his father's criminal enemies with a remote-controlled racing car. Speed's overriding sense of justice prompts him to intervene, which he does successfully. Flash Marker Junior and the surviving criminals surrender to the police. The next chapter, which includes fantastic and supernatural elements, focuses on a race in Central America. To save a remote tribe's independence, Speed impersonates the tribe's injured champion, Demon Kabala, and wins a race inside a volcano.

Back in Japan, Speed and Racer X are pitted against a young racer who is supported by organized criminals. The private match between Speed and Racer X from chapter 2 is repeated, in almost identical panels, before the official race begins. The race is won by Speed, but only because Racer X lets him pull ahead.

The three subsequent chapters shift the focus from car racing to outlandish capers in exotic settings. First, Speed battles both a young prince and a court conspiracy in Arabia. In the desert, Speed and his trusty Mach 5 survive sandstorms, attacks by rifle-wielding camel riders, and the crumbling of the Palace of Doom. The next chapter features a group of criminals trying to

find the last secret of Henry Ford, which is hidden in a Ford Model T. In another chapter, the Kante Race in northern Mexico is a pretext for a story in which a gang of international criminals tries to steal a doomsday atomic element. Speed and Racer X, who enters the race as Chinese driver King Hu, defeat the criminals and save the world.

Next, Speed becomes a test pilot for engineer Mr. Otto, whose son, Speed's friend Swifty, was killed by thugs working for Mister Condor, a shady businessman. Speed completes the test run, and the criminals are defeated and handed over to the police. The series ends with a chapter in which Speed must complete a three-island racecourse to save a tiny Pacific Island nation. Donning the garb of the injured crown prince, himself a racer, Speed fights evil Prince Sauna and a Japanese racer in his pay, the heinous Reaper. Reaper is killed in an accident he causes, and Sauna is double-crossed by his doctor before the race is over. As Speed wins, his family and friends arrive. They include Racer X, who finally reveals himself to be Speed's older brother, Rex Racer. Six years before, he left the family in anger over Pops' refusal to let him race. At the series' end, the family is reconciled.

Volumes

- *Speed Racer: Mach Go Go Go*, Volume 1 (2008). The English translation of the first four chapters of the series, based on the 2000 Fusosha edition, introduces the key characters and features three races in Japan before moving to a fantastic Central American setting.
- *Speed Racer: Mach Go Go Go*, Volume 2 (2008). The English translation of the final six chapters, based on the 2000 Fusosha edition, focuses on fantasy adventure stories, introduces the Mach 5's new capabilities, and resolves the Racer family conflict.

Characters

- *Speed Racer*, the protagonist, is a boyish-looking eighteen-year-old Japanese man with an Elvis Presley-style pompadour and heavy black eyebrows. Completely committed to winning every car race, he also has a strong sense of justice and is fiercely loyal to his parents, girlfriend, and younger brother. His races and other adventures fuel the plot of each chapter.

- *Racer X*, a.k.a. *Rex Racer*, is Speed's older brother and secret mentor. He is a tall Japanese man in his twenties with strong facial features partially hidden by his black mask, which bears a white *X* and covers much of his face. An accomplished racer, he fell out with his father six years before the start of the narrative but still feels protective of his younger brother.
- *Pops* is Speed's father, a portly, middle-aged Japanese man with a short moustache. He is a stubborn engineer who tries to prohibit his sons from racing. He designs the engine of Speed's Mach 5.
- *Trixie* is Speed's girlfriend, an attractive young Japanese woman with a 1960's-style chignon. Resourceful and devoted to Speed, she is an accomplished helicopter pilot and rescues Speed at critical moments.
- *Sprtle Racer* is Speed's younger brother, a preteen boy often accompanied by the chimpanzee Chim-Chim. They join Speed in his adventures but often cause trouble, providing comic relief.
- *Duggery* is a young, arrogant, and ungrateful Japanese car racer whom Speed defeats.
- *Captain Terror* is a middle-aged Japanese racer who wears a white feather on his helmet and a flowing black robe. He dreams of joining man and machine to create a superior entity. Proud and willful, he loses to Speed.
- *Flash Marker Junior* is a young man obsessed with avenging his father. His vigilantism is opposed and overcome by Speed.
- *Demon Kabala* is a middle-aged Central American man who races roughly and unfairly to save his traditional tribe from forced assimilation.
- *Zoomer Slick* is a young Japanese racer. Arrogant, greedy, and in cahoots with criminals, he is defeated by Speed.
- *Kim Jugger* is a young Arabian racer. He is arrogant and ungrateful but is saved by Speed from a palace intrigue.

- *Tongue Blaggard* is a middle-aged man of indeterminate ethnicity. He sees car races purely as opportunities to win money.
- *Belda Danke* is a young European racer dressed in black. Her maternal love for her blind daughter, Emily, turns her away from evil.
- *Mister Otto* is a middle-aged Japanese engineer who resembles actor Toshirō Mifune. He is a proud nationalist who refuses to sell his engine patents to international corporations. Speed avenges the death of his son, Swifty.
- *Crown Prince* is a young Pacific Islander racer. He has a gentle spirit, and Speed impersonates him to secure his royal succession.

Artistic Style

Yoshida drew *Speed Racer* by himself, without the support of assistants typical of later manga. As a result, his panels tend to focus on the essential, typically featuring a character or machine. Yoshida's style was influenced by the artwork of the American *Superman* comics, and this influence is particularly apparent in Yoshida's drawings of the various villains of the series. Speed Racer and his friends are drawn in a style Japanese critics call *mukokuseki*, or nationless, appearing more European than Japanese. In contrast with the earlier chapters, the final chapter is drawn in a somewhat blunt, sloppy style.

Speed's car, the Mach 5, is drawn in great detail and from many perspectives. With its rocketlike fenders and pointy central hood section featuring a stylized *M*, the Mach 5 resembles cars from the late 1950's rather than the mid-1960's, when the manga was first published. Other cars are drawn to resemble actual racing cars of the period, including those produced by Mercedes, Ford, and Aston Martin.

The relative visual realism of the cars is juxtaposed with scenes of fantastic crashes and surreal racecourses. The Mach 5 seems to survive major crashes depicted in bold, occasionally full-page panels. After most crashes, the car is virtually intact when the story continues in the next panel. There is an abundance of graphic depictions of violence—from car crashes to gun battles and fistfights—that shocked readers outside Japan in the 1960's. Every race depicted in the series features thugs and vicious opponents who resort to violent tricks that send cars crashing into each other or spinning off the track.

Themes

A major theme of the series is Speed Racer's unbending will to win every race he enters. However, this is juxtaposed with his innate sense of fairness and compassion for his fellow racers. As a consequence, Speed always acts to help others in need, even if they are his arrogant or ungrateful opponents.

Another key theme is Speed's relationship with Racer X. Long before the final revelation that Racer X is Speed's older brother, Speed finds himself in many situations in which he joins forces with this other well-respected professional driver. The bond between these two true racers is celebrated throughout the manga.

The series also celebrates individualism. Speed and his father stand up to and confront bullies, be they criminals or representatives of large corporations. Often, Speed must fight opponents who fight in groups, including a horde of evil bikers and the Car Acrobatic Team. Speed's individual skill triumphs over the mass of attackers.

The manga includes a number of references to Japanese popular culture. For example, the Japanese surname of the protagonist, Mifune, pays homage to Japanese actor Toshirō Mifune, who was famous for playing samurai roles. At the same time, it demonstrates the post-World War II American influence on Japanese culture. Speed's helmet and the hood of the Mach 5 are adorned with the Western letter *M*, rather than a Japanese character. The series' Japanese title also plays on Japanese-English interaction: The word *go* means "five" in Japanese and is also an appropriate racing command in English.

Impact

Yoshida developed *Speed Racer* in the tradition of early post-World War II Japanese manga. This tradition was primarily established by the influential work of Osamu Tezuka and is best exhibited in Tezuka's *Tetsuwan atomu* (*Astro Boy*), first published between 1952 and 1968. Tezuka's influence on Yoshida's earlier works is pronounced, and as Yoshida based *Speed Racer* on his earlier racing manga, Tezuka's influence is apparent in the later series as well.

Eventually, though the manga developed a loyal, international fan audience, the anime proved much more popular and influential. It was one of the first color anime and mixed a family story with a car-racing plot in a way that appealed to many viewers. The anime became one of the first to be adapted into English and broadcast in the United States, and its success prompted US companies to dub additional anime into English.

The enduring success of the anime led to the development of three *Speed Racer* video games in the 1990's. These in turn fueled a short-lived revival of the manga in 1997, with new, noncanonical chapters created by manga artist Toshio Tanigami. Additional animated adaptations followed, introducing Speed Racer and his family to a new generation of fans. The original manga continued to be revered as one of the most important early manga to reach an international audience.

Films

Speed Racer. Directed by Andy Wachowski and Lana Wachowski. Warner Bros., 2008. This film adaptation stars Emile Hirsch as Speed and Christina Ricci as Trixie. The film differs from the manga by developing an original story line focused on racing. It also gives Speed an additional car, the Mach 6. At the end of the film, Racer X does not reveal his identity to Speed.

Television Series

Speed Racer. Directed by Hiroshi Sasagawa. Tatsunoko Productions, 1967-1968. This animated series stars the voice of Katsuji Mori (Peter Fernandez in English) as Gō Mifune (Speed Racer). The anime series follows the manga quite closely. However, its fifty-two episodes include events, characters, and cars not featured in the manga. Racer X and Speed do not unite at the end of the anime. The English adaptation was directed by Fernandez.

Speed Racer X. Directed by Hiroshi Sasagawa. Tatsunoko Productions, 1997. This animated series, a remake of the original anime, stars the voice of Koichi Tochika (Dave Wittenberg in English) as Gō Hibiki (Speed Racer). Characters were renamed and changed, with new ones added and old ones dropped. The series was canceled after thirty-four episodes. The English version was stopped after episode 11 because of licensing problems.

Speed Racer: The Next Generation. Directed by John Holt, Jay Surridge, Frank Rivera, and Matt Rodriguez. Lions Gate Entertainment, 2008-   . This American animated series features the voice of Kurt Csolak as Speed, the son of Speed Racer. The series continues the original story of Speed Racer, replacing his car with the new Mach 6.

R. C. Lutz

Further Reading

Graton, Jean. *Michel Vaillant* (1957-   ).

Tezuka, Osamu. *Astro Boy* (1952-1968).

Bibliography

Gravett, Paul. *Manga: Sixty Years of Japanese Comics.* New York: Harper Design, 2004.

Kelts, Roland. *Japanamerica: How Japanese Pop Culture Has Invaded the U.S.* New York: Palgrave Macmillan, 2007.

Maynard, Senko K. "Sources of Emotion in Japanese Comics: Da, Nan(i), and the Rhetoric of Futaku." In *Exploring Japaneseness,* edited by Ray T. Donahue. Westport, Conn.: Ablex, 2002.

See also: *Astro Boy*; *Phoenix*; *Dragon Ball*

T

TO TERRA. . .

Author: Takemiya, Keiko
Artist: Keiko Takemiya (illustrator)
Publisher: Asahi Sonorama (Japanese); Vertical (English)
First serial publication: *Terra e. . .*, 1977-1980
First book publication: 1980 (English translation, 2007)

Publication History

Science fiction was a new genre for *mangaka* Keiko Takemiya when she began publishing *Terra e. . .* (*To Terra. . .*) in the pages of the *Gekkan Manga Shōnen* magazine starting in January, 1977. By that time, Takemiya had established her reputation as a member of manga's Year 24 Group, which consisted of innovative female artists born around 1949, the twenty-fourth year of Japan's Shōwa era (Takemiya was born in 1950). Before *To Terra. . .* Takemiya invented, and subsequently specialized in, the *shōnen-ai* manga subgenre, which featured young boys in love with each other and was targeted to young-adult female readers.

In the magazine installments, *To Terra. . .* ran until May, 1980. Because of its popularity it was published in three paperback volumes in August, 1980, when the anime movie based on the graphic novel was released in Japan. Over the years, *To Terra. . .* built a considerable fandom. This persuaded a producer's consortium led by Mainichi Broadcasting System to launch an anime television series based on Takemiya's manga. Upon the series launch in 2007, Japanese publisher Square Enix reprinted the three volumes of *To Terra. . .* on April 6, 2007. In the same year, in the United States, Vertical published the three volumes in English, originally issued from February 20 to June 26, 2007.

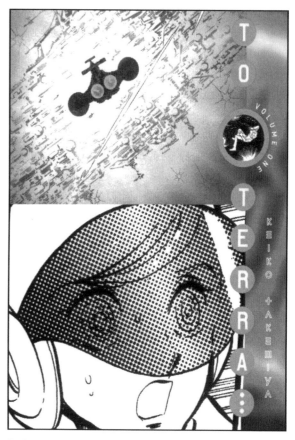

To Terra... (Courtesy of Vertical)

Plot

After her success with tender *shōnen-ai* manga, drawn for young girl audiences in Japan, Takemiya turned to the science-fiction genre targeted to young male readers. *To Terra. . .* introduces a dystopian future. In the fourth millennium, humanity worries that human nature has led to the destruction of Earth. Human planners believe that this problem can be mitigated only by humanity's voluntary submission to computer control. Thus begins the era of Superior Domination, a political order in which humans are ruled by computers.

To set up and maintain this rule, a group of giant computers comes to control humanity, which has spread across the galaxy. The biggest threat to this system stems from the Mu—short for mutant children with paranormal abilities. The Mu gather around their leaders, Soldier Blue and the blind woman Physis, and commandeer a giant spaceship. Among humans, children are born in vitro and raised by foster parents on special planets such as Ataraxia. There, Jomy Marcus Shin readies himself for his maturity check, to be performed at age fourteen. The check is designed to identify and kill teenagers with extrasensory powers, which would make them Mu children. But Jomy, a latent Mu, is saved by the Mu and teleported to their spaceship, where he is groomed to succeed Soldier Blue upon the death of this Mu leader.

Next, the manga shows the grooming of the new human leader, Keith Anyan. He is an exceptional student from the moment he sets foot on the educational space station E-1077, after passing his maturity check on Ataraxia. Keith bonds with down-to-earth Sam Houston. Keith engages in a fierce rivalry with Seki Ray Shiroe. He proves his ultimate loyalty to the computers, personified by the avatar Mother Eliza, when he shoots the dissident Shiroe out of space.

Forty-three years later, with none of the characters having aged visibly at all, the Mu are led by Jomy and settle on Naska. For the first time in recent human history, Mu mothers give birth to children naturally. One of them is Tony, born of the nurse Carina. Just as the Mu get comfortable on Naska, the humans decide to attack them there.

The leader of the strike force is Keith Anyan. He wears an earring bearing the blood of Sam, who was captured by the Mu and rendered an imbecile as a result of their interrogation and then released to Terra as an idiot. As Keith arrives on another planet in the Naska system, he is suddenly attacked by his valet, Jonah Makka, who is a Mu in hiding. Makka keeps secret his unrequited homoerotic love for Keith. Keith forgives Makka for his attack, which he covers up to shelter Makka from the military police.

Keith descends in a space shuttle on Naska but is brought down by Mu paranormal powers. After his interrogation, Keith kidnaps Physis and Tony. With the help of Makka's psychic powers, however, Keith is returned to the human forces. After most of the Mu flee Naska, the humans destroy the planet. Jomy seeks a showdown on Terra.

Under Captain Harley, the fleet of combined surviving Mu manages to defeat the human spaceships around Pluto. This happens despite Keith Anyan's training of anti-Mu forces, which cause the death of Mu special mutant forces. Among the dead Mu warriors is the woman Artella, who dreamed of a happy future with Tony. Jomy demands a personal meeting with Terra's central computer, called Grandmother, despite worries of his staff that this would lead him into a trap. Finally arriving on Terra, Jomy destroys Grandmother at the price of his own life (at the hand of Keith).

The Mu girl Twellen assumes command of the Mu fleet dominating the solar system. Surprisingly, Keith Anyan rebels against Grandmother's backup, a computer called Terra. Destroying the computer, Terra nevertheless kills Keith, too, and wreaks havoc on Earth. But this frees humanity from computer control. The epilogue shows two humanoid families returning to Terra from outer space, with their children bonding for a happy future.

Volumes

- *To Terra. . .*, Volume 1 (2007). Jomy Marcus Shin joins the Mu at age fourteen. The volume also includes a full introduction of the antagonist, Keith Anyan, and his world. Mu establish a colony on Naska.
- *To Terra. . .*, Volume 2 (2007). Mu settle on the planet Naska but are not left alone by the humans. Keith Anyan leads the strike force that destroys Naska. Mu escape to seek a final decision on Terra.
- *To Terra. . .*, Volume 3 (2007). After the Mu win the battle of Pluto against the humans, the computer Grandmother agrees to a meeting with Jomy. Jomy destroys Grandmother but is killed by Keith, who in turn destroys Grandmother's backup before his own death. This sets humans free and ends their war with the Mu.

Characters

- *Jomy Marcus Shin*, the protagonist, is a pretty-looking, male adolescent with blow-dried hair. His youthful physical appearance never changes even as he reaches the biological age of fifty. He leads the Mu in the groups' quest to Terra and dies in his final duel there.

- *Keith Anyan*, the antagonist, is a teenage boy with black hair who is tall and has distinctive facial features. Like the other characters, he never ages as decades pass and as he becomes the leader of the humans on Terra. He tolerates the homoerotic adulation of his boy servant Makka and defeats Jomy only to turn against Terra's computer, dying in the cataclysm he causes.

- *Physis* is a psychic woman of the Mu race, a blind prophetess with long hair reaching to the floor. She comforts the Mu leaders and is revealed to be the biological mother of Keith Anyan.

- *Soldier Blue*, the original leader of the Mu, is a frail person trapped in a boy's infirm body. He dies on the bed from which he telepathically directs the rescue of Mu children from the clutches of Terra's computers.

- *Grandmother* is the computer that controls human destiny. At times, she appears as a benign older woman; she is also called Mother Eliza or Mother. On Ataraxia, her hardware shell looks like a primitive idol with immense black breasts and a crystal head. She is destroyed by Jomy and the Mu.

To Terra... (Courtesy of Vertical)

- *Captain Harley* is the commander of the Mu mother ship. He is a young adult leader with a commanding presence characterized by his cape-clad uniform. He is loyal to Soldier Blue and Jomy.
- *Sam Houston* is a blond-haired childhood friend of Jomy and then an adolescent companion of Keith. He ends up a babbling idiot after his spacecraft is intercepted by the Mu and he undergoes psychic interrogation. He dies of pneumonia in Keith Anyan's custody on Terra.
- *Seki Ray Shiroe*, a rebellious human boy on E-1077, has dark hair and lanky features. He is killed by Keith Anyan when he tries to flee to Terra on his own.
- *Tony*, the first natural born Mu and heir apparent to Jomy, has long wavy hair and wears a black uniform. His immense paranormal powers make him the leader of the Mu strike force.
- *Jonah Makka*, a Mu boy in love with Keith, has slender features and a subservient character. He sacrifices his life for Keith.
- *Artella*, a Mu girl born on Naska, wears her hair in two braids. Tony's love interest, she dies during the Mu attack on Pluto.
- *Twellen*, a Mu woman, looks like a sixteen-year-old girl with fluffy hair. She becomes leader of Mu star fleet after Jomy's death.

Artistic Style

As is typical for manga, Takemiya draws on the artistic support of subordinate artists, nine of whom are thanked on the final page of the graphic novel. Thus, the backgrounds—whether of space scenes, computer rooms, or full-page images of futuristic cities and violent spaceship battles—are drawn in amazing detail. The manga is drawn in black and white, as is common for the genre. Key characters are drawn in loving detail, such as Physis, with her long, flowing hair, or Keith Anyan with his square features and ear stud.

There is great variety among the panels of each page. Any traditional arrangement of nine square panels per page is virtually absent. Instead, panels overlap, are adjusted to the pace of the story, and often occupy full and overlap pages. Takemiya's panels thrive from the kinetic energy that they display at moments of crisis and battle, and the lyricism of interludes when a temporary solution has been reached.

Almost all key characters are drawn as young adults. This is typical of the *shōnen* genre directed toward young-adult men in Japan. Only minor characters are middle or old aged. Occasionally, however, the side characters appear more as comical caricatures than as realistically drawn persons. The lead characters share the characteristics of manga: wide, expressive eyes, small noses, large mouths, and youthful features. There is an androgynous element to characters such as Tony, who has long, wavy blond hair, and Makka, who has feminine features. Physis is drawn as an idealized young woman. The embryos growing in test tubes have full bodies of hair.

Spaceships, computers, and other futuristic hardware are drawn in loving detail. For a manga created in the late 1970's, the future depicted does not look dated at all, if occasional levers and analog dials can be overlooked. A persistent motif is the impressive graphic depiction of deep space. There is fantastic variation in the

---

Keiko Takemiya

Keiko Takemiya, born around 1950, is one of the earliest female figures in Japanese comics. She is best known outside Japan for her science fiction series *To Terra . . .* and *Andromeda Stories*, the latter a collaboration with famed writer Ryu Mitsuse. Takemiya is closely associated with the *yaoi*, or boys' love, genre of manga; it is said that her story *Song of the Wind and Trees* set the groundwork for these tales of impossibly beautiful homosexual young men whose tantalizing romantic experiences are intended for female readers. She is the originator of Genga Dash, a movement to digitize the original manuscripts of manga so as to document the full production process. Takemiya helped create the manga department at Kyoto Seika University, and later became the school's dean.

panels, ranging from small-detail scenes to large crowd assemblies drawn in amazing detail.

Themes

The key theme of *To Terra. . .* is that of free human will versus social engineering to ensure ecological order. The manga questions the legitimacy of subordinating individual human desires to the requirements of an apparently harmonious social order and a life of equilibrium with nature. The issue of social conformity, from childhood through adulthood, is addressed blatantly. By depicting a future in which humanity has abrogated individual decision making to submission to total social control, Takemiya highlights the boundaries of social engineering and a government's right to prescribe the desired behavior of its citizens. Given Japanese society's traditional preference for social harmony, Takemiya's vision of the dangers of total control and conformity is particularly significant.

The paranormal activities of the Mu mutants can be read as symbols of the unique capabilities of humans that fall outside the grid of strict social control. It is interesting that aside from the adult character Captain Harley all leading Mu are drawn to look like adolescents. This stresses the idea of youthful desire for nonconformity and the pain adolescents feel from the imposition of absolute social norms.

The theme of boy-to-boy love, proven enticing for adolescent female readers in Japan, is subtly hinted at in *To Terra. . .* Soldier Blue embraces Jomy Marcus Shin in lovingly depicted panels, and the same is true for Keith Anyan and Jonah Makka, even though their embraces are not of a definite sexual nature. In addition, key characters keep their adolescent physiques, even as they age into their fifties. In the science-fiction genre, this can be explained through advances in medical science, but it gives rise to the visual depiction of young boys sharing moments of vaguely erotic tenderness. American readers may overlook these occasional panels, or be startled by them.

Impact

In Japan, *To Terra. . .* immediately created a huge, loyal fan base. The Mu's rebellion against conformity rang true among adolescent readers. This was so par-

ticularly in the age of Japanese economic expansion during the 1990's, when the so-called bubble economy finally burst. In the previous decades, when conformity seemed to lead to an assured albeit boring life as a salaryman or a homemaker, *To Terra. . .*'s rebellious characters, such as Jomy Marcus Shin or the mysterious Physis, appealed strongly to young readers. The super-achiever Keith Anyan looks like a definite foil, a character easy to hate. Keith's liaison with Sam, however, whose blood he wears in an ear stud, and his ultimate self-sacrifice to free humanity from computer control make him an interesting, likable character.

For young Japanese female readers, the spectacle of boys sacrificing themselves for boys they love, as in Makka's death for Keith, proved attractive. *To Terra. . .* solidified the fame of Takemiya and was turned into successful film and television anime movies. In the United States the graphic novel found many fascinated readers as well.

Films

Terra e. . . (Towards the Terra). Directed by Hideo Onchi. Toei Animation, 1980. This animated film stars the voices of Junichi Inoue as Jomy Marcus Shin, Masaya Oki as his opponent Keith Anyan, and Kumiko Akiyoshi as Physis. The film differs from the manga in that Jomy and Keith are reborn on a rebuilt Terra, and the Mu find a new leader in Tony. This gives these characters a more definite happy end than the graphic novel.

Television Series

Terra e. . . (Towards the Terra). Directed by Osamu Yamazaki. Mainichi Broadcasting System, 2007. This animated series stars the voices of Mitsuki Saiga as Jomy Marcus Shin, Takehito Koyasu as Keith Anyan, and Sanae Kobayashi as Physis. The series differs from the manga in some details and introduces some new characters, taking into account fan feedback about the manga. The most important changes are that both Jomy and Keith are reincarnated and become friends, and Tony becomes leader of the Mu.

R. C. Lutz

Further Reading

Shirow, Masamune. *Ghost in the Shell* (1989-1991).

Takemiya, Keiko. *Andromeda Stories* (2007-2008).

Bibliography

Johnson-Woods, Toni, ed. *Manga: An Anthology of Global and Cultural Perspectives*. New York: Continuum, 2010.

Raiteri, Steve. "*To Terra. . .*" *Library Journal* 132 (May 15, 2007): 75.

Welker, James. "Beautiful, Borrowed, and Bent: 'Boys' Love' as Girls' Love in Shojo Manga." *Signs* 31 (Spring, 2006): 841.

See also: *Ghost in the Shell*; *Battle Angel Alita*

TOWN OF EVENING CALM, COUNTRY OF CHERRY BLOSSOMS

Author: Kouno, Fumiyo
Artist: Fumiyo Kouno (illustrator)
Publisher: Futabasha (Japanese); Last Gasp (English)
First serial publication: *Yūnagi no machi*, 2003; *Sakura no kuni*, 2004
First book publication: *Yūnagi no machi, Sakura no kuni*, 2004 (English translation, 2007)

Publication History

In the summer of 2003, Kouno was a rising manga artist, and her editor at Futabasha's *Weekly Manga Action* magazine suggested that she write a manga about the atomic bombing of Hiroshima during World War II. The September 30, 2003, issue of *Weekly Manga Action* featured *Yūnagi no machi* (Town of evening calm), the first story of her project. In July, 2004, the two stories of *Sakura no kuni* (Country of cherry blossoms) were published.

Based on the success of the three stories, Futabasha published them in a single volume (*tankōbon*), *Yūnagi no machi, sakura no kuni*, in October, 2004. In 2007, Last Gasp, a small American press specializing in unusual and underground comics, published the first English edition as *Town of Evening Calm, Country of Cherry Blossoms*. Naoko Amemiya and Andy Nakatani supplied the translation. A second American printing came out in November, 2007, as the first printing sold quickly. In Japan, a *bunkoban* edition was published in 2008. In the United States, Last Gasp published a hardcover edition in 2009.

Plot

At first glance, *Town of Evening Calm, Country of Cherry Blossoms* appeared an unusual choice for the *Weekly Manga Action*. Born in Hiroshima, but not a descendant of atomic-bomb survivors, Kouno approached her Hiroshima manga with some reluctance. Its tender story of three generations of survivors of the atomic blast over Hiroshima seemed oddly placed in a manga magazine that features covers of bikini- or underwear-clad young women; *Weekly Manga Action* is primarily marketed as a *seinen* manga, sold to mostly

Town of Evening Calm, Country of Cherry Blossoms. (Courtesy of Last Gasp)

male readers between eighteen and thirty years old. But during this time, Kouno's manga series *Nagai Michi* (*Long Road*, 2001-2004), about the experiences of a young married couple, was running in the magazine.

"Town of Evening Calm" begins in Hiroshima in the summer of 1955. Minami Hirano is a young office worker who helps her female coworker Furuta sew a copy of a pretty summer dress that they spotted in a shop window. When Furuta asks their male coworker Uchikoshi if the dress would suit Minami too, it causes both him and Minami some embarrassment. On her way home, Minami takes off her dress shoes to save them from wear as she walks to the post-World War II makeshift hut where she lives with her mother, Fujimi.

Later, Uchikoshi visits Minami, who had missed work because she had to take her mother to the hospital. When Uchikoshi suggests Minami would make a good wife someday, Minami chases him away. That evening, in the women's communal bath house, Minami looks sadly at the radiation burns covering her arms.

Minami goes home with Uchikoshi one week later, and their first kiss triggers Minami's flashback to the day the atomic bomb fell. She runs from Uchikoshi and relives that day and its immediate aftermath. Back at work, she and Uchikoshi make up, but Minami falls ill with fatigue. As Minami dies from the long-term effects of radiation sickness, she wonders if her death makes happy the people who dropped the bomb.

Part 1 of "Country of Cherry Blossoms" opens in the spring of 1987. Tomboy Nanami Ishikawa has just entered fifth grade in Tokyo. Nanami's mother Kyoto has died, and she lives with her younger brother Nagio, her father Asahi (the brother of the late Minami), and her grandmother Fujimi. A latchkey child, Nanami is a passionate baseball player. She is hurt during practice, so both she and her friend Toko go to the hospital, where her grandmother Fujimi and brother Nagio have been receiving treatment.

In the hospital, the personnel welcome Nagio, who is being treated for asthma, and drop cherry blossoms on his bed because he cannot go outside for them. Scolded by her grandmother for disturbing Nagio, Nanami is taken home. That summer, Fujimi dies from her radiation poisoning.

Part 2 begins in the summer of 2004. The retired Asahi worries his two children, who are in their twenties. They fear that he has become senile. When Asahi leaves suddenly, Nanami follows him. At a bus station, Nanami is greeted by Toko, whom she has not seen for seventeen years. They trail Asahi to Hiroshima.

While Toko visits the Peace Memorial Park, Nanami follows Asahi. Her father visits old friends and prays at his family grave. As Asahi sits by the riverbank, the story flashes back to the years after Minami's death, when Asahi returned to Hiroshima. He falls in love with young Kyoko Ota, an atomic-bomb survivor who helps Asahi's mother with her sewing business. Nanami

Fumiyo Kouno

Fumiyo Kouno was born in Hiroshima, Japan, in 1968. She is best known for her manga *Town of Evening Calm, Country of Cherry Blossoms*, a work that deals with the emotional and literal fallout of the nuclear attacks synonymous with her hometown. The manga was serialized between 2003 and 2004 in the *seinen* (or young men's) magazine *Weekly Manga Action*, published by Futabasha. It was later adapted as a live action motion picture. Kouno subsequently produced another series that deals more directly with World War II. Titled *Kouno sekai no katasumi ni* (*To All the Corners of the World*), it tells the story of a young bride persevering during wartime. Kouno is the winner of many major industry awards, including the 2004 Japan Media Arts Festival Grand Prize, the 2005 Tezuka Osamu Cultural Prize Creative Award, and the 2009 Japan Media Arts Festival Excellence Prize.

then remembers the sudden death of Kyoko, her mother, when she was young.

In the present, Nanami arranges for Nagio to meet them in Tokyo, furthering the nascent romance of Nagio and Toko. On the train home, father and daughter have a heart-to-heart talk. Asahi insists that he is sane, and that his daughter reminds him of his late sister Minami.

Characters

- *Minami Hirano*, the protagonist, is a pretty, cheerful twenty-three-year-old Japanese woman whose arms still bear radiation marks from the Hiroshima atomic-bomb blast. She initially denies a tender romance with a male coworker out of guilt for having survived the blast when so many died. Her unexpected death signals both criticism of the war and a new beginning.
- *Furuta*, Minami's pretty coworker, is identified with a white barrette in her black hair, and involuntarily initiates Minami's tender romance.

Forty-nine years later, she is visited by Asahi on his remembrance trip to Hiroshima, helping to bring closure to the narrative.

- *Uchikoshi* is Minami's shy male coworker and romantic interest. When Asahi meets him in 2004, he has turned just as bald as Minami jokingly foretold.

- *Fujimi Hirano* is Minami's mother. Her face is wrinkled from early aging and grief over losing her husband and, eventually, her three daughters as a result of the Hiroshima bombing.

- *Nanami Ishikawa*, the tomboy niece of Minami, wears her hair short like a boy and dresses in a baseball uniform at eleven. At eighteen, she is an office worker with longer hair, but she still has an independent attitude. She trails her father to Hiroshima and learns more about her family history.

- *Toko Tone* is the light-haired, feminine-attired teenage classmate of Nanami in 1987. Seventeen years later, she has become a nurse and is the possible love interest of Nanami's brother Nagio.

- *Asahi Ishikawa*, Minami's brother and Nanami's father, a salaryman dressed in a coat and tie in 1987, is a spry, restive retiree in 2004. His memorial trip to Hiroshima reveals the full extent of the Hirano family tragedy, but ends in hope for the future.

- *Kyoto Ota*, demure and starry-eyed, is a Hiroshima bomb-blast survivor. She admires, loves, and marries Asahi. She is the mother of Nanami and Nagio. She dies of radiation poisoning.

Artistic Style

The U.S. edition of *Town of Evening Calm, Country of Cherry Blossoms* preserves the original Japanese format, in which the book is bound on the right side and the story is read from right to left. Even though this implies having to read the book from the back, it avoids the unfortunate mirroring done to other manga, in which right becomes left, distorting the original visuals.

Kouno's drawings are detailed and convey a fine picture of Japan from 1955 to 2004. Minami's eating utensils, Asahi's traditional wooden geta sandals, Nanami's cell phone, and her coworker's laptop are drawn in detail, as are the interiors and exteriors of their domestic and urban environment. Full-page panels introduce each story. The bombing is alluded to in a graphic manner through a full-page image of Hiroshima's ruined Genbaku Dome (which becomes the center of Peace Park). In the upper left-hand corner of the scene, in which Minami views Genbaku Dome in 1955, Kouno adds two cherry trees that were not actually planted until 1956, foreshadowing a future her character would not live to see.

The realism of Kouno's artistic style captures the visual reality of the changes in Japan in five postwar decades. When Minami dies, the panels become white, featuring only the letters of her last thoughts. This color choice is particularly appropriate because white is the traditional color of death and mourning in Japan and other Buddhist Asian countries.

Themes

The physical and psychological effects of surviving the atomic bombing of Hiroshima are key themes of *Town of Evening Calm, Country of Cherry Blossoms*. Text and pictures address issues of nuclear catastrophe, survival, the long reach of radiation poisoning, and the effects of the bombing on families. Nonetheless, Kouno finishes her story on notes of hope (strongly tied to the Buddhist idea of reincarnation) and on the importance of remembrance.

The theme of humanity's resilience is visualized through the serenity of the manga's opening pages, which feature a cheerful Minami walking barefoot along the river canal. Ten years after the catastrophe, a modicum of normalcy has returned, as depicted in the office scene with Minami and Furuta. But this normalcy is a transitory moment of respite, alluded to in the title. The *yunagi*, or evening calm, provides Hiroshima with a brief interlude between the afternoon's sea breeze and the evening's inland winds.

Minami cannot escape the past. She cannot even wear a short-sleeve shirt similar to the one she helps her friend sew. Minami's arms bear scars from the radiation burns, indicated by patchy lines and seen in panels such as those in which she examines herself in the public bathhouse. Her death signals the impossibility of escaping fate.

There is hope, however, that life will carry on. As Minami's brother marries Kyoko Ota, who survived the atomic bombing, the two newlyweds are shown standing on a rebuilt bridge in Hiroshima in a two-page panel. An undisclosed speaker, clearly Minami, says that she has decided to be (re)born as their child. Later, Nanami's father remarks how much his daughter reminds him of his late sister.

Impact

In Japan, Kouno's manga was celebrated for artistically delivering a personal, humane, and subtle antiwar message. When *Town of Evening Calm, Country of Cherry Blossoms* came out as a book in 2004, it quickly sold more than 180,000 copies. The manga helped Japanese readers to talk more about the issue of the atomic bombing of Hiroshima and Nagasaki, a controversial subject in postwar Japan. Earning two major Japanese art awards, the graphic novel established Kouno's rep-

utation as major manga artist. It was even adapted into a literary text-only novel by Kei Kunii.

In the United States, Last Gasp Books published the manga in English in 2007. The manga's ongoing success in Japan also accounted for a second, even more prestigious paperback edition in 2008. From April 24 to September 5, 2010, the Hiroshima Children's Museum commissioned a fifty-minute planetarium show. Indicative of *Town of Evening Calm, Country of Cherry Blossoms*' wide cultural appeal, the show combined animation and special effects with 130 frames from Kouno's manga.

Films

Yunagi City, Sakura Country. Directed by Kiyoshi Sasabe. Fukuoka Broadcasting Systems, 2007. A live-action film, *Yunagi City, Sakura Country* adheres closely to the manga. The year in which Minami's story takes place was changed from 1955 to 1958.

Town of Evening Calm, Country of Cherry Blossoms. (Courtesy of Last Gasp)

The film premiered at the 2007 Cannes Festival. It opened for general release in Japan in July of that year. Kumiko Aso, portraying Minami, won three "Best Actress" awards for her role, from the Hochi Film Awards, the Mainichi Film Awards, and the Blue Ribbon Awards.

Radio Series

Yunagi City, Sakura Country. Directed by Kenji Shindo. Japan Broadcasting Corporation (NHK), 2006. On August 5, 2006, the eve of the anniversary of the Hiroshima bombing, Japan's premier public radio station, NHK-FM, broadcast a radio play adaptation of Kouno's graphic novel. Hirofumi Harada's script followed the graphic novel closely, foregrounding the stories of Minami and Nanami. Popular Japanese television actor Kenji Anan was the voice-actor for Minami's love interest, Uchikoshi, who, as in the film and novel version, was given the first name Yutaka, which was missing in the original graphic novel.

R. C. Lutz

Further Reading

Asano, Inio. *Solanin* (2008).

Tezuka, Osamu. *Ayako* (2010).

Bibliography

Johnson-Woods, Toni, ed. *Manga: An Anthology of Global and Cultural Perspectives*. New York: Continuum, 2010.

Lunning, Frenchy, ed. *War/Time*. Minneapolis: University of Minnesota Press, 2009.

Macwilliams, Mark, ed. *Japanese Visual Culture: Explorations in the World of Manga and Anime*. Armonk, N.Y.: M. E. Sharpe, 2008.

Mihalsky, Susan. "*Town of Evening Calm, Country of Cherry Blossoms.*" *Library Media Connection* 29, no. 5 (March/April, 2011): 76.

See also: *Solanin*; *A Distant Neighborhood*; *Four Immigrants Manga*

TSUBASA: RESERVOIR CHRONICLE

Author: Clamp

Artist: Mokona Apapa (illustrator); Tsubaki Nekoi (illustrator); Satsuki Igarashi (illustrator)

Publisher: Kodansha (Japanese); Random House (English)

First serial publication: *Tsubasa: Rezaboa kuronikuru,* 2003-2009

First book publication: 2003-2009 (English translation, 2004-2010)

Publication History

By 2002, the four-woman manga artists' collective known as Clamp (which includes Nanase Ohkawa, Mokona Apapa, Tsubaki Nekoi, and Satsuki Igarashi) decided to create a new series that would bring together some of their previous characters from other series. These characters were given new backstories, though, making them quite different from their originals.

Tsubasa: Reservoir Chronicle began publication in Kodansha's *Weekly Shōnen Magazine* in May, 2003. The manga's two main characters came from Clamp's previous series, *Cardcaptor Sakura* (1996-2000); however, they were both aged to late adolescents and featured completely new origins.

At the same time, Clamp began the series *xxxHolic* (2003-2011) in *Young Magazine.* Its two main characters were given important supporting roles in *Tsubasa,* encouraging readers to follow both series. The four artists of Clamp managed to deliver the weekly output of both series.

The success of *Tsubasa* led to the collection of its 232 episodes into twenty-eight books. Unique for manga, Kodansha offered both regular and deluxe editions of the books. The deluxe version featured additional colorized pages. The two book editions were published simultaneously from August, 2003, to November, 2009.

In the United States, Random House published the twenty-eight-book regular volumes under its imprint Del Rey Manga from April, 2004, to November, 2010. The American version stayed faithful to the manga

---

Clamp

Clamp is not a single artist but a collective of female manga artists and writers. The group began as a self-publishing enterprise in the mid-1980's and became a commercial force after joining up with mainstream publishers. The magazine *Nakayoshi,* published by Kodansha, serialized Clamp's *Cardcaptor Sakura* and *Magic Knight Rayearth,* and *Jump Square,* published by Shūeisha, serializes *Gate 7.* Especially popular are Clamp's series *Chobits* and *xxxHolic,* both of which appeared in Kodansha's *Young Magazine.* Clamp consists of Satsuki Igarashi, Mokona Apapa, Tsubaki Nekoi, and Nanase Ohkawa. Ohkawa is recognized as the group's leader, and she has likened her role to that of a film director. In 2006, she told the *New York Times,* "I decide who does the characters, and what she's going to do with them. . . . I assign the roles. . . . I also choose the visual style" (Solomon).

---

format, reading from right to left, with the book spine on the right.

Plot

With *Tsubasa: Reservoir Chronicle,* Clamp wanted to create a manga for young boys from elementary school to middle school. Midway through the series, major plot twists turned it into a manga for somewhat older readers.

Tsubasa opens in the fantasy Kingdom of Clow. Syaoran is a young archaeologist who continues the work of his late father. He is friends with Princess Sakura, who is in love with him. On a trip to ruins that are the subject of an archaeological dig, Sakura looks at a strange seal on the ground. Suddenly, she is attacked by a horde of black clad men, who steal her wings (wings representing her soul and memories). She is left in a coma. The next few panels reveal that a strange man and his female assistant are behind the maneuver. Much later, the series reveals them to be the evil wizard

Fei-Wang Reed, the antagonist of the series, and his helper Xing Huo.

To save Sakura, Syaoran lets himself be transported to another world in another dimension by Clow's High Priest Yukita; the world is actually Japan. There, Syaoran meets the space-time witch Yuko Ichihara. The witch helps people for the price of what is most dear to them. Syaoran gives up Sakura's memories of him in return for a chance to save her. During the quest, he is joined by two young men from two other worlds. One is an uptight young ninja, Kurogane, who was sent away by his queen, Tomoyo, to cure him of his eruptions of violence. The third associate is a young wizard, Fai D. Flowright, who wishes to travel as far away from his king as possible. To facilitate their travels, Yuko creates a cute little creature that looks like a happy rabbit, called Mokona Modoki.

To save Sakura, the band of three unlikely allies must collect as many of the white feathers that contain fragments of Sakura's soul as possible. They travel to many strange worlds in different dimensions. Each world provides the setting for an individual story arc. Typically, all worlds feature strong fantasy elements.

When the first white feather is secured, Sakura wakes up. Each new feather brings back more of her memory, excluding those of her love for Syaoran. Sakura begins to develop new feelings for Syaoran independent of her past memories.

After a series of feather-hunting subplots on different worlds, Clamp shocks readers with the first of many major plot twists. On a world resembling a post-catastrophic Tokyo, it is revealed that Syaoran is actually a clone. At the root of all the problems is the evil sorcerer Fei-Wang Reed. Jealous of the magic powers of his antagonist, Clow Reed, Fei-Wang Reed imprisoned the original Syaoran and cloned him. This happened when the original Syaoran first visited Clow and tried to rescue Sakura from a death curse placed on her by Fei-Wang.

The original Syaoran managed to endow the clone with part of his heart, sealed behind the clone's right eye, to humanize him. As this seal breaks during a fight, the clone becomes the unthinking tool of Fei-Wang Reed. Just before this happens, the original Syaoran

managed to escape, travel to Japan, and have Yuko unite him with the clone's group around Sakura.

The original Syaoran fails to kill the evil clone. Under a spell from Fei-Wang Reed, Fai Flowright tries to kill the original Syaoran. Sakura takes Fai's blow instead. This splits her body and soul, sending the two parts into two different dimensions. The clone kills Sakura's soul to get at her feathers, which was his mission all along. Just before her soul dies, Sakura reveals that she, too, is a clone of the original Sakura, now in Fei-Wang's power.

The original Syaoran and his allies travel to an alternate version of the Kingdom of Clow. There, they face Fei-Wang Reed. In the course of battles, Fei-Wang destroys both clones. Fei-Wang also revives Yuko, whom Clow Reed froze in time to prevent her death. This means Fei-Wang's magic has become stronger than Clow's.

Before dying again, Yuko uses her new life to revive the clones of Syaoran and Sakura. These clones give birth to a boy who turns out to be the original Syaoran, creating a time paradox. Finally, the original Syaoran, Kurogane, and Fai Flowright confront Fei-Wang Reed. The original Sakura awakens and joins the fight. Kurogane kills Fei-Wang. As their price for this, Syaoran must continue to travel through space and time. Only occasionally can he meet the original Sakura, who must stay in Clow to keep chaos at bay. The clones turn into two feathers as Fei-Wang dies. Kurogane and Fai decide to accompany Syaoran on his journeys.

Just as he is about to depart, Syaoran tells Sakura that his real name is Tsubasa, the word for "wings" in Japanese. This finally explains the title of the series, *Tsubasa: Reservoir Chronicle*. All the worlds visited serve as a reservoir for the feathers of Sakura's wings stolen in the beginning.

Volumes

- *Tsubasa: Reservoir Chronicle*, Volume 1 (2004). Collects the first five episodes. Introduces Syaoran and Sakura and launches the series.
- *Tsubasa: Reservoir Chronicle*, Volumes 2-14 (2004-2007). Each volume collects from eight to nine episodes, up to episode 108. The protagonists travel from one fantastic world to the next to

recover feathers of Sakura's soul. Her personality grows back with each feather.

- *Tsubasa: Reservoir Chronicle*, Volume 15-16 (2007, 2008). Collect episodes 109 to 124. Clamp surprises their readers with the major plot twist that Syaoran is actually a clone made by Fei-Wang Reed. This completely upsets the story.
- *Tsubasa: Reservoir Chronicle*, Volumes 17-27 (2008-2010). Collect episodes 125 to 219. The story turns to the fight against Fei-Wang Reed. Clamp adds twist after twist to the plot, including the fact that Sakura is also a clone. The series moves from a young-male-adult to an older–male-adult audience.
- *Tsubasa: Reservoir Chronicle*, Volume 28 (2010). The final volume collects episodes 220 to 232, and resolves all plot twists. Syaoran must continue his journey, but his two male friends join him, making for an open ending.

Characters

- *Syaoran*, the apparent protagonist, is an adolescent boy with light brown hair that is drawn as white when not featured on color covers. He is of medium height, making him the shortest of his friends. He is in love with Princess Sakura. In the beginning, he wears trademark goggles to protect him from the sands of Clow, and he often wears a trench coat. The manga reveals that he is a clone of the original Syaoran. Destroyed but resurrected by the space-time witch, he and clone Sakura become parents of the original Syaoran.
- *Syaoran*, a.k.a. *Tsubasa*, the true protagonist. He is a teenager who looks and dresses just like his clone. In the middle of the manga, he escapes his imprisonment to hunt down his clone. His price for being part of killing Fei-Wang is to travel the universe forever. He can see his true love, the original Sakura, only occasionally.
- *Sakura*, love interest of Syaoran, is the teenage Princess of Clow. She has red hair that is drawn as white in the manga. She often wears a short-sleeved blouse with round chest ornaments, a short skirt, and sometimes a long cape. She is robbed of her memories, represented by white

wings. Later revealed to be a clone, she dies, is resurrected, and gives birth to the original Syaoran. She dies again when Fei-Wang does.

- *Sakura*, original princess of Clow, is the same age as her clone and is dressed like her as well. She awakens during the final fight against Fei-Wang. She waits on Clow for Syaoran's visits.
- *Fei-Wang Reed*, the antagonist, is an evil wizard. He is an older man and wears a monocle. His hair is black with long sideburns and two strands of white hair that look like devil's horns. His quest for power triggers and fuels the plot.
- *Kurogane*, supporter of Syaoran, is a young ninja dressed in black. He has a short, fierce temper and comes from the world of medieval Japan. He is sent on his journey by his mistress, Queen Tomoyo, to protect him from Fei-Wang Reed. Kurogane kills the evil sorcerer and volunteers to accompany the original Syaoran on his eternal journey.
- *Fai D. Flowright*, supporter of Syaoran, is a gangly young wizard with blue eyes, the source of his magic powers, and a white-blond mane of hair. Good-natured and a steady friend of Syaoran, he loves to tease Kurogane. As a child, he was given the identity of his twin, who has been killed by Fei-Wang. Fai resumes his original name of Yui as he accompanies Syaoran in the end.
- *Yuko Ichihara* is a powerful sorceress called the space-time witch. She appears to be in her twenties but is of indefinite age because of her magic background. She wears black. At her shop in Tokyo, she grants people their wishes for what is most dear to them.
- *Mokona Modoki*, the comic sidekick of the three protagonists, is a funny-looking, rabbitlike creature with a jewel on its forehead, drawn like a Pokémon character.

Artistic Style

When the four-woman *mangaka* collective Clamp began work on *Tsubasa: Reservoir Chronicle*, the weekly series was designed for a young male audience. Clamp decided to simplify their typical panel layouts and use broader strokes in the drawings of characters and backgrounds. The characters were drawn in classic manga style. The alien worlds, particularly the ruins and palaces of Clow, tend to look roughly executed.

The interplay between the major characters drawn by Apapa, and the supporting cast and backgrounds created by Nekoi and Igarashi, worked well visually, showing no stylistic breaks. Clamp maintained its fluid organization of panels. Panels rarely correspond to the classic arrangement, almost breaking out of the page at climactic moments.

The drawing of wings and feathers, to support the series' key theme, is prevalent throughout. The wings tend to be rather stylized and can be observed in various architectural elements, such as the palace and ruins of Clow. Evil Fei-Wang Reed sports an emblem of two dark wings on the front of his black robe.

At times, readers were confused by the detail and exuberance of the manga's many fight scenes. It requires some careful scrutiny to figure out the exact movements of a battle, what weapon hits where and with what impact. Stark contrast of black and white is often used for fight scenes. Romantic interludes tend to rely on shades of gray.

As the series progressed, Clamp reverted to its more mature, trademark artistic style. Combined with a more complex plot, the artwork became more chiseled. Close-ups of characters appeared to take up central space.

Themes

As *Tsubasa: Reservoir Chronicle* begins, the key theme is the journey of three unlikely companions to save the soul of the woman one of them loves. It is a classic quest story. The series presents the idea that through a strong, communal effort, mishaps can be reversed, and a bad situation can be rectified.

The plot around Yuko concerns the theme that to gain one's ideal one has to be ready to make a major sacrifice. All three characters on the journey to save Sakura must separate from what they hold most dear. The themes of self-sacrifice, self-discipline, and goal orientation are highlighted.

The manga is also a classic adventure story. Working from the plot premise of collecting Sakura's

feathers from different worlds, the creation of each new world allows Clamp to visualize strange, fantastic environments that often bear some thematic connections to modern Japan. The first world visited, the Republic of Hanshin, can be read as a satire of Japanese obsession with perfection. The postcatastrophic Tokyo exemplifies the popular theme of life after an apocalypse.

Finally, the theme of life as a journey is used to close the series. In a fashion not untypical of a manga series, there is little closure; instead, there is the promise of new beginnings. Ironically, the new start does look somewhat like a continuation of the old. It seems that the theme of the circularity of life is given more prominence than in Western comics.

Impact

In Japan and the United States, *Tsubasa: Reservoir Chronicle* was welcomed because it promised to include many of Clamp's popular characters from their other series, albeit in a new story. In the beginning, readers liked Syaoran's commitment to save Sakura. The series proved popular because of the different adventures of the three protagonists.

The manga became famous for its dramatic plot twists. The more plot twists Clamp offered in the second half of the series, the more they astounded, and mostly delighted, their readers. There was some criticism that the plot twists were too many. Some critics complained that the twists were insufficiently motivated and executed, and that they merely led to confusion.

But Clamp's audacious experiment paid off well. Also successful was their idea to link the fantasy world of *Tsubasa and xxxHolic*, set in contemporary Japan. Yuko's magic shop, which links the two series, was well liked by fans. Since Clamp began as a fan enterprise, they kept an astute eye on the series' appeal among readers. At one point, story writer Ohkawa admits that the focus of the series was shifted from horror to mystery to keep in tune with audience preferences. As a result of the series' popularity, the original Japanese run of the *Tsubasa* book volumes, both in the normal and deluxe edition, exceeded a remarkable twenty million copies sold.

Films

Tsubasa the Movie: The Princess in the Country of Birdcages. Directed by Itsurō Kawasaki. Clamp/Dentsu/FUNimation Entertainment, 2005. This thirty-five-minute animated film stars the voices of Miyu Irino as Syaoran and Yui Makino as Sakura. The film features the key characters of the manga in an original story about searching for a feather containing Sakura's memory on a different world. The film was not written by Clamp and received mixed critical reviews.

Television Series

Tsubasa: Reservoir Chronicle. Directed by Koichi Mashimo, et al. Bee Train/Clamp/FUNimation Entertainment, 2005-2006. The series starred the voices of Irino as Syaoran and Makino as Sakura. It ran for two seasons, with a total of fifty-two episodes. It was written by Hiroyuki Kawasaki and stayed fairly close to the original manga. The episodes cover the search for Sakura's feathers on different worlds, before the revelation that Syaoran is a clone.

Tsubasa Tokyo Revelations. Directed by Akiko Honda, Shunsuke Tada, and Hideyo Yamamoto. Production I.G., 2007. One of two original video animation series. This was not aired on television but was sold straight to video. It was written by Clamp author Ohkawa. It comprises three episodes, which reveal that Syaoran is a clone and feature his fight with the original Syaoran.

Tsubasa Chronicle: Spring Thunder. Directed by Shunsuke Tada. Clamp/FUNimation Entertainment/Kodansha, 2009. Created by the same team as the first direct-to-video release, this film takes the story forward to the apparent death of clone Sakura and ends just before the climactic battle against Fei-Wong Reed.

R. C. Lutz

Further Reading

Clamp. *Cardcaptor Sakura* (1996-2000).

_____. *xxxHolic* (2004-2011).

Bibliography

Johnson-Woods, Toni, ed. *Manga: An Anthology of Global and Cultural Perspectives.* New York: Continuum, 2010.

Raitery, Steve. "*Tsubasa: Reservoir Chronicle* Vol. 1." *Library Journal* 129 (September 1, 2004): 128.

Reed, Calvin. "Comics Bestsellers." *Publishers Weekly* 254 (July 9, 2007): 16.

Solomon, Charles. "Four Mothers of Manga Gain American Fans With Expertise in a Variety of Visual Styles." *The New York Times*, November 28, 2006.

See also: *Cardcaptor Sakura*; *Ghost in the Shell*

20TH CENTURY BOYS

Author: Urasawa, Naoki

Artist: Naoki Urasawa (illustrator)

Publisher: Shogakukan (Japanese); VIZ Media (English)

First serial publication: *20 seiki shōnen*, 1999–2007

First book publication: 2000-2006 (English translation, 2009-   )

Publication History

20th Century Boys was originally published by Shogakukan in *Big Comic Spirits*, a weekly *seinen* manga magazine. Shogakukan also reprinted the series as a twenty-two-volume set. The last two books of the series were reprinted with the title *21st Century Boys*. In 2009, an English-language version of *20th Century Boys* was published in the United States by VIZ Media. VIZ originally licensed the series in 2005, but creator Naoki Urasawa requested the books be published after the English translation of *Monster* (2006-2008), as his artwork had undergone dramatic improvements.

Plot

20th Century Boys tells the story of Kenji Endo, a middle-aged man who has resigned his fate to managing a mediocre convenience store and raising his infant niece Kanna. When not working, he reminisces about his childhood and his grand dreams of being a mighty hero.

After it is reported that his friend Donkey has committed suicide, Kenji notices a peculiar symbol on a note left for him. The symbol was originally associated with a secret base and group of childhood friends for whom Kenji wrote a book called the "Book of Prophecy." He gradually discovers a shadowy group, whose leader is named Friend. While some people feel the organization is harmless, others are suspicious of its motives.

Dissenters of the group are eliminated one by one. At the same time, a mysterious virus has emerged that leaves its victims drained of blood. The more Kenji investigates, the more convinced he becomes that Friend is someone from his childhood. He gradually recruits

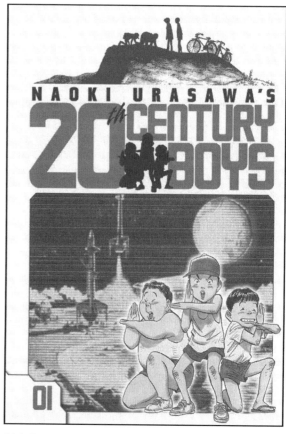

20th Century Boys. (Courtesy of VIZ Media)

his friends Otcho, Yukiji, Maruo, Mon-chan, and Yoshitsune to piece together what the "Book of Prophecy" contains and to stop Friend.

The group's first attempt to halt Friend's actions is December 31, 2000, when a giant robot attacks Tokyo. Kenji tries to blow up the robot, but the plan backfires. Friend takes full credit for destroying the robot and curing the virus; in reality, his group created the virus and kept a vaccine in reserve until the moment to seize power was right.

The story then skips ahead fourteen years. The Friendship Democratic Party has become the dominant political party in Japan, bringing rampant corruption. Kenji and his friends have been branded terrorists. During this time, Kanna begins to sow the seeds of rebellion against Friend by allying herself with the Chinese and Thai mafias. Also revealed is that Kanna is Friend's daughter.

During this time, Friend decides to enact the next stage detailed in his "New Book of Prophecy," which calls for the death of all but 3 million people on Earth. He gradually shifts from a political figure to a religious icon. His plan is thwarted, however, by his chief scientist, Dr. Yamane, who kills Friend. After this, a massive worldwide funeral is held for Friend, during which the pope arrives from the Vatican to deliver a speech in his honor. Kanna and the others learn that the real plan is to assassinate the pope, and they race to thwart this plot.

However, nobody predicts that Friend will rise from the dead to protect the pope from the assassin's bullet. After this event, the story skips ahead three years, to the Year 3F. During this time, Friend has instituted numerous bizarre policies, including one that sets up the Earth Defense Force, a group commissioned to protect the planet from alien invasion. At this point, Kanna leads a rebel faction under the moniker the Ice Queen, and Kenji reappears with his guitar. The story ends with Friend's death and the collapse of his cult's empire, and Kenji and Kanna save the world from destruction by an antiproton bomb.

Volumes

- *20th Century Boys*, Volume 1 (2009). Collects chapters 1-10. Kenji reminisces after a friend's suicide. A strange cult emerges in Japan.
- *20th Century Boys*, Volume 2 (2009). Collects chapters 11–21. Features the growing power of Friend's influence, a mysterious virus, and Kenji's efforts to uncover Friend's identity.
- *20th Century Boys*, Volume 3 (2009). Collects chapters 22-32. Features Kenji's struggle to follow the trail to the truth about Friend.
- *20th Century Boys*, Volume 4 (2009). Features the introduction of Kenji's friend Otcho, living in Thailand under the moniker "Shogun," and Friend's infiltration of the Japanese government.
- *20th Century Boys*, Volume 5 (2009). Collects chapters 33–43. Features Kenji's niece Kanna, a teenager living in a world drastically changed by the events of the Bloody New Year's Eve.

- *20th Century Boys*, Volume 6 (2009). Collects chapters 44-54. Features a young manga artist's incarceration in a maximum-security prison, which would be a death sentence were it not for his closest cellmate.
- *20th Century Boys*, Volume 7 (2010). Collects chapters 55-65. Features Otcho's efforts to plot an escape from Umihotaru Prison to reach a girl he calls the "final hope," Kanna.
- *20th Century Boys*, Volume 8 (2010). Collects chapters 66-76. Reveals the truth behind the events of the Bloody New Year's Eve.
- *20th Century Boys*, Volume 9 (2010). Collects chapters 77-87. Features Kanna's decision to take a stand against Friend, while ordinary teenager Koizumi Kyoko experiences the reeducation camp, Friend Land.
- *20th Century Boys*, Volume 10 (2010). Collects chapters 88-98. Features Koizumi's efforts to reach Kanna to tell her everything about Friend Land, before the Friends reach Kyoko first.
- *20th Century Boys*, Volume 11 (2010). Collects chapters 99-110. Features Koizumi's escape with the help of another former classmate, Sadakiyo, "the Lie of 1970," and Kanna's discovery that Friend is her father.
- *20th Century Boys*, Volume 12 (2010). Collects chapters 111-122. Features a message from the past left by Kiriko Endo and Otcho's search for Dr. Yamane.
- *20th Century Boys*, Volume 13 (2011). Collects chapters 123-134. Features Friend's death and mounting evidence suggesting a deadlier threat on the horizon.
- *20th Century Boys*, Volume 14 (2011). Collects chapters 135-146. Features Friend's memorial and Yoshitsune's trip through Friend's mind to deduce what will happen next.
- *20th Century Boys*, Volume 15 (2011). Collects chapters 147-159. Features the discovery of a book of prophecies that puts a young Catholic priest's life in grave danger. Also, in the streets of Tokyo, Friend is seen walking again.
- *20th Century Boys*, Volume 16 (2011). Collects chapters 160-170. Features the story of Fukubei's

lonely childhood, before flashing forward to the third year of the Friendship Era.

- *20th Century Boys*, Volume 17 (2011). Collects chapters 171-181. Features a dystopian future in which Friend rules the world; rumors persist of a growing resistance lead by a figure named the Ice Queen.
- *20th Century Boys*, Volume 18 (2011). Collects chapters 182-192. Features Joe Yabuki, a man traveling Japan on his motorbike with a guitar and a song.
- *20th Century Boys*, Volume 19 (2012). Collects chapters 193-203. Features Joe's efforts to pass a checkpoint to Tokyo without clearance.
- *20th Century Boys*, Volume 20 (2012). Collects chapters 204-214. Reveals that Joe Yabuki is really Kenji, and features his efforts to return to Tokyo in time to thwart Friend's latest plan.
- *20th Century Boys*, Volume 21 (2012). Collects chapters 215-225. Features clues to the identity of the current Friend and the countdown to the final battle.
- *20th Century Boys*, Volume 22 (2012). Collects chapters 226-238. Features both Friend's plan to destroy the world in seven days and Kanna's efforts to save lives with a music festival.
- *20th Century Boys*, Volume 23 (2012). Collects chapters 239-251. Features the death of the second Friend and an eerie peek into his childhood.
- *20th Century Boys*, Volume 24 (2012). Collects chapters 252-259. Features the final battle at the place where it all began, the boys' secret base.

Characters

- *Kenji Endo,* the protagonist, is a middle-aged Japanese man. A laid-back dreamer, he runs a convenience store and raises his niece, Kanna. As the series progresses, he accepts his responsibility of stopping Friend. He goes missing for twenty years and reemerges as a man named Joe Yabuki.
- *Friend,* the primary antagonist, is thought to be two people in the series. The first is a megalomaniac named Fukubei. The other is another former

classmate of Kenji named Katsumata. Both incarnations of Friend are charismatic, deceitful, and selfish.

- *Kanna Endo* is Kenji's niece and the protagonist beginning in 2014. Intelligent and charismatic, she later leads a rebel faction against Friend. She struggles with her identity after discovering she is Friend's daughter.
- *Kiriko Endo* is Kenji's older sister. Beautiful, kind, and intelligent, she is a gifted bacteriologist. She later ends ups involved in Friend's plans. She spends the rest of the series trying to atone for her association with Friend.
- *Chouji Ochiai,* a.k.a. *Otcho*, is Kenji's childhood friend, who designed the symbol Friend uses for his organization. After the death of his son, he leaves to seek enlightenment and lives in Asia's seedy underground under the nickname "Shogun."
- *Yukiji Setoguchi* is a childhood friend of Kenji, first introduced as a customs official at an airport. A tomboy in her youth, she becomes more professional as an adult. She joins Kenji in the fight against Friend and later becomes Kanna's guardian.
- *Yoshitsune* is the timid and quiet friend of Kenji. During the Bloody New Year's Eve, he fakes his death. Over the years, he grows into a capable, inspiring leader.
- *Maruo* is a friend of Kenji, who joins in the fight against Friend. Overweight and not particularly clever, he is nevertheless a loyal ally and friend. He survives the Bloody New Year's Eve to become a successful manager in the music industry.
- *Keroyon* was an old friend of Kenji, who got his nickname because of his frog-like appearance. Unlike the others, he initially declines to help on Bloody New Year's Eve. He later resurfaces in the United States during the plague of 2015.
- *Donkey* is another member of Kenji's group who grew up to be a high school science teacher. His death is what first prompts Kenji to investigate Friend's mysterious group.

Artistic Style

As with *Monster*, Urasawa relies on a realistic style for his character designs and settings in *20th Century Boys*. While the bulk of the story takes place in Tokyo, the occasional chapter in Europe or the United States features starkly different settings. When a new narrative begins at the Vatican, Urasawa displays the classical architecture. His threads running in the United States are set in small towns in New Mexico and Kansas, which heightens the tension felt about Friend. When a group can wipe out rural towns in the United States and infiltrate the Vatican, one wonders where a safe place to hide could be.

Urasawa portrays people in a realistic style, with a wide variety of facial features, body types, and ages. He even depicts several of the characters aging through the years; in the case of such characters as Yukiji, the effect is subtle. Others, such as Otcho, age quite drastically; the stress of time shows clearly, from hairstyles to pronounced features. Friend appears ageless, however, which emphasizes how much his behavior resembles that of a child playing games.

Like *Monster*, the action scenes tend to be tight and fast, likely because many of the most violent scenes are caused by soldiers. Unlike previous series, Urasawa does not hesitate to show readers sudden acts of violence. By showing the callous deaths of the innocent and guilty alike, Urasawa stresses that Friend is not so much good or evil as uncaring and selfish.

Themes

20th Century Boys' overarching themes concern childhood, and how people's pasts shape their futures. The many side characters use their memories not only to remember what they created but also to try to figure out their enemy. They wonder who among them has become the mysterious and menacing Friend, and if it is possible to recognize the motives of an adult from his behavior as a child.

The story toys with Friend's identity throughout the series. In the end, Urasawa implies two separate individuals played the role. The first is Fukubei, who longed to be the center of attention among his peers. He is especially jealous of Kenji, who wrote the "Book of Prophecy." This is reflected in the first era of Friend (ending in 2015); in these times, Friend is seen as a hero, a beloved protector of the people. Kenji and the others are portrayed as terrorists who tried to murder innocent civilians. At last, Friend had bested Kenji and become the person other people admire the most.

The second Friend, Katsumata, has different ambitions. Unlike Fukubei, Katsumata's motivations are driven by hatred, first for Kenji and later for humanity in general. During his reign, over half the world's population dies from a plague, and Japan regresses to a feudal society. People are subject to Katsumata's fantastical whims, including the construction of the Earth Defense Force to combat aliens.

There is a related theme: The dreams and desires that people nurture as children shape the adults they become. The future is the past, and vice versa. Yoshitsune doubts himself a capable leader in Kenji and Otcho's absence, until he remembers one summer he took the initiative to rebuild their secret base. Kenji becomes the musician he dreamed of being during the hot afternoons of his childhood. Yukiji spends her life protecting everyone she loves, and Maruo's loyalty to his friends never wavers. Some of these arcs take years to come full circle, but by holding on to the child inside the characters are true to themselves.

Lastly, in addition to shaping one's own dreams and actions, one can shape those of the people around him or him. Kenji realizes that his childhood actions shaped not only his future but also the futures of his classmates. Had he treated Fukubei and Katsumata differently, the future might have been quite different. Had he been more forthright about his feelings for Yukiji, he might have married her. His sister Kiriko could have led a much happier life by not being involved with Friend. In the case of the latter, however, Kanna would have never existed. Thus, Urasawa reminds readers that the past cannot be changed, so it is best to not dwell on "what if" scenarios. In summation, *20th Century Boys* documents the tricky, difficult job of growing up and dealing with the trials of life, and it stresses the importance of every decision one makes along the path of life.

Impact

Urasawa draws on his own childhood to create the setting for *20th Century Boys*. Characters reference comics such as *Tetsujin-28* (1956-1966), *Astro Boy* (1952-1968), *Phoenix* (1954-1988), and *Ashita no Jō* (1968-1973), all titles published before or during the 1970's. The "Book of Prophecy" is woven from the threads of these and other classic comic story lines. The construction of a bowling alley on the boy's beloved secret base inspires them to create an "evil emperor" to defeat. The boys even have a traditional haunted-house adventure, which Urasawa uses to give readers a peek into the mind of Friend.

Kenji falls in love with rock and roll and spends his days listening to bands and musicians such as Creedence Clearwater Revival, Jimi Hendrix, and Janis Joplin. The song "20th Century Boy" by T. Rex also features prominently in the series. Readers of *20th Century Boys* will notice that the story is tied to nostalgia but deftly uses childhood memories to explain adult characters' motivations, relationships, and personalities.

Films

20th Century Boys 1-3. Directed by Yukihiko Tsutsumi. Nippon Television Network Corporation, 2008-2009. These film adaptations star Toshiaki

Karasawa as Kenji Endo, Tokako Tokiwa as Yukiji, and Etsushi Toyakawa as Otcho. Aside from the compression of certain plot points, the trilogy is fairly faithful to the comic.

Lyndsey Nicole Raney

Further Reading

Ohba, Tsugumi, and Takeshi Obata. *Death Note* (2003-2006).

Tezuka, Osamu. *MW* (1976-1978).

Urasawa, Naoki. *Monster* (1994-2001).

Bibliography

Raiteri, Steve. "*20th Century Boys*." Review of *20th Century Boys*, by Naoki Urasawa. *Library Journal* 134, no. 12 (July, 2009): 78.

Sanders, Joe Sutliff. "*20th Century Boys*." Review of *20th Century Boys*, by Naoki Urasawa. *Teacher Librarian* 37, no. 4 (April, 2010): 27.

Yadao, Jason. *The Rough Guide to Manga*. New York: Rough Guides, 2009.

See also: *Death Note*; *MW*; *Monster*

U

Usagi Yojimbo

Author: Sakai, Stan
Artist: Stan Sakai (illustrator); Tom Luth (colorist)
Publisher: Fantagraphics Books; Mirage Comics; Dark Horse Comics
First serial publication: 1987-
First book publication: 1987-

Publication History

Usagi Yojimbo originated in small-press comics of the 1980's, first appearing in the anthropomorphic-animal anthology series *Albedo Anthropomorphics*. The series moved to Fantagraphics Books, which first included *Usagi Yojimbo* in its anthropomorphic-animal anthology *Critters* and later showcased the comic in its own series. The series rode the wave of success of black-and-white independent comics through the 1980's, until changes in the marketplace led creator Stan Sakai to take his samurai rabbit to Mirage Comics for a full-color run. When Mirage folded after sixteen issues, Sakai moved his series to Dark Horse Comics, which began carrying the title in 1996. The character of Miyamoto Usagi has also appeared as a guest star in a number of other titles. In 2011, Dark Horse released *Usagi Yojimbo: Yokai*, the only all-original *Usagi Yojimbo* graphic novel.

Although Sakai is a Japanese American artist creating comics in English for publication in the United States, he has noted in interviews that he is often considered a manga artist because *Usagi Yojimbo* is set in Japan and strongly influenced by Japanese culture and folklore.

Plot

Usagi Yojimbo is constructed as a slice-of-life picaresque. A samurai without portfolio, Usagi has no other agenda than to act according to his best judgment and to continue to improve himself as a person and a

Usagi Yojimbo. (Courtesy of Dark Horse Comics)

swordsman. Although there is an overarching plot of the series, in which Usagi opposes the schemes of the evil Lord Hikiji and other tyrannical or criminal figures, the real goal of the story is to provide a window into the history and culture of seventeenth century Japan while telling bittersweet stories of heroism and humanity.

The two major elements that drive the world of *Usagi Yojimbo* are time and death. Unlike the characters in other anthropomorphic-animal comics, who tend to be immortal clowns or unchanging whimsical figures, the characters of *Usagi Yojimbo* live, age, and die. Wars and duels have casualties, characters have children who grow, and every character can learn and change with time and experience. Over the course of the series, Usagi evolves from a rather simple, stern figure whose behavior is guided by rigid Bushido principals into a well-rounded protagonist who offers commentary on many aspects of life. He progresses from early manhood to something approaching middle age.

Seventeenth century Japan, the other "star" of the series, was a pivotal era. Japan unified as a nation during that time and greatly restricted the use of gunpowder until the nineteenth century, ensuring the value of swordsmen like Usagi until contact with the West.

Volumes

- *Usagi Yojimbo: The Ronin*, Volume 1 (1987). Collects short stories from *Albedo* and *Critters*.
- *Usagi Yojimbo: Samurai*, Volume 2 (1989). Collects issues 1-6 of the Fantagraphics series.
- *Usagi Yojimbo: The Wanderer's Road*, Volume 3 (1989). Collects issues 7-12 of the Fantagraphics series, along with other materials.
- *Usagi Yojimbo: The Dragon Bellow Conspiracy*, Volume 4 (1990). Collects issues 13-18 of the Fantagraphics series, along with other materials.
- *Usagi Yojimbo: Lone Goat and Kid*, Volume 5 (1992). Collects issues 19-24 of the Fantagraphics series, along with other materials.
- *Usagi Yojimbo: Circles*, Volume 6 (1994). Collects issues 25-31 of the Fantagraphics series, along with other materials.
- *Usagi Yojimbo: Gen's Story*, Volume 7 (1996). Collects issues 32-38 of the Fantagraphics series, along with other materials.
- *Usagi Yojimbo: Shades of Death*, Volume 8 (1997). Collects issues 1-6 of the Mirage series.
- *Usagi Yojimbo: Daisho*, Volume 9 (1998). Collects issues 7-14 of the Mirage series.
- *Usagi Yojimbo: The Brink of Life and Death*, Volume 10 (1998). Collects issues 15-16 of the Mirage series and issues 1-6 of the Dark Horse series.
- *Usagi Yojimbo: Seasons*, Volume 11 (1999). Collects issues 7-12 of the Dark Horse series.

- *Usagi Yojimbo: Grasscutter*, Volume 12 (1999). Collects issues 13-22 of the Dark Horse series.
- *Usagi Yojimbo: Grey Shadows*, Volume 13 (2000). Collects issues 23-30 of the Dark Horse series.
- *Usagi Yojimbo: Demon Mask*, Volume 14 (2001). Collects issues 31-38 of the Dark Horse series, along with other materials.
- *Usagi Yojimbo: Grasscutter II—Journey to Atsuta Shrine*, Volume 15 (2002). Collects issues 39-45 of the Dark Horse series.
- *Usagi Yojimbo: The Shrouded Moon*, Volume 16 (2003). Collects issues 46-52 of the Dark Horse series.
- *Usagi Yojimbo: Duel at Kitanoji*, Volume 17 (2003). Collects issues 53-60 of the Dark Horse series.
- *Usagi Yojimbo: Travels with Jotaro*, Volume 18 (2004). Collects issues 61-68 of the Dark Horse series.
- *Usagi Yojimbo: Fathers and Sons*, Volume 19 (2005). Collects issues 69-75 of the Dark Horse series.
- *Usagi Yojimbo: Glimpses of Death*, Volume 20 (2006). Collects issues 76-82 of the Dark Horse series.
- *Usagi Yojimbo: The Mother of Mountains*, Volume 21 (2007). Collects issues 83-89 of the Dark Horse series.
- *Usagi Yojimbo: Tomoe's Story*, Volume 22 (2008). Collects issues 90-93 of the Dark Horse series, along with other materials.
- *Usagi Yojimbo: Bridge of Tears*, Volume 23 (2009). Collects issues 94-102 of the Dark Horse series.
- *Usagi Yojimbo: Return of the Black Soul*, Volume 24 (2010). Collects issues 103-109 of the Dark Horse series.
- *Usagi Yojimbo: Fox Hunt*, Volume 25 (2011). Collects issues 110-116 of the Dark Horse series.
- *Usagi Yojimbo: Traitors of the Earth* (2012). Collects issues 117–123 of the Dark Horse series as well as stories from *Dark Horse Maverick 2001* and *MySpace Dark Horse Presents*, issue 35.

Characters

- *Miyamoto Usagi*, the protagonist, is an anthropomorphic male rabbit and a samurai with a powerful sense of honor and decency.
- *Ame Tomoe* is an anthropomorphic female samurai cat modeled on a historical figure. She is a recurring character in the series and often an ally of Usagi.
- *Murakami Gennosuke* is an anthropomorphic male rhinoceros *ronin* with a severed nasal horn. Modeled on actor Toshiro Mifune, he is some-

times an ally of Usagi and sometimes an opponent.
- *Jotaro* is an anthropomorphic male child rabbit who is the unacknowledged son of Usagi by Mariko.
- *Zato-Ino* is an anthropomorphic blind male pig based on the main character of the Japanese *Zatoichi* film series. He is a masseur and swordsman.
- *Yagi* and *Gorogoro* are anthropomorphic goats who are based on the main characters of the manga series *Lone Wolf and Cub* (1970-1976), a

Usagi Yojimbo. (Courtesy of Dark Horse Comics)

disgraced samurai-turned-assassin and his infant son.

- *Mariko* is an anthropomorphic female rabbit from Usagi's home village and the lost love of his life. She maintains the masquerade that young Jotaro is her husband's son.
- *Jei*, a.k.a. *the Black Soul*, is an anthropomorphic male samurai wolf armed with a black-bladed spear. He is an almost unkillable psychopath and religious fanatic who has battled Usagi on numerous occasions.
- *Lord Hebi* is an anthropomorphic male samurai snake and the vassal of Lord Hikiji.
- *Lord Hikiji* is the ruthless and ambitious primary villain of the series. He has never been depicted "onstage" in the later series, though he crosses over with other Sakai stories. In his one appearance, he is drawn as a human.
- *Lord Noriyuki* is an anthropomorphic male panda cub who is a young daimyo (feudal baron) Bottom of Form struggling to learn to do his noble duty.
- *Kitsune* is an anthropomorphic female fox and a thief whose path has crossed Usagi's on more than one occasion.
- *Sensei Katsuichi* is an anthropomorphic male samurai lion and swordplay trainer who has been a part of Usagi's adventures several times, generally as an ally. He was the rabbit's sword-training master.
- *Inspector Ishida* is an anthropomorphic male cat and a police detective who sometimes adventures alongside Usagi. He is based on Chinese Hawaiian police officer Chang Apana.
- *Sanshobo* is an anthropomorphic male bear who appears in a handful of Usagi stories. He is a monk/priest and a former samurai.
- *Sasuke the Demon Queller* is an anthropomorphic male fox who travels the land as an itinerant ghost- and monster-hunter. He sometimes shares adventures with Usagi.
- *Neko*, *Mogura*, and *Komori Ninja* are, respectively, anthropomorphic cat, mole, and bat ninja clans. They are generally both cannon-fodder opponents for Usagi and homages to the Japanese

Stan Sakai

Stan Sakai is synonymous with his manga *Usagi Yojimbo*, whose title character is a mercenary bunny rabbit: have sword, will hop. He introduced the character in 1984 and continues to publish it. Born in 1953 in Kyoto, Japan, Sakai has spent most of his life in the United States, first in Hawaii, where his family moved when he was two years old, and later in California, where he has long lived in Pasadena. Though raised in the West, he acknowledges ties to his native country, having noted that Hawaii in particular has a strong Japanese culture. He has said that he is not much of a manga fan and has regularly distanced his own stories from manga. The Japanese cultural claims he makes are more filmic, notably Akira Kurosawa's *Seven Samurai*, which Sakai lists as his favorite film. Sakai got his start in comics as letterer for Sergio Aragonés's comic adventure, *Groo the Wanderer*.

and American tradition of stagehand, garb-clad ninja assassins.

- *Tokage lizards* are small, ubiquitous lizard creatures doodled into many panels of the stories, offering lightly humorous nonverbal counterpoints to the goings-on. They are Sakai's most obvious tributes to cartoonist Sergio Aragonés.

Artistic Style

Although Sakai's work is classified as manga by some, there is little of the Disney-influenced manga style to his art. Sakai's early work in fanzines demonstrates his love of many comics figures of the 1960's and 1970's, including some of his peers. However, in *Usagi Yojimbo*, his art is primarily inspired by the work of collaborator Aragonés (best known for his work in *MAD* magazine and his series *Groo the Wanderer*, 1982-1984) and the visual styles of classical Japanese painters and filmmakers. Despite clean, spare lines and neatly symmetrical compositions, every panel is packed with detail and action, a Harvey Kurtzman-esque touch that has been a comedic trademark of *MAD* artists such as Aragonés. However,

Sakai uses this bustling sea of detail less for laughs and more to emphasize the living, breathing world he creates.

Despite Sakai's considerable skill working with color, most of these stories are presented in black and white. The power of this visual choice is used to strong effect, though with far greater restraint than is seen in the often melodramatic Japanese-influenced artwork of Frank Miller. Much of Sakai's work resembles classic "funny animal" comic books and cartoons (down to the absence of blood amid the frequent violence), and he has continued to use narrative captions and thought balloons long after most mainstream superhero comics abandoned these "outmoded" storytelling devices. Because it uses such straightforward methods, the art of *Usagi Yojimbo* perfectly complements the scripts, contributing to the series' unpretentious, highly successful method of storytelling.

Themes

To a certain extent, *Usagi Yojimbo* is an exploration by a third-generation American, examining the culture of his ancestors and showing it through his eyes. As Sakai's own Web site points out, *Usagi Yojimbo* is not an international success: It faces a tremendous uphill battle in Japan, where stories of samurai and of Miyamoto Musashi have burgeoned for centuries.

The samurai code of Bushido, and the ways in which it does or does not reflect the real lives of samurai (and others), is integral to the stories, as is the way everyday life works amid the seemingly rigid nature of feudal Japanese culture. Sakai seems to point out both the essential humanity behind all cultures and the fact that no set of ideas (samurai honor or other ideology) can completely explain all the modes of human expression. Sakai's characters are both Japanese and cartoon animals; above all else, however, they are people. Sakai achieves this empathic link for the reader, bringing his world to vivid life.

Usagi Yojimbo is a graphic narrative that examines what it is to live and be human, and, incidentally, it expresses wonder at the heroism of a long-ago place and time. Readers learn who Usagi is and what his place is in his world, which helps them understand more of their own life and world.

Impact

Standing at the intersection of traditional "funny animal" comics and the hypersexualized "furries," bridging the gap between 1980's black-and-white independent comics and modern mainstream comics with circulations almost as small, and joining East and West, *Usagi Yojimbo* is a graphic narrative that takes its comfortable place between worlds. Feted by both genre-only institutions such as the Cartoon Art Museum and broader cultural institutions such as the Japanese American National Museum (which hosted the 2011 exhibit "Year of the Rabbit: The Art of Stan Sakai's *Usagi Yojimbo*"), *Usagi Yojimbo* offers readers a mingling of "low" and "high" culture, with "funny books" that address everything from language to crafts, social mores, and personal responsibility.

The whimsical nature of *Usagi Yojimbo* puts it comfortably in the company of both *Groo the Wanderer* and *Teenage Mutant Ninja Turtles* (1984-1993), the latter of which has crossed over with *Usagi Yojimbo* on many occasions. Sakai's work is a smart, introspective take on Japanese culture, especially popular culture, with tributes to Godzilla, Gamera, and Akira Kurosawa. Although *Usagi Yojimbo* was preceded by both Mark Rogers' Samurai Cat stories (first published in 1984) and Larry Hama and Michael Golden's *Bucky O'Hare*, a series about an anthropomorphic rabbit warrior created in 1981, the comic owes no particular debt of influence to either of these. Perhaps the strongest influence *Usagi Yojimbo* has exerted on other creations is in its creator's quiet dedication to solid storytelling and painstaking research.

Richard A. Becker

Further Reading

Laird, Peter, and Kevin Eastman. *Teenage Mutant Ninja Turtles* (1984-1993).

Sim, Dave. *Cerebus* (1977-2004).

Smith, Jeff. *Bone* (1991-2004).

Bibliography

Sakai, Stan. *The Art of Usagi Yojimbo: Twentieth Anniversary Edition*. Milwaukie, Oreg.: Dark Horse Books, 2004.

_____. *Usagi Yojimbo: The Special Edition*. Seattle: Fantagraphics Books, 2010.

Solomon, Charles. "Don't Get Between the Rabbit and His Sword." *Los Angeles Times*, November 25, 2005. http://articles.latimes.com/2005/dec/18/books/bk-solomon18.

See also: *Lone Wolf and Cub*; *Fist of the North Star*; *Blade of the Immortal*

UZUMAKI
SPIRAL INTO HORROR

Author: Ito, Junji

Artist: Junji Ito (illustrator); Steve Dutro (letterer); Izumi Evers (cover artist)

Publisher: Shogakukan (Japanese); VIZ Media (English)

First serial publication: 1998-2000

First book publication: 1998-2000 (English translation, 2001-2002)

Publication History

Junji Ito's *Uzumaki* (whirlpool) was originally serialized in *Weekly Big Spirits* and *Weekly Big Comic Spirits* from 1998 to 2000. English translations of individual chapters were released in issues 5.2 to 6.8 of *PULP* magazine, a defunct publishing imprint of VIZ Media specializing in alternative, experimental manga series aimed at adult audiences. Yuji Oniki's English translation of *Uzumaki*, published by VIZ, was republished in three bound volumes between 2001 and 2002. Because the English translation of *Uzumaki* is laid out in the traditional Western reading format, Ito's artwork is printed in reverse, differentiating the artwork from that seen in the original Japanese iteration of the series. Like the majority of serialized manga publications, *Uzumaki*'s visual content is primarily black and white, although each volume contains introductory pages with full-color images.

Plot

Uzumaki depicts the collapse of a Japanese coastal community called Kurozu-cho, which falls under a hypnotic curse. The series begins as protagonist Kirie Goshima sees the father of her boyfriend, Shuichi Saito, observing a snail crawling along a wall. When she asks Shuichi why Mr. Saito was acting oddly, he explains that his father is becoming obsessed with helix-shaped objects. Soon afterward, Mr. Saito commits suicide by locking himself in a washing machine and contorting his body into a spiral. When he is cremated, a helix-shaped cloud forms in the sky. Before

Uzumaki. (Courtesy of VIZ Media)

is dissipates it forms an image of Mr. Saito's corpse, driving Shuichi's mother insane; she commits suicide soon after.

Convinced that Kurozu-cho is a cursed place, Shuichi asks Kirie to leave town with him, but she is unwilling to abandon her family. The couple encounters a multitude of spiral-related horrors: Kirie's friend Azami Kurotani develops a spiral-shaped scar on her head that literally consumes her, Mr. Goshima's pottery is warped by spirits from the ash clouds that descend into Dragonfly Pond, two lovers from rival families twist their bodies together so that they can never be separated, and Kirie's hair becomes possessed and starts draining her life force. Shuichi cuts off Kirie's hair, saving her life.

The events in Kurozu-cho grow stranger. Kirie's classmate Mitsuro becomes obsessed with her and jumps in front of a car to declare his love. Some of Kirie's classmates transform into snail people. The black lighthouse overlooking the city emits a monstrous glow, and anyone who enters is burned to death. Kirie rescues her brother, Mitsuo, from the lighthouse and is badly injured. While recovering in the hospital, she encounters mosquitoes that fly in hypnotic spiral patterns and discovers pregnant women who are drinking human blood to feed their unborn children. In the final chapter of the volume, Kirie is pursued by a hurricane that hovers over Kurozu-cho, howling her name. Like the smoke clouds from the crematorium, the hurricane soon disappears into the center of Dragonfly Pond.

Eventually, Kurozu-cho is leveled by hurricanes. Kirie and her family move into a ramshackle row house infected with a virus that causes spiral-like growths to form on their skin. Eventually, Kirie's family vacates the row house, and their skin soon heals.

The rest of Japan loses contact with Kurozu-cho, and a group of television reporters comes to investigate. As the crew drives through a tunnel toward the town, its vehicle is pursued and destroyed by a twister; only Chie Maruyama survives. Chie finds three children tied to stakes near the pond. She frees them, but they turn on her, displaying an ability to manipulate the wind. Chie screams, and the children are carried away in a hurricane. Chie encounters Kirie, who explains that the atmosphere of Kurozu-cho has become warped and that sudden movements can create whirlwinds. Kirie takes Chie to an old row house where she lives with her family and a crowd of townspeople, including Shuichi.

Chie, Kirie, and Mitsuo leave the row house to search for food and are attacked by a gang of men who ride whirlwinds. Back at the row house, they find an old map of Kurozu-cho that depicts the town as a spiral. A fight breaks out over who owns the map, and Kirie's family (along with Chie and Shuichi) is ejected from the home. Desperate for food, they approach the gang of twister riders and learn they survive by eating snail people. Kirie's father confronts them and is blown away by strong winds.

The group discusses leaving town. Chie reveals that the tunnel exit has turned into a spiral. They encounter and join up with a group of volunteers led by Tanizaki. Some of the volunteers begin transforming into snail people, and the group theorizes incorrectly that only people inside the row houses are safe from the curse.

Kirie's group grows so hungry that they are forced to eat dead snail people to survive. When Kirie returns to her mother and brother's shelter with snail-person meat, she learns that her mother has been blown away by the wind and her brother is transforming into a snail person. Kirie, Shuichi, Mitsuo, and Chie resolve to leave town, while Tanizaki stays behind to build shelters. The group becomes lost in the woods and encounters more of Tanizaki's volunteer friends, who want to eat Mitsuo. Kirie carries her transformed brother to a cliff and tells him crawl to safety while the volunteers' bodies contort into spirals.

When Kirie, Shuichi, and Chie emerge from the forest, they find that Kurozu-cho has been reconstructed into a spiral labyrinth. They encounter Tanizaki, who has grown older and claims not to have seen them in years; clearly, time is warped in the forest. Ta-

---

Junji Ito

Junji Ito is one of Japan's manga masters of horror. Ito was born in 1963, and is best known outside of Japan for a pair of short series, *Uzumaki* and *Gyo*. Both were first serialized in the markedly adventurous *seinen* (or young men's) anthology magazine *Big Comic Spirits*, which is published by Shogakukan. *Uzumaki* is a paranoid fantasy in which spirals transform a small town into a claustrophobic nightmare; *Gyo* imagines an invasion of mechanized aquatic life. Ito's work is marked by an almost languorous sense of inevitability, and he roots his often nightmarish visions of corpuscular, metastasizing organisms in a stark realism. That is to say, his depictions rarely follow the manga mode in which characters' faces and bodies contort, often comically, to match their moods. He has published numerous short manga, many of which have been collected outside Japan in the *Museum of Terror* series.

nizaki tells them Kirie's parents are at the center of the labyrinth. As they travel to the center, Chie becomes trapped in a building and is never seen again.

Kirie and Shuichi eventually reach the center of the labyrinth and find Dragonfly Pond drained, revealing a spiral staircase leading underground. On the way down, a spiral person attacks Shuichi and drags him over the edge. Kirie continues her descent and finds a massive spiral city beneath Kurozu-cho. The ground is made of the petrified corpses of the town's residents, including Kirie's parents. Kirie finds Shuichi alive, and the two twist their bodies together, completing the cycle of the spiral. The staircase raises and seals Dragonfly Pond, fulfilling the curse.

At the end of the final volume there is an additional "lost" chapter that takes place before Kirie's hair is possessed by spirals in chapter 6. Shuichi discovers a new galaxy and reports his findings to local astronomer Mr. Torino. Soon, many people in Kurozu-cho discover new and unseen galaxies. Mr. Torino goes insane and tries to kill Kirie and Shuichi so he can take credit for discovering the galaxies. The couple is saved when the galaxies communicate with Mr. Torino simultaneously, causing his head to swell to a massive size and explode into a galaxy.

Volumes

- *Uzumaki*, Volume 1 (2001). Collects chapters 1-6. Kirie Goshima first encounters the spiral, which kills her boyfriend's parents and possesses her hair.
- *Uzumaki*, Volume 2 (2002). Collects chapters 7-12. The spiral becomes more prevalent, affecting Kirie's classmates and family members and culminating in the manifestation of a massive hurricane.
- *Uzumaki*, Volume 3 (2003). Collects chapters 13-19 plus "lost" chapter "Galaxies." Kurozu-cho is destroyed by hurricanes, and the ruins transform into a gigantic spiral.

Characters

- *Kirie Goshima*, the protagonist, is a female high school student with light-colored hair. Despite her serious countenance, she is kind-hearted and conscientious. She is described as hypnotic, which may be why so many of the horrors in Kurozu-cho occur in her presence. She is the last resident of the town to succumb to the spiral's curse.
- *Uzumaki*, though more of a force than a character, is the manga's antagonist. The spiral's curse pervades Kurozu-cho and is responsible for the town's destruction. It manifests in numerous ways, taking control of helix shapes and other natural phenomena such as hurricanes, dust devils, and whirlpools. Uzumaki can physically transform people. Uzumaki's final incarnation is as a monstrous spired city beneath Dragonfly Pond.
- *Shuichi Saito* is a tall teenager with short black hair, sunken cheeks, and dark circles around his eyes. He is Kirie's boyfriend. Having lost both his parents to the curse, he is sensitive to the dangerous presence of spirals in the town, using this awareness to protect Kirie from harm. He grows increasingly distant and paranoid.
- *Mr. Saito* is Shuichi's father and the first victim of the curse. He is an older man with glasses and a receding hairline. He mangles himself in a washing machine. Both Shuichi and his mother see his twisted form in numerous spiral objects, including clouds, whirlpools, dead millipedes, and tree growth rings. During these hallucinations, he invites them to join him in the spiral.
- *Mitsuo Goshima* is Kirie's brother. He is a strong-willed but immature boy with straight black hair. Although he often teases Kirie, the two grow closer as the situation in Kurozu-cho worsens. Eventually he turns into a snail person.
- *Chie Maruyama* is a young reporter with shoulder-length black hair who comes to investigate Kurozu-cho after the rest of Japan loses contact with the town. She is horrified by what she discovers but bravely accompanies Kirie and Shuichi in the search for Kirie's missing parents. She becomes trapped in the row-house maze on the way to Dragonfly Pond and is never seen again.

- *Tanizaki* is a volunteer trapped in Kurozu-cho after coming to help clean up wreckage left by the hurricanes. Prior to Kirie and Shuichi's trip into the forest, Tanizaki is a young man with a glowering expression; when they return, he is older and has grown a beard. He is willing to do anything to survive, even if it means eating the meat of the snail people, who used to be human. He is last seen disposing of bodies in the row-house labyrinth.

Artistic Style

Uzumaki is collected in three volumes, each beginning with four pages of watercolor plates painted in muted tones that establish Kurozu-cho's gloomy atmosphere. Following these plates are densely packed black-and-white images dark with Ito's heavy line work, which is a crucial aspect of *Uzumaki*'s oppressive atmosphere. VIZ Media's English translation of *Uzumaki* uses the traditional left-to-right reading sequence seen in Western comics.

Ito is known for his highly realistic manga artwork. The images in *Uzumaki* are claustrophobic in their level of detail, heightening the manga's looming sense of dread. The skies over Kurozu-cho are often darkened by heavy cross-hatching, and as the story progresses, spiral-shaped cloud formations drawn in thin, close lines (reminiscent of Vincent van Gogh's *The Starry Night*) begin to appear. Buildings and other human-made structures are drawn in precise, razor-sharp black lines that contrast with the wispy, free-flowing lines of trees and ferns permeating the town. Appropriately, these twisting, curved forms become increasingly widespread as Kurozu-cho falls further under the spiral's spell.

A primary contributing factor to *Uzumaki*'s chilling atmosphere is Ito's ability to depict the internal emotional states of his characters. Kirie Goshima rarely smiles and is usually seen with a worried expression on her face. Often, characters' physical appearances signify their moral compunctions: "good" charac-

ters' faces are symmetrical and drawn with minimal lines and white space, while the various antagonists are drawn with close, hard lines, their exaggerated features signifying evil intentions. Characters cursed by the spiral are often first depicted as traditionally beautiful. However, as the curse takes hold, their beauty fades, and they transform into monsters. This visual trope becomes increasingly prevalent in *Uzumaki* as the curse infiltrates the town.

Themes

Uzumaki deals primarily with supernatural themes. Kirie encounters an array of otherworldly beings during the manga's progression, including ghosts,

Uzumaki. (Courtesy of VIZ Media)

zombies, snail people, and vampiric mosquito women. Supernatural occurrences in Kurozu-cho are so commonplace that they become almost comical. Ito highlights the underlying humor in *Uzumaki* through mini comic strips at the end of each volume. These amusing semiautobiographical strips are not strictly part of *Uzumaki*'s narrative; instead, they provide a tongue-in-cheek, fictionalized account of Ito's experiences writing the series.

One of the major themes in *Uzumaki* is obsession. The manga begins with Mr. Saito's disturbing fascination with helix-shaped objects. As the narrative progresses, the obsession spreads and literally spirals out of control. The curse usually begins with a character demonstrating an unhealthy fixation. Kirie's friend Sekino becomes totally absorbed by her desire for attention, and her hair turns into spirals. Numerous male figures declare their undying love for Kirie and end up stalking her. The antagonists in *Uzumaki* generally begin as good people who become hypnotized by spirals, falling prey to the curse. This is also demonstrated by characters who have the opportunity to leave the town but choose not to, such as Kirie's father, who wants to stay to dedicate himself to the art of the spiral.

Uzumaki is a fatalistic horror manga because the characters cannot escape the curse's vortex. While Kirie and Shuichi fight to the end in their attempts to survive, Ito's narrative is structured and presented in such a way that readers realize the townspeople of Kurozu-cho are doomed from the beginning. Events become increasingly violent and bizarre as the town spirals into destruction. Ito's already densely packed illustrations grow darker and more disturbing, emphasizing the foreboding nature of the curse as the world spirals out of control.

Impact

Ito is most famous for his flagship title, *Tomie* (first published in an English collection in 2001), which spawned multiple films. Although *Uzumaki* was also made into a feature film, the manga retains a degree of "cult" status and is not as popular as the longer-running *Tomie* series. Nevertheless, the VIZ Media edition of *Uzumaki* was nominated for the Eisner Award for Best U.S. Edition of Foreign Material, and in 2009, the Young Adult Library Services Association included *Uzumaki* in its Top Ten Great Graphic Novels for Teens. *Uzumaki* has received favorable reviews in literary magazines such as *Rain Taxi* and on book-review Web sites such as *PopImage* and *Ninth Art*. Because of the series' sheer strangeness and apocalyptic themes, *Uzumaki* is often compared to the works of Edgar Allan Poe and H. P. Lovecraft, indicating its potential to become a classic of the horror genre.

Films

Uzumaki. Directed by Higuchinsky. Omega Micott, 2000. This film adaptation, cowritten by Ito and Kengo Kaji, stars Eriko Hatsune as Kirie Goshima and Fhi Fan as Shuichi Saito and covers most of the events in *Uzumaki*'s first volume. Plot differences mainly involve shifting the order of events to fit the script; major changes include Kirie's father's suicide by drill and Shuichi's possession by spirals during the film's conclusion. Many shots in the film are directly based on the manga's framing, and the film camera's blue lens filter re-creates the washed out, mournful tones seen in Ito's watercolors at the beginning of each volume. The film is more intentionally comedic than the original manga.

Fergus Baird

Further Reading

Furuya, Usamaru. *Suicide Circle* (2002).
Ito, Junji. *Tomie* (2001).
Umezu, Kazuo. *The Drifting Classroom* (1972-1974).

Bibliography

Ito, Junji. "A Conversation with the Creator of *Uzumaki*." Interview by Akiko Iwane. *PULP* 5, no. 2 (July, 2001).

McRoy, Jay. "Spiraling into Apocalypse: Sono Shion's *Suicide Circle*, Higuchinsky's *Uzumaki*, and Kurosawa Kiyoshi's *Pulse*." In *Nightmare Japan: Contemporary Japanese Horror Cinema*. New York: Rodopi, 2008.

See also: *Drifting Classroom*; *Death Note*; *Mai the Psychic Girl*

WE WERE THERE

Author: Obata, Yuki

Artist: Yuki Obata (illustrator); Inori Fukuda Trant (letter)

Publisher: Shogakukan (Japanese); VIZ Media (English)

First serial publication: *Bokura ga ita*, 2002-2012

First book publication: 2002-2008, 2009-2012 (English translation, 2008-2012)

Publication History

In May of 2002, the Japanese *shōjo* manga magazine *Betsucomi*, published by Shogakukan and targeting a young-adult female audience, published the first chapter of Yuki Obata's new series, *Bokura ga ita*. In English, the title has been published as *We Were There*. The success of the series led to publication of the first *tankōbon* book volume by Shogakukan in October, 2002.

The series enjoyed considerable success, and the magazine installments were regularly collected in new *tankōbon*. However, in early 2008, the series suddenly stalled following the publication of chapter 51, which ended with a cliff-hanger. After more than a year, the series resumed with the publication of chapter 52 in June of 2009. The book publication continued, with Volume 13 published in October of that year. Obata ended the series in February of 2012, and the sixteenth and final volume was published in the spring.

VIZ Media began to publish an English translation of the series under the title *We Were There* in November of 2008. The English volumes collect the same chapters as the Japanese originals. VIZ also kept intact the Japanese right-to-left reading order, the original black-and-white interior artwork, and the color covers.

We Were There. (Courtesy of VIZ Media)

Plot

Obata began her artistic career by creating manga for a young female audience, and she felt comfortable in this *shōjo* genre. Four years after her debut, in 2002, she developed *We Were There*, a series that follows the key characters from high school to early adulthood, focusing on the effects of first love on a person's emotional development. As an initial setting, Obata chose her own hometown of Kushiro on Hokkaidō, Japan's northernmost island.

We Were There begins on fifteen-year-old Nanami Takahashi's second day of high school. The cheerful, sunny Nanami tries to make friends with her bookish homeroom desk mate Yuri Yamamoto. Like many girls at school, Nanami develops a crush on the sixteen-year-old Motoharu Yano.

The plot quickly introduces a dark element that complicates the story and ties the key characters together. It is revealed that Motoharu's girlfriend, Nana Yamamoto, the older sister of Yuri, died the previous summer in a car crash. To make matters worse, she was riding with her former boyfriend, whom Motoharu had thought was no longer part of her life.

Despite these ghosts from the past, Nanami and Motoharu develop a powerful high school romance that overcomes a variety of challenges. This idyll is shattered when Motoharu moves to Tokyo with his mother. At the end of Volume 8, Motoharu promises Nanami that their relationship will continue despite the distance between them. However, Motoharu reneges on his promise. His troubled mother has committed suicide in Tokyo, causing Motoharu to sever his ties to Nanami and his friends. Assuming Nanami and the others will attend Tokyo colleges, Motoharu moves back to Hokkaidō for a while.

Obata moves the plot to a climax in Tokyo. At age twenty-three, Nanami works at the same publishing company as her fellow high school classmate Akiko Sengenji. Nanami is dating Masafumi Takeuchi, also from her high school. By accident, Akiko rediscovers Motoharu, now using the last name Nagakura, in Tokyo. Akiko urges Nanami to see Motoharu one last time on the eve of her engagement to Masafumi, but Nanami refuses. A flashback reveals that Motoharu had slept with Yuri Yamamoto once after Nana died. Later, she followed Motoharu back to Hokkaidō after dropping out of college in Tokyo. Out of pity, even though he dislikes Yuri, Motoharu lets her move in with him when he returns for a job in Tokyo.

On her twenty-fourth birthday, Nanami refuses Masafumi's marriage proposal. Instead, she hurries to the airport to try to see Motoharu, who is on his way to Sapporo. At the same time, Masafumi confronts Yuri at Motoharu's place. Nanami finally confronts Motoharu at the airport. It seems that for Motoharu, their love is finished, and Nanami attempts to let go of the past.

The next two volumes reveal that neither Nanami nor Motoharu can really let go of the other. Leading up to the final volume, Nanami falls into a coma, and Motoharu rushes to the hospital to see her.

Volumes

- *We Were There*, Volume 1 (2008). Collects chapters 1-4. The key characters of the series are introduced, and the central, troubled romantic relationship between high school students Nanami Takahashi and Motoharu Yano is established.
- *We Were There*, Volumes 2-8 (2009-2010). Collects chapters 5-31. The romance between Nanami and Motoharu develops further. At the end of Volume 8, after graduation, Motoharu moves to Tokyo but promises to remain in a romantic relationship with Nanami.
- *We Were There*, Volume 9-11 (2010). Collects chapters 32-44. In Volume 9, Nanami is stunned when Motoharu stops contacting her, apparently severing their romantic bond. The ensuing chapters explore Nanami's near obsession with her love for Motoharu and gradually reveal that Motoharu has turned to a solitary life because of his mother's suicide. Motoharu returns temporarily to Hokkaidō without letting Nanami know. Nanami flashes back to visions of her high school romance.
- *We Were There*, Volume 12 (2011). Collects chapters 45-48. The series moves on a trajectory to its conclusion with the rediscovery of Motoharu in Tokyo. Three chapters flash back to explain Motoharu's relationship with Yuri. The volume also includes a bonus story, a spoof on the Little Red Riding Hood tale that features the series' key characters in cutely drawn disguises.
- *We Were There*, Volume 13 (2011). Collects chapters 49-53. Unwilling to marry Masafumi, Nanami meets Motoharu and appears ready to let go.
- *We Were There*, Volumes 14-16 (2012). The outcome of Nanami and Motoharu's relationship is revealed.

Characters

- *Nanami Takahashi*, the protagonist, is a petite young Japanese woman with light brown hair who grows from a fifteen-year-old high school student to a twenty-four-year-old professional. She is cheerful, a bit shy, and anxious to make friends and falls hopelessly in love with Motoharu Yano. Her unwillingness to give up on Motoharu despite years of separation drives the plot to the climax of the series.

- *Motoharu Yano*, a.k.a. *Motoharu Nagakura*, is a lanky Japanese man with light brown hair and a big smile who grows from a sixteen-year-old student to a young professional. He appears extremely self-confident, wins all challenges with his teachers, and later becomes friendly with his bosses. His tragic relationship with Nana Yamamoto makes him somewhat distant emotionally; he rejects the love of Nanami and becomes the focus of many young women's romantic attention.

- *Yuri Yamamoto* is the younger sister of Motoharu's first love, Nana, and a rival for his affection. She is a pretty young Japanese woman with brown hair who appears somewhat mousy in high school but becomes rather stylish in her early twenties. She is driven to win Motoharu's love even though she knows he dislikes her.

- *Masafumi Takeuchi* is Motoharu's high school friend and later a rival for Nanami's love. A serious, good-looking young Japanese man with light brown hair, he is career- and family-oriented. Nanami's rejection of his marriage proposal finally makes him reject Motoharu as a friend.

- *Akiko Sengenji* is a high school classmate of Nanami and Motoharu. A young Japanese woman with straight black hair, she is sincere and cares for Nanami, with whom she works in Tokyo. She also had a crush on Motoharu in high school, and her discovery of him in Tokyo launches the climax of the series.

Artistic Style

Obata's artistic energy is focused on her key characters. They are drawn in classic manga style, with pointy chins, exaggerated eyes, tiny or sometimes absent noses, and mouths often drawn to reveal the characters' emotions. To highlight scenes from Nanami's memories of her happy times with Motoharu, Obata includes some watercolor panels, which convey well a sense of vague but powerful nostalgia. Similarly, Obata's color covers for the book volumes also use watercolors and often feature Motoharu's trademark wide, bright smile. This image of Motoharu's face consistently appears throughout the manga and is in deliberate contrast with his increasingly cold and emotionally detached behavior.

We Were There. (Courtesy of VIZ Media)

To indicate a character's thoughts and feelings, Obata styles her lettering differently than the main text, a feature that is preserved in the English lettering. In addition to regular dialogue and internal thoughts, the manga includes some authorial commentary on the characters, which is expressed in small, cursive lettering and accompanied by an arrow or line pointing at the character being described. As the series moves from the high school romance of Nanami and Motoharu into darker terrain, black boxes with white lettering express the characters' most painful thoughts.

Obata's drawings are generally sparse and concise. Characters are often shown in a highly stylized fashion, with just a few key facial or body features depicted and more detail left to the reader's imagination. People, particularly their faces, come first, and backgrounds are filled in sparingly. The characters' physical environment is drawn unobtrusively. The Japanese setting, including the style of homes and characters' school uniforms, for example, is drawn to emerge as a matter of fact. The backgrounds generally have an unspectacular, everyday feeling to them. There are occasional large panels depicting special, particular scenes, such as the mountains of Hokkaidō during a high school hike or the wide, oppressive Tokyo sky hovering over a dwarfed, disconsolate Nanami suffering from her unfulfilled longing for Motoharu.

Themes

The key theme of *We Were There* is the lasting effect of a powerful first love. The series explores the various challenges to such a love both in the initial high school setting and later with the characters as young professionals. When Nanami falls in love with Motoharu, her emotions can be seen on her face in the form of big smiles and deep blushes. Indicative of the relative formality of a Japanese high school, Nanami often refers to Motoharu by his last name, Yano, just as he often calls her Takahashi.

Obata complicates her plot through Motoharu's past. Because of his popularity and charisma, he was able to steal Nana Yamamoto from her former boyfriend, even though she was one year his senior. The theme of deep suffering caused by romantic disappointment is explored through the depiction of the pain

Motoharu feels. Behind his bright smile, his heart is cold as a result of Nana's betrayal (she died in a car driven by her former boyfriend, implying that she was cheating on Motoharu on the day of her death). In turn, Motoharu becomes a rather difficult boyfriend for Nanami. His reluctance to talk about his past, together with his one-night stand with Nana's younger sister, Yuri, causes Nanami to break up with Motoharu at times. However, Nanami is shown, sometimes in special watercolor panels, to hold on to memories of all the happy times with Motoharu. She cannot accept the love offered by Motoharu's friend and later rival Masafumi.

Obata brings the theme of high school love to a close when Motoharu moves with his mother to Tokyo. In a panel often repeated to show its importance in Nanami's memory, she and Motoharu link their pinkies together in the Japanese style of sealing a promise, in this case, to stay lovers. However, Obata goes on to explore the theme of a love lost. Because of his mother's suicide, Motoharu decides to forgo all deeper romantic attachments and effectively breaks off contact with Nanami. As both Nanami and Yuri seek to win Motoharu's lasting love, *We Were There* focuses on the related theme of an intense romantic rivalry between two different young women for the same difficult, elusive man. This theme carries the series to its conclusion.

Impact

We Were There quickly developed a large, loyal readership among *Betsucomi*'s teenage female audience. Its story of a difficult high school romance fit right in among the popular themes of the genre. Obata's decision to keep strictly to realism and not to include any magic or fantastic elements also proved a successful

---

Yuki Obata

Yuki Obata is the creator of *We Were There*, a romance manga aimed at teenage girls. It ran for a decade, beginning in 2002, in the Shogakukan-published *shōjo* magazine *Betsucomi*. Obata has said that the manga helped her to explore the emotions of her youth, and indeed many of her series have been set in high school.

decision. The somewhat unusual initial setting of a high school in Hokkaidō distinguished *We Were There* from more common Tokyo-based series.

As a sign of the series' success, five month after the series was launched in *Betsucomi*, its first four chapters were collected in a *tankōbon* book volume. This volume ranked among the top ten manga best sellers following its publication, as did many of the subsequent volumes. By 2006, the first nine volumes of the series had sold 4.5 million copies in Japan. At the end of 2011, more than 10 million copies of the first fifteen volumes had been sold.

The series survived its sudden one-and-a-half year hiatus, with readers returning quickly to chapter 52. The series' conclusion in March of 2012 was timed to coincide with the theatrical release of the first part of the live-action film based on the series.

Films

Bokura ga ita. Directed by Takahiro Miki. Toho Films, 2012. This live-action film stars Yuriko Yoshitaka as Nanami Takashi and Ikuta Toma as Motoharu Yano. It was released in two parts and follows the manga faithfully up to the series' ending.

Television Series

Bokura ga ita. Directed by Akitaro Daichi. Artland, 2006. This animated television series comprises twenty-six episodes, which cover the story of Nanami Takashi and Motoharu Yano during their high school romance, ending with Yano's departure for Tokyo.

R. C. Lutz

Further Reading

Motomi, Kyousuke. *Dengeki Daisy* (2007-   ).

Shina, Karuho. *Kimi ni Todoke: From Me to You* (2005-   ).

Bibliography

Ashcraft, Brian, and Shoko Ueda. *Japanese Schoolgirl Confidential*. New York: Kodansha, 2010.

Prough, Jennifer S. *Straight from the Heart: Gender, Intimacy, and the Cultural Production of Shojo Manga*. Honolulu: University of Hawaii Press, 2011.

Thompson, Jason. *Manga: The Complete Guide*. New York: Del Rey, 2007.

See also: *Nana*; *A Distant Neighborhood*

Y

YOTSUBA&!

Author: Azuma, Kiyohiko
Artist: Kiyohiko Azuma (illustrator); Terri Delgado (letterer)
Publisher: Media Works (Japanese); ADV (English); Yen Press (English)
First serial publication: *Yotsubato!*, 2003-
First book publication: 2003-   (partial English translation, 2005-2007)

Publication History

Kiyohiko Azuma's *Yotsuba&!* was first serialized in the monthly *seinen* magazine *Dengeki Daioh*, published by Media Works, in 2003. The first bound collection of *Yotsuba&!* was published in Japan that same year.

In 2005, ADV published the first U.S. version of *Yotsuba&!*, translated into English by Javier Lopez. Even though the comics in *Dengeki Daioh* are written for men, specifically those who are interested in stories about young girls, ADV gave *Yotsuba&!* an all-ages rating, and the series was accepted as a children's manga. ADV published five volumes at an erratic rate, and the promised Volume 6 was never printed.

In February of 2009, manga publisher Yen Press licensed Volume 6, releasing it in September of that year. Yen also rereleased Volumes 1-5, with new translations by Amy Forsyth and Stephen Paul, and went on to publish additional English-language volumes of the manga.

Plot

Yotsuba&!'s has a slice-of-life storytelling style. Each chapter focuses on five-year-old Yotsuba interacting with or learning about some aspect of her world. Though the series mostly consists of stand-alone chapters, the chapters build on one another, and some stories even bleed into two or more chapters.

Yotsuba&!. (Courtesy of Yen Press)

The story begins with Yotsuba and her adoptive father, Koiwai, moving to the town of Emaimachi. They are met at their new home by Koiwai's friend Jumbo. When Yotsuba wanders off while Koiwai and Jumbo are unpacking, she is found by two of the Ayase sisters, her new next-door neighbors. Yotsuba and Koiwai soon become friends with Fuuya, her sisters Asagi and Ena, and their mother. As Koiwai and Yotsuba settle into their new home and the Ayase sisters enjoy their summer break, Yotsuba learns about global warming, goes shopping, catches cicadas, and plays in the rain.

In Volume 2, Yotsuba meets Ena's friend Miura, whose tomboy looks hide a strong fear of frogs and bugs. More summer fun is had when Koiwai, Jumbo, and Fuuya take Yotsuba and Ena swimming. The Ayase family wonders about Yotsuba, trying to determine who her parents are and where she is from. She does not have a mother; Koiwai says he just started taking care of her one day. Yotsuba knows only that she came "from the left."

The summer theme continues in Volume 3 as Yotsuba learns about the practice of giving souvenirs after a trip, visits the zoo, celebrates Obon (the Japanese summer festival honoring ancestors) by giving away flowers, and goes to see a fireworks show. Jumbo has a crush on Asagi, so he is willing to treat Yotsuba, Ena, and Miura to goodies at the festival, partially so they will report to Asagi on his generosity and soft-heartedness.

In Volume 4, Jumbo takes Koiwai and the girls on a fun fishing trip. Fuuya's luck at love is as hopeless as Jumbo's, and Yotsuba tries to comfort her when Fuuya sees the boy she likes with a new girlfriend; instead, Yotsuba ends up blabbing Fuuya's troubles to the entire Ayase family when she writes her own newspaper. By this time, summer is ending, and Yotsuba dreams of being the *tsukutsuku boshi*, which she thinks is a summer fairy. She is surprised to find that it is just a type of cicada.

A nemesis is introduced when Yotsuba meets Yanda, Koiwai's junior at work. The two hate each other on sight and behave increasingly childishly around each other, even when Jumbo takes the gang stargazing. The volume ends on a high note when Koiwai agrees to take Yotsuba, Ena, and Fuuya to the beach.

As school starts, Yotsuba learns that Ena and Miura have to do homework. Yotsuba is still too young for school, but she creates a recycling project of her own and tries to "work" while Koiwai does. Koiwai decides that Yotsuba is old enough for her first bicycle, but she gets in trouble when she goes by herself to deliver milk to Fuuya at school.

In Volume 5, Yotsuba gets a fever and has to stay in bed all day. Later, she gets to play with a cup-and-

string telephone with Ena, talk to her grandmother over a real phone, and help Fuuya bake a cake. Best of all, she, Koiwai, and Jumbo go to a ranch to see cows.

Yotsuba has a few more "grown-up" experiences in Volume 8. She goes to Fuuya's cultural festival, and she and Ena help pull the dashi float during a festival. Also, she looks for acorns and plays in the rain during a typhoon. In Volume 9, Koiwai and Yotsuba go shopping. He gets a new coffee grinder, and she gets a teddy bear that she names Juralumin. Koiwai, Asagi, Asagi's friend Torako, Ena, and Yotsuba later go to see a hot-air balloon festival. They watch the balloons take off, get to ride in one, and enjoy spending the day outside together.

Volumes

- *Yotsuba&!*, Volume 1 (2009). Collects chapters 1-7. Yotsuba and Koiwai are introduced, as is the standard chapter format.
- *Yotsuba&!*, Volume 2 (2009). Collects chapters 8-14. Ena's friend Miura is added to the cast of characters.
- *Yotsuba&!*, Volume 3 (2009). Collects chapters 15-21. Asagi's friend Torako is introduced.
- *Yotsuba&!*, Volume 4 (2009). Collects chapters 22-27. In between chapters 24 and 25 is a collection of four-panel comic strips reminiscent of Azuma's previous series, *Azumanga Daioh* (2000-2004).
- *Yotsuba&!*, Volume 5 (2009). Collects chapters 28-34. The summer arc ends. Yanda, Koiwai's younger coworker, is finally seen.
- *Yotsuba&!*, Volume 6 (2009). Collects chapters 35-41. Yotsuba receives a bike.
- *Yotsuba&!*, Volume 7 (2009). Collects chapters 42-48. Yotsuba visits a farm.
- *Yotsuba&!*, Volume 8 (2010). Collects chapters 49-55. Yotsuba attends a cultural festival.
- *Yotsuba&!*, Volume 9 (2010). Collects chapters 55-62. Yotsuba goes to a hot-air balloon festival.
- *Yotsuba&!*, Volume 10 (2011). Collects chapters 63-69. Yotsuba learns to make pancakes.

Characters

- *Yotsuba Koiwai*, the protagonist, is a five-year-old girl whose name (meaning "four-leaf," as in clover) reflects her ponytailed green hair. Her irrepressible nature and avid curiosity get her into scrapes, but her infectious cheerfulness makes her friends and family smile. She often misunderstands things, which provides much of the humor for the series.

- *Koiwai* is Yotsuba's adoptive father. He has long, shaggy hair and is something of a slacker, preferring to lounge around the house in a T-shirt and boxers, though his competitive nature shows through at times. He tries to teach Yotsuba proper behavior and takes her on many outings, but he also allows her to wander freely throughout their town. He works from home as a translator.

- *Jumbo*, a.k.a. *Takashi Takeda*, is Koiwai's friend. His nickname is a reference to his extreme height. He has short, spiky hair, wears glasses, and sports a goatee. His fun-loving personality meshes well with Koiwai's laid-back tendencies. Jumbo works in his father's floral shop and has a crush on Asagi Ayase.

- *Fuuya Ayase* is the middle daughter of the Ayase family. She is in her second year of high school, where she is vice president of her class. She is sensible, levelheaded, dependable, and has excellent manners. She runs errands for her mother and helps Koiwai with Yotsuba. She has short dark hair and likes to wear T-shirts with cute pictures on them.

- *Ena Ayase* is the youngest daughter of the Ayase family. She has long dark hair and is in elementary school. She is smart and hardworking and tries to help keep an eye on Yotsuba, with whom she sometimes plays.

- *Asagi Ayase* is the oldest daughter of the Ayase family. She is pretty and has long hair and a teasing personality.

- *"Mommy" Ayase* is the mother of the Ayase family. Having three daughters of her own, she is charmed rather than bothered by Yotsuba's quirks. She is often annoyed by Asagi but is proud of how responsible Fuuya is.

- *Miura Hayasaka* is Ena's friend. She has short hair and often dresses like a tomboy. She is afraid of bugs and frogs. She is intelligent, has a sar-

Kiyohiko Azuma

Kiyohiko Azuma, born in 1968, is largely known outside of Japan for the comedy *Yotsuba&!*, about a cheerful girl with green hair. It has run in the magazine *Dengeki Daioh* since 2003. In Japan, he gained fame first for an earlier *yonkoma* (four-panel) series titled *Azumanga Daioh*, a light comedy set in high school; it spawned several video games, among other adaptations. Azuma has said he first drew manga at age sixteen, which is somewhat late for future manga creators. He has also done character designs for animations and games. He also won the Excellence Award at the Japan Media Arts Festival.

castic streak, and is easily annoyed by Yotsuba's cluelessness and Jumbo's showmanship.

- *Torako* is Asagi's friend. She is quieter and more cynical than Asagi and likes to take photographs. Though Yotsuba's oddities can overwhelm her, she cannot help but be charmed by them.

- *Yanda Yasuda* is Koiwai's junior at work. He and Yotsuba do not get along, and when she acts childish, he quickly stoops to her level.

Artistic Style

One of the more obvious artistic choices in *Yotsuba&!* is the contrast between realistic backgrounds and cartoonish characters. The sharp geometrical lines of the settings highlight the softer curves of the characters, allowing them to take center stage. Though some reviewers have criticized Azuma's backgrounds, feeling that he relies too much on photo references, others have found that the settings bring a sense of grounded reality to Yotsuba's imaginative life. The use of real backdrops allows characters to indulge in over-the-top expressions without kicking readers out of the story or reminding them that they are reading a manga rather than living the tale.

Yotsuba is the most unrealistically portrayed of all of the characters, with her odd ponytails, overly large head, and cartoonish face. The other young children

(Ena and Miura) are also cartoonlike, though slightly more realistic than Yotsuba. As the characters get older, they become more true to life. Azuma has been praised for making each character distinct. Each has his or her own quirks, opinions, and desires, and his depictions of each reflect that.

Though Azuma's previous work, *Azumanga Daioh*, was drawn in a four-panel comic strip style, which necessarily limited storytelling potential, *Yotsuba&!* has a more traditional layout. Azuma mostly uses rectangular panels, often five or six per page, but having more panels available on a page and in a chapter allows him to take his time setting up a scene or a joke. This technique gives *Yotsuba&!* a somewhat luxurious pace that is broken up by comedic action. The pace also allows Azuma to turn small events into adventures, which fits with the theme of finding joy in everyday life. Within each panel, Azuma varies how his scenes are laid out, what the perspective is, and whether or not the backgrounds are fully fleshed out. By changing elements as needed, he keeps the comedy fresh and keeps readers engaged in what could otherwise be a collection of nonevents.

Themes

The main theme of *Yotsuba&!* is stated on the last page of each volume: "Enjoy Everything." Each chapter in the series gives Yotsuba a chance to explore something new and gives the other characters the chance to enjoy the exploration along with her. At the end of Volume 1, Koiwai comments about Yotsuba, "That kid always finds enjoyment in everything. Nothing can ever get Yotsuba down." This zest for life is what makes Yotsuba a delight even when she is breaking the rules. Her curiosity and joy allow her to find wonder in the most mundane tasks.

Humor is also a major element in *Yotsuba&!*. Azuma plays up the odd behavior, vivid imagination, and over-the-top responses and emotions of a young child. By making the older characters just as likely to act silly, Azuma keeps the series from being just about Yotsuba's strangeness. He shows readers the humor in everyone's actions, whether intended or unintended. Also, he explores the many varieties of humor, from situational to physical and teasing.

Yotsuba&! gives readers a look at life in modern suburban Japan, and there are many aspects of the series that are distinctly Japanese. The realistic and highly detailed settings and the use of puns and dry humor bring to life the cultural details added to the story. From the tatami mats and futons in Koiwai and Yotsuba's bedroom to the sights of a cultural festival, Japan is practically a character in the story.

Tied in with the theme of Japanese culture is the idea of nostalgia. *Yotsuba&!* is an idealized look at the joys of childhood. The Japanese idea of *natsukashii*, or nostalgia for a nonexistent time, is reflected in Azuma's focus mostly on the joys of childhood, rather than on the sadness, frustration, or annoyance. Yotsuba is only rarely shown throwing a tantrum, and even that is portrayed with humor, not irritation. She is allowed to wander unchaperoned without fear that anything will happen to her, an example of how only the good elements of the past are recalled.

Impact

Azuma's series received critical acclaim when it debuted in Japan. *Yotsuba&!* was awarded an Excellence Prize in the Manga Division at the 2006 Japan Media Arts Festival. In 2008, it was nominated for the first ever Manga Taishō award and was a nominee for the Tezuka Osamu Cultural Prize. *Yotsuba&!* has had strong sales both in Japan and in the United States. Librarians in the United States were pleased to have an all-ages manga title that they could add to their children's collections. Reviewers in library journals praised its genuinely sweet cuteness and loved both its cross-gender and cross-age appeal and genuine humor. Volume 1 was included in *Library Journal*'s Best Graphic Novels of 2005 list and was also on the Young Adult Library Services Association's (YALSA's) 2007 Popular Paperbacks "What's So Funny?" list. Volume 4 was on YALSA's 2008 Great Graphic Novels for Teens list. The series as a whole was featured in several other lists of recommended graphic novels for libraries.

However, many online fans and bloggers who knew of the series' origin in *Dengeki Daioh* wondered how a manga written for an adult male audience in Japan could be considered family friendly in the United States. Some bloggers were not able to get past the "moe" and "lolicon" (sexualization of underage girls) qualities of other *Dengeki Daoih* titles, while other fans doubted that *Yotsuba&!* would appeal to children since its focus seemed to be on adult nostalgia for childhood's joys.

Yen Press's retranslation of the series caused some controversy. Some fans and reviewers did not like the company's decision to put cultural notes in the margins and to retain both the original sound effects with added pronunciations and translations and the use of honorifics, feeling the choices cut into the humor of the series. However, even when reviewers acknowledge Azuma's occasional tendency to draw out a joke for too long or the series' avoidance of any weighty issues, fans appreciate the series for its feel-good nature.

Snow Wildsmith

Further Reading

Konami, Kanata. *Chi's Sweet Home* (2004-   ).
Ragawa, Marimo. *Baby and Me* (2006-   ).
Thompson, Richard. *Cul de Sac* (2004-   ).

Bibliography

Alverson, Brigid. "Review: *Yotsuba&!*, Vol. 6." Review of *Yotsuba&!*, by Kiyohiko Azuma. *Manga-Blog*, September 12, 2009. http://www.mangablog.net/?p=5474.

Brenner, Robin. "Manga Movable Feast: *Yotsuba&!* and the Question of Appeal." *School Library Journal*. September 3, 2010. http://blog.schoollibraryjournal.com/goodcomicsforkids/2010/09/03/manga-movable-feast-yotsuba-and-the-question-of-appeal.

Kimlinger, Carl. "Review: *Yotsuba&!* GN 8." Review of *Yotsuba&!*, by Kiyohiko Azuma. *Anime News Network*, July 28, 2010. http://www.animenewsnetwork.com/review/yotsuba&/gn-8.

Leavitt, Alex. "*Yotsuba&!*—The Adult Comic Comic." *Department of Alchemy*, September 1, 2010. http://doalchemy.org/2010/09/yotsuba-the-adult-comic-comic.

See also: *Amulet*; *A Distant Neighborhood*

Appendixes

BIBLIOGRAPHY

Allison, Anne. "Fierce Flesh: Sexy Schoolgirls in the Action Fantasy of *Sailor Moon*." In *Millennial Monsters: Japanese Toys and the Global Imagination*. Berkeley: University of California Press, 2006.

———. "Sailor Moon: Japanese Superheroes for Global Girls." In *Japan Pop! Inside the World of Japanese Popular Culture*, edited by Timothy J. Craig. Armonk, N.Y.: M. E. Sharpe, 2000.

Allison, Brent. "Interviews with Adolescent Animé Fans." In *The Japanification of Children's Popular Culture: From Godzilla to Miyazaki*, edited by Mark I. West. Lanham, Md.: Scarecrow Press, 2009.

Alverson, Brigid. "Review: *Yotsuba&!*, Vol. 6." Review of *Yotsuba&!*, by Kiyohiko Azuma. *Manga-Blog*, September 12, 2009. http://www.mangablog.net/?p=5474.

Arnold, Andrew D. "Coming to America." *Time*, February 19, 2005. http://www.time.com/time/columnist/arnold/article/0,9565,1029794,00.html.

Ashcraft, Brian, and Shoko Ueda. *Japanese Schoolgirl Confidential*. New York: Kodansha, 2010.

Berndt, Jaqueline, ed. *Comic Worlds and the World of Comics: Towards Scholarship on a Global Scale*. Kyoto: International Manga Research Center, Kyoto Seika University, 2010.

"*Berserk*: Book 1." Review of *Berserk*, by Kentaro Miura. *Publisher's Weekly* 251, no. 10 (2004): 52.

"Best Sellers: Graphic Novels." *Library Journal* 1 (October, 2004): 126.

Bird, Lawrence. "States of Emergency: Urban Space and the Robotic Body in the Metropolic Tales." *Mechademia* 3 (2008): 127-149.

Born, Christopher E. "In the Footsteps of the Master: Confucian Values in Anime and Manga." *ASIANetwork Exchange* 17, no. 1 (Fall, 2009): 39-53.

Brenner, Robin. "Manga Movable Feast: *Yotsuba&!* and the Question of Appeal." *School Library Journal*. September 3, 2010. http://blog.schoollibraryjournal.com/goodcomicsforkids/2010/09/03/manga-movable-feast-yotsuba-and-the-question-of-appeal.

———. *Understanding Manga and Anime*. Westport, Conn.: Libraries Unlimited, 2007.

Bryce, Mio, and Jason Davis. "An Overview of Manga Genres." In *Manga: An Anthology of Global and Cultural Perspectives*, edited by Toni Johnson-Woods. New York: Continuum, 2010.

Bunche, Steve, "Tezuka: Discovering a God of Manga." *Publishers Weekly*, November 24, 2009. http://www.publishersweekly.com/pw/by-topic/new-titles/adult-announcements/article/26010-tezuka-discovering-a-god-of-manga-.html.

Buronson and Kentarou Miura. *Japan* (1992).

Buronson and Ryoichi Ikegami. *Fist of the North Star* (1983-1988).

Cavallaro, Dani. *Magic as Metaphor in Anime: A Critical Study*. Jefferson, N.C.: McFarland, 2010.

Ceglia, Simonetta, and Valerio Caldesi Valeri. "Maison Ikkoku." *Image [&] Narrative* 1 (August, 2000). http://www.imageandnarrative.be/inarchive/narratology/cegliavaleri.htm.

Cha, Kai-Ming. "Sports Manga Gets in the Game." *Publishers Weekly* 252 (April 18, 2005): 25-26.

Choo, Kukhee. "Girls Return Home: Portrayal of Femininity in Popular Japanese Girl's Manga and Anime Texts During the 1990's in *Hana yori dango* and *Fruits Basket*." *Women: A Cultural Review* 19, no. 3 (2008): 275-296.

Clements, Jonathan, and Helen McCarthy. *The Anime Encyclopedia: A Guide to Japanese Animation Since 1917*. Berkeley, Calif.: Stone Bridge Press, 2001.

Cohn. Neil. "A Different Kind of Cultural Frame: An Analysis of Panels in American Comics and Japanese Manga." *Image [&] Narrative* 12, no. 1 (2011): 120-134.

Cools, Valérie. "The Phenomenology of Contemporary Mainstream Manga." *Image [&] Narrative* 12, no. 1 (2011): 63-82.

Cornog, Martha. "*From Eroica with Love*." Review of *From Eroica with Love*, by Yasuko Aoike. *Library Journal* 133, no. 15 (September 15, 2008): 39.

———. "Monster." *Library Journal* 134, no. 12 (July, 2009): 78.

Cornog, Martha, and Steve Raiteri. "Japan's J. K. Rowling." *Library Journal* 132 (May 15, 2007): 73.

Cubbison, Laurie. "Anime Fans, DVDs, and the Authentic Text." *Velvet Light Trap* 56 (Fall, 2005): 45-57.

Dacey, Katherine. "*Solanin*." Review of *Solanin*, by Inio Asano. *Pop Culture Shock*, November 19, 2008. http://www.popcultureshock.com/manga/index.php/reviews/manga-reviews/solanin.

Davis, Jason, Christie Barber, and Mio Bryce. "Why Do They Look White?" In *Manga and Philosophy: Fullmetal Metaphysician*, edited by Josef Steiff and Adam Barkman. Chicago: Open Court, 2010.

Diaz, Junot. "The Psychotic Japanese Monster." *Time* 172, no. 4 (July, 2008): 50.

Drazen, Patrick. *Anime Explosion! The What? Why? and Wow! of Japanese Animation*. Berkeley, Calif.: Stone Bridge Press, 2002.

"*The Drifting Classroom*." Review of *The Drifting Classroom*, by Kazuo Umezu. *Publishers Weekly* 253, no. 25 (2006): 46.

Drury, Molly. "Manga Review: *Solanin*." Review of *Solanin*, by Inio Asano. *UK Anime Network*, December 15, 2009. http://www.uk-anime.net/manga/Solanin.html.

Eiji, Ōtsuka. "Disarming Atom: Tezuka Osamu's Manga at War and Peace." *Mechademia* 3 (2008): 111-126.

Ellis, Bill. "Folklore and Gender Inversion in Cardcaptor Sakura." In *The Japanification of Children's Popular Culture: From Godzilla to Miyazaki*, edited by Mark I. West. Lanham, Md.: Scarecrow Press, 2009.

Exner, Nina. "Basic Reader's Advisory for Manga: Select Popular Titles and Similar Works." *Young Adult Library Services* 5 (Spring, 2007): 13-21.

Fleming, Michael. "VIZ Media Enters Movie Biz." *Daily Variety*, July 20, 2008, p. 8.

Fujie, Kazuhisa, and Onno van't Hot. *Nana Essentials: The Ultimate Fanbook*. Tokyo: DH, 2008.

Gallacher, Lesley-Anne. *The Sleep of Reason: On Practices of Reading Shōnen Manga*. PhD diss., University of Edinburgh, 2010.

Gardner, Jared. "Autography's Biography, 1972-2007." *Biography: An Interdisciplinary Quarterly* 31, no. 1 (Winter, 2008): 1-26.

Garner, Dwight. "Manifesto of a Comic-Book Rebel." *The New York Times*, April 14, 2009. http://www.nytimes.com/2009/04/15/books/15garn.html.

Goldberg, Wendy. "The Manga Phenomenon in America." In *Manga: An Anthology of Global and Cultural Perspectives*, edited by Toni Johnson-Woods. New York: Continuum, 2010.

Goldsmith, Francisca. "*Japan Ai: A Tall Girl's Adventures in Japan*." Review of *Japan Ai: A Tall Girl's Adventures in Japan*, by Aimee Major Steinberger. *Booklist* 104, no. 15 (April 1, 2008): 39.

Gravett, Paul. *Manga: Sixty Years of Japanese Comics*. London: Collins Design, 2004.

Groensteen, Thierry. *The System of Comics*. Translated by Bart Beaty and Nick Nguyen. Jackson: University Press of Mississippi, 2007.

Halverson, Cathryn. "'Typical Tokio Smile': Bad American Books and Bewitching Japanese Girls." *Arizona Quarterly: A Journal of American Literature, Culture, and Theory* 63, no. 1 (Spring, 2007): 49-80.

Handa, Issei, and Daniel Komen. *The Bleach Breakdown: The Unofficial Guide*. Tokyo, Japan: Cocoro Books, 2007.

Hart, Christopher. *Mangamania Shonen: Drawing Action-Style Japanese Comics*. New York: Chris Hart Books, 2008.

Hong, Christine. "Flashforward Democracy: American Exceptionalism and the Atomic Bomb in *Barefoot Gen*." *Comparative Literature Studies* 46, no. 1 (March, 2009): 125-155.

Humphrey, Robert L. "Book Notes." Review of *The Four Immigrants Manga: A Japanese Experience in San Francisco, 1904-1924* by Henry Yoshitaka Kiyama. *American Studies International* (June, 1999): 107-108.

Ichioka, Yuji. *The Issei: The World of First Generation Japanese Immigrants, 1885-1924*. New York: Free Press, 1988.

Inuhiko, Yomota, and Hajime Nakatani, trans. "Stigmata in Tezuka Osamu's Works." *Mechademia* 3 (2008): 97-111.

Ishii, Anne. "Medical Manga Comes to America." *CMAJ: Canadian Medical Association Journal* 180, no. 5 (March, 2009): 542-543.

Ito, Junji. "A Conversation with the Creator of *Uzumaki*." Interview by Akiko Iwane. *PULP* 5, no. 2 (July, 2001).

"*Japan Ai: A Tall Girl's Adventures in Japan*." Review of *Japan Ai: A Tall Girl's Adventures in Japan*, by Aimee Major Steinberger. *Publisher's Weekly* 254, no. 50 (December 17, 2007): 40.

Johnson, Mark Dean. "Uncovering Asian American Art in San Francisco, 1850-1940." In *Asian American Art: A History, 1850-1970*, edited by Gordon H. Chang, et al. Stanford, Calif.: Stanford University Press, 2008.

Johnson-Woods, Toni, ed. *Manga: An Anthology of Global and Cultural Perspectives.* New York: Continuum, 2010.

Kan, Kat. "Pirates, Zombies, Racing, and Being a Stranger in a Strange Land." *Voice of Youth Advocates* 31, no. 1 (April, 2008): 36.

Kawamoto, Saburo. "The Nightmarish Imagination." In *The Drifting Classroom, Volume 11*. San Francisco, Calif.: VIZ Media, 2008.

Kelts, Roland. *Japanamerica: How Japanese Pop Culture Has Invaded the U.S.* New York: Palgrave Macmillan, 2007.

Kershaw, Ian. *Hitler, 1889-1936: Hubris.* New York: W. W. Norton, 1999.

Kimlinger, Carl. "Review: *Yotsuba&!* GN 8." Review of *Yotsuba&!*, by Kiyohiko Azuma. *Anime News Network*, July 28, 2010. http://www.animenews network.com/review/yotsuba&/gn-8.

Kishimoto, Masashi. *The Art of Naruto: Uzumaki.* San Francisco: VIZ Media, 2007.

Klady, Leonard. "Crying Freeman." Review of *Crying Freeman*, by Kazuo Koike. *Variety* 360, no. 10 (October 9, 1995): 63.

Koike, Kazuo. "Kazuo Koike: The Dark Horse Interview." Interview by Carl Horn. *Dark Horse Comics*, March 3, 2006. http://www.darkhorse.com/Interviews/1261/Kazuo-Koike--The-Dark-Horse-Interview-3-3-06.

Kubo, Tite. *All Colour but the Black: The Art of Bleach.* San Francisco: VIZ Media, 2008.

Lamarre, Thomas. "Born of Trauma: Akira and Capitalist Modes of Destruction." *positions: east asian cultures critique* 16, no. 1 (Spring, 2008): 131-156.

Leavitt, Alex. "*Yotsuba&!*—The Adult Comic Comic." *Department of Alchemy*, September 1, 2010. http://doalchemy.org/2010/09/yotsuba-the-adult-comic-comic.

"The Legacy of *Astro Boy*: A Discussion between Naoki Urasawa and Makoto Tezuka." In *Pluto: Urasawa ´ Tezuka Volume 1*. San Francisco: VIZ Media, 2009.

Lunning, Frenchy, ed. *War/Time*. Minneapolis: University of Minnesota Press, 2009.

Lyga, Allyson A. W., and Barry Lyga. *Graphic Novels in Your Media Center: A Definitive Guide.* Westport, Conn.: Libraries Unlimited, 2004.

Macias, Patrick. "Manga and the NANA Phenomenon." *Kateigaho: Japan's Arts and Culture*, 2006. http://nana-nana.net/news69.html.

_____. "About the Artist: Kazuo Umezu." In *The Drifting Classroom, Volume 1*. San Francisco, Calif.: VIZ Media, 2006.

MacWilliams, Mark W. "Japanese Comic Books and Religion: Osamu Tezuka's Story of the Buddha." In *Japan Pop! Inside the World of Japanese Popular Culture*, edited by Timothy J. Craig. Armonk, N.Y.: M.E. Sharpe, 2000.

_____, ed. *Japanese Visual Culture: Explorations in the World of Manga and Anime.* Armonk, N.Y.: M. E. Sharpe, 2008.

Martinez, D. P., ed. *The Worlds of Japanese Popular Culture: Gender, Shifting Boundaries, and Global Cultures.* New York: Cambridge University Press, 1998.

Mautner, Chris. "Chris Mautner Reviews *Pluto*, Volumes 1-3 by Naoki Urasawa." *The Comics Journal*, December 29, 2009. http://classic.tcj.com/manga/chris-mautner-reviews-pluto-vols-1-3-by-naoki-urasawa.

Maynard, Senko K. "Sources of Emotion in Japanese Comics: Da, Nan(i), and the Rhetoric of Futaku." In *Exploring Japaneseness*, edited by Ray T. Donahue. Westport, Conn.: Ablex, 2002.

McCarthy, Helen. *The Art of Osamu Tezuka, God of Manga.* New York: Abrams ComicArts, 2009.

_____. *Hayao Miyazaki: Master of Japanese Animation.* Berkeley, Calif.: Stone Bridge Press, 2002..

McCloud, Scott. *Making Comics: Storytelling Secrets of Comics, Manga, and Graphic Novels.* New York: Harper, 2006.

_____. *Understanding Comics: The Invisible Art.* New York: HarperPerennial, 1993.

McRoy, Jay. "Spiraling into Apocalypse: Sono Shion's *Suicide Circle*, Higuchinsky's *Uzumaki*, and Kurosawa Kiyoshi's *Pulse*." In *Nightmare Japan: Contemporary Japanese Horror Cinema*. New York: Rodopi, 2008.

Mihalsky, Susan. "*Town of Evening Calm, Country of Cherry Blossoms.*" *Library Media Connection* 29, no. 5 (March/April, 2011): 76.

Miller, John Jackson, and Maggie Thompson. *Warman's Comic Book Field Guide*. Iola, Wisc.: Krause, 2004.

Misiroglu, Gina, ed. *The Superhero Book*. Detroit: Visible Ink Press, 2004.

Mockett, Marie Matsuki. "Head over Heels for *Boys over Flowers*." *National Public Radio*, April 15, 2011. http://www.npr.org/2011/04/15/134563204/ head-over-heels-for-boys-over-flowers.

Molotiu, Andrei. "Masashi Tanaka's Gon Series." *The Comics Journal* 242 (April, 2002): 71-74.

"*MW*." Review of *MW*, by Osamu Tezuka. *The Complete Review*, n.d. http://www.complete-review. com/reviews/comics/tezukao2.htm.

Nagasaki, Takashi. "Postscript." In *Pluto: Urasawa ´ Tezuka Volume 8*. San Francisco: VIZ Media, 2010.

Nakazawa, Keiji. "A Note from the Author." In *Barefoot Gen: A Cartoon Story of Hiroshima*. San Francisco: Last Gasp Books, 2004.

_____. *Hiroshima: The Autobiography of Barefoot Gen*. Translated by Richard H. Minear. Lanham, Md.: Rowman & Littlefield, 2010.

Napier, Susan J. *Anime from Akira to Howl's Moving Castle*. New York: Palgrave Macmillan, 2005.

_____. *Anime from Akira to Princess Mononoke: Experiencing Contemporary Japanese Animation*. New York: Palgrave, 2000.

_____. *The Fantastic in Modern Japanese Literature*. New York: Routledge, 1996.

_____. "Vampires, Psychic Girls, Flying Women, and Sailor Scouts: Four Faces of the Young Female in Japanese Popular Culture." In *The Worlds of Japanese Popular Culture: Gender, Shifting Boundaries, and Global Cultures*, edited by Dolores P. Martinez. New York: Cambridge University Press, 1998.

Natsume, Fusanosuke. "Akira Acclaimed." *Look Japan* 46, no. 481 (April, 1996): 20-21.

_____. "Postscript: Why Is *Pluto* So Interesting?" In *Pluto: Urasawa ´ Tezuka Volume 3*. San Francisco: VIZ Media, 2009.

Navok, Jay, and Sushil K. Rudranath. *Warriors of Legend: Reflections of Japan in "Sailor Moon."* North Charleston, S.C.: BookSurge, 2005.

Oda, Eiichiro, and Akira Toriyama. "Monochrome Talk: Eiichiro Oda X Akira Toriyama." In *One Piece: Color Walk 1—Art of Shonen Jump*, edited by Elizabeth Kowasaki. San Francisco, Calif.: VIZ Media, 2005.

Ohba, Tsugumi, et al. *Death Note, Volume 13: How to Read*. San Francisco: VIZ Media, 2008.

O'Luanaigh, Cian. "Osamu Tezuka: Father of Manga and Scourge of the Medical Establishment." *The Guardian*, July 21, 2010. http://www.guardian. co.uk/science/blog/2010/jul/21/medical-manga-osamu-tezuka.

Onoda Power, Natsu. *God of Comics: Osamu Tezuka and the Creation of Post-World War II Manga*. Jackson: University Press of Mississippi, 2009.

Orbaugh, Sharalyn. "Busty Battlin' Babes: The Evolution of the Shojo in the 1990s Visual Culture." In *Gender and Power in the Japanese Visual Field*, edited by Joshua S. Mostow, Norman Bryson, and Maribeth Graybill. Honolulu: University of Hawaii Press, 2003.

O'Rourke, Shawn. "*Lone Wolf and Cub* Part 1: History and Influences." *Popmatters*, December 2, 2009. http://www.popmatters.com/pm/feature/ 116502-lone-wolf-and-cub-part-1-history-and-influences.

Ōtsuka, Eiji. "Disarming Atom: Tezuka Osamu's Manga at War and Peace." Translated by Thomas LaMarre. In *Mechademia* 3, edited by Frenchie Lunning. Minneapolis: University of Minnesota Press, 2008.

Patten, Fred. *Watching Anime, Reading Manga: Twenty-Five Years of Essays and Reviews*. Berkeley, Calif.: Stone Bridge Press, 2004.

Pellitteri, Marco. *The Dragon and the Dazzle: Models, Strategies, and Identities of Japanese Imagination*. London: John Libbey, 2010.

Petersen, Robert. *Comics, Manga, and Graphic Novels: A History of Graphic Narratives*. Santa Barbara, Calif.: Praeger, 2010.

Phillipps, Susanne. "Characters, Themes, and Narrative Patterns in the Manga of Osamu Tezuka." In *Japanese Visual Culture: Explorations in the World of Manga and Anime*, edited by Mark W. MacWilliams. Armonk: M.E. Sharpe, 2008.

Power, Natsu Onoda. *God of Comics: Osamu Tezuka and the Creation of Post-World War II Manga*. Jackson: University Press of Mississippi, 2009.

Prough, Jennifer S. *Straight from the Heart: Gender, Intimacy, and the Cultural Production of Shojo Manga*. Honolulu: University of Hawaii Press, 2011.

Raiteri, Steve. "*20th Century Boys*." Review of *20th Century Boys*, by Naoki Urasawa. *Library Journal* 134, no. 12 (July, 2009): 78.

_____. "Crying Freeman." Review of *Crying Freeman*, by Kazuo Koike. *Library Journal* 131, no. 15 (September 15, 2006): 44.

_____. "*Graphic Novels.*" *Library Journal* 130 (May 15, 2005): 98-103.

_____. "Graphic Novels." *Library Journal* 130 (November 15, 2005): 51.

_____. "*Ranma 1/2: Vol. 1.*" *Library Journal* 128 (September 1, 2003): 144.

_____. "*To Terra. . .*" *Library Journal* 132 (May 15, 2007): 75.

_____. "*Tsubasa: Reservoir Chronicle* Vol. 1." Library Journal 129 (September 1, 2004): 128.

Reed, Calvin. "Comics Bestsellers." Publishers Weekly 254 (July 9, 2007): 16.

"The Rise and Fall of *Weekly Shōnen Jump*: A Look at the Circulation of *Weekly Jump*." ComiPress, May 6, 2007. http://comipress.com/article//1923.

Rubin, Lawrence. "Big Heroes on the Small Screen: Naruto and the Struggle Within." In *Popular Culture in Counseling, Psychotherapy, and Play-Based Interventions*. New York: Springer, 2008.

Rust, David. "Like Nothing Else Going: Gon." *The Comics Journal* 201 (January, 1998): 41-42.

Ryberg, Jesper, Thomas S. Petersen, and Clark Wolf. *New Waves in Applied Ethics*. New York: Palgrave McMillan, 2007.

Sakai, Stan. *The Art of Usagi Yojimbo: Twentieth Anniversary Edition*. Milwaukie, Oreg.: Dark Horse Books, 2004.

_____. *Usagi Yojimbo: The Special Edition*. Seattle: Fantagraphics Books, 2010.

Sanders, Joe Sutliff. "*20th Century Boys*." Review of *20th Century Boys*, by Naoki Urasawa. *Teacher Librarian* 37, no. 4 (April, 2010): 27.

Schodt, Frederick L. *The Astro Boy Essays: Osamu Tezuka and the Manga/Anime Revolution*. Berkeley, Calif.: Stone Bridge Press, 2007.

_____. *Dreamland Japan: Writings on Modern Manga*. Berkeley, Calif.: Stone Bridge Press, 1996.

_____. "Henry Kiyama and *The Four Immigrants Manga*." In *The Four Immigrants Manga: A Japanese Experience in San Francisco, 1904-1924*. Berkeley, Calif.: Stone Bridge Press, 1999.

_____. *Manga! Manga! The World of Japanese Comics*. 12th ed. Tokyo: Kodansha, 2001.

Shamoon, Deborah. "Situating the Shōjo in Shōjo Manga: Teenage Girls, Romance Comics, and Contemporary Japanese Culture." In *Japanese Visual Culture*, edited by Mark W. MacWilliams. Armonk, N.Y.: M. E. Sharpe, 2008.

Shimatsuka, Yoko. "Do Not Pass Go." *Asiaweek* 27 (June 29, 2001): 54-55.

Smith, Zack. "An Amulet Update: Checking In with Kazu Kibuishi." *Newsarama*, July 6, 2009. http://www.newsarama.com/comics/070906-Amulet2-Kazu.html

_____. "Searching the Clouds and Taking Flight with Cartoonist Kibuishi." *Newsarama*, November 10, 2010. http://www.newsarama.com/comics/amulet-flight-kazu-101110.html

Solomon, Charles. "Don't Get Between the Rabbit and His Sword." *Los Angeles Times*, November 25, 2005. http://articles.latimes.com/2005/dec/18/books/bk-solomon18.

_____. "For Manga, a Novel Approach." Los Angeles Times, April 29, 2007. http://articles.latimes.com/2007/apr/29/entertainment/ca-manga29

_____. "Four Mothers of Manga Gain American Fans with Expertise in a Variety of Visual Styles." *The New York Times*, November 28, 2006, E5.

Spies, Alwyn. *Studying Shōjo Manga: Global Education, Narratives of Self and the Pathologization of the Feminine*. PhD diss., University of British Columbia. 2003. https://circle.ubc.ca/handle/2429/15104.

Stephanides, Adam. "Adam Stephanides Reviews *Solanin* by Inio Asano." Review of *Solanin*, by Inio Asano. *The Comics Journal*, January 15, 2010. http://classic.tcj.com/manga/adam-stephanides-reviews-solanin-by-inio-asano.

Stevenson, Jason. *Yoshitoshi's Strange Tales*. Amsterdam: Hotei, 2005.

Suter, Rebecca. "Japan/America, Man/Woman: Gender and Identity Politics in Adriane Tomine and Yoshihiro Tatsumi." *Paradoxa: Studies in World Literary Genres* 22 (2010): 101-122.

Suzuki, Kazuko. "Pornography or Therapy? Japanese Girls Creating the Yaoi Phenomenon." In *Millennium Girls: Today's Girls Around the World*, edited by Sherrie Inness. Lanham, Md.: Rowman, 1998.

Swanson, Paul L. "Osamu Tezuka's *Buddha*." Review of *Buddha*, by Osamu Tezuka. *Japanese Journal of Religious Studies* 31, no. 1 (2004): 233-240.

Takada, Mayumi. "The Four Immigrants Manga and the Making of Japanese Americans." *Genre: Forms of Discourse and Culture* 39, no. 4 (Winter, 2006): 125-139.

"Taniguchi Jirō." In *Manga: Masters of the Art*, edited by Timothy Lehmann. Scranton, Pa.: Collins Design, 2005.

Taylor, Stephen. "Urasawa's Mesmerizing *Monster*." *The Daily Yomiuri*, April 13, 2008, p. 13.

Tezuka, Makoto. "Postscript." In *Pluto: Urasawa x Tezuka Volume 2*. San Francisco: VIZ Media, 2009.

Tezuka, Osamu. *Phoenix Volume 2: A Tale of the Future*. San-Francisco: VIZ Media LLC, 2002.

Thompson, Jason. *Manga: The Complete Guide*. New York: Ballantine Books, 2007.

Thorn, Matt. "Shojo Manga—Something for the Girls." *The Japan Quarterly* 48, no. 3 (July-September, 2001).

Toku, Masami. "Shojo Manga! Girls' Comics! A Mirror of Girls' Dreams." *Mechademia* 2 (2007): 19-33.

Tomine, Adrian. Introduction to *The Push-Man and Other Stories* by Yoshihiro Tatsumi. Montreal: Drawn and Quarterly, 2005.

Tong, Ng Suat. "A Swordsman's Saga: Blade of the Immortal." *The Comics Journal* 228 (November, 2000): 42-45.

Toriyama, Akira, and Rumiko Takahashi. "Toriyama/Takahashi Interview." Translated by Toshiaki Yamada. *Rumic World*. http://www.furinkan.com/takahashi/takahashi4.html.

Tse, David. "Crying Freeman." Review of *Crying Freeman*, by Kazuo Koike. *Sight and Sound* 7 (May, 1997): 40.

Vollmar, Rob. "Frédéric Boilet and the Nouvelle Manga Revolution." *World Literature Today* 81, no. 2 (March/April, 2007): 34-41.

Watsuki, Nobuhiro. "Free Talk." In *Rurouni Kenshin*, by Nobuhiro Watsuki. Vol. 5. VIZBIG Ed. San Francisco: VIZ Media, 2009.

_____. "Rurouni Secrets: An Interview with *Rurouni Kenshin* Author Nobuhiro Watsuki." In *Rurouni Kenshin Profiles*, edited by Kit Fox. San Francisco: VIZ Media, 2005.

Welker, James. "Beautiful, Borrowed, and Bent: 'Boys' Love' as Girls' Love in Shojo Manga." *Signs* 31 (Spring, 2006): 841.

_____. "Flower Tribes and Female Desire: Complicating Early Female Consumption of Male Homosexuality in Shōjo Manga." *Mechademia* 6 (2011): 211-228.

Whitlock, Gillian. "Autographics: The Seeing 'I' of the Comics." *Modern Fiction Studies* 52, no. 4 (Winter, 2006): 965-979.

Wong Kin Yuen. "On the Edge of Spaces: *Blade Runner*, *Ghost in the Shell*, and Hong Kong's Cityscape." *Science Fiction Studies* 27, no. 1 (March, 2000): 1-21.

Wong, Wendy Siuyi. "Globalizing Manga: From Japan to Hong Kong and Beyond." *Mechademia* 1 (2006): 23-45.

Wyman, Walt, and Kazuhisa Fujie. *The Rurouni Kenshin Companion: The Unofficial Guide*. Denver, Colo.: DH, 2006.

Yadao, Jason S. *The Rough Guide to Manga*. New York: Rough Guides, 2009.

Zaleski, Jeff. "Fist of the Northstar." Review of Fist of the Northstar, by Buronson and Tetsuo Hara. Publishers Weekly 250, no. 20 (May 19, 2003): 55.

TIMELINE

c. 700's	Woodblock printing is brought to Japan from China.
c. 1100's	*The Tale of the Genji*, by Murasaki Shikibu (early eleventh century), is adapted into an illustrated scroll. This era also marks the development of kamishibai, or a "paper drama," often enacted on the street with the aid of illustrated scrolls.
c. 1600's	This century marks the development of ukiyo-e, consisting of woodblock prints depicting scenes from history, literature, and the environment.
1814	The term "manga" is employed in the title of a collection of sketches by Japanese artist and printmaker Katsushika Hokusai, creator of the famous *The Great Wave off Kanagawa* print.
1868	The Meiji period begins in Japan, ushering in the modern era, including a more open stance toward foreign nations.
1874	The first manga magazine published in Japanese, *Eshinbun Nipponchi*, appears.
1909	Future manga publishing powerhouse Kodansha is founded.
1918	Artist Rakuten Kitazawa founds the Manga Kourakuki, an association for Japanese illustrators.
1922	The major publishing company Shogakukan is founded.
1925	Shueisha, an early manga publisher, is founded. Along with Shogakukan, it is now part of the Hitotsubashi Group.
1928	Osamu Tezuka, creator of *Astro Boy* and a major influence in the manga medium, is born.
1930s	A depressed economy leads to the revival of kamishibai, which continues until after World War II. Many manga creators will get their start drawing kamishibai toward the end of and after the war.
1930s	Ippei Okamoto introduces Japanese audiences to Western comics, including *Bringing Up Father*, *Katzenjammer Kids*, and *Mutt and Jeff*.
1947	The monthly magazine *Manga Shōnen* is founded and is published through 1955.
1949	Many trailblazing female *mangaka* (manga creators) are born, including Moto Hagio, Yumiko Oshima, Keiko Takemiya, Riyoko Ikeda, and Ryoko Yamagishi; collectively, these female *mangaka* are known as the "Fabulous Forty Niners."
1951	*Astro Boy*, or *Tetsuwan Atom*, by Osamu Tezuka is first published, setting the tone and structure for young boys' (*shōnen*) manga.

1954	*Princess Knight*, or *Ribon no Kishi*, by Tezuka is first published, setting the tone for young girls' (*shōjo*) manga.
1954	The *shōjo* magazine *Nakyoshi* begins publishing. One year later, in 1955, the *shōjo* magazine *Ribon* begins publishing.
1956	The magazine *Weekly Manga Times* debuts. It is widely considered the first weekly manga publication.
1957	Yoshihiro Tatsumi reportedly coins the term "*gekiga*" to distinguish mature manga from what manga has come to mean—comics for kids.
1959	Two influential monthly manga anthologies, Shogakukan's *Shōnen Sunday* and Kodansha's *Weekly Shōnen Magazine*, are launched in the same month (May).
1961	The first anime series, *Manga Calendar*, is broadcast on Japanese television.
1964	*Garo* magazine is founded to support adventurous comics for mature readers. It is published through 2002.
1968	The magazine *Weekly Shōnen Jump* first publishes. It eventually becomes the best-selling manga magazine in Japan —which is to say, the world—giving birth to *Slam Dunk*, *Dragon Ball*, *Naruto*, *One Piece*, and countless other popular titles.
1969	Doraemon, a robotic cat and one of the most popular characters in Japanese pop culture, makes its debut in six different magazines.
1975	The first Comiket convention is held for creators of self-published manga (*dōjinshi*).
1982	Katsuhiro Otomo's *Akira* begins serialization in *Young Magazine*. It runs through 1990.
1983	Frederik L. Schodt's *Manga! Manga! The World of Japanese Comics*, which presents a history of manga, is published.
1983	Frank Miller creates the American comic *Ronin*, which is strongly influenced by manga. He goes on to draw covers for the translated editions of *Lone Wolf and Cub*.
1986	*Dragon Ball* by Akira Toriyama begins serialization in *Weekly Shōnen Jump*.
1986	The company VIZ (now known as Viz Media) is founded in the United States with the purpose of bringing translated Japanese manga to English readers.
1989	Marvel Comics, home to such popular superheroes as Spider-Man, begins its full translated edition of Otomo's *Akira*.
1991	The *shōjo* manga *Sailor Moon* is first published.

1997	Mixx, later known as TokyoPop, is founded in Los Angeles to license manga and anime. Eventually, the company will produce non-Japanese comics inspired by manga.
1999	*Pokemon* debuts on American television.
2002	*Shōnen Jump* magazine debuts in America.
2003	*Spirited Away*, directed by manga creator Hayao Miyazaki, wins the Academy Award for Best Animated Feature.
2008	The Japanese publisher Kodansha forms an American company, based in Manhattan.
2010	The Japanese Digital Comic Association announces a joint venture with American publishers to fight online piracy.
2011	Borders Books and Music, which served a substantial amount of manga's American readership, closes its last U.S. store.
2011	TokyoPop closes its publishing division.
2012	*Shōnen Jump* magazine in America closes its print edition and moves online.

WORKS BY ARTIST

WORKS BY AUTHOR

Works by Publisher

INDEX

Note: Page numbers in **bold** indicate main discussion. Character page numbers reflect their description only. Additional information about the character can be found in the plot section of the referenced article. Most names below are characters. Artists, authors and publishers can be found in separate indexes. * indicates real person with sidebar.

background style and setting *(continued)*: *Sanctuary*, 286–287; *To Terra . . .,* 307; *Tsubasa: Reservoir Chronicle*, 318; *20th Century Boys*, 323; *We Were There*, 339; *Yotsuba&!,* 343, 344

Bai Ya Shan (a.k.a. White Ivory Fan): *Crying Freeman*, 77

balloons. *See* speech bubbles; thought bubbles

Banana Fish, **20–24**

Band of Seven: *InuYasha: A Feudal Fairy Tale*, 166

bank manager, the: *MW*, 206

Barefoot Gen, **25–30**

Bat: *Fist of the North Star*, 117

Batou: *Ghost in the Shell*, 143

battle and fight sequences: *Akira*, 8; *Blade of the Immortal*, 50; *Bleach*, 56; *Dororo*, 91; *Dragon Ball*, 96; *Fist of the North Star*, 118; *Gon*, 154; *Nausicaä of the Valley of the Wind*, 225–226; *Pluto*, 256; *Ranma 1/2*, 261; *Rurouni Kenshin*, 271; *Saint Seiya: Knights of the Zodiac*, 282, 283; *Tsubasa: Reservoir Chronicle*, 318

Battle Angel Alita, **31–34**

Battosai, Hitokiri. *See* Himura, Kenshin

Belldandy: *Oh My Goddess!,* 235

Benta: *Phoenix*, 249

Berserk, **35–40**

Bertie: *Sailor Moon*, 276

*Big Comic, 206

*Big Comic Superior, 286

Biwamaru: *Black Jack*, 44

Black Jack: *Black Jack*, 43

Black Jack, **41–46**

Black Knights: *Saint Seiya: Knights of the Zodiac*, 282

Black Moon: *Sailor Moon*, 276

Black Queen: *Black Jack*, 44

Black Soul. *See* Jei

Blade of the Immortal, **47–51**

Blanca: *Banana Fish*, 23

Bleach, **52–57**

blind monk: *Dororo*, 90

Blue Warriors: *Saint Seiya: Knights of the Zodiac*, 282

Boma: *Ghost in the Shell*, 143

Bonaparta, Franz: *Monster*, 202

border style: *Blade of the Immortal*, 50; *Cardcaptor Sakura*, 71; *Dororo*, 90, 91

Boyer, Dr.: *Monster*, 201

boy manga. *See shōnen* manga style

Boys Over Flowers, **58–63**

Brando, Dio: *JoJo's Bizarre Adventure*, 174

Brando of Turkey: *Pluto: Urasawa Tezuka*, 254

Braun, Richard: *Monster*, 202

Brook: *One Piece*, 245

brushwork: *Lone Wolf and Cub*, 180

bubbles. *See* speech bubbles; thought bubbles

Buddha, **64–68**

Buddhism: *Buddha*, 67; *InuYasha: A Feudal Fairy Tale*, 167; *Lone Wolf and Cub*, 180; *Mai, The Psychic Girl*, 197; *Phoenix*, 250; *Saint Seiya: Knights of the Zodiac*, 283; *Town of Evening Calm, Country of Cherry Blossoms*, 312

Bugnug (a.k.a. Dark Eyes): *Crying Freeman*, 76

bullying, as core theme: *Boys Over Flowers*, 62

Bulma: *Dragon Ball*, 95

Bunny (Chibi Usa, a.k.a. Rini): *Sailor Moon*, 275

*Buronson, 114

Byakuya: *InuYasha: A Feudal Fairy Tale*, 166

Callenreese, Aslan. *See* Lynx, Ash

Capek, Petr: *Monster*, 202

Captain Harley: *To Terra . . .,* 307

Captain Tennille's Impersonator: *JoJo's Bizarre Adventure*, 174

Captain Terror: *Speed Racer: Mach Go Go Go*, 301

captions. *See also* dialogue; speech bubbles: *Akira*, 8; *Berserk*, 39; *Ghost in the Shell*, 143; *Usagi Yojimbo*, 329

Caramel Man 004: *Dr. Slump*, 100

Cardcaptor Sakura, **69–73**

caricatures: *Dragon Ball*, 96

cars: *Speed Racer*, 301–302

cartoonish style: *Adolf*, 2–3; *Amulet*, 13; *Black Jack*, 44–45; *Buddha*, 67; *Drifting Classroom, The*, 108; *Dr. Slump*, 100

Catzi: *Sailor Moon*, 276

Cerberus (a.k.a. Kero): *Cardcaptor Sakura*, 71

Chairman, The: *Barefoot Gen*, 28

change. *See* transformation and change, as core theme

Chaos: *Sailor Moon*, 276

characters. *See plot within specific articles;* specific characters; specific titles

Charlie: *Four Immigrants Manga, The*, 122

Charnon, Silas: *Amulet*, 12

Charuka: *Nausicaä of the Valley of the Wind*, 225

Chi-Chi: *Dragon Ball*, 95

Chigusa, Mr.: *Maison Ikkoku*, 191